EARLY BUDDHISM
AND ITS ORIGINS

EARLY BUDDHISM AND ITS ORIGINS

by

Vishwanath Prasad Varma

Munshiram Manoharlal
Publishers Pvt. Ltd.

ISBN 81-215-0326-4
This edition 2003
First published 1973

Printed in India.
Published by Munshiram Manoharlal Publishers Pvt. Ltd.,
Post Box 5715, 54 Rani Jhansi Road,
New Delhi 110 055.

Dedicated to my ancestors

KANHAIYA PRASAD

and

LALA AMRITA PRASAD

and

RAJAKESHWAR PRASAD (NUNUJI)

CONTENTS

Page

A NOTE ON TRANSLITERATION

Generally the methods and symbols used in Monier-Williams' *Sanskrit-English Dictionary* have been used in this book.

Several words have been written in their more familiar Sanskrit forms than in the more obscure Pali ones. For example *Nirvāṇa* (nibbāna), *Karma* (Kamma), *Dharma* (Dhamma) have been preferred. In the use of proper names also the Sanskrit forms have been generally preferred.

ABBREVIATIONS

AB	Aitareya Brāhmaṇa
AN	Aṅguttara Nikāya
AV	Atharvaveda
BAU	Brihadāraṇyaka Upaniṣad
BRU	Brihadāraṇyaka Upaniṣad
BB	Bibliotheca Buddhica
BG	Bhagavadgitā
BS	Brahma-Sutra
BST	Buddhist Sanskrit Texts (Darbhanga)
CU	Chhāndogya Upaniṣad
DB	Dialogues of Buddha
DN	Dīgha Nikāya
EB	Encyclopaedia Britannica
ERE	Encyclopaedia of Religion and Ethics
ESS	Encyclopaedia of Social Sciences
ET	English Translation
HOS	Harvard Oriental Series
IA	Indian Antiquary
IC	Indian Culture
IHQ	Indian Historical Quarterly
JAOS	Journal of the American Oriental Society
JBRS	Journal of the Bihar Research Society
JPTS	Journal of the Pali Text Society
JRAS	Journal of the Royal Asiatic Society
KN	Khuddaka Nikāya
MN	Majjhima Nikāya
MSS	Mahabodhi Society, Sarnath
PTS	Pali Text Society
RV	Ṛgveda
SBB	Sacred Books of the Buddhists
SBE	Sacred Books of the East
SBH	Sacred Books of the Hindus
SN	Samyutta Nikāya

SU	Śvetasvatara Upaniṣad
TB	Taittirīya Brāhmana
TS	Taittirīya Samhitā
TU	Taittirīya Upaniṣad
VS	Vedānta Sutra
UP	Upaniṣad
YS	Yogasutra
YV	Yajuraveda
ZDMG	Zeitschrift für Deutsche Morgenlandische Gesellschaft

PREFACE

THE WORLD IS being linked up together in several respects, both ideologically and technologically. The tremendous release of industrial and technological forces and energy has sought to annihilate distance and has helped to build the material bases of a united world. At the theoretical plane also, the concept of unity is being strengthened. The electro-magnetic theory of matter has revealed that behind all diversities there lies the same energy. This concept of unity behind all material and phenomenal manifestations shows that the density, rigidity and hardness of the different elements in nature are only the external aspects of all-pulsating energy. Spiritual idealism as well as the various humanistic and humanitarian movements harp on the concepts of fraternity, co-operative mutuality and the unity of human beings at the psychic and spiritual planes. But unfortunately, a contradictory trend has also made its appearance. There is a crisis of civilization brought about to-day by imperialistic rapacity and the threatened possibility of nuclear annihilation is indeed alarming. Hence, it is required that the notions of unity, compassion and love fostered by early Buddhism be re-studied and imbibed in our lives. The studies of comparative religions, as a whole, can bring to light the truths hidden therein and can vitalise even our present life.[1]

Apart from accentuating the moral foundations of contemporary civilization, the study of comparative religions, provides insight into the working of the human mind and thus helps in a genuine appreciation of the dominant forces that have been operative in world history. Hegel regarded history as the march of the world-spirit (*Welt-Geist*) and religion, for him, was the representation of the absolute mind. Marx, on

[1] Stanley A. Cook, *The Study of Religions* (London, Adam & Charles Black, 1914), pp. 426-27. George Grimm, *The Doctrine of the Buddha: The Religion of Reason*, (Leipzig, 1926). W.L. King, *Buddhism and Christianity* (London, George Allen & Unwin, 1962).

the other hand, wanted to stress the almost causally determining role of the relations of production on the 'superstructure' of religion. There are also other philosophies of religion — of Schleiermacher, Pfleiderer, Pringle Pattison, Schweitzer, Edward Caird and others. An attempt has been made here to study early Buddhism in the light of the concepts and propositions of modern philosophies of history and religion. In this book not only the philosophical tenets of Buddha have been analysed but the philosophical bases and socio-political implications of his religious tenets have also been considered. Hence along with a discussion of the ontology, epistemology and psychology of Buddhism, a historical study of its philosophical background as well as the discussion of its religious, ethical and social teachings have also been undertaken. In this study of the philosophy and sociology of Buddhist religion, not only the Hegelian methodology as outlined in the three volumes of *Philosophy of Religion* but also the concepts and propositions of more recent studies on the subject have been present in the author's theoretical framework.

Comparative studies of Indo-European literature, philology, mythologies and religions began in the last quarter of the eighteenth century and have been carried forward in the nineteenth and the twentienth centuries.[1] Buddhism also has been studied considerably in the nineteenth and the twentieth centuries. In this book, Buddhism has been discussed from the critical, comparative, historical and sociological points of view. It is true that Buddha obtained some deep and profound illumination (*bodhi*) in the state of mystic absorption. But the philosophical formulation of the *pratityasamutpāda* and the four Aryan truths can only be studied with reference to the various currents and cross-currents of India's religious history from about the 10th century B.C. onwards. The picture of early Buddhistic teachings that we get in the *Vinaya* and the *Sutta Piṭaka* can be, in several aspects, shown to be influenced by the process of the decline of the Vedic religion also. Early Buddhism has been studied here as a system of teachings for the emancipation (*vimutti*) of man but simultaneously, through-

[1] M. Monier-Williams, *Buddhism : In its connexion with Brahmanism and Hinduism and its Contrast with Christianity* (London, John Murray, 1889) *Indian Wisdom*.

out this book, the point of view has been maintained that a great religious movement is not ushered in the world all at once. Sometimes it may be that for centuries dominant ideas incubate and thus the background is being prepared for a very long time. But the stress on the situational background of a big religious movement does not imply that we should neglect the *determining* influence of the world-moving personality of Buddha on the genesis of early Buddhism. It would be an example of extreme objectivism to say that the general currents and cross-currents in the social and religious history of India from the 10th century BC were working in a direction which, by the inevitable law of historical causation, culminated in the Buddhistic movement. In this book, the religious, social, economic and political background of early Buddhism will be emphasized, but the commanding personality of Buddha will also be taken into full consideration. Early Buddhism was simultaneously a school of religion and a system of philosophy. It did contain profound psychological doctrines and elements of abstruse metaphysics but these were to be cultivated not for the purpose of abstract intellectual delight but for emancipation. Hence it will be dfficult to prepare two separate boxes and put its religious elements in the one, and its philosophical elements in the other.

A study of the situational background is indeed essential. It helps us to appreciate the forces amidst which a great religious personality flourishes and with reference to which his teachings are oriented. Hence along with the study of the philosophy and ethics of early Buddhism, the historical evolution of ancient Indian religion should also be shown. The movement of the Semitic races between 2500 to 2000 BC has been considered to be an important factor in the development of the Egyptian, Hittite, Babylonian and Assyrian religions. The historical method has also been applied to the study of the Sumerian and the Mosaic religions. The Decalogue has been studied in its social context and its agrarian background pointed out. Early Christianity has been studied with reference to its Jewish and non-Jewish sources. Islam also has been the theme of such a critical and historical enquiry.

It is essential to apply the historical method to the study of early Buddhism at three levels. First, the growth of moral, philosophical and religious concepts and propositions from the Vedic days onwards has to be studied.[1] To some extent, the historical method has been applied by Oldenberg and Benimadhav Barua. Barua has tried to trace the philosophical background of Buddhist thought in his *A History of Pre-Buddhistic Indian Philosophy*. But his work is mainly devoted to an elaborate elucidation of the thought of the individual teachers of the Upaniṣads. He is busy in reconstructing the philosophical personalities of the later Vedic and Upaniṣadic sages. He does, at times, refer to Buddhist works. But, by and large, his work is on the Upaniṣadic philosophy and not on Buddhism. Th. Stcherbatsky[2] and A.B. Keith[3] have also tried to trace the philosophical background of early Buddhism. But their attempts are very sketchy and fragmentary. They, nonetheless, have also, recognized the necessity of the pursuit of the historical method in the study of religious and philosophical developments.

Second, a textual study of the early Buddhist scriptures can be made for a determination of the successive layers of the contents of the books. C.A.F. Rhys Davids, one of the important authorities on early Buddhism, has recognized the necessity of a work of this type. She says: "A higher criticism of Buddhism, that is, historical research, such as has been wrought in Christian scriptures may accomplish great things. Will the next generation carry on a higher torch ?"[4] In several learned papers written since 1927 and in her book *Sakya or Buddhist Origins*, she has pursued this historical-critical method with reference to the Buddhist scriptures.

[1] A.K. Coomaraswamy, *Buddha and the Gospel of Buddhism*, (London, George G. Harrap & Co., 1916), p. 219 : "Just as with the history of the various Brahmanical darshanas, so with Buddhism as a sect there remains much to be accomplished in historical elucidation and in exegesis and interpretation. But a more important task has hardly been envisaged: the connected historical study of Indian thought as an organic entirety."

[2] Th. Stcherbatsky, "Pre-Buddhaic Buddhism", *The Central Conception of Buddhism*, (First ed., London, Royal Asiatic Society 1923; Third ed. Calcutta, Susil Gupta Ltd., 1961), pp. 55-62.

[3] A.B. Keith, *The Religion and Philosophy of the Veda and the Upaniṣads*, (Harvard Oriental Series, Vols. 31 and 32: Cambridge Harvard University Press, 1925), pp. 535-551.

[4] C.A.F. Rhys Davids, "A Basic Conception of Buddhism" *Indian Culture*, Vol. II, 1935-36, pp. 749-754.

A third way to apply the historical method to early Buddhism is to analyse the entire social, political and economic background of the movement and thus to discover the important forces which helped to determine the crystallization and growth of Buddhism as a religious association and movement.

In this book the dominant aspects of the Buddhist religion and thought have been analyzed in the context of the prominent features of ancient Indian culture, religion and ethics.[1] A detailed study has been made here of early Buddhist religion and philosophy but throughout an attempt has been made to integrate them, wherever possible, with the strands of previous thought and culture. The historical study of ancient Indian religions and philosophies is an important step in finding out the original elements in Buddha's teachings. Max Müller, Deussen, Oldenberg, Schayer, Keith and Barua[2] have undertaken a study of the influence of the Upaniṣadic teachings on Buddhism. But my attempt is more comprehensive. I have tried to stress the roots of Buddhism in the Vedic Samhitās themselves. In the study of the evolution of ancient Indian religious concepts, the ideas of the Indus Valley civilization, to the extent that it is possible to infer them from their religious remains, have also been taken into consideration. The attempt to trace, wheresoever possible, Buddhist concepts to the Vedas may be claimed as one of the contributions which this book may make to knowledge. The Vedas contain several types of thought and different layers of poetic[3] collections. Although polytheistic, monotheistic and monistic elements are found in them, it is possible to trace sceptical and critical notions also there. Even during the days of the Upaniṣads there are references to the doctrines of *asadvāda*. Buddha seems to continue the critical, rational and protestant elements in ancient Indian thought. There must have been a continuity from the later Vedic days, in the succession of teachers who sponsored a critical and sceptical attitude against

[1] The *Kalahavivāda Sutta, Culaviyūha Sutta* and *Mahaviyūha Sutta* of the *Sutta Nipāta* mention the contemporary philosophical problems and categories of discussion.

[2] Benimadhav Barua, *A History of Pre-Buddhistic Indian Philosophy*, (University of Calcutta, 1921), pp. vii-viii (Preface).

[3] cf. the views of Kaegi, Lanman, Arnold (*The Vedic Meter*) and Macdonell.

ritualism. Gautama Buddha belongs to this school.

Buddhism, as stated above, has been represented in this book as a revolt against the tradition of the Vedas, the Brāhmaṇas and the Upaniṣads. It is a mistake, in the opinion of the author, to represent early Buddhism as a philosophical carrying forward of the streams of Upaniṣadic thought. Buddha was an ethical teacher who stressed *dhyāna*, *samādhi* and *nirvāṇa* but he also challenged some of the essential propositions of Brāhmanism. But although early Buddhism was critical in its attitude to contemporary Brāhmanism, and although it used some negative phraseology as *anātman*, *nairātmya* and *nirvāṇa*, possibly to differentiate and to keep its system apart from the Brāhmanism of those days, it had solid positive teachings of its own. The ethical and pietistic element was dominant in its teaching. The lofty structure of the ethico-religious idealism of early Buddhism emphasized rigorous moral endeavours and Yogic practices. This was a deep positive note of the teaching. But the stress on the positive[1] elements in Buddhism certainly does not mean that early Buddhism should be represented as another branch of the Upaniṣadic teachings.

I have also tried in this book to emphasize the higher aspects of the religion and thought of the Vedas and the Upaniṣads. I marvel at the monumental intellectual industry of the Western Indologists but I am constrained to think that their conclusions are sometimes vitiated by biases and prejudices. They have failed to appreciate the significance of such important concepts of ancient Indian culture as *brahmacarya*, *tapas* etc. Without being narrowly nationalistic, I have tried to reveal the more sublime aspects of ancient Indian thought and philosophy from the days of the *Ṛgveda* to the *Tripiṭakas*. It will be inadequate to consider external ritualism as the only significant element in Indian culture. The Yogic and mystical sides of religion have also been pointed out. But I am not fond of idealizing the aspects of ancient religions. Thus, it will not be correct to represent the ancient practice of sacrifices as the media for the attainment of unity with the cosmic powers and to neglect the

[1] An ancient lost Buddhist Pali *sutta*, rediscoverd in China and translated by J.B. Pratt, and referred to in one of his books also substantiates the positive aspects of early Buddhism. J.B. Pratt, *The Religious Consciousness: A Psychological Study*, (New York, The Macmillan Co., 1921.)

magical and animistic character of the sacrifice.

In this book, besides the historical study of religious and philosophical ideas, the methodology developed by the school of Sociology of Religion has also been pursued to some extent. This method has been pursued here at two levels. First, the social, economic and political background of early Buddhism has been investigated. Secondly, the explicitly laid down as well as the implied and ancillary teachings of early Buddhism with regard to the problems of society and political organization have also been studied. But it cannot be lost sight of that in spite of having social, economic and political consequences, Buddha's movement was primarily ethical and religious.

The psychological factors in the origin of religions have also been considered in this book with special reference to Buddhism. The correlation between religious truths and the psychological trends of the people cannot be neglected. If the Indian national mind did accept the teachings of the Vedānta and Buddhism, it does indicate that some important individuals and groups must have had the deep desire to make a search after immortality and must have believed that through the acquisition of supernormal Yogic powers immortality could be obtained. In one of the Buddhist Suttas we find reference to Yassa and the fifty-four associates of his. Even in his meeting for the first time with Buddha, Yassa expresses a sense of disgust and despair at the prevalence of pain and misery in the world. It is an important problem of psychology of religion to study the motivations that led people like Bimbisāra and Prasenajit to become so deeply attached to this new gospel of Buddhism. What were the motivational compulsives that led rich bourgeois magnates to accept Gautama's teachings? Were they thus seeking 'compensations' for guilty conscience at their being rich while the masses suffered or were they anxious to unravel the mysteries of the beyond because the present was seized with the prospect of death? Why of all people in the world, the phenomenon of death has made only the Indians so nervous about it, and this, in spite of their formal adherence to the concepts of transmigration of the soul and immortality of the *ātman* ? These fundamental problems of racial psychology require a deeper probe than has been made at present. Psychological factors are present not only in the acceptance of moral and metaphysical truths but also in the interpretations that are put upon religious and metaphysical notions in successive ages. In the nineteenth and twentieth centuries, India has been subjected to the cultural confrontations with the West and hence unconsciously and sometimes half-consciously scholars have attempted to read Western notions in ancient Indian thought. Early Buddhism has been supposed to contain doctrines analogous to Kant's categorical imperative, Comte's positive philosophy and positive polity, socialism and democracy. The simple statement of the Upaniṣads, *annam brahman,* has been interpreted to be a forecast of Alexander's notion of matter as the first stage of emergent evolution. Thus, both in the acceptance of religious doctrines as well as in the interpretations that are put upon them, psychological factors are present. The dichotomy evolved in modern psychology between the introvert-extrovert types, shows that the introverts have more inclination to religion and philosophy while the extroverts lean to action and hardihood. In this book along with the methodologies of the philosophical and sociological approaches to religion, the psychological approach to religion has also been partly referred to. The psychological approach has been indicated in the chapters discussing the life and personality of Gautama Buddha and the concept of *dukkha.*

Every significant intellectual adventure in the career of an author, at least in the realm of the humanities and the social science, is linked, howsoever remotely, with his internal life. I took to the study of Buddhism in a period of deep emotional and spiritual disquiet. At the age of eighteen, I had to experience a major tragedy in our family and since then the basic problems for my thought have been death, soul, God and eschatology. The eternal problem of Indian thought — is there a way to conquer death ?, became also my personal problem. The traditional emphasis of Indian thought on the realization of God or on the realization of the immortality of the soul, seemed unsatisfying to me because I began to wonder as to how could Gautama Buddha, traditionally venerated as a very great holy man, attain phenomenal spiritual greatness and not accept the doctrines of God and soul in their conventional sense. Some of my teachers whom I approached for a straight answer to Buddha's views on God and soul did not give adequate answers.

Hence towards the end of 1944 I proposed to embark upon a detailed study of early Buddhism and its relations to the ancient systems of Indian thought beginning from the Vedas onwards.

The main bulk of the materials incorporated here were collected by me as a Research Scholar in the department of History, of the Patna University, from May 7, 1945 to April 9, 1947. During this period Acharya Dr. Dhirendra Mohan Datta taught me both Western and Indian Philosophy. For several hours at a stretch, on numerous occasions, in course of a period of two years, he trained me in the concepts and notions of Indian and Western thought. Prof. Ganga Nath Bhattacharya taught me Greek Philosophy. Dr. Tarapada Chaudhry looked over a few of the first drafts of the chapters. Dr. Kali Kinkar Datta (at present Vice-Chancellor, Patna University), who was my thesis supervisor, encouraged me and also listened to my reading of a few chapters. Some of the materials of the thesis were published in 1945 and 1946 in *The Journal of the Bihar Research Society* and *The Patna University Journal.* I am grateful to the late Dr. S. C. Sarkar, Pandit Brahmānanda and the late Pandit Ayodhyā Prasad for encouraging me in my Buddhistic researches.

When I was in the United States the late Prof. Pitirim Sorokin of Harvard advised me in 1947-48 to give a sociological orientation to my Thesis which I had written at Patna and whose title at that time was *The Origins of Buddhism.* But I could not do that then, because of being engaged in fulfilling the requirements for advanced degrees in Political Science. In 1950 I had some discussions with the late Prof. Joachin Wach of the University of Chicago on this problem and I also attended a few of his post-graduate classes on Sociology of Religion. I had also discussions with several Western Indologists like Walter Eugene Clark of Harvard and the late F. Edgerton of Yale. I met Dr. Stede and Miss Stede in London. Dr. Stede favored a sociological approach to the study of Buddhism.

In December 1951 and January 1952 I made some further studies in the field of Buddhism and read the works of Nāgārjuna and Candrakīrti and also some critical treatises written by modern Western scholars like Poussin and Stcherbatsky. In December 1952 I again critically read portions of the *Brahma-Sutra Bhāsyam* of Śamkara and the *Tattvasamgraha*.

In February 1956, my revered father passed away and once again the problems of death, soul and God became uppermost in my mind and I slowly turned again to the study of religion and spiritualism. In that year *The Journal of the Bihar Research Society* brought out two special volumes on the occasion of the twenty-fifth centenary of Buddha and, through the courtesy of Dr. K. K. Datta, the editor, I got the opportunity of getting published some parts of the thesis in a thoroughly revised form. From 1956 to 1963, I undertook a thorough re-drafting of the whole of the thesis as written from 1945 to 1947.

The book, as it finally emerges, incorporates three types of reflections which are rooted in my experiences of life. First, the deep emotional longing to get some anchor in a forlorn world full of destruction and culminating in the final death of the individual participants has been ever present. The deaths of near and dear ones has sharply brought out before me the evanescence of physical and material elements. Secondly, as a former student of ancient Indian history and philosophy I have a keen interest in the evolution of ideas. The period from the *Ṛgveda* down to the close of the ancient Hindu age has formed a subject of my absorbing theoretical interest. Thirdly, since 1947 I am a student and teacher of Political Science. Hence, necessarily, the problem of the social and political thought of ancient Buddhism has also preoccupied me.

In some form or other the subject of this book has been present in my mind since 1945 till today. I am not a Buddhist but I have an immense veneration for Gautama Buddha. In this book I have tried to be critical and have incorporated the concepts and proposition of Western social sciences and philosophy in the analysis of Buddhist philosophy and religion. But I am also of the opinion that Western Indologists like Oldenberg, Keith and C.A.F. Rhys Davids have failed to understand the essential spirit of ancient Indian thought inspite of their gigantic scholarship. I claim to have combined criticism and appreciation. I hope this study of ancient Buddhist religion and philosophy will further the cause of the study of religions from the multi-disciplinary and integrated standpoints of modern philosophical and social scientific developments.

November 25, 1969.
Rajendranagar, Patna-16 VISHWANATH PRASAD VARMA

PART ONE

THE PHILOSOPHY AND SOCIOLOGY OF EARLY BUDDHISM

SECTION ONE

INTRODUCTION

Chapter 1

THE LIFE, PERSONALITY AND PROPHECY OF BUDDHA

1. *The Life and Personality of Buddha*

The study of ancient religions is important for obtaining an insight into the social psychology of the antique races.[1] In the prevailingly secular atmosphere of modern times, religion is only one of the fields where the social consciousness finds its expression and manifestation but in the older civilizations it (religion) had almost an universal and comprehensive sway over the lives and minds of people.[2] In ancient times even political battles were fought in the name of religion. When the old Aryans, Israelites and other Semitic tribes proclaimed battles against their contestants, they used to do so in the name of sacred deities and even their victories were proclaimed as the triumphs of the gods. In Egypt and Babylonia the king had connexions with the temples. In ancient India also, the priesthood was the custodian of the entire sacred literature and was the prime factor in the preservation of intellectual culture. Hence for a sociological study of ancient history and culture it is essential to obtain a knowledge of the prevailing priestcraft, religious systems and ceremonies, cults and sacrifices. That is the way to obtain a knowledge of ancient socio-religious consciousness and character.

[1] B. K. Sarkar, *The Sociology of Races, Cultures and Human Progress.* It is not possible to accept any longer Hopkins's hypothesis, that Buddha's conventional head-dress of curly locks and his clan name (Sākiya) would indicate descent from a Northern, perhaps Scythian race.—E. W. Hopkins, *History of Religions* (Macmillan, 1928), p. 83.

[2] With occasional exceptions, we find that before the French Revolution, almost all the social and political movements centred round religion. N. Schmidt, "Problems Concerning the Origin of Some of the Great Oriental Religions", *Journal of the American Oriental Society*, 1933, pp. 191-214.

The historical and sociological approaches to the study of religions seek to trace the social, economic, political, cultural and intellectual background of a religious movement. The past legacy and the impact of the environment cannot be minimised. A study of the diverse types of situational trends and the network of ideas current at the time when the founder of a religion appears is essential for a historical investigation. The different religions of the world like the Egyptian, the Babylonian, the Greek, the Jewish and the Christian have been studied from this historical point of view and significant propositions have been arrived at. The historical and sociological methods may be applied to the study of ancient Indian religions also. Hegel has familiarized us with the notion that great men are only the spokesmen of the 'ideas' of the age. The nebulous ideas of the day find their crystallization in the great man. But Hegel is mistaken in minimizing the creative role of the world-historical individual by stressing too much their being the embodiment of the world-spirit. A great historical personality does have significant and superior vision to understand and sometimes to fight successfully the forces of the age. Hence a world-historical individual cannot be regarded as the mere product of the age. There seems to be truth in the saying that great men are as much the creators of their era as created by them. There is interaction between both. It is said by historical objectivists that if there would have been no Luther, someone else would have produced the Reformation but the subjectivists retort that if there would have been no Charles the Great, there would have been no Coronation and the history of the Middle Ages would have been different.

Buddha was a creative personality of a very high order. The political works and exploits of Alexander, Caesar, Changhiz and Napoleon have proved ephemeral but the gigantic personality of Buddha[1] continues to mould the lives and conduct of thousands and perhaps even millions of people. The followers of Buddha trace the roots of his teachings in the profound super-sensuous realizations of the great prophet. They regard Buddha almost as a super-historical personality who revealed

[1] Contrary to Western practice, in this book only Buddha has been used and not "the Buddha".

a noble way of emancipation on the basis of his deep and rigorous austerities, meditations and *samādhi*. It is only natural for the believers in a particular sect to credit the founder of their faith with supernormal (*uttarimanussa*) powers of insight and penetration into the nature of truth and reality. But the historical and sociological approaches to the origins of religions have made us aware of the tremendous influence of the ideas and notions that are current in an epoch upon the minds of the greatest of thinkers. Even the most original of thinkers and seers do not operate in an isolated realm of abstractions. A great man is the spokesman of his age. The period from *c.* 600 B.C. to 400 B.C. was one of the intellectually and politically most vital epochs in human history both in the West and the East. Some of the senior and junior contemporaries of Buddha were Bimbisāra, Ajātaśatru, Prasenjit, the six Tirthaka teachers, Solon, Cleisthenes, some of the Sophists in Greece, Nebuchadnezzar Nabonidus, Cyrus and Zoroaster. The concrete social and political universe with its values, beliefs, cultural norms, concepts and proposition does leave indelible impress on the way the great teachers and original geniuses frame their basic questions. It also imparts to them the linguistic framework through which they perform the morphological processes of thought and which leaves its unmistakable influence even on the final conclusions of their analysis. The dominant concepts and symbols of the social and cultural universe influence the ways and styles of thought. Perhaps it will not be an exaggeration to say that even the notion and criterion of what constitutes an element of originality in our thought is also socially conditioned. Some cultures would not be appreciative of the notion of originality. They would favour traditional adherence to the old norms of ego-integration and social conformity. Even in the case of Buddha an attempt was made to interpret his teachings as being only the re-affirmation of what had been stated by the previous Buddhas like Vīpassī.[1]

It is true that the historical and sociological approach with its emphasis on environmental and social determinism and the consequent diminution of the creative role of the great reli-

[1] In this book all references to the numerous volumes of the texts and translations of the Tripiṭakas, unless otherwise stated, are to the Pali Text Society, London editions.

gious leaders seems to destroy the organic unity of a religious teaching and it also tends to wound the feelings and emotions of the devout religious soul. The pursuit of this method is essential, nonetheless, in the interest of higher knowledge and comparative criticism. But the resort to this method should not imply the minimization of the genius of the great founders of religions. A great personality does powerfully respond to the social, economic and political forces and sentiments of the day and does incorporate into his teachings many elements from the preceding and contemporary network of ideas but the final shaping and the explicit mode of formulation of the system do bear the impress of his genius. Buddhism also was a product of the times and it does derive many of its concepts and propositions from the previous thinkers and the prevalent corpus of ideas and it does also expressively react to the forces current in the environment of the day but no one can deny that the Buddhistic movement does bear the most powerful impress and impact of the personality of Buddha. The derivation of ideas from different sources is not the primary thing. What is important is the dynamic definition and evaluation of the specific elements taken from different sources for the role they are to play in the new sub-systems and systems. The impact of personality is shown in the final shape that the several ideas assume in the organic structure of the thought-system and there can be no doubt that Gautama Buddha, the founder of Buddhism, was not only the greatest figure produced by the Asian world but was also an epoch-making world leader and prophet.[1]

The life, personality and prophecy of Buddha indicate the profound impression made on his mind by the way of living of the ascetic monk dedicated to *pravrajyā*.[2] Both Gautama on the one side and Plato and Aristotle, on the other, would

[1] Paul Dahlke, a great admirer of Buddha, says in his *Buddhist Essays*, p. 19 : "... already, almost two and a half milleniums ago, the supreme summit of spiritual development was reached, and that at that distant time, in the quiet hermit groves along the Ganges, already had been thought the highest man can think...For higher thought there is not more than that Buddha-thought which wipes out the world, and with it its bearer".

[2] R. Spence Hardy, *A Manual of Buddhism* : *In its Modern Development* (London, Williams and Norgate, 1880).

condemn the appetitive sensuous life led by the vulgar (*pṛthag-jana* of Buddhism). But while the Greek thinkers are content only with a philosophic contemplation of ideas or an intellectual contemplation of God (*theos*), Buddha was far more trenchant in his advocacy of the austere code of life and *samādhi* for a person who wanted to attain *nirvāna*. The best and virtuous life, according to the Greeks, could be realized only in the perfect polity. But Gautama stressed the significance of *arhattā* for its own sake. He is far more individualistic in his attitude than Plato. Whilst the perfect guardians are trained in dialectics and take a keen interest in the defence of the country, the *arhat* is an expert in the art of the four (or sometimes five) *arūpa dhyānas*. The key concept, however, in the Buddhist way of life is not God-realization or identity with the supra-cosmic *brahman* but emancipation. There is no doubt that some of the fundamental elements of the contemporary Brāhmanical cult and philosophical ideas were subjected to destructive criticism by Gautama Buddha but his personal life of renunciation of the comforts of home life at the early age of twenty-nine shows that in his emotional and cathectic make-up he was a Hindu of Hindus. The prospects of rulership in the land of the Sakyas (Sākiyas)[1] failed to attract Gautama and he embarked on the path of homeless wandering, contemplation and asceticism, thus dedicating himself to the pursuit of emancipation and obtained final cognitive enlightenment at the age of thirty-five. It would have been possible for Gautama to combine political rulership and philosophical pursuits and adopt a career similar to that of Janaka, Aśvapati Kaikeya and Ajātaśatru of Kāśi. But his disenchantment with the ways of the mundane sphere was deeper. He renounced his ancestral inheritance, hearth and home, wife and only son for the realisation of the path to the deliverance from the miseries of 'birth, old age, sickness and death.' He became a wandering ascetic. In the later Buddhist literature we get moving descriptions of his cutting his locking hair with a sword, his parting

[1] D. B. Spooner regarded Buddha to be of Iranian descent while V. A. Smith (*Oxford History of India*, p. 49) held that the Lichchavis and the Sakiyas were Mongolians.—Noted in K. J. Saunders, *Gautama Buddha* (Calcutta, Y.M.C.A. Publishing House, 1959, first published in 1922), p. 6.

with his charioteer Channa and his first visit to the town of Rājgir (Pāli Rājagaha). Like the students of spiritual wisdom of the day he sought knowledge from two teachers Ālāra Kālāma and Uddaka Rāmaputta. In the Upaniṣads one comes across some famous teacher-student relationships. Yama instructs Naciketā, Sanatkumāra instructs Nārada and Aṅgiras seeks instruction from Bhāradvāja. In one of the Upaniṣads, Uddālaka instructs his son Śvetaketu and according to another, Śvetaketu questions his father about *brahman* and, when the latter fails to answer him, they both go to Ajātaśatru for knowledge. These seekers are satisfied with the revelation of the supreme esoteric secret. Gautama never comes across any acknowledged champion of Advaita wisdom during the course of his studentship. His own previous teachers could not win his intellectual adherence although he gave a place to their teachings in his elaborate eightfold methodology of *rūpa* and *arūpa dhyāna*. But the contemporary philosophical gnosis did not satisfy him and hence he took to the path of physical askesis. *Tapas* as a path to knowledge has a long history in this land and Gautama turned to that.

The Buddhist records indicate that the six years (535 B.C.—529 B.C.) spent by Gautama in serious self-castigations and penances were almost entirely useless and that they only convinced him of the futility of that path. According to these records, supreme enlightenment dawned on Gautama on the very first night of the forty-nine days spent beneath the sacred tree. In the Upaniṣadic tradition also we find that for the pure in heart the mere utterance of the supreme truth is enough to secure final realisation. According to the *Kaṭha Upaniṣad*, Naciketā obtains enlightenment even while Yama is narrating to him the mystic transcendental truths. But it seems more logical to hold that slowly the mind and heart are prepared for the reception of illumination than to think that a sudden dawn of spiritual knowledge is possible. It may, however, be pointed out that mystics, not only in India, but in several other countries have recognized that physical askesis and even deliberate self-torture is a path to immediate spiritual enlightenment. The Jaina prophet Mahāvīra also attained omniscience due to the practice of *tapas*.[1] The *Muṇḍaka Upaniṣad* also refers to *tapas* as one of the four (the others being *satya*, *samyak jnāna*, and *brahmacarya*) technics for the realisation of supreme reality. Thus it appears more logical and psychologically convincing to hold that the vital elements of the cardinal Buddhistic truths must have been dawning upon Gautama's mind during this long period of six years of self-discipline and beneath the sacred Bodhi tree only the final crystallization was obtained. H.G. Wells has recognized this psychological fact and says : "When the mind grapples with a great and intricate problem, it makes its advances, it secures its position step by step, with but little realisation of the gains it has made, until suddenly, with an effect of abrupt illumination, it realises its victory."[2]

Describing the illumination of Gautama the early Buddhist records (*Bodhikathā*, *Mahāvagga*) say :

"When the conditions (of existence) reveal themselves
To the ardent contemplating Brahmin,
To earth he casts the tempter's hosts,
Like the sun, diffusing light through the air."

This comparison of the illumined person to the sun is also found in Plato's *Republic*, Book VIII and the *Bhagavadgitā* (*teshām ādityavat jnānam*).

After the attainment of illumination, for forty-five years, till the attainment of *mahāparīnirvāṇa* at the ripe age of eighty, Buddha devoted himself to teaching the populace the truths that he had found out. This programme of constant itinerary that Buddha took up after his final enlightenment is somewhat comparable to the life of the Greek Sophists and the Yāyāvaras and Parivājrakas of the Indian tradition.[3] In the

[1] The six years of intense asceticism undergone by Buddha have their parallel in the one hundred and one years of rigorous *brahmacarya* of Indra spent at the Aśhrama of Prajāpati.—(*Chāndogya Up.*, VIII, 9-11).

[2] H.G. Wells, "The Rise and Spread of Buddhism", *The Outline of History*, p. 392.

[3] There are many common points between his teachings and the contemporary Brahmanical philosophy. T. W. Rhys Davids, *Buddhism* (London, 1925, Ist. ed., 1877), pp. 83-84, says : "Gautama was born and brought up, lived and died a Hindu ... There was not much in the metaphysics and principles of Gautama that cannot be found in one or other of the orthodox systems, and a great deal of his morality could be matched from the earlier or later Hindu books. Such originality as Gau-

Upanishads there is the recognition of the monastic life but regular spiritual tours are not contemplated there. Even if the Vrātyas of Eastern India are considered to be the prototype of Sādhus and Yogins, it is not certain that they carried on intellectual and spiritual propaganda. But in the Tripiṭaka literature we certainly find some Parivrājakas who led a wandering monastic life.

Even if we may find some evidences for individual wandering monastic teachers in the Upaniṣads, the overwhelming pattern there is that seekers of spiritual truth, as for example, the Brahmacārins of Yājnavalkya, study and meditate under a particular teacher. Mahāvīra and Buddha, on the other hand, are the great exemplars of wandering monastic life. Except for the four months of the rainy season (cāturmāsya), Gautama was constantly on tour and his life was absolutely dedicated to the dissemination of truth and wisdom. The famous places associated with his wandering career are Sarnath, Rājgir,[1] Gayā, Śrāvasti etc. Once he made a visit to his home town Kapilavastu. At Sārnath he delivered his first sermon to the five disciples—Kaundinya, Vappa, Bhaddiya (or Bhadrika), Mahānaman and Assaji (Aśvajit). At Rājgir there lived Sañjaya the wandering heterodox ascetic. His two disciplies, Sāriputta and Moggallāna were converted to Buddhism, or better, accepted the discipleship of Gautama. At Uruvelā, in Gaya, the three Jatila brothers were received into Gautama's fold. They were Uruvela Kassapa, Nadi Kassapa and Gaya

tama possessed lay in the way in which he adopted, enlarged, ennobled and systematised that which had already been well said by others; in the way in which he carried out to their logical conclusion principles of equity and justice already acknowledged by some of the most prominent Hindu thinkers. The difference between him and other teachers lay chiefly in his deep earnestness and in his broad public spirit of philanthropy". Oldenberg, *Buddha*, p. 52, also says : "... it is certain that Buddhism has acquired as an inheritance from Brahmanism not merely a series of its most important dogmas, but what is not less significant to the historian, the bent of its religious thought and feelings which is more easily comprehended than expressed in words."

[1] At Rājgir the famous First Council (*samgati*) after Gautama's death was also held.—Jean Przyluski, *Le Concile De Rajagrha* [*Introduction to the History of the Canons and Sects of Buddhism*] (Paris, 1st Part, 1926; 2nd Part, 1927).

Kassapa. They were fire-worshippers.[1] His father and aunt accepted his teachings. The latter, even joined the Samgha. While at the ancestral palace, in his home town, he visited also his wife. She apparently bore no grudge against him, although it is very possible, that she must have harboured a grievance against him for his having stealthily escaped from that place. His only son Rāhula asked him for his patrimony and Buddha ordered a Bhikkhu to admit him to the Samgha.

Not only did Buddha deliver sermons and hold conversations generally with seekers of knowledge and sometimes also with adversaries, most of whom are recognized in the Buddhist literature as having eventually accepted his path (*mārga*), but he also organized the Samgha. K.P. Jayaswal holds that the Buddhist Samgha was an association based on the application of the ideals and practices of political republicanism to a religious group.[2] C. A. F. Rhys Davids has emphatically elaborated the distinction between Śakya-ism and Monastic Buddhism which developed two or three centuries after Gautama and represents the views of the editors of the Piṭakas.[3] Sakya-ism would have been represented by the oral teachings of Buddha and his co-workers. She has pointed out three fundamental distinctions between Sakya-ism and Monastic Buddhism :

(i) Dharma meant to Gautama an inner guide.
Dharma meant to the monks external doctrines.

(ii) Mārga meant to Gautama a way for personal elevation.
Mārga meant to the monks the eightfold path.

(iii) Nirvāṇa meant to Gautama the extinction of passions.
Nirvāṇa meant to the monks the extinction of a man's self.

Gautama Buddha had a very austere but magnetic personality. According to the Buddhist records, his physical person

[1] Fire-worship is referred to in the *agni-vidyā* of the *Kathopaniṣad*. Fire-worship was also practised by the Zoroastrian priests.

[2] K. P. Jayaswal, *Hindu Polity* (Bangalore Publishing Co., 1955, 3rd ed.), p. 42, considers the birth of the Buddhistic movement as the birth of organized monasticism in the world. C.A.F. Rhys Davids thinks, on the other hand, that originally the Sākya movement was a lay movement and monasticism is a later development.

[3] C.A.F. Rhys Davids, *Sakya or Buddhist Origins* (London, Kegan Paul, Trench Trubner & Co., 1931).

was robust. He had the thirty-two marks of the 'great man' on his person. In the later Buddhist tradition, Gautama is considered to be *lokottara* (Pali = *lokuttaro*), extraordinary, above all worlds, and even superior to the gods. In his adolescent years also he is represented in the *Buddha-carita* of Aśvaghosha, to be a powerful warrior and archer. His vigorous and powerful physique enabled him to undergo the severe strain of penances and asceticism. Even after he had attained enlightenment he continued to lead a very active life although not as hard as during the years when he was between twenty-nine to thirty-five years old. He roamed throughout the regions of Magadha, Vaiśalī and Kośala which roughly represent a considerable portion of modern Bihar and Uttara Pradesha. He maintained full physical vigour till the age of fifty-six. At fifty-six, some strain of advancing age was felt and he sought the assistance of Ānanda, the beloved disciple and also a cousin. His walking tours, nevertheless, continued and even at the age of eighty he could undertake the journey from Rajagir to Kuśinagara via Nālandā, Pātaligrāma, Vaiśalī and Bhoganagar, on foot. It is evident, thus, that a powerful and strong body did immensely aid Gautama in the pursuit of his religious preaching. In the Buddhist accounts Gautama is credited with *riddhibala* or extraordinary miraculous power. He certainly rebukes his disciples for the display of superhuman powers. But he himself displays miraculous powers at Śrāvasti to vanquish the six heretical teachers. He is credited with having made a three-month stay in heaven.

Gautama Buddha had a serious and dignified bearing. Never in the Buddhist scriptures is he ever represented as indulging in excess of emotions. He never laughs and never does he yield to tears. He speaks only a little and always speaks in set measured terms.

But in spite of his deep austerity and exalṭed bearing, there were, certainly, human touches in him. He has a soft corner for Ānanda, he goes to visit his father and his wife and son at Kapilavastu and he accepts the exhortation of his aunt and foster-mother Mahāprajāpati Gautami, after Ānanda had intervened on her behalf, to open a female branch of the Saṃgha (*bhikkhuni saṃgha*).

At the time of his death, his attitude is absolutely unperturbed. To the anxious importunities of Ānanda not to give up his physical body, he answers by a short discourse on the inevitable dissolution of all constituted entities.

As a teacher, he resorted, to a certain extent, to argumentation and discussion. The Upaniṣadic teachers like Pippalāda, Bhāradvāja, Mahidāsa Aitareya and Uddālaka also engaged in such discussions. But besides the dialectical method of advancing propositions and counter propositions, he also resorted to lecturing or delivering a full-length discourse, as for example, the *dharmacakrapravartanasūtra*, the *ādīptaparyaya* etc. This method of delivering discourses, he, probably, either himself discovered or borrowed from the practice of the speakers in the republican mote-halls (*santhāgāra*) of the day. The Vedic Samhitās employ the method of enunciating in verse, statements about the gods, cosmos and man. The Brāhmaṇas like the *Śatapatha*, contain elementary expositions of the sacrificial system. The Upaniṣads employ the method of argumentation but they suffer in point of methodological dialectics to the dialogues of Plato. The Buddhist dialogues are short in comparison to those of Plato. They are also more cryptic and dogmatic than the compositions of Plato. Hence, in spite of a deeper spiritual and mystical appeal, the Upaniṣads and the Tripiṭakas do not give that evidence of sustained intellectual creativism as do the dialogues of Plato.

Because of his critical attitude towards the popular and Brāhmanical religion of the day, Gautama is, at times, regarded as a rationalist. His rationalism, however, is fundamentally different from that of Kant. The Kantian rationalism originated as a reaction against the empiricism of Bacon, Hobbes and Locke and the scepticism of Hume. But early Buddhist rationalism was aimed against the revelatory and institutional foundations of sacrificial Brāhmanism.

Gautama Buddha was not primarily interested in the social and political problem of the day. He did not deliberately embark upon the mission of social reform but, since he operated in a socio-political-economic framework, social, political and economic teachings did occasionally emanate from him. Some of his ethical concepts also had significant social and political implications. But essentially he was an ethical and religious teacher, inculcating a psychological method of moral reformation and a way of emancipation from suffering. He rejected the ritualism and the ceremonialism of the day, he found unsatisfying the path of the ascetics who insisted on physical austerities and he maintained silence regarding the metaphysical doctrines of unity with the *brahman*.

It is wrong, however, to characterize early Buddhism as merely "ethical idealism."[1] It is true that ethically-oriented right conduct is praised in this system, but *śila* is only one element in Buddhism. Gautama, himself, did not attain enlightenment merely by the meticulous observance of the minutest rules of conduct. He engaged in deep contemplation and meditation. He stressed that the way to the cessation of suffering is the *nirodha* of *avidyā* and *nirvāna* is attained by *samādhi* and *prajnā* and not merely by *śila*. Hence along with moral purification, psychological gnosis and meditation are considered the technics of emancipation (*vimutti*).[2]

Gautama did learn some significant processes of meditation from two of his teachers—Ālāra Kālāma and Uddaka Rāmaputta. But he claimed to have gone, deeper in that path. Hence, when, on his way to Sārnath from Gayā, Upaka Ājivaka asked him, as to who was his teacher, Buddha said that he had attained supreme enlightenment (*bodhi*) by his own efforts. Hence in his teachings he constantly stressed self-culture, personal endeavours and self-devclopment and wanted people to be *ātma-dīpa* and *ātma-śaraṇa*. In the contemporary social and religious systems too much emphasis had been placed upon

[1] According to Albert Schweitzer, *Indian Thought and its Development* (E. T. by Charles E. B. Russell. New York, Henry Holt & Co., 1936), p. 116, the greatness of Gautama Buddha consisted not in his theoretic insight but in his spiritualization of world-and-life-negation and in his breathing into it a spirit of ethics. He also says that Buddhism makes its own the ethical acquisition of Jainism. According to tradition, Buddha took recourse to a double language — to the simple man he taught moral doctrines and he propounded philosophy and even esoteric teachings to the more learned.

[2] A. A. Macdonell, *Lectures on Comparative Religions* (University of Calcutta, 1925), pp. 74-75, regards Buddhism as an offshoot of Brahmanism and says that philosophically, Buddhism might have derived ideas from the S imkhya but "it is really on what may be called its religious side that Buddhism is original". The first, second and third Aryan truths are philosophical while the fourth is religious.

dependence on external godheads. Although the Upaniṣads proclaimed the doctrine of monistic idealism, in practice, the people must have been dependent on their chosen deities and rendered worship to them. Upon such a people much too prone to dependence on external gods, Gautama Buddha inculcated absolute reliance on personal gnostic endeavours and a devoted pursuit of rigorous ethical discipline. He was of the view that by sustained and dedicated efforts at the attainment of *prajñā*, man could reach a status higher than that of even the gods. From this stress on personal endeavours it appears that Buddha was a very clean and honest prophet and did not intend to initiate any personality cult of his own. Neither did he claim to act as an intermediary between man and God.

So long as Gautama lived, his presence was the greatest bond holding the disciples together. If they sought to surrender themselves to him that required only a formal declaration that they accepted the *dhamma* as propounded by the Buddha.[1] But, later on, after the passing away of Buddha, acceptance of the supremacy of the Samgha was also made vitally essential.[2]

1 Louis de la Vallee Poussin, seems incorrect in saying that the Buddhists from the beginning regarded Buddha as a god although Gautama taught other doctrines. Poussin, *The Way of Nirvana* (Cambridge University Press, 1917), p. 30. says, "Buddhism has been, from the beginning, a religion, a religion properly so called, that is, there have been, from the beginning, Buddhists for whom Buddha was a god and who did not hope for a better state than rebirth in Buddha's heaven, but this Buddhist religion has nothing or little to do with the most authentic teaching of Sakyamuni. Old Buddhism is essentially a discipline of salvation".

2 Benimadhav Barua, *A Prolegomena to the History of Buddhist Philosophy* (University of Calcutta, 1918), has discussed the six stages of the development of early Buddhism as a religion :

(i) The organisation of the Samgha. Hence two sets of teachings were required : (a) *lokottara* and (b) *lokiya* ;

(ii) Rules of conversion were laid down. Hence religious sanction was provided to Pātimokkha.

(iii) Seniority by age was admitted. Formerly there was only the acceptance of seniority by merit.

(iv) There was the organisation of *bhikkhus* in something like a caste.

(v) *Pindadāna* was justified.

(vi) Ghost-stories were composed as stored, for example, in the *Vimāna Vatthu* and the *Petta-Vatthu*.

It, seems, possible, nevertheless, that the formula of triple surrender is a part of original Buddhism.[1]

Sometimes it is said that although a great ethical teacher, Buddha did not venture into the field of deep and subtle metaphysics. In the *Aggivaccagotta Sutta* of the *Majjhima Nikāya*, Vaccagotta raises ten questions :

A. Referring to Matter (*Loka*)	(1) The worlds are eternal. (2) The worlds are non-eternal. (3) The worlds are finite. (4) The worlds are infinite.
B. Referring to Soul	(5) The soul is identical with the body. (6) The soul is different from the body. (7) Tathāgata is re-born after death. (8) Tathāgata is not re-born after death.
C. Referring to Rebirth	(9) There is both re-birth and not re-birth. (10) There is neither re-birth nor non-re-birth.

Buddha refuses to answer these questions which are called *avyākṛta*.[2] His refusal to answer them, is not simply based on the ground that they do not foster moral growth (*nirveda* and *upaśama*) as is ordinarily supposed, but also on the ground that they do not lead to *abhijñā* and *sambodha* and *nīrvāṇa*, that is, they do not foster illumination. In other words, the refusal is based on the non-relevance of the answers to enhance morality and emancipation. Gautama claims that he reveals only the *dṛsta* (his realisation) and disclaims having any dogma (*dṛstigata*).[3] During the course of the discussion, at one place Vaccagotta says that he has been caught by ignorance and delusion (*sammoha*). But eventually he agrees that the tenets of

[1] Even in the *Iti-vuttaka*, Gautama is regarded as a saviour—"One who sees me sees the truth". Western scholars are puzzled by the simultaneous acceptance in later Mahāyānism of the concept of *anātman* and the worship of the Buddha.

[2] Sometimes the Ten *Avyākṛtas* are compared to the Kantian Four Antinomies and the concept of the unknowability of the *Ding-an-sich*.

[3] S.M. Melamed, *Spinoza and Buddha : Visions of a Dead God* (University of Chicago Press, 1933), p. 262, complains against Buddha's "lack of outspokenness about metaphysical principles" which earned him (Buddha) the reputation of being an atheist.

Gautama are free from branches, external forms or solid material forms but are existent only in pure essence.

But although Vaccagotta is silenced it can be pointed out that even if the answers to the first four and the last four questions may not be ethically profitable and that these questions may even be unanswerable from the metaphysical standpoint, still the fifth and the sixth questions do demand an answer from the ethical standpoint. A discussion of the question whether the soul is identical with the body or different from the body does have considerable ethical relevance and meaningfulness. The hedonism of the Cārvakas and the sensationalism of some other materialistic philosophers are based on the identification of the body and the soul. The Jaina stress on extreme asceticism and non-injury (*ahimsā*) is based on the metaphysical belief that all substances are animated by souls, the only exceptions being *dharma*, *adharma*, *pudgala* and *ākāsa*. Thus the examples of the Cārvakas and the Jainas are enough to point out that the ethical doctrines of the day were rooted in implicit or explicit metaphysical notions.[1] Hence I do not think that Gautama was justified in ruling out the discussions of the identity or otherwise of the soul and the body. Ethical distinctions get a firm root only when the separation of the body and the soul is posited. A settled conviction on the immortality of the soul is a dominant foundation of the belief in the efficacy of moral action because it teaches that no wicked action would ever remain unpunished and no good action would lapse unrewarded. Hence it is not sound from the standpoint of ethical enquiry to rule out discussions of these *avyākṛta* problems. They have significant connections with the analysis of problems of ethics and emancipation. The refusal to answer them, unfortunately, does give rise to an occasional suspicion that either Gautama was an agnostic[2] or that he did not have any settled metaphysical notions[3] or that

[1] Melamed, *Spinoza and Buddha*, p. 259, refers to the deep metaphysical roots of Buddha's concept of suffering.

[2] A. Berriedale Keith, *Buddhist Philosophy in India and Ceylon* (Oxford University Press, 1923), pp. 45, 63, regards Buddha as a "genuine agnostic" who did not have a clear conclusion regarding metaphysical questions.

[3] A.B. Keith, "The Buddha as a Master Mind", *Indian Culture*, Vol. V. pp. 229-238 ff., says that Buddha did not have "definite views" and

he was not an expert in the discussion of abstruse problems of ontology.[1] According to the *Lalita-Vistara*, however, which is a later account. and hence not very reliable for the period of early Buddhism, Gautama had studied the Sāṁkhya-Yoga, the Vaiśeshika, Hetuvidyā, Nyāya and the Bārhaspatya. But there is no mention of his having studied the Karma-Mimānsa and the Upaniṣadic Vedanta.

Gautama Buddha's life, personality and prophecy have been variously interpreted.[2] But I regard it inadequate to consider him merely a social and democratic revolutionary who acted as the declared spokesman of the Kshattriyas against the Brāhmins and also as the great supporter of the downtrodden and suppressed section.[3] By and large, his personality impresses me as that of a profound spiritual and moral teacher who wanted to transmit the holy Aryan path leading to *nirvāṇa.*

We cannot regard Buddha as a mere Sophist.[4] The Greek sophists had no faith in the system of idealism promulgated by Parmenides, Xenophanes and Zeno. They also ridiculed the external religious ceremonialism of the Greek religion. Buddha also was silent regarding the central tenet of Upaniṣadic idealistic metaphysics. He also condemned the external Vedic ritualism and the social system based on paying esteem and deference to birth and caste. But although he is silent regarding the spiritual values of the Upaniṣads and is a hostile critic of the

he had failed to achieve positive convictions even for himself. Gautama accepted the doctrine of 'Indeterminates' and hence he preached an ethical and meditative way of Dhyānas (ecstasy).

[1] Stressing the spirit of "metaphysical" construction and classification of Buddha, H. Oldenberg, *Buddha* (Translated from the German text of the first edition by William Hoey, 1882) p. 180, compares him to the Christian Scholastic Origen. Th. Stcherbatsky compares him to Descartes and Spinoza.

[2] Melamed, *Spinoza and Buddha*, p. 258, considers Gautama Buddha as a great synthesiser of the same type as Spinoza who synthesized formal modern thought.

[3] Albert Schweitzer, *Indian Thought and its Development*, p. 93, regards Buddha as a free thinker because he opened his monastic order even to the Sudras.

[4] For the growth and nature of Indian "sophistic" movement, see Oldenberg, *Buddha*, pp. 67-70. B.C. Law, "Wandering Teachers of Buddha's Time", *Journal of Asiatic Society of Bengal*, Vol. XIV. No. 7, 1918, pp. 399-406.

contemporary ritualistic cult, he is never a negative dialectician like the Greek sophists Gorgias and Thrasymachus. In the words of Plato, the sophists were not dialecticians because they did not use the art of contradiciton for eliciting truth. They were, on the other hand, followers of the 'eristic' method because they used the art of contradiction for the sake of contradiction. Buddha had a far deeper and more moral approach to life and its problems than the Greek sophists Protagoras and Alcidimas. Although not a constructive and erudite metaphysician, he was a great ethical teacher who inculcated piety, contemplation and self-abnegation and his way of life is sharply different from that of the sophists who taught the art of political success by accepting payments.

Although in its later manifestations Buddhism became a separate religion and even a separate Church, in the beginning it worked within the fold of the contemporary religious systems of the day. Nevertheless, it is clear from the Tripiṭakas that Gautama had dreams of the ever-increasing propaganda of his religion. He was a spiritual giant, and although he was humble enough to say that he had only revealed the ancient Aryan way[1] and not initiated any new gospel, it cannot be denied that his behaviour-pattern was that of a missionary. He was not confined to his cloister and did not lead the life of an isolated monk and philosopher. The band of his monastic preachers went out preaching. Gautama had great zeal for religious propaganda and was not a mere spiritual sage calmly preaching the gospel of ethical idealism to an intellectual elite. According to the accounts of the Tripiṭakas he is constantly on the move and is filled with a great amount of religious elation and harmonious affections and institutes formal ceremonies for the initiation of monks and laymen into the 'order' founded by

[1] Gautama only claims to have seen an ancient road trodden by Buddhas of bygone ages. The *Saṃyutta Nikāya*, "The City", referring to an ancient road and an ancient palace says : "...he were to invite the king to rebuild that city, and that city were to become flourishing and populous and wealthy once more. Even so brethren, have I seen an ancient path, an ancient road trodden by Buddhas of a bygone age...which being followed I understand life, and its coming to be and its passing away...I have declared same to the fraternity—so that holy life flourishes and is spread once more."

him. We find that along with a keen interest in psychology and ethics, Buddha prescribed rules with minute and meticulous details about the conduct of bhikkhus and bhikkuṇis. Thus it is clear that his was a very comprehensive and many-sided religious and moral personality.

2. *Buddha's Leadership*

In a religious system the personality of the founder is very important both philosophically and sociologically. The transcendent and cosmic truths inwardly perceived and intuitively realized by the founder constitute the basis for any religion. A mere coherent arrangement of some cosmological and moral propositions would not constitute the religious framework. Buddha is supposed to have had the ralization of some essential truths—*Sammā Sambuddha.* He himself believed in his 'enlightenment' and his followers and disciples also accepted it and regarded him as a lion of Dharma and the embodiment of illumination. This type of superintellectual perception[1] and vision of some transcendent—cosmic truth differentiates the personality of the religious leader from that of the statesman, party leader, warrior or chief. A basic element in the pattern of distinctive characteristics of the religious leader is this fact of intuitive apperception of trans-empirical truth and reality. It is essentially rooted in the conception of a spiritual and evaluative teleology. Religion is oriented to the acceptance of an ordered, organic and spiritual nature of the universe. This organic teleology is conceived as being not merely functional but is supposed to be the consequence of the presence of a supreme divine reality and truth. For the ancient Indian mind, the celibate or monastic anchorite commanded a special veneration because he had turned his back upon the allurements of the world and had taken a decided step to initiate himself through meditative contemplation into the superior mysteries. Since the time of the *Atharvaveda* we have the picture of the *muni* dominating the Indian mind. The *Ṛgveda* constantly refers to the power of *tapas*. Yājnavalkya is the arch-leader of monastics. The teachers who flourished in the seventh and sixth centuries

[1] Cf. D. T. Suzuki, *Mysticism: Christian and Buddhist* (London, George Allen Unwin, 1959), pp. 37-75.

B.C., although some of them were sceptics, materialists and atheists, essentially were "religious" in the sense that they had left the household and led the lives of wanderers.[1]

Buddha was a prophetic religious leader. He had renounced the pleasures of a royal home and had accepted the begging bowl. Hence by this supreme example of self-abnegation he had confirmed the traditionally venerated path of religious men. Thus the reverence, prestige, respect and status associated with this vertically superior status of the Muni and the Tāpasa became associated with him and his disciples. He had in this life and in previous existences as a *bodhisat* fully cultivated the ten *śila* of a bhikkhu, had attained the seven kinds of wisdom (*bodhyanga*), had successfully transcended the ten *samyojana* (fetters) and was an expert master of the technics of *dhyāna*, *samāpatti* and *samādhi*. He sanctified a life of poverty, self-conquest and holiness. Buddha, thus, obtained authority by the acceptance of the path of self-abnegation. This authority is not based on the institutional dynamics of the exercise of legitimate political control but is a symbolic type of authority. At occasions it can become coercive in a tradition-bound society rooted in static *mores* and customs. But normally it operates in a non-penal way. In the words of Max Weber we can regard the prophecy of Buddha as an example of the exercise of *charismatic* authority. The princely birth and the aristocratic associations of Buddha further intensified his *charismatic* authority and he was venerated by his followers as a compassionate super-sage. Durkheim has pointed out the importance of the "sacred" in religious authority. This stress on the sacred can be expressed in diverse ways.[2] The revelation

[1] Devamitra Dharmapala, *Buddha* (Madras, Natesan & Co., 5th ed., 1943), pp. 34-35. Edward Conze, *Buddhism : Its Essence and Development* (New York, Harper & Bros., 1959, 1st ed., 1951), pp. 54-55 : "Poverty, celibacy and inoffensiveness were the three essentials of monastic life. A monk possessed almost no private property at all. . . The begging-bowl was the Buddha's badge of sovereignty."

[2] R. H. Lowie, *The History of Ethnological Theory* (New York, Rinehart & Co., 1937), p. 208 : "He [Durkheim] asserts that all societies dichotomize the universe into a sacred and a profane half, the sphere of religion coinciding with that of the 'sacred, *i.e.* segregated, forbidden thing' (*choses sacress, c'est-a-dire separees*; *interdites*) recognized as such by the community of believers. Now such an antithesis is, indeed, reported

of the sacred character of Buddha through the presence on his body of the thirty-two marks of a transcendent personality is only one aspect of the manifestation of this reverence for the sacred and the supernormal. Furthermore, in the Tripiṭakas we get numerous stories about the demonstration of superhuman feats by Buddha. The acceptance of the veracity of these legends is only an illustration at a more popular level of the metaphysical proposition accepted since the Upaniṣadic times that access to the superior, intuitively cognitive heights and depths of truth imparts control over the processes and events of the physical world. This is the famous theory of *yathākāmacāra* of the Upaniṣads which was also accepted in Buddhism.[1] Hence it can be said that the acquisition of enlightenment is not merely a matter of profound inner experience but is associated, in a sociological sense, with the manifestation of *charismatic* authority which may imply the transcendence of institutional sanctions. In both the Upaniṣadic and Buddhist literature, therefore, spiritual realization is conceived as conferring power.

The foundation of the Samgha was another aspect of this *charismatic* authority. The power which was manifested at an individual level in the case of the other religious wanderers became now scrutinized and institutionalized. The Samgha accentuated the social power of Buddha in two senses. It, being an association, was based on the organization of discipline, control and order. In spite of persistent denials by Buddha of his supermanhood or of his being in any sense divine or supramundane and transcendent, the disciples regarded him with profound awe and veneration. The formation of the Samgha necessarily gave to the founder the prestige and authority of the head and leader of the association. In spite of the Samgha being based on the concept of equalitarianism, Buddha enjoyed the authority of a supreme patriarch, as if he were the head of an association organised on the principle of subordination and

from Polynesia, where "noa" and "tabu" express precisely the antagonism between secular and holy things." J. E. Carpenter, *Comparative Religion* (Oxford Univ. Press, 1913, Reprint of 1944), pp. 133-134.

1 The Buddhist would emphatically plead that gnostic illumination (prajña) is the only antidote to the dreads, anguishes and inhibitions of a forlorn world.

pyramidal hierarchy. Thus the power of intuitional and prophetic *charisma* was accentuated by this institutional leadership of a social and ecclesiastical fraternity. In a different sense also, the Samgha strengthened the foundations of Buddha's leadership. For purposes of survival in the struggle for competitive existence an association is compelled to exalt the personality of the founder. It becomes almost essential to transform the personality of the founder who considered himself only as a 'physician' curing the sick and a 'ploughman' ploughing the field of immortality (*Sutta Nipāta*, 80) into a symbol of superhuman wisdom, power and greatness. As time passes myths and legends begin to accumulate. New tales are fabricated which are calculated to put the founder at a "chosen" place. The general orientation of these tales, myths and symbols is to remove the personality of the leader beyond the pale of ordinary criteria and to etherealize him into the concentrated essence of super-normal greatness, perfection and omniscience. This aspect of divine transmutation of Buddha's personality, partly begun during his life-time attained almost a climax with the growth of Mahāyānism. The rise of Mahāyānism resulted in the absolute divinization of the personality of Buddha and this was an example of the tendency of the human mind to have a concrete apotheosis of beneficent kindness, compassionate goodness and comprehensive power to bring about the liberation and salvation of the believers. Thus we find that from the standpoint of religious sociology the transformation of the path-finder, the revealer of the way and the cogniser of the truth into the divine embodiment of power, goodness and bliss, and an Absolute rather than a historical figure and teacher is indicative of the trend of the mass mind and of religious followers to stress the aspect of the "sacred" in the social psychology of world religions.

CHAPTER 2

THE ORIGINS OF RELIGION AND EARLY BUDDHISM

1. *The Origins of Religion*

MODERN ANTHROPOLOGICAL and sociological researches into the origins of religions have brought to light astounding propositions and conclusions. The old orthodox view has been that religious truths were revealed by some supracosmic divine agency at the beginning of creation or at some particular time to some chose prophets. Dayānanda held that in the primordial beginning of creation, the Vedic Samhitās were revealed to the four pristine rishis—Agni, Vāyu, Āditya and Angirā. The Hebrews believe that Jehova revealed the Ten Commandments to Moses. Christianity and Islam also accept the revelation of their religious teachings to Jesus and Muhammad. But philosophers of religion in the eighteenth and nineteenth centuries began to challenge the authenticity of revelation at a specific time and place. They felt that the eternally perfect Being could not be conceived to have engaged in such a mundane task because it amounted to the acceptance of spatial and temporal determinations even for the infinitely perfect substance.

Modern cosmology has destroyed the foundations of the physical world-view of religions. To conceive that the creation of the world took place at a certain date appears unreliable to students of physics. Darwinian evolutionism has delivered a tremendous shock to the believers in the special creation of a chosen pair or group of human beings by the Almighty. Freudian psycho-analysis is another terrific challenge to traditionally venerated heroes, gods, legends, and myths. Freud would be repelled by the notion that God created man in his own image. He, to the contrary, would sponsor that religious symbols are the projections of man's psychic demands. Modern anthropological, sociological and psychological researches also seriously challenge the notion and historicity of revelation. They emphasize totemism, or fetishism or ancestor-worship or magic or the fear of the known and unknown forces of nature or the fear of capital (in Lenin's view) as the source of religious beliefs and practices. Not divine illumination or the awakening of the super-conscious but fears of various kinds are being regarded as the source of religious belief. Religion is now considered as a "compensation" for the feelings of human helplessness and providing the need of "dependence" and support, for man, on something bigger and vaster than himself. Durkheim regarded God as only the symbolic magnification and transfiguration of society and in his view the clan is identified with an animal or a plant conceived as the totemic divinity.[1] Social scientists have tried to find out elements of kinship between some of the religious practices and notions of the savage tribes of New Zealand, Pacific islands and Africa and the Aruntas in Australia on the one hand, and the old religious tenets and legends recorded in the Vedas, Scandinavian mythology and the wonder tales of ancient Greece and ancient Rome on the other. Thus the problem of the origins of religions is one of the main controversial issues of the social sciences.

Religion has been variously defined. Broadly speaking, it can be defined as a belief in the spiritual value of things. Some scholars see in totemism the origin of religion and some in magic. Spencer hit upon ancestor worship as the source of religion. It is true that primitive religions did not distinguish between spirituality and superstition but it would be correct to say that the primitive mind had a belief in something supernatural or supra-individual. This native apprehension of a "force", external and superior to man, was later on provided a more rational and spiritual dimension and got conceptualized as the *brahman* of Vedantism. This same "force" has been provided a philosophical dimension in Western idealism in the shape of the notion of the Absolute. So far as early Buddhism is concerned it does not present the essential aspects of antique religions, as illustrated in ancient Egypt, Babylon and Mohen-

[1] E. Durkheim, *The Elementary Forms of Religious Life*, (E.T. by J. W. Swain, London, 1915).

jodaro ; it is developed form of religion. Hence the anthropological investigations into the origins of religions are more applicable to the Indus Valley religion and the earliest strata of the Vedic religions than to the Tripitaka Buddhism. There are some elements, however, in Buddhism which can be studied anthropologically.

If we study the Buddhist Tripiṭakas we do find in them remnants of elements of folk-culture and the primitive notions and practices of the masses of northern India. But early Buddhism does contain considerably vaster elements of a higher metaphysics and a lofty moral idealism also. The ideas and sermons of Zoroaster in Persia, of Lao-Tse and Confucious in China, of the ethically-oriental prophets in Palestine and of Gautama and Mahāvīra in India contain exalted moral and spiritual teachings which show a sufficient degree of theoretical sophistication and maturity. Buddha was a teacher of great renown[1] and philosophical illumination dawned upon him after he had undergone physical, mental and moral austerities of an extreme kind for six years. This central fact of Buddhahood—the prophetic vision of Buddha—must not be lost sight of. Buddhists do not accept any superconscious perfect reality as the source of liberating gnosis but in their view the dawn of a super-intellectual vision of the highest truth through *samādhi* is recognized and certain fact of experience. The *charismatic* leadership of Gautama Buddha was accepted because he was acclaimed to have had an authentic grasp of superior truth. He himself also always proclaimed that he had the thorough intuitional apprehension of truth.

But even if we accept this intuitional source of religion, we do have to acknowledge that the Buddhist movement operated in a definite social, economic and political background. This background does have some influence on a religious movement although it may not 'determine' or 'condition' the movement. Edward Caird says that the Indian Aryans could produce no

[1] Gautama Buddha was the acknowledged leader of the Samgha. According to M. Monier-Williams, *Buddhism*, pp. 71 ff., the samgha was not a hierarchy, nor an ecclesiastical organization under a centralized authority. As the first Head of the Samgha, Gautama had no successor. Nor was the Samgha the repository of theological or a meditating caste of priests.

higher social organisation than that of an aggregation of subject tribes under a despotic ruler. This social organisation, according to him, had both religious and ethical implications.[1] He says that for the same reason their polytheism did not develop towards the comparative order of the Greek pantheon. Hence also the growing consciousness of a unity beneath the multiplicity of the gods could only take an abstract form, the form of an undefined Being or substance, out of which all was supposed to come out and to which everything must return. Furthermore, he points out that the ethics which could spring from such a faith was only the negative ethics of an asceticism which renounced the world and withdrew from it as an empty illusion. If Edward Caird, a confirmed Hegelian idealist, can accept these religious and ethical consequences of the social structure of the ancient Indians, it appears that he is perilously, although unconsciously, near the Marxist historical materialist view of the origin and evolution of religious in response to the demands of the relations of production. Social, economic and political factors do have a vital influence on the growth and spread of a religious movement. Buddhism was not a purely intellectual or philosophical movement having the sole intention of controverting the idealism of the Upaniṣads. Buddha's aim was to indicate the moral and mystical path of emancipation to tormented humanity. But if he was not a philosopher of the cloister, withdrawn and isolated from human confrontations, neither can he be regarded as a radical reformer imbued with the sentiments of utilitarianism or democracy. The modern notions of social idealism, social justice and humanitarian solidarity were not his motivating factors and guiding forces. Nevertheless, he was concerned with the people and was pained at the sad plight of misery-stricken, anxious and desperate wayfarers. Furthermore, he did work for the success of his movement in a political and economic setup. Hence although he was concerned with the doctrines of *anātman* and *pratītyasamutpāda* he was also busy with the organisation of a large number of *bhikkhus* and *bhikkhunīs*. Thus there can be no denial of the fact that Gautama Buddha operated in a politico-economic framewokr and willingly or unwillingly he did have to deal with some

[1] Edward Caird, *The Evolution of Religion*, Vol. I, pp. 262-63.

social, political and economic problems.[1] Hence, it may be said that the personality of Buddha has more in common with that of Moses and Christ than of Kant. A study of the Tripiṭakas is essential to obtain a comprehensive picture of the environment in which Gautama lived and worked.

My own view with regard to the origin of religion may be called a synthesis of the Vedantic, Hegelian and Marxian methodologies. From the Vedanta I accept the fact of the personal illumination of the founder of a religion. I am not propounding here the ontological substantialistic reality of personal illumination in itself. What I want to state is that the founder of a religion does accept that he has obtained some significant illuminating experience. This personal belief which is psychologically objective for the founder, because of its dominating influence on him, is a factor with tremendous import. Unless he is a fake, this belief results in the tansformation of his life and character and his acceptance in the minds and hearts of his disciples is largely a consequence of *their* belief in their teacher having attained that supreme religious experience. In Vedāntism, the centrality of the transforming religious experience (*anubhava* and *sakshātakāra*) is very much emphasized. Buddhism, early Christianity and the mystic sects in India, China, Islam and the West do also accept the reality of this transforming experience. I have called this trend Vedantic only in order to highlight the importance of intuitional experience realised in *samādhi*, in this system. I do, however,

[1] The Buddhist Tripiṭakas contain references to various institutional practices which would indicate that some common features characterized the contemporary republican states and the Buddhist Samgha. B. K. Sarkar, *Political Institutions and Theories of the Hindus*, p. 149, refers to these features like majority decision, predominance of the voice of elders in a civic or public meeting and trial by jury (*uvvahika—the Cullavagga*, IV. 14, 19-21). Many of the provisions and regulations of the Buddhist Samgha were identical with those which were prevalent among other religious groups — S. Dutt, *Early Buddhist Monachism*, pp. 16, 28. But since there is no mention of any pre-Buddhistic order of nuns it may be a Buddhist innovation. Ātreyī (in the Ṛgveda), Maitreyī and Gārgi are isolated examples of learned women but there is no information regarding the evangelisation work done by any band of female ascetics. Hence the organisation of the Samgha for female monks (*bhikkhunī* and *therī*) seems to be an original contribution of Buddha to group organisation in ancient India.

acknowledge that this mystic experience is not the monopoly of the Vedanta.

I agree with Hegel in holding that there is a close connection between religion and the political principle. Religion, according to Hegel, is the sphere in which the nation defines its basic notions of Truth and God. Hegel regards absolute truth as the content of religion and as intuition, feeling and representative knowledge it aims to comprehend God. Everything else is to be seen in this light and depends on it for justification. He says in his *Philosophy of History* :

"The conception of God, therefore, constitutes the general basis of a people's character. In this aspect, religion stands in the closest connection with the political principle. Freedom can exist only where individuality is recognized as having its positive and real existence in the Divine Being. The connection may be further explained thus : Secular existence, as merely temporal—occupied with particular interests—is consequently only relative and unauthorized ; and receives its validity only in as far as the universal soul that pervades it—its principle—receives absolute validity ; which it cannot have unless it is recognized as the definite manifestation, the phenomenal existence of the Divine Essence. On this account it is that the State rests on Religion . . . While, however, the correct sentiment is adopted, that the State is based on Religion, the position thus assigned to Religion supposes the State already to exist ; and that subsequently, in order to maintain it, religion must be brought into it—in buckets and bushels as it were—and impressed upon people's hearts. It is quite true that men must be trained to religion, but not as to something whose existence has yet to begin. For in affirming that the State is based on Religion—that it has its roots in it—we virtually assert that the former has proceeded from the latter ; and that this derivation is going on now and will always continue ; *i.e.*, the principles of the State must be regarded as valid in and for themselves, which can only be in so far as they are recognized as determinate manifestations of the Divine Nature. The form of Religion, therefore, decides that of the State and its constitution. The latter actually originated in the particular religion adopted by the nation ; so that, in fact, the Athenian or the Roman State was possible only in connection with the specific form of Heathenism existing among the respective peoples ; just as a Catholic State has a spirit and constitution different from that of a Protestant one."[1]

Marx is correct in stressing the importance of the forces and relations of production in a religious movement. But his friend Engels is wrong in only referring to the legacy of primitive notions on religious ideas. They (Marx and Engels) are absolutely blind to the significance of the religious experience and they are also wrong in thinking that the relations of production have a 'determining' role on religious ideas. I do accept that the constellation of economic forces and economic institutions does play a significant part in the growth of a religious movement. In this book I myself have tried to indicate the influence of economic forces on the growth of Buddhism. But I do never uphold a theory of the causal or even conditioning role of the economic structure of society on a religious movement. Religious movements, in their turn, do initiate social and economic teachings also. Even mystically-oriented religions like Vedanta and Buddhism do inculcate social and economic precepts and propositions. Hence it is the process of a two-way impact between religion and economy.

Thus the methodology which I have pursued may be regarded as a critique of Marxism. I do accept that Buddha had undergone a vital phase of spiritual transformation. By asceticism and meditation he had obtained some super-normal experience. This personal intuitional experience is a very momentous element in studying the institutional and historical growth of Buddhism. I accept the conjoint role of the contemporary social, political, economic and cultural factors of the period, and not solely of economic factors. A comprehensive historical study of the political, social, economic and cultural factors has to be undertaken and their role indicated in the institutional development of Buddhism. Furthermore, the social, economic and political teachings of early Buddhism also have to be studied although it is true, we cannot get there a systematic theory of state and sovereignty or a sophisticated theory of Economics and Sociology.

[1] Hegel, *The Philosophy of History*, (E.T. by J. Sibre, Wiley Book Co., New York, 1944), pp. 50-51.

2. *Philosophical and Sociological Analysis of Buddhism*

Buddha was a great teacher of the ethical way. His basic problem was to obtain emancipation from the entanglements of the world because these are infected with transitoriness. There is no anchor or place of safety and refuge against the elemental sway of the primordial dark powers of total destruction and negation. From the dismal and satanic sway of death, the seers of the Upaniṣads had prescribed a return to the superior spiritual ultimate—the *brahman*. There are a few stray references in the Tripiṭakas which may, indirectly, indicate the possible belief of Buddha in an Absolute. But the overwhelming evidence of the general bulk of the Tripiṭakas is against the ascription to Buddha of any belief in absolutism. He starts in his famous formula of the *pratityasamutpādā* with the basal factor of ignorance. It is possible to argue that this monumental power of ignorance postulates the eventual, although remote, presence of some spiritual and truthful being, unmindfulness of whose existence results in the process of the chain of psychic becoming. But in original Buddhism, ignorance is not a cosmic power of creative becoming as in the Samkarite Vedantic metaphysics but is a subjective non-awareness of the four Aryan truths about the existence and removal of sufferings from the world. Since the force of ignorance is not a cosmic power of illusory creation, hence it is not possible to say that original Buddhism is a philosophy of illusionism. If *nirvāṇa* could mean the absolute extinction of all manifested phenomena, then it could have been possible to say that Original Buddhism is illusionism because against the mighty reality of an imponderable nihil the concrete processes and phenomenal becomings would be utterly non-existent and would be only illusory appearances. Hence I think that from the philosophical standpoint, original Buddhism is neither absolutism nor illusionism.

In all the great religions of the world we find that the acceptance of a transcendent and cosmic Godhead is a vital principle. The monotheistic religions frankly preach obedience to and firm devout faith in a great personal anthropomorphic Godhead. Even the polytheistic religions of Greece accepted some sort of a head in a divine pantheon. There can be no organized religious system and belief without a Godhead because the basis of religion is the rejection of the temptations of the lower selves for the sake of the realization of some superior realm of being. Buddha ridicules the theistic conceptions of his time. Thus early Buddhism is perhaps the only example in the history of religions to be constructed on the basis of the negation of a Godhead.[1] Sometimes it has been said that the silence of Buddha about metaphysical questions was an indirect indication of his view about the non-comprehensibility of superior truth by the ordinary intellect. Gandhi said that the purity and perfection of the personal life of Buddha are enough evidence to confirm his belief in a supreme divine principle. But regardless of such indirect, and to my mind, weak arguments to prove the belief of Buddha in a Godhead, the early Buddhist scriptures are consciously marked by the absence of any devout fervour for the majesty and providence of God which we find in the *Rgveda* or the Old Testament. Early Buddhism thus poses a serious problem for philosophy of religion. For the consummation and perfectibility of the religious life what is needed is not merely a primordial God as pure activity or a God as the foundation and guarantee for a moral life. Religion is postulated on the acceptance of a God who is all-merciful and compassionate and who can make responses to a life of devout communion. The theistic view of the world alone can make the world meaningful for a sensitive soul repelled by the transitory and evanescent character of worldly phenomena. It there is no feeling of responsive divine communion and fellowship and no assurance of an infinite immortality there can be no religious life. A materialist, a sceptic or a nihilist could criticize some of the degenerations of the theistic conceptions of pre-Buddhistic India. But in spite of some truth in these criticism, it is to be stated that no system of religious faith and discipline could be found in an atheistic world. We can have social and moral rules to organize our social relations in the absence of God, but it is absolutely meaningless and futile to plead for a religious life of inner fellowship in the

[1] W. B. Selbie, *The Psychology of Religion* (Oxford, Clarendon Press, 1923), pp. 109-110, 112, 119. C. C. Josey, *The Psychology of Religion* (New York, Macmillan & Company, 1927), pp. 52, 64.

absence of God. Religion without God, may sometimes be a mockery of words and a supreme example of self-deception. Hence in spite of great veneration for the personality and lofty character of Buddha, I do not regard Early Buddhism as a religion in the theistic and devout sense of the term.[1] But although early Buddhism may not be considered to be a religion in the traditionally accepted sense of a path to divine realization and communion and cultivation of a sense of dependence on God, it is to be deemed a religion in the sense of teaching a transcendence of the passions of the empirical ego and affirming the mystical quest for the raptures of contemplation (*jnāna*). Its elevated code of austere morals and its emphasis on the obliteration of sorrow and deliverance (*vimutti*) from all pain also impart to it the character of a religion.

Sometimes it has been said that Buddha was opposed to metaphysics because he was preoccupied with the problem of immediate release from the sufferings of the world. His stress on the healing of a wound caused by the arrow and not dialectical discussions about the structure of the arrow is supposed to indicate his pragmatic and positivistic temper. But he was not a pragmatist in the sense of stressing the factual contents of concrete sensuous experience. Modern Comtean positivism makes a fetish of science and believes in the regeneration of the world by the formation of a positivist society under the management of the priests of science. It is wrong to class Buddha as a Comtean positivist. Buddhist positivism does not aim to exalt physical science at the cost of speculative metaphysics. Buddha's insistence on the impermanence of worldly phenomena is completely antithetical to the ascription to him of the positivistic world-outlook. The pragmatism of Pierce, James, Dewey and others and the positivistic sociology of

[1] C. P. Tiele, *Outlines of the History of Religion* (E. T. from the Dutch by J. E. Carpenter. London, Trubner & Co., 1877) p. 137 : "Primitive Buddhism ignored religion." William James, *The Varieties of Religious Experience* (London, Longmans, Green & Co., 1941), pp. 31. F. B. Jevons, *An introduction to the Study of Comparative Religion* (New York, Macmillan & Co., 1920) pp. 247-49, refers to the denial of teleology in Buddhism. He says : "In Buddhism we have a developed religion—a religion which has been developed by a system of philosophy, but scarcely, as religion, improved by it."

Auguste Comte are utterly rooted in this world. They want to utilize the resources of human ingenuity and science for the transformation of the world. The temper of Buddha was absolutely and permanently permeated with the sense of complete disenchantment and utter sense of the insignificance of the cosmos. He is completely removed from the modern belief in the incorporation of bureaucratic and technological rationality in the social and economie structure of mankind. The problem of Buddha is a personal and an eternal problem. He was disillusioned with the world because there was no sense of stability in it. Although the problem of Buddha starts at a psychological level, it is eternal in the sense that death, disease, dismay and final disaster are in the permanent destiny of all human beings. Modern phenomenologists, Freudians, existentialists and neuro-psychologists also substantiate the view-point of early Buddhism in their stress on a fundamental "anxiety" as the impelling basis of man's existence.

Buddha wanted a way of escape and he found the way in the theory and practice of the negation and neutralization of the human ego. The ego is the root of all anxieties, neuroses, impeded impulses, deviant and psychopathic behaviour and compulsive strivings proceeding from the unconscious. Hence Buddha wanted the extinction of egohood which is the root of all *dukkha.* There is no apparent casual relation, nor perhaps any relation between the pursuit of an ascetic way of life and the ever-mighty fact of death because like a physical demoniac colossus, death equally reduces the noble and the unjust, the saint and the criminal to nullity. In a theistic system, which Buddhism is not, there is the belief in the conservation of moral efforts which finally results in a realization of spiritual fellowship and communion with God. The only rational connexion between an austere living and moral emancipation is the psychological feeling that by rejecting the things which lead to pleasure and comforts in life, man achieves a vicarious conquest over the all-negating, all-destroying power of death. The terror of death arises from the fact that it pulverizes all that a man holds dear. If it were possible to make a voluntary abandonment of these things which a man holds dear then to that extent the terror of death would be eliminated. Hence according to Buddha an ascetic negation and rejection of the things of the world and a steady, devoted pursuit of pure life are meant to provide emancipation. The uncertain and accidental character of death provides the justification of the passionate urgency with which Buddha and his disciples pleaded with the people to accept the Buddhist way and to seek salvation.

Buddha refused to accept the concept of the soul as a spiritual monadic substance. The Upaniṣadic conception of the identification of the psychic self and the cosmic-transcendent self also failed to satisfy him. The Sāmkhya-Yoga conception of the multiplicity of transparent selves did not evoke his sympathetic response. In her researches after 1927, Mrs. C.A.F. Rhys Davids had been desperately trying to give a positivistic and absolutistic interpretation of the message of early Buddhism. She even fabricated the fantastic thesis of the "unknown co-founders" of Buddhism. But in the philosophical and sociological study of religions we are not concerned with the dialectical play over obscure and insignificant words relegated to some, rather unimportant, corners of the scriptures, but we emphasize the vitality of the gospel. We mean to put the stress on one point : What is the message that has been promulgated with repeated emphasis ? To what points does the teacher constantly return and what elements does he constantly reiterate? If this standpoint is taken into consideration, we are constrained to think that early Buddhism emphasizes the neutralization and negation of subjectivism. It reduces the being and the personality of man into a psycho-physical complex of the five elements—*rupa*, *samjñā*, *vedanā samskāra*, and *vijñāna*. The negation of the human self as a spiritual and immortal principle shows the dangerous recoil of subjectivistic psychology on itself. In the Vedic religion the external world was regarded as of great ontological significance and the great Vedic deities were supposed to have physical and real existence. This ontological speculation received a check with the exaltation of the psychic principle in man. The Upanisads preach the glories of the mighty splendours of the *ātman* that is identical with *brahman*, which is the originating and the energising principle of the cosmos. But the critical and devastating attacks of early Buddhism were levelled not only against the supreme Absolute, the infallibility of the Vedic scriptures and the sanctity of the ritualistic cult but the concept of the self as an eternal principle was also pulverized. The use of the introspective method had thus attained its climax in the reduction of the spiritual self almost to utter nihil. This negation of the subjective entity shows the combined action of the philosophical and sociological principles in the formation and crystallization of the religious confraternity. By the denials of the Godhead and of the reality of the human spirit and by refusing to offer any coherent and systematic answers to the problem of the origination, the procession and the destiny of the universe, early Buddhism entirely negated those philosophical elements which constitute the essence of any religious system. Science tries to view the things of the world in terms of the manifestation of some primal material or vital principle. It tries to explain the cosmic in terms of the cosmic. But the distinctive criterion of religion is to explain the cosmic in terms of the supra-cosmic. If the physical sciences explain history in terms of the concatenation of physical processes and phenomena, the religious spirit seeks to understand history in terms of super-temporal eternity. The basic principle of the idealistic philosophy of religion is the acceptance of the revelation of eternity in the phenomenal modes of spatiotemporal location. From this standpoint the philosophical foundations of early Buddhist religion were weak but for what it lacked philosophically, it compensated sociologically. The exalted and inspired character of Buddha accentuated the notion of religious *charisma* associated generally with the personality of the founder of a religion. In spite of Buddha's negation of the eternal and immutable principles of the Upaniṣadic metaphysics, his inculcation of the moral way and his emphasis on the worthlessness and vanity of the things of this world, the foundation of a powerful order of monastic confraternity accentuated the belief in the transcendent character of the founder. Sociologically speaking, one of the basic principles of religion is the exaltation of the founder who is looked upon as the human centre of awe and reverence. The magnification of the religious leader is a cardinal element in the institutionalization of religion. Thus if from the philosophical standpoint Buddhism tends to negativism and nihilism, from the sociological standpoint it presents to us the picture of the accentuation of the reverence for the sacred personality of the leader. The reverence for the sacred leader is perhaps a legacy from the remote anthropological past of man.

SECTION TWO

EVOLUTION OF INDIAN RELIGION AND BUDDHISM

Chapter 3

THE VEDIC RELIGION AND THE ORIGINS OF BUDDHISM

1. *Introduction* : *Vedic Roots of Spiritual Idealism*

Since the beginnings of the rationalistic enlightenment in France with Diderot and Voltaire and the Kantian-Hegelian idealistic movement in Germany[1] the philosophical approach to religion became an organised branch of study and analysis.[2] Furthermore since the middle of the nineteenth century the sociological approach[3] to the problems of religion has also become significant in the works of Comte, Marx and Spencer. In the twentieth century Max Weber, Durkheim and Troeltsch are important names in this field. I will try to utilize in this book some of the concepts and notions made familiar by both philosophers and social scientists to study early Buddhist religion.[4]

[1] C. C. J. Webb, *Kant's Philosophy of Religion* (Oxford, Clarendon Press, 1926).

[2] Otto Pfleiderer, *Philosophy and Development of Religion* (Gifford Lectures at Edinburgh for 1894. Edinburgh, William Blackwood, 1894), 2 vols. Rudolf Otto, *The Idea of the Holy* (Oxford Univ. Press, 1928). A. Seth Pringle-Pattison, *Studies in the Philosophy of Religion* (Gifford Lectures at Edinburgh for 1923. Oxford Univ. Press, 1930).

[3] Hans Kelsen, *Society and Nature*, (London, Kegan Paul, 1946).

[4] Andrew Lang, *Myth, Ritual and Religion* (London, Longmans, Green & Co., 1899), 2 vols. Vol. I, pp. 206-245 ; Vol. II, pp. 148-183. P. Masson-Oursel, *Comparative Philosophy* (London, Kegan Paul, 1926). A.G. Widgery, *The Comparative Study of Religions* (London, Williams & Norgate, 1923). J.E. Turner, *Essentials in the Development of Religion* (London, George Allen, 1937), pp. 67-75. Raphael Karsten, *The Origins of Religion* (London, Kegan Paul, 1935), pp. 11-21. Willem F. Zuurdeeg, *An Analytical Philosophy of Religion* (London, George Allen, 1959), pp. 301-302. N. P. Jacobson, *Buddhism* (London, George Allen, 1966), Ch. VI. "The Buddhist Analysis of Culture", pp. 124-143.

The religion of the *Ṛgveda* and the *Atharvaveda* is concerned with reverence (*sraddhā* ; *havīshā vidhema* etc.) paid to external objective entities of nature like fire, earth, lightning, heavens, etc. But it is not correct to say that the religion of the Vedas can be regarded as only objective, as Edward Caird does. He accepted the Hegelian dialectical thesis of the sequential progression of religion from the objective stage to the subjective and from the subjective to the absolute stage. He interpreted the evolution of ancient Indian religion according to this scheme and regarded the Vedic religion as the example of objective religion, the Upaniṣads as representing subjectivism, and Buddhism as exemplifying the highest example of subjective religion.[1] Caird could not find any manifestation of the absolute stage of religion in India. It is possible, nevertheless, to locate in the Vedas traces of the concept of an Absolute, transcending the subject and the object, although the dominant theme is the worship of external objects of nature which symbolize power, strength, immensity and lustre and evoke sentiments of fear and awe.[2] The *Purusha Sūkta* represents the *purusha* as both transcendent and immanent and as the source of the entire cosmic procession, both subjective and objective. The long hymn ascribed to *Dirghatamas* in the first *manḍala* of the *Ṛgveda* contains the doctrine of *ekam sat* according to which the several deities are considered to be, in essence, the same as the primal pure spiritual existent.[3] The *Nāsadiya Sūkta* perhaps represents the culmination of the cosmological speculations of the Veda and the *ānidavātam svadhayā tadekam* contains the roots of the later concept of the Vedantic Absolute.[4] In it even the gods are said not to have known the secret of the cosmic and super-cosmic spirit. The *svadhā* is regarded as the conceptualization

[1] Edward Caird, *Evolution of Religion* (Gifford Lectures at St. Andrews, Glassgow, James Maclehouse & Sons, 1907, 2 vols), Vol. I. pp. 40, 42, 43-44, 53.

[2] Macdonell, *Vedic Mythlogy.*

[3] A. K. Coomaraswamy, "An Essay in Vedic Ontology", *J.A.O.S.*, 1935. W.N. Brown, "Creation Myth of the Ṛgveda", *J.A.O.S.*, 1942.

[4] V.P. Varma, "Decline of the Vedic Religion" *Journal of the Bihar Research Society*, December 1945, pp. 169-74.

of superior creative potency and the prototype of *māyā*.[1] Thus the *Nāsadiya* doctrine of Being (*ekam*) reveals to us an atmosphere different from the naive realism of the external worship paid to gods like Indra, Agni, Varuṇa, Soma and Vishnu. Nevertheless it remains true that the predominance of the worship of external nature-gods is the pervasive picture that we obtain of the Ṛgvedic religion.[2]

2. *Some aspects of the origins of the Upaniṣadic Religion and Philosophy in the Vedas*[3]

Since the time of Bādarāyaṇa, scholars and thinkers have been engaged in elucidating the secrets of the supra-sensible monistic idealism of the Upaniṣadic philosophy and the character of the monotheistic religion of the Upaniṣads. But the question of the relation of these words of knowledge to the Vedic wisdom has not yet been adequately taken up because the true import of the Vedic knowledge still remains to be finally deciphered and decided. The sacrificial-liturgical, polytheistic, mythological interpretations of Sāyaṇa, Mahidhara, and their followers, as also the naturalistic-historical interpretations of the European scholars backed up with numerous references to comparative religion, linguistic paleontology and anthropological researches into primitive social psychology are not adequate, although these contain a great amount of truth. The great vitiating factor in the matter of Vedic cultural research, so far, has been the unwarranted conscious and half-conscious predilection that the Veda contains only the remnants of an old quasi-enlightened civilization and hence one must not expect to embark thereupon any profound truth. Another source of

[1] A peculiar theory of the origin of Māyāvada, based on the juxtaposition of *brahman* as the regular and orderly procedure, and Māyā as the unregulated self-determined intervention of a god, is presented in Schayer's *Mahayamistische Erlosungslehre*. It has been criticized by A. B. Keith, *Religion and Philosophy of the Veda*, Vol. II, p. 532. There are references to mechanical and naturalistic conceptions of the universe in *Ṛgveda*, X, 81, 4.

[2] J. Muir, "Progress of Vedic Religion towards Abstract Conceptions of the Deity", *J.R.A.S.*, 1865.

[3] Section two was read at the session of the Indian History Congress at Patna, 1946.

misrepresentation of the Vedic wisdom has been the hasty application of the evolutionary methodology of Darwin and Spencer in the realm of history and culture. It is argued that because evolution means the development of the more differentiated, heterogeneous and complex types from the less differentiated, homogeneous and simple ones, in an uninterrupted straight line, and because we find in the Brāhmaṇas a developed mechanical sacerdotal ritualism, hence according to the evolution theory the pre-Brāhmaṇa age (the age of the Vedic Saṁhitās) must be an age of simple ritualism and unsophisticated worship of nature-powers with no advance in high thoughts. But history, sometimes, does provide data for a cycle-view of evolution with intermittent breaks and declines.[1] Great periods of cultural advance are sometimes followed by periods of retrogression. Hence if we maintain the thesis that the Vedic Saṁhitās contain some words of philosophic and cultural worth, higher than the sacrificialism of the Brāhmaṇas, this view should not be objected to on grounds of a false view of evolution theory. The infiltration of the Kassites brought down a decline of the previous magnificent Sumero-Semitic Babylonian culture and the penetration of the Barbarians spelled the downfall of the Hellenic-Roman legacy. On the analogy of these historical examples it should not be surprising to find that the advances made in thought and culture in the Vedic age receive a check during the period of the Brāhmaṇas, and are only taken again for further researches and comments with the emergence of the Upaniṣadic seers.

The religion of the Veda presents a composite and complex character. In this respect it is comparable to the Indus Valley culture. Just as the Indus Valley culture shows on the one hand crude religious conceptions and notions, but at the same time advances to a meditative subjective religion in the conception of the Yogi Siva, so also in the Vedas we find monotheistic descriptions emphasizing an ethical idealism as also glorifications of Soma-drinking and the feats of the warrior-gods. Between the philosophic achievements of the Vedas and the Upaniṣads there is the hiatus of the sacrificial mechanism and polytheism of the Brāhmaṇas. The Brāhmaṇas accept many of the Vedic

[1] Cp. Aristotle, Nietzsche and the Purāṇas.

notions and present them as legacies to the Upaniṣadic teachers. But generally we feel that during the Brāhmaṇa age the genius of the race had given up its philosophical and mystical pursuits and was exclusively absorbed in and had concentrated itself upon the rather lower task of sacrificial details.

We shall not concern ourselves here with the elucidation of the Upaniṣadic teaching—whether it is the monistic supra-rational mystic idealism of Śankara, or the pantheistic theism of Rāmānuja, or the absolute idealism of the type of Hegel, Bradley or McHaggart. Our problem here is historical—the elucidation of the philosophic origins and cultural derivations of the Upaniṣadic religion. Is the Upaniṣadic thought a reaction against sacrificial polytheism, formulated by the enlightened Kṣatriya class[1] or is the Upaniṣadic monism a crystallization out of the vague mysticism surrounding the sacrificial magic ? The Upanisadic philosophy of emancipation is regarded by some as indicating the world-disenchanted temper of the Aryans due to their migration from the Punjab, farther east. Others take to the fancy of a racial admixture as the cause of the vital changes in the Upaniṣadic thought in comparison to the Vedic thought.[2]

In accordance with the famous Hegelian formula of the historical development of religions—objective, subjective and absolute—Edward Caird considers the Vedic religion to be the example of the objective and the Upaniṣadic, of the subjective one. If this point of view is maintained then there seems to be a great difference between the two great religions—the one fundamentally concerned with nature and the other with the *psyche* and spirit. But we find that the Vedas had already advanced in the direction of the glorification of the subjective emotions like *manyu*, *sraddhā* etc. The highest Vedic god was not a cold featureless anthropomorphic deity, but was endowed with feelings and passions, as we see in the descriptions of Indra, Rudra and Usaṣ. The "soul" of the Upaniṣads is described in an exalted fashion in some of the Atharvan hymns and the *Sivasaṁkalpa-sūkta* of the *Yajurveda* shows advance in the

[1] This view of Deussen and others has been criticized by Dr. A.B. Keith, *Religion and Philosophy of the Vedas*, Vol. II.

[2] *Infra*, Chap. VI.

direction of higher psychology. The analysis of Caird is not quite correct, because the Upaniṣads conceive of the unity of the spirit and nature in the Brahman or Ātman and the Upaniṣadic 'Ātman' is not the subjective ego of western thinkers, but is the name of the highest reality.

The fundamental conceptions of the Upaniaṣdic religion and philosophy can be traced to the Vedas. We need not grope in the dark to seek the origin of the vital thought of the Upaniṣads—the unity of the cosmos and the psyche. The Nāsadīya hymn formulates the idea of the everconscient absolute reality wherefrom the cosmic procession starts, and this principle is carried to its logical point of development in the Vedantic formulas enunciated in the *Chhāndogya*, the *Brihadāraṇyaka*, the *Aitareya* and some of the other pre-Buddhistic Upaniṣadic texts.

Even in the famous *Dīrghatmas* hymn (Rv. 1. 164) we find the concept of *ekam sat* and this connotes not only a unity among the various gods as is apparent by the names of the several deities mentioned there, but it signifies also a unity of the entire creation—that there is only one existence. The Upaniṣads are anxious to preserve this concept of Unity and in their cosmological accounts we find a great solicitude to maintain the notion of unity lest it should suffer a dualistic attack from the cosmological side. Hence we find in the *Muṇḍaka* the metaphor of the *ūrnaṇābhi* (spider), and in the *Chhāndogya* the causal formula of *satkarya-vāda* maintained by the examples of earth, the iron-mass etc. The Vedic concept of the unity of the gods and of existence was not a mere haphazard poetic flash or a sudden temporary intuition. No doubt, the logical ratiocinative processes are not found here as we find in the later metaphysical Vedantic works or even in the Upaniṣads, but the manner of presentation shows that the Vedic seers were dimly conscious of the revelation that had dawned upon them.

We feel that this concept of unity was attained in three stages. First, the total supremacy of the individual godheads like Indra, Agni or Varuṇa and visualised,—the stage of 'henotheism' as Max Müller calls it. But this henotheism is not the highest pronouncement upon the Vedic religion and philosophy. The second stage was reached when all the great gods were identified. The third stage was reached when the unity of the gods was expanded to cover the unity of the entire cosmos, — the transition of the notion of unity from the realm of religion to the realm of philosophy. Some of the hymns of the *Atharvaveda* and the *Ṛgveda* contain such notions. The other ancient religions of Egypt, Western Asia and South-Eastern Europe stopped with an anthropomorphic monotheistic supreme deity, — Amen-Ra or Marduk or Zeus. In those countries the religion of the monistic absolute did not develop. The Upaniṣads, specially the *Kaṭha* and the *Śvetāśvatara* contain references to monotheism. In the Upaniṣads, when Brahman is contemplated mystically, we find that in the empiric sphere the way is naturally being prepared for a monotheism which the general mind will associate with cosmic functions. Thus in the Upaniṣads we find both monotheism and monism.

The development of monistic thought in the Veda and the Upaniṣads, not merely for the purposes of logical abstraction but also for the purposes of meditation shows the psychic advance of some of the priestly families of the Vedic Aryans during these early times. Compared to this the Chinese Tāo — which shows great approximations to the impersonalistic absolutistic ideal — is a late development.

In the Vedic cosmological accounts we occasionally find the notion of monotheism. The cosmological argument for theism we find maintained in many of the great religions, and although it has been criticised on philosophical grounds by Kant, it has been advocated by other thinkers. The later Nyāya philosophy unfolds it. The Vedic conception of Viśvakarman is the incipient crystallization of the cosmological argument for theism.

These Vedic cosmological accounts are the real sources of the Upaniṣadic cosmology. In the *Chhāṇdogya* and the *Taittirīya* we find the cosmological arguments for theism. Śaṅkara says that the cosmological arguments applies to the monotheistic godhead in the empiric phenomenal sphere.

Some aspects of the Upaniṣadic immanental pantheism also find Vedic parallels, although in the Vedas and the Upaniṣads the transcendental godhead is equally mentioned along with the immanental concept. In the dialogue of Nārada and Sanatkumāra in the *Chhāndogya* we find the *Bhūman* conception. In the *Ṛgveda* we come across a hymn, and the remarkable similarity, both terminological and conceptual, between this hymn, and the Upaniṣadic passage about the *Bhūman* must be pointed out.[1] It is strange why so long this Vedic hymn has not attracted the attention of Vedic savants.

The *Puruṣasūkta*, which occurs in the *Ṛgveda* and the *Yajurveda*, provides the inspiration for many of the Upanisadic conceptions. In the *Bṛhadaraṇyaka* we find the description of the sacrificial horse cosmically conceived. The various parts of the universe are taken to be various limbs of the sacrificial horse. In the *Muṇḍakopaniṣad* the different physical elements are regarded as the different limbs of the Brahman. These conceptions bear a remarkable parallelism with the Puruṣasūkta conception of the personal godhead; the latter may have provided the impetus to the *visvarūpadarsana* of the Gītā and also may be the original source of the Purāṇic conception of the manifestation and emanation of the totality of the cosmic phenomena from Śiva and Viṣṇu.

If we analyse in details we find that a considerable part of the Upaniṣadic terminology is taken from the Vedas. The same gods, the same Yajna and Tapas, Ātman and Brahman figure in both. We do accept that the Upaniṣads have modified and expanded the connotation of these terms.

The philosophic and religious meaning of the term Upaniṣad may be connected with the Vedas. According to Śaṅkara the term has the sense of elimination of sorrow and the realisation of ultimate reality. A.B. Keith illogically and unsuccessfully tries to refute this view. He emphasises only the sense of 'session' contained in the term, which (the session) led to the ascription of an esoteric character to the teachings propounded because of the secrecy involved. According to Oldenberg the term *Upaniṣad* connotes *upāsanā*—worship and reverence. The interpretation of Oldenberg emphasises the empirical aspect of the worship of the highest reality (of course when the highest reality is looked at from the point of view of Māyā), and it is similar to the view of Śaṅkara. Apparently, the act of worship involving a dualistic metaphysics runs somewhat counter to the monistic teaching of the Upaniṣads. But this interpretation can be justified in the sense that the Vedāntic contemplation is the culmination of worship. In the writings of the ancient and

[1] *Rv.* X, 36, 14.

medieval Christian theists and mystics we find the religion of contemplation emphasised. The contemplation of the Absolute is only the next higher step of the worship of the monotheistic god. The Chhāndogya says, *tajjalān iti sānta upāsīta*—the supreme energy of the world—creative, preservative and destructive—is to be calmly worshipped. Furthermore we get numerous references to the symbolical worship of the Absolute as the mind, the Āditya (sun), etc. This tradition of mystic absorption and meditation and also the worship of the highest godhead has a Vedic origin.

There was a time when the higher aspects of the Vedic religion and thought were not recognised, one of the main reasons being prejudice. The Vedic civilization may be contemporaneous with the great civilizations that flourished around the Mediterranean, but perhaps these latter did not attain the philosophic and literary height of the Vedic. Of the insistence of the Upaniṣadic religion and philosophy on worship, meditation and contemplation we find roots in the Vedic emphasis on Bhakti and Yoga and mysticism. The inspired hymns to Varuṇa are full of devotional emotionalism. The famous Gāyatrī hymn emphasises the collective practice of meditative abstraction. The picture of the inspired *muni* in the tenth Maṇḍala of the *Ṛgveda* shows acquaintance with supernormal powers associated with Yoga. The *Atharvaveda* and the *Yajurveda* contain many references to the various Prāṇas and their control, a feature of Yoga referred to in the *Kaṭha, the Śvetāśvatara* and even in the Pātañjala Darśana and the *Bhagavadgītā*. Even in the Mohenjodaro days we find this aspect of Yoga emphasized in the representation of Śiva. This figure of the proto-Śiva also shows a high ethical advancement because of the tender fervour displayed for the animal kingdom (in the figure). It seems that the Indus valley and Vedic associations of Śiva with the animal kingdom, as also the prophylactic character of Pūṣhan may have been the inspiration for the Buddhistic idea of representing the Buddha as deeply concerned with the sufferings of the animal world—a feeling which we find depicted in the Buddhistic artistic figures and in legends.

The Vedic religion is a composite one. It is, in Hegelian words, an example of the reconciliation of the religions of nature, of law and of spirit. The ritualistic side of this religion was emphasized by the Brāhmaṇas and the higher contemplative side by the Upaniṣads. But the period between the end of the Samhitā age and the Upaniṣads was not only one of sacrifice and ritual but was also rich in the development of thought. The certitude which characterises the philosophic assertions of the Upaniṣads presupposes a long antecedent past. This is also apparent from such phrases as *eke āhuḥ* and *ṛchābhyuktam.* There also was a development of sophistical teaching in the pre-Upaniṣadic period, which may trace itself to the references to scepticism found in the hymns. This sophistical teaching reached its climax in the teachings of the "six heretical teachers" and even in some aspects of the teachings of Buddha.

3. *Vedic scepticism as one of the roots of Buddhism*

But even in the days of the *Ṛgveda* a spirit of doubt about the existence and potency of gods had begun to infiltrate into the thought of some Vedic singers—*kasmai devāya havishā vidhema.* Some modern exponents interpret the word *kam* (in *kasmai*) as meaning blissful and hence regard this Ṛgvedic hymn as inculcating the necessity of the worship of the blissful Godhead. But the historical and comparative methodologists of Vedic interpretation regard this hymn as a definite indication of the emergence of scepticism. There are other hymns which also contain sceptical views. The growth of scepticism[1] in the Vedic period is immensely significant from the standpoint of the origins of Buddhism. Buddha launched a protest movement against the contemporary systems of worship, ritualism and Brahmaṇical sacerdotalism. It may well be suggested that the thinkers and poets who began critical reflections on the Vedic religious ideas and practices and expressed sceptical notions are the precursors of the heterodox systems of Buddhism and Jainism.[2] Yaska's *Nirukta* refers to Kautsa who regarded the Vedas as *nirarthakāh* (meaningless). In the

[1] For sceptical notions see *Ṛgveda,* VIII, 96, 13-15 ; II, 1, 5 ; VIII, 3, 103 ; IV. 24, 10.

[2] The *Mahābhārata,* XII, 218, contains references to heretical teachers at the courts of ancient kings. According to Pandya, *Intelligent Man's Guide to Indian Philosophy,* p. 123, the atheistical notions referred to in the *Mahābhārata,* produced the doctrines of the Cārvakas, the Jainas, the **Sāmkhyas** and the Buddhists.

dialogue of Pañcaśikha and Janaka Janadeva in the *Śāntiparva*, the former refers to atheistical views. The Buddhist scriptures refer to twenty-three previous Buddhas who preceded the historical Sākyamuni.[1] Buddha himself claimed to be only an expounder of the old norm. Hence it may be legitimate to attempt to find the roots of the Buddhist revelation and teachings in the later Vedic tradition of quest, criticism and scepticism. Buddha is not only silent regarding the monistic and pantheistic metaphysics but is also indifferent, if not explicitly hostile, to the conception of a monotheistic Godhead. Almost all the Semitic religions like Hebraism, Christianity and Islam, the Egyptian and the Mesopotamian religions, and the Aryan religions believe in a supreme deity. But Gautama Buddha appears to be an atheist. The source of Buddhist atheism must be sought in the Vedic traditions of scepticism.

Since the Vedic days there were rationalistic and sceptical thinkers. In the *Ṛgveda*, II, 12, 5 and VIII, 100, 34, there is a denial of Indra's existence. In the *Ṛgveda* X, 117, there is stress on benevolence without the solicitation of the help of any gods. In the *Ṛgveda*, X, 151, 5, Śraddha *Kāmāyani* is asked to make men faithful and this is perhaps an indirect indication that men were losing faith. Sometimes it has been held that there is a note of scepticism and doubt in the *Nāsadiya hymn* (*ko addhā veda*) and in the famous strain—*kasmai devāya havisha Vidhema.* There is a note of humour in the *Ṛgveda* IX, 112, and of satire in the *Ṛgveda*, VII, 103. Perhaps the people who advocated one or other of such views are called exponents of the Āsura views in the *Chhāndogya*, VIII, 8, 4-5.

A study of the genesis of religious reforms points out that the founder of a religion is not an isolated genius but he synthesizes and brings to a united focus the inchoate insights that have been attempting to permeate the intellectual climate for quite sometime. The great teachers are not the accidental freaks of history unrelated to the trends and ethos of the age but can be said to be the explicit crystallizations and authentic expressions of the implicit and latent forces that have been

[1] S. Beal, *Romantic History of Buddha*. R. S. Hardy, *The Legends and Theories of the Buddhists* (London, Frederick Norgate, 2nd ed. 1881), p. 154.

struggling to receive an audible voice. Hence the roots of some dominant elements of the Buddhistic protest have to be traced to the antecedent historical conditions and intellectual forces that were slowly becoming strong since the later Ṛg-vedic times.[1] A similar evolutionary hypothesis is relevant for the genesis of the other historical religions as well. There are elements in Judaism which point out its affiliations with the earlier Sumerian and Egyptian religions. Christianity owes a substantial portion of its ethics and theology to Judaism. Islam has borrowed from Christianity and Judaism.[2] Buddhism has derived not only a number of philosophical categories from the Upaniṣads but its mood of criticism and protest are possibly derived from those teachers of the later Ṛgvedic and Upaniṣadic period who failed to obtain any consolation from the complicated mechanism of the sacrificial religion.[3] Thus the spirit of philosophical speculation which generated an inner and subjective orientation and which failed to be satisfied with the invocation to the deities of a pluralistic pantheon found its expression in the personality of Buddha who exalted the sentiments of anti-Brāhmanical protest.[4] In pre-Buddhist and

[1] For references to materialistic doctrines in ancient India see *Sarvadarśanasamgraha*, *Shaddarśana-samuccaya*, *Nyāyamanjari* and *Tarkarahasyadīpikā*, D. Sastri. *A History of Indian Materialism, Sensationalism and Hedonism*, points out four stages in the development of Indian materialism : (i) the Bārhaspatyas (ii) *Svabhāvavāda* or *Lokāyata*. Ajita Kesakamabala, Purana Kassapa and Kaṃbalāsvatara belonged to this school, (iii) the extreme hedonism of the Cārvakas and (iv) the reaction against spiritualism leading to the identification of the self with mind, thought etc. But Sastri lamentably fails in analysing the elements of naturalism, mechanism and scepticism in the Vedas. See V.P. Varma *Bhartiya Darśana*.

[2] For the influence of the Cretan and Homeric religion on the Hellenic religion and related topics, see Hall, *History of Ancient Near East*.

[3] H. Oldenberg, *Buddha*, p. 18 says : "...the process of the self-destruction of the Vedic religious thought which has produced Buddhism as its positive outcome." Max Müller, *Ancient Sanskrit Literature* (Allahabad, Panini Office, 1912), p. vii, refers to traces of the "Buddhistic Crisis" in the latest productions of the Vedic literature. He also says : "It is possible to discover in the decaying literature of Vedic Brahmanism the contemporaneous rise of a new religion, of Buddhism." (*Ibid*, p. 135.)

[4] Max Müller, *Ancient Sanskrit Literature*, p. 17, says that people in India were prepared by centuries of thought and meditation and by the corruption of the Brahmanical system to embrace the religion of Sākya.

Buddha's times there were several teachers who protested against the Vedic authority. The nature of their protest can be compared to that of the protest of Pratardana and Bhāradvāja. The Tirthaka teachers did not care even to know the Brahmanical literature and system. Certainly some aspect of their protest against Vedicism was as outspoken as that of Buddha. The protest of these monastics, ascetics, dialecticians, sophists and sceptics sought to subvert the theological and ritualistic foundations of Brāhmanism.

In this chapter the hypothesis sought to be proved has been that Buddhism was no accidental creation in the history of Indian thought. Several European Indologists have been content with tracing the roots of Buddhism to the Upaniṣads. But I have accepted the hypothesis that it is possible to trace the germs of the Buddhistic protest in some of the hymns of the Vedas. From the later Vedic times there were thought-currents which protested against the priestly sacrificial ritualism and the pluralistic pantheon. Buddha's was the most eloquent expression of protest against the traditional theology, priestcraft and sacerdotal ritualism.

But in emphasizing a long pre-Buddhist history of the forces and trends which served as the foundations of Buddhism, I do not mean to minimize the great eminence of Buddha's personality. The greatness of a world-historical personality lies in his accurate perception of the declining and dominant forces of an age and in his singular imagination in making some of his own notions and propositions serve as the symbols of the forces with which he identifies himself. No great man operates in isolation or in sheer imagination. As a religion and as an ethical philosophy, Buddhism was concerned with the problems of moral perfection, emancipation from sorrow, and the attainment of gnosis and illumined *noesis* (*prajñā*). But Buddha's gospel would not have been able to attract large adherents unless directly or indirectly it would have associated itself with some of the contemporary social forces. Thus it should not appear strange that along with the discussions of Abhidhamma psychology and the concepts of *ānantyāyatana*, *dhyāna* and *atakkāvacara*, the Tripiṭakas also address themselves to the problems of social philosophy

CHAPTER 4

THE POST-VEDIC RELIGION AND THE ORIGINS OF BUDDHISM

1. *The Development of the Yajña in the Brāhmaṇas : Cult and Myth*

DIFFERENT PERSON and societies have stressed different aspects of religions and hence the connotation of this word has also varied in the different cultures. The Vedantists emphasize supernormal mystic consciousness and higher inward experience as the basis of religion. Yogins and sages testify to the authenticity of supramental experience. But the masses and priests have been fundamentally concerned only with the ceremonial and ritualistic aspects of religions. They devote their attention and energies primarily to the several rites and sacrifices. The application of the critical and comparative method to the study of the sacrifices and rituals would reveal the positive mundane aspects of mass psychology and popular religious consciousness. Sacrifices formed an integral part of religion among the ancient Jews, Egyptians, Phoenicians and Cretans and possibly also among the Sumero—Semitic Babylonians and the Hittites. Among these people animals were killed in the sacrifices. Even among the Vedic Aryans sacrifices to Agni, Soma, Indra and Vishnu formed an important aspect of the contemporary religion.[1] So for as the people of Mohenjodaro and Harappa are concerned it is not possible to state anything definite about the prevalence of sacrifices amongst them.

The ritualistic aspects of the Vedic religion were expounded in the Brāhmaṇas, the principal of which is the *Satapatha.* This is a monumental book and contains the detailed formulas

[1] Ragozin, *Vedic India*, p. 382ff.

of the sacrificial mechanism of the Vedic cult. Regarding the ancient Vedic compositions one can never make positive statements about their dates but so much is sure that the 8th century B.C. may be regarded as the lower limit of the date of the composition of the *Śatapatha Brāhmaṇa.*[1] Perhaps the upper limit of the date of the composition of the literature of the Brāhmaṇas may go as far back as the 12th century B.C. Jacobi regards 1,000 B.C. as the end of the Brāhmaṇa period. Besides the *Śatapatha*, the *Taittirīya Brāhmaṇa* is also of importance. The central feature of the Vedic religion is the ritual or *yajña*. The deities who are invoked and worshipped in the process of the sacrifices naturally become the centre for the fabrication of numerous legends and myths. Thus during the days of the Vedas and the Brāhmaṇas the cults and myths are very much interrelated. It would be an exaggeration, however, to assert that the cult is the source of myths.[2] So much, however, can be said that in spite of their reciprocal influence, the cult is the more dominant aspect of the Vedic religion. The various types of sacrifices constitute the centre of Vedic ritualism. In the *Yajurveda* and the *Śatapatha Brāhmaṇa* is found the classic description of the Vedic sacrifices. The priests were so much obsessed with the potency of the sacrifice that the Vedic demiurgos Prajāpati, was identified with the sacrifices.[3] The *Śatapatha* goes to the extent of identifying Vishnu and the *yajña*.

2. *Upaniṣadic Idealism and Pantheism*

The dominant theme of the Upaniṣads is the inculcation of the supremacy of the brahman.[4] It is regarded as the prin-

[1] According to Jacobi, referred to in Th. Stcherbatsky, "Pre-Buddhaic Buddhism", *Central Conception*, the *Kaṭha Upaniṣad* which belongs to the 8th century B.C. contains roots of pre-Buddhaic Buddhism and also traces of pre-Jina Jainism. Stcherbatsky also regards the *Kaṭha* as pre-Buddhistic.

[2] Ernst Windisch, *Buddha's Geburt Und die Lehre von den Seeldenwanderung* (Leipzig, 1908), holds that although Buddhism borrows from Brahamaṇism a mythology, it has also a mythology of its own.

[3] *SB.*, 1,5,1,16 ; VI, 3.5. *Panchavimśa Brāhmaṇa*, VII, 2, 1.

[4] H. Oldenberg, *Die Lehre der Upanishaden*. R.D. Ranade, *A Constructive Survey of Upaniṣadic Philosophy*. Jacobi "Early History of Indian Philosophy", *Indian Antiquary*, 1918. U. C. Bhattacharya, "Pre-Upaniṣadic Teachers of Brahmavidyā", *Indian Historical Quarterly*,

ciple which provides the rational justification for the manifold plurality.[1] Paul Deussen is of the view that the doctrine of *brahman* was formulated in an atmosphere different from that of the sacrificial mechanism.[2] He regards it as a legacy of the Kshattriya cosmologists like Pravāhaṇa Jaivali, Ajātaśatru and Janaka[3] and says that the Brāhmins, later on, appropriated this concept.[4] The Kshattriya thinkers and kings are said to have made some notable contributions to ancient philosophy of India. (i) Pravāhaṇa Jaivali imparts the doctrine of transmigration (*panchagnī vidyā*) to Uddālaka; (ii) according to the *Chhāndogya*, 1, 8 and 9, Pravāhana imparts the doctrine of ether as the *arche* to the Brahmins and (iii) there are instructive conversations between Ajātaśatru Kāśya and Drīpta Bālāki, and Aśvapati Kaikeya and Uddālaka. Oldenberg holds that the concept of *brahman*, the idea of the essence of reality, gradually became distinct from the heaps of confusions of the notions of those days. He says : "...the farther thought goes, the more clearly

Vol. III, 1927, refers, definitely unconvincingly, to a *shloka* class of literature as the predecessors of the Upaniṣadic literature.

[1] A.B. Keith, *Religion and Philosophy of the Veda*, Vol. II, p. 469, says that parallel with this recognition of the principle of absolute all-containing unity was the decline from power of Varuna.

[2] Some scholars tend to think that *brahman* represents the abstraction of the force of the sacrifice ; *e.g.* S. N. Dasgupta, *Indian Philosophy*, I, pp. 35-37. He lists three meanings of *brahman* ; (i) *mantra*, (ii) duly performed sacrifice and (iii) power of sacrifice.—*Indian Phil.*, I, pp. 210-11. According to Hillebrandt, *brahman* signifies a mysterious power.

[3] J. Hertel, *Weisheit der Upanishaden*, also accepts the Kshattriya origin of the doctrine of *brahman*. Keith A.B., *Religion and Philosophy of the Veda and the Upaniṣads*, Vol. II, p. 447. S. Radhakrishnan, *Indian Philosophy*, Vol. I, p. 439, says. "Both Upaniṣads and Buddhism allowed the highest spiritual dignity to the poor and the humble... "But this statement is absolutely unwarranted so far as the Upaniṣads are concerned. If we apply the modern criteria of sociological investigations it would be clear that the Upaniṣads, in spite of their theosophic flights and monistic speculations contain an atmosphere of caste arrogance and preach the superiority of the two higher orders. It is incorrect to interpret the Upaniṣadic teachings in terms of the ethical idealism of the Christian Gospels.

[4] According to Garbe, quoted in Keith, *Religion and Philosophy*, II, 494, there is a four-fold contribution of the Kshattriyas : (a) monistic metaphysics, (b) *Karman* ethics, (c) the Sāmkhya doctrines and (d) Kshattriya doctrines at the basis of Buddhism.

do they [*i.e.* the powers and symbols on whose working is fancied the system of the universe to rest] appear to rest on great fundamental forces, from which their existence is principally derived..."[1] But he denies that we can trace the genesis of the conception of unity in the Vedic text. To me, the views both of Deussen and Oldenberg appear far-fetched. Keith has refuted the thesis that the *brahman* cosmogony is a creation of the Kshattriya heads of the then clans and kingdoms. I have stated earlier that it is possible to trace the roots of the concepts of a primordial spiritual existent in the *nāsadiya* hymn. This Ṛgvedic notion of a primal omnipotent spirit was further developed and received its classic exaltation at the hands of the Upaniṣadic teachers.[2] Thus it is possible to state that the doctrine of *brahman* is the natural development, at the hands of the writers of the Āraṇyakas and the Upaniṣads, of the notions of *ekam sat* and *ānidavātam svadhayā tadekam* which are formulated in the *Ṛgveda*. Sometimes it is said that the very word *brahman* has a monotheistic origin. *Brahman* signifies great, that is great in relation to the other deities and devas. In origin, the basic notion behind *brahman* may be the same as in the Polynesian word *taboo* (*tabu* or *tapu*) and the Melanesian word *mana*. Among the primitive tribes the king and the priest were regarded as possessing the taboo which was regarded as the heralder of a portent once some forbidden things were done.

3. *The Religion of the Upaniṣads*

The Upaniṣads contain references to the absorptive contemplation of the absolute or *brahman*. The prevalent view about ancient Indian religion has been that either it implies a polytheistic objective religion or there is the stress on the realization of the monistic Absolute in a state of ecstatic calm. In this absolutist conception the aspect of the worship of a monotheistic Godhead is neglected. It is possible, nevertheless, to find in the Upaniṣads numerous passages which teach the

[1] Oldenberg, *Buddha*, p. 23.

[2] The word "Upaniṣad" is interpreted in three ways : (i) It means the destruction (*viśaraṇa*) of innate ignorance ; (ii) It means the path (*gati*) of *brahman* and (iii) It signifies spiritual and metaphysical concourse.

worship of one supreme God and it may even be said that the Spirit which is reflected upon at the philosophic level is also worshipped at the religious level. The worship of a monotheistic Godhead must have been prevalent in the Upaniṣadic period. Our view that during the Upaniṣadic days there was the inculcation of the worship of a monotheistic Godhead[1] should not appear surprising because even in the later periods of Indian religious history we find that the *Vishistādvaitavāda* of Rāmānuja was based on the worship of one supreme Godhead. The *Chhāndogya* proclaims *tajjālaniti śānta upāsīta*[2]—the God who is the creator, the sustainer and the destroyer of the cosmos should be worshipped peacefully. Hence it is possible to state that while the highly educated and spiritually-oriented individuals would engage themselves in philosophical meditations, the less educated would be told to worship the one supreme God,[3] the masses being content with their pluralistic pantheon. This worship of the one great Godhead is akin to the worship of the Mahā Brahmā referred to, in the *Brahmajāla Sutta.* Thus it is possible to point out two layers in the religious thought of the Upaniṣads. While the spiritual aspirants are to practise *śravaṇa*, *manana*, and *nididhyāsana* as steps towards the realization of the supreme *brahman*, the philosophically-oriented religious devotees would, at a more empirical plane, perform the worship of the monotheistic Godhead and would practise the *japa* of *Om*[4] and *udgītha*.[5] In

[1] Cf. *SB.*, I, 1,6,14 : He who sacrifices to the gods does not gain so great a world as he who sacrifices to the *Atman.*

[2] Deussen, *Phil. of the Upaniṣads*, (Eng. trans. by A.S. Geden, Edinburg, T. & T. Clark, 1906) pp. 180-181, thus explains this cosmological formula :

(i) *tad—brahman*,
(ii) *ja*—the universe has developed,
(iii) *li*—disappears,
(iv) *ana*—in *brahman*, at the time of its origin, the universe lives and moves.

[3] S.N. Dasgupta, *Indian Philosophy*, Vol. I, p. 430.

[4] Cf. the Uktha of the *mahāvrtta* ceremony described in the *Aitareya Āranyaka*, II, I, 3. In the *Chhāndogya*, II, the *Udgīttha* is identified with the absolute.

[5] According to Oldenberg, *ZDMG*, Vol. 1, 457 ff. and *Die Lehre der Upanishaden*, pp. 37, 348, the real sense of the word *Upaniṣad* is reverence or worship—*upāsanā*. S.N. Dasgupta, *Indian Philosophy*, I, p. 45 also

medieval times in India we find that Śamkara, although one of the greatest teachers of Vedantic monism, worshipped, as tradition has it, the great God Śiva as the supreme Godhead.

4. *Monism and the Origins of Monasticism*

Brahman also signifies the unity of the microcosm and the macrocosm or of the psychic and the cosmic principles. This thesis is expounded in the discourses of Uddālaka and receives its classic statement in the *Brihadāraṇyaka Upaniṣad* which is a part of the *Śatapatha Brahmaṇa*. Yājnavalkya formulates the doctrine of the cosmic Absolute who is also supra-cosmic. He teaches one of the cardinal tenets of idealism[1]—the unknowability of the subject. The practical and moral implication of this metaphysics of *brahman* is the exaltation of the monastic ideal.[2] Yājnavalkya states: "Knowing him, the *Ātman*, Brāhmaṇs relinquish the desire for posterity, the desire for possessions, the desire for worldly prosperity and go forth as mendicants." Thus philosophical idealism and ethical monasticism are vitally linked up in the teachings of Yājna-

refers to the theistic element involved in the conception of *brahman* as *antaryāmin* holding the universe in his *praśāsana*. Even the Vedic Varuṇa, Mitra and Aryaman contain elements of being pure benevolent deities. Indra is also worshipped as a mighty God and saviour according to *Ṛgveda*, IV, 17, 17 ; X, 112,10 ; V, 3,9. Saunders, *Gotama Buddha*, p. 106, is needlessly critical of the Vedas and pre-Buddhistic teachers for not having formulated the conception of a supreme, righteous and loving God. In the *Chhāndogya*, Sanatkumar admits that various entities could be worshipped symbolically but in the case of the masses these symbols could become idols. See Deussen, *Philosophy of Upaniṣads*, pp. 113ff.

[1] Yājnavalkya's statement, '*na pretya sanjñā asti*' (*BAU*, II, 4,12) however, prepares the ground for materialism according to some ancient thinkers. Barnett, attempts a compromise by saying that Yājnavalkya's expression is of a materialist but his argument is that of an idealist.

[2] Oldenberg, *Buddha*, p. 49 "...the dualism of impermanence and permanence which influences all thought in this age, here imposes from the first on the idea of deliverance and on the ethical postulates which flow from it, this negative character : morality is not a form of active participation in the world but a complete severance of self from the world." The examples of Krishna, Buddhna, Śamkara and others would, however, show that the Indian ethical ideal has always *also* insisted on a full participation in temporal activities for the uplift of the veil of sorrow, although renunciation and isolation have been no less lauded. *Lakasangraha* and *sarvalokānukampā* have also been regarded as vital formulas of the Indian ethical life.

valkya. Oldenberg thus comments upon this development. "This is the earliest trace of Indian monasticism ; from those Brahmans who knowing the *Ātman* renounce all that is earthly and become beggars, the historical development progresses in a regular line up to Buddha, who leaves kith and kin, and goods and chattels to seek deliverance wandering homeless in the yellow garb of a monk.[1] According to Oldenberg there were two important factors in the development of pre-Buddhaic monasticism : (i) The cohesion of monks and ascetics into organized fraternities and (ii) the emancipation of at least a majority of them from the authority of the Vedas. It is true that the monasticism of the Buddhists and Jains has its roots in the practice of the pre-Buddhist monks,[2] one of whom was Yājnavlkya.[3] But Oldenberg does not seem to be correct in his statement that this is the earliest beginning of the monastic movement. In the *Ṛgveda* there are reference to *munayah* whose pattern of life was radically different from that of the common people.[4] Moreover, the *Atharvaveda* contains a *sūkta* extolling the *brahmacārin*. The Vedic *brahmacārin* is not a mere seeker of mental knowledge but has to be thoroughly trained in the control of his senses and has to lead a life of discipline, fervour and meditation. It is true that he is not a life-long monk but,[5] nevertheless, his way of life is almost that of a

1 Oldenberg, *Buddha*, p. 31.

2 B.M. Barua, "The Ājivikas", *Journal of the Department of Letters*, Calcutta University, Vol. II, 1920, pp. 1-80, opines that the Ājivikas derive their origin from an ancient *vānaprastha* or *vaikhānasa* order, which was founded 117 years before Makkhalī Gośāla.

3 There is one difference between Yājnavalkya and Buddhą. The former renounced the world after having gained knowledge. But the renunciation of Buddha is for the sake of knowledge—*vividisā sannyāsa*. The question of Upaka Ajivaka to Buddha : "whom do you follow friend in leaving the world ?" Would indicate that acceptance of a teacher by a monastic disciple was a common practice during the time of Buddha.

4 *Ṛgveda*, X, 136.

5 *T.B.* III, 12. 3, says that the gods attained divine rank by asceticism. It may be pointed out here that European scholars like Hertel and Keith have entirely failed in grasping the moral dignity of the life of the ascetic. It is an example of cultural differences making the mind pre-disposed to minimizing the significance of a way of life which is not one's own. In the use of the words "foolish asceticism", Keith, *Religion and Philosophy of the Vedas and the Upaniṣads*, Vol. II, p. 594, has only shown the pettiness of his mind.

monastic. The *Chhāndogya Upaniṣad* also sings the glories of *brahmacarya* as the highest *yajnā*. According to the *Muṇḍaka* and the *Praśna Upaniṣads*, *brahmacarya* is one of the most necessary requirements for initiation into spiritual esotericism. Furthermore, the Vedas exalt the practice of *tapas* and state that through its systematic cultivation it is possible to conquer death.[1] Even the entire cosmos is regarded as having proceeded from the creative potency of *tapas*.[2] The Upaniṣads mention the *tāpasa*. It may be inferred that the ascetic is a Vedic figure because the Upaniṣadic statements do not indicate that they are referring to some new institutional innovation. Hence it may be possible that in all likelihood the ascetic (*tapasvi*) is a Vedic institution. In the utterances of Yājnavalkya are found the philosophical advocacy of the doctrine of the eternal spiritual real and the inculcation of the ethical teaching of monasticism.[3] But monism and monasticism are not irrevocably associated. In the Upaniṣads there are teachers who preach spiritual monism and monistic idealism but who lead the lives of householders. Uddālaka, the father of Śvetaketu, formulates concepts of spiritual metaphysics, perhaps as important as those of Yājnavalkya but he is a householder. Aśvapati Kaikeya, Ajātśatru of Kāśi and Pravāhaṇa Jaīvali are important champions of monistic idealistic metaphysics without being advocates of *sannyāsa*.[4] Thus Oldenberg appears to be wrong in generalizing perhaps

[1] *Ṛgveda*, X, 90.

[2] Cf. R. Mehta, "Asceticism in pre-Buddhist Days", *Indian Culture*, Vol. 3. 1936-37, pp. 571-84.

[3] O. Pfleiderer, *Philosophy of Religion*, Vol. IV, p. 104 and Vol. III. pp. 59-66 points out that the Brahmanic ideal of redemption was esoteric, scholastic, idealistic and monistic and hence it never passed beyond the Philosophical circle. But Buddha gave a new turn to the doctrine of salvation because (i) he severed the scholastic portions from the ethical parts : (ii) he typified the ideal of salvation in his own person and (iii) he organized the holy life. Hence there appear great differences between the teachings of Yājñavalkya and those of Buddha.

[4] The Taittirīyas, Gautama, Baudhāyana, Āpastamba and Vaśishtha advocate marriage. According to Baudhāyana, II 6,11,26-27,34 originally only one order of the householders existed. The other three orders were introduced by Kapila, son of Prahlāda, who disagreed with the gods *i.e.* Brahmins. See B. M. Barua, *A History of Pre-Buddhist Philosophy*, pp. 246-47.

from the solitary example of Yājnavalkya that monism and monasticism are associated in the Upaniṣadic thought. I have earlier pointed out that monism has its rudimentary beginnings in the *Ṛgveda.* If the word *munayah* in the Ṛgveda is a correct reference to wandering ascetic thinkers and anchorites then it is possible to hazard the hypothesis that Buddha, Mahāvira, and even Yājñavalkya himself were rather following a way of life that had its roots in the later Vedic period.[1] Thus just as in the matter of philosophic attitude, the roots of Buddhism lie in Vedic scepticism, so also it is possible to find the roots of its monasticism in the Vedas.[2] Hence in tracing the origins of Buddhism we have to rest content not only with the Upaniṣads but have to go back still earlier to the Vedas. Thus it is possible to state that the Vedic literature contains the roots of three types of later developments: (i) The ritualistic sacrificialism of the Brāhmaṇas and the Sutras has its Ṛgvedic roots. (ii) The Upaniṣadic spiritual absolutism has its roots in the cosmogonic and theosophic speculations of the *Ṛgveda* and the *Atharvaveda.* (iii) The protestant movements of Jainism, Buddhism and Sāmkhya have their roots in the Vedic sceptical hymns. The Vedas are the miscellaneous works of different types of minds belonging to various schools of thought and religious practice and it is not at all surprising that the roots of three types of religious and philosophical movements should be found in them.

5. *The Attitude of the Upaniṣads and Buddhism towards the Vedas.*

The Upaniṣads adopt an ambivalent attitude towards the

[1] The *Muṇḍaka Upaniṣad* also refers to a class of monastic monks, the *muṇḍa*. The Vedic *munayah* and *yatayah* appear to be the earliest prototypes of monks and wanderers. The *Śatapatha Brāhmaṇa* contains the words *arhat* and *śramana.* E.J. Rapson, *Ancient India,* (Cambridge University Press, 1916, 3rd ed.), p. 57, states that there is close connexion between the *Śatapatha Brāhmana* and Buddhism and one point referred to by him in this connexion is that, this work lists the Gautamas as teachers and the patronymic Gautama was adopted by the Kshattriya family in which Buddha was born.

[2] According to C.A.F. Rhys Davids there were two non-Brahmanical doctrines in Buddhism—(i) The study of mind-ways as apart from the man and (ii) the growth of monasticism in which the standard of manhood was lowered to mean not something capable of becoming Godhead but something it was better to end.

Vedas. At some places they relegate the Vedas to the department of inferior knowledge but at some other places they would accord to them a place of honour. Some passages of the Upaniṣads even adopt an attitude of mild reverence for the Vedas. One *Brihadāranyaka* passage (II, 4, 19) ascribes infallibility to the Vedas and holds that they have a supernatural origin from the great Being.[1] In the *Chhāndogya*, (III, 5, 4), the Veda is considered to be a nectar and the Upaniṣads are held to be the nectar of nectar. In the *Kena Upaniṣad*, the Vedas are regarded as the "sum of the parts"—*Vedāh sarvāngāṇi.*[2] The Upaniṣads call themselves as Vedanta[3] and this also is an indirect testimony to the fact that they were anxious to maintain some kind of affinity in nomenclature between their mystic wisdom and the old literature of India.[4]

If the passages referred to above, indicate that the Upaniṣadic teachers had accorded a place of honour to the Vedas, there are numerous other paragraphs and verses where they adopt a critical, condemnatory and ridiculing attitude towards them. The famous dialogue between Nārada and Sanatkumar brings out the insufficiency of the Vedic literature and in general, of all the empirical arts and sciences. Sanatkumara, the *rishi*, who possibly belonged to the Kshattriya group,[5] considers the entire range of literature and wisdom studied by

1 *Mahato bhutasya nihsvaśitam.*

2 Deussen says that in this passage the Vedas are regarded as the 'secret doctrine of the Brahma' (*brāhmim vāva ta upaniṣadam*). But I do not agree with this opinion because here the mystic wisdom conveyed by Umā Hemāvatī is called *Brāhmi Upaniṣad* and is not a reference to the Vedic knowledge.

3 Cf. *Muṇḍak, vedāntavijñānasuniscitārathāh.* But the term Vedānta as applied to the Upaniṣads has nothing to do with Vedanta-Sutras (*VS.*) of Bādārāyāna. Some Indian scholars would ascribe the *VS.* to 500-200 B.C. Max Müller holds it to belong to the period before the *Mahābhārata.* Jacobi would ascribe it to 200-150 A.D., while Keith says that it is not earlier than 200 A.D.

4 The Upaniṣads are called Vedānta because they marked the close of the period of Vedic studies.

5 Carlo Formichi. "Upaniṣads", *Journal of the Department of Letters,* Calcutta Univ. X, V, 1927, pp. 82-130, says that Sanatakumar was either the god of war or a person bearing his name. He also says that there was a lay and dynamic movement in ancient Indian society which accounts for the stupendous outburst of Buddhism.

Nārada as '*nāma eva*'—mere verbal knowledge or a study only of names and nomenclature.[1] Thus even the Vedas are regarded by Śanatkumara as dealing only with names and it is apparent that the supreme theosophic knowledge of emancipation was regarded as being beyond the ken of the Vedas. This text of the *Chhāndogya* definitely holds that the Vedas are insufficient to provide the knowledge that can lead to the extinction of sorrow. Hence Nārada prays to Sanatkumara—*Bhagavān śokasya pāram tārayatu*. The *Taittirīya Upaniṣad* also declares the Vedas to be insufficient to pierce the ultimate reality and hence inadequate to comprehend the supreme secret about the blissful Being. The *Kaṭha Upaniṣad* declares unequivocally and emphatically that *pravacana* (Vedic learning) and *bahunā śrutena* (much knowledge of Vedic books) are incapable of revealing the supreme secret.[2] In the *Muṇḍaka Upaniṣad* it is stated that the imperishable eternal reality cannot be known by the four Vedas and the six Vedāngas. They are said to be relevant only to the phenomenal and the empirical realms and hence they are inferior to the extent that the utter transcendent is beyond their comprehension. Only the occult mystic knowledge conveyed by the Upaniṣadic teachers can reveal the ultimate reality. In another passage also of the *Chhāndogya* the same verdict of insufficiency is passed on the Vedas. Śvetaketu studies the Vedas for full twelve years but still he fails to answer the query of his father regarding that fundamental principle through the gnosis of which "the unheard becomes the heard, the unthought becomes the thought and the uncognized becomes the cognized." When the son Śvetaketu indicates his failure, Āruni imparts to him the knowledge of the essential unity of the cosmic (*tat*) and the psychic (*tvam*) entities. Thus one main weapon in the Upaniṣadic attack upon the inadequacy of Vedic literature is the emphasis on the failure of the latter to provide the key to spiritual liberation.

A second ground for the inadequacy of the Vedic literature is its failure to answer deep questions of eschatology. Some of

[1] Cf. also the view of Yājnavalkya, in *Brihadāraṇyaka*, IV, 1, 2, that Vedic literature as also the other sciences are only "Vāchaiva".

[2] Contrast, however, the *Brihadāraṇyaka* passage, IV, 4, 22 where it is said: "*esa atmā yoyam vijñānamayah...tametam vedānuvachanena brāhmanāh vividishanti yajñena dānen tapasāpnāshakena*".

the Upaniṣads contain a discussion of *panchāgni vidyā.*[1] Śvetaketu who had been trained in the Vedas (*anuśista*) fails to provide the answers to the five eschatological questions put to him by Pravāhaṇa Jaivali and returns in disgust to his father and says : "so then without having really done so, you have claimed to have instructed me...it was imagination, then, when you previously declared that my instruction was complete." Thus it appears that the failure of Śvetaketu to answer the eschatological questions put to him by Pravāhaṇa Jaivali is at least an indirect indication of the fact that the teachers of Upaniṣadic metaphysics considered the Vedas to be inadequate to provide the knowledge about the destiny of the soul when the body would be dead. In the *Brihadāraṇyaka* also we find that Janaka who had studied the Vedas (and heard the teachings of the Upaniṣads) is unable to answer the questions regarding the fate of the soul after death and the adequate answer to them is provided only by Yājnavalkya who has realized the supreme truth and reality inculcated by the Upaniṣads.[2] It may be pointed, however, that from the standpoint of the advancements in metaphysical speculations that had been made during the days of the Upaniṣads, the theosophical and eschatological passages of the Vedas require considerable amendment and enlargement.

To the extent that Buddha totally repudiated any appeal to the Vedic scriptures he was a rationalist.[3] Although he claimed to have realized some truths through the process of superior cognition and even supra-rational intuitive realization, nevertheless, in his career as a teacher he appealed to the dialectical method of argument and discussion.[4] There is similarity

[1] *Chhāndogya*, V. 3-10 ; *BRU*, VI, 2 ; *Kaushītaki*, I. According to the *Chhāndogya*, 4, 15, a knowledge of the "Five-fold Fire" is regarded as the road to *brahmapatha*.

[2] *Brihadāraṇyaka*, IV, 2, 21. Some Vedic scholars say that it is abundantly clear from these passages that during the Upaniṣadic days the true import of the Veda was being lost. It is conceivable that the answers to the philosophical and eschatological questions raised here could have been provided from the Vedic standpoint, *e.g. Ṛgveda*, X, 129 ; and I, 164.

[3] The *Aṅguttara Nikāya*, III, 653, contains an important passage in refutation of reports (*anuśravaṇa*), traditions and past authority.

[4] There does not seem to be much foundation for B.M. Barua's views that Bhāradvāja. the propounder of the *Muṇḍakopaniṣad*, prepared the way

between the scoffing and ridiculing attitude of Buddha towards the Vedas and the Upaniṣadic view that contemplation is on a more exalted plane than Vedic ritualism. Buddha denied the hypothesis of the revelatory character of the Vedas and he ridiculed the practice of invoking the Vedic deities.[1]

6. *The Upaniṣadic and the Buddhistic Revolt against the sacrificial system* (800 B.C.-500 B.C.).

Some interpreters of the Vedic religion have exalted the aspect of sacrifice as a mechanism of moral purification through the propitiation of higher powers. Sri Aurobindo considers it a mystical and symbolical rite of purification and a dominant element in the conceptions of the ancient mysteries.[2] But an impartial historical enquiry would reveal that the sacrifices did contain elements of barbarism and savagery.[3] and the motivation behind them (sacrifices) in several cases was mean and sordid.[4] Even if the original motive of some of the religious

for Buddha's rationalism. He says that the anti-Brahmanic crusade is old but the first definite theoretical attempt made against the Brahmanical system was that of Bhāradvāja whom he regards as a transcendentalist, not in the Kantian but in the Emersonian sense. See pp. 237-253 of B.M. Barua, *Pre-Buddhistic Philosophy*.

[1] The *Silavimarśa jātaka* says : "Of no value are the Vedas, of no value are birth or kinsmen for the future world ; only one's own pure virtue brings him happiness in the next world." (*Jātakas*, Vol. III, no. 362).

[2] Sri Aurobindo, *Heraclitus*, p. 56.

[3] E.W. Hopkins, *History of Religions* : "Sympathetic magic, rites of expiation, an all-souls feast, expulsion of demons by satisfying them with blood poured on the ground, by noise, spells and fire...sacrifice as a communion, a bargain, a piacular and as aptropiac ; a gradual change from an underground pit as ghost-home to the place of torment for sinners, a resurrection but of shining bodies, and a sensuous paradise for the gods in Yama's later in Indra's heaven, these are the prominent features of the decadent Vedic age."

[4] E.J. Rapson, *Ancient India*, pp. 47-48, points out that in the *Yajurveda* all the moral elements in religion seems to fade out and are overwhelmed by a complicated system of ceremonial which is no longer regarded as a means of worship but as an end in itself. In the *Ṛgveda* sin had a moral connotation but in the *Yajurveda* sin signified the transgression of some details of the sacrificial system. Rapson also indicates that the sacrifice had developed into a system of magic through which supernatural powers might be obtained and those could be utilized either for temporal or spiritual purposes and 'even to coerce the gods themselves'. The

teachers who were partly responsible for the initiation of the sacrificial cult might have been pure,[1] the system as a whole as presented in the *Śatapatha Brāhmaṇa* is not an elevated piece of psychological and religious ceremony but is full of dull and tiresome details which leave the heart cold and dry.[2] If the Buddhistic records are to be relied upon, the picture that they give of the contemporary rituals and sacrifices is very dismal and indeed terrible.[3]

The Vedic civilization was primarily a rural[4] one but in the later Vedic days towns began to grow and the fighter aristocracy was getting prosperous through colonization. The contemporary kings as well as the pugnacious aristocrats wanted to

Kauśika Sūtra, ed. by Bloomfield, 102, 1-5 and *Hiraṇyakeśi Gihyasutra*, ed. by J. Kirste, (Vienna, Alfred Holder 1889), I, 16-17, contain reference to the magical elements in the sacrifice. *The Kauśika Sūtra*, XV. 7,6 and XVII, 12, 7, contains reference to Brahmanical supremacy obtained through the sacrifice, S.N. Dasgupta, *Indian Philosophy*. I, p. 80, refers to the magical elements in the sacrifice and even states that in the time of Buddha philosophy had come to a deadlock in the sacrificial schools. See also A.B. Keith, *Religion and Philosophy of the Veda*, II, 471, for magical elements in the sacrifice, and S.N. Dasgupta, *Indian Idealism*, p. 2.

1 In an arrogant tone, the *Paidva Brāhmaṇa*, VI, 1, 11, says that the slave has no god and no sacrifice.

2 According to the *Sāmkhya Kārika*, no. 21, the Vedic rituals are defective on three grounds : (i) They are impure because there is bloodshed in sacrifices like the *aśvamedha* ; (ii) they are non-eternal because gods like Indra have passed away and (iii) there is unequal distribution of results, *e.g.*, the *jyotishtoma* leads to heaven while the *vājapeya* leads to sovereignty of heaven. See Harrison, *Philosophy of the Sāmkhya Kārika*. Sylvian Levi, *Doctrine du sacrifice*, p. 9, says that the sacrificial system has no place for morality. Hopkins, *Hindu Ethics*, contradicts this statement.

3 The *Aitareya Brāhmaṇa*, VII, 3, contains the story of Śunahśepa. E.J. Rapson, *Ancient India*, p. 54, points out that there was a transition from human sacrifice in which at first some animal and subsequently a cake of rice was substituted. The *purashamedha* would involve the sacrifice of 184 persons. According to Winternitz and Oldenberg, it was symbolical but Hillebrandt opines that the *purushamedha* involved real human sacrifice. Keith, *Religion and Philosophy*, pp. 379-80, discuss the mixture of religion and magic in the notions of the *Atharvaveda* and the *Brāhmaṇas*. Animal sacrifice was practised even in the Eleusinian mysteries.—Van Hook, *Greek Religion*. There was an important sacrificial cult in Rome demanding elaborate attention. See M. Winternitz, *Indian Literature*, (Calcutta Univ., 1927), Vol, I, p. 198n.

4 Eliot, *Hinduism and Buddhism*, (Routledge and Kegan Paul, 1921, Reprint of 1954), p. 89 : "It was in village life that Brahmanism grew up."

consolidate their power and one significant method of strengthening the emotional and sentimental foundations of their power was to placate the priesthood and give it huge fees (*dakshiṇa*)[1] in the different sacrifices.[2] The simple primitive Vedic sacrifice had grown elaborately complicated in later times and almost assumed the appearance of a protracted mechanical cult. Even a cursory glance at the *aśvamedha* and *vājapeya* sacrificial formulas would indicate that they are meant for a leisured wealthy class. The priests relished evolving new methods and formulas for the sacrifice.[3] The leadership of the Brahmins in the sacrificial cult to which heightened magical powers were attributed enhanced the social power and prestige of the priesthood. It is true that the priesthood in India was never as solidified an ecclesiastical organization as in medieval Europe or ancient Egypt and ancient Babylon.[4] In these two latter countries the temples even sent candidates for accession to the imperial throne. Since the Indian priesthood was not internally as solidified a group as that of the above-mentioned countries and civilizations[5], hence it did not and could not evolve a mechanical elaborate ritualism for their own personal sake. They needed patrons for whom these costly and elaborate rituals were to be performed. They found their patrons in the contemporary kings and nobles. Thus a natural relationship grew between the kings and aristocratic magnates on the one side and the more or less individualistically-oriented self-seeking Brāhmin priests on the other.[6] The *Śatapatha Brāhmaṇa*

1 *SB*, II, 2,2,2.

2 Sometimes the priest was treated with contempt as in *Ṛgveda*, VII, 103, 1,7-8 ; X, 88,19.

3 In *Śatapatha*, II, 2, 2, 6, the *anucāna* Brahmiṇs are being called *manusyadevāh*.

4 H. Oldenberg, *Buddha*, p. 14, grossly exaggerates the solidarity of Brahmanism when he says : "...the Brahmanas, standing without the pale of the state, bind themselves together in a great confederacy..." L.W. King, *A History of Babylon*, (London, Chatto and Windus, 1915), pp. 61,62,78-79,191.

5 Melamed, *Spinoza and Buddha*, pp. 237-238, takes a different view. He says : "In no other country of the world has the priest attained such a high estate, such despotic power, such an invulnerable position."

6 According to Richard Garbe, *Ancient Indian Philosophy*, the Brahmins did not establish ecclesiastical rank or hierarchy. But they were interested in being appointed as household priests in the king's family.

constantly stresses the combination of the *brahma* and the *kshattra* powers.[1] The tremendous elaboration of the sacrificial cult took place in middle India and, centuries later, Manu also says that Āryāvarta was the sacred land where sacrificial religion prevailed in its most glorious form. But the elaborately complicated character of the sacrifices,[2] which, among other things, had been brought about by the power-based alliance of the Brāhmins and some of the Kshattriyas, became a factor for the decline of the system because it became too complicated to survive long.[3]

Another factor responsible for the decline of the sacrificial mechanism was the rise of the absolutistic philosophy of the Upaniṣads. Deussen states that the period of the Upaniṣads is from 1000 B.C. to 500 B.C. S.N. Dasgupta regards 700-600 B.C. as the date of the oldest Upaniṣads. Even if this view were correct, it would certainly prove that about 700 B.C. a movement of protest against the contemporary system of sacrifices had begun. The principal Upaniṣads contain cosmogonic and eschatological speculations. According to Deussen, the development of the doctrine of *ātman* was independent of the mystical and allegorical speculations upon the rituals as carried on in the Āraṇyakas and all the different Vedic schools tried

But Garbe does not seem to be correct in his statement that the household priesthood gave to the Brahmin the position of prime minister. Describing the situation of Brahmanism in the Gangetic Valley during the early Buddhist period C.A.F. Rhys Davids says : "It [Brahmin teachers] was a sort of magnificent tribe of Levi in Judaism. It attached value to hereditary descent comparable to what may be found in an exclusive aristocracy. It claimed monopoly in the right of teaching and repeating the (orally) fixed hymns and mantras of authoritative religious doctrine. It claimed the right of training in such teaching the sons of nobles and its own children. It claimed a monopoly of conducting such ritual as was in accord with its body of oral sayings on the subject."

[1] There are some hints of opposition also between the *brahma* and the *kshattra powers*. —*Śatapatha* VIII, 1,4,10.

[2] Macdonell, *Lectures on Comparative Religion*, *op. cit.*, p. 64, says that in the age of the Brāhmaṇās the sacrifice became the dominant centre of all intellectual and religious operations.

[3] There were three fourth-month offerings : (i) the Vaisvadeva, (ii) the Varuṇapraghāsa and (iii) Sākamedha : Sometimes the *agnicayana* would extend for a whole year and would involve the arrangement of 101800 bricks. A mystical-symbolical meaning was attached to it. Cf. S.N. Dasgupta, *Indian Philosophy*, Vol. I, pp. 13-14.

to incorporate the new doctrine. Although they do not openly preach a crusade against the Vedic sacrificial cult, still some of the Upaniṣads, like the *Muṇḍaka*, ridicule the Vedic liturgy. Some of them preach that philosophic contemplation on the nature of the absolute is a higher sacrifice than the concrete formalism of the contemporary sacrificial system.[1] The highest element in the Upaniṣadic philosophy is the notion of the Absolute, the supreme *brahman*, untouched by the relativism and sorrow of the empiric phenomenal existence. This doctrine of the Absolute exalts philosophical gnosis at the expense of routine formulas and mechanism of sacrifice and worship. The minimization, in the scale of values, of the Vedic external religion that is thus engineered indirectly prepares the ground for the emergence of heterodox philosophical systems which openly challenged the efficacy of the Brahmanical religion in the name of a higher ethical culture. The Upaniṣads contain references to teachers and schools whose views are not systematically expounded there. It is possible to hold that those teachers who accepted the supremacy of *asat* do not have their views discussed in the extent Upaniṣads.

The sacrificial ritual obtains wide acceptance only when people adhere to the belief in heavens and hells. The rise of a philosophical protestant system which preaches emancipation and salvation through cognition and meditation tends to undermine the belief in the heavens and hells of the priestly conception.[2] The Upaniṣadic theory of the absolute, with its identification of the psychic, the cosmic and the transcosmic principles was an almost indirect death-blow to all beliefs in the popular gods who inhabited the heavens or who aided people in going to heaven. The Upaniṣadic absolutism and spiritualism as enunciated by Yājnavalkya and Uddālaka amounts to a neutralization of all kinds of dualism which is the basis of any worship or any ritualism. One point becomes very clear from the Upaniaṣdic protest against the contemporary

[1] S.N. Dasgupta, *Indian Idealism*, p. 50.

[2] In early Buddhism there is also reference to hell (*niraya*) and worlds of gods. The *Brahamajāla Sutta* refers to fall from the *ābhāsvara brahmaloka* to the *śunya brahma vimāna* and fall from the latter to the earth. There is mention of fall from *manahpradushika devaloka* and *kridāpradushika devaloka*.

rituals. Rituals indicate that stage of religion when the resort to realism and objective concepts is the dominant aspect of human thought. But advance in philosophic endeavours implies a recoil therefrom and that naturally results in the opposition to mythologies and external worship and rituals. Thus concentration upon philosophic self-consciousness amounts to a turn away from objective consciousness. Sacrifices were taken recourse to because they were thought to be efficacious in the production of desired targets and results. According to the Upaniṣadic cosmogony, the omnipotent self is the creator of the universe. Before the awful majesty of this supreme being all external deities lose their splendour. Thus philosophical cognition of the Absolute is regarded as the prime factor and all kinds of objective worship are accorded the second place. Consequently sacrificial ritualism loses its glamour. Although the thought of the Upaniṣads was highly philosophical and hence confined to the intellectual elite, its emphasis on meditation and contemplation could not but minimize the dominating influence the sacrifices had during the immediately preceding age.

An important weapon in the Upaniṣadic armoury against the Vedas is the critical and even condemnatory attitude adopted against the Vedic sacrifices.[1] According to Deussen, the older the Upaniṣads are the more marked is their opposition against the Vedic sacrificial cult. In the section on *Śauva Udagītha* the Sāma singers are ridiculed and indirectly the contemporary priesthood with its Vedic wisdom is condemned.[2] This "dog *Udagītha*" is definitely reminiscent of the Ṛgvedic hymn to the frog which is one of the earliest satirical hymns aimed against the contemporary Brahmanical religion and social system. In the *Muṇḍakopaniṣad* also the sacrifices were openly condemned.[3] This attitude of mocking and ridiculing the Vedic sacrifices received its culmination in the defiant and sarcastic anti-Vedic propositions of Buddha which is expressed in the *Tevijja Sutta.*[4]

[1] *BAU,* I. 4,10.

[2] *Chhāndogya* I, 12, This *śauva udagītha* is an invective against Brahmanical external sacrificialism. According to some interpreters it asserts the supremacy of the spiritual over the materialistic objectives of life.

[3] *Muṇḍaka,* I, 27 and 28.

[4] Oldenberg, *Buddha,* p. 171.

Some of the Upaniṣads tried to humanize the bloody sacrifices by preaching moral substitutes.[1] The Upaniṣadic conception of *pancāgni vidyā* is, to some extent, an attempt to replace the external mechanism of sacrifice by a consecrated pure life itself being regarded as a sacrifice.[2] Sometimes the Upaniṣads would take a favourable attitude to the sacrifices by conceiving it in a philosophical way. Thus the *vaiśvānara vidyā* regards the entire cosmos as a sacrifice. The *Chhāndogya* would regard human life itself as a sacrifice. These references would point out that in the original sacrificial system an insistence must have been there on pious religiosity and devotion. This aspect was later on abstracted from the sacri• cial religion and attributed to the cosmos or to the human life itself. This kind of moderate reformism[3] assumed greater proportions when the Buddhists, the materialists and the naturalists made bitter criticisms of the sacrificial system. Sometimes the sacrificial system was sought to be replaced by other practices and formulas. Great importance was attached to *tapas* and it was said that only through *tapas* were the great truths of the universe revealed.[4] The Upaniṣads stress the self-introspective meditative side of *tapas*. In Buddhism also there is references to extremes of self-castigations. Thus the method of *tapas* came to some extent to replace the prevalent technics of

[1] The *Chhāndogya*, V, 19-24, insists on inner sacrificet o *prāṇa*. See also the *Kaushitaki* which refers to the *antara agnihotra* of Pratardana. The *Samyutta*, I, 167 and 169 also insists on the inwardness of the sacrifice.

[2] For the origins of this notion see *Śatapatha*, XI, 3,1,4. The *Muṇḍaka Upaniṣad* frankly accepts the efficacy of the sacrificial creed in some of its hymns. See *Muṇḍaka* I,2,1 and I,2,6. The *Praśnopaniṣad* IV, 4 contains some concession to the sacrificial cult and says that by fruit of sacrifice there is the daily conveyance of the *mana* to *brahman*.

[3] In the *Muṇḍaka Upaniṣad* I, 2,1-5, the efficacy of Vedic sacrifices is taught but in I, 2, 6-10, the sacrificers are seriously deprecated as *rāgātura*, *bāla*, and *pramudha*. These two kinds of statements not only in this Upaniṣad but also in the *Brihadāraṇyaka* and the *Chhāndogya*, indicate, no doubt, the moderate reformism of the Upaniṣads but they also indicate a hopeless and irreconcilable confusion and indefiniteness of thought regarding the relevance of sacrifices for higher *noesis*, gnosis and liberation.

[4] The enormous significance attached to the *yajña* in the Brāhmaṇas began to be attributed to *tapas* during the period of the Purāṇas.

sacrifices and rituals. Later on, the *Gitā* also says that sacrifices could be performed with the help of physical things (*dravya*), as opposed to the sacrifice of animals. This quest for the substitutes of the animal sacrifices which begins in the Upaniṣads is, in itself, an indication of the fact that the system was on the decline and had substantially ceased to command the allegiance of thinking men.

During the Upaniṣadic days it appears that both the kings and some of the philosophically-minded Brahmin teachers were against the sacrificial cult although the average man and his family priest might have delighted in the external worship and rituals. Enlightened kings like Janaka, Pravāhaṇa Jaivali and Aśvapati were engaged in speculations upon the absolute. The contemporary Brahmin teachers and philosophers like Uddālaka[1] and Yājnavalkya were also engaged in similar enterprises. Thus it would be wrong to interpret the anti-sacrificial philosophical movement as one directed by the Kshattriyas.[2] It would be safe to take it as a movement of philosophic rationalism which was led by Brahmins, Kshattriyas and also by such "casteless" man as Satyakāma Jābāla.

Buddha, in common with some of the Upaniṣads voiced his emphatic protest against the contemporary bloody sacrifices.[3] His disapproval, certainly, was more pronounced, more

[1] According to the *Brihadāranyaka*, III, 3, 1-2 and III, 7,1-2, Bhujyu Lahyāyani and Uddālaka Āruṇi reside in the Madra country and make a study of the sacrificial culture. This fact is mentioned in the assembly that met at the court of King Janaka. The decline of the sacrificial cult was bound to occur when there was no certainty about the fate of the performers of the sacrifice. The question of Bhujyu Lahyāyani to Yājñavalkya would indicate the growing spirit of scepticism with reference to the sacrificial cult (*kva pārikshitā abhavan*) Yājñavalkya tries to evade answering the question—(*yatrāshvamedha yājinobhavan*),

[2] Vidhushekhar Bhattacharya, *The Basic Conception of Buddhism* (University of Calcutta, 1934), pp. 1-9, distinguishes six streams of pre-Buddhistic views : (i) the sacrificers, (ii) the Upaniṣadics, (iii) the synthesizers of *vidyā* and *avidyā*, (iv) the Sāmkhyans, (v) the free thinkers and (vi) the ascetics.

[3] In the Vedic literature the *Shamitri* is referred to as being concerned with the slaying of the sacrificial animal. A.M. Hocart, *Ritual and Emotion*, p. 202, says that emotionalism began to corrode the ritual in the Upaniṣads and in the shape of Buddhism to destroy it. Buddhism wanted to provide mental healing to those who were suffering from world-

radical and more condemnatory of the sacrifices than that of the Upaniṣads.[1] The picture of the contemporary sacrifices that one finds depicted in the Tripiṭakas may be taken to be also generally relevant for the period from *c.* 800 B.C. to 500 B.C. and some of the details referred in the Buddhist scriptures are corroborated also from the Brahmanical records. The *Kuṭadanta Sutta* (the *Dīgha Nikāya*) points out that in Magadha, a revered teacher, along with three hundred disciples, was performing a great sacrifice.[2] He had been given plenty of land and wealth by Bimbisāra. For the sacrificial purpose, seven hundred bullocks, seven hundred calves, seven hundred she-calves, seven hundred goats and seven hundred rams had been brought to the sacrificial ground. This gigantic preparation for blood-spilling in the name of religion is indicative of the dismal degeneration of the contemporary cults.[3] The *Tevijja Sutta* of the *Dīgha Nikāya* contains reference to the practice of invoking deities like Indra, Ishāṇa,

weariness and 'desirousness' and emotional disturbances and hence it discarded a ritual which had been worked out for external purposes. For Buddha's protest against the cruelty of the sacrificial cult, see *Majjhima Nikāya* I, 342, *ff*., and *Aṅguttara*, II, 205. The *Bhuridatta Jātaka, The Jātaka* E.T. by Cowell and Rouse, Vol. VI, No. 54), pp. 110-11 says :

"If he who kills is counted innocent
* * * * *
Let Brahmins, Brahmins kill — so all were well—
* * * * *
To veil the post, the victim and the blow
The Brahmins let their choicest rhetoric flow ;
* * * * *
These cruel cheats, as ignorant as vile,
Weave their long frauds the simple to beguile."

[1] Winternitz, *Indian Literature*, II, pp. 37-58. In the *Majjhima Nikāya* (Hindi translation, p 411), Buddha says that a professional priest is not a Brahmin but a *yājaka*.

[2] The *Kuṭadanta Sutta* indicates the relation between Brahmanism and Buddhism. The *Tevijja Sutta* contrasts the Brahmin culture and the Buddhist ideals. The *Ambaṭṭha Sutta* brings out Buddha's attitude to caste.

[3] According to the *Yajña Sutta, Saṃyutta Nikāya* (Vol. I, pp. 74-75, Nalanda ed.) the Vedic sacrifices which involve violence do not bring about the intended consequences and hence great sages do not perform them. Those sacrifices which do not involve violence to animals like the goat or the sheep or the cow bring great benefits and hence should be performed by the wise.

Prajāpati, Brahmā, Maharddhi, Yama etc.[1] Thus it appears that the elaboration of the sacrificial cult which began in the later Vedic age and the days of the Brāhmaṇas had reached almost its culmination during the pre-Buddhaic and Buddhaic days and this implies that, in fighting this complicated ritualism, the philosophic protest of the Upaniṣads had not been sufficiently effective and hence opposition to the cult needed more radical and more effective efforts. Buddha inculcated the doctrine of the middle path between extreme luxuries and extreme austerities. He taught a system of ethical-philosophical discipline and sacrifices were of least concern to him.[2] Once a Brahmin, named Sundarikāyana, came to meet Buddha and he had in his hands the remaining portions of the oblations of sacrifice. Buddha thus spoke to him : "Do not deem Brahmin, that purity comes by mere laying wood in fire, for it is external. Having therefore left that course, I kindle my fire only within, which burns for ever, and on that I have my mind rightly fixed for ever". He vehemently protested against bloody sacrifices but it appears that the stalwarts of contemporary Brahmanism did not oppose him as strongly and as doggedly as the Popes had resisted the advancing tide of Luther and Lutheranism. One possible reason of this weak resistance might have been that the philosophic protest earlier levelled by the Upaniṣads might have slowly prepared the ground, to some extent, for the Buddhist protest. Buddha was a man of deep compassion and love for all—*maitrī* and *karuṇā* and his opposition to the sacrificial cult proceeded from his universalistic concern for the good of all living beings. Some Christian critics and interpreters seem to minimize the significance of the love and altruism of Buddha and they state that Buddhist non-violence was born out of the consciousness of a common share in the final Nothingness. This amounts almost to a denial of the great love for all living beings that characterized the prophetic personality of Buddha.[3]

Buddha inculcated the necessity of ethical endeavours in

[1] The description given here is parallel to the one given in the *Bhagavadgītā — Kāmātmānah svargaparāh.*

[2] The *Sundarika Sutta, Samyutta Nikāya,* 1, 168.

[3] For a different view, H.C. Warren, *Buddhism in Translations,* (Harvard University Press, 1915), pp. 86-87.

place of the sacrificial system. He succeeded in converting the Kassapa brothers of Gayā with their devoted band of one thousand Jatilas. They formed a group of ascetics who used to perform sacrifices for the attainment of supernormal powers. The *Mahāvagga* contains the story of their conversion and says that this was effected after Buddha displayed on that occasion far more gigantic supernormal feats. Buddha protested vehemently against the bloody sacrifices and in the *Kuṭadanta Sutta* he refers to a mythic *yajña* that had been performed in the past and had been finished only with common articles like ghee, oil, etc.[1] Buddha's prime concern was with moral reforms. Hence he was bound to attack the violent sacrificial cult.[2] He stressed virtuous living and meditation. Hence he pointed out the inadequacy of the contemporary ceremonies and rituals. Buddha also formulates the conception of alternatives to animal sacrifices, like *dāna-yajña* (which also occurs in the *Gitā*), *trisaraṇa-yajña* and the *shikshāpada-yajña*. *Shikshāpada-yajña* and *śila-yajña* stress moral endeavours, while *samādhi-yajña* and *prajñā-yajña* emphasize spiritual efforts at mediation.[3] To

[1] This is the reference to Māhāvijīta's sacrifice. In it oxen, goats, fowls, fatted pigs or any other living creatures were not put to death ; no trees were cut for *stambha* or yupa ; no *darbha* grass was arranged for seat. But the sacrifice was completed with butter, ghee, oil, milk, sugar and honey (*shashtha-parka*).

[2] Cf. Buddha's utterance in the *Samyutta Nikāya*, Vol. I, E.T. by C.A.F. Rhys Davdis, pp. 102-03 when he is informed of the performance of a bloody sacrifice by Prasenjit of Kośala :

"The sacrifices called" 'the Horse', the Man,
The Peg—thrown Site, the Drink of Victory,
The Bolts withdrawn, and all the mighty fuss :
These are not rites that bring a rich result.
Where diverse goats and sheep and kine are slain,
Never to such a rite as that repair
The noble seers who walk the perfect way.
But rites where is no bustle nor no fuss,
An offerings meet, bequests perpetual,
Where never goats and sheep and kine are slain,
To such a sacrifice as this repair
The noble seers who walk the perfect way.
These are the rites entailing great results.
These to the celebrant are blest, not cursed.
The 'oblation runneth o'er', the gods are pleased."

[3] *Kuṭadanta Sutta*, *Dīgha Nikāya*.

provide some concession to the empirical consciousness of men, Buddha, in common with the traditions of the *Bhagavadgitā*, formulated the scheme of an ethical spiritual system of *yajña* and it was so provided that if any body were to insist on the performance of sacrifices he could perform them with ordinary and common food materials and could absolutely avoid blood. The historical accounts of the subsequent ages indicate that Buddha had been effective in his protest and the ardour of the sacrificial cult did decline considerably.[1] When once more the sacrificial cult revives during the days of the Śungas and the Guptas it could never assume the same complicated and obscene character that it had in the later Vedic and Brāhmaṇa days.[2]

[1] N. Datta, "Internal Forces in the Spread of Buddhism", *Proceedings of the Second Oriental Conference*, (University of Calcutta, 1923) pp. 535-47, recognizes that Buddhist stress on *maitrī* and *ahimsā* and its revolt against sacrificial ritualism, caste dominance. Vedic revelation and Atharvan magic were signficant factors in its success.

[2] Cf. the *Aśvamedha*.

CHAPTER 5

THE PHILOSOPHY OF THE UPANIṢADS AND THE ORIGINS OF BUDDHISM

1. *The Fundamental differences between the Upaniṣadic and the early Buddhistic Philosophy*

FROM VERY old times the view of there being deep affinities between the Upaniṣadic and the Buddhist[1] gospels has persisted. Gaudapada held the view that the main ideas of the Upaniṣads tallied with those of Buddha. The *Śraddhotpāda Sutra* of Aśvaghosa, has a strong resemblance to the teachings of the Upaniṣads. Sadānanda and Kumārila have believed in the closeness of the relation between these two powerful streams of thought.[2] Max Müller[3], Bloomfield, Rhys Davids, C.A.F. Rhys Davids and Oldenberg adhere to the view that the gospel of the Sākyamuni has been deeply influenced by the teachings of the Upaniṣads. Stcherbatsky who interprets the central conception of Buddhism as a radical pluralism traces the concept of Dharma, meaning vital essential super-subtle elements, in the *Kathopaniṣad.*[4] Keith regards Buddha as an agnostic

[1] In the *Mahāpadāna* Sutta of the *Digha Nikāya* there is the mention of previous Buddhas like Vipāsyi. Śikhi, Visvabhu (Vessabhu), Krākuchhanda (Kakusandha), Konāgamana and Kaśyapa. A more comprehensive list of the previous Buddhas is given in the *Buddhavamśa.*

[2] In the *Vedantasāra* of Sadānanda, the Cārvākas, the Naiyāyikas and the Bauddhas are referred to as accepting the validity of the Upanishads. The *Tantravārtika*, 1, 32.

[3] According to Max Müller, *Ancient Sanskrit Literature*, p. 134. Buddhism in its original form was only a modification of Brahmanism. It grew up slowly and imperceptibly and its very founder could hardly have been aware of the final results of his doctrines.

[4] Th. Stcherbatsky, "The Dharmas of the Buddhists and the Gunas of the Sāmkhya". *The Indian Historical Quarterly*, Vol. X. pp. 737-60.

with no definite opinions on metaphysics but even he compares the Buddhist concept of *Nirvāṇa* with the Upaniṣadic Absolute and affiliates the doctrine of the "original pure underfiled radiant consciousness" of the *Anguttara Nikāya* with the Upaniṣadic *prajnānam brahman*.[1] B.M. Barua has made an attempt to trace the Upaniṣadic sources of Buddha's ideas at great length.

It is not certain that Buddha had any deep knowledge of the Vedas[2] and Upaniṣads. In the six years which he spent as a wanderer and seeker, previous to his enlightenment, he does not confront any profound spokesman of idealistic wisdom. Some of his later biographies speak of him as being fully conversant with the schools of metaphysical philosophy. But from a study of the Tripiṭaka literature this claim is not substantiated. He, however, must have had some acquaintance with the fundamental theme of the Upaniṣadic thought which is to expound the metaphysics of the absolute spiritual real. Buddha derides the Vedic and Upaniṣadic theological and theosophical conception but he does not engage in an abstruse psychological and metaphysical examination of the bases of the old teachings. He adopts a pragmatic orientation and is content with relegating the 'indescribable' or *Avyākṛta* questions as examples of empty and futile intellectual jugglery.[3] He was perfectly free to minister as a pragmatic doctor and healer of the existing wounds of society. I am only stating that there is nothing in

According to Stcherbatsky the originality of Buddhism consists in its *anātmavāda —dharmavāda —samskāravāda —pratityasamutpāda.* But Stcherbatsky's interpretation of *dharma* in *Kaṭha*, IV. 14, *evam dharmāns-prithagpaśyan tānevānuvidhāvati*, seems highly imaginative and fanciful. There is no validity for interpreting the word *Dharma* or *Dhamma* as occurring in the Pali literature as element.

[1] A.B. Keith, "Pre-canonical Buddhism", *The Indian Historical Quarterly*, Vol. XII No. 1, March 1936, pp. 1-20. In the *Anguttara Nikāya* I, 10, it is stated : *Prabhāsvaramidam Chittam.*

[2] In the *Samyutta Nikāya* 1, 168 and the *Sutta Nipāta*, 463, Buddha is called *Vedajna* and *Vedāntajna.* A.K. Coomaraswamy, "Rebirth and Omniscience in Pali Buddhism", *Indian Culture*, Vol. III. 1936-37, traces similarities between the characteristics of Buddha and the Vedic god Agni. Both Buddha and Agni are omniscient and both are very precocious. Furthermore the statement *bahudhā pi hotwāseko homi* of the *Samyutta Nikāya* is comparable to the Ṛgvedic *ekam vā idam vivabhuva sarvam.*

[3] The *Potthapāda Sutta* of the *Digha Nikāya.*

the Tripiṭa ka literature to prove that Buddha had any profound acquaintance with the metaphysical teachings of the Vedas and the Upanisads.[1] It is not possible to identify the sixty-two schools of thought and experiences mentioned in the *Brahmajāla Sutta* of the *Dīgha Nikāya* with the Upaniṣadic concepts. Nor is there any record of any deeply learned discussion between him and any acknowledged authority on the Upaniṣadic metaphysics. Aristotle repudiates the Platonic doctrine of universals and Hegel repudiates the Fichtean doctrine of subjectivism. But their repudiation is at a philosophical level. On the other hand, Buddha's main and uppermost concern was with the elimination of pain and sorrow and as an ethical pragmatist he found metaphysics to be unnecessary for this purpose.[2] His concrete and immediate concern for the cessation of suffering is illustrated in his exhortation to Māluṅkyaputta. He says :

> "A man is hit by a poisoned arrow. His friends hasten to the doctor. The latter is about to draw the arrow out of the wound. The wounded man, however, cries : "stop : I will not have the arrow drawn out until I know who shot it, whether a warrior or a Brahman, a Vaiśya or a Sudra, to which family he belonged, whether he was tall or short, of what species and description the arrow was', and so on. What would happen ? The man would die before all these questions were answered. In the same way the disciple who wished for answers to all his questions about the beyond and so on, would die before he knew the truth about suffering, the origin of suffering, the cessatlon of suffering and the way to cessation of suffering."[3]

It is difficult to characterize the entire thought of the Upaniṣads with any particular 'ism'. Śamkara interpreted the Upaniṣads as a gospel of spiritual monism. Deussen found deep similarities in the ideas of Parmenides, Plato, Kant,

[1] According to H.G. Wells, *Outline of History*, (New York, 1931), p. 391, after his departure from home Gautama became versed in all the metaphysics of his age. But his acute intelligence was dissatisfied with the solutions offered him. It is difficult to find corroborations for the opinion of Wells in the Tripiṭaka literature.

[2] The *Sutta-Nipāta* : "The different schools of philosophy contradict each other, they proclaim different truths but the truth is only one. As long as the disputations are going on, so long will there be strife in this world."

[3] *Majjhima Nikāya*, No. 63 : *Chula-Mālunkyaputta Sutta.*

Schopenhauer and the Upaniṣads. According to Jacobi, Keith and Sukthankar the true import of the Upaniṣads is pantheism. It should be stated that the supreme quest of the Upaniṣads is for the *bhumā*—the stupendous comprehensive being. The seers of the Upaniṣads attempt to make a transition from the surface materialistic standpoint to the vital sphere and thencefrom successively to the mental and the intellectual spheres and finally arrive at the notion of the supreme, delightful and blissful sphere of the transcendent reality. In the *Chhāndogya Upaniṣad*, Prajapati leads Indra from the materialistic physical point of view of the identification of the corporeal being with the self, to the empirical standpoint of the identification of the self with the dreaming being. Thenceforward an ascent is made to the idealistic standpoint of the dreamless self and the final culmination is conceived as the realisation of the highest spiritual self in the super-conscious layer of profound spiritual awareness. The deepest and profoundest reality, according te the Upaniṣads is not a contentless, featureless, indeterminate abstraction. But it is said to be identical with the inmost self of man himself. But whatever be the central gospel of the Upaniṣads—monistic idealism or pantheistic spiritualism—the dominant concern of early Buddhism is not at all with any such metaphysical theory. There is no sanction in early Buddhism for the acceptance either of spiritual idealism or divine immanence. The great discourses of Buddha do not refer to any substantial spiritual existent. It is true that Buddha does not openly and categorically refute monistic metaphysics. Sometimes it has been stated that Buddha's supreme indifference to metaphysical disquisitions might have had its remote roots in the Upaniṣadic view that the Absolute is not amenable to the grasp of empirical knowledge. But to argue that because he was silent about the supreme spiritual real, he believed in that in his heart of hearts, is an absurd conclusion. It will be attributing a charge of gross infidelity and betrayal to Buddha if we regard him as a mighty teacher and prophet and in the same breath credit him with the cunning and the ingenuity to have hid from the vast number of his disciples the deepest secret for nearly forty-five years. The great evangelists are anxious to give out the highest result of their endeavours even at the cost of endless repetitions. A great teacher does not reserve the end product his supreme realization to an obscure mention in the course of a discourse, which is liable to different interpretations, but repeats it almost *ad nauseam*. Thus the supreme theme of the Upaniṣadic philosophy is conspicuous by its absence in the early Buddhist literature because Buddha did not subscribe to them in any way. It unmistakably points out the deep rupture in the two systems of the Upaniṣads and early Buddhism.

It is possible that at the religious level the Upaniṣads advocate the worship of one monotheistic God—the *tadvanam* in the *Kena Upaniṣad*[1] and the *tajjalān* in the *Chhāndogya*. In the Upaniṣads the cosmological argument for the existence of God as the creator is found. There are some incipient references also to the ontological argument for theism. Towards the end of the Vedic period the worship of one supreme Godhead, for example, the Hiraṇyagarbha, the Visvakarman etc., was advocated. In some of the metrical Upaniṣads like the *Muṇḍaka* and the *Śvetāśvatara* there are references to a supreme personal God. In some of the Upaniṣads there is the advocacy of meditation on spiritual symbols. Buddha emphatically repudiates every kind of external worship. In some of the Suttas he ridicules the traditional method of invocation to Vedic deities. In the *Tevijja Sutta* of the *Dīgha Nikāya* Buddha mocks at the attempts of the Brahmins to invoke Indra, Ishāna, Prajāpati, Brahmā, Mahardhi, Yama etc...He mocks at the idea of reaping fruits and rewards through propitiating the gods. He never prescribes the use of symbols for the purposes of concentration although the early Buddhist scriptures contained a detailed categorized scheme of mystic and supra-psychic experiences. There is no mention of symbols in the Buddhist scheme of Jnānas. Thus there is no place in early Buddhism either for the personal God of the Upaniṣads or for the symbolic method of concentration.

Buddha's hostility to the Upaniṣadic *Brahman* and the Vedic and Brahmanic God and deities is in line with the ideas of some of the contemporary teachers. All the six Tirthaka teachers like Ajita Keśakambala, Prakuddha Katyāyana, Sanjya Belathaputta, Nigganatha Nātaputta, Makkhali Gośāla and Purṇa Kaśyapa

[1] *Kena Upaniṣad*, 31.

repudiated the conceptions both of a monistic impersonal indeterminate absolute and a theological personal God. Atheistic ideas are present in the views of Virochana as reported in the *Chhāndogya Upaniṣad* and called as the *Āsuropaniṣad.* Perhaps the ideas of the original atheistical Sāmkhya which might have been prevalent at that time had strengthened the anti-theological intellectual trends. The *Ahirbudhnyasamhitā* contains references to an early Sāmkhya work the *Shashtitantra.* Possibly the Sāmkhya of the *Shashtitantra* was theistic and resembled the theism of the Pancarātra Vaishnavas.[1] According to the *Ahirbudhnyasamhitā*, the Samkhya system of Kapila was Vaishnava. Buddha's atheism remains a permanent antithesis of the Upaniṣadic teachings. Although the dominant trend of the Upaniṣads is to inculcate some type of transcendental—immanentistic metaphysics of a spiritual kind, they contain references to heterodox views which have been mentioned there for the purpose of being refuted. Thus we find that there were schools which believed in the origination of existence, *sat*, from non-existence, *asat.*[2] Since the Vedic days there were sceptics who did not favour the contemporary pantheon of gods. There seems to be a persistent tradition of sceptics, pseudo-rationalists and free thinkers who did not favour the dominant theology and spiritual metaphysics of that age. Buddha belongs not to the tradition of the Vedas, Brāhmanas and the Upaniṣads but to this critical anti-Vedic tradition whose views are occasionally referred to in the sacred literature but never elaborated upon.[3] Just as the foundations of the Reformation movement of Luther were laid by Wycliffe and just as John the Baptist prepared the background of the ethical movement of Jesus Christ, similarly the tremendous intellectual stir and freedom of thought created by the researches, opinions and investigations of teachers and leaders of heterodox thought in the seventh and sixth centuries

[1] Dasgupta, *Indian Philosophy*, Vol. I, pp. 220-221, says that most of the schools of Vaishnava thought accepted the cosmology of the Sāmkhya. This may possibly justify the assumption that "Kapila's doctrine was probably theistic." *Ibid.*, p. 221. According to Dasgupta, *Indian Idealism*, p. 68, the Pāncharātra theology is contemporaneous with the development of the thought of the sophistical teachers.

[2] *Chhāndogya*, VI, 2, 1, *tasmādasatah sajjāyāta.* Cf. the *Ṛgveda, devānam prathame yuge asato sadajāyata.*

[3] A.M. Pizzagalli, *Cārvaka Nastika e Lokayatika*, Pisa. 1907.

B.C. prepared the atmosphere for the rise and development of the movement of Buddhism. It is essential to realise the point that the genesis of Buddhism has to be sought not so much in the idealism and spiritualism of the Upaniṣads as in the critical, sceptical, rationalistic and heterodox schools of thought that were contemporary with the Upaniṣads and which had their beginnings even in the period of the Samhitas. Buddha's opposition to the Vedic theology and the Upaniṣadic absolutistic metaphysics would appear to be a definite and monumental step in the advance of the heterodox ideology. Buddha may safely be taken to be the spokesman of the section that failed to receive consolation in the confused motley of the numerous gods or who failed to obtain intellectual and emotional response in the concept of a static primordial absolute reality utterly aloof in its archetypal supernal abode from the anguishes and sufferings of humanity. To the sensitive heart of Buddha deeply moved by the pervasiveness of human discomforts, disease, and death it was downright betrayal to harp on the uncontaminated bliss of the absolute being in the context of a world infected by tragic contradictions and fatality.

The denial of the soul in the Buddhist philosophy of *anātmavada* was a great break from the Upaniṣadic tradition. The very term *anātman* is deliberately designed to assert the great break from the Upaniṣadic tradition. There is no place for a soul in the teachings of Buddha.[1] There can be three possible conceptions of the soul. There is the primitive conception of the soul as almost a physical entity and a counterpart of the body. All objects in the world are supposed to have a soul according to the panpsychic conceptions of animism. In ancient Egypt, for example, there was the conception of a 'double' of the human being. After the death of the man this 'double' was supposed even to eat and drink and hence in the tombs of relations people used to put objects of food and drink for this departed double.[2] A second conception of the soul is psychological. The soul is regarded as the resultant of the total physical and psychical structure of a man. In modern terminology the

[1] For Buddhist Anātmanism see the verse of Vajirā in the *Therigatha*; The *Simha Sutta* of the *Samyutta Nikāya*; the *Samyutta Nikāya,* 1, 42 the *Majjhima Nikāya*, I, 138.

[2] Cf. *Chhāndogya*, VIII, 8.

soul as a psychological conception may be equated with a man's personality. This soul is sometimes supposed to be extinguished at the cessation of the physical being of the man.[1] The *Samyutta Nikāya* contains reference to a school—the *Ukkalavassabhanna*—which rejected the persistence of individuality after death. One of the schools of the Cārvakas accepted this psychological view of the soul.[2] There is the third or the metaphysical concept of the soul. In this sense there can be two sub-variants of the theory. One metaphysical view of the soul regards it as a spiritual substance. In this sense the Jainas, the Mimānsakas, the Naiyāyikas and the Sāmkhya accept the existence of a super-physical entity. This substance is supposed to transmigrate to other corporeal existences after the death of the physical body.[3] A second metaphysical view of the soul conceives of it as the limitation or unique particularisation or modalization of an absolute spiritual reality. The Upaniṣads generally tend towards this view of the soul. Buddha repudiates the metaphysical view of the soul. There is no place in his teachings for the anthropological and psychological conceptions of the soul either. Against the dominant *Ātmanism* of the period he stands for *anātman*. Sometimes relics of the anthropological view of the soul have been traced in the Buddhist conception of a *gandharva* which is an operative

[1] Cf. the *Katha. nāyamastīticaike.*

[2] For the views of the Dhūrta Cārvākas who absolutely denied a soul and the Suśikshita Cārvakas who held that there is a soul but is destroyed at death, see S.N. Dasgupta, *Indian Philosophy*, Vol. I, pp. 78-79.

[3] According to H. Jacobi, *Die Entwicklung der Gottesides bei den Indern* (1923), pp. 19ff., the middle Upaniṣads like the *Katha, Isa, Śvetāśvatara, Muṇḍaka* and *Mahānarāyana* and the younger Upaniṣads like the Praśna, the *Maitrāyani* and the *Māṇḍukya* have traces of Sāmkhya influence upon them. In these groups of Upaniṣads the doctrine of the personal immortality of monadically conceived soul appears, most probably under the influence of the Sāmkhya philosophy. This concept of the immortal soul was later accepted by the Nyāya, the Vaiśesika, the Mimāmsa and Jainism. But Jacobi's contention seems to be unfounded. As early as the *Śivasamkalpa Sūkta* of the *Vājasaneyi Samhitā* we find reference to *ajaram manah* or immortal mind. The occurrence of the word *me* would indicate that the Vedic poet has in mind a psychic and not a cosmic entity. Here at least there are germs of an incipient monadic conception of self. A monadic concept of the self may also be traced in the account of transmigration given in the *Brihādāaraṇyaka* where the analogy of the *triṇajalāyukā* is mentioned.

factor in the rebirth of man's personality. Sometimes the *vijnāna* which is one of the five factors in the *nāmarupa skandha* of the Buddhist psychological scheme has been interpreted as a parallel to the spiritual self. Sometimes the concept of the *pudgala* held by some of the Hīnayāna schools has been regarded as some kind of a spiritual soul. According to the Vātsiputriyas the *pudgala* is neither identical with nor different from the five *skandhas*. According to Stcherbatsky, all schools of Buddhism repudiated *ātmavāda* or the theory of a soul corresponding to a psycho-physical individual but the Sāmmitiyas and the Vātsiputrīyas adhered to the theory of *pudgalvāda* or the doctrine of permanent soul. Vasuvandhu attacked the *pudgalavādins*. But inspite of these speculations which interpret early Buddhism as some form of a soul-metaphysics, the dominant all-pervasive note of the Buddhist teachings as found in the Tripiṭakas is one of the negation of the soul as a substantial reality. This neutralization of the spiritual soul, as inculcated in the Upaniṣads, by reducing it to a complex of five psychophysical processes[1] as maintained in the doctrine of the *nāmarupa skandha* represents a frontal attack of Buddhism on the prevailing absolutist metaphysics. Sometimes it is stated that the concept *nāma* in *nāmarupa skandha* might have been taken from the *Atharvaveda* and the pre-Buddhistic literature. In the Upaniṣads the *nāmarupa* is the phenomenal appearance and the real substratum is behind that. But according to the Sarvastivādi school *nāmarupa* signifies the acceptance of a radical form of pluralistic realism. Jacobi wants to trace the roots of the five skandhas in the five Pranas of the Upaniṣadic tradition. C.A.F. Rhys Davids would like to trace their roots in the five *Indriyas*. But these are wild conjectures. There is not the least ideological affinity between them. There seems to be more truth in the view which would point out the affinity between the five skandhas and the five *Kosha* referred to in the *Taittiriya Upaniṣad*. The negation of the soul as a substance was a revolutionary doctrine in many sense.[2] It indicated

[1] In his famous sermon at Sārnatha, Buddha denied that *rupa, samjñā, vedanā, samskāra* and *vijñāna* could be regarded as the *attā*.

[2] It does not seem correct to trace the roots of the Buddhist conception of *anātman* in the notion of the *Shodasakala purusha* developed in the *Praśnopaniṣad*.

that the challenge represented by Buddhism was far more radical than that of the Jainas because the latter believed in the habitation by the soul in all kinds of substances. It made also, the further question of the identity of the psychic self and the cosmic and the trans-cosmic *brahman* meaningless because if the soul itself was a non-entity there was nothing worth-while to be gained by useless speculations about its future eschatological destiny. There are some passages in the Buddhist literature which however take a cautious attitude on the problem of the *attā*. In one of the dialogues Buddha says :

"If I, Ānanda, when the wandering monk Vacchagotta asked me : "is there the ego ?' had answered : 'the ego is,' would that have served my end, Ānanda, by producing in him the hnowledge ; all existences (*dhamma*) are non-ego ?' That it would not, sire'. But if I, Ānanda, when the wandering monk Vacchagotta asked me : 'Is, there not the ego ?' had answered : 'The ego is not,' then that [would lead] Vacchagotta to be thrown from the bewilderment into another : 'My ego, did it not exist before ? But now it exists no longer !'"[1]

The Buddhist concept of the *anātman* marked a more radical departure from the Brahmanical theology[2] than the mild and moderate protests of the Upaniṣads against the sacrificial liturgy.[3] No sacrificial cult could stand on the basis of 'a psychology without a soul.' Bhattacharya says that the sacrificers had such supreme faith in the power of the sacrificial mechanism that there was no need of God in this school of thought. But Bhattacharya is wrong in ascribing the later view of the Mimānsakas to the ritualists and sacrificers flourishing in the period

[1] *Ānandasuttam, Samyutta Nikāya*, Vol. II, (—Nalandā ed., Vol. III, p. 343), quoted in Oldenberg, *Buddha*, pp. 272-273.

[2] "Mahāvijita Jātaka" in the *Kuṭadanta Sutta, Dīgha Nikāya* (*Dīgha Nikāya*, Hindi Trans. pp. 50-55). According to A.M. Hocart, *Ritual and Emotion*, p. 203, the period of the Brahmanical liturgical books was the culmination of ritual complexity. An intellectual preoccupation with religious ceremonies is generally followed by an emotional reaction. Emotionalism began to comode the ritual in the Upaniṣads and in the shape of Buddhism to destroy it. According to Max Müller the *Muṇḍaka Upaniṣad* is the work of a Muṇḍaka or Buddhist monk who was yet faithful to the Brahmanic law. *SBE*, Vol. XVI, XXVII.

[3] For the relation between the Brahmanas and the Upaniṣads, F. Edgerton. "The Upaniṣads : What do they Seek, and Why," *Journal of American Oriental Society*, 1929, pp. 97-121.

previous to and contemporary with the rise of Buddhism.[1] It is true that in some of the Upaniṣads we find some kind of condemnation of the sacrificial creeds and formulas. In the Upaniṣads some attempts were made to allegorize and spiritualize the sacrificial cult but they (the Upaniṣads) accepted the validity of the traditional Vedic liturgy and ritualism as a path to the lower realm of *pitṛyāna*. Thus the sacrificial *karmakānda* received at least a subordinate place in the scheme of the Upaniṣadic thought. It is true that by the inculcation of the overwhelming superiority of a transcendental metaphysics, the Upaniṣads had tried to put before the people a goal higher than the dry mechanism of a credal and ritualistic sacrament.

There was no institution like the priesthood under Buddhism. There were no priests in the Samgha. Even among the lay Upāsakās of Buddhism, the far greater probability is that there would absolutely be no place for a priesthood in a religious system which believed in the surrender to Buddha and not to any God or deity. The Buddhist monks did not perform any religious ceremony and had no sacerdotal functions. The rejection of the priesthood was more trenchant in the Buddhistic than in the Upaniṣadic traditions.[2] The Upaniṣads had tolerated the priesthood. Aśvala, one of the teachers mentioned in the *Brihadāraṇyaka*, is a *Hotā*. In the *Chhāndogya Upaniṣad* we find that the esoteric doctrine of *pancāgni vidyā* is symbolically represented in terms of a sacrificial rite, thus indirectly implying that the services of a priest might possibly be required for the consummation of some of the processes mentioned there. Buddha's break with the institution of priesthood was far more fundamental than that of the Upaniṣads.[3]

[1] Vidhusekhara Bhattacharya, *The Basic Conception of Buddhism*, *op. cit.*, refers to the *Ṛgveda*, VIII, 48, 3, where the Vedic poet states that they have drunk the Soma juice, become immortal and known the gods.

[2] According to Rapson, *Ancient India*, p. 14, Jainism and Buddhism were revolts against Brāhmaṇa tradition.

[3] There is no foundation for B.M. Barua's view, *A History of Pre-Buddhistic Philosophy*, p. 244, that Bhāradvaja's transcendentalism prepared the way for the rationalism of Buddha. The only common point

Although Buddha is represented in the Tripiṭakas as being deliberately silent about the concept of an absolute spiritual existent and once or twice scoffingly treats the entire theme, there is the recognition in early Buddhism of the concept of *avidyā* which is an important instrument in the dialectics of gloom and spiritualism. Both the Upaniṣads and early Buddhism accept the concept of *avidyā*. But there is one important difference in the connotation of this term. The Upaniṣads tend to conceive *avidyā* at a cosmic level also, although this tendency receives its final crystallization only in later Vedānta. Early Buddhism, on the other hand, recognizes *avidyā* only at the psychological level. At best *avidyā* is conceived as the basis of individual existence—*bhāva* and *jāti*.

Thus we see how deep, radical and fundamental was the gap between the traditional religious system of thought and liturgy and that of the Buddhists. Buddha repudiated monistic metaphysics, ridiculed monotheistic and polytheistic conceptions and utterly pulverized the concept of a soul as a self-subsistent reality. By challenging the validity of the sacrificial cult and the institution of priesthood he drew himself further away from the conservative Brāhmanical elite who were the repositories and conservers of the contemporary religious tradition.

The concept of *nirvāṇa* is also a doctrine which hits at the roots of the Upaniṣads. Buddha's refusal to say anything about the future destiny of the Tathāgata is persistent. The eschatological problem of the existence of one who has attained *nirvāṇa* is a great mystery. The nature of nirvāṇa according to Buddhist authors is controversial. There is a school which regards *nirvāṇa* as tantamount to utter extinction. The other school would interpret *nirvāṇa* only as an annihilation of pain and sorrow.[1] Even if this later interpretation were true and

is that both refused to accept the sacrificial cult. But there is no logical transition from transcendentalism to rationalism.

[1] Poussin, *The Way of Nirvāṇa*. Poussin, "A Few Words on Sukha," *K.B. Pathak Commemoration Volume* (Poona, Bhandarkar Research Institute, 1932), pp. 55-56. According to H.G. Wells, *Outline of History*, p. 393, nirvāṇa signifies serenity of soul. *Nirvāṇa* does not mean extinction. It only means the extinction of future personal aims that necessarily make life base or pitiful or dreadful. When the first-personal pronoun has vanished from his private thoughts, then he has reached the higher

nirvāṇa was only the absolute neutralization of suffering, it is never possible to equate it with the Upaniṣadic conceptions of emancipation. According to Caird, the early Buddhist religion treats the whole objective world as an illusion from which it is the highest duty of man to free himself. The religion of Buddha begins with the negation of all the objective gods of earlier Hinduism or the reduction of them to parts in the great illusion of outward existence, and which at last finds the divine, if anywhere, only in the self-negating process of the finite mind and the *nirvāna* which is supposed to be its result.[1] The ultimate spiritual destiny of the men of knowledge, according to the Upaniṣads, is a positive state of fullness of being and the attainment of absolute delight. This goal of final bliss can provide a great impetus and teleological incentive to the spiritual endeavours of men. Even a lady like Maitreyī hankers after immortality and refuses to be satisfied with mundane prosperity. The teleology of immortality is indeed, blissful and inspiring. At a few places in the Tripiṭaka literature *nirvāṇa* is interpreted as an indeterminate predicateless something. Thus even if *nirvāṇa* were not total extinction but some kind of positive absolute reality, its conceptualization in terms of negative predications is possibly aimed as a deliberate counterpoise to the Upaniṣadic characterizations of the blissful nature of the supreme status of the man of knowledge. There can be no doubt that from the terminological standpoint the concept of *nirvāṇa* is an antithesis to the concept of *brahmaloka* of the Upaniṣads. It is true that at times the Upaniṣads also tend to characterize the supreme reality in negative terms—the terms *neti neti* are supreme example of this negative methodology, but notwithstanding these negative characterizations, there is no doubt in the minds of the Upaniṣadic teachers that the final spiritual goal of man is positive plenitude of bliss. In some of the later Mahāyāna teachers like Aśvaghosha we do find some formulations of the concept of an Absolute. There is a passage in the *Iti-Vuttaka* which might imply belief in an Absolute. "There is O monks ! something not born, non-exis-

wisdom, *nirvāṇa*, serenity of soul. According to the *Samyutta Nikāya*, III, 109, it is a wicked heresy to interpret *nirvāṇa*, as extinction. Dahlke and Oldenberg accept a negative view of *nirvāṇa*.

[1] Edward Caird, *Evolution of Religion*, Vol. I, pp. 33-34.

tent, not made, not compounded. If there were not this something not born, non-existent, not made, not compounded there would not be known here deliverance from what is born, existent, made and compounded".[1] But even if at the metaphysical level there may be some passages which assert a more positive and absolutist conception of reality, it remains true that at the religious level the concept of *nirvāṇa* might not evoke the same emotional response as perhaps the concept of *mukti* as propagated in the traditional metaphysics of the day, can do. If Buddha had the slightest certainty about the reality of a permanent spiritual existent, the concept of *nirvāṇa* would be the most unfortunate depict the state of realization of that indeterminate ultimate.[2] A negative concept could not evoke the sympathy of the masses which is the desideratum of a popular religious movement as distinguished from an aristocratic metaphysical conceptualism meant for the select coterie of thinkers and intellectuals. I am constrained to believe that just as the concept of *anātman* is deliberately designed to challenge the concept of the self as propounded in the Upaniṣads, so also the concept of *nirvāṇa* is deliberately chosen as a conceptual antithesis to the Upaniṣadic notions of *ānandam brahman*. If Paṇini belongs to the pre-Buddhistic days and if the word *nirvāṇa* occurring in the *Ashtādhyayi* is pre-Buddhistic, still the appropriation of this concept in the metaphysics of early Buddhism would imply a definite protest against the notions of contemporary absolutist metaphysics and the ideas of traditional religious systems. Thus we see the radical, almost unbridgeable gap between the Upaniṣads and early Buddhism.

[1] *Iti-Vuttaka*, E.T. by J. H. Moore (New York, Columbia University Press, 1908), p. 43.

[2] There is no foundation for Radhakrishnan's statement (*Gotama Buddha*, p. 49) that the Upaniṣadic *brahman* is called by Buddha as *Dharma* "to indicate its essentially ethical value for us on the empiric plane." According to Buddha, *Dharma* is the moral norm and never a supreme primordial reality. Nor is there any foundation for W.S. Urquhart's statement (*Vedānta and Modern Thought*, Oxford University Press. 1928, p. 94) that there is a good deal in favour of the view that Buddha without stating his attitude "implicitly admitted an ultimate reality." Similarly baseless is Melamed's contention, '*Spinoza and Buddha*, p. 274, that Buddha often referred to union with the cosmic principle and this is identical with Spinoza's *amor Dei intellectualis*.

2. *The Influence of the Upaniṣads upon Buddhism*

But although in some of his dominant philosophical conceptions Buddha's attitude was a radical departure from the Upaniṣadic system of thought, still there are some unmistakable evidences of the influence of the Upaniṣads upon early Buddhism. Buddha was inspired by the contemporary monastic ideal of life. In the *Ṛgveda* there is the picture of the inspired *muni* which some Jaina scholars regard as a reference to their Sadhus.[1] The word *yatayah*, also occurs in the Vedic literature. But the institution of an organized monasticism cannot be proved for the Vedic time. There was no organized monastic institution in the ancient civilizations of Egypt, Assyria and China although in the Sumerian culture we find references to the existence of sacred virgins dedicating their lives to intellectual and commercial pursuits. The Vedic attitude towards life and its problems is one of strength and conquest, hope and optimism. But with the Upaniṣads the clouding veil of gloom and pessimism makes its appearance.[2] The phenomena of the world come to be regarded as full of sorrow.[3] In the *Kaṭha Upaniṣad* we find reference to the prevalence of cosmic misery —*lokadukha*.[4] But although the Indian philosophical schools accept the immensity of cosmic suffering, they also prescribe a way of release and emancipation from suffering. According to the Buddhist system, the first and the second truths assert the existence of cosmic suffering which is explained through the formula of *pratityasamutpāda.* The third and the fourth truths indicate the possibility of the complete cessation of suffering through the pursuit of the Aryan eight-fold path. A similar philosophy of the existence and extinction of suffering is propounded in other systems like the Nyāya, the Yoga and the

[1] *Ṛgveda*, X, 136. The word *muni* also occurs in the *Brihadāraṇyaka*, III, 5, 1.

[2] Paul Deussen, *The Philosophy of the Upaniṣads* (Edinburgh, 1906), pp. 140-146.

[3] *Brihadāraṇyaka*, III, 4, 2 ; III, 5, 1 ; III, 7, 23 ; *ato 'nyad ārtam*, — what is distinct from him that is full of suffering."

[4] *Kaṭha*, II, 2, 11 ; *na lipyate lokadukhena bāhyah.* According to Brihadratha, as reported in the first Prapāthaka of the *Maitrāyani, sarvam chedam kshayishnu* and *nihsāre asmin sarire kim kamopabhogaih.* Naciketa says in the *Kaṭha, api sarvam jivitamalpameva*

Sāmkhya. Yājnavalkya fails to find happiness in a householder's life and finally renounces the world. In the case of Yājnavalkya, monasticism might be a social corollary to the concept of a supreme spiritual Absolute whose overwhelming majesty and dominance is a direct contrast to the transitory, painful and ephemeral character of the worldly phenomena. Hence his quest for the supernal absolute is postulated upon the belief in the eventual hopelessness of all earthly endeavours.[1] But although monasticism makes its appearance in the Upaniṣadic age, it is conceived primarily at an individual level. Perhaps Yājnavalkya is a monumental but isolated example of a monastic figure. Angirā and Pippalāda appear to be heads of educational establishments and are not peripatetic monastic preachers. Ushasta Cākrāyaṇa, Raikva and Uddālaka Āruṇi are men of the world. Some of the celebrated figures of the Upaniṣads like Janaka, Ajātaśatru and Pravāhaṇa Jaivali are householders. But if monasticism is an isolated phenomenon in the Upaniṣads, the organized monkhood of early Buddhism is a great and vital social reality.[2] The widespread movement of monasticism that we find associated with the religion of Buddha is inexplicable if considered only as based on the Upaniṣadic parallel and model.[3] There must be some deeper causes of this monastic movement. Analysing the origin of the concept of *mukti* Deussen says :

1 Edward Caird, *Evolution of Religion*. Vol. I, p. 361, says with reference to Buddhism : "The strange faith in which...India found healing for its pains, and deliverance from the aimlessness and meanness of a life in which men were no longer bound together by effective national bonds or animated by worthy social ambitions. The nobler spirits of India—thrown back upon themselves from a world in which they could no longer see any divine power revealed, but only a vain cycle of meaningless change ...sought to find peace [in nirvāṇa]......Hence the Buddhist rises to an all embracing love or charity for all beings, immersed like himself in the pains of existence......Such an attitude of mind is experienced only as the extreme of a religion of subjectivity, in which even subjectivity loses its meaning."

2 In the *Anguttara Nikāya*, III, 451, however, there is reference to twenty-one laymen who had been Arahats. There is special mention there of Shuddhodana, the father of Buddha.

3 According to I.B. Horner, *The Early Buddhist Theory of Man Perfected* (London, Williams & Norgate, 1936), pp. 55-56, the Buddhist concept of the *arahat* is not influenced by any Upaniṣadic legacy.

"The attempt has often been made to understand man's longing for deliverance from another side as the result of the heavy pressure upon the Indian people of the Brahmanical system. Thereby, according to the view suggested, the ancient delight in existence had been ruined and lost in consequence of the subservience of the mind to the Brāhmaṇas, and the body to the Kshatriyas. But not to mention that the conditions of life in the rich valley of the Ganges were in all probability hardly worse than formerly in the Panjab, and that the idea of emancipation had certainly arisen not in the circle of the oppressed but rather in that of the oppressors, a disposition to pessimism, such as the theory assumes, was not at all peculiar to the times in which the doctrine of emancipation arose. It is true that by emancipation suffering also with all its possibilities was removed ; but Buddhism was the first to transform that which was a mere consequence into a motive, and by conceiving emancipation as an escape from the sufferings of existence, to make selfishness the ultimate mainspring of existence,—even if not to the extent that was done later by Islam, which is never weary of depicting to the people the glories of heaven and the terrors of hell."[1]

The Upaniṣads inculcate a life of meditation and contemplation of the great truths but they do not emphasize withdrawal from the mundane pursuits of a householder's life. In Buddhism, on the other hand, the stress on the renunciation of all ties of the home life is dominant. The occasional disgust expressed in the Upaniṣads at the contemptible character of worldly existence is transformed into the Buddhist gospel of permanent recoil from the sorrowful and evanescent nature of mundane life. It is possible that the renunciation of Mahāvira, the Jaina prophet, might have been of some inspiration to Buddha. Mahāvira also organized his band of monastic disciples. There were other monastic congregations also at the time Buddha flourished.[2] The germs of the monastic movement which began in the days of the Upaniṣads assume tremendous proportions under the leadership of the new Śramaṇa teachers like Mahāvira and Buddha.[3] In the personal psychological make-up of

[1] Paul Deussen, *The Philosophy of the Upaniṣads*, p. 341.

[2] Pāṇini, *Ashtādhyayi*, V, I, 94 : *Tadasya brahmacharyam.* Rhys Davids refers to Tāpasas as spiritual wanderers.

[3] Hermann Jacobi, *Jaina Sutras*, *SBE*, Vol. XXII, pp. XXIV-XXV. "Our foregoing inquiry suggests where we have to look for the originals of the monastic orders of the Jainas and Buddhists. The Brahmanic ascetic was their model, from which they borrowed many important practices and institutions of ascetic life. This observation is not an entirely new one. Professor Max Müller has already, in his *Hibbert Lectures*

Buddha there seems to be a supreme fascination for the bliss and glories of the monastic life.[1] In the *Rāshtrapāla Suttanta* of the *Majjhima Nikāya* there is a categorization of four factors which ordinarily impelled people to adopt the monastic life : (i) *jarāhāni*, old age, decrepitude, (ii) *vyadhihāni*, fatal disease, (iii) *bhogahāni*, loss of fortune and (iv) *jnātihāni* : loss of relations. But the monasticism of Rāshtrapāla, the son of Agra Kulika is based on a different motivation. Rāshtrapāla is a Buddhist Bhikkhu and he became a monk because he found that the world of becoming did not have any sound basis. Buddha's admiration for the life of the ascetic Bhikkhu makes him condemn in unmeasured terms the evils of sense gratifications. He says :

"A butcher throws before a dog tormented by hunger, a bare and fleshless bone with which he cannot satisfy his hunger — like such a bare bone are the sensual pleasures, full of torment and sufferings, out of which only evils arise. As a bird of prey pounces upon a piece of meat and other birds attack him and illtreat him —so only suffering and evil arise from sensual pleasures. The sage shrinks back before sensual pleasures as from a pit filled with glowing coals. Sensual pleasures are like a beautiful dream vision, which vanishes when one awakes, like a borrowed treasure, on account of which one is envied by those who do not know that it is only borrowed. A man comes into a forest, sees a tree laden with fruit, and climbs up in order to eat till he is satisfied : then a second man comes along, sees the same tree, and in order to gain possession of the fruit, sets about felling the tree : evil will befall the man up in the tree : thus only suffering and torments and all kinds of evil arise from the gratification of sensual pleasures."[2]

Buddha's great renunciation permanently added a sacramental halo to the monastic ideal of life and gave to monasticism immense esteem and reverence. In the Buddhist stress on the monastic ideal of life, however, we may accept some degree of Upaniṣadic influence.

The concept of *karman* reveals the immense debt which early Buddhism owes to the previous philosophical tradition. According to the Upaniṣads a man's personality is constituted by his

(p. 351), stated a similar opinion ; likewise Professor Buhler, in his translation of the Baudhāyana Sutra (passim) ; and Professor Kern, in his *History of Buddhism in India*. [*Manual of Indian Buddhism*.]"

1 The *Dhammika Sutta* of the *Sutta Nipāta*.

2 *Potaliya Sutta Majjhima Nikāya*, No. 54.

actions. It is true, however, that the ultimate primacy belongs according to the teachings of the Upaniṣads to philosophical gnosis and not to noble actions. The belief, nevertheless, in the operative efficacy of a spiritual law of *karman* is strong. The future births of a person are determined by his actions.[1] In Buddhism also the knowledge of the four Aryan truths is emphasized but *karman* has a fundamental importance in Buddhist thought. Due to the great importance of ethics in early Buddhism *karman* has necessarily been emphasized.[2] It is surprising that although Buddhism repudiated the concept of soul as a substance it could not do away with the notion of rebirth. But according to Buddhism there is the rebirth not of any substantial spirit but only of character or personality which is constituted by *karman*. According to Paul Deussen, *karman* must have in every case an individual bearer and that is what the Upaniṣads call *ātman* and what the Buddhists inconsistently deny. Hiriyanna criticizes Deussen and says that according to Buddhism there is rebirth not only at the end of this life as in other Indian systems but at every instant. Buddhism denies a 'stable self' but accepts a 'fluid self'. Sometimes it is said that the concept of *karman* was a new addition to Upaniṣadic thought. This is indicated by the confidential character in which Yājnavalkya and Jāratkārava speak about the matter.[3] Although the roots of the theory of *karman* as a moral law lie in the Vedic concept of *rita* it is possible that the implications of *karman*

[1] *yathā karma yathā śrutam.*

[2] According to M. Hiriyanna, *Outlines of Indian Philosophy*, p. 154, the rationalisation of the doctrine of *karman* brought about by Buddha can be understood in contrast to the other schools of thought because in the traditional Hindu doctrine the allotment of pain and pleasure was in supernatural hands and in the Jaina theory of *Karman* there is reference to subtle matter adhering to and pulling down the soul from its natural spiritual height.

[3] *Brihadāraṇyaka*, III, 2, 13. There is no foundation for Hume's view (*Thirteen Principal Upaniṣads*, p. 6) that the theory of *karman* stated here and the further view of Yājnavalkya that after death the *ātman* goes to *ākāśa* — *ākāshamatmā* — are "out and out the Buddhist doctrine." In order to substantiate his queer thesis of the influence of Buddhism upon the Upaniṣads, Hume refers to the occurrence of the word *sarvāvato* in the *Brihadāraṇyaka*, IV, 3, 9. This word *sarvāvato* is found in the *Brihadāraṇyaka* and in northern Buddhist writings.

had not been yet sufficiently generalised.[1] Buddha imparted a very wide and comprehensive significance to *karman*. Karman constitutes the being of a man. One's action is one's fate.[2] One is the maker of one's destiny. At the time Buddha flourished there were dialectical antagonistic tussles going on between the respective protagonists of actionism and non-actionism. Makkhali Gośāla and Purāna Kassapa (Kaśyapa) were fatalists.[3] They did not believe that good and bad actions lead to good and bad results. Buddha foresaw the disastrous consequences for moral life that would follow from a non-adherence to the law of *karman*. It is possible that the Upaniṣads might not have been the sole roots of the Buddhist theory of *karman*. Jainism also strongly adheres to the belief in the concept of *karman*. Nevertheless the great influence of the Upaniṣadic concept of *karman* on early Buddhism has to be accepted.

The famous formula of the *pratityasamutpāda* or the *dvādaśāyatana* is a great example of the use of the category of causation, or more technically, dependent origination, to explain individual life and destiny. Several of the terms in the *dvādaśāyatana* are also used in the Upaniṣads. It is possible to find the germinal roots of the *dvādaśa nidāna* in the *Brihadāraṇyaka* notion that a man's being is constituted by his *karman*, his *karman* is determined by his will (*kratu*), and his will is impelled

1 According to A.K. Coomaraswamy, *Buddha and the Gospel of Buddhism*, p. 93, it is due to Gautama to say that the abstract concept of causality as the fundamental principle of the phenomenal world is by him far more firmly grasped and more clearly emphasized than we find it in the Upaniṣads, Nevertheless the thought and the word "Becoming" are common to both and both are in agreement that this becoming is the order of the world, the mark of organic existence.

2 The *Silavimarśa Jātaka* (*Jātakas*, Vol. III, pp. 292-93).

3 The Ājivikās denied freedom of will. Hoernle, "Ājivikās", *Encyclopaedia of Religions and Ethics*. D.R. Bhandarkar, "Ājivikās, *The Indian Antiquary*, Vol. XLI, 1912, pp. 286-292, refers to Nanda Vachcha and Kisa Samkichcha as the predecessors of Gośāla. Buddha criticized Gośāla's conception of there being neither action nor consequence. Purana Kassapa believed in the passive (*nishkriya*) character of the soul and hence denied the consummation of the fruits of actions. Ajita was a believer in destructionism (*uchhedavāda*) and hence denied the law of moral causation. According to B.M. Barua, "The Ājivikās", *Journal of the Department of Letters*, Calcutta University, Vol. II, 1920. Sarbhanga Kaundanya and Udayi Kundiyāyana were original Ājivikā teachers.

by his fundamental desire or Eros (*Kāma*).

The dominant note of the spiritual teachings of the Upaniṣads is the inculcation of the immanence of the spirit and the identity of the human self with the universal and transcendent reality. But contrasted to the mechanical and dogmatic ritualism of the Brāhmaṇas, the Upaniṣads also emphasize the ethical note. Some of the Upaniṣads like the *Taittirīya*, the *Muṇḍaka* and the *Kaṭha* emphatically assert that without absolute adherence to the path of piety, it is not possible to realize the spirit. The supreme truth can be realized only by the strictest observance of the moral norms.[1] According to the *Brihadāraṇyaka*, it is imperative to renounce the egoistic desire for wealth, family and progeny in order to be a true aspirant for the supernal reality. Among the Orphics and the Pythagoreans also, there was great stress on the pursuit of the ethical way as a prerequisite for spiritual realization. The neo-Platonists, the medieval Christian monastics and the Sufis also believed in the sanctity and supremacy of moral endeavours. Buddha subscribes to the supremacy of the moral norm. He condemns the undue importance of physical askesis. He would not advocate the practice of Yoga for obtaining supernormal powers. He believes in an ethical *tapasyā* and inward meditation. He was a wise, humane and compassionate teacher. His stress is on holy life.[2] As a fulfilment of the ethical endeavours, he inculcates the filling in of the mind with pure feelings. It is true that in early Buddhism we have dialectical discussions about the psychology of *anātman* and the metaphysics of *pratityasamutpāda* but the overwhelming stress is on the conquest of pain and sorrow through a pious life. Thus it can be stated that the ethical discipline which is mentioned in the Upaniṣads is made the dominant theme in early Buddhism.[3] In Greece

[1] *Chhāndogya*, II, 23 ; V. 10, 1. *Brihadāraṇyaka*, IV, 4, 22 : V, II. *Taittirīya*, 1, 9, III.

[2] According to John Mackenzie, *Hindu Ethics*, Oxford University Press, 1922, p. 103, there is insistence on love in Buddhist ethics and with the recognition of the virtue of love, the social gospel for relief to mankind enjoys a greater prominence in Buddhist ethics than in the Hindu ethics. Love is more in conformity with the *ārya ashtāngika mārga* than with the Upaniṣadic way of gnostic salvation.

[3] According to B.G. Tilak, *Gitā-Rahasya* (Hindi edition, 1950), pp. 570-585. Buddhism is a descendant of Vedism. He thinks that the methodo-

Socrates stressed the ethical and humanistic orientation in philosophy as opposed to the previous stress on cosmogonic speculations. Instead of the *arche* and the *apeiron*, Socrates called attention to virtue as knowledge. Buddha also stood for the ethical way. He taught that a dedicated pursuit of the Aryan eight-fold way was the sure means to trans-mundane illumination and even super-rational consciousness.

The theory of Yoga is also mentioned in the Upaniṣads. Yoga is sometimes recognized as a possible way for the realization of the Absolule but it is true that the greatest emphasis in this system is on philosophic and mystical contemplation. Buddha himself was a Yogi.[1] In early Buddhism there is an elaborate theory of the different stages of meditative cognition.[2] But according to both—the Upaniṣads and Buddhism, Yoga is not the pre-eminent path to the cessation of suffering. However, it can be said that the emphasis on the technics of Yoga is one of the common points between the Upaniṣads and early Buddhism. The *Satipatthāna Sutta* refers to the various kinds of exercises of *praṇayāma*. Sometimes it has been maintained that Buddha had learnt from his teachers the method of *samādhi* but the technic of *prajñā* (wisdom) has been his particular contribution to the science of meditation The advocacy of Yogic practices and the references to the attainment of some form of superior transcendent wisdom (*prajñā*)

logy of emancipation outlined in the Upaniṣads is similar to the fourth Aryan truth as formulated in Buddhism. Although Buddha did not adhere to the Upaniṣadic concepts of *ātman* and *brahman*, still the stress on making the mind peaceful, disinterested and passionless is similar in both the systems.

[1] After the attainment of enlightenment Buddha performed some magical feats or *yamaka-pāṭihāriya*. Kern, *Manual of Indian Buddhism* (Encyclopaedia of Indo-Aryan Research, Strassburg, Karl J. Trubner, 1898), p. 21, finds kinship between *yamaka* and *yoga* ("*yamaka*, double, being nearly synonymous with Yoga, conjunction"). According to Kern, the practice of Yoga was hardly less developed in the time of Buddha than in the time of Patanjali.

[2] Senart *Origines Bouddhiques* (Paris, Ernest Leroux, 1907), translated into English by M. Roy, *Indian Historical Quarterly*, Vol. VI, 1930. In view of the elaborate discussion of *jnāna* in early Buddhism Max Müller (*Last Essays*, *second series*, 1901, p. 121) is mistaken in his statement that Buddhism is "the highest Brahmanism popularised, everything esoteric being abolished."

and enlightenment makes early Buddhism a rather confused system of thought. It is possible to accept the efficacy of meditation even in a non-theistic system. The Sāmkhya provides an example. But the theory of mystic vision obtains its rational justification only when some form of absolute spiritual real is posited which is to be intuitively realized. Early Buddhism accepts the transcendence of normal rational criteria, it adheres to the efficacy of the path of Yogic concentration and contemplation but it repudiates, even if it be by silence and by a deliberate indifference, the concept of a spiritual Existent. But, at least the partial acceptance of the technics of Yoga by early Buddhism, is a testimony to the fact that as a religious movement, although the latter could dispense with an Absolute and a personal God, it dare not go against the socially prevalent criteria of some of the accompaniments of a holy man.

3. *Conclusion : The Decline of Vedic Religion and The Rise of Early Buddhism*

According to Windelband there are three factors operative in the appearance and success of any system—(i) the "logic of things"—the pragmatic demands of the existing types of speculation, (ii) the Cultural Complex—the general ethos of time and the complication or interweaving of problems—and (iii) the Individual—the personality of the thinker.[1] It has to be remembered that the greatness of a genius consists in providing an original synthesis of the dominant ideas of the age Genius is not another name for mere exercise in novelty or eccentricity. The important point is not the derivation of an idea from this or that source. What is of significance is the final form provided and the impact of an idea on the social forces and movements.

There are differences of opinion as to the true nature of the Vedic religion. But even the acutest critic testifies to the growth of cosmological speculations and pantheistic and even monotheistic conceptions towards the end of the Saṁhitā period. The seers of the Upaniṣads inherited the philosophical legacy

[1] Wilhelm Windelband, *A History of Philosophy* (E.T. by James H. Tufts, New York, The Macmillan Co., 1901. 2nd ed., tenth printing, 1953), pp. 8-18, has discussed the conception of the history of philosophy as the product of a great variety of factors. For him the history of philosophy is both a philological-historical and critico-philosophical science.

of the Saṁhitā period as is clear from phrases like *ṛchābhyuktam*. But the Vedic religion had also a practical ritualistic side. This tradition was extended and carried to a logical finish in the Brāhmaṇas.

Anthropologists and ethnologists trace in the Vedic religion an amalgam of conceptions of different races. The *Ṛgveda* represents the religion of the nature-worshipping Brahmin priests and Indo-Aryans. The *Atharvaveda* shows a stage when the Indo-Aryans were in contact with the other Easterners and were absorbing elements of folk-religion. The legacy of the Indus valley people—the Proto-Australoids, the Mediterraneans and the Mongoloids was also there. It seems to be clear, hence that the religion prevalent in India from c. 2000 B.C. to 1000 B.C. was a complex structure. Because it was influenced by different races, it can be easily understood that other racial contacts and movements also, in their turn, could change it.[1]

The Brāhmaṇas, the exegetical literature concerning the Vedic sacrifices, carried to great extremes the ritualistic details. The *Aitareya Brāhmaṇa* contains the story of the sacrifice of *Śunaḥśepa*. The *Śatapatha* is a monumental classic of the science of the sacrifice, far more detailed than the Babylonian liturgy. The Israelite and Phoenician religions also contained sacrificial traits. There are vital difference between the Vedic and the West Asiatic systems of sacrifice. But sacrifice, as the supreme concern of human life, was cultivated only in the period of the Brāhmaṇas. The interpretations of Mahīdhara point out that the Vedic texts of *Yajurveda* were interpreted to support violently horrible practices. Violence and slaughter characterized the sacrifice in the Brāhmaṇa period. The *Kuṭadanta Suttra* of the *Digha Nikāya* contains testimony for this. Hence there appears to be a two-fold cause of the reaction against the sacrificial system—(1) Its complication and mechanisation were bound to evoke rationalistic[2] and philosophical criticisms. (2) Its violence was bound to lead to an ethical and pietistic revolt. As times showed, the Upaniṣads heralded the intellec-

[1] There are some historical parallels,—*e.g.* changes in Buddhism due to Hellenic contact and changes in Israelite religion due to Semitic-Babylonian and Zoroastrian-Persian contact.

[2] Rationalism, not in the Kantian sense, but in the Voltairean and the French enlightenment philosophical sense.

tual protest, and the ethical humanitarian ground of reaction was prepared by the great sage of the clan of the Sākyas.

The speculative tendency is uppermost in the Upaniṣads. The Upaniṣadic Absolute was the supracosmic parallel of the psychic *ātman*. According to Western notions this is the culmination of subjective religion, because the notion of soul is carried to the highest immanental and transcendental levels. The various deities who might have been worshipped by the people then *i.e.*, in the Upaniṣads, as is clear from the *bhāṣya* of Śamkara, are the imperfect manifestations of the Absolute. The conception of the Absolute marks the death of all religions,[1] provided we exclude from the contents of religions the deepest and highest mystical vision. Religion or *upāsanā* as Śamkara says proceeds on the duality of the worshipper and the worshipped. The monistic idealistic teaching demonstrates that even the creator, cosmic God is an inferior impermanent reality. The *Māṇḍukya Upaniṣad* contains a distinction between the God of religions (the third stage of consciousness), and the Absolute of mysticism (the fourth stage of consciousness). The doctrines of Uddālaka Āruni and Yājnavalkya are a severe challenge to all objective religious conceptions.

The popular objective foundations of the Vedic religion were sought to be destroyed by the Upaniṣads. The various *devalokas* were all subordinated to the non-spatial psychic Brahmaloka. A new hypothesis may here be pointed out. The various opinions of the various Upaniṣadic teachers as to the location of the Absolute in the sun, moon, *vidyut*, etc., may be actual historical references in the sense that these deities might have been worshipped then as supreme deities. The *Brahmajāla Sutta* of *Dīgha Nikāya* contains allusions to such worship. Instead of supporting the popular religious notions and practices, as has been done for Christianity in the Middle Ages by scholastic philosophers, the Upaniṣads carried an indirect revolt against all objective religious practices.

They also protested against the aristocracy of birth. Highest knowledge of spirituality was being imparted to Satyakāma of low birth. Hence the superiority of the Brāhmaṇas, which is

[1] Hegel, *Philosophy of Religion*, Vols. I and II. Caird, *Evolution of Religion*, Vol. I, pp. 316-376.

so prominent in the Brāhmaṇa texts, in so far as they even claimed exemption from royal control, was undermined. The Vedantic knowledge is stated to have descended from the Kṣatriyas to the Brāhmaṇas. Pravāhaṇa Jaivali, the Kṣatriya, imparts education to both Śvetaketu and his father Uddālaka Āruṇi.

The Upaniṣads tried to minimise the importance of Yajña in a two-fold way. (1) The *Muṇḍaka* outspokenly derides the ritualistic system as futile and as being preached by the ignorant people.[1] (2) Sometimes they show that study and meditation are the highest kind of *Yajña.* At times the pure life is conceived as Yajña, as in the Orphic and the Pythagorean sects. Thus the ritualistic sacrifice is substituted by intellectual sacrifice.

The attitude of the Upaniṣads towards the Vedas is one of compromise. As is clear from the *Muṇḍaka* and from the speech of Sanatkumāra, the Vedas were given an honoured place, though not accepted as the final word for emancipation. But anyhow the traditions of Vedic scholarship were continued in the various residences of the Upaniṣadic Āchāryas and their *antevāsins.* These centres were economically very potent, as is clear from the munificent offerings to Raikva and Yājnavalkya. If in the case of the later Buddhistic religion it is argued that the economic prosperity of the Vihāras was a corrupting influence, if in the case of Christianity it is argued that the growing secularisation and wealth of the church was a factor of clerical decline necessitating various monastic reforms ; it may be probable that the Vedic religion too would have suffered a decline due to the enervating influence of the economically almost self-sufficient Vedic scholarship centres and a priesthood rich in cattle. There is a tone of sarcasm in the statement of Yājnavalkya—*gokāmā eva vayam* (which may be called eudaemonistic ethics).

The Upanisaḍs thus attacked the strongholds of Vedic religion. Another attack came from the Sophistic and ethical movements of the 7th and 6th centuries B.C. Just as Socrates and his successors Plato and Aristotle attacked the Greek religion and wanted to set up an ethical and idealistic standard, so also Buddha tried to establish his Aryan truths on the inalien-

[1] Cf. the intellectual protest of Heraclitus against Greek religious sacrifice. Plato emphasises intellectual contemplation of the Ideas.

able foundation of a very profound concern for human miseries. Buddha wanted to remove the sufferings of the masses not by carrying on a wholesale political and economic revolution, but by providing the psychological remedy of a deep unconcern for the world and its allurements. He wanted the eradication of *tṛṣṇā* and the destruction of the five *upādānaskandha*. The teachings of Buddha may have been partly idealistic, being constructed against the background of the Upaniṣadic metaphysics, but so far as the Tripiṭakas and their actual teachings are concerned, the doctrines of *nirvāṇa* Anātmanism, dynamic nature of the transitory world characterised by the *Pratityasamutpāda* were in no way favourable to the Vedic religion. Buddha did not carry on an open crusade against the Vedic savants and their cherished beliefs and dogmas. He tried to ennoble the prevalent violent sacrificial system. He provided for sacrifice of grains, etc., and tried to moralise the sacrifices like the Hebrew Prophets by giving the highest importance to ethical acts. He opposed the contemporary renowned scholars of Brāhmaṇism on three-fold bases : (1) He severely challenged the claim of attainment of unity with *brahmā* (m.) of the Brahmins. He also derided the search after *brahman* as a futile endeavour. He propounded that neither the ṛṣis nor their ancestors up to the seventh in ascending order had a glimpse of *brahman*. He condemned the invocation of gods and the enchanted songs sung in their praise at the time of sacrifices. (2) He claimed that he preached the way to supracosmic vision, to supreme knowledge and to *nirvāṇa*. It is mentioned in the Upaniṣads and occasionally even in the *Ṛgveda* that the supreme end of human life is not study or reflection, but self-realisation. Buddha always claimed to have been the realised and enlightened Arhat and Tathāgata. According to legends and myths, the brahmanic scholars paled into insignificance due to the supernormal powers and prowess manifested by Buddha. Further, the latter was a keen dialectician and debator and it was very difficult to corner him. (3) Buddha hit at the gross worldliness of the contemporary Brahmin scholars and priests. Even the king Ajātaśatru and Prasenajit were struck with the purit and holy living of the Buddhist monks and their austere med tations continued lifelong as distinguished from the small duration of the *brahmacarya* of the other religious systems.

The teachings of Buddha were in consonance, to a certain extent, with the teachings of the Veda and Upaniṣads in the ethical spirit, although ethics were greatly preponderant in his system. As contradistinguished from him were the grossly materialistic and hedonistic Cārvākas, the nihilistic and deterministic teachers like Kaccāyana, Keśakambala, Gośāla, and the relativists Mahāvira, Belatthaputta, and some others.[1] These had absolutely no connexion with the Vedic religion. The Cārvākas derided the Vedic texts as works of cheats. According to the naturalists (*svabhāvavādi*) and the mechanists there was no purpose in nature. But Buddha held that there was some superior rationality in the world-process and hence he taught that good and evil bore their respective fruits. Gośāla's determinism meant the fruitlessness of all actions, vicious or virtuous. Makkhali said :

> "Beings become depraved without cause or conditions ; they become morally pure also without cause. Our attainments do not depend on efforts or action, either of our own or of others. There is no human energy or power that is effective. All things that have life, creatures, and souls, are without inherent force. They are bent this way and that by the necessity of their specific nature."[2]

This meant a challenge to the Brāhmanical claim of good actions being the equipments for heaven. According to the Upaniṣads actions constitute the essence of a man and survive him as Yājnavalkya narrated to Jāratkārava.

Ajita Keśakambala denied the value of charity, sacrifices and oblations to fire. He denied the existence of a hereafter. The Vedic and the Upaniṣadic thoughts accept a hereafter, be it in the sense of an emancipated transcendental state or a heaven of the popular conception. Ajita condemned deities, ridiculed the Brāhmaṇas and Śramanas who claimed to have realised the

[1] M. Hiriyana, *Outlines of Indian Philosophy* (London, George Allen & Unwin, 1932), pp. 103-104, says that the *Mahābhārata* is the major source of heretical doctrines like *yadrichhāvada* (the source of the doctrines of the Cārvākas) and *svabhāvvada*. But the difficulty is the exact determination of the date of the *Mahābhārata*.

[2] See *Sāmañña-phala Suttanta* of the *Dīgha Nikāya* Cf. A.B. Keith, *Buddhist Philosophy in India and Ceylon* (Oxford University Press, 1923), p. 136.

truth and in the spirit of utter materialism he reduced the human existence to the four elements.[1]

Pūrṇa Kāsyapa's doctrines, represent gross epicureanism, and were entirely destructive of Vedic and Upaniṣadic ethics.

Prakruddha Kaccāyana taught the existence of seven groups ——Earth, Water, Fire, Air, Happiness, Misery and Life. The acceptance of "life" shows Kaccāyana was not materialistic. He advances to the vitalistic conception in the Bergsonian spirit. Of course, vitalism is greatly enunciated in the Upaniṣads (cf. the supremacy of the Prāṇas over senses and the elements) and in the Taittiriya (prāṇam brahman).

The sceptical and problematic doctrines of Sañjaya are comparable to the *syādvāda* of the Jainas as based on a conception of the manifold nature of Reality. It is to be noted that the Upaniṣads and the Vedic sacrificial formulae inculcate the notion of faith as vitally essential for success in the domain of spiritual wisdom.

An important factor in this critical and sophistical movement was seen in the teaching of Mahāvira. The substitution of an omniscient God by powerful omniscient Tirthaṅkaras, and the formulation of a scheme of evolution of the world essentially different from Vedic and Upaniṣadic cosmology show that Jain tenets are antithetical to the traditional system.

In its classic form of a realistic dualism the Sāmkhya is anti-Vedic in the sense that it tries to construct a system of evolution instead of accepting the existence of a supracosmic creative agency as accepted in the form of Hiraṇyagarbha or Prajāpati in the Vedas and the Brāhmaṇas. As distinguished from the Buddhists, the Sāmkhya accepted the validity of the Veda as a *pramāṇa* and is anxious to establish its Vedic origin, a claim which has been seriously challenged by Śamkara.[2] We have tried to show later that the Sāmkhya system of thought had a Vedic origin and developed alongside with the Upaniṣads and was a potent factor for the rise of Buddhism. But the *Sāṁkhya Karikā* is very critical of Vedic sacrifices and calls them impure. It regards, not sacrificial works, but discriminative knowledge,

[1] Ajita lays the foundation of a popular materialistic philosophy different from the modern ideas of Haeckel in *The Riddle of the Universe*.

[2] Śamkara's Bhāsya on *Vedānta Sūtra*, 2.2.10.

as the true means to liberation. Thus, besides the Brahmanical sacrificial mechanism, Upaniṣadic Absolutism, Buddhist and the contemporary rationalism, another source of attack against the Vedic religion came from the Sāmkhyas.

Although it is possible to trace the roots of the Buddhist concepts of *karman*, Yoga and *tapas*, and of the Buddhist theory of monastic life and of rebirth in the Upaniṣads, it cannot be doubted that the system of early Buddhist thought bears the indelible stamp of the unique and powerful personality of Buddha. The ethical idealism and monasticism of early Buddhism testify to the moral temperament and austere personality of the founder. One of the greatest factors in the success and spread of Buddhism was the noble, sublime and compassionate character of the founder of the faith. Buddha is comparable in the mode of his life to the prophets who brought about an ethical reformation in Judaism in the sixth and fifth centuries B.C. and to Zoroaster who brought about a moralization of the ancient Persian religion. According to Edward Caird, other subjective religions like philosophical Stoicism and the Ethical Monotheism of the Jews in the days of the Prophets and the Psalms, represent the divine being who is the unity of object and subject under the guise of an abstract subject. Buddhism carries the opposition of the subject and the object to such an extent that it cannot admit their unity under any guise whatever and hence it is a religion without a God.[1] Against the concept of the scriptural revelation as maintained by the Vedic and Upaniṣadic teachers Buddha stood for the sanctity of personal life.[2] Against the creed of dull and complicated sacrificialism Buddha advocated the dedicated pursuit of moral endeavours. Against the superficial moral code of some of the Tirthaka teachers Buddha championed the cause of superior ethical idealism and rigorism by basing his moral teachings on the creed of collective sadness and universal malady which characterize the real nature of the phenomenal world.

Buddha was to a great extent an individualist. He stood for vindicating the claims of moral endeavours or the *ashtān-*

[1] Ed. Caird, *Evolution of Religion*, Vol. I, pp. 355. ff.

[2] According to Pischel, *Leben Und Lehre des Buddha*, the *Sutta Nipāta* which is one of the significant books on Buddhist ethics is modelled upon the Upaniṣads.

gika mārga. He did not believe in surrender to any scriptural code or to any priesthood. He did not accept the notion of doctrinal revelation. He refused to acknowledge any person as his preceptor. He was an individualist because he claimed to have found out a way of deliverance by virtue of his own efforts. He claimed himself to be his own teacher. Upaka Ājivaka was surprised to see the lustre and calm on the face of Buddha and he enquired of him about his teacher. Buddha replied that he himself was his own teacher. He exhorted the people to concentrate their efforts for the extinction of suffering. He was an individualist who taught the immense importance of personal efforts against the mediation of any priesthood.[1] It is certainly true that the roots of spiritual individualism are contained in the Upaniṣads because the latter also do not enshrine the role of a priesthood for the attainment of emancipation but that individualism of the Upaniṣads is tempered by the overwhelming stress on the revelatory character of the mystical formulas through repetition of which the aspirant is supposed to attain the supreme reality. Buddha was an individualist to the extent that he taught a norm of emancipation free from the influence of any theistic godhead or any divine doctrinal scripture or any priesthood. He himself claimed to be not a dispenser of salvation but a teacher of the moral creed and the way of emancipation. Buddha's individualism was more radical than that of Martin Luther and John Calvin. The latter only dispensed with papal interference in the matter of Biblical interpretation. Buddha taught the sanctity of personal effort to a much greater degree because he dispensed with the Vedic scriptures altogether. Buddha's radical individualism was a further break away from the Upaniṣadic tradition.

Sometimes attempts have been made to exaggerate the legacy of the Upaniṣads upon Buddhism. Radhakrishnan ascribes to Buddha the role of a democratic teacher of ethical universalism. He says:

> "Buddhism helped to democratise the philosophy of the Upaniṣads, which was till then confined to a select few... It was Buddha's mission to accept the idealism of the Upaniṣads at its best and make it available for

[1] H. Oldenberg, *Buddha* [E.T. by W. Hoey], 1882, p. 52.

the daily needs of mankind. Historical Buddhism means the spread of the Upaniṣad doctrine among the people... Such democratic upheavals are common features of Hindu history. When the treasures of the great sages were the private property of a few, Rāmānuja the great Vaishnava teacher proclaimed the mystic texts to even the pariahs."[1]

It is not necessary to controvert the ascription of this role of a democratic populariser of Upaniṣadic idealism to Buddha because Radhakrishnan himself contradicts this statement of his at another place. He says: "... the religion of Buddha is an aristocratic one. It is full of subtleties that only the learned could understand, and Buddha had always in view the Samanas and the Brahmaṇas... Democracy is a modern motive of social reform."[2] We have seen that the fundamental theme of the Upaniṣadic teachings,—*brahmātmāikyavāda*—is repugnant to Buddha. Some of the conceptions and propositions which are common to the Upaniṣads and Buddhism receive a great extension in the later schools of thought.[3] Hence it is not correct to hold that early Buddhism is only a restatement of the doctrine of the Upaniṣads from a new standpoint. If the primary mission of Buddha was to democratize the spiritual idealism of the Upaniṣads it would mean that the whole historical evolution of the philosophy and religion of Buddhism which is a story of steady drift away from the Upaniṣadic religion and philosophy is a tragic epitaph on his tomb. But such stupendous mistakes history seldom makes.

Buddha was conscious that he had discovered a new way of emancipation. His supreme quest was for the extinction of pain and suffering. His system is characterized by the insistence on an ethical norm. It does incorporate vital elements from the contemporary systems of thought. Some of the schools from which Buddhism borrows might not have assumed the crystallized intellectual shape in the sixth and fifth centuries B.C., which they did later. It is certainly true that some dominant

1 S. Radhakrishnan, *Indian Philosophy*, Indian edition, Vol. I, p. 471.

2 *Ibid.*, p. 439.

3 Poussin, "Vedānta and Buddhism", *Journal of the Royal Asiatic Society*, 1910 pp. 129-140. In the later developments of Indian philosophy, some of the writers of the *advaita* school incorporated the dialectical form of criticism which was developed by the Buddhists. Śamkara was influenced by the methodology of the subjectivistic and nihilistic schools of Buddhist thought.

conceptions of Indian culture which are contained in the Vedas and the Upaniaṣds are taken up and incorporated by Buddha in his system. But it is not only a gross exaggeration but a mistake to state that early Buddhism is only the extension and fulfilment of the teachings of the Upaniṣads. In spite of some common concepts and ideas, the difference in the orientations of the Upanisads and the Tripiṭakas is immense and vital.

SECTION THREE

EXPOSITION AND ANALYSIS OF EARLY BUDDHISM

CHAPTER 6

BUDDHIST PESSIMISM

1. *Introduction*

THE CONCEPT OF Dukkha represents one of the dominant aspects of Buddhist religion and philosophy.[1] It is a significant expression of the incongruities, contradictions, frustrations and unhappiness that meet an individual if he is sensitive and cares to interpret his experiences. Dukkha is born out of the never-ceasing tension between the subjective aspirations of the individual—the *upādāna*, and the limitations and inhibitions imposed by the concrete objective external set of situations. Dukkha is an expression of the gloom, despondency and privations produced by the impediments to human ideation, identifications and interests. There is a constant struggle between the multiplicity of human expectations and desires and the niggardliness and restrictions of nature in their fulfilment. Hence human life is full of pain, grief and sorrow. The eternal enigma and the perpetual threat of death always pervades the expressions of philosophical thinkers and poets. In several cultures the stupendous helplessness and utter extinction symbolized by death has appeared as a grim reality and a constant source of philosophizing. Marcus Aurelius once defined philosophy as meditation over death. Confucius, the Chinese

[1] C.A.F. Rhys Davids, *Buddhism*, p. 157, says that the Buddhist word *dukkha* like the Christian word sin is the widest possible concept for the unideal. But I feel that there is great difference between the two because while in Christianity sin refers to the debasement or fall from a primordial innocence and is to be traced to tasting the fruit of the tree of knowledge, in Buddhism *dukkha* is to be traced not to knowledge but to its precise opposite, *avijjā*. For the difference between the Egyptian, Vedic-Buddhistic and Zoroastrian ideas of sin, *Life of Swami Vivekananda*, Vol. II, p. 712.

sage, was also deeply perturbed over the death of his mother and found solace in the performance of altruistic actions.[1]

The Buddhist theory of *dukkhavāda* is an expression of the helplessness of man in face of the calamities and severe deprivations brought about by natural phenomena like disease, old age and death. Man's capacities for fulfilment and realization are limited and when his ambitions and aspirations are not realized, he undergoes an experience of 'baulked dispositions'. He begins to question the bases of his existence and seeks to find a possible explanation of his discouragement, desperation and miseries in some universally operative law. Buddha saw an old man, a diseased man and a corpse and the futility of all earthly endeavours thoroughly gripped his whole being. He discovered that all living creatures are subjected to this immediate, compulsive, universally operative, lamentation, despair and suffering. Nothing in the shape of worldly gains could satisfy him, so great and intense was the force with which the aspect of nihil and extinction had caught his mind and heart. He was deeply impressed with the phenomenon of what an existentialist philosopher like Karl Jaspers would call "foundering". He found out, therefore, a moral and psychological way of escape for the conquest of this *dukkha*[2]. He did not teach dumb acceptance of suffering but propounded a way of transcendence of it by robust ceaseless efforts.

2. *Pessimism in Pre-Buddhist Indian Culture*

The picture of the culture-mentality that we obtain from the remains of the Mohenjodaro and Harappa civilizations is one of worldly quests and material satisfactions. There is nothing to indicate the beginnings of illusionism and pessimism. The people at these places were a mercantile community and were interested in architectural perfection, street construction, arts and crafts, tools and toys. They relished the joys and satisfactions of the world. Unfortunately, there are no literary

[1] Cf. also the utterances and writings of Hesiod, Job (the *Book of Job* in the *Old Testament*), Leopardi, Heine, Schopenhauer (*Welt als Wille und Vorstellung*), von Hartmann, Thomas Hardy etc.

[2] Otto Pfleiderer, *Philosophy of Religion*, Vol. IV, p. 8, says that to the pessimistic mood of the Buddhist evil is the true kernel of existence to be removed by the cessation of the finite.

works of the period available to show the trend of their reflections on the nature and destiny of man. But the figure of the god Śiva that has been found at Mohenjodaro shows that this mercantile community was capable of conceiving the image of a god who later became the embodiment of benignity, calmness, propitiousness and austerity. Śiva is possibly represented here in the posture of a Yogi. If it is true that a people conceive of their gods in terms of the conceptual framework dominant in their minds then it will not be an exaggeration to hold that even in this civilization some very elementary elements of otherworldliness begin to appear in the notion of Śiva, the Yogi.

The Vedas breathe a spirit of harmony and fulfilment. They vibrate a spirit of emotional warmness and are characterized by a vital desire for conquest, advance, longevity and material prosperity. The Vedic gods are powerful, beneficent and keenly interested in mundane affairs. Indra is the favourite popular god of the Aryans.[1] He receives praise from his devotees and his immense prowess is constantly lauded so that he may be pleased to bestow his succour on the devotees. The other gods of the period also represent titanic strengh and power. They are characterized not so much by austere moral perfection and a spirit of quiet or resignation as by vigour, strength, capacity, fervour, revengefulness and pugnacity. Whenever the priest or his *yajamāna* would be afflicted he would seek the support of the gods. The shafts of Rudra are powerful and malignant and constant prayers are offered to this god to bestow help and assistance.

The Vedic people wanted a fullness of life.[2] They prayed to the gods to grant the operative efficacy to the different human limbs and organs for one hundred years and more. One of the hymns in the *Yajurveda*, as interpreted by Swami Dayānanda Saraswati, contains the prayer for a longevity extending up to three hundred years. These hymns show that life and the world were regarded as pleasant and the desire for self-preservation was immense.[3] The Vedic Aryans prayed to the gods

[1] In *Ṛgveda*, X, 119, Indra expresses his feelings of exhilaration as a result of Soma drink.

[2] For Vedic optimism, see *RV*, 1, 104, 8 ; 1, 114, 7-8 ; 1, 136, 15.

[3] Cf. the Vedic prayer : "Sight and light and joy do thou give us, long may we see the sun as it rises"—*RV*, X, 14, 8 ; X, 59, 6.

to save them from contranatural extinction.[1] Keith appears wrong in his guess that the Vedic prayers for longevity are a reflection upon the early mortality of the people. The all-pervasive spirit of the Vedas is one of glee, joy and mirthfulness. As yet there is no sense of disenchantment and despair. The Vedas represent the idcals and aspirations of an agrarian tribal civilization and they are full of the sentiments of satisfaction in the realization of health, progeny, riches and cattle. The *Atharvaveda* contains allusions to the use of charms, incantations and various forms of magic for the preservation of the physical body.

The Vedic period represents primitive nature-engrossment. The Vedic people found delight in nature. They lived with and amidst nature. There were no systematic attempts made as yet to create an intermediate wall of technological civilization between man and nature. There was the use of some tools and implements and artifacts but nevertheless it may broadly be said that the pastoral and agrarian Vedic Aryans lived in and amidst nature. Hence in their spirit there is a naturalness, unsophisticated childishness, freshness and vivacity. Air, earth, water, fire and the high heavens engross their attention and provide them happiness. Their life was simple, unostentatious and unsophisticated. Their gods were nature-gods and their (of the gods) lives were the representations of the pattern of lives of the people. A simple prayer and the libations of food and Soma-juice were enough to elicit the mercy and graciousness of the gods. Meditation and contemplation, to arouse a sense of identity with the gods, were not yet common. The parallelism between the pattern of lives attributed to the gods and the actual modes of existence of the people indicates that the nature-gods are to some extent the typifications also of social processes and forces. The bodies, dress, food, morals and manners of the gods are conceived on the basis of the actual concrete social life of the people. Thus the Vedic religion is partly based upon the model of the Vedic society and in both we find a sense of joy and happiness.

The Vedic religion was a natural counterpart of the Vedic

1 Even after death the Vedic people expected life and joy as the rewards of merit earned in this world. See E.W. Hopkins, *Hindu Ethics*, p. 42.

society. The priests who were the custodians of religion were occupants of great social esteem and prestige. They were immensely interested in their fees or *dakshiṇā*. The association of religion with the spiritual sense of transformation of life and the attainment of supra-mundane illumination was still far off. Religion, as yet, was, so to speak, only an extension of social life and was not the reflection of any sense of deep anguish and disquiet at the presence of cosmic contradictions. Religion, so far, was only an element in the natural and contented life of peace and simple joy.[1]

The picture of religion and society that we get in the Brāhmaṇas is more or less akin to what we find in the Vedas. There is a pronounced growth of sacrificial rites and a sacerdotal caste, however. The rituals also serve a social purpose. They are either means for the propitiation of the gods or are intended as counteracting forces against malignant powers. The zest and ardour evinced in the performance of sacrifices show that the priests and the people are interested in the realization of mundane values. They prayed to the gods to give them power. They relish longevity, honour, progeny, cattle and the glories of heaven or *svarga* which also is conceived as modelled upon the elements and constituents of the social structure. During the period of the Vedic Saṁhitās, the sacrifices were simple but in the age of the Brāhmaṇas they become detailed, elaborate, complicated and protracted. This testifies to the fact that in those days religion reinforced the cohesive elements of a tribal and agrarian civilization. Religion in the shape of rituals had a great social meaning and a social purpose. It was a mechanism to enhance the pleasure and joys of the world. So long as the norms, institutional patterns and commands of the society are strong, the world-renouncing tendencies of pessimism do not appear. The individual inspite of some personal miseries and tragedies becomes adjusted to the society through accommodation to its commands and prohibitions. The religious system of the Vedic and Brāhmanic days reinforced the integrative elements of the contemporary society by emphasising the performance of rites and rituals which involved participation in those activities

[1] Cf. P. Regnaud, "Le Pessimisme Brahmanique", *Annals du Musee Guimet*, (I, 101 ff), quoted in M. Winternitz, *A History of Indian Literature*, Vol. I, p. 263n.

by members of the group. The religion of those days had thus a significant social function. It acted also as a deterrant against the rise of social alienation, distrust and individualism. Pessimism, on the other hand, with its stress on the miseries of life in society is, in one sense, a challenging individualistic creed. It means the assertion of the interpretation of the individual against the traditionally dominant modes of structured, institutionalized and norm-set action. Pessimism may seek to release the sensitive individual from the performance of many social duties and obligations by revealing their ultimate futility and the absence of any meaningful dimension in them in face of the dominant stupendous inexorability of death and extinction. The religious system of the age of the Vedas and the Brāhmaṇas was full of socio-religious compulsiveness and that acted as a deterrant to the generalization of any extra-social or trans-social implications from philosophic reflection upon the nature and destiny of man. With the breakdown of the unifying patterns of society there is a loosening of the bonds of social cohesiveness and instead of performing their socially-conforming duties, sensitive souls, impelled by world-flight begin to meditate upon the nature, sanction, standards and ideals of duties.

With the Upaniṣads we land in an atmosphere of philosophic exaltedness and somewhat sustained intellectual ardour. In the Vedas and the Brāhmaṇas we obtain glimpses of the popular religion besides the hieratic, manipulative and supplicative ritualism of the priests. But in the Upaniṣads we are faced with the earnest cosmological quests of isolated individual souls. The dominant theme of the Upaniṣads is the inculcation of the reality of an infinite spiritual being which can be experienced by super-intellectual perceptions. If the supreme real is a super-phenomenal being and is utterly free from the contaminations of diversity and plurality, it follows almost as a corollary that the world of perceptual space and time is comparatively of less worth. Sanat Kumara in the *Chhāndogya Upaniṣad* in ringing words stresses the happiness associated with the infinite or *bhumā* and thus condemns the quest for perfection in the petty objects of the world. But one must not jump to the conclusion that during the Upaniṣadic age the people as a whole were seized with a spirit of despair, woe, ruin and futility of the world. The Upaniṣads are metaphysical and mystical productions of the sages and seers and hence their elevated tone of intellectual earnestness and philosophic seriousness is not a representation of the actual world-view of the masses. The only plausible conclusion that can be drawn is that with the Upaniṣads the theme of the burden of the world with its fatalities and contradictions begins to weigh heavily upon the minds of the thinkers of the age. So deeply imbued with the concept of the infinite happiness of the ultimate *brahman* the teachers of the Upaniṣads were, that they regarded everything else as full of sorrow—*anyad ārtam*. From the assertion of the sorrowful character of mundane phenomena, it is only the next step to say that they should be rejected as being illusory and painful.[1]

The gospel of world-despair of the Upaniṣads has to be viewed, however, in the framework of two vital limiting propositions. True it is that the world is full of death, incapacity and pettiness but this has to be seen in the background of the plenitude of bliss of the *brahman*.[2] The transcendent perfection and delight of the Spirit is a challenge to the engrossments in the joys of the world. The blissful character of the *brahman* is a guarantee of ultimate peace and repose. In the Upaniṣads there is a call to realize the bliss of *brahman*. Hence from the psychological standpoint there is ground for hope.[3] In a materialistic cosmological scheme there are greater chances for the growth of a sense of weariness and despair. Thus the spiritual metaphysics of the Upaniṣads is an antidote to the concept of absolute despair. The dominant theme of the Upaniṣads is the overwhelming majesty of the spiritual infinite. The mundane is not so much rejected and condemned as made to derive its limited and partial significance and worth from the *brahman* itself. The world is sometimes regarded as being

[1] M. Winternitz, *A History of Indian Literature*, Vol. I, p. 264. The Upaniṣad declares — *brāhmano nirvedamāyāt*.

[2] The Upaniṣadic attitude to life may be partly compared to the Stoic philosophy. Edward Caird, *Evolution of Religion*, Vol. I, pp. 325. ff.

[3] Swami Vivekananda, *Vedānta Philosophy At The Harvard University* (Udbodhan Office, Calcutta, 1929), p. 33, says that in the Vedāntic conception there is the denial of sensuous optimism and the assertion of real super-sensuous optimism.

created by the *brahman* and at times is conceived as an emanation of the *brahman.* The divine real and the mundane world are not so much regarded as polar contradictories as the continuity of the same real.[1] Hence there is not much scope for the total stress on the miserable nature of the world. Yājnavalkya renounces the world but he does not make any fetish out of the sorrowfulness of the world. Naciketas, the principal figure in the *Kaṭha Upaniṣad*, is a young boy and has highly developed religious sensibilities. But even he is in quest of spiritual immortality and does not totally condemn the world as a place of sin, suffering and sorrow. Moreover, the *Kaṭha* is a late production in the field of Upaniṣadic literature.

A second reservation to the pessimistic interpretation of the Upaniṣads is that the passages which refer to the miserable character of the world are not many. The *Kaṭha Upaniṣad* contains the word *lokadukkha* which means the misery, wailing, mourning and bemoaning prevalent in the world but this Upaniṣad is a fairly late composition.[2] There are pessimistic strains even in the *Maitrāyaṇī*[3] which is regarded as post-Buddhistic.[4]

It is true that monasticism with its rejection of the joys and satisfactions of the world is a reflection of the acceptance of a pessimistic view of the world,[5] but for the Upaniṣadic period it can be said that monasticism is not yet generalized or universal. Some of the greatest names in the Upaniṣads are those of householders and kings. They engage in philosophical disquisition but they feel no urgency to renounce the world. Other teachers like Ushasta Cākrāyaṇa, Uddālaka Āruṇi and Satyakāma Jābāla lead the normal lives of peaceful householders. The Greek exponents of philosophical idealism like Xenophanes, Parmenides, Zeno and Melissus of Samos are also

[1] The *Taittirīya Upaniṣad*, II, 7 and III, 6, states that Bliss or *ānandam* is the ether in which we all dwell. It regards *ānandam* to be the origination, source of preservation and final place of return of all beings.

[2] For the insistence on suffering see *Kaṭha Upaniṣad*, I, 1, 26. The *Kaṭha*, II, 4, 2 refers to the net of death — *mrityor yanti vitatasya pāśam*.

[3] *Maitrāyaṇī Upaniṣad*, 1, 2-4.

[4] In VII, 8 ff. The *Maitrāyaṇī Upaniṣad* contains allusions to Buddhists as heretics.

For monasticism in Chinese Culture, B.K. Sarkar, *Sociology of Races, Cultures and Human Progress*, p. 101.

dwellers in the world and participants in its joys and sorrows. Plato in the *Republic*, sings the glories of the 'Idea of the Good' but he never feels any desire to renounce the 'Cave' of the city for the bliss of the beyond. The spirit of the Upaniṣadic teachers is somewhat akin to that of the Greek philosophers. They feel that the pessimistic rejection of the world is not the necessary accompaniment of an idealistic philosophy. A few of the Upaniṣadic teachers are quite commonplace in their modes of action. Sayugvā Raikva is notorious for his love of gifts and fees. Yājnavalkya accepts plenty of cows and gold from king Janaka. It has to be noted, however, that although monasticism may not be praised or universally practised by the Upaniṣadic teachers, the philosophic spirit of questioning the world and its claims is certainly fully present there. Monasticism is more pronounced in the *Muṇḍaka Upaniṣad.*

3. *The Truth of Suffering* : *Pessimism*

The first Aryan truth in Buddhist metaphysics is the reality of sorrow.[1] Buddha was persuaded to renounce the world because the element of all-encompassing pain had made him absolutely restless. He stresses the poignancy of sorrow and frustration in human life.[2] He has rightly pointed out the psychological and physical havocs to which human life is subjected. In the *Samyutta Nikāya* Buddha asks :

> "What think ye, disciples, whether is more, the water which is in the four great oceans, or the tears which have flown from you and have been shed by you, while ye strayed and wandered on this long pilgrimage and sorrowed and wept, because that was your portion which ye abhorred and that which ye loved was not your portion."

In the *Dhammapada* we have some of the most poignant passages in the whole of world's literature. Buddha draws pointed attention to the changes, vicissitudes and tragedies of life. He condemns the charms of the body. He says that nowhere, neither in the heavens nor in the recesses of mountains

[1] The *Dhamma-Cakka-Pavattana Sutta*. Cf. also the *Mahādukkhakhanda Suttanta* of the *Majjhima Nikāya*.

[2] *Mahādukhaskandha Suttanta* of the *Majjhima Nikāya*. Also the *Anattasutta* delivered at Sarnatha.

nor in the depths of the sea, is there any spot where one could be saved from the ravages of death. Buddha says :

"If three things were not in the world, my disciples, the Perfect one, the holy, supreme Buddha, would not appear in the world, the law and the doctrine, which the Perfect one propounds, would not shine in the world. What three things are they ? Birth and old age and death ?"

According to Buddha, the grim fateful reality of the world is constituted by ceaseless mutation, death and destruction.[1]

"Whether Buddhas appear in the world or whether Buddhas do not appear in the world, it remains a fact, an unalterable condition of existence and an eternal law, that all karmic formations (*sankhār*) are impermanent (*anicca*). This fact a Buddha discovers and masters, and when he has discovered and mastered it, he announces, proclaims, preaches, reveals, teaches and explains thoroughly that all sankharas are impermanent. Whether Buddhas appear in the world, or whether Buddhas do not appear in the world, it remains a fact, an unalterable condition of existence and an eternal law, that all karmic formations are subject to suffering (*dukkha*). This fact a Buddha discovers and masters, and after having discovered and mastered it, he announces, proclaims, preaches, reveals, teaches and explains thoroughly, that all sankharas are subject to suffering. Whether Buddhas appear in the world, or whether Buddhas do not appear in the world, it remains a fact, an unalterable condition of existence and an eternal law, that all that exists (*sabbe dhammā*) is non-absolute (*anattā*, *i.e.*, without an unchangeable or absolute ego-entity). This fact a Buddha discovers and masters, and after having discovered and mastered it, he announces, proclaims, preaches, reveals, teaches and explains thoroughly, that all that exists is non-absolute (without a permanent ego)."[2]

The dominant purpose of Buddha is to bring home to the sensual and appetitive souls the immense tragedy enacted by "birth, old age, death, sorrow, lamentation, misery, grief and despair". Our evanescent life is regarded as only a drop in the everflowing sea of constant change and transformation. The easy, contented, childish, fantasies of the goodness of the world are shaken by Buddha. He teaches the grimness of sorrow, death and extinction. According to the *Bhikkhunī Samyutta*, "The whole universe is consumed with flames, the whole universe is enveloped in smoke, the whole universe is on fire,

[1] Edward Caird, *The Evolution of Religion*, Vol. I, p. 33, states that the Buddhist religion treats the whole objective world as an illusion from which it is the highest aim of the devotee to free himself.

[2] *Aṅguttara Nikāya*, II, 134.

the whole universe trembles."[1] The insistence of Buddha on the cardinal tenet of suffering is a testimony to the searching character of the philosophical thought of the times which refused to be satisfied by the traditional accounts of cosmology and ethics in which the gods were propitiated to grant favors and boons. So deep is the sense of hopelessness aroused by this first Aryan truth of suffering that it seems a little strange that Buddha who was destined to take up the conquering political career of a *Cakravartī* should have such a poignant realization of the depth and pervasiveness of cosmic and human sorrow.

But although the concept of *dukkha* has such an overwhelming importance in the early literature of Buddhism, there is no attempt to make a fetish of misery. Buddha is not a misery-mongering psychopathic intellectual. Melamed draws a distinction between the universalism, pessimism, acosmism and asceticism of Buddha and the individualism, theism, optimism and the anthropomorphic world-picture of the Old Testament. He puts Buddha and Spinoza, more or less, in the same group. To both Buddha and Spinoza, human life was an eligiac episode in the cosmic order. Both believed that human life is a typographical error of eternity, purposeless, useless, meaningless. To both, human life was a minus, an irrational magnitude.[2] But to any serious student of Buddhism, Melamed's statements would appear more rhetorical than correct. He is still persisting in the old identification of Buddhism with the pessimism of Schopenhauer. Unlike Schopenhauer, Gautama would not consider this world as a horrible place. He harps on the theme of the prevalence of misery to make people take up the quest of emancipation. He refuses to invite bodily tortures for their own sake, unlike the medieval Christian ascetics. St. Teresa said that only suffering could make life meaningful to her. Buddha, on the other hand, does not advocate the blissfulness of suffering. In the *Majjhima Nikāya* he condemns the attitude of inviting suffering for its own sake in the hope of getting emancipation.

4. *The Origin and Extinction of suffering : Optimism*

If the first Aryan truth asserts the concrete existence of

[1] Quoted in Oldenberg, *Buddha*, p. 219.

[2] Melamed, *Buddha And Spinoza*, pp. 274-275.

suffering as a fact, the second Aryan truth asserts the psycho-physical dynamics of suffering. While according to Karl Jaspers, radical and inevitable guilt is derived from the primitive unchosen condition of *Existenz*, Buddha's originality is indicated in his determined attempt to provide a scheme of the origin of suffering. While meditating under the Bodhi tree, Gautama is said to have cognized the twelve-linked formula of the explanation of pain. This concept of *pratītyasamutpāda* has a two-fold implication.[1] First, at the cosmic level, it asserts the law of the operation of dependent origination.[2] There is nothing isolated and disparate in the universe. The whole universe is regarded as a chain of interdependent events in the process of fluxional mutation. Sometimes the Buddhist concept of *Pratītyasamutpāda* is differentiated from the concept of *adhityasamutpāda*. The latter accepts the hypothesis of fortuitious origin (*ahetu apacaya*) and was sponsored by the sophist teacher, Pūrna Kaśyapa. Viewed in this way, *pratityasamutpāda* is an expression of the universal law of dynamic causation.[3] It categorizes both the ultimate and the immediate precipitant roots of actions and events.[4] Instead of the operativeness of the laws of the gods, it

[1] There is a concrete picture of the twelve nidānas in Ajanta. See Waddel's article, "Buddha's Secret from a Sixth Century Pictorial Commentary and Tibetan Tradition", in the *Journal of the Royal Asiatic Society*, 1894.

[2] Paul Oltramare, *La Formula bouddhique des douze causes* (Geneva, University Library, 1909).

[3] The *Samyutta Nikāya*, 12,53 and 12,5, states that existence depends on *upādāna*. According to the *Abhidhamma*, the law of causation is developed as the theory of relations (*paccaya*) or a system of correlation (*patthāna naya*). Elliot, *Hinduism and Buddhism*, Vol. I, p. 208n, points out that according to the latter theory phenomena are not viewed merely in the simple relation of cause and effect but one phenomenon can be the assistant agency (*upakāraka*) of another phenomenon in twenty-four modes. Elliot is of the opinion that though the Buddhist Piṭakas insist on the universality of causation they have no concept of the scientific uniformity of nature.

[4] The following table represents the causational formula of the *pratītyasamutpāda* :

1. Those of the past lives :	*Avidyā*, or ignorance.
	Samskāra, or predispositions or tendencies.
2. The present life :	*Vijnāna*, or consciousness of self.
	Nāmarūpa, or mind and body.

asserts the effective action of auto-dynamic forces of ceaseless propulsion and mutation.

Secondly, *pratītyasamutpāda* is also interpreted at a psychological level to explain the origination of suffering. The teacher and leader of the Ājivika sect, Makkhalī Gośāla taught that suffering had no cause. Buddha's attitude is totally different from his. The second Aryan truth emphatically enunciates that suffering has a cause. The formula of *pratītyasamutpāda* is thus explained in the *Mahāvagga* :

> "From ignorance come conformations (*sankhāra*) ; from conformations comes consciousness (*viññana*) ; from consciousness come name and corporeal form ; from name and corporeal form come the six fields ; from the six fields comes contact (between the senses and their objects) : from contact comes sensation ; from sensation comes thirst (or desire) ; from thirst comes clinging (to existence : *upādāna*) ; from clinging (to existence) comes being (*bhava*) ; from being comes birth ; from birth come old age and death, pain and lamentation, suffering, anxiety and despair. This is the origin of the whole realm of suffering... But if ignorance be removed by the complete extinction of desire, this brings about the removal of conformations ; by the removal of conformations, consciousness is removed ; by the removal of consciousness, name and corporeal form are removed ; by the removal of name and corporeal form, the six fields are removed ; by the removal of the six fields, contact (between the senses and their objects) is removed ; by the removal of contact, sensation is removed ; by the removal of sensation, thirst is removed ; by the removal of thirst, the clinging (to existence) is removed ; by the removal of the clinging (to existence), being is removed ; by the removal of being, birth is removed ; by the removal of birth, old age and death, pain and lamentation, suffering, anxiety, and despair are removed. This is the removal of the whole realm of suffering."[1]

But in the theory of *pratītyasamutpāda* there is no attempt to answer the ontological problem of the ultimate existence of suffering—*why* is there suffering at all in the world ? This question is not touched at metaphysical levels in Buddhist

		Shadāyatana, or the sense organs.
		Sparśa, or contact.
		Vedanā, or emotion.
		Tṛshṇā (*Tanhā*), or craving.
		Upādāna, or clinging or attachment.
3. Of the future lives	:	*Bhava*, or coming-to-be.
		Jāti, or rebirth.
		Jarāmaraṇam, old age and death.

[1] ***Bodhikathā, Mahāvagga.***

philosophy. Only the dialectical processes of the origin of suffering in individual life are indicated in the formula of *pratītyasamutpāda*. Warren says that there is some repetition in the formula of *pratītyasamutpāda*. (i) At one place, *avidyā* and *samskāra* are regarded as responsible for the emergence of *vijnāna* and *nāmarūpa*. (ii) Later, *jati* and *jarā* are considered to be dependent on *tṛshṇā* and *upādāna* and *bhava*.[1] According to Buddhaghosa, the repetition is for practical purposes. Warren states that the twelve-fold formula in its present shape is a patchwork of two or more formulas that were then present, put together by Buddha and made into one —perhaps expanded, perhaps contracted. Hence the human being is "brought into existence twice".

Avidyā or the ignorance of reality is regarded as the root of pain and evil according to the Vedānta, Sāmkhya and Buddhism. In the Vedāntic philosophy, the sublation of the false sense of egoistic delusion is held to be the path to the acquisition of the knowledge of *brahman*. Buddhism traces the roots of suffering consequent on birth and existence to a twelve-fold link of causal concatenation.[2] The ignorance of the four Aryan truths or *avidyā* is the root of suffering in early Buddhism. *Avidyā* generates all kinds of malformation, defects and pain both at the physical-vital and the psychic levels. The transcendence of *avidyā* is the way to the attainment of the status of the *arhat*. Thus it appears that in Buddhism the gospel of pain and suffering is not the expression of occasional effusions of poetic sensitiveness. Buddhism, in a sense, is the science of suffering. It makes a radical probe into the ways that can be resorted to for the extinction of suffering after it has found out the roots of suffering. This scientific attitude of analysis and investigation is different from any *ad hoc* assertion of pain and sorrow. Thus the Buddhistic standpoint is differentiated from the poetic and romantic effusions about world-sorrow—*Weltschmerz*. Buddhism is not content to poetize about suffering but it prescribes an effective and radical moral path for the

[1] H.C. Warren, *Buddhism in Translations* (Harvard Oriental Series No. 3, 1915), p. 115.

[2] According to Kern, *Manual of Indian Buddhism*, p. 46, the relation between the Aryan truths and the twelve nidānas is comparable to the relation between medical science and pathology.

conquest of suffering. It does not envisage the prospect of a never-ceasing battle between the two mighty principles of good and evil. Furthermore, it does not sponsor the idealistic approach of reconciling oneself to the existence of terrrestrial evil which would be considered an integral element in the comprehensiveness of a divine dialectic. It does not hold that by the attainment of a reconciling universal vision, evil and suffering would appear only as elements in a more perfect spiritual synthesis. It also rejects the popular view of the devotee that evil and suffering are the mechanisms of providence to test people and thereby strengthen their character.[1] On the other hand, it makes available in the formula of the *pratīty-asamutpāda* a psychological explanation of suffering in terms of individual motivation. Individual longing and clinging is regarded as responsible for evil and suffering. Buddhism does not erect an ontological absolute of *dukkha* either.[2] It conceives of *dukkha* in terms of psychological and physical experience.

Early Buddhism cannot be described as the religion of mere gloom, despair and sorrow.[3] If the first truth enunciates the law of suffering, the second truth probes into the psycho-physical origin and dynamics of suffering[4] and the third and fourth inculcate the moral means of the subjugation of suffering. Pfleiderer says that the non-theological, softly sensitive, Buddhist way of thinking could not attain to the conquest of evil and its transmutation into good ; all that it could think was the alleviation of pain either by individual charity or by *nirvāṇa*. But I do not think that it is correct to interpret Bud-

[1] For the ancient Greek views regarding suffering and evil see James Adam, *The Vitality of Platonism* (Cambridge University Press, 1911), pp. 190ff.

[2] S.K. Maitra, *Ethics of the Hindus*, p. 309, seems wrong in ascribing the theory of ontological pessimism to Buddhism.

[3] According to P.L. Narasu, *Essence of Buddhism*, p. 119, (noted in C.A.F. Rhys Davids, *Buddhism*, p. 171), the imputation of pessimism to Buddhism is due to the claim of Schopenhauer of there being affinity between his system and Buddhism. According to Schopenhauer, *ratio* or reason is the factor which contaminates human will and thus results in suffering. He prescribes a derationalization of human will and a turning back to the Idea. Buddha, on the other hand, prescribed an elaborate moral and psychical discipline for the conquest of suffering.

[4] Contrast Makkhali Gośāla.

dhism as a mere metaphysics of gloom. Buddhism may not preach the glorification and sanctification of individual existence and the social structure but, nevertheless, it is emphatic in stating the doctrine of the strenuous and energetic application to the task of conquering death and sorrow. Hence, suffering, in spite of all its overpowering character, is not the essence of the Buddhist philosophy. To Buddha the taint of sin and the contamination of transition, misery, impermanence and insubstantiality can be transformed into the conscious realization of the glories of a moral and psychological conquest. Hence Buddha is not satisfied with "the painful, misery-laden wheel" of birth and death. He is a prophet of the Nirvanic consciousness which implies an extinction of pain, sorrow and suffering. A religion, to win the acceptance of a large section of mankind, must offer some positive consolation. It must provide a way to resolve the contradictions of life. It must offer hope, fulfilment and positive realization. Hence in place of the objective concrete facts of sorrow and destruction, Buddha offers the joyous hope of mendicancy. He has discovered an ethical-psychological path which leads to "aversion, absence of passion, cessation, quiescence, knowledge, wisdom and Nirvāṇa." He prescribes the method of the cessation of the finite complexes of the *samkhāras* which results in the nullification of suffering and evil. Ajātaśatru, the king of Magadha, testifies that while the monks belonging to other sects and denominations looked pale and dejected, the faces of the Buddhist bhikkhus were lit with great luminousness. This points out that the monks of the Buddhist confraternity were deriving some kind of super-sensuous pleasure. The early Buddhist poetry contains the record of the joyous and pleasant feelings of the Buddhist ascetics and female nuns. The rapturous delight given expression to by the monks and nuns is a testimony to the realization of some kind of positive fulfilment of conquest of evil by members of the early Buddhist confraternity. Hence even a critic like C.A.F. Rhys Davids had to acknowledge the vitality of the gospel of perfectibility as sponsored by Buddhism. She says :

"If the critic would dwell more on the positive tendencies in Buddhist ethics, he might discern under the outward calm of mien of the Buddhist sage, in literature and art, a passion of emotion and will not paralysed or expurgated but rendered subservient to and diffused around deep faith and high hope. For there is no doctrine, not even excepting Platonism, that sees in life, in the life that now is, greater possibilities of perfection. Nor is there any system, not excepting that of the Christian, which sees in the evolution of human love a more exalted transcendence of the lower forms of that emotion."

Buddha claims that although he had voluntarily renounced most of the good things of life which are so dear to the common folks, none lived more at ease (*sukhena seti*) than himself.[1] In the *Alavaka Sutta* of the *Aṅguttara Nikāya*, Buddha says that in spite of economic prosperity the merchant suffers from *paridāha*—groanings and tribulations which arise from three sources, (a) *rāga* or lust, (b) *dvesha* or aversion or hatred and (c) *moha* or delusion. He himself claims to have transcended the sorrow, consequent upon these psychological privations and anguishes. This means that sorrow and disquiet are not accepted as the final gospels in Buddhism. Certainly, there is extreme sensitiveness to the least presence of suffering in the early stages, but he who has embarked upon the ethical path conquers the sting of sorrow. It has to be stressed that Buddha's gospel does not end with the assertion of suffering but is a potent technic for the conquest of sorrow. Hence the *Sutta Nipāta* says :

"What other men call Sukha, that the Saints
Call Dukkha ; what the rest so name,
That do the Ariyans know as happiness."[2]

The true Brahmin, according to Buddha, is one who has brought about a psychological revolution in his character—he who is emancipated (*vimutta*), *gentle* (*śitala*), free from contaminations (*upādhi-rahita*) has conquered fear and is full of

[1] *Aṅguttara Nikāya* I, 136 ff. and *Samyutta Nikāya* 4, 127. The *Aṅguttara Nikāya* contrasts the delight of renunciation (*pravrajyāsukha*) to the pleasures of home life (*grihasukha*), the delight of actionlessness (*naishkarmyasukha*) to the pleasures of the senses (*kāmasukha*) and the indeterminate delight (*nirupādhisukha*) to the pleasures of mundane determinations (*upādhisukha*).

[2] *Sutta-Nipāta*, Verses 759 ff. Cf. *SN*, 4, 127. Poussin, "A Few Words on Sukha", *K.B. Pathak Commemoration Volume*, points out that according to the school of Asanga, *nirvāna* is *sukha* without being *sukhasamvedana*, while *bodhisukha* is both beatitude and the conscisousness of beatitude. This definition is found in the *Buddhabhumiśāstra*.

peace.[1] Thus it is evident that in Buddhism the central gospel is the extinction of pain and sorrow and not the absolutization of pain and sorrow.

6. *The Sociological Study of Buddhist Dukkhavāda*

Five hypotheses are generally advanced as explanatory propositions for the emergence of the theory of *dukkhavāda*. The first is the psycho-analytic theory. According to this, the roots of the theory of *dukkha* are to be found in the psychological neuroses of Buddha himself. He was an extraordinarily sensitive personality and the all-pervasiveness of sorrow which appeared to reveal itself to him through the old man, the diseased man and the corpse was only an exaggerated interpretation put upon a commonplace phenomenon. There is partial truth in this hypothesis. Buddha had led a sheltered and quiet life.[2] He suffered a nervous breakdown almost, to see the painful fact of disease, old age and death. He was perhaps over-tender and extremely sensitive.[3] He failed to be

[1] According to Paul Deussen, *The Phil. of the Upaniṣads*, p. 341, while the elimination of suffering was a secondary consequence of the attainment of emancipation, Buddhism made the escape from sufferings (*dukkha-upaśama*) as equivalent to emancipation and hence rendered the consequence into the motive.

[2] H.G. Wells, *The Outline of History* (New York, 1931), p. 390, says : "It was not a very satisfying life intellectually. There was no literature except the oral tradition of the Vedantic epics, and that was chiefly monopolized by the Brahmins ; there was even less knowledge. The world was bound by the snowy Himalayas to the north and spread indefinitely to the south. The city of Benares, which had a king, was about a hundred miles away. The chief amusements were hunting and love-making. All the good that life seemed to offer, Gautama enjoyed. He was married at nineteen to a beautiful cousin. For some years they remained childless. He hunted and played and went about in his sunny world of gardens and groves and irrigated rice-fields. And it was amidst this life that a great discontent fell upon him. It was the unhappiness of a fine brain that seeks employment. He lived amidst plenty and beauty, he passed from gratification to gratification, and his soul was not satisfied. It was as if he heard the destinies of the race calling to him. He felt that the existence he was leading was not the reality of life, but a holiday—a holiday that had gone on too long. While he was in this mood he saw four things that served to point his thoughts."

[3] B.H. Streeter, *The Buddha And The Christ* (London, Macmillan & Co., 1932), p. 62, points out that the experience of 'disillusionment' makes Buddha more of a "modern" man than Jesus Christ. Jesus had

reconciled to his normal fashionable, comfortable princely life after having seen these painful phenomena. Perhaps this peculiar personality of Buddha which, on principle, is sharply sensitive to the grimness and havoc-creating aspects of pain and sorrow may be responsible for the vehemence and zeal with which Buddhism announces the theory of *dukkha.* C.A.F. Rhys Davids has pointed to the prevalence of emotional, impulsive, nervous and eager men in North-east India in those days. This psychosomatic structure revealed itself in the increased stress on "fealing". She thinks that there was an element of exuberance in the sensuous responsiveness of the people. Thus she traces the emphasis on the element of suffering in early Buddhism to the reactions of the psychological types prevalent in north-east India.[1] The psychological roots of Indian pessimism have also been accepted by Griswold.[2] He holds that in Indianthought there is great stress on cognition—*jñāna*, and feeling—bhāvanā, but there is inadequate stress on volition. This results in the production in Indian thought of extravagant thinking and morbid feeling.

The second explanation of Buddhist pessimism is geographical.[3] It is said that the Vedic Aryans who lived in Panjab had a more cheerful temperament. Their migration to the eastern regions is supposed to be responsible for the change in their temperament. Thus the dulling and enervating effects of the eastern regions are supposed to be responsible for the philosophy of Upaniṣadic idealism and illusionism and the Buddhist gospel of suffering.[4] But this environmental

first hand experience of poverty and oppression. But Buddha knew these things only by sympathy.

[1] C.A.F. Rhys Davids, *Buddhism*, p. 65.

[2] H.G. Griswold, "Indian Pessimism", *Encyclopaedia of Religion and Ethics*, Vol. IX, p. 812.

[3] Bloomfield, *The Religion of the Veda*, p. 264 and W. Crooke, *Natives of Northern India*, p. 14 ff. uphold this view.

[4] The geographical, topographical and climatological explanation of Indian pessimism has found favour with several Indian and foreign critics. See Rabindranath Tagore, *Sadhana* (chapter 1). Melamed, *Spinoza and Buddha*, p. 235, states that in the midst of the tropical environment of India, with its abundance of life and colour and its superabundance of heat and humidity, man, humbled by the overpowering forces of nature surrendered his initiative and turned slowly away from the attractions and pleasures of existence. According to Keith, *The Religion and Philosophy of the Veda and Upaniṣads*, Vol. II, p. 469 : "In India

explanation is inadequate. The regions in eastern India gave birth to such vigorous imperial systems as those of the Mauryas, the Guptās and the Pālas. Chandragupta Maurya and Khārvela who drove away foreign hordes from the country also came from eastern India. Hence it does not appear plausible to trace the roots of Buddhist *dukkhavāda* to the enervating effects of the damp climate of the Terai jungles or the regions of Rājgir and Gayā.

A third, anthropological, explanation of Buddhist *dukkhavāda* is found in the theory of racial admixture. According to Griswold the racial fusion of the Aryans and Dravidians may have been the cause of the melancholy temperament of the Indians.[1] It is sometimes said that the optimistic buoyancy of the primitive barbaric Vedic Aryan tribes was lost when they came into contact with the aborigines and other dark-skinned inhabitants. But this statement implying the pessimistic character of the world-view of the tribal population or of the Dravidians is also an unfounded assertion. This theory was popularized by the rabid chauvinistic exponents of Nordic superiority and lacks scientific corroboration.

A fourth, sociological, explanation of the theories of idealism, illusionism, pessimism and mysticism is offered by the Marxist school of political science. Marxism regards idealism as a distortion of reality and an attempt at the clogging of class-contradictions. It believes that the pessimistic gospel of despair and nullity is preached by the exponents of the interests of the dominant classes in order to benumb the zeal and revolutionary fervour of the suppressed strata.[2] It is true that to a certain extent Buddhism was associated with princes and mercantile magnates. The kings and the financiers supported this movement but there are no concrete evidences to establish any correlation between the Buddhist concept of *dukkha* and the

under...conditions of climate and life and racial admixture, thought turned to speculation rather than to action and inclined to see unity in lieu of regarding life as a struggle between the good and the bad."

1 "Indian Pessimism", *ERE*, IX.

2 Rahula Sāmkrityāyana, *Darshana Digdarshana* (In Hindi), pp. 382 ff. has discussed the social origins of the Upaniṣadic gloom and pessimism. He categorizes three factors: (a) The suppressed sense of revolt of the exploited; (b) Social inequalities; and (c) The internal quarrels among the exploiting sections.

support rendered to Buddhism by Bimbisāra or Anāthapiṇḍika.

A fifth, political, line of investigation of the Buddhist gospel of suffering emphasizes the elements of unhappiness brought about by the political upheavals and vicissitudes of the period. In the seventh and sixth centuries B.C., the northern and eastern portions of India were convulsed by intermittent political wars and bloodshed. It was a period of nervous excitement and tensions from the political standpoint. Some of the passages in the Tripiṭakas refer to the havoc brought about by wars, tyranny, lawlessness and immorality.[1] They also contain references to the ravages consequent upon famines and disease. To a certain extent it is possible that these political and economic factors might have revealed to the people the pettiness and miseries of the world and hence they might have become psychologically attuned to a gospel of the evanescence and utter misery of temporal phenomena. In those days of undeveloped technology it was impossible to advocate any philosophy of collective material perfection or progressive meliorism. The vast multitude had no rosy comfortable future for them. The women did not have social and political roles to perform. The Sudras and the slaves were objects of exploitation. Only the few top families, and there also the males, had some brilliant prospects before them. Hence it has been said that the notion of *dukkha* emphasized in Buddhism and other contemporary systems was a theoretical formulation of an actual concrete miserable situation and therefore it could be accepted by its adherents.

According to Sinclair Stevenson, the sixth century B.C. was an epoch when constant wars between various little kingdoms must have made the lot of the common people hideous with suffering and oppression and hence people ardently desired to escape from such a sorrowful world.[2] Men hoped to evade the avaricious fingers of the king or fortune by renouncing everything that could be taken from them. But this is a wrong and

[1] Political factors were responsible for the Jewish stress on suffering. Because of the exile in Babylonia and centuries of foreign domination, the Jews had deep experience of political anguish and hence suffering was for them a national problem.—Streeter, *The Buddha and the Christ*, pp. 67-68.

[2] S. Stevenson, *The Heart of Jainism* (New Delhi Munshiram Manoharlal, 1970), p. 3.

far-fetched guess on the part of Stevenson. The monastic and lay adherents of Buddhism were not tax-ridden and oppressed proletarians but opulent princes, revered Brahmin teachers like Āśvalāyana, Uttara, Śaila, Brahmāyu, and great mercantile magnates like Anāthapiṇḍika. Furthermore, the volitional and emotional elements involved in renunciation are not adequately explained by any theory of economic deprivation as the incentive to renunciation or *sannyāsa.*

From the Vedas and the Brāhmaṇas to the Tripiṭakas is a long story of immense mental change and psychological transformation. Greek religious thought, to some extent, has a similar development.[1] In Homer, gods are also subjected to fate. According to Hesiod there are five historical ages,—(i) The golden age, (ii) the silver age, (iii) the bronze age, (iv) the age of heroes and (v) the age of iron. If in the golden age, men after death become spirits, in the silver age they are destroyed through their sins. Pindar asserts that those who will keep the faith will be happy. Aeschylus stresses the idea of fate and nemesis. Orphism believes in pre-natal sin and redemption. It pointed out that virtuous conduct could shorten the cycle caused by sin. Thus Homer and Hesiod are parallel to the Vedic optimistic thought. Orphism comes near the Upaniṣadic mysticism and pantheism. Sophocles answers to the first Aryan truth of Buddhism. Stoicism contains some points similar to the teachings of Buddhist ethics.

In Buddhism the insistence on the gloom, misery, sorrow and afflictions of the world is supreme. The Upaniṣads contain the record of philosophical abstractions and mystical discipline. The evangelisation of the people and forming them into a specific separate association is not a part of their mission. In a sense they can be called aristocratic productions. But Buddhism was, from the beginning, characterized by a missionory orientation. Hence it was compelled to harp on the miseries of the world in order to make the people come to its fold.[2]

[1] See Van Hook, *Greek Religion* ; Farnell, *Higher Aspects of the Greek Religion* ; Harrison Themis, *Social Origins of the Greek Religion.*

[2] O. Pfleiderer, *Philosophy of Religion*, Vol. IV, pp. 236-37, points out that Buddhism made a principle of the religious nothingness of the world and hence was able to cross the barriers of race and nation. A.B. Govinda, *The Psychological Attitude of Early Buddhist Philosophy,*

Although Buddhism was not a mass movement, its membership was constituted by the middle classes and the lower middle classes. It sought its recruits from amongst the Kṣatriyas and the Vaiśyas if not from amongst the Śudras. The middle classes which constituted the bulk of its members and supporters could not be made to give up the old traditional patterns of religious and social life by the disquisitions regarding the twelve-fold causal formula of *pratītyasamutpāda* or the mystical raptures of the four-fold *dhyāna* and the dogmatics of *nirvāna*. The missionary character of Buddhism is apparent from the very beginning. Unlike Buddha, Yājnavalkya in the Upaniṣads had made no attempt to get a band of followers. Buddha, from the beginning, is anxious to make public the truths he had discovered by hard austerities and meditations. He could obtain followers only if he taught the evanescent character of the world. He did not offer the solace of a theistic superior agency. Hence only by preaching the existence of extreme sorrow in the perceptual world could he make people take such a decisive step in their lives— to renounce the traditional joys and pleasures of home life and accept the hard life of a *bhikkhu*. Only the deep and dominant realization of the painful character of worldly phenomena would make the people give up their homes, father and mother, wife and children.[1] The aim of Buddha was to indicate the terribly shaky and hopeless character of everything to which a man may like to cling. It has been said that on the day of his enlightenment, Buddha was beseeched by Brahmā Sahampati and other gods to broadcast his noble teachings for the good and salvation of the world. Buddha was immensely reluctant because he found that people were engrossed in lust and pleasures and he felt a terrible disinclination to reveal his

pp. 6?-63, says that Buddhist *dukkhavāda* is the essential basis of a comprehensive philosophy because it starts with suffering than which there is no experience more universal.

[1] Cf. The *Viśṇu Purāṇa*, Part 6, Chapter V, where the evils of existence are acutely depicted and the conclusion is the stress on the necessity and worth of deliverance :

Adhyātmikādi Maitreya jnatvā tāpatrayam budhah Utpannajnāuavairagyah prapnotyāntikam layam

supreme discovery to these wretched folks.[1] He was persuaded, however, to take up a preaching career. As a counterpoise to the engrossments of the people in petty gratifications and sensual satisfactions, Buddha had to paint the miseries of birth, old age, pangs of separation and death. If this was the best of all possible worlds and if there was a pre-established harmony in it, then there was no need of a rejection of it. Hence the assertion of the doctrine of sorrow has a justifiable place in a popular religion like Buddhism. Buddha rightly felt that the people were sunk in apathy, ignorance and luxuries and only by exalting the element of *dukkha* into a vital immanental norm could he hope to wean people away from their appetitive and vegetative path of apparent happiness but real tribulation and misery. Thus from the sociological standpoint the element of pessimism was an integral factor in the popularization of Buddhism. Buddha had to preach *dukkhavāda* to make his movement popular.

Besides these sociological factors advanced as being responsible for the Buddhist theory of *dukkhavāda*, I will also advocate the philosophical approach.[2] A philosophic probe into the nature and procession of the world does indicate the immensity of suffering.[3] It reveals to man the depths of despair to which he is subjected because everything that he holds dear and precious is bound to come to an end.[4] A sense of world-weariness and dejection emerges as the natural product of the unhappy consciousness which is the necessary and significant phase of philosophical phenomenology. A philosophy that teaches that everything is all right and things are as they should be is no philosophy. It proceeds either from a naive unreflecting theodicy or shows the absence of deep reflection.

[1] Cf. A.B. Keith, *Buddhist Philosophy in India and Ceylon* (Oxford, 1923), p. 59.

[2] Cf. A.B. Govinda, *The Psychological Attitude of Early Buddhist Philosophy* (Patna University Readership Lectures, 1936-1937), p. 69.

[3] A.K. Coomaraswamy, *Buddha And The Gospel of Buddhism*, p. 180, points out that the pessimism of Vedanta or of Buddhism is the result not of a decline of material civilization but of the accumulation of experience.

[4] The thoroughly pessimistic tone of the *Yoga-Sutras*, II, 15-17, has also a philosophic basis—*pariṇāmatāpasamskāradukhaih gunavritivirodhācc dukhameva sarvam vivekinah* and *heyam dukkhamanāgatam*.

The apprehension of the painful character of the world is a recognition of the fact that the spirit has arisen from its natural slumber of peace and ease and has begun to reflect upon the contradictions and anguishes of existence. In this sense the gospel of pain is a recognition of the advance of spiritual reflection. In some of the positivistic and quantitative schools of social research, an attempt is made to measure the amount of happiness of individual human beings. This appears, to some extent, to be a ludicruous attempt at the application of quantitative technics in fields where they are not germane. Bentham and his school also accepted the ideal of a balancing of pain and pleasure. Buddha's stress on the dark and shadowy character of the phenomena of the world is not a proposition based on the empirical and quantitative study of pain and pleasure in the lives of people selected by "area sampling" or "random sampling" but is an intuitive and philosophical statement founded upon his own perceptions and experiences. Thus the basis of early Buddhist *dukkhavāda* is basically intuitional. Leibnitz was worried at the existence of evil in this best possible of all worlds. He accepted three types of evil. (i) Metaphysical evil emerges from the finiteness of things and is unconditionally willed by God. (ii) Physical evil, pain etc. is often a retribution for the eventual improvement of man. (iii) Moral evil or wickedness cannot be attributed to divine will. According to the *Mahāvagga*, (*The Vinaya Piṭaka*) Buddha says that everything is on fire because of the operations of lust, hatred, infatuation, death, disease, old age, birth, cries, misery, unrightmindfulness and worries. Of these birth, old age, disease, death and cries are physical phenomena while, lust, hatred, infatuation, sorrow ete. are mental. Due to the overpowering forces of these agencies, Buddha insists on detachment or *nirveda*. According to Leibnitz, God could not eradicate evil and wrong without eliminating the potency of self-determination which is the root of moral action. Leibnitz's *Theodicea* in some senses is an example of naive optimism. While Leibnitz does not prescribe any remedy for the elimination of evil except belief in a *theodicea*, Buddha prescribes the radical way to the conquest of pain and sorrow.

CHAPTER 7

ANĀTMAVĀDA

1. *Introduction*

ONE OF the most difficult problems of the history of philosophy has been to decipher the real meaning of Buddha's gospel.[1] The devout Buddhists of China, Japan and Tibet regard him (Buddha) as the personal embodiment of the highest metaphysical reality— something like the *avyaktam vyaktimāpannam* of the *Bhagavadgītā*. In the later phases of medieval Hindu tradition, Buddha was regarded as an *avatāra* whose compassion was universalistic. Dharmakīrti considered him a heralder of a critical revolt against Vedicism, traditionalism and philosophical absolutism. Since the middle of the nineteenth century kinship has been sought to be established between early Buddhism and the developments of modern Western thought. Buddhist *dukkhavāda* has been compared to the cosmic pessimism of Schopenhauer and Hartmann ; the notions of *anityatāvāda* and *kshaṇikvāda* have been compared to the Bergsonian conception of dynamic reality and even to the phenomenalistic and "energetistic" schools of physics ; and the Buddhist emphasis on *maitrī* and *karuṇā* in a non-theistic context, has inspired some of the social idealists, humanists and humanitarians. The Buddhist *anātmavāda* has also been regarded as a remarkable precursor of the conception of "psychology without a soul."[2] and hence as comparing favourably with the advance of German philosophy up to Brentano, French philosophy upto Bergson

[1] K.J. Saunders, "The Quest of the Historic Sakya-Muni", Chap. VI in *Buddhistic Studies*, edited by B.C. Law (Calcutta, Thacker, Spink & Co., 1931), pp. 178-185 ; H. Kern, *A Manual of Indian Buddhism*, pp. 46-73.

[2] Th. Stcherbatsky, *The Central Conception of Buddhism* (Calcutta, Susil Gupta, 1961, 3rd, Indian edition), p. 23.

and British philosophy up to Bertrand Russell.[1]

The problem of the soul has been ever present since the beginnings of human speculations.[2] According to the ancient Egyptians, man was not an individual unity but a compound consisting of the body and of several immaterial parts called souls— the *Ka*, the *Ba*, the *Sekhem*, which continued to exist separately even after death. The Vedas refer to *manas*, *asu*, *prāṇa* and *ātman*. In the Vedas the notion of a substantial human soul independent of the body which could survive bodily death began to develop. The dualism of the body and the soul,is a persistent part of the Indian philosophical tradition. In the Israelite, Zoroastrian, and Islamic religions also, the question of a perdurable non-corporeal entity which will enjoy eternal felicity has been investigated. The Greek philosophers examine the nature of the *nous* and the *psyche*. The Patristic and Scholastic philosophers were busy with the problem of the nature and destiny of the *anima*.

It is difficult to accept that there is an immediate, universal intuition of the soul or of the self,[3] as the spiritual entity which expresses itself through mental phenomena like thinking,[4] feeling and willing. It is true that some philosophers state that everybody experiences his "I-ness", but I think that this self-experience refers not to the direct experience of an autonomous spiritual substance but to the whole personality of a man which is a composite formation of bodily and mental phenomena. The acceptance of the human soul or self as a spiritual entity is not based on direct experience but is inferred on various grounds. It is a convenient hypothesis to explain the differences among

1 Th. Stcherbatsky, "The Dharmas of the Buddhists and the Gunas of the Sāmkhya", *The Indian Historical Quarterly*, Vol. X.

2 Eliot, *Hinduism and Buddhism*, Vol. I, p. 218. The ancient Egyptians who had great interest in problems of after-death believed that fate after death depended on actions of present existence. See *Precepts of Ptaḥhetip* and *Book of the Dead*.— Cf. H. R. Hall, *The Ancient History of the Near East*, (London, Methuen & Co., 1913), pp. 132-33.

3 In this chapter the words *soul* and *self* have been almost interchangeably used.

4 The nature of the soul has been variously described in systems of Indian Thought. According to the Nyāya it is unconscious, consciousness being only an intermittent quality. The Sāmkhya holds that the *purusha* is of the nature of pure consciousness.

men's fortunes. Furthermore, it provides a psychological solace to man who somehow wants to endure beyond death.

2. Views Regarding the Ātman in the Upanisadic Literature

(i) *Absolutism* : The ancient Upaniṣads are a vast corpus of philosophical views. On the problem of the human self it is possible to point to at least four different kinds of views in them. The most important philosophical standpoint of the Upaniṣads is an absolutistic spiritualism which inculcates the identity of the human psychic entity[1] and the immanental cosmic and trans-cosmic *brahman.* The Upaniṣadic texts like *tattvamasi* regard the self as a spiritual principle which, although it energises the human body, is not a separate independent entity but is only a particularization or delimitation of the supreme spiritual real. Some of the schools of Indian philosophy like Sāmkhya-Yoga, Nyāya-Vaiśeshika and Jain-Mimānsa accept the multiplicity of selves but according to the Upaniṣadic spiritual monism, only the one supreme *brahman* is real and in its inmost essence the human being is identical with that. Some interpreters of Buddhism like Ananda Coomaraswamy say that in his discourses Buddha does not refer to this absolutist view but I think that it is possible to allude some reference to this monistic view in the Tripiṭakas.[2]

(ii) *Animism* : In the first view of the Upaniṣads, mentioned above, the human *jīva* is considered to be only the personalized and individualized form of the supreme self as is evident from the statement—*anena jivenātmanānupraviśhya nāmarūpe vyākarvaṇīti.*[3] But there is present an entirely animistic conception of the word *jīva* in another statement of the *Chhāndogya* : *jivāpetam vāva kiledam mṛyate na jivo mṛyate* and also *yadekām shākhām jivo jahāti atha sā śushyati dvitīyām jahātyatha sā śushyati.*[4] Here the word *jīva* is used in an

[1] In the *Ṛgveda* the word *ātman* first meant the vital spirit (from- $\sqrt{an}$ to breathe), then it signified the self of the world (*RV* 1. 164,4) and finally it connoted the self of man. Besides *ātman* the other terms that signified the soul in the *Ṛgveda* are *manas* and *asu.*

[2] In Buddha's second discourse there is a reference to this view. See *Vinaya Texts*, pp. 100 ff.

[3] *Chhāndogya*, VI, 3, 2.

[4] *Chhāndogya*, VI, 11, 2-3.

animistic sense and is attributed the capacity of transmigration.[1] This view I have called animistic[2] since here the tree is regarded as having the *jīva.*[3] It appears that the popular primitive conception of *jīva* has been given here a literary recognition. Thus it appears that even after the emergence of metaphysical monism, some place was provided in the Upaniṣadic literature to animistic notions which were current among the populace and which might have been taken from the tribal population.

(iii) *Quasi-Materialism* : The Upaniṣads also contain reference to materialstic views. In the *Kaṭha*, which is a later poetical composition, we get the following verse :

yeyamprete vicikitsā manushye astīteyeka nāyamstīti caike. Etadvidyāmanuśishtastvayāham varānāmesh varastṛtiyah. Devairatrāpi vicikitsitam purā... (*Kaṭha*, 1, 1, 20-21). This Upaniṣadic passage shows that in those days there were two standpoints regarding the destiny of the soul—one view maintained that the soul continued to exist as an entity even after the extinction of the body and the other held that with physical death there was the disintegration of the soul also. Here there is the explicit mention of the view that according to one school of thinkers, after death, the soul ceased to exist. Thus it is held by this school that the soul existed only as long as the body did. This opinion resembles the belief of the Suśikshita Cārvākas (as distinguished from the Dhūrta Cārvāka) that the soul survived so long as the body did. To some extent the Upaniṣadic view mentioned here may also be compared to the view of the principal Semitic religions— Christianity and Islam, according to which the soul lasted as long as the body but

[1] There are animistic notions even in the *Ṛgveda.* "There seems to be a belief in the Vedas that the soul could be separated from the body in states of swoon, and that it could exist after death... In a hymn of the *RV*, (X/58) the soul (*manas*) of man apparently unconscious is invited to come back to him from the trees, herbs, the sky, the sun etc." S.N. Dasgupta, *A History of Indian Philosophy* (Cambridge, 1922), Vol. I, p. 25.

[2] For the Dravidian character of animism, G.W. Brown's art. in *Studies in Honour of Bloomfield*, pp. 75ff.

[3] The views of Aristotle and Descartes regarding the residence of the soul in specific portions of the human body are also animistic. Descartes in his *The Passions of the Soul* thinks that in the pineal gland the soul resides. The *Chhāndogya Upaniṣad* says that there is a pond in the heart and therein the soul resides.

the vital difference between the above materialistic view (as mentioned in the *Kaṭhopaniṣad*) and the Semitic view is that although the latter repudiates the notion of a beginningless soul, it upholds that at the time of Resurrection[1] the souls would miraculously rise. The dogma of resurrection (Latin *resurrectio*) is first foreshadowed in the *Old Testament*. In the *New Testament* it becomes an accepted tenet. The Upaniṣadic view, although partly resembling the materialistic standpoint in its advocacy of the notion that with death there is the disintegration of the soul, is immensely different from materialism to the extent that the latter (materialism) would not sponsor the notion of anything like the soul as an entity even during the living state of the body.

(iv) *Radical Pluralism* : A peculiar meaning of the word *Dharma* which implies that the Upaniṣadic literature even sanctions 'soullessness' has been put forward by the Russian academician Stcherbatsky. According to Stcherbatsky early Buddhism is a radical pluralistic philosophy accepting the reality of seventy-five elements which are called *dharma* in that system. Although only the Sarvāstivādins explicitly maintain this doctrine, there is sanction, according to Stcherbatsky, for this view, even in the early Buddhist literature. He even goes on to say that this meaning of *dharma* as element which would imply the repudiation of a substantialistic soul is contained in a passage of the *Kaṭhopāniṣad*. He says :

"In the *Kaṭhopaniṣad,* which belongs to this class, a doctrine is mentioned that is evidently strongly opposed to the monistic view of an immortal soul (*ātman*), and favours instead a theory of separate elements (*pṛthag-dharmān paśyati*). This theory is repudiated with the following remarks : 'Just as rain-water that has fallen down in a desert is scattered and lost among the undulations of the ground, just so is he (philosopher) who maintains the existence of separate elements lost in running after nothing else but these (separate elements).' Professor H. Jacobi has shown that unorthodox opinions, opposed to the accepted soul-theory, are alluded to even in the oldest set of the Upaniṣads. These indications are made in the usual Upaniṣad style and [are] anything but precise. What emerges from the passage of the *Kaṭhop.* cited above is that there was a doctrine opposed to the reigning soul-theory, that it maintained the existence of subtle elements and separate elements (*pṛthag dharmān*) and that such a doctrine, in the opinion of the author, did not lead to salvation. Śamkara, in his commentary, agrees that Buddhism is alluded to, but,

[6] See also Hodgson, *Resurrection of Human Body*, 1853.

very bluntly, he interprets *dharma* as meaning here individual soul. As a matter of fact, *dharma* never occurs with this meaning in the Upaniṣads. Its occurrence in the *Kaṭhop*. leaves the impression that it is a catchword referring to a foreign and new doctrine, some *anātma-dharma* theory."[1]

The assertion of Stcherbatsky with reference to 'soullessness' in the *Kaṭhopaniṣad* is too ingenious and even artificial. I have mentioned it, however, as an alternative hypothesis which was maintained with great seriousness by that Russian scholar.

3. *Buddha's Theory of Anattā*

The difficulty with early Buddhist philosophy is that Buddha does not make categorical statements. Some teachers and reformers express themselves in explict and clear terms and we exactly know where they stand. Dayānanda Saraswati is one such example. On the other hand, there are teachers who adopt positions of compromise and speak at different levels. Buddha, Śamkara and Kant are examples of this second type. At the absolute metaphysical level Śamkara repudiated God but accepted theism at the theological and devotional level. In the realm of pure reason there is no place for God according to Kant, but he accepts God in the field of practical reason. Buddha was a cautious teacher and although sometimes he would claim that he had given out his teachings unreservedly, it appears that at other times he would make a distinction among his listeners and would refuse to disseminate some esoteric teachings to the unregenerate multitude. Sometimes he would list certain questions as *avyākṛta* and would not say either yes or no in answer to them. Thus it becomes most embarassing to ascribe any explicit metaphysical position to him. This uncertainty is further increased by the difficulty of putting an uniform interpretation on the vast literature of the Tripiṭakas which have been composed by different authors at different times. Thus Buddha has been regarded as an agnostic, a radical pluralist, an ethical idealist and a psychological negativist. Whatsoever a position be ascribed to him, it can always be countered by citing some clear or obscure passage from the Tripiṭakas.

During the Upaniṣadic period, keen discussions were going on

[1] Th. Stcherbatsky, *The Central Conception of Buddhism* (Calcutta, Susil Gupta, 1951, Indian edition), p. 58.

regarding the nature and destiny of the *ātman*.[1] It is possible that the remote root of Buddhist *anātman* may be found in the statement of Indra to Prajāpati (where the former says) that the *ātman* in the deep dream state unrelated to the empirical consciousness appears like 'annihilated' (*vināśamevāpito*). But in place of abstract metaphysical speculations, Buddha evinced a tremendously urgent concern for the elimination of the positive concrete fact of suffering. It is true that there are cosmological and eschatological discussions in the early Buddhist scriptures but the everwhelming burden of all these writings is sorrow and the end of sorrow. The realistic approach to the cessation of suffering through an austere and disciplined life is ascendent in Buddhist thought. But although on account of his ethical pragmatism and anti-transcendental positivism Buddha could dismiss enquiries into the nature of the Absolute, he could not remain silent on the problem of the human self because all questions of moral perfectibility and the extinction of suffering are concerned with the nature of the human personality and hence ethical discussions could not afford to ignore the problem of the human self.

Sometimes it is said that Buddha never denied the transcendent-immanent self[2] as inculcated in the Upaniṣads and his immediate purpose was merely to clear the ground for the triumph of the Upaniṣadic view which had been out of focus because of the revolt led by scepticism, agnosticism, determinism and materialism.[3] By denying to the empirical phenomenal psychic-physical *nāmarūpa* the character of selfhood he was preparing the ground for the emergence of the absolutistic view of the self. Radhakrishnan ascribes such a role to the founder of Buddhism. He says : "Buddha clearly tells us what the self is not, though he does not give any clear account of what it is. It is however wrong to think that there is no self at all according to Buddha... Buddha is silent about the Ātman enunciated in the Upaniṣads. He neither affirms nor denies

[1] *Chhāndogya*, VIII, 11, 1.

[2] In the *Samyutta Nikāya*, III, 17, ff., there is a denial of immanence. According to *Alagaddupamn Suttanta* of the *Majjhima Nikāya* the notion that world and soul are one has been repudiated.

[3] Cf. The revolt of the six Tirthaka teachers, V.P. Varma, "The Decline of Vedic Religion", *Journal of the Bihar Research Society*, December, 1945.

its existence... Buddha consistently refuses to deny the reality of the soul."[1] Radhakrishnan, at one place, even categorically ascribes to Gautam Buddha the role of a Upaniṣadic teacher and says : "The Upaniṣads arrive at the ground of all things by stripping the self of veil after veil of contingency. At the end of this process they find the universal self, which is none of these finite entities, though the ground of them all. Buddha holds the same view, though he does not state it definitely."[2] The "Vedantification" of early Buddhism attempted by Radhakrishnan appears untrue. If in his heart of hearts Buddha did adhere to the concept of a spiritual real, why was he shy of saying so ? It must have been a stupendous task of self-deception (or hypocricy ?) for Buddha to adhere to a monistic spiritualism and keep mum over it for forty-five years. If the Tripiṭakas are to be considered the basis for the views of Buddha, then the concept of 'Soullessness' seems to me to be the view of the founder of Buddhism.

There are three cardinal conceptions of early Buddhism—impermanence, non-soulism (*anattā*) and the gospel of sorrow. Since there is nothing permanent, it almost automatically follows that the soul or self as an abiding self-subsisting entity does not exist.[3] Soon after the *upasampadā* of the Pancavargiya Bhikkhus (which included Kondanya) Buddha delivered a sermon to them on *anātman* and emphatically stated that *rūpa*, *sanjñā*, *vedanā*, *samskāra* and *vijñāna* do not constitute the self. The question, however, of anything besides this *nāma-rūpa-skandha* being the self is an open one. One school of interpreters would argue that Buddha only meant to deny that the phenomenal categories are the self but he silently meant to assert the selfhood of something super-phenomenal. This positivistic interpretation derives partial strength from the last sermon of Buddha in the *Mahāparinirvāṇa Sūtra* where he exhorts his disciples to be *ātmadīpa* (a light unto oneself) and *ātma-śaraṇa* (a refuge unto oneself).

There are several references in the early Buddhist scriptures to the denial of the soul or self. In the *Aṅguttara Nikāya* it is

[1] S. Radhakrishnan, *Indian Philosophy*, Vol. I (Indian edition), pp. 386-89.

[2] *Ibid*, p. 388.

[3] The *Aṅguttara Nikāya*, III, 359.

stated : "Even so do men of true creed declare the gnosis they have won— they tell of their gain (*artha*) but they do not bring in the ego."[1] *The Samyutta Nikāya* contains similar repudiations of the ego :

> "When one says 'I', what he does is that he refers either to all the *khandhas* combined or any one of them and deludes himself that that was 'I'. Just as one could not say that the fragrance of the lotus belonged to the petals, the colour or the pollen so one could not say that the *rupa* was 'I' ; that the *vedanā* was 'I', or any of the other *khandhas* was 'I'. There is nowhere to be found in the Khandhas 'I am'."[2]

In the *Simha Sutta*[3] of the *Samyutta Nikāya* it is stated that Buddha taught the doctrine of the recomposition and dissolution of matter and he taught to Baka that even the *brahmaloka* was not eternal. In this same *Samyutta Nikāya* it is stated that the world "is empty of a self or of anything of the nature of a self." When Ānanda asks Gautama Buddha the meaning and significance of the phrase 'the world is empty' the latter says :

> "That it is empty Ānanda, of a self, or of anything of the nature of a self. And what is it that is thus empty ? The five seats of the five senses, and the mind, and the feeling that is related to mind— all these are void of a self or of anything that is self-like."[4]

In the *Majjhima Nikāya*[5] the doctrine of the permanence of the soul or self is regarded as a foolish doctrine. Thus it is clear that there are several explicit statements with reference to *anattā*.

Sometimes it is said that Buddhist *anattāvāda* is directed not so much against the metaphysical notions of the self as formulated in the Upaniṣads but against the primitive animistic views prevalent in popular circles.[6] But it is also true that some

[1] Cf. N.K. Bhagavat, *Early Buddhist Philosophy of Theravad School*.

[2] *Samyutta Nikāya*, III, 13.

[3] *Samyutta Nikāya*, III, 85.

[4] *Samyutta Nikāya*, IV, 54.

[5] *Majjhima Nikāya*, I, 138.

[6] There are some passages, however, in the early Buddhist literature which should like denials of the Upaniṣadic notions of the self. The *Majjhima Nikāya*, I, 138, contains the following : "Since neither self, nor ought belonging to self, brethren ! can really and truly be accepted, is not the heretical position which holds : 'this is the world and this is the self, and I shall continue to be in the future, permanent, immutable, eternal, of a nature that knows no change, yea, I shall abide to eternity,' is not this simply and entirely a doctrine of fools ?"

of the Upaniṣads themselves contain primitive and animistic notions. The *Kaṭhopaniṣad* twice refers to the human soul as being of the size of the thumb (*angushthamātrah*).[1] The *Śvetāśvatara* says that the human soul is of the same subtle size as the ten thousandth part of the tip of the hair. But Buddha would give no quarter to such conceptions.

Neither would he seriously consider the Jain conception of the soul as *śarīraparimāna*. Beyond the psycho-physical organism or the *nāmarupa-skandha*, Buddha would refuse to acknowledge any other subtler metaphysical entity.

Buddha also says that the *vijnāna* is not seif.[2] This statement has been interpreted as being directed against two schools of thought— the Upaniṣadic and the Jaina. Buddha has no sympathy with the conception of the soul as an abstract cogniser and he wants to repudiate the Upaniṣadic notion of the *vijñāna* as *brahman*.[3] He also repudiates the Jain conception of the soul as one having consciousness as its essence. Buddha's view that the *vijnāna* is not the self is further reinforced with the view that in the fourth and fifth stages of *dhyāna* there is the experience of *naivasamjnānāsamjnāyatana* and *samjnāvedayitanirodha*.

Besides the animistic and the Jaina notions of the soul, a third contemporary school repudiated by Buddha was that of Ālāra Kālām. In his early wanderings, Buddha approached the renowned sage Ālāra Kālāma and became his disciple learning the successive degrees of ecstatic meditation. Ālāra taught the view that the individual soul when it absolishes itself is set

[1] In the "Savitri" section of the *Mahābhārata* also it is said : *angusthamatram purusham niscakarsha Yamo balāti* See B.G. Tilak, *Gita-Rahasya* (Hindi edition, p. 191).

[2] In the *Tanhāsamkkhya Sutta* of the *Majjhima Nikāya* (M.N. No. 38) it is maintained that *vijnāna* is not only not to be regarded as the *attā* or the soul but is not to be conceived as even a life-long immaterial substance. C.A.F. Rhys Davids, "Soul Theory in Buddhism", *Journal of Royal Asiatic Society*, 1903, says that *vijñāna* is not an abstract entity but a series of intellectual processes or force-moments. But his statement that vijñāna 'hypothetical quasi-noumenal continuum of self-induced flash-points of consciousness' is over-sophisticated. There seems, to me, no reason as to why *vijñāna* should be regarded as hypothetical. Stcherbatsky has interpreted *vijñāna* as the fundamental element of pure undifferentiated empty consciousness.

[3] In the *Śatapatha Brāhmana*, X, 3, 5, 13, the self is defined either as mind or as consciousness.

free. "...having abolished himself by himself, he sees that nought exists and is called a nihilist ; then like a bird from its cage, the soul escaping from the soul escaping from the body is declared to be set free ; this is that supreme Brahman constant, eternal and without distinctive signs, which the wise who know reality declare to be liberation."[1] Buddha objected to this doctrine on the ground that the liberated soul was still a soul, and whatever the condition it attains, must be subject to rebirth, and "the absolute attainment of our end is only to be found in the abandonment of everything."[2]

4. *Textual References to Attā in the Pali Scriptures*

The overwhelming refrain of the Tripiṭakas is that there is no soul or self as a substance. In the preceding pages we have cited explicit references which negate any notion of a transcendent 'I'. Nevertheless, there are certain passage and statements which mention the word *attā*. These do create a problem. Either it has to be accepted that there is inconsistency in the Tripiṭakas, which, considering the great bulk of this literature and also the fact that its different portions were composed at different periods, by several disciples, is not surprising, or it has to be accepted that the references to *attā* are to the empirical personality of man and not to a metaphysical substance.

(i) In the *Mahāvagga*[3] Buddha asks the thirty Bhadravargiyas to make a search after the soul— *attānam gaveseyyāmā*. Sometimes it is said that the word *attā* used here is merely taken from the current terminology and its sole purpose is to strengthen the resolve of men to follow the path leading to the extinction of sorrow and there is no implication of the definite positing of a spiritual entity as a self-subsistent being.

(ii) In the *Dhammapada* it is said *attā hi attano nātho ko hi nātho paro siyā*. Here the word *attā* which is a Pali form of *ātman* is used.[4] This statement has a complete resemblance to

[1] Quoted in A. Coomaraswamy, *Buddha and the Gospel of Buddhism* (Indian edition, Bombay, Asia Publishing House, 1956), p. 21.

[2] *Ibid.*

[3] *Mahāvagga*, 1, 14 (Nālandā Ed.).

[4] The word *attā* is used in the sense of moral consciousness in the *Saṃyutta Nikāya*, III, 120 ; IV, 47 ; I, 169 and in the *Aṅguttara Nikāya*, III 255, 267 ; 1, 149, III ; 65 and I, 53.

this *shloka* of the *Bhagavadgitā* (VI, 5) :

uddharedātmanātmānam nātmānamavasādayet
ātmaiva hyatmano bandhurātmaiva ripurātmanah

(iii) Besides the use of the word *attā*, the *words āṭmadīpa* and *ātmaśaraṇa* are also used in the *Mahāparinirvāṇa Sūtra*. The bhikkhus are exhorted to regard the *attā* as their light and refuge. Thus Gautama Buddha makes an emphatic and righteous protest against the doctrine of grace which is sponsored in some of the Upaniṣads as the *Kaṭha.*[1] Buddha recognizes the dignity and worth of human personality and human efforts. Hence he repudiates the notions of the prophetic and mediating role of the Saviour. Buddha, thereby denies having any pretension to supernatural authority or to kinship with any extraordinary immortal principle (although there are some other passages in the Tripiṭakas which may support such claims). It may be pointed out, however, that these words *ātmadīpa* and *ātmaśaraṇa* cannot be taken as enunciations of the positive concept of the soul as substance. Their aim is to stress individual efforts but no metaphysical soul seems to be implied here.

(iv) In the *Samyutta Nikāya* (III, 25) it is said : "O ye mendicants ! I am going to point out to you the burden as well as the bearer of the burden : the five states are the burden and the *pudgala* is the carrier of the burden ; he who holds that there is no soul is a man with false notions". In this statement the duality of the *pudgala* (self) as the subject and the matter-stuff as the object is posited. Later on, this *bhāravāhi* conception as formulated in the *Samyutta Nikāya* was taken up by the Sammittiyās and the Vātsiputriyās and they adhered to the notion of a soul as distinct from the *nāmarūpa*.[2] This passage of the *Samyutta* does sanction the notion of a soul as a self-subsistent entity and unless it is explained away, as by A.B. Keith, as a reference not to any transcendental substance but only to the popular empirical view, it is bound to prove a stumbling-block to the negativistic interpretation of early Buddhism.[3] I think that this is a very intriguing passage and it

[1] The *Kaṭhopaniṣad*, I, 2, 23.

[2] According to Stcherbatsky, there is a difference between the *attā* and the *pudgala*. *Attā* connotes the psychical-physical self while the *pudgala* means a permanent soul. This distinction seems far-fetched.

[3] Th. Stcherbatsky, *The Central Conception of Buddhism*, p. 22.

definitely sanctions the notion of a substantive psychic entity. But perhaps it is alone in so categorical an assertion with regard to the reality of the *pudgala*. It might be taken as a later interpolation in view of its incongruence with the vast majority of other passages which sanction *anātmavāda*.

(v) There is a further passage in the *Samyutta Nikāya* which reads :

"Then the wandering monk Vachchagotta spake to the Exalted One, saying. 'How does the matter stand, Venerable Gautama, is there the ego ?' When he said this, the Exalted One was silent. 'How then, venerable Gautama, is there not the ego ? And still the Exalted One maintained silence. Then the wandering monk Vachchagotta rose from his seat and went away. But the venerable Ananda said to the Exalted One : Wherefore sire has the Exalted One not given an answer to the questions put by the wandering monk Vachchagotta ? If I, Ananda, when the wandering monk Vachchagotta asked me : 'Is there the ego ?' had answered, 'The ego is, then that Ananda would have confirmed the doctrine of the Sramanas and Brahmanas who believe in permanence. If I, Ananda, when the wandering monk Vachchagotta asked me 'Is there not the ego ? had answered 'The ego is not', 'then that Ananda would have confirmed the doctrine of the Sramanas and Brahmanas who believe in annihilation."

Oldenberg draws a negativistic conclusion from this dialogue and says that this passage leads to the Buddhist teaching 'the ego is not'.[1] But this means that Oldenberg is committing the same fallacy of annihilationism which Buddha was anxious to avoid. Buddha inculcates the middle path between eternalism and annihilationism and as in his conception of *aniccāvāda* so also in his conception of *anattāvāda* he steers a middle path but Oldenberg puts an extreme view in his mouth. But although I agree that generally Buddha had a negativistic approach to the concept of the *attā*, I differ from Oldenberg since I think that this particular passage does not sanction *anattāvāda*.

5. *Indirect Evidence and Implications in Support of Buddhist Attāvāda*

(i) Although the general impression that has been left on my mind from a study of the Tripiṭaka literature is that Buddha did not believe in any self-subsistent human self or in any non-corporeal soul-entity, there are some literary references as well

[1] H. Oldenberg, *Buddha*, pp. 272-73.

some indirect arguments to show that Buddha might have had belief in some kind of a spiritual entity that dwelt in the human body and which was an eternal immutable self.[1] In the *Samyutta Nikāya* occurs : "When one says 'I' what he does is that herefers either to all the *skandhas* combined or any one of them and deludes himself that that was 'I' "[2] Here the empirical psycho-physical complex (*skandhas*) is denied the character of a permanent spiritual self but some positivistic interpreters of Buddhism argue that by denying the character of self to empirical categories Buddha is indirectly arguing for a meta-empirical self.[3] In the famous *Dharma-cakra-pravartana Sutra* delivered at Sārnath, everything, subjective and objective, is denied the character of a self. Buddha says that what is evil and painful cannot be the *ātman*. With reference to this passage also, advocates of a spiritual self have put forward the interpretation that Buddha is only repudiating the character of selfhood to the empirical and phenomenal categories but is indirectly sponsoring his belief in a meta-empirical self. But I think that the question is still problematic and it is difficult to argue categorically that the denial of selfhood to the phenomenal modes implies the indirect positing of the reality of a transcendent superior 'I'.

(ii) The Buddhist monk is advised to view the objects of the world as 'This is not mine, I am not this'. This statement may imply that the denial here refers only to the empirical elements and there is still a transcendent self which remains when the worldly entities pass away.

(iii) One of the grounds in support of *ātmavāda* is the belief in heavens and hells. If after death the soul goes to heaven or hell in accordance with its merit or demerit then it necessarily follows that there must first be a soul. If there is first such a

[1] Poussin, "The Ātman in the Pali Canon", *Indian Culture*, Vol. II, 1935-36, pp. 821-824, does recognize that in the Pali literature there are many passages supporting *anātman* but few passages which support *attā*.

[2] *Samyutta Nikāya*, II, 13 : "It is no fit question to ask, who experiences contact ? Who is it that feels ? This is the right way to question : *conditioned by what* is there contact ? *Conditioned by what*, is there feeling ?"

[3] Locke argued that there must be an enduring soul or self wherein the various mental operations of thinking, feeling and willing have their substratum.

substance as the soul, only then does the question of its final destiny come up.[1] If a system believes in heavens and hells, then to be consistent it must adhere to the belief in the existence of a soul. The mythology of the Tripiṭakas is full of the mention of heavens and hells. Various gods, Yakṣas and Gandharvas[2] are also referred to. According to the *Dhammapada* Buddha condemns a liar to hell. Buddha himself refers to his visits to the various *loka.* Such an enormous mythology looks meaningless if there is no substantialistic soul. There is radical incongruity in believing in different kinds of heavens and hells and at the same time in denying any entity as the self or the soul. If it were to be said that the 'character' or 'impressions' of a man transmigrate, then the stay of such shapeless subtle essences in heavens and hells is calculated neither to satisfy the critic nor to offer solace to the multitude.

(iv) Another indirect argument to substantiate a positive interpretation of Buddhist *attā* is the emphasis on *dhyāna.*[3] Without positing a spiritual principle it is impossible to explain the ascending scales of mystical consciousness. The adherence to the canons of *śila* prepares an aspirant for *samādhi* and *samādhi* results in the attainment of *prajnā* or discriminative vision. This *prajnā* is the great attribute of the *Samyak sambuddha* and gives to him *dharma vipaśyanā.* Commenting on the four-fold *dhyana* of early Buddhism C.A.F. Rhys Davids has stated :

"First, the attention by way of sense-cognition is hypnotically stimulated and concentrated, till mind working through sense is arrested. Then intellectual zest or keen interest dies away ; and then mind as happy, easeful emotion ceases, and a sort of zero-point is attained, leaving the vaguer consciousness of wide abstraction : infinity of space ; next, infinity of receptive consciousness (*vinnāna*), a potentiality of emotion and sensation, but with no actuality ; then as it were a negative conscious-

[1] The Egyptian mythology was built upon the peculiar conception of the soul prevalent there.

[2] A peculiar significance is attached to *gandharva* in some parts of Buddhist literature. According to the *Majjhima* Nikāya, I, 265 and the *Aṅguttara Nikāya*, I, 176 the *nāmarupa* can only develop if the *gandharva* descends in the womb.

[3] Dr. Heiler, *Die Buddhistische Versekung* ; C.A.F. Rhys Davids, "Dhyana in Early Buddhism", *Indian Historical Quarterly*, Vol. III, 1927, pp. 689-715.

ness, or awareness that the preceding stage, so far from revealing any persistent unity was 'nothing whatever' (*natthi kinci*). Finally, a stage is reached described as neither conscious nor unconscious, faint and delicate mentality fading into complete trance. And the expert Jhānist could so predetermine this self-hypnosis as to induce it and emerge from it when he chose."[1]

These grades of superior mystical illumination receive their ontological significance only if a positive interpretation is put on *attā* and belief in an ultimate spiritual reality of which the human soul is a particularization is attributed to Buddha.

(v) There are some references in the Buddhist scriptures to a blissful *nirvāna*. In the *Dhammapada*, *nirvāṇa* is regarded as the state of highest happiness. In the *Theragathā* and the *Therīgathā* one finds poetic descriptions of the rapturous and ecstatic state of nirvanic bliss. In the *Mahāvagga* it is said that after enlightenment, Buddha enjoyed the bliss of that exalted state for a long time. These statements do not fit in with a negativistic notion of the final destiny of man. It is to be emphasized that if moral life has a purpose,[2] if mystical realization is not a myth and if the funeral pyre is not the final platform of the human personality then there must be an infinite spiritual principle in the cosmos and human life. Without ardent belief in the reality of the self as a substance, a man may become a giant hero and a gigantic intellectual but spiritual life seems difficult and even meaningless and purposeless. The deep serenity and contemplative life of Buddha, his stress on the attainment of super-rational truth which was the sure means to the cessation of suffering and his perfect peace in the face of his approaching end do not receive their satisfying meaning in the context of a philosophy of non-soul. If only the gospels of soullessness and annihilationistic *nirvāṇa* are the final consequences of the most rigorous ascetic and ethical discipline, then early Buddhism would appear to be most unsatisfying both as a popular religion and as a true metaphysic. The dissatisfying character of early Buddhist

[1] C.A.F. Rhys Davids, "The Quest of the Ideal", *Buddhism*, pp. 214-15. See also Suttas numbers 43 & 44 of the *Majjhima Nikāya*.

[2] In the *Samyutta Nikāya* it is stated, however, that *brahmcaryavāsa* is not possible on the supposition of the identity of the body and the soul, neither is it possible on the supposition of the difference of the body and the soul. (R. Samkrityayana, *Bauddha Darshana*, in Hindi, pp. 22-23).

negativism led, as a reaction, to the growth of popular ceremonialism and idolatry and also to philosophic absolutism in the latter developments of Mahāyāna religion and philosophy.

(vi) In the famous Buddhist formula of *triśaraṇa* there is the surrender to Buddha, Dharma and Samgha. So far as surrender to Buddha is concerned, during his life time it meant the acceptance of his spiritual leadership although he himself never made such claim. Anyway, it can be argued that if Buddha was completely extinct after the *parinirvāṇa* then there was no sense in making a surrender to him. The element of surrender has a significance only if Buddha was subsisting as a spiritual being, may be, in some super-terrestrial regions.

These indirect evidences in support of *ātmavāda* are indeed significant. A religion is a whole and it has not only to provide certain abstract propositions of cosmology but has to give a philosophy of life to the people. Hence a number of compromises have to be made with popular views and prejudices and some of them are also incorporated in the religious system itself. Thus although I hold that at a philosophical plane, Buddha expounded the notion of soullessness I think that he was constrained, by the force of the environmental matrix wherein he operated as a religious leader, to include many notions and conceptions which appear crude from the standpoint of abstract soullessness. Unless we are prepared to regard the Tripiṭakas as a conglomeration of incongruent notions, we should say that although from the rigid canons of philosophical exposition Buddha adhered to soullessness, still, to provide energetic inspiration to the people he had to speak at times in linguistic symbols which are more consonant with a positive belief in a soul.

6. *Western Interpreters of Buddhist Non-soul Doctrine*

Western interpreters specially in the nineteenth century and the earlier part of the twentieth century put a negativistic interpretation on early Buddhism. Hegel regarded Buddhism as a creed of final negation.[1] Edward Caird interpreted Buddhism as a doctrine of recoil upon the subjective entity and as a gospel of nirvāṇic extinction. Streeter in his *Buddha and Christ* and

[1] Hegel, *Philosophy of History*, pp. 167-72.

Melamed in his *Spinoza and Buddha* interpret Buddhism as a negative creed which denied the soul and the world. It is true that the Christian interpreters feel glory in contrasting the affirmative stress on the blessedness of the soul in Christianity from the nihilistic extinction of the soul which is all that Buddhism has to offer to man. But if this, rather extreme, interpretation has been put upon Buddhism, the early Buddhist scriptures, which are the sole sources for knowing what Gautama Buddha taught and which have been so regarded by Buddhists for over two thousand years, are themselves to blame for that. There is no clear linguistic evidence to indicate that Buddha ever adhered to the notion of a transcendent self as the inmost essence of a man. The attempt to attribute a positive belief in some kind of a spiritual self to Buddha, on logical and philosophical grounds of consistency, is always problematic. For making early Buddhism look like a positive creed of spiritual fulfilment, I would not sanction an interpretation which clearly goes against the letter of the Tripiṭakas. The Tripiṭakas, I would regard, as far more authentic for knowing the inner meaning of the gospel of Buddha than any modern neo-Hinduist attempts at "Vedantification" of Buddhism as attempted by Ramakrishna, Vivekananda, Gandhi and Radhakrishnan.

7. *Change in the view of C.A.F. Rhys Davids Regarding the Interpretation of Anātman*

Mrs. C.A.F. Rhys Davids has perhaps made the most wide-spread contributions in the field of early Buddhism. In her earlier publications like *Buddhism* and *Buddhist Psychology* she puts a negativist interpretation on Buddhist *anattā* and wrote : "The anti-attā argument of Buddhism is mainly and consistently directed against the notion of a soul, which was not only a persistent, encouraging, blissful, transmigrating superphenomenal being, but was also a being wherein the supreme *Ātman* or world soul was immanent, one with it, in essence and as a bodily or mental factor issuing its fiat."[1]

[1] The fundamental basis of Buddhist *anātmavāda* was to challenge the supposed exemption of the *ātman* from the universal laws of causation and impermanence. C.A.F. Rhys Davids, *Buddhist Psychology*, p. 32.

But in her later writings she almost absolutely changed her standpoint[1] and began to propound that *anattā* is a later accretion[2] of monastic origin and is an imposition on the original gospel of Sakya Buddha which (the original gospel) was more or less constructed on the Upaniṣadic pattern. Referring to the *Samyutta Nikāya* (Kosala : *Udānam* 1.5.)[3] which she compares with the *Brihadāraṇyaka* refrain *ātmanas tu kāmāya sarvam priyam bhavati* she says : "I believe it is far more likely, that the original speaker of the verse used *attā* in the sense in which the original speaker of the Upaniṣad utterance used *ātman*. I believe it is far less likely that the Sakyan used *attā* in the sense in which Piṭaka compilers came to use it, much later. For those two older speakers, the *ātman*, *ātta*, was that More in each man who was potentially the Most in him,"[4] According to the interpretation of C.A.F. Rhys Davids, the insistence on "becoming" would mean not an ontological via media between being and non-being but an ethical discipline for the realisation of the "potential" in man. The change of stand of C.A.F. Rhys Davids who had spent nearly fifty years of her life-time in the study of Buddhism is significant. But my own

[1] C.A.F. Rhys Davids, "A Vanished Sakyan Window", *Indian Culture*, Vol. II, 1935-36, pp.115-124. C.A.F Rhys Davids, "The Relations between Early Buddhism and Brahmanism", *Indian Historical Quarterly*, Vol. X, 1934, pp. 274-87, says that the concept of immanence as taught in the Upaniṣads is never attacked by Buddha. C.A.F. Rhys Davids. "The Unknown Co-founders of Buddhism", *Journal of Royal Asiatic Society*, 1927, pp. 193-208. C.A.F. Rhys Davids, "A Dynamic conception of Man", *Indian Culture*, Vol. VI, 1939-40, pp. 235-39, and "Buddha and not Buddhists." *Indian Culture*, Vol. III, 1936-37, pp. 515-17.

[2] C.A.F. Rhys Davids, "History of the Doctrine of Skamdhas", *Indian Culture*, Vol. III, 1936-37, pp. 405-11, 653-662, says that the doctrine of the five Skamdhas is an editorial increment quite out of date for and unworthy of the first Buddhist missionaries.

[3] "The whole wide world we traverse with our thought,
And nothing find to man more dear than self
Since aye so dear the self to others is
Let the self-lover harm no other man".
(Spoken by Buddha to Prasenajit)

This verse also occurs in the Tibetan *Dhammapada* translated by Rockhill (but not in the *Pali Dhammapada*).

[4] C.A.F. Rhys Davids, "Amity", *K.B. Pathak Commemoration Volume*, *op. cit.*, (pp. 57-67), pp. 60-61 ; *Sakya or Buddhist Origins* (London, Kegan Paul, 1931), pp. 235-256.

impression about the researches of C.A.F. Rhys Davids is that they are full of hair-splitting verbal dialectics and rely on imagination. She is willing to stretch words and phrases to yield meanings at which the original speakers would be staggeringly surprised. Her fantastic thesis of an original positive Buddhism and a later monkish asceticism is ridiculous. Furthermore, she has not brought forward any single authentic passage which would convincingly show that Buddha believed in the spiritual and substantialistic character of the soul.

8. *Conclusion*

Buddhism is unique among the religious systems of the world in having denied the substantial character of the soul. No other religion, Aryan or Semitic, has dispensed with the soul. If the Tripiṭakas have to be followed, there is no doubt that *anattā* means the radical denial of the soul. The psycho-physical empirical categories have been denied the character of soul in early Buddhism. The overwhelming silence about and even the occasional denial of the Upaniṣadic conception of the soul are almost conclusive to prove that Buddha did not subscribe to any soul—empirical or transcendent. It is a surprising phenomenon as to how such a negativistic creed could attain so much vigor and vitality and spread in so many areas of the world.

But although Buddhism denies the perpetually abiding character of any ego or self, it cannot be regarded as being a materialistic creed. Its essential conception is the conditioned or dependent character of all phenomena. What was called the self or the *ātman* in pre-Buddhist literature is stated by Buddhism to consist of sensations and conformations. Buddha is an *anātmavādi* but not a materialist. If Buddhism were corporeal materialism, it would have repudiated an enduring soul and preached the reality of the body. But according to early Buddhism the body is no abiding reality.[1] It is a cluster of certain elements of physical phenomena and nothing more. Hence what exists is a mere process, a complex manifold interdependent phenomenal aggregation subject to origination, maturation and eventual extinction. It can be said that the aim of Buddhism is to teach the contingent character of all physical

[1] According to the *Samyutta Nikāya* III, 157, body and mind "are impermanent, are liable to suffering, and without soul."

and mental phenomena and to repudiate any permanent, abiding, etarnal self or substance. In place of the self-determined and self-sufficient character of simple entities, *anātman* is a registration of the flowing, relative and 'devoid of any soul' character of the physical-psychical complex.[1] The detailed categorization of matter, perception, feeling, conformation and consciousness in the *nāmarupa-skandha* has been done only with a view to preach the soullessness of any of the possible material and mental factors.

[1] Cf. The *Samyutta Nikāya*, V, 10, 6. The statement in the *Samyutta* has also been quoted in T.W. Rhys Davids, ***The Questions of King Milinda***, ***SBE***, II, 1, 11.

CHAPTER 8

THE PHILOSOPHY OF REBIRTH

1. *Introduction*

THE DOCTRINE of rebirth has a prominent place in the ancient systems of Indian thought.[1] The Vedantic and Buddhist systems adhere to it in some form or other. Perhaps this notion of rebirth is the sole important distinguishing feature of Hinduism from the Semitic religions like Judaism, Christianity and Islam.

The concept of rebirth has been interpreted in two ways. In the most popular form it means that man is a spiritual monadic soul and after the disintegration of his body he would assume another form. He may assume either a human form again or may be compelled to assume even an animal form. Secondly, this doctrine of rebirth has sometimes meant birth in some super-terrestrial region. According to the Hindu popular tradition there are other regions besides this earth where there are living beings. Hence it is possible that the soul may assume some physical form or other in some super-terrestrial regions. In both these forms of this doctrine the common point is the acceptance of the continuity of the existence of the soul.

The theory of rebirth is an answer to the persistent and deep desire of man for self-perpetuity.[2] Sometimes the desire for self-preservation seeks satisfaction in the continuation of oneself, through one's progeny. But that alone would not satisfy a man. The egoistic propensity of man loves to relish the prospects of endless continuity through numerous births. Even in some countries and civilization outside India, this doctrine of rebirth has been upheld. Pythagoras was an

[1] For the classic statement of the doctrine of rebirth see the *Bhagavad-gitā*, II, 23 and XV, 8-10.

[2] It is possible that the doctrine of metempsychosis arose to account for the tragic and terrible lot of man in the world.

ardent believer in transmigration of souls[1] and it is reported that once in the barking of a dog he discovered the agonizing cries of one of his dead friends. Plato accepted the notion of the previous existence of souls. He adopts the theory of "recollection" by the soul of its previous existences. Bruno in the Middle Ages accepted this notion. The German poet Goethe although greatly inclined towards science loved to play with the idea of metempsychosis.

In modern times it is difficult to believe in a notion which demands so much of credulity on our part.[2] Even if one is not an atheist or a materialist, still he finds it difficult to believe in the concrete perpetuation of a monadic supra-atomic spiritual substance through endless births and deaths. The scientific procedures of observation, quantification, mensuration and controlled experimentation do not have the least chance of application in this realm. One has either to believe in this doctrine or to reject it. There can be no objective and dispassionate argumentation about it. There may be, however, something to be said for this doctrine in finding some plausible explanation of the phenomenon of genius. The exceptional intellectual achievements of the great geniuses cannot be explained only by the three-fold factors of heredity, environment and nurture. Geniuses appear as freaks, as deviations, from the normal course of human achievements. The theory of rebirth comes as a handy explanation of this phenomenon. Hence it is not possible to dismiss this theory as entirely fantastic. It may have some meaning and relevance in a region which is beyond the cognizance of human faculties. For those who believe in a non-mechanical universe the doctrine of rebirth has provided strengthened energy to face the trials of this life.

2. *History of the Doctrine of Rebirth in India*

On anthropological evidence it has been stated that the tribal population of India holds the notion of continuity of the dead person in some form or other. It is possible that even in the third millenium B.C. the ancestors of these tribal people

[1] Cf. Sri Aurobindo, *The Problem of Rebirth* (Sri Aurobindo Ashrama, Pondicherry, 1952), p. 8.

[2] For a contemporary formulation of the concept of rebirth see Sri Aurobindo, *The Riddle of This World* (Pondicherry, Sri Aurobindo Ashrama, 1951, fourth edition), pp. 83-86.

believed in some such notions. It is not far-fetched to hold that the universally prevalent belief in ghosts is a part of the tribal belief in some kind of continuity of the departed ancestors. The acceptance of several kinds of genie is also a part of that same tradition. This primitive belief in the persistence of the ancestors is partly responsible for the later evolution of the doctrine of rebirth. Poussin says :

> "The belief in reincarnations was a purely savage surmise, liable to be organized in what is called totemism, an unprogressive and absurd paganism, and no more. To be sure of it, we have only to open the books of Tylor or Durkheim. Brahmans and Buddhists borrowed this belief, which was altogether new to the Aryan tradition ; but they found no difficulty in adapting it either to the dogma of the reward of good and evil deeds or to a monism as rigid as that of the Eleatic 'school'."[1]

We do not have any evidence about the beliefs and conceptions of the Mohenjodaro people regarding metempsychosis. It is possible to hold that the crude notions regarding the continuity of the soul after death may be a part of a widely prevalent tradition in which the aboriginal remote ancestors of the modern Indian tribes as well as the people who built the foundations of the civilization at Harappā and Mohenjodaro might have shared. The *Atharvaveda* may partly contain the remnants of the beliefs and notions of the aboriginal tribes.

Western Indologists generally tend to hold that in the Vedas there is no conception of rebirth of the soul upon earth.[2] According to Böhtlingk, Ernst Windisch, Pischel and Geldney, the concept of *punarjanam* is found in the *Ṛgveda* and the *Brāhmaṇas*. But according to Oldenberg, Macdonell, Sylvain Levi, Bloomfield and Hopkins, the idea of *punarjanam* is developed only in the Āraṇyakas and the Upaniṣads. After death. according to the Vedic poets and bards, the souls are supposed to have residence in the world of Yama. But Swami Dayananda holds that in the Vedas the doctrine of transmigration is present.[3] In one of the hymns of the *Ṛgveda* there is a

[1] Louis Vallee de la Poussin, *The Way of Nirvāṇa*, p. 18.

[2] A.B. Govinda, *The Psychological Attitude of Early Buddhist Philosophy*, p. 33.

[3] Bothlink has found allusion to the doctrine of rebirth in the *Ṛgveda*, 1, 164, 30-32 R.D. Ranade in *A Constructive Survey of Upaniṣadic Philosophy* has emphatically supported Böhtlingk and finds great logic in

prayer for the acquisition of sense-organs, the body—the *tanva* and the animating spirit or the *asu.* In the *Yajurveda* there is a prayer for the re-acquisition of *ātma.*[1] In the *Atharvaveda* also there is a similar prayer.[2] The word *ātman* in the Vedic Samhitās, however, is interpreted as referring only to the *animus.* It is not a reference to the spiritual soul-substance of the later metaphysical Vedānta. Originally the word *ātman* meant the animating principle. It signified the breath. It is, thus, an indication of the great significance of air or breath in ancient thought. The basic root in both the words *ātman* and *prāṇa* is similar — $\sqrt{at}$ or $\sqrt{an}$.

Towards the end of the Vedic period, some of the seers accepted the notion of an indeterminate absolute immanental power. During the Vedic age it will be far-fetched to seek the roots of the conception of a spiritual soul-substance attaining identity with this primal infinite power.

The germs of the concept of transmigration of the soul appear in the Brāhmaṇas.[3] The priests of those days adhered to the concept that through good works, birth in a good family could be obtained.

It has been maintained that the doctrine of the transmigration of the soul is a late development in the Upaniṣads and is different from the Vedic and Brāhmaṇic idea of retribution in the other worlds. Some Christian Scholars have gone to the extent of maintaining that the doctrine of transmigration of the soul has been much influenced by the savage belief in the passage of the human soul into plants and animals. The doctrine of transmigration accepts a realistic and pluralistic view of the soul and hence it fits in more with the Vedic doctrine of the soul as a separate substance than with the Upaniṣadic monism. Hence, it may be, that the Upaniṣadic view of transmigration is an old Vedie legacy which is maintained alongside with the acceptance of the Upaniṣadic absolute by being relegated to the empiric sphere. If some of the Upaniṣads

his arguments. J.W. Hopkins, *Hindu Ethics*, p. 44 also says : "...metempsychosis which is also known in a vague form to the Ṛgveda."

1 *YV.* IV, 15 : "*punaratmā me āgan*".

2 *AV.* VII, 6, 67, 1 : "*punaratmā*".

3 The *Śatapatha Brāhmaṇa* 1, 5, 3, 4, contains a dubious allusion to the concept of transmigration.

do not believe in a total merging of the individual soul in the absolute at the time of liberation, but impart some sort of separate consciousness to it, we can very well find an origin of this notion in the Vedic quest for immortality.

In the Upaniṣadic age three conceptions of the destiny of the soul were present. (I) At a philosophical plane, the soul was supposed to gain identity with the Absolute through deep meditation and intuitive consciousness. (II) It was also held that through good works, specially sacrificial rituals, the soul could attain heaven. (III) The souls of the dead persons were supposed to attain birth in human or animal bodies according to their actions. This rebirth could be attained either immediately after death or after some period of residence either in heaven or hell in accordance with the merits acquired by it, the soul could assume a human or an animal form.

In the *Kaṭha Upaniṣad* there is a clear statement regarding the belief in the transmigration of the soul. Rebirth is regarded as being determined by one's intellectual and moral attainments. It is stated that a person of debased character would be reduced even to an existence in the trees or other substances. This conception of the attainment of the status of trees (*sthāṇu*) may appear very crude but in one sense it is a testimony to the concrete unity of all existence. The peculiarity of the ancient Hindu philosophy of rebirth is the notion of the possibility of descent from a higher scale of life to the lower, and this indicates the great importance attached in Hindu thought to moral causation and the power of human efforts.

The essence of the Upaniṣadic concept of rebirth is the stress on the determination of character and personality not merely by the mechanical terms of heredity and environment but by the impact of the concentrated essence and potency of the actions performed in previous lives. This element of Upaniṣadic thought has also been accepted by Buddhism.[1] In the Jātakas it is elaborately laid down that Buddha had to undergo almost unbearable rigors of penances in previous existences before he could attain the exalted heights of Buddhahood.

1 A.K. Coomaraswamy, *Buddha and the Gospel of Buddhism*, p. 200, says : "We are told, for example, that Buddhism differs from Brāhmanism in its refutation of the 'then current pessimistic idea that salvation could not be reached on earth, and must therefore be sought for in rebirth in

Buddhism accepts the concept of rebirth.[1] But there are two momentous differences between the Upaniṣadic and the Buddhistic theories. The first theoretical difference proceeds from the rejection by Buddhism of the monadic and substantialistic view of the human soul. It may appear ridiculous at first sight to uphold the notion of rebirth without the acceptance of any transmigrating spiritual entity.[2] According to Buddhism there is the rebirth of personality or of the psycho-physical complex— the *nāmarūpa skandha*. In the *Milinda Panha* the notion of the rebirth of the *nāmarūpa skandha* has been illustrated with numerous examples. They are, however, not proofs but analogies. For illustrating the notion of rebirth without transmigration, the *Milinda* gives the analogies of (i) the lighting of one lamp from another and (ii) the transmission of verses from the teacher to the disciple. The acceptance by Buddhism of the concept of rebirth[3] even after the repudiation of the spiri-

heaven'. (T.W. Rhys Davids, *Early Buddhism*, p. 55). But if this idea was 'current' as a motif of the sacrificial ritual, it certainly was not maintained by the Brāhman idealists."

[1] Warren, *Buddhism in Translations* (Harvard Oriental Series), p. 234, says that in Buddhism there is the concept of rebirth and not of transmigration. According to C.A.F. Rhys Davids, *Buddhism*, there is the concept of a migration of character but not of the soul. Referring to the later tradition, Louis vallee de la Poussin, *The Way of Nirvana*, p. 49*n* refers to the *Abhidharmakosa*, III, 324 where there is mention of transmigration of *karman* alone.

[2] Sometimes in the Buddhist scriptures consciousness or *vijñāna* is regarded as the transmigrating entity. H. Oldenberg, *Buddha*, points to the appearance of Māra at the time of the death of Godhika. "When the venerable Godhika has brought about his own death by opening a vein, the disciples see a dark cloud of smoke moving to and fro on all sides round his corpse. They ask Buddha what the smoke means. "That is Māra, the wicked one, O disciples," says Buddha : 'he is looking for the noble Godhika's consciousness : where has the noble Godhika's consciousness found its place ?' But the noble Godhika has entered into Nirvāna; his consciousness nowhere remains". Quoted from the *Samyutta Nikāya*, Vol. I, in H. Oldenberg, *Buddha*, pp. 266-267.

[3] Cf. The *Lankāvatāra Sūtra*, iii, quoted in D. T. Suzuki, *Outlines of Mahayana Buddhism*, p. 41 :

"In a combination of causes
The vulgar seek the reality of self.
As truth thy understand not,
From birth to birth they transmigrate."

tual substantialistic view of the soul is a testimony to the enormous power of persistence of notions which have been accepted in the cultural tradition. The sway of the concept of rebirth must have been overwhelming over the national mind of northern India in those days to compel its acceptance by Buddhism in some modified form.

A second important difference between the Upaniṣadic and the Buddhistic theories of rebirth lies in the rejection by the latter of the possibility of lapse from the human status to birth in the trees. This seems to be an advance in the evolution of thought. It means that the immense qualitative difference between the human personality and the trees must have been recognised. So great is the difference between a man and a tree that in spite of terrific moral misbehavior the possibility of birth in the trees has been ruled out by Buddhism. But in common with the Upaniṣadic tradition, Buddha does seriously uphold the possibility of birth among the animals. According to the Jātakas, he himself had previous births among the animals before he became ready for his incarnation as Buddha. This implies that the ancient Indian thinkers would be opposed to the concept of evolutionary progression confined only to human beings. They upheld the view that if a man took recourse to the path of evil and untruth there could be retrogression and he would have to take birth among the animals. Thus in ancient Indian philosophy there is the acceptance both of evolution and retrogression. This is in contrast to the sentimental optimism of the idealists and views of the spokesmen of materialistic science.

3. *Sociological Analysis of the Concept of Rebirth*

According to the advocates of the theory of historical materialism, the concept of rebirth was generated and popularized by the ideological supporters of the interests of the ruling and propertied sections. The latter popularized this notion in order to provide spiritual and moral rationalization of the social and economic disproportionalities in society. The concept of rebirth is thus supposed to have put a moral meaning into the existing fact of social tyranny and exploitation. It is supposed to make the people reconciled to their fate because even the greatest evils which could be checked by social action become rationalized as divinely ordained sanctions for demerits and evil actions performed in past existences.

I do not agree with this sociological explantion. What grounds is there for imputing base and sordid motives to the exponents of the theory of rebirth ? This explanation assumes the existence of the counterpart of modern "ideological" writers and advocates in very ancient times.

I uphold an anthropological and a philosophical approach to this problem of the origin of the concept of rebirth. From the anthropological standpoint it seems that to hold that the dead relation continues to live in some form is a part of the psychological aspiration of the people. The tribe or the family was regarded so important in those days that even after death the dead person was considered as in some ways connected with the life of the tribe or the family either in the form of a ghost or a prophylactic ancestor. The idea of transmigration of the soul is a refinement of this crude notion.

Besides anthropological roots, the idea of the transmigration of the soul or rebirth has a philosophical origin. It is related to speculations regarding the conservation of the merits acquired and the penalization for the evil deeds committed. An elementary notion of rectificatory justice demands that the good and evil of this world should be properly dealt with.[1] This is the *prospective* conception of justice. The human mind, further seeks some kind of explanation for the disparities, contradictions and incongruities prevalent in the world. To explain the anomalies of the present day world the concept of rebirth appears as a ready moral instrument. This is the *retrospective* conception of justice. The philosophy of rebirth is thus built on this two-fold foundations of prospective and retrospective justice and is related to philosophical reflections on the nature of moral action. Thus I think that although the elementary germs of the concept of rebirth may be found in the ideas of the prolongation of the life of the departed soul among the primitive tribes, the final philosophical explantion given to it is the work of philosophers who speculated on the moral destiny of man.

[1] According to the Vedic belief, life and joy after death were regarded as the reward of virtue. See E. W. Hopkins, *Hindu Ethics*, p. 42.

In the earliest periods of civilization, the tribe or the clan or the sib (German *sippe*) or the blood-based family was the primary unit. The idea of distinct specific separate individuality was not yet born. The individual sought significance in the preservation of the clan. The formulation and acceptance of the notion of rebirth is a revolutionary inroad upon the cohesiveness of the group. In place of seeking the roots of individual action in the compulsive norms and commands of the group, the theory of rebirth proclaims an unusually prominent notion of individuality. It proclaims that each soul monad inhabiting a physical body is a distinct person with a prolonged history in time. It teaches the conservation of accumulated experiences. It proclaims that the centre of gravity of individual life is to be found in one's own self. Thus just as the emergence of the concept of 'Daemon' in Socratic philosophy has been the precursor of a theory of individualism in Greece so also the concept of rebirth was the proclamation of the notion of spiritual and moral individuality in India. Its emergence in one sense symbolizes the break of the old tribal community and the kinship structure. The old tribal community had been exposed to the corrosive attacks of social stratification by the solidification of the caste endogamy. The caste system was a social-institutional attack on the primitive community and sundered its old organic bonds. The concept of rebirth was a further significant philosophical attack on the cohesiveness of the primitive community because it introduced the principle of distinct continuing separate individuality. It definitely asserted that the individual is not lost in the group. His spiritual existence transcends the confines of the group. Thus the doctrine of rebirth has a very great sociological and political importance in the history of Indian thought.

Chapter 9

EARLY BUDDHIST ETHICS

1. *Ethics in the Pre-Buddhistic Thought*

For some critics of Indian philosophic thought there is no important place for ethics in it inasmuch as the philosophy of *māyā* or world-illusionism involves the reduction of all actions, good or bad, to nullity[1] and the transcendent Absolute, removed from all cosmic dualities and ethical conflicts is to be attained not by the perfection of moral character but by the knowledge of the identity of the immanental and psychic entities.[2] It is thus implied that in the Indian systems of thought moral perfection is regarded as belonging to the mundane spheres which are a product of *māyā*. It is further emphasized that at best morality according to Indian thought is only a way— *mārga* or *naya* or *yāna*, to produce knowledge and is not something of absolute worth in itself.[3] Schweitzer has criticized Hindu ethics as being world-and-life-negating. Melamed writes :

> "In Western religiosity ...man and God are pictured as being in opposition to each other. The myths of Prometheus and of Heraclitus in ancient Greece, as well as the myth of the flood in the Bible, testify to an intense conflict between man and God. Even Christianity stresses the contradistinction between man and God. In the individualistic West, God is endowed with personality, which creates a state of tension between Himself and man. This conflict between God and man gives birth to ethics. In ancient India, however, God, constituting only eternal being

[1] C.R. Lanman, *Beginnings of Hindu Pantheism* (Cambridge, Mass : Charles E. Sever, 1890), p. 24 : "What a prospect— dark and void— this Supreme Spirit before whom all human endeavour, all noble ambition, all hope, all love is blighted : What a contrast, a relief, when we turn from this to the teachings of the gentle Nazarene."

[2] A.B. Keith, *The Religion and Philosophy of the Veda and Upaniṣads*, Vol. II, pp. 598, 596.

[3] Paul Deussen, *The Philosophy of the Upaniṣads*, p.362. Also *Muṇḍaka*, III, 2, 2 ; *Kaṭha*, VI, 11 ; *Brihadāraṇyaka*, IV, 4, 23.

and bereft of all personality, does not contain the possibility of ethics."[1]

But this is not a correct representation of the place of ethics in ancient India. The Vedāntic realization is regarded as the culmination of the most rigorous ethical discipline. Moral preparation for spiritual life is thoroughly emphasized in the *Praśnopaniṣad*, and in the *Chhāndogya* in course of the dialogue of Prajāpati and Indra, as well as in the teachings of Satyakāma to Upakośala Kāmalāyana. The *Kaṭhopaniṣad*[2] states in emphatic terms :

Nāvirato duścaritāt nāśānto nāsamāhitaḥ
nāśāntamānaso vāpi prajnānenainamāpnuyāt (1, 2, 24)

The Hindu thinkers never confounded the highest absolute view with the relative empirical standpoint. The positing of a transcendent utter being is not tantamount to the sanctioning of an impure way of life. If it were so, a similar charge could be made against physical realism, positivism and materialism. Because scientific materialism would preach the ultimate and sole reality of electrons and protons, no body can pretend to be indifferent to good and evil, on the ground that in the final analysis everything is the quantitative and qualitative representation of electronic movements.

It will be wild to believe that the ancient Hindus, who fought the battle of Mahābhārata, who created the Maurya and the Gupta empires, and whose achievements in art and logic, sculpture and architecture, poetry and positive sciences still strike the imagination of the world were mere speculators engrossed in the subtleties of *māyā* and neglected the imperative demands of a sane and sober life and social order. Buddha who instructed his disciples to spread his message of evangelisation to the whole humanity was not a mere *māyāvādi*. The philosophical standpoints of the Hindus—illusionism or mentalism, idealism or solipsism, scepticism, naturalism or realism —never collided with the active pursuit of a vigorous morally-oriented social life. Hence Indian thought cannot be loosely regarded as being only world-and-life-negating.

[1] Melamed, *Spinoza and Buddha*, p. 243.

[2] The *Kaṭhopaniṣad*, I, 3, 7 also stresses the combination of knowledge and ethics and condemns one who is *avijnānavān*, *amanaskaḥ* and *aśuchiḥ*.

The Vedas contain moral injunctions.[1] The insistence of the Vedic seers is on *rita*[2] and *satya.* The *Ṛgveda says* that the immensest austerities (*abhīddhāt tapaso*) have led to their (*ṛta* and *satya*) generation. *Ṛta* is a cosmic immanental force of righteousness.[3] It indicates the belief of the Vedic seers in a teleological conception of the universe because moral perfection is regarded as the aim of the human being.[4] The *Ṛgveda* says that the good man deviates not from the path of truth.[5] The *Yajurveda* prescribed a graduated course of moral evolutionism:

Vratena dikshāmāpnoti dikshyāpnoti dakhiṇām
Dakshinā sraddhāmāpnoti śraddhyā satyamāpyate (*V.S.* XIX, 30)

Sometimes *satya* is regarded not merely as an individual moral attribute but as a cosmic force (*satyena uttabhitā bhumih*). The famous *Prithivī Sūkta* of the *Atharvaveda* also regards *satya* and *ṛta* as cosmic forces upholding the earth.

The *Ṛgveda* recognizes social virtues as well (*nāryamaṇam pushyati no sakhāyam kevalāgho bhavati kevalādī*). Conformity to the divine dictates constitutes moral life according to the Vedic notions. It is true that the gods of the Vedas are not all very moral, but still ethical elements are emphasized. Certainly Indra is prone to drink and Rudra is revengeful but Varuṇa

[1] Cf. Kaegi, *The Ṛgveda*, p. 18 : "...the hymns strongly prove how deeply the prominent minds in the people were persuaded that the eternal ordinances of the rulers of the world were as inviolable in mental and moral matters as in the realm of nature, and that every wrong act, even the unconscious, was punished and the sin expiated."

[2] E.J. Thomas, *The Life of Buddha*, p. 173, thus describes the anthropological roots of the notion behind *rita*: "The possibility of such a conception must have arisen very early in the formation and growth of the association of individuals in societies. A member of a tribe must act in certain ways supposed to be advantageous to his fellow individuals and himself, and certain other actions are forbidden."

[3] The word *Artamanya* in the Amarna letters (*c.* 1380-1350 B.C.) is comparable to the Sanskrit *Ritamanya.* The Mitannian evidence (1475-1280 B.C.), may be also cited in this connexion ; *Artasumara* is comparable to the Sanskrit *Ṛtasmara* (mindful of right) and *Artatama* is parallel to the Vedic *Ritadhaman.*

[4] According to Macdonell, *Vedic Mythology*, p. 11, 26 *ṛta* signifies two kinds of order : (i) order in the moral world as truth and right, and (ii) order in the religious world — sacrifice and rite.

[5] *Ritasya panthāmanveti sādhu vijānatīva na diśo minā̆ti.*

(who, like Buddha, is regarded as omniscient) is the great guardian of the moral life and his spies traverse in all quarters to find out the guilty. Varuṇa is *dhṛtavrata*, and the upholder of physical and moral order.[1] At one place, Agni also is called *vratapati*—the lord of the great vows.[2] In the *Ṛgveda*[3] moral virtues like beneficence and righteousness are attributed to Dyauh and Prithivī. The *Ṛgveda* also condemns the great moral vices.[4] These notions had great influence on the Upaniṣadic and Buddhistic thought also. There are some vital affinities in the moral characteristics attributed to the Vedic god Varuṇa and Buddha. But there are differences also. Varuṇa forgives the sins of the implorers. In the Upaniṣads and early Buddhism the notion of forgiveness of sins is not present. The later theistic cults again adopted this idea.

The predominant impression which the Vedic religion leaves, however, is of the power and buoyancy of the gods. Some moral sentiments and notions are inculcated there but they do not occupy that tremendous importance there which they do in Buddhism and Jainism. It must be stated, nonetheless, that the one legacy which the Veda leaves is the belief in the prevalence of order and truth in the world.

The *Brāhmaṇas* are mainly concerned with ritualism and sacrifice and, hence, they stress the social aspects of morality.[5] The Upaniṣads, on the other hand, stress the emancipation of the individual brought about by the realization of the ultimate reality through gnosis and moral perfection. Buddhism, although it adheres to the gospel of *nirvāṇa* which is obtained by the individual, also sanctioned social elements of morality. The *Brāhmaṇas* recognize the three "debts" of a man. The debt to the gods can be redeemed by religious life and sacrificial ritualism.[6] The debt to the ancestors (*pitarah*) can be redeemed by procreating sons who would continue the family-line. Through study and meditation it is possible to get freedom

[1] A.B. Keith, *The Religion and Philosophy of the Veda and Upaniṣads*, pp. 433-34.

[2] The God Savitā has also a lofty moral side.

[3] *Ṛgveda*, I, 159, 1 ; VI, 70, 6 ; I, 160. I ; IV, 56, 2.

[4] *Ṛgveda*, VII, 104, 8ff ; IV, 5, 5ff.

[5] S.N. Dasgupta, *Indian Philosophy*, Vol. I, pp. 25-26.

[6] According to the *Śatapatha Brāhmaṇa*, I, 9, 3, 2 the dead pass between two fires which burn the evil-doers but let the good go by.

from the debt to the seers. In continuance of the Vedic tradition, the *Brāhmaṇas* also lay insistence on speaking the truth. One important point in the ethical code of the *Brāhmaṇas* is the inculcation of the confession of evil deeds performed.[1] Surprisingly enough, the Upaniṣads do not mention confession. But in the Buddhist monastic code confession of sins assumes an exaggerated predominance. In conformity with the Vedic tradition, in *Brāhmaṇas* also, there was stress on asceticism. The gods were regarded as having attained their position, potency and power by means of austerities.[2] This is a significant notion and its influence can be seen not only on Buddhism but also on Purāṇic Hinduism. Buddhism regarded 'devahood' as a rank to be gained by individual moral efforts. In the later books of Hinduism also, the status of a *deva* is not regarded as a permanent position but is supposed to last only so long as the merits of the righteous deeds last. Thus it can be said that the *Brāhmaṇas* inculcated a notion which had tremendous influence on Indian thought and which contains stress on moral endeavours by the individual because they can lead one to the status of a god.

2. *Evolution of Buddhist Moral Ideas*

Howsoever intuitively perceived and experienced and transcendentally-oriented a system of ethical philosophy might be, it does have some social foundations and social implications. How much so ever a man might try, he cannot remove himself from the organic structure of society. It is true that Buddha received enlightenment under the Bodhi tree as a result of intense austerities and deep contemplations but he had flourished amidst a social, economic and political context whose conscious and unconscious influences were cast on his personality and thought. A great man represents the explicit flowering of the dominant forces of his particular age. The insistent and compulsive urgency with which the problem of pain and suffering represented itself to the sensitive mind of Buddha was a consequence of the social ethos and spirit of that age which was pulsating with pessimism and monasticism and of a society in which wandering preachers were many. Buddha

1 *Śatapatha Brāhmaṇa*, II, 5, 2, 20. Cf. also Christianity.
2 *Taittirīya Brāhmaṇa*, III, 12, 3.

himself was conscious that his teachings were bound to have social influences. The *Dhammapada* says : "A supernatural person (a Buddha) is not easily found, he is not born everywhere. Wherever such a sage is born, that race prospers."[1] In the process of acquiring an institutional framework, ethical teachings more and more demonstrate their social influence. The teachings of Buddha although oriented to the acquisition of final emancipation from misery, have, in the course of Indian history, cast profound social influences. A sociological study of early Buddhist ethics receives added justification today when responsible leaders of peoples and nations are saying that the Buddhist concepts of *avaira* and *maitrī* can alone save humanity from the threatening holocaust and catastrophe. Mahatma Gandhi's political success in modern India is an additional substantiation of the view that the Buddhist ethics of *ahimsā* can have social and political implications. The movement of Gandhi was a vindication of the practical applicability of the Buddhist concept of non-violence on a national political scale. Hence it is essential that a sociological study of Buddhist ethics should be undertaken. In the West, Westermarck, Max Weber, L.T. Hobhouse, Durkheim, Albion Small, Joachim Wach, Pitirim Sorokin and others have undertaken significant steps in the development of a sociological study of religious and ethical ideas. A sociological study of early Buddhist ethics would involve the discussion not only of the social origins of the ethical ideas, but also of the implications of those ideas for the social structure.

If Buddhist ethics stressed the development of moral rectitude and uprightness for the growth of meditative self-concentration and contemplative insight, still it had a social aspect in the sense that the Buddhist Bhikshu had to lead his austere life in the Samgha. He was not residing in complete isolation. Even if he could, for some time, live in a cave or some riverside retreat, he had to come in touch with people for his food and some other needs of his physical self. The Samgha was a type of a religious community and the deep affectual bonds of a primary group had their operation there. The *Theragāthā* refers to the ethics of brotherliness in the Samgha :

[1] *Dhammapada*, XIV, 193.

"Behold the company who learn of him—
In happy concord of fraternity...
The noblest homage this to Buddhas paid."

The Samgha provided an institutional basis to the ethical life of the Buddhist monks. It also generated an atmosphere of the direct and indirect suggestion of the primacy of moral values. The individual desire to lead a moral life thus received reinforcement and intensification becauee of the existence of a social fraternity. The individual monk was a cell in the organic confraternity of the Samgha. The teachers and saints who were advanced in the moral and meditative path (the *arhat*, the *anāgami* and the *sakṛdāgami*) were the loci of sympathetic radiation. They encouraged the initiates (the *srotapanna*) in the path of the redemption of the sins and sorrows of the world. The senior monks had attached to them the prestige and social status associated with age, wisdom and holy living. Thus it is possible to state that although the members of the Samgha had made a deliberate withdrawal from the great lay and agrarian society, the formation and organisational structure of the Samgha tended to give a social and collective appearance to the dominant ethical norms to adhere to which the members had taken a vow. Thus the Samgha tended to give even to moral and meditative life the impress and cast of an associational existence. It made possible a group life in quest of moral and virtuous activity and meditation.

The great religions of the world ascribe a superhuman origin to their ethical conceptions. The religious leader is regarded as only the medium through whom the divine being reveals the moral and sacred path. This tendency to ascribe a superhuman origin to their teachings and conceptions is an aspect of the dominant trend of world religions to obtain adherence and following by claiming a super-social source for their theology and ethics. There is no explicit recognition of any superior divine agency in Buddhism. Nevertheless, Buddhists believe that the great truths dawned on Buddha in a super-intellectual stage of deep absorption. Hence, Buddhism in spite of the non-acceptance of a theistic agency ascribes an intuitional if not a revelatory origin to its moral ideas.

But we find that several non-intuitional sources have contributed to the growth of the Buddhistic ethical ideas.

Early Buddhism believed that if one had developed the sentiment of universal all-comprehensive compassion (*maitrī*), then one could obtain the capacity to tame not only robbers and enemies but even wild animals. Buddha is able to subdue the furious elephant Nālāgiri by the force of compassion. The Jātaka tales depict the early lives of Buddha, prior to the attainment of final Buddhahood and they state that the Bodhisat used to live in perfect amity with even furious animals. This is another illustration of the operative force of compassion. From the sociological standpoint, it is a corroboration of the magical potency of ethical virtues. It is possible to see behind such beliefs the heritage of old pre-historic magical conceptions which ascribed power and potency to the chief and the sorcerer. The *Atharvaveda* is a great storehouse of such magical beliefs and elements. In Buddhist literature also we find innumerable instances referring to the acquisition of super-normal powers of Buddha consequent upon the dawn of enlightenment. Hence the primitive connexion between magic and ethics is, to some extent, retained in Buddhism. The magical potency which in olden times was supposed to adhere to the chief is now transformed to the *arhat* and the Buddha.

Besides revelation and magic, there is a third source for the growth of moral ideas and that is pragmatic consideration for social adjustment and welfare. Every individual has in him the egoistic propensity to self-preservation. But the equally operative tendency of egoistic self-preservation present in all individuals can lead to a regime of anarchy and chaos, if there are not rules of adjustment to settle conflicts. Hence in the processes of social accommodation, adaptation and adjustment, there is the evolution of socio-moral rules. The concept of *ahimsā* must have evolved as a remedy to solve individual tensions and struggles. In the later processes of intellectual refinement, these socio-moral rules of adjustment and management of conflicts and tensions are given an idealistic appearance. This idealistic colour is essential to instil in people a feeling of attachment for and obligation to obey the moral rules. The rigors of social penalization and external constraint are also employed to obtain conformity to these idealistically-coloured moral rules to the extent that adherence to them is regarded essential for social cohesion. *Asteya* or non-thieving is a great moral notion but since its maintenance is vitally essential for social preservation, hence the agency of constraint and institutionalized coercion is taken recourse to for its application. Thus it is possible to realize that the problems of social adjustment have also contributed to the evolution of moral ideas.

But it has to be borne in mind that this desire for social cohesion does not explain the total meaning and significance of ethics. The psychological growth of man also results in a chastening of his emotions. Thus we find the development of what Westermarck calls "moral emotions". According to him, moral disapproval is a way of expressing individual resentment against a specific way of action and moral approval is a form of retributive, sympathetic and altruistic emotion. The psychological growth of men leading to the emergence and flowering of moral emotions is not something mechanical. It is highly subjective. In the same society or even in the same family there may be persons of the most diverse temperaments. Early Buddhism accepts the concepts of *karma* and *samsāra.* These have psychological foundations. The ethical orientations of men and their capacity to progress in the path of moral endeavours are determined by their past emotional heritage. Even Buddha himself had to practise penances and austerities in several previous lives before he could attain the cognitive, volitional and emotional maturity and egoistic non-affectivity which Buddhahood typifies. The concept of *bhāvanā* or emotional apperception is lauded in early Buddhism as an ingredient for the attainment of truth. Thus we find that the emotional factor has also to be stressed in indicating the origin of moral ideas. In studying the evolution and development of Buddhist moral ideas, these four factors have to be stressed — intuition, magic, social adjustment and moral emotions.

As stated earlier, during the Vedic age ethical ideas were evolving. What was not *Ṛta* was *anṛta* and the Vedic seers prayed for being led to the path of *satya*, in place of the path of *anṛta.* There was great stress on moral virtues like *vrata* (vows), *dikhsā* (initiation into the moral way), faith (*śraddhā*) and *dāna* (beneficence). Gifts were to be imparted not only to the sacrificial priests but to all the needy and the *Ṛgveda* categorically states that one who eats alone is eating sins. Agni is also called the protector of vows— *vratapati.* The Vedic gods and goddesses like Savitā, Dyauh and Pṛithivi have also moral attributes applied to them. The fact that during the Vedic period there was an emphatic and explicit distinction between good and evil is clearly brought out in the opposed juxtaposition of *bhadra* (the noble and good) and *durita* (the evil or bad). The Vedas speak of the evils associated with the transgression of the divine law or the moral immanental law of *ṛta*. These evils are regarded as *vrijina*.[1] The God Varuṇa is regarded as the forgiver of sins and evil. There is an advanced notion of ethical evolution involved in the idea that Varuṇa knows the motives of men. The *Ṛgveda* also accepts the distinction between moral sin and sacrificial sin. The latter refers to a violation of the exact methodology of the sacrificial mechanism, while the former involves a reference to the violation of the laws of human conduct. The Vedas indicate the social aspects of morality in the condemnation of sorcery, seduction, adultery, witchcraft, and gambling. The concept of *dāna* (gifts) has a foremost place and in the *Ṛgveda* we find mention of gifts without involving any mediation of the gods : this forestalls the Buddhist ethic of beneficence.

The fundamental theme of the Upaniṣads is the all-pervasiveness and inclusive immanence of the supreme spirit. The cosmic self is identical with the psychic essence in its inmost being. The cosmic *brahman* is also transcendent. It has been said that since the human being can realize the identity with the absolute by cognitive contemplation and since the supreme being is beyond the application of the criteria of good and evil, hence the Upaniṣads teach a transcendent supermoralism. But the Upaniṣads stress the ethical path both as a preparatory discipline for the acquisition of supreme knowledge and as a natural consequence of spiritual gnosis. The *Muṇḍakopaniṣad* points out that supreme knowledge cannot be attained without rigorous conformity to the moral path. The *Kaṭhopaniṣad* also stresses the moral disciplines as a preparation for the attainment of the liberating knowledge. The *Brihadāraṇyaka Upaniṣad* also stresses beneficence and asceticism. The *Taittirīya Upaniṣad* gives us the categorical imperatives of the virtues essential for a householder. The *Chhāndogya* gives us the ethic of the

[1] The *Atharvaveda*, xi. 8, 19 and vi, 26, refers to *pāpman* or an impersonal evil.

Three D's (*Da*)— beneficence (*dāna*), self-restraint (*damana*) and kindness (*dayā*). It has sometimes been stated that the Upaniṣads inculcate the despotic imperialism of the man of knowledge in the ethical realm because they teach the irrelevance of ethical canons for the man who possesses liberating knowledge. Melamed says that since the Upaniṣads teach pantheistic immanence hence there is no place for the imperativeness of the ethical norms for the man who has obtained the final knowledge of the Spirit.[1] It is true that the Upaniṣads teach the identity of the *brahman* and the human soul but this type of realization leads to the growth of an attitude of moral identification with the entire order of living beings. The realised saint developes an attitude of equality and philosophic equanimity. Nevertheless, it is correct that the conception that the man of knowledge goes beyond the applicability of the criteria of sin and merit is at least formulated in a fashion which can have, sometimes, socially damaging implications. At times this ideal can be exploited by hypocrites. From the standpoint of social cohesion and organization what we need is the inculcation of the absolutism of moral virtues. It is certainly true that the Absolute Spirit is not touched by the criteria of morals evolved by human beings at a certain time and place. But no embodied human being can ever concretely attain complete identity with the supreme spirit. How much soever his spirit might be developed and enlightened, so long as the seer is physically alive he is faced with problems of social adjustment. Even when he is dead it is society that takes care of his dead body. Hence the complete immersion in the Absolute, even if possible on a purely mental and philosphical plane, can never be a concrete total actuality. Although in modern times Vivekananda, Rama Tirtha, Tilak and Aurobindo have tried to defend the Upaniṣadic metaphysics from the charge of ethical irrelevance, I consider that the Upaniṣadic ethical code is not happily phrased from the social standpoint. If it is imperative to preserve society and to better it, then for no human being, regardless of his saintly and spiritual acquisitions, the prescription of the canon of ethical irrelevance should be permitted. Wheresoever the saint comes

[1] Melamed, *Spinoza and Buddha*, p. 243.

in conflict with the accepted moral canons and criteria of correct and right citizenship, he should be adequately dealt with by the established institutions.

3. *The Sociology of Early Buddhist Ethics*

The ethics of Buddhism preaches a middle way between the extremes of sensuous appetitive hedonism and utter and absolute self-abnegation and asceticism. This *Madhyamā pratipadā* (middle way) is categorized as the eight-fold moral way— the *ārya āshtāṅgika mārga*. But although Buddhist ethics avoids the extreme concepts of chastisement and penalization of the body associated with the teachings of the Jains, the monkish ethics of Buddhism is definitely and pronouncedly ascetic and rigorous from any utilitarian and eudaemonistic standpoint. However, Buddha showed great courage of spirit in denouncing the grosser and harsher forms of asceticism. He claims that he had propounded a moral way that is noble, and oriented to the realization of the supreme enlightenment. There are eight great concepts in his moral way–- right opinions (*samyak dṛsti*), right aspirations or volition (*samyak samkalpa*), right speech (*samyak vāk*), right actions (*samyak karmānta*), right means of livelihood (*samyak ājiva*), right efforts (*samyak vyāyāma*), right mindfulness (*samyak smṛti*), and right contemplation (*samyak samādhi*).

Right opinions refer to the acceptance of correct metaphysical views. Although Buddhism is silent about transcendental metaphysics, nonetheless, it prescribes certain metaphysical schemes of the origination and extinction of suffering. The formula of *pratītya-samutpāda* (conditioned generation) is one such illustration. This stress on right opinions shows that, according to Buddha, ethical norms cannot have mere pragmatic foundations. They should be rooted in the apperception of some fundamental truths. The sanction of ethics in early Buddhism lies not in the existence of a mechanism of external social and political constraint but in the sovereign imperative of the perception of the pervasiveness of sorrow and pain in the world. If moral rules are regarded as rooted only in the cult of individual expediency, then it is possible that man may like to exploit the world to the maximum. The only bar to immoral action in that case is the fear of detection and punishment. But the criterion of morality, according to Buddhism, lies in the growth of an inner sense of the necessity of virtue in a world where all constituted creatures are equally governed by the inexorable law of sorrow and pain. Hence the community of suffering-fraught populace must traverse the moral way.[1]

Right aspirations are also essential. They are needed for the growth of renunciation, benevolence and kindness to all living beings. The stress on right aspirations and volitions indicates the inwardization of morality in Buddhism. The *Dhammapada* says :

> "All that we are is the result of what we have thought : it is founded on our thoughts, it is made up of our thoughts. If a man speaks or acts with an evil thought, pain follows him, as the wheel follows the foot of the ox that draws the carriage. If a man speaks or acts with a pure thought, happiness follows him, like a shadow that never leaves him."[2]

The emphasis on right aspirations is an important advance in the direction of ethical intuitionism. It is an attempt to found the roots of morality in the chastened conscience of man. As Socrates and Plato preached against the external conventionalism of Cephalus and Polemarchus and the operational pragmatism of Glaucon, so also in place of the traditional ritualism of the *Brāhmaṇas* and the formal asceticism of the wandering teachers, Buddha heralded the application of inner reason and volition to moral life. He taught the ennoblement and purification of human intentions. This concept of right aspirations has great social implications also. Modern psychologists are trying to examine the emotional foundations of tribal, social and national conflicts and they also advocate some kind of psychological integration and remaking of man. If our aspirations are right, not only can social tensions and international conflicts be resolved but we can build a better and happier world. It is true that in the framework of Buddhist ethics, right aspiration was oriented to the cultivation of those sentiments which could lead to the realization of the state of *nirvāṇa*, still socially beneficial sentiments are not excluded from

[1] Cf. *Dhammapada* I, 7, "The world does not know that we must all come to an end here ; —but those who know it, their quarrels cease at once."

[2] *Dhammapada*, I, 1 and 2.

its purview. "It is longing for aspiration, the hope to live in love with all ; the aspiration of true humanity."

Right speech is cultivated by abstaining from lying, calumination, abuse and fruitless conversation. An aspirant must abstain from back-biting and from harsh language. A good deal of social conflict is generated by the absence of restraint over the use of language. The avoidance of harsh language leads not only to the growth of inner peace but it is also a solid virtue which imparts social esteem and prestige. The great success of Buddha, Christ and Gandhi was, in part, a consequence of their modest and pacifying language. We have to beware of confusing strength of character with offensive speech.

Buddha lays great emphasis on right deeds. Right actions lead to the formation of virtuous character. Buddha repudiates the concept of a substantial soul monad but he was committed to the conception of the causal operativeness of the acts performed. "To say one (person) acts, another reaps the fruits of those acts is not true. And to say : one and the same both acts and is affected by the result is not true." But although there is no concept of the soul as an unchanging spiritual being, nevertheless, we find in Buddhism the concept of the continuity of character and personality. According to Buddhism, it is essential to perform right deeds because they lead to the formation of the right type of character. Right actions involve abstention from destruction of life. It is essential not to grasp and take what is not given to one and the concept of purity is also extremely essential. "He who destroys life, who speaks untruth, who in this world takes what is not given him...even in this world digs up his own root."[1] In Buddhism we find the distinction between good actions and bad actions. Good actions are characterized by the absence of covetousness, jealousy and delusion (*alobha, advesha* and *amoha*). Hence only he can perform right actions who has conquered the lower passions and is free from the desires and illusions of the ego. Egoism is the cardinal evil because it generates false attachments and perversities. Good actions have two consequences. They eventually lead to the realization of the supreme goal of final extinction of all pain, evil and

1 *Dhammapada*, 246 and 247.

sorrow. This is their individual aspect. They also lead to the welfare and good of other human beings. This is their social aspect. It is true that in early Buddhism the physiological and psychological aspects of actions have been emphasized because it is a religion of redemption but the social aspects of action are not altogether neglected. If good works are performed, then social adaptation and harmonious functional adjustments are bound to result. But the concrete performance of good works is a very difficult enterprise because it is the resultant of diverse factors. Modern science stresses the concept of heredity which has a significant role to play in the development of character and personality which are the efficient causes of good actions but according to the Buddhist theory the parents and the family through whom and in which a person is born are also determined by his own actions. A second significant force for the concrete eventuation of good works is the compulsive mechanism and demand of the physiological and psychological structure of man. There are some actions whose performance is impelled by this physiological and psychological structure. This structure is built up by the accummulated heritage and impressions of the actions of past lives. It leads to the generation of Samskāras which constitute the uniqueness of individual hnman nature. There are also some social factors which are operative. Education is such a factor. There may be certain ideals which are significant in some societies. They also exercise a moulding influence. The specific environmental situation wherein certain actions are to be performed is also an important factor to be reckoned with. The interaction between the psycho-physical organism of the individual participants in the action-arena and the social ideals takes place in a definite situational field. Thus it is clear that in a sociological study of the concept of right actions we cannot be content with only a psychological analysis of the individual personality. The situational field and the dominant social ideals can not be denied their role. It is very true that the supreme quest for a Buddhist was the attainment of the way of emancipation. But this perfectionist quest, in order to become interiorized in the human psyche and to be operative as a force of purposive propulsion towards the acceptance of the Buddhist way, had to become socially expressed. Ideas do not have a ghost-like existence in space and time. Before ideas can become operative forces they want some form of social habitation in the minds of men. Hence, in a sociological study of the concept of action this social side constituted by the adherence to some ideals and the physical and social environmental field of operation should be taken into consideration.

The concept of right livelihood has pronouncedly a social orientation. "Life is easy to live for a man who is without shame, a crow hero, a mischief-maker, an insulting, bold and wretched fellow. But life is hard to live for a modest man, who always looks for what is pure, who is disinterested, quiet, spotless, and intelligent."[1] The concept of right livelihood excludes many kinds of mean and vulgar activities. It can have diverse social implications. Aristotle condemned large-scale trade, monopolies and the use of money as capital. He called them to be unnatural "chrematistic" activities as distinguished from natural finance which is to foster moral living. The Buddhist concept of right livelihood will also imply a condemnation of these acquisitive economic operations. If we were to stress the economic implications of this concept, it will help us in substituting the profit motivation of modern bourgeois industrial economy by the motivation of service. The economic ethics of Buddhism is opposed to the individualistic notions of the self-interest of man and the maximization of returns as morally valid criteria of economic action. It refuses to consider the realm of business as a separate compartment of, life which has its own professional ethics, different from the ethics of the other departments. According to Buddhism, life is one integral whole and ethical norms seeking to control deviance and evil have universal sway. The Buddhist ethical way conceives of right living as a preparation for right concentration and meditation and hence, according to Buddhism, economic activities have only an instrumental reality. They are, at best, means. Economics does not assume for itself the structure of a preponderant substantive reality in Buddhist ethical philosophy. Economic action, according to Buddhism, is a means and it has to be moralized in order that it may not impede the attainment of *nirvāṇa*. The idea of the

1 *Dhammapada*, XVIII, 244-245 Max Müller's translation.

moralization of economic activities is brought out in this statement of the *Sutta Nipāta* : "Those who in this world are wicked, and such as do not pay their debts, are slanderers, false in their dealings, counterfeiters, those who in this world being the lowest of men commit sin."[1] Although, according to the scheme of the eight-fold way, the concept of *samyak ājiva* is a norm for the ascetic seeking the goal of emancipation, still it is possible to extend the sphere of its operation.[2] Thus this ideal depicted in the *Sutta Nipāta* : "Waiting on mother and father, protecting child and wife, and a quiet calling, this is the highest blessing. Giving alms, living religiously, protecting relatives, blameless deeds, this is the highest blessing"[3]— would be in consonance with the concept of right living.

Right efforts imply a systematic psychological training. They imply the suppression of the rising of evil states and the eradication of those evil states which have already arisen. They also include the stimulation of good states and the perfection of those which have come into being. *Samyak vyāyāma*, thus we see, is definitely a psychological and moral scheme of training and it has no affinity with the Platonic and Aristotelian notions regarding gymnastics.

Right mindfulness indicates the constant mental presence of the dominant goals of existence. It is opposed to any inertia and lethargy with regard to the supreme quest of Nirvāṇa. It implies a conquest of all kinds of false cravings and hankerings. It stresses a strenuous desire to overcome dejection. The aspirant has to train his body and mind in such a way that he will be ardent, self-possessed and mindful. "The disciples of Gotama are always well awake and their thoughts day and night are always set on Buddha, on the law, on the Samgha,

[1] *Sutta Nipāta*, *Āmagandhasutta*, 245.

[2] *Tevijja Sutta*, *Dīgha Nikāya*, E.T. by Rhys Davids in *Buddhist Sutta's*, *SBE*, Vol. XI, p. 191 :

"He abstains from the getting of silver or gold... He abstains from the getting of bondmen or bondwomen... He refrains from buying and selling. He abstains from tricks with false weights, alloyed metals, or false measures. He abstains from bribery, cheating, fraud and crooked ways. He refrains from maiming, killing, imprisoning, highway robbery, plundering villages, or obtaining money by threats of violence." These are the principles for the guidance of the conduct of a Buddhist.

[3] *Sutta Nipāta*, 261-262.

on their body (*kāyagatā sati*), in compassion and in meditation (*bhāvanā*)."[1] The operations of death are inexorable and hence it is essential that immediate efforts should be made to attain the supreme knowledge. "Death carries off a man who is gathering flowers and whose mind is distracted, as a flood carries off a sleeping village."[2] "Well-makers lead the water (wherever they like) ; fletchers bend the arrow ; carpenters bend a log of wood ; wise people fashion themselves."[3] It is essential to cultivate the path of earnestness leading to immortality, because thoughtlessness is the path of death. The Buddhist concept of *apramāda* has heen differently interpreted. Fausboll translates it by '*vigilantia*', Childers by 'diligence', and Max Müller by earnestness. It is an essential supplement to the concept of right mindfulness.

Right contemplation is the culmination of the ethical process. Morality, according to Buddhism, receives its consummation in the attainment of the serene concentration of the mind. *Samyak samādhi* stresses inward cognition and reflective abstraction. *Samādhi* is a state of mind consequent upon deep meditation and absorption. According to the Buddhist scheme there are four meditations which lead to the attainment of perfect concentration. The first *dhyāna* results in the attainment of gladness and joy. The second *dhyāna* leads to the attainment of elation and inner peace and silence. By the third *dhyāna*, a person is able to neutralize all his passions and false presuppositions and assumptions. The fourth and the final *dhyāna* results in the attainment of perfect tranquillity and self-realization. Hence the *Dhammapada* says :

> "The Bhikshu who acts with kindness, who is calm in the doctrine of Buddha, will reach the quiet place (*nirvāṇa*), cessation of natural desires and happiness. O Bhikshu, empty this boat ! if emptied, it will go quickly ; having cut off passion and hatred, thou wilt go to Nirvaṇa... Meditate, O Bhikshu, and be not heedless ! Do not direct thy thought to what gives pleasure, that thou mayest not for thy heedlessness have to swallow the iron ball (in hell), and thou mayest not cry out when burning, 'This is pain'. Without knowledge there is no meditation, without

[1] *Dhammapada*, 296-301.
[2] *Ibid.*, 47-48.
[3] *Ibid*, 80.

meditation there is no knowledge : he who has knowledge and meditation is near into *nirvāṇa*."[1]

Samādhi as obtained by the four types of meditations is a state of deep absorption. It is the attainment of knowledge by identity with the great principles of truth. It goes beyond the conceptual cognition of thought. In a sense, it transcends the Kantian conception of the free will willing the free will, because it is a process of unitive absorption in which both cognition and volition attain their maturest perfection. It is true that this perfection of concentration is highly personal and subjective in character. But even this self-contemplation has also a sociological side. The processes and technics of contemplation result in the development of an integrated, steady and self-possessed personality. The early Buddhist writings always refer to the delight and radiance that are spread over the face of a true disciple of Buddha. This kind of integrated personality is in itself a social gain. Modern social psychologists have made us aware of the dangerous explosions and conflicts which are the consequences of the frustrations and psychoses of individuals. The schizophreniac or the divided personality is a great social problem. Hence if some person is able to attain a sense of delight, calm and happiness he not only realizes a great personal goal but is also rendering a great social service. His personality emits sparks of happiness and peace. Hence it is clear that the existence of such a personality has a great social value. "Whatever place a faithful, virtuous, celebrated ... man chooses, there he is respected. Good people shine from afar, like the snow of mountains ; bad people are not seen, like arrows shot by night."[2] By stressing the notions of morality and contemplative concentration, early Buddhism preached a deepening of the sense of morality. It provides an ethical teaching which inculcates profund purity and holiness.

The Aryan eight-fold way is a signal contribution to the evolution of moral ideas. It removes the subject of ethics from the domain of supernaturalism and transcendentalism. It preaches a moral way in which the individual is required to confirm to the path of ethics not out of the fear of an external agency.

1 *Dhammapada*, 368-372.
2 *Dhammapada*, "Miscellaneous," 15.

Morality has an inner source and impulsion and its efficacy lies in the purification of intentions. The Buddhist "way" is a comprehensive code and it preaches a path which leads to the integration of personality and the attainment of calm, peace and silence. But although not supernaturalistic in its foundations, there is an element of the *a priori* in Buddhist ethics. *Samādhi* and *nirvāṇa* are super-intellectual categories and we cannot obtain a rational analysis of them. They do involve at least an initial faith in their certainty before the aspirant can take up the path.

But although there is an element of the *a priori* in Buddhist ethics because it is oriented to the path of individual perfection and the attainment of *nirvāṇa*, the eight-fold ethical way is calculated to promote the ongoing of the social process and structure. The adherence to the concepts of right speech, right actions and right means of livelihood introduces better community relations not only in the Buddhist Samgha but in the greater society with which the Bhikshus come in contact. The modern school of ethical sociology believes in the betterment of society and the maximization of satisfactions by the rational realization of human interests. But Buddhist ethics advocates the realization of social peace and communal fraternity by recourse to self-abnegation. There is no Fichtetan conception of the perfection of society or of social justice in early Buddhism but the concept of right means of livelihood, if practised on a collective scale, can provide the basic value for solving the social and economic problems of an underdeveloped and poor country. In several countries we have seen the rapacities and plundering activities of industrialists who have brought havoc on society by mercilessly tampering with the social and natural resources. Hence modern economists are advocating the concept of conservation. If an extended social application is made of the Buddhist notions of right action and right means of livelihood, we shall get that incorporation of the moral element in economic activity which is the dream of sociological economists like Tawney.

Sometimes it has been said that the Buddhist eight-fold path is purely introspective and contemplative and is not adequately dynamic. It is true that the eight-fold path is regarded as significant because it culminates in the attainment of contemplation. But we should emphasise its dynamic character to the extent that it preaches the cultivation of will, striving, patient courage and an earnest and immediate application to the moral path. It should not be forgotten that the action-orientation of ethics is implicit in the very name *mārga*. Buddhist ethics is not a matter of formal intellectual acceptance but it emphasizes the leading of a moral life. Man can be saved not by blind belief and passive faith but by the dynamic adherence to the path of ethics.

Besides the Aryan eight-fold path, the early Buddhist scriptures refer to another ethical categorization—the four *brahma vihāra*. *Maitrī*, *karuṇā*, *muditā* and *upekshā* constitute the four *brahma vihāra*.[1] They are also referred to in the *Yoga-Sutras* of Patanjali and are possibly derived both by Buddhism and Patanjali from a common source. *Maitrī* or *mettā* is one of the most important concepts of Buddhist ethics. It comprehends both non-hatred and loving kindness. Hatred does not cease by hatred, only non-hatred can overcome hatred. This, according to Buddha, is the eternal law. "Victory breeds hatred, for the conquered is unhappy. He who has given up both victory and defeat, he, the contented, is happy." Buddha exhorts his disciples to live happily, not hating those who hate them. But the absence of hatred, arrogance and resentment is only one side of the picture. The wanderer who wants to attain final emancipation must practise non-violence. Hence the *Udāna* says:

> "The whole wide world we traverse with our thought
> Nor come on aught more dear to each than self.
> Since aye so dear the self to other men,
> Let the self-lover harm no other man."

Buddha affirms that he who strikes or insults others is not an anchorite. According to the *Dhammapada* one who inflicts pain on innocent and harmless persons meets with one of these ten states: "He will have cruel suffering, loss, injury of the body, heavy affliction or loss of mind, or a misfortune coming from the king, or a fearful accusation, or loss of relations, or destruction of treasures, or lightening—fire will burn his houses,

[1] These four terms are referred to in the *Bojjhaṅgasamyuttam* of the *Samyutta Nikāya* (Nalanda Ed., IV, pp. 115-16).

and when his body is destroyed, the fool will go to hell."[1] The social implications of non-hatred and non-resistance are obvious. The tremendous sociological orientation of Buddhist ethics and perhaps of the whole of Hindu ethics is clearly brought out by the immense moral and spiritual significance attaching to the concept of *ahimsā*.[2] *Ahimsā* is the signal way to attain fraternity and even identity with the entire realm of created beings. But Buddhism is not content only with the negative way of formulation by emphasising non-violence. It also preached the positive fullness of kindness. In profoundly moving utterances the *Sutta Nipāta* declares :

> "Even as a mother watcheth o'er her child
> Her only child, as long as life doth last,
> So let us, for all creatures, great or small,
> Develop such a boundless heart and mind.
> Ay, let us practise love for all the world,
> Upward and downward, yonder, hence,
> Uncramped from ill will and enmity."[3]

The Buddhist believer is expected to be extremely solicitous for the well-being and happiness of all creatures. "Whatever living beings there are, either feeble or strong, all, either long or great, middle-sized, short, small or large, either seen or which are not seen, and which live far or near, either born or seeking birth, may all creatures be happy-minded." The Buddhist stress on kindness and love seeks to emphasize a notion which is essential both for social well-being and for *nirvāṇa*. The *Itivuttaka* says : "All the means that can be used as bases for doing right are not worth one-sixteenth part of the emancipation of the heart through love. That takes all those up into itself, outshining them in radiance and in glory." This stress on the universality of compassion by Buddhism had great social consequences and it provided an exalted norm for action.

In early Buddhist literature, the cultivation of kindness and love is sometimes associated with the acquisition of magical

1 *Dhammapada*, X, 137-140.

2 A.B. Keith, *The Religion and Philosophy of the Veda and the Upaniṣads*, II, p. 476 : "The doctrine of Ahimsā is one which has never even in India received full sanction."

3 *Sutta Nipāta*, "*Mettasutta*", 148-149.

powers. Even dumb animals and furious beasts are caught by the dynamic spark of *maitrī* and become absolutely tame and follow the saint. Thus the superior efficacy of love is clear. From the sociological standpoint *maitrī* is the concept of social accommodation and adjustment because it profoundly transforms the character of the wicked and the violent. In the Jātakas we find numerous stories which indicate the transmutation of the concept of *maitrī* into the dynamic principle of self-sacrifice for others. The Jātakas constantly reiterate the theme of self-sacrifice for the good of other beings. In the older ethical systems of the Vedas and the Upaniṣads and the law codes, kindness and sympathy were stressed but Buddhism excels Brahmanism in the immense emphasis it put on "loving kindness, wide, ample, expanding, free from enmity and ill-will." From the sociological viewpoint *ahimsā* and *maitrī* are principles of rational harmony and universal love. *Maitrī* is a creative force of social development and it can safely act as a deterrant and counterpoise to the dissimilar and disharmonious forces of social tensions, contradictions and struggles. *Ahimsā* and *maitrī* not only lead to the growth of internal harmony but they also result in the growth of spontaneous sympathy and a sense of dynamic identification with all living beings in their sorrow and suffering. Thus the cultivation of *ahimsā* and *maitrī* can generate also a sense of inner fraternity. This kind of brotherliness is needed in the growingly impersonal civilizations of the modern industrial world.

Several Western critics have tried to distinguish the non-hatred and friendly sentiments inculcated in Buddhism from the stress on love in Christianity. According to Oldenberg, Buddhism emphasizes not the emotion of a world-embracing love but the peaceful feeling of friendly harmony. In the reiterated emphasis on the cultivation of universal *maitrī*, Oldenberg finds "not the groundless enigmatic self-surrender of love, but rather intelligent reflection, the conviction that it is thus best for all and not least, the expectation that the natural law of retribution will allot to such conduct the richest reward."[1] Schweitzer also has drawn a distinction between the Buddhist negativism of *ahimsā* and the active love of

[1] Oldenberg, *Buddha*, p. 292.

Christianity, From the standpoint of social psychology it is essential to distinguish between non-hatred and friendliness on the one side and positive love on the other. But two reservations have to be made. First, from the standpoint of social relations, the difference does not appear very substantial because even in the *Sutta Nipāta*, *maitrī* has been illustrated by the boundless love of the mother for the child. Secondly, in the Jātakas we find numerous stories of the overflowing love of Buddha for all living creatures. Nevertheless, it seems correct to maintain that the supreme goal of the Buddhist is the realization of philosophic detachment and indifference, while Christianity has stressed love for all human beings because all are children of the same providential Father. In the early Buddhist literature, the reconciling and harmonizing power of *maitrī* has been illustrated by the story of the son who forgave the assassin of his father even when the former had the ready weapon in his hand to finish the wicked assassin.[1] This story is a supreme illustration of the transforming power of *maitrī* when it is sincerely accepted as a norm of action. But Keith is guilty of unnecessarily reading the Aristotelian concept of prudence (*phronesis*) in this greatly edifying tale. He says : "The element of calculating prudence is ever present."[2] Prudence is a cardinal concept in Aristotle's *Nicomachean Ethics* but it has no worthy place in Buddhist morality.

Besides *maitrī*, the theory of the four *Brāhma Viharas* also stresses *karuṇā*. *Karuṇā* signifies a feeling of universal sympathetic identity with all living creatures. The Indian mind has always regarded Buddha as an embodiment of kind sympathy. *Muditā* or cheerfulness is also a moral category. Loving kindness, universal compassion and cheerfulness have great social functions and roles. They are oriented to the realization of a sense of fraternal identity which goes beyond the Greek concept of intelligent co-operative interdependence in a community (*koinonia*). The life of Buddha typifies for all time the radical eradication of all socially disorganizing sentiments. The concepts of *maitrī* and *Karuṇā* can alone strengthen the foundations of any political and social group. The concept of self-

[1] *Mahāvagga*, X, 2.

[2] A.B. Keith, ***Buddhist Philosophy in India and Ceylon*** (Oxford, 1923), p. 117.

interest alone is inadequate. *Maitrī* and *karuṇā* are the foundations of universalistic solidarity They replace the notions of reciprocity by the idea of universal compassion. The fourth category in the *Brahma Vihāras*, *Upekshā* is more individualistic in its orientation. It stresses the development of utter non-attachment to the ills, pains, pleasures and tragedies of the world. *Upekshā* is the characteristic of the man of vision, who refuses to be enchanted by the allurements of the evanescent world. The *Sutta Nipāta* thus defines a calm Muni : "Without desire for pleasant things and not given to conceit, and being gentle, intelligent, not credulous, he is not displeased with anything. Not from love of gain does he learn, and he does not get angry on account of loss, and untroubled by desire he has no greed for sweet things. Equable (*upekha*), always thoughtful he does not think himself equal to others in the world, nor distinguished, nor low ; for him there are no desires (*Ussada*)". Thus the attribute of the monk is the cultivation of supreme indifference. It is clear that this indifference can be acquired only by prolonged concentration and mental austerities. The stress on indifference shows the ascetic other worldly orientation of Buddhist ethics.

In early Buddhism there were three concepts which comprehended the ethical quest and the philosophic achievement. *Śīla, samādhi* and *prajñā* are famous categories in the Buddhist literature. *Śīla* is a comprehensive code of moral life. *Samādhi* is of deep mental training culminating in contemplation. Morality and contemplation result in the attainment of deep wisdom. These three concepts are integrally inter-connected : "As hand washes hand and foot washes foot, so uprightness is purified by wisdom, and wisdom is purified by uprightness. Where there is uprightness, there is wisdom : where there is wisdom, there is uprightness. And the wisdom of the upright and the uprightness of the wise, have of all uprightness and wisdom in the world the highest value." Concentration is the intermediate category in the transition of ethical purification into the attainment of profound philosophical vision and wisdom. "Pervaded by uprightness, self-concentration is fruitful and rich in blessing ; pervaded by wisdom the soul becomes wholly freed from all infirmity, from the infirmity of desire, from the infirmity of becoming, from the infirmity of error, from the infirmity of ignorance." Sometimes two other categories, *vimutti* (emancipation) and *vimutti-jñāna-darśana* (insight into the knowledge of emancipation) are also added to the triology of *śila*, *samādhi* and *prajñā*.

There are five elements in *śila* — non-violence, non-thieving, non-adultery, not to indulge in falsehood and non-drinking. The prohibition of violence is socially very significant. "A monk abstains from killing living creatures ; he refrains from causing the death of living creatures. He lays down the stick ; he lays down weapons. He is compassionate and tender-hearted, he seeks with friendly spirit the welfare, of all living beings." There are additional restrictions on the monk who joins the confraternity of brethren. There are three conditions for the attainment of truth—*śraddhā* or faith, *darśana* or philosophic insight and *bhāvanā* or cultivation and meditation. The practice of truth has a great part to play in the moralisation and harmonisation of social relations. "What he has heard here he does not repeat there, to separate that man from this ; what he has heard here he does not repeat there, to separate this man from that. He is the uniter of the separated, and the confirmer of the united. He enjoys concord ; he seeks to promote concord ; he takes delight in concord ; he is a speaker of concord-producing words."

In the Buddhist literature we find repeated references to numerous moral categories[1] and although we do not find a systematic philosophy of ethics, certainly these categories have great social implications. Sometimes the ideal virtues are categorized as ten in number — charity, purification of conduct, patience, earnest endeavours, contemplation, intelligence, use of right means, resoluteness, strength and knowledge. We also find references to fear of committing sins (*Ottapa*), to *purity of conscience* (*anavajja*) and to sympathy (*samgaha*). Buddhism lays great stress on gifts. This positive social ethic of *dāna* is immensely lauded in early Buddhism. A gift bestowed on those who are passionless, who do not hate, who are free from vanity and lust brings great reward. But in the interest of the right allocation of the economic resources of the society it is essential

[1] CAF Rhys David's article on "Amity" in the ***K.B. Pathak Commemoration Volume, op. cit.***

that the virtue of gift should be wisely exercised "Better it would be to swallow a heated iron ball, like flaring fire, than that a bad unrestrained fellow should live on the charity of the land." Self-control in all its aspects has profound social implications also. Early Buddhism emphasizes sympathy (*samgaha*). It includes charity and gifts, gentle and unassuming conversation, kind acts and a dynamic sense of all-identification with the totality of living creatures. According to Buddhism the moral way of living, culminating in philosophic wisdom, is higher than the attainment of heaven or the establishment of imperialism over the earth and all the worlds. Hence it is evident that in the Buddhist scheme of values, the economic, social and political spheres are rated inferior to the moral and spiritual spheres.

Early Buddhism takes special delight in the detailed categorization of the sins and evils from which a person has to guard himself. Murder, stealing and sexual impurity are the three sins of the body. Lying, slander, abuse and fruitless talks are the four sins of speech. Acquisitiveness, hatred and error are the three sins of the mind. These ten transgressions, if refrained from, are bound to have an ennobling effect on the pattern of social adjustment. Early Buddhism also condemns sensuality, the desire for rebirth, ignorance and metaphysical dialectics removed from the ethical way. There are five hindrances to ethical perfection : appetitive sensuality (*kāmachanda*), evil desires (*vyāpāda*), sluggish activity and lethargic dullness (*thinamiddha*), nervous excitement (*uddhachha*) and scepticism (*vichikitsā*). Sometimes we get references to the seven fetters or impediments to moral realization : lustful indulgence (*anumaya*), abhorrence (*paṭigha*), unfounded philosophical beliefs (*drishti*), scepticism (*vichikitsā*), vanity (*māna*), attachment to the prolongation of physical existence (*bhava-rāga*) and ignorance (*avidyā*). At other places we find mention of the roots of evils (*akuśala mulāni*) : lying, delusion, hatred, attachment and lust. It is true that the orientation of these moral categories is towards individual perfection. But it is fundamentally incorrect to conceive of individual perfection as totally removed from the mechanics and dynamics of the social structure. The moral and spiritual purification of the individual does powerfully affect the feelings and sentiments of other human beings. There are numerous tales in Buddhist literature to illustrate the deep and profound transformation wrought in the lives of those who were once socially destructive like thieves, robbers and criminals.

4. *Critical Reflections and Conclusion*

Buddhist ethics is more comprehensive than the traditional Brahmanical identification of ethics with duties relevant to professional calling. It goes beyond the conception of ethics as caste duties. Hence the content of virtuous conduct so long confined to caste obligations and sacrificial performances is definitely extended. The *Dhammapada* provides a summary of Buddhist ethics in these terms : "Not to blame, not to strike, to live restrained under the law, to be moderate in eating, to sleep and sit alone, and to dwell on the highest thoughts, — this is the teaching of the Awakened."[1] In Buddhism, morality does not consist only in the performance of external action but it is imperatively laid down that intentions should be purified. Even when Buddhism accepts the traditional and conventional elements in ethics it teaches the incorporation of a moral element in them. Thus the abstractness and externality of action is suffused with the concreteness of pure sentiments.

Buddhist ethics is not founded upon the command of a divinely inspired primordial law-giver. Hence the sanction behind the moral imperatives of Buddhism is not the authentic revelation of the divine will by an angelic prophet. Buddha is a great teacher but he is not expressing the divine will. Hence the Buddhist ethical code is not rooted in the pre-existent conceptual pattern of the divine mind. According to early Buddhism the actions performed by an individual have a causal efficacy and the consequences of the acts performed are brought forth almost by an automatic inexorable vehemence. So long as evil actions do not begin to bring havoc upon the doer he relishes them. So also, so long as meritorious deeds do not begin to shed glory the doer is not inclined to their performance. Early Buddhism teaches the almost cosmic operation of the law of *karma*. There is no conception of a Leibnizean theodicy and pre-established harmony. Buddha stresses the cosmic operativeness of the law of karma and this provides the

[1] *Dhammapada*, 185.

categorical imperative of the ethical path. The belief in this law amounts to the visualization of social reform and innovation not on an institutional pattern and organised planning but by effecting a transformation in human character. The central theme is to purify human motivation.

There is a definite strain of individualism in Buddhist ethics. The final goal of an individual human being is the attainment of emancipation. The realization of *nirvāṇa* which is the complete extinction of all pain and misery is the ultimate destiny of man. *Nirvāṇa* can be attained by all individuals, provided the right type of means are employed. Even Buddha himself had to make tremendous efforts involving prolonged therapeutics of will and intelligence for its attainment. There is no concept of predestination in Buddhist ethics. *Nirvāṇa* is not the monopoly of a selected or a chosen group It is capable of being universally realized. To this extent, Buddhism reacts against the aristocratic element involved in the theodicy of predestination. The *Kaṭhopaniṣad* states that the Atman can be realized only by him whom it chooses. But Buddhism teaches individual responsibility for the attainment of salvation. Although Buddha is the supreme teacher and leader and the revealer of the norm and although surrender to him is one of the cardinal tenets of Buddhism, still Buddha emphasizes one's own efforts for spiritual realization. He wants the disciples to be a light unto themselves and to rely on themselves. "Self is the lord of self, who else could be the lord ? With self well-subdued, a man finds a lord such as few could find. The evil done by oneself, self-begotten, self-bred crushes the foolish as a diamond breaks a precious stone. By oneself the evil is done, by oneself one suffers : by oneself evil is left undone, by oneself one is purified. Purity and impurity belong to oneself, no one can purify another."[1] This type of vigorous stress on individual efforts generates a profound sense of optimism. Buddhism explains the sinful and irrational structure of the world in terms of the deeds committed by individuals. Thus it teaches the individuals not to supplicate some external agency but it stresses to the utmost degree self-efforts. Thus it prepares the foundations of an ethic of healthy

[1] *Dhammapada*, 160 and 165.

and robust individualism. The idea that the individual can make or mar his destiny is one of the greatest contributions of Buddhism to social ethics. It is a great challenge to all pretentions to automatic and aristocratic monopoly of the final wisdom.

According to Buddhism the moral fact has two dimensions. The morality of action leads to the attainment of heaven. Early Buddhism derived from traditional Brahmanism the belief in heaven and hell. The doer of evil actions suffers twice. He suffers in this world and also in the next. The Jātakas refer to eight great hells and sixteen minor hells. Sometimes this figure of hells is raised up to one hundred and more. The *Dhammapada* would condemn the liar to hell. "The virtuous man delights in this world, and he delights in the next ; he delights in both. He delights and rejoices, when he sees the purity of his own work."[1] Thus one incentive to moral action is the attainment of heaven. Sometimes a better status in a future rebirth is regarded as the fruit of good deeds performed on earth. But the final goal of the moral fact including both actions and intentions is the attainment of *nirvāṇa.* When once this final goal is realized, "Even thus, Bhikkhus, understand that ye must put away moral rules, let alone immoral rules." This conception of the moral way as a "raft" would run counter seriously to the immense significance attributed to the ethical code in Buddhism. However, the general and overwhelming trend of Buddhism is to emphasize the supremacy of the moral norm even when they teach the ultimateness of *nirvāṇa* and *prajñā.*

Buddhism teaches the vast significance of *samādhi* and *nirvāṇa. Samādhi* is a state of deep and intense concentration. When it is engaged in, not at intermittent intervals but as a matter of frequent duration, then it involves the element of adjustment to a super-normal world. This means that the more the transcendent aspects of ethics and metaphysics are emphasized, the more the elements of withdrawal and ascetic rejection of the world would become pronounced. There is no question of identification with the norms accepted in the society. Thus the final ethic of Buddhism is oriented to the ascetic realization of other-worldly goals.

1 *Dhammapada,* 16.

Although the lay ethics of Buddhism are based on accommodation and compromise with the world and although common ideas, common interests and customs and mutual sympathy are stressed for the common people, the final and dominant note is withdrawal from the duties, sanctions and obligations of the social life. Thus we find a vast difference between Buddhist ethics and Greek ethics. Although Plato sings of the "Idea of the Good", and although Aristotle refers to the contemplation of the pure activity of God, both of them teach the concept of reform of the *polis*. But the final quest of Buddha is for *nirvāṇa* and all elements of lay adjustment with and adaptation to the community are of secondary significance. "How is there laughter, how is there joy, as this world is always burning ? Why do you not seek a light, ye who are surrounded by darkness ? This body is wasted, full of sickness, and frail ; this heap of corruption breaks to pieces, life indeed ends in death."[1] Hence the supreme vocation is renunciation of the dark state of the householder's life and to make efforts for that realization which led to the extinction of all sorrows and whence there is no return again to this tragedy-stricken world.

Buddhism stresses resolute endurance, forbearance, beneficence, benevolence and sympathy. It is true that all ethical preparations are oriented to the attainment of enlightenment but this does not really amount to the total devaluation of the mundane values and temporal interests of the lay people. There is no condemnation of the norms and technics and processes associated "with the adjustments of family and social lives. Buddha did not preach social chaos and disorganization. Nevertheless, it is true that in his scheme of values the life of the ascetic who had renounced the home life was rated vastly superior to the life of the householder. Hence the life of the householder, highly praised in the traditional Brahmanical code of social ethics, is now regarded with an eye of critical suspicion. Early Buddhism marks the tendency to accentuate the monastic trends that were visible towards the end of the Upaniṣadic age. By exalting the life of the ascetic in quest of emancipation, Buddhism tends to build up a separate sphere of spiritual ethics removed from the profane cult of those who

[1] *Dhammapada*, 146 and 147.

were still immersed in the pleasures of the world. This premium on asceticism and the supremacy of the moral virtues associated with the life of the Bhikshu creates a sense of psychological tension for the average believer. On one side there is the deep-seated desire of man to found a family and lead a comfortable existence. On the other side there is the teaching of Buddhist ethics which preaches the evanescence of temporal goods and mundane values.[1] The constant emphasis on the inexorability of death leads at times to a sense of nihilistic despair and utter illusoriness in the minds of men. The natural quest for self-preservation is subjected to a series of devastating onslaughts by the hymns in praise of the conquest of egoism. Hence the final conclusion of Buddhist ethics, in spite of the occasional discussions of lay morality, is the quest of a system of soteriology and emancipation. The stress is not on social adjustment and the realization of rational common good as in Greek ethics but on the development and cultivation of an attitude of philosophic quiet and indifference.

The dominant stress on an other-worldly orientation in quest of the extinction of pain and sorrow led to the neglect of the conception of social rationality as the criterion of the good life. All action impelled by the calculation of self-interest is suspected in Buddhism. Desire, in anticipation of any experience of pleasurable feeling, is regarded as the root of evil and hence individual economic activity in quest of the maximization of individual profit can never find any theoretical foundation in the economic ethics of Buddhism. It is true that most of the psychological and moral attributes which are highly praised in early Buddhism do have direct and indirect social implications but the absence of the conception of the primacy of social good and its rational realization lead to the absence of any theory of social and economic justice. In early Buddhism individual hardships and privations are explained in terms of individual action and there is no attempt at the institutional and sociological analysis of the foundations of

[1] Max Weber, "Religious Rejections of the World and their Directions", *Essays in Sociology*, p. 323 : "It is also in India that the technique which corresponds to such abnegation has been most highly developed. Monkhood, as well as the typical ascetic and contemplative manipulations, were not only first but also most consistently developed in India."

social irrationalities and contradictions. There is no elaborate attempt in early Buddhism to apply critical ethical judgments to the state and society. Hence Buddhism did not prescribe any thorough program of social reform. Only individuals can be conceived as capable of moral action. Buddha does not sponsor any program of the incorporation of morality and rationality in the structure of the state. Early Buddhism has no belief in an Ethical State to be realized in the future. Nor could the transcendentedly-oriented Buddhist ethics ever regard the political structure as the embodiment of freedom or the actualization of the ethical substance. According to the Buddhist scheme emancipation is to be attained not by the performance of good, socially-conforming, works but by righteous mendicancy, intuitive perception and contemplative insight. Socially-conforming works can at best lead to the attainment of heaven and good birth in the future. Hence there can be no ultimate motive for any definite interest in secular ends and positive programmes of social amelioration and betterment. Instead of stressing the performance of good works, *nirvāṇa* is oriented to rending asunder the wheels of *karma.* This transcendental stress implies the dissociation from all direct mundane interests. But this quest for *nirvāṇa* does not mean any anti-social egoistic hedonism. It is a mistake to regard transcendental ethics as anti-social. The quest of transcendental values is absolutely removed from being anti-social. The only charge from a sociological standpoint that can be levelled against a scheme of transcendental ethics is that it does not adequately stress social good. It is perfectly correct to hold that a transcendentally-oriented ethieal system relegates the pursuit of secular values to a subordinate realm. But the realization of *nirvāṇa* can never be consonant with the doing of any deed that can have socially devastating implications and consequences. The charge of egoistic hedonism is not correct because, after all, the goal of the extinction of suffering has to be attained by the individuals themselves. There can be no vicarious atonement and no realization of truth by proxy. The individuals are the loci of all those works and austerities which lead to the realization of truth and emancipation. But a person who has become enlightened can serve the fellow-seekers after truth in two ways. First, he can impart teachings to them. He can be of help in resolving their doubts and solving their problems. Secondly, he helps in setting standards of an exalted excellence of moral character. Hence the seer can become a centre of inspiration and he can radiate moral and spiritual vigour and strength.

Buddhist ethics has certainly set before itself a transcendent ideal. Social, political and economic ethics have a subordinate place here. The supreme and final goal is individual redemption from sins and sorrows and sufferings. The attainment of *nirvāṇa* is the supreme imperative. But although the teachings of the realization of *nirvāṇa* are introspective, subjective and deeply personal, still the spiritual and ethical quest is regarded not in terms of quietistic passivity or the vacuum of resignation but in terms of a mighty conquering adventure. Hence the *Dhammapada* says : "Who shall overcome this earth, and the world of Yama and the world of the gods ?... The disciple will overcome the earth, and the world of Yama, and the world of the gods."[1] The interpretation of the spiritual efforts towards emancipation in terms of conquest indicates the dynamic and powerful aspect of Buddhism and it should remove any association of weakness or sluggishness with the ethical and spiritual life.[2]

Early Buddhism has set before us an exalted code of moral living. It certainly is a rigorous code but there can be denial of or doubt about its elevated tone and nature. Buddha's unblemished life is one of the greatest events in the ethical advance of humanity. Early Buddhism has rendered a signal service to humanity by preaching the moralization of human conduct and by stressing universal nobility, compassion, benevolence and sympathy. It may not be possible to imitate the life of Buddha for ordinary individuals but the ideal that he has set can be a worthy goal for achievement. Society will certainly benefit if these ideals and especially the concept of non-hatred and loving kindness are incorporated not only in any one civilization but in the world as a whole. The pure, serene and elevated life of Buddha is a challenge to our lives engrossed in petty satisfactions and is a light for solving the neurotic discontents and crisis of

[1] *Dhammapada*, 44.

[2] Cf. F. Edgerton, "The Upaniṣads : What do they seek and why ?", *Journal of the American Oriental Society*, 1929, pp.97-121.

civilization.

5. *The Gospel of Buddha as a Philosophy of Life*

The intellectuality, the luminous and exalted nobility and serenity, the invincible will-force, a deep and profound sense of universal sympathy and compassion, titanic moral strength and an austere gravity—these aspects of the personality of Gautama Buddha are writ large upon the history and thought of Asia. "The Light of Asia" was the ideal man for Schopenhauer. The work of Buddhist evangelisation in the far eastern countries is an undying testimony to the immense dynamic energy released by the powerful moral personality of Buddha. Like all great prophets Buddha taught more by the impact of his personality than by his expressed utterances.

All scepticism that emerged out of dialectical analysis of moral teachings was silenced in the aura of his radiant personality. Hence we find that the teachings of the Tripiṭakas, which have lent themselves to the most diverse interpretations — from spiritual absolutism to scientific materialism and from idealistic mysticism to a fore-running of the theory of "psychology without a soul" like that of James, Russell and Brentano, did not cause the least confusion in the minds of personalities like Sāriputta, Kassapa and Ānanda.

Buddha has attempted to solve the problem of the choice between a contemplative, speculative life, and an energetic, philanthropic life. The *Bhagavadgitā* has also tried to reconcile the two ideals, but we find in the later commentators of the Gitā that either philosophic contemplation or devotional surrender was pronounced to be the final verdict on the teachings of the book. Buddha also wanted to solve this problem. He had the idealism of a Yājnavalkya and the renunciation of a Janaka. His doctrine of *pratityasmutpāda* would challenge comparison with the metaphysical researches of Pravāhaṇa Jaivali and Uddālaka, but at the same time he worked ceaselessly for full forty-five years for the redemption of suffering-stricken people.

He, who constantly harped on the impermanence of the cosmic phenomena and condemned all earthly pleasures to dust was also busily anxious to perfect the organisation of his Samgha. The person who had made a sacrifice of his political heritage was a few times consulted on questions of politics by the contemporary potentates and he offered his best advice. The ideal of *nirvāṇa* which he had realised connoted the complete extinction of lower passions and motives and the attainment of supersensible calm and peace, but simultaneously it was consonant with great and dynamic work for the moral uplift of the people. The controversialists and sophists of those times like Pūrna Kassapa and Ajita engaged in useless wranglings and discussions, but did not concern themselves with the eternal prob'em of all religious and ethical quest — the extinction of misery. Hence Buddha condemned them. His own ideal was the synthesis of an intellectual culture with moral development culminating in *nirvāṇa.* He was deeply sensitive to the cosmic pervasiveness of misery. After superhuman efforts he had discovered the secrets of existence under the sacred tree and he wanted to disseminate them everywhere. Hence we find him demonstrating through his subsequent career the ideal for a man of knowledge.

A perusal of world history shows us that this is, in a way, the ideal of all prophets. The greatest action must be backed by the greatest idealism. Hence we find a Kautilya behind Chandragupta, an Aristotle behind Alexander, a Ramdasa behind Shivaji and Rousseau behind Robespierre. The idealism of Buddha culminated in great action. Plato and Aristotle emphasised the superiority of a contemplative life. In the works of modern idealistic philosophers like Green and Bosanquet, on the other hand we find emphasis on participation in national and civic activities. But the Buddhist Bhikshus had many centuries ago attempted to practise to a certain extent the ideal of the combination of knowledge and action. Even Śamkara, the exponent of the philosophy of non-action (*naishkarmya*) was also a titan in the field of action. By the adoption of a synthetic ideal Buddha gave a great challenge to the contemporary deterministic and relativistic thinkers like Gośāla and Sanjaya Belatthaputta who had taught the futility of action and thereby could endanger moral life. By his categorical emphasis on moral action Buddha rendered a tremendous service to Indian ethics. He, in a way, pronounced the freedom of the human will but at the same time he enunciated the inexorable law of *karma.* Hence we find that the *Weltanschauung* of Buddha is not annihilationistic but it is an emphatic assertion of the energetic application of the human will to moral action. Consequently, progressive moral perfectionism is reiterated in the verses of the *Dhammapada.*[1]

Besides formulating and realising the goal of a man of knowledge, we find Buddha reconciling ethics and metaphysics. The British utilitarians formulated the creed of the greatest good of the greatest number. Auguste Comte's positivism made a plea for a universal scheme of human development. The Upaniṣadic ideal taught the empiric character of ethical action, as concerned only with the phenomenal world, the ontological reality being beyond good and evil. In the face of these different creeds we find Buddha setting up the scheme of the *Ashtāngika Mārga* which synthesises moral action and spiritual realisation.

In the aryan eight-fold way we find that the development of mystic concentration (*dhyana* and *sāmādhi*) is consequent upon a rigorous conformity to an ethical discipline—(*ājiva*, *vyāyāma*, and *samkalpa*). In the *Muṇḍakopaniṣad* (3.1.4) also we find such an ideal— the realisation of the soul is said to be consequent upon a thoroughly truthful life, ascetic discipline, self-restraint and integral knowledge, but the later metaphysical Vedanta and also the principal Upaniṣads make knowledge the *sine qua non* of ultimate realisation. The Buddhistic ethical code is not destructionistic but it is a universalistic theory which places before man the ideal of self-negation for a greater ethical self-fulfilment and thus may provide the real moral foundation and background for modern humanitarianism and internationalism. Modern idealistic thinkers also want the negation of the egoistic interests of the individual man for the total good of the community. Buddha placed before man a rigorous ethical code to prepare him for the realisation of nirvāṇa. Buddhist metaphysics is not based merely on a pure intellectual analysis but it has recourse to the subliminal psychology of man as we find in the Abhidhamma texts and it wants to create an integrated personality not baffled by the conflicts of the conscious and sub-conscious. Buddha believes in the dawn of supernormal vision to man which would enable him to know things comprehensively, by identity, as Bergson would say. But for this a true apprehension of the Buddhist metaphysics is

[1] ***Dhammapada*, 21-24.**

necessary ; hence the constant insistence is on '*smṛti*' *and* '*dṛshti*'—the knowledge of Buddhist teachings and scriptures.

Christian critics have tried to criticize Vedantic ethics as being relegated to the empiric sphere only. Although this criticism is not fully justified, still it is apparent that no such criticism is possible of the Buddhist teachings. Even if Buddha constantly distinguishes between the transcendental vision of a Tathāgata (*lokottara dṛshti*) and the apprehension of a normal man, his utterances always regard the *mārga* as the central pivot of his system. Although according to the Buddhist metaphysics there is the sublation of *avidyā* in the Nirvanic state and although the *Upādāna-skandha* ceases to exist, before the realised comprehension of an Arhat, still the Buddha teaches constant vigilance in the moral path. Revealing his personality to Upak Ājivaka, Buddha claims moral perfection and trans-empirical gnosis, but still almost every evening throughout his career we find him meditating on the nature and truth of the metaphysical teachings. H.G. Wells makes the following remark in criticism of the Buddhist *mārga* :

> "Gautama had no knowledge nor vision of history, he had no clear sense of the vast and many-sided adventure of life opening out in space and time ...... The idea of mankind as a great brotherhood pursuing an endless destiny under the God of Righteousness, the idea that was already dawning upon the Semitic consciousness in Babylon at this time, did not exist in his world."

We would like to point out that it would have been better if before making a statement like this, Wells would have gone through the hundreds of *Jātaka* tales which emphasise the progressive perfectionism of Buddha in numerous phases of life as Bodhisattva, before his final descent, into terrestrial consciousness as the historic Buddha. The idea of rebirth of personality and insistence on *ahimsā* are the true bases of the realisation of the truth of a man's being and also for the identification of his partial and limited consciousness with the entire cosmos.

Buddha tried to reconcile the rival claims of spirit and matter. He never denied the ontological existence of the world. According to the later radical pluralism of the Sarvastivadins with their seventy-five "elements", the cosmos is in an endless and beginningless commotion. The early Buddhists can be regarded as realists in their epistemological analysis (relation between *rūpa* and *vijnāna*). Stcherbatsky contrasts the half-way illusionism of original Buddhism with the radical illusionism of Śamkara and Nāgārjuna. It is difficult to find in Buddhism the parallel of the will of Schopenhauer. Some stray statements in the Tripiṭakas are parallel to Barkeleyanism and are the foundation of the later Yogācāra philosophy. Because Buddha does not admit an absolute, hence he cannot uphold the view that nature is the teleological manifestation of the Supreme Being. His view about the changing world is that it is real, although in constant motion, and hence his philosophy has been compared to that of Heraclitus and Bergson. By the formula of the *Nāma-rupa-skandha* it seems clear that he wants to emphasise both *rūpa* (matter) and *vijnāna* (consciousness). The *avidyā* of original Buddhism is not a creative potency, nor does it spring from the Tathatā as in Aśvaghosa.

The insistence of Buddha on the existence of matter is also apparent in the "*Aggañña Sutta*" where he describes a realistic cosmogonic scheme and a psychological theory of social development. But although he gave an important place to matter, he never identified the cosmic objectivity with any immanental godhead in the Spinozistic way. He criticises the cosmological argument for theism and ridicules the idea of a primal creative agency. Matter to Buddha is uncreated like the *Prakṛti* of the Sāmkhya and the immutable seven-fold categories of Prakuddha Kaccāyana. By freeing the analysis of matter from a theistic and theological basis he rendered a service to positive science as was done by Democritus and Empedocles in ancient Greece.

But the Buddhist position is not materialism or naturalism. The Chārvākas taught materialism to support a gross egoistic hedonism. Buddha, to the contrary, believed in the rebirth of personality, thus formulating the creed of progressive moral evolution from birth to birth. He, thus, taught the transitive efficacy of moral causation. The later Pali exegesis puts moral causation as having the same certitude and deterministic finality as natural causation has in the organic and inorganic kingdom. But, Buddha's insistence on *karman* did not deny the initiative of the human will.

Buddha's stress on the attainment of supernatural powers in the path to *nirvāṇa* shows he is in line with the traditional and orthodox Yoga of Patanjali. But unlike the separate soul-substance of the Pātanjala Yoga, in original Buddhism there is no one soul entity, although recent scholars like C.A.F. Rhys Davids, and Radhakrishnan wrongly think that Buddha accepted a soul of the Upaniṣadic type.

The Upaniṣads put before the world the principle of the identity of the object and the subject : the brahman is identical with the *ātman*. But the insistence of Buddhism on ethics is greater than that of the Upaniṣads. The modern world, shaken by ideological conflicts, can look to the early Buddhist standpoint for a moral integration because the ethical absolutism of Buddha is a permanent vindication of the central worth of the moral being of man.

Buddha was a keen analyst and he proclaimed the supremacy of human reason by subjecting the scriptural wisdom to a searching scrutiny. He never posed as a divinely appointed prophet dispensing a deliverance to those who believed in him. He taught *Vibhaājjavāda* — analytical wisdom. He wanted people to come and look into his doctrines. He was ready to subject his standpoint to discussion. But in spite of his philosophic rationalism, in his Yoga he was also an upholder of transcendental mysticism and contemplation. Even in European thought we find that discursive analytical rationalism and intellectualism have been subjected to criticism by Kierkegaard and Bergson. According to the Buddhist tenet *prajña* is the culmination of the concentrated application of *vijñāna*.

To what extent was Buddha a democratic champion of the rights of the down-trodden and exploited ? Was he the Kshatriya spokesman against the tyranny and monopolistic claims of the Brahmans ? It is clear that he does not put forward a concrete programme for the socio-economic and political rehabilitation of the demos. His whole temper of thinking was in the direction of a moral and spiritual uplifting of the human race. He speaks not a word against slavery. He could anticipate Abraham Lincoln by hundreds of years. He is only content with giving equality to a slave, turned monk, in his Sangha. Even Asoka simply wants better treatment of the slaves and hired labourers.

Buddha's insistence on Ahimsā charmed the people of all

races and climates. His burning compassion has always been the source of permanent solace. No doubt the numerous religious and philosophical developments of Buddhism show that the original teachings of the Master (Śāsta) were variously understood, but still the guiding principles and the persistent spirit of philosophical and ethical quest were kept intact to a great degree.

CHAPTER 10

KARMAN, MORAL DETERMINISM AND FREEDOM

1. *Theory of Determinism*

DETERMINISM IMPLIES not only a check upon and regulation of the operative efficacy of the human will but it also holds that the life of man is subjected to powerful forces which are almost beyond his control. These forces not only influence and condition his life but even *determine* it. Although determinism is different from the religious and popular conception of fatalism which implies the total futility almost of the endeavours of a man, it (determinism) does also seriously enunciate a vital domination over the actions and life of man. It does not absolutely neutralize the spontaneity and freedom of man but it does emphasize that human efforts and will work in a framework which is mighty and even uncontrollable. Some thinkers have pleaded for the philosophy of climatological or economic determinism while others advocate a theological or absolutistic determinism.[1] In the dominant systems of Indian thought it has been held that the merits or demerits of the actions performed by a man and the psychological impulsions behind them accumulate, and in course of time they acquire such a vital potency that they determine the life itself of the man. Determinism serves to counter the tendency of explaining the facts in the universe and history in terms of the random conglomeration of atoms or an arbitrary fiat of an omnipotent God who dispenses predestination. It pleads for the acceptance of a law-governed world and seeks to establish the determination of cosmic and historical operations in terms of mighty laws.[2] There is also

[1] V.P. Varma, *The Political Philosophy of Sri Aurobindo* (Asia Publishing House, Bombay, 1960), pp. 92-104.

[2] The *Aṅguttara Nikāya*, IV, 77, forbids speculation on four subjects and two of these are, *karma vipāka* and *lokacintā*. Eliot, *Hinduism and Buddhism* (London, Edward Arnold & Co., 1921, 3 Vols. Re-issued by

a form of determinism which is called psychological determinism which implies that the human will is not free in its volitional activities but is determined by previous accumulations of the influences of psychic energy. Thus it seeks to account for the formation of choice and decisions among alternative possibilities through antecedent psychical and physical conditions.

The concept of *karman* as expounded in Indian thought stressed the notion of justice based on individual retribution but it was not usually expanded to imply the scientific notion of universal uniformity and cosmic causality. Hence it will not be proper to compare the old concept of *karman* and the notions of Galilean-Newtonian physics. Sometimes, however, it is said that the conceptions of *niyantā* and *dhammatā* upheld in Buddhism answer to the notions of natural law of the Stoics. Moral determinism (*karmavāda*) accepts the operation of a law of just recompense in the world. It is opposed to the two trends of materialistic accidentalism and divine election. Materialistic accidentalism seeks to explain the phenomena of the world as well human suffering and enjoyment by the working of chance or sheer arbitrariness—*yadṛichā.* There is no proportion, according to it, between the actions we perform and the amount of misery and happiness which is our lot. The notion of divine election is based on the acceptance of the dogma that God in his superior will has decreed that only some persons will attain salvation and thus be redeemed from sin and sorrow. Moral determinism, on the contrary, does not accept that man's life is the mere translation of the arbitrary promulgations of God but it seeks to establish a commensurability between his actions and the consequences he reaps. The enunciation of the concept of moral determinism is a landmark in the ethical evolution of man because it not only accepts the operation of an infinite law of conservation of moral energy in the world but, in the form that it has had in Indian thought, it states that a man's ancestry. his station in life, his sorrow and happiness and even

London, Routledge & Kegan Paul Ltd., 1954) Vol. I, p. 221-22, says that Buddha may have felt that an attempt to transform the law of causation into a cosmic law would turn into 'speculation' and would go dangerously near fatalism.

his death are determined by his own actions. Buddhism is a staunch advocate of moral determinism and its *karmavāda* is a mighty exemplification of it. In some schools of Buddhism it is accepted that the actions of men not only influence their personal lives but have even enormous general influences.[1]

The concept of *karman* represents one of the prime themes in Indian philosophical speculations and social life. It definitely indicates the prevalence of the belief in a universal harmonious pattern. The ordinary meaning of *karman* is action. At a more comprehensive level it also connotes the motivation behind the action and the objective set of consequences following from it. Thus three factors are important in the study of *karman*. First, the motivational impulsion which determines the course of action ; second, the specific physical and instrumental steps followed ; and third, the process of consequences—*vipāka* and *saṁskāra*,[2] that ensue from the action. In terms of Samskrit terminology they can be respectively called *saṁkalpa*, *karman* and *pariṇāma*. In Buddhist philosophy, the term *vijñapti karman* refers to external objective acts, while *avijñapti karman*[3] refers to the inner psychic motivation behind the act

1 L.V. Poussin, "Karma", *Encyclopaedia of Religion & Ethics*, Vol. VII, pp. 673-77 : "Acts have also a fruit of a general kind. Towards the end of the little cosmic period (*antarakalpa*), plants etiolate, are crushed by stones and rain, and bear little fruit ; this is the result of a superabundance of murder, theft etc. ... the fruit of *karman* as sovereign (*adhipati*). The creation of the universe is the result of the acts of all beings together, the hells are created by the acts that require to be punished in hell and so on..."

2 *Majjhima Nikāya*, "*Saṁkhāruppati Suttanta*", for the Buddhistic theory of *saṁskāra*. H. Oldenberg, *Buddha* (Translated by W. Hoey, London, Williams & Norgate, 1882) p. 242 : "We might translate *saṁskāra* directly by actions, if we understand this word in the wide sense in which it includes also at the same time the 'internal actions,' the will and the wish." According to the *Saṁyutta Nikāya*, III, 87, *saṁskāra* has the function of synthesis, *saṁkhātamabhissanaṁkharonti*. There are fifty-two *saṁskāra* states according to Buddhism. Sometimes *saṁskāra* is translated as "restless, substanceless procession."

3 *Avijñapti* is the lasting moral result of our actions. Th. Stcherbatsky, *The Central Conception of Buddhism* (London, Royal Asiatic Society, 1923). p. 99 : "It (*avijñapti*) constitutes a link between the act and its future retribution, it is, therefore, the same as *saṁskāra*, *apūrva*, or *adṛshta* of the Brahminic systems". According to Poussin, *Avijñapti* is a thing of particular nature which is subtle although derived from the four

as well as the consequences following from it. The resultant chain of consequences can be further analyzed at two levels : consequences accruing to the doer or the participant and environmental consequences.[1] Almost all schools of Indian thought, orthodox or heterodox, theistic or atheistic, adhere to the philosophy of *karman*. It is expounded at great length in Jainism and Buddhism, in the Nyāya-Vaiśeshika, in the Sāmkhya and Yoga and in the two schools of Mimānsa. In some schools of Indian thought the accumulated potency of actions is believed to operate with such transcendental efficacy that there is no place therein for the concept of the overruling majesty of God. *Karmavāda* obtained an almost universal philosophical adherence. It has also powerfully influenced the popular mind of India. Suzki points out the differential manifestation of karman : (a) as the principle of conservation of energy at the *physical* level ; (b) as the principle of evolution and heredity at the *biological* level and (c) as the principle of immortality of deeds at the *moral* level.

2. *The Concept of Karman in the Vedas, Brāhmaṇas and the Upaniṣads*

The Vedic poets and singers adhered to the belief in *ṛta* (*ṛta*)[2] — the cosmic law of harmony and order. This order was recognized not merely as a mechanical uniformity but as proceeding from a superior moral and beneficent force[3] symbolised by the god Varuṇa. In the Vedas we also find reference to the *vrata* of *ṛta* (or *ṛta*) followed by the gods.[4]

great material elements. It is produced by a voluntary and conscious bodily or vocal act but when produced it develops of its own accord irrespective of whether the man is sleeping, working or meditating.

[1] D.T. Suzuki, *Outlines of Mahayana Buddhism*, (London, Luzac & Co., 1907), pp. 181-82. Elaborating the concept of *dharmadhātu* (spiritual universe), Suzuki, *ibid.*, p. 189, stresses the collective influence of a moral deed and states that deeds once committed leave permanent effects on the "general system of sentient beings."

[2] Cf. the Avestic word *Asa* (*Urta*). The word *ṛta* has been written as *rita* in this book for simplicity.

[3] According to A.A. Macdonell, *Vedic Mythology* (Strassburg, Verlag von Karl J. Trubner, 1897), pp. 11, 13, 26, 101, 120., *rita* contains in it the germs of the law of *karman* or the unalterable law of producing effects.

[4] *RV*, I, 65, 3.

Vrata is the law of effective austere living[1] and through the cultivation of the vows in one's life can alone man testify to his sincere belief in cosmic moral harmony. Thus the idea of universal order and rhythm at the physical level was substantiated by the law of moral order. The concepts of *ṛta* and *vrata* effectively demonstrate the prevalence of the teleological conception of the world.

The ritualistic cult of the sacrifices was an exemplification at the religious and practical level of the belief in a universal moral order of *ṛta* and *satya*.[2] The sacrificers had some specific goals to achieve and the external act was regarded as the physical process for the realization of those goals. The belief was widely prevalent that accuracy in the performance of the sacrificial deed would necessarily produce the intended consequences both here and hereafter. Everybody could obtain the desired goals if only he stuck to the exact sacrificial formula. The belief was dominant that the sacrifice is a powerful instrument which has tremendous potency.[3] It was only a demonstration at the religious level of the conception that to every action there is necessarily a reaction.[4] In the *Ṛgveda* the germs of the philosophy of moral determinism are found.[5] It is stated that the person who makes sacrificial gifts

[1] In view of the Vedic emphasis on *vrata, tapas, brahmacarya* ; S.N. Dasgupta, *Indian Idealism* (Cambridge University Press, 1933), p. 9, seems to be inaccurate when he constantly harps on the "non-moral and non-ethical" character of the law of *karman*.

[2] A.B. Keith, *The Religion and Philosophy of the Veda and the Upaniṣads*, Vol. II, p. 464, says that there was no doctrine of a divine judgment in the Vedic literature.

[3] S.N. Dasgupta, *Indian Idealism*, p. 3, holds that the later moral theory of *karman* developed from the magical belief in potency of sacrifices to produce the intended consequences. He says : "The law of *karman* was thus rooted in the Indian mind from the earliest days in the tribal belief in the efficacy of magical operations, incantations and the like, and it was only extended at a later stage into the ethical field."

[4] In the Babylonian religious conceptions which almost arose in the same period as the Vedas, world-events were regarded not as the consequences of natural forces nor due to human spontaneous will but, due to the decision (*Piristu*) of gods. S. Langdon, "Babylonian Mysteries", *The Encyclopaedia of Religion and Ethics* (ed. by James Hastings, 13 Vols, New York, Charles Scribner's Sons, 1908-26), Vol, IX, pp. 70-72. These volumes have been referred to in an abbreviated form as E.R.E.

[5] According to R.D. Ranade, *A Constructive Survey of Upaniṣadic*

re-acquires them after death. This is akin to the primitive conception of recompense according to which death is no impediment to the operation of the law of rewards and vengeance. The *Ṛgveda* mentions the term *ishtāpūrta* which indicates the merit won by making offerings to gods and gifts to the priests. In the funeral hymn it is stated that the dead person would be able to unite himself with the fathers (*pitaraḥ*) through the fruits of his offerings and gifts.[1] In the *Taittirīya Saṃhitā* also the gods are prayed for uniting the dead man with his *ishtāpūrta* when he attains their abode. The *ishtāpūrta* symbolises the concentrated essence of the ritualistic ceremonies and to this is attributed great efficacy in producing the desired consequences. This concept also serves as the germinal background for the theory of moral determinism or *karmavāda* as it is formulated later in the Upaniṣads and Buddhism.

The Vedas exalt the concept of *karman*. There are references to the powerful exploits of Indra which have great influences on both the physical-terrestrial and the atmospheric regions. The Vedas also inculcate the supremacy of *tapas* - Originally *tapas* meant fervour and physical heat. But soon it became inclusive enough to comprehend also endeavours in the direction of moral restraint and voluntary suffering of pain. In the *Atharvaveda* (*brahmacāri sūkta*) it is stated that through sensual restraint and disciplined life (*tapas*), a Vedic student can attain immortality. Thus even in the Vedic literature, *tapas* had a moral connotation. *Tapas* is sometimes regarded as the source of the entire cosmic manifestation. Thus it is held as a creative force of singularly great potency. This concept further accentuates the notion of moral determinism because the determination of cosmogonic phenomena is attributed to the power of accentuated (*abhīddha*) *tapas*. *Tapas* also is a kind of *karman* and, as expounded in the Upaniṣads, it includes both

Philosophy (Poona, Oriental Book Agency, 1926), p. 148, the Ṛgvedic (X. 16.3) *prithiviñca dharmanā* is the beginning of the law of *karman*. John Mckenzie, *Hindu Ethics* (Oriental Reprint, 1972) p. 15 :"... though the *karman* doctrine is not yet formulated, its ethical principles are already in evidence. Thus suffering is recognized as the fruit of previous sin, and when a good man dies he goes to the next world carrying his merit with him."

[1] *RV*, X, 14, 8.

[2] *AV*, X, 7, 11.

physical restraint and austerities as well as moral rigor and philosophic contemplation.

During the days of the Brāhmaṇas, the growth of the sacrificial cult helped in bringing out the implications of the concept of *karman*.[1] There grew the idea that through his actions man makes out a world for himself and after death he is born into it.[2] The idea of the impershableness of *karman* is also developed in this period.[3] The *Kauśitakī Brāhmaṇa* refers to the person who knowing "in me there is imperishableness, sacrifices, his sacrifice perishes not."[4] The *Taittirīya Brāhmaṇa* also subscribes to the view of the of the imperishableness of good deeds. The *Śatapatha Brāhmaṇa* states that punishment is inflicted according to one's deeds.[5]

The Upaniṣads contain as their principal theme the philosophy of spiritual idealism. Although as a corollary to absolute monism, they sometimes contain statements which indicate the ethical indifference of the person who has attained the realization of the *brahman*, still there are other passages also in them which teach the belief in good following out of noble actions,[6] thereby subscribing to the Vedic notion of the omnipotence of an eternal order in the universe.[7] The *Brihadāraṇyaka*

[1] The *Śatapatha Brāhmaṇa*, 1,9,3,2, mentions that there are two fires on route to heaven which burn whom they should burn and let pass those whom they ought to let pass. *Supra.*

[2] The *Śatapatha Brāhmaṇa*, XI, 2, 7, 33, states that a man's fate after death is determined by weighing his good and evil deeds. Paul Deussen, *Philosophy of the Upaniṣads*, p. 319, points out that the Ṛgvedic hymns teach for the good a continued existence with the gods under Yama's control and for the evil a journey into abyss. The standpoint of the *Atharvaveda* and the *Brāhmaṇas* is the same, only the conception of recompense for works is carried out in detail. Deussen, *ibid*,, pp. 317-28, for ancient Vedic eschatology).

[3] In the *Taittiriya Āraṇyaka*, VI, 5, 13, there is reference to the idea of judgment.

[4] *KB*, VII. 4. (the *Kaushītaki Brāhmana* is abbreviated as *KB*) Contrast E.W. Hopkins, *Ethics of India* (Yale University Press, 1924), p. 43 : "The view that the gods direct men's thought and action was not worked out [in the Vedas] into any system of determinism but rested on the ... thought may we not do what ye punish".

[5] *Śatapatha*, VI, 2,2,27 and X, 6,3,1.

[6] *Brihadāraṇyaka*, III, 2,13. In the *Muṇḍakopniṣad*, I, 2.1, *karmāni* is used in the sense of sacrificial action.

[7] H ·Griswold, "Indian Pessimism", *The Encyclopaedia of Religion and*

(IV. 3.33) contains a reference to *karmadeva* which implies the reality of men who have attained to the status of gods by their actions. The *Ishopaniṣad* which is taken from the fortieth chapter of the *Yajurveda* promulgates the concept of disinterested action, a gospel which has been expounded in great details in the *Bhagavadgitā*.[1]

3. *A Sociological Study of the Origin and Development of the Theory of Karman*

There are three views about the origin and development of the concept of *karman*. The first is the anthropological view which would trace its roots in the notions of the primitive tribes regarding the potency of certain 'sacred' actions, formulas and incantations in bringing about the intended consequences. To the primitive mind there was not much of a radical difference between the living and the dead. The old tribes held that even after physical death, in some form or other, the spirits were hovering in the dark house-corners or roofs or on the tops of the neighbouring big trees and continued to participate in the welfare of the living progeny. Some roots of the theory of *karman* can be traced in the belief in the magical character of the sacred acts.[2] The belief that the performance of certain forbidden acts, the 'taboo', would produce disaster was only the reverse side of the same belief. The law of *karman* is postulated on the belief that physical death does not mean any damage to the power of the past actions done by the individual to produce their results. The adherence to the notions of the sacred and the taboo and to the belief in the continuity of the personality of the ghost-

Ethics, IX, p.813 : "It was only when the personal gods of the Ṛgveda had become merged more or less completely into the pantheistic and impersonal 'one' and 'all' of the Upaniṣads that the doctrine of an automatic principle of retribution arose. The passing of the Vedic gods left a place for *karman*."

[1] The teachings contained in *Kurvanneveha karmāni* of the *Ishopaniṣad* (*mantra* no. 2), is interpreted in different ways according to the philosophical predilections of the commentators. Śamkara stresses only knowledge (*vidyā*), Kumārila emphasizes both *vidyā* and *avidyā* (*karman*), while Prabhākara exalts *karma*, as the pathway to salvation.

[2] L. Thorndike, *A History of Magic and Experimental Science* (New York, 1923, 2 Vols.), Vol. II.

ancestors prepare some of the fundamental framework for the emergence of the theory of *karman*, though it cannot be denied that the later developments ascribing a transcendental efficacy to the *apūrva* and the *adṛsha* or the conception of God as *karmādhyaksha* represent further refinements of the old notions. In the Ṛgvedic period we find that the worship of the various deities is carried out in such passionate reverential mood that the notion, that the gods were mere passive spectators and the sacrificial mechanism had powers of auto-dynamic operation does not seem convincing. In the Mimānsa philosophy, the autonomous potency of the sacrificial cult was exalted to the height.

The anthropological study of the genesis of the notion of *karman* which traces its roots in primitive magical ideas and ghost-worship receives some additional substantiation from the later developments of the theory of *karman*, where also significant vestiges of old primitive notions are discovered. In the philosophy of the Jainas we find the maintenance of belief in subtle *karman*-matter which is supposed to pour into the the soul and stick to that. This process of sticking is aided by the passions of men.[1] The *karman*-matter that adheres to the soul generates a colouration like white, black etc. This colouration is termed *leshya* in Jaina philosophy. This primitive notion of colouration by the efficacy of *karman*, as the determinant of the character of the soul, that is elaborated in Jainism, is also maintained in the *Dhammapada* which says : *kanham dhammam vippahāya sukkam bhāvetha pandīto.*[2] This notion of *karman*-colouration thus appears to be a part of a general tradition which was accepted both by Jainism and Buddhism.[3] The Yoga system of Patanjali also accepts this

[1] Cf. the view of Leibnitz that *materia prima* clouds and mystifies the representations of the monads.

[2] *Dhammapada* (87). It means that a wise man should renounce 'black' actions and stick to 'white' ones.

[3] Some primitive notions regarding *karman* also appear in the Buddhist cosmological speculations, *e.g.*: "at the beginning of the re-creation of the world there arise in the vast void of the universe 'winds born of acts' which heap up the clouds from which the creative rain will pour". (Quoted in Poussin, "Karma", *E.R.E.* Vol. VII, pp. 673-75). According to the *Śarabhanga* (*Jātaka Jātaka*, No. 522), the lurking deed *karman*, is said to wait long to catch a man and in his last birth gets its opportunity.

view. Thus the anthropological standpoint regarding the origin of *karman* receives additional substantiation from the primitivism implicit in the notion of the *karman*-matter and its adhesion to the soul.

The second view traces not the origin of the concept of *karman* but seeks to analyze the process of its development. It is possible to trace some kind of a correlation between the ethical doctrine of *karman* and the political processes of expansion and territorial settlement that were going on in the country. Since the later Ṛgvedic days there began the process of the eastward migration and settlement of some of the Aryan tribes. This migration and settlement was going on in various parts of the country and specially in northern India. The process of empire-building in Magadha, Kośala, Vatsa and Avantī was the culmination of the political process of adventurism and conquest. Political action of an organized character was the need of the hour if the various kingdoms and the several republican polities were to maintain their existence. Political competition and strifes were rampant and only by the resort to constant intrigues, diplomatic manoeuvres, successful adjustments and even military preparedness could the territorial integrity of a political entity be safeguarded. Hence the social and political reality presented the aspect of constant struggle and action. It will not be considered far-fetched if some kind of a correlation is established between the actual processes of hectic action going on in the social and political world and the emphasis on actions in the moral and religious world.[1] After all, the participants, both in the political process and the moral and religious process, were recruited from the same social environment and hence it is not unrealistic to hold that the Upaniṣadic and Buddhistic emphasis on *karman* in the moral world might have as its partial background the tremendous urgency of action in the political world. Marxists have stressed that the notion of the activistic nature of the subject in epistemology is specially fostered by the

There is no foundation, however, to point out that Buddhism borrowed the doctrine of *karman* from Jainism. It was a part of the contemporary world-view.

[1] K. Marx, *Theses on Feuerbach* and K. Marx & F. Engels, *The German Ideology*.

proletariat because it alone is in contact with the production-process. They thus establish a thorough correlation between the social reality and theory of knowledge. I have hazarded some kind of correlation between the political reality and moral theory.

The third view regarding the development of the theory of *karman* is more sociological. It is postulated upon the acceptance of a social conflict between the Brahmins and the Kshattriyas. The conflict between these two sections expressed itself also at an intellectual level and the Kshattriyas were the spokesmen of more enlightened notions against the traditional theology and conservative dogmatism of the hieratic sections. Some Western Indologists, like Garbe, are of opinion that the doctrine of *karman* was a new addition to the philosophical world-view of the Upaniṣads and was a formulation of the Kshattriyas. The newness of the doctrine is testified to by the confidential manner in which Yājṇavalkya reveals this esoteric doctrine to Ārtabhāga. He takes hold of the hand of Ārthabhāga and takes him away from the assembly and there tells him about this doctrine as if he wanted to conceal it from the audience.[1] Garbe holds that in opposition to the Brahmanical systems, the Kshattriyas formulated two dominant conceptions — the metaphysics of monistic absolutism and the ethical law of *karman*. Emphasizing the peculiarity of the Yājṇavalkya-Ārthabhāga dialectics, Western Indologists say that the newness of the doctrine is indicated by the almost hesitant manner in which Yājṇavalkya reveal this doctrine to Ārthabhāga.

But I do not think that this view of the Western Indologists is warranted by the facts. In the period subsequent to the Upaniṣads, the doctrine of *karman* acquired immense significance. The Buddhistic concepts of *dvādaśa nidāna* and *ashtāngika mārga* exalt the efficacy of action both in the

[1] Carlo Formichi, "Upaniṣads", *J. Of Dept. Of Letters*, Calcutta Univ., 1927. Vol. XV (pp. 83-130), says that in the *Chhāndogya*, V, 2, 4, Pravāhaṇa propounds that *śraddhā* is the vital surviving element after death. This represents the Brahmanical point of view. But instead of *śraddhā*, Yājnavalkya stresses *karman*. Formichi says that Yājnavalkya spoke in private because he knew he was propounding something heretical. It appears, according to him, that Yājnavalkya and Ārtabhaga spoke as if they had been two Buddhists (p. 129, *Ibid.*).

origination and in the liberation of men. At the time when Buddha flourished there were serious strifes in the philosophical world with regard to determinism and moral autonomy. The Ājivikas were determinists.[1] The Jainas were extreme advocates of the concept of *kriyāvāda*. The thorough adherence to the concept of *karman* by Jainism and Buddhism indicates that, since these movements were not confined to the aristocratic elite but wanted to influence the middle classes and the agricultural population also, the people also must have been predisposed to the acceptance of this doctrine. During the time of Buddha the theory of *karman* was a popular creed. If the hypothesis of the doctrine of *karman* being a popular one at the time when Buddhism and Jainism flourished, that is in the sixth and fifth centuries B.C., is correct, then it can be legitimately argued that some centuries must have elapsed during which the concept of *karman* was being popularized. In those days of absence of mass education it would certainly take a long time before a philosophical concept could be popularly accepted. Hence to account for the inconsistency in the concept of *karman* being a novel philosophical secret during the age of the *Brihadāraṇyaka Upaniṣad* as it is fancied by some of the Western Indologists, and a popular belief in the Jaina-Buddhistic period, two factors may be considered as being responsible. First, a long period of several centuries must have intervened between Yājṇavalkya and Mahāvira-Buddha during which the concept of *karman* was being popularized. But since this hypothesis is not historically tenable, the only reasonable alternative to hold is the second hypothesis, that Yājṇavalkya was not expressing something novel, unique and unheard of by the people, and his desire for communicating this doctrine in secret is only in the general Upaniṣadic fashion according to which conceptions which have esoteric implications are to be discussed in secret. Thus I subscribe to the ancient Vedic origin of the concept of *karman* which was only being maintained and developed by the Upaniṣads. The *Bhagavadgitā* also says that the doctrine

[1] Cf. "In the ninety-one aeons, O Vātsya, which I [Buddha] recall, I remember but one single Ājivika who attained to heaven and he acknowledged the truth of *kamma* and the efficacy of works". *Anguttara Nikāya*, II, p. 227 (London, Pali Text Society edition).

inculcating liberation through actions is an ancient one.

The eschatological[1] ideas of the Vedas and the Upanișads also substantiate the thesis of the Vedic origin of the theory of *karman* and the implied moral determinism. The Upanișads and the *Bhagavadgitā* contain reference to the two eschatological yāna — the *devayāna*, the path of the man of knowledge, and the *pitriyāna*, the path of the man of action. Even the Samhitās refer to these two paths.[2] The two-fold *yāna* involves a theory of moral determinism because it is a specification of the fate of a person in accordance with his attainments. Thus personal achievement is regarded as the prime force which determines the future abode of a man. The idea of "as a man does so he reaps" is contained in the theory of *yāna* because a man's worth determines his future station. This doctrine of the commensurability of a man's station in the future life with the merits and demerits attained in the present life is a substantiation of the belief in moral determinism. The *Chhāndogya Upanișad* refers to the disparate destinations of the well-merited, (*ramaṇiyacharaṇāh*) and evil-merited (kapuyacharaṇāh)[3] Thus the study of Vedic and Upanișadic eschatology would dispel the unwarranted hypothesis of some western Indologists which ascribes the formulation of the concept of *karman* to the Kshattriyas.

4. *Modificatians of the Individualism of Karman in the Upanișads*

The concept of *karman* is highly individualistic. It seeks to explain the destiny of an individual in terms of his own efforts.

1 For the elucidation of eschatological notions in general, J.A. Macculloch, "Eschatology", *Encyclopaedia of Religion and Ethics*, Vol. V., pp. 373-91. Cf. Plato's views on eschatology discussed in the last book of the *Republic*. There are references in Plato to spheres for passage of dead men.

2 S.N. Dasgupta, *Indian Philosophy* (Cambridge University Press, 1922), 5 vols., Vol. I, pp, 23-42, is grossly mistaken in attributing the origin of the notions of *devayāna* and *pitŗyāna* to Pravāhaṇa Jaivali because the roots of them go back to the *Yajurveda*, IX, 47. For the terms *devayāna* and *pitŗyāna*, the *Praśnopnișad* used the terms *uttarāyaṇa* and *dakshināyaṇa*.

3 According to the Upanișads, *karman* is the set of means and instruments which serve as the link between will and the concrete achievement of the willed consequences. Thus the cause of rebirth is not *karman* but desires. Cf. S.N. Dasgupta, *Indian Philosophy*, I, pp. 56-57.

It repudiates the conception of God as an irresponsible arbitrary omnipotent being who dispenses misery and happiness in his whimsical promulgations. *Karman* asserts the prevalence of order in the world and is antagonistic to any conception like that of Calvinist predestination. It is opposed also to the notions of natural determinism of a mechanical order which explains human fate in terms of the motions of atoms and electrons. The theory of *karman* is the first significant attempt in the history of human speculations to explain a man's destiny in terms of his own personal endeavours. The stress on one's own efforts as the sure path to moral purification and personal illumination is the first significant protest against the tribal notions of collective responsibility. *Karman* heralds the theory of individualism and if, at the religious level, it is opposed to divine predestination and despotism, at the social level, it is opposed to the tribal notion of morality which emphasizes the "gens" (the *communitas*) as the unit and does not concern itself with the apportionment of justice according to one's deserts. Thus it can be said that the theory of *karman* is a great individualistic protest against the tribal canons of morality.

But the individualism of *karman* was not definite and rigid in the days of the Upaniṣads. Several other conceptions which were prevalent in that period challenged the individualistic character of *karman* and made concessions to divine grace on the one side and to the interests of family and social solidarity on the other.

Although the Upaniṣads uphold the view that a man's destiny is made by the actions done by him, still the theory of determinism through *karman* has been modified to some extent by some alternative conceptions which appear at times inconsistent. The later Upaniṣads which have a pronouncedly theistic orientation exalt the conception of grace.[1] The *Kaṭha Upaniṣad* contains the classic statement that the *ātman* is attained not by intellectual acumen or scholastic profundity but by grace. Thus the conception of divine elect, — *yamaive-*

[1] In Japan one sect of Buddhists upholds that faith in Amita (Amida) secures salvation and transcends the effects of actions.— J. Takakusu, *The Essentials of Buddhist Philosophy* (Asia Publishing House, Bombay, 1956), pp. 174-180 ; J.B. Pratt, *The Pilgrimage of Buddhism* (New York, Macmillan Co., 1928), pp. 661-62.

shah vṛnute, is maintained. This amounts to the maintenance of pre-determination or the notion of the primacy of divine will (*voluntas*) which would choose whomsoever it pleases for final emancipation. This notion of grace is inconsistent with that doctrine which believes in the possibility of emancipation only through one's own efforts for the acquisition of moral purification and philosophical gnosis. In Mahāyana Buddhism, Christianity and Islam there is the acceptance of the notion of grace but Jainism and early Buddhism emphatically repudiate this creed (of grace).

In the interests of social structural continuity, the Upaniṣads propound the view that the son takes over the actions of the father.[1] This detracts from the otherwise serious adherence to moral determinism which is found in the Upaniṣads. The concept of moral determinism is individualistic because it isolates the person from the tribal or familistic background and seeks to explain his personality and destiny with sole reference to his *karman* and the resultant *samskāra.* But the notion that the merits and demerits of the father are shared by the son infringes upon the rigor of the individualism of the theory of moral determinism. Perhaps this notion of the inheritance of the actions of the father by the son was advocated by some teachers of the Upaniṣads to bolster the declining sacrificial system. The monistic philosophy of the times tended towards the minimization of the significance of the ritualistic liturgy. Monasticism was also in the air. The sacrificial ritualism for its continuance required the stability of the family system. For the preservation of the sacrificial cult against the joint attacks of philosophical absolutism and ethical monasticism it was essential to insist once again on the importance of the progeny. The *Brihadāraṇyaka Upaniṣad* says that the son provides relief from all difficulties.[2] The social distributivist aspects of the notion of *karman* are further emphasized in the *Kauśitaki Upaniṣad* which says that the previously committed good and evil works of a dead person are shared by his friends and enemies respectively.[3]

[1] *Brihadāraṇyaka*, I, 5, 17 and *Kaushitaki*, II, 15.

[2] *Brihadāraṇyaka Upaniṣad*, 1, 5, 17.

[3] The *Ṛgveda*, VII, 86, 5, refers to the doctrine of inherited sin (*drugdha — amghasa —* sin). According to the *ManicoraJātaka*, (*Jātaka*,

Anotner detraction from the individualism of the theory of moral determinism is the view contained in some of the Upaniṣads that the last thoughts of a man determine his future station.[1] This view is also contained in the *Bhagavadgitā* and the later theistic Bhakti literature constantly harps on the theme that in the last moments a man should keep his mind and soul attuned to a personal Godhead. In one sense, however, it may be possible to reconcile the deterministic character of the theory of *karman* and the arbitrary voluntarism of the notion that the last thoughts determine one's station after death, by holding that even the purity and nobility of last thoughts is determined by the holiness of life throughout. It is not possible to imagine that a person of deviant character would at once revolutionize his personality and begin to think of holy thoughts if that had not been the pattern of his life for a considerable period.

5. *The Buddhist Philosophy of Moral Determinism* (*Karman*)

In early Buddhism there is a three-fold specification of *karman* — (a) mental, (b) vocal and (c) physical. The *Dhammapada* (1), lays the greatest emphasis on the mind as the instrument controlling action — *manopubbamgamā dhammā manosetthā manomayā*. At the time of enlightenment under the sacred Bodhi tree Buddha had three visions. In the second vision, "he saw the whole universe as a system of *karma* and reincarnation, composed of beings noble or mean, happy or unhappy, continually passing away according to their deeds, leaving one form of existence and taking shape in another." Buddha taught the momentous vitality and significance of *karman*[2] with such vehemence and fervour that it has been said that he almost put this concept in place of the Upaniṣadic *brahman*.[3] In the

No. 194), famines, floods etc. are brought about by the faults of the king. See E.W. Hopkins, "Modifications of the Karman doctrine", *JRAS.*, 1906, pp. 581-593. (JRAS. — *Journal of Royal Asiatic Society*) In the *Santiparva*, 1,29 and the *Manusmriti*, IV, 170, also, there is mention of the *karman* of the forefathers affecting the children.

1 *Chhāndogya*, 3.14.1 ; *Praśna*, 3.10 : *Brihadāraṇyaka*, 4.4.5.

2 Charles Eliot, *Hinduism and Buddhism*, (London, Edward Arnold & Co., 1921), 3 Vols. Vol. I, p. 139.

3 C.A.F. Rhys Davids, "Man as Willer", *Buddhistic Studies* (ed. by B.C. Law Calcutta, Thacker, Spink & Co., 1931), pp. 587-611, p. 587,

period of the Upaniṣads, the two-fold operation of the law of *karman* as a physical force in the natural world and as a moral force in the realm of human personality was regarded as being almost under the superintendence of a primordial Absolute. But, according to Buddha, this law of *karman* was regarded as operating with almost autonomous deterministic finality. Gautama Buddha holds that men are the inheritors of *karman* (*kammadāyāda*), *karman* is their very own (*kammassaka*), *karman* is the cause of their rebirth (*kammayoni*) and *karman* is their refuge (*kammapaṭisarana*). He was very emphatic in upholding the commensurability between actions and their consequences, in this life and in lives beyond. In those systems of thought which maintain the persistence of the soul as a substance, this view of commensurability through continuity is legitimately sponsored. But Buddha did not accept the conception of a substantial soul monad which persists between lives. Nevertheless, he maintains the continuity of cause and effect.[1] He does not even refer to the conceptions of an astral or subtle sheath which could be the receptacle of the essence or the consequences of *karman* and which would persist till liberation is attained.[2] Nevertheless, Buddha is perhaps the greatest prophet of the sanctity of actions. At a time when cunning Brahmin priests were exploiting the superstitious credulity of the populace and in the name of pleasing gods and demons were inviting them to perform numerous rituals, ceremonies and sacrifices, Buddha taught the autonomy and potency of human efforts. Buddha's insistence on the nobility of actions gains pointed significance when analysed in the background of the radical nihilism implied in the deterministic teachings of

says that the triplet, action of mind *manokamma*), action of word and action of body is a contribution of the Buddhist and Jain scriptures. She credits Zarathustra for having taught a similar view in Persia. Cf. the term *Manasikāra*, *The Compendium of Philosophy* (of Anuruddha, E. trans. of *Abhidhammatha-Sangaha* by S.Z. Aung and edited by C.A.F. Rhys Davids, *PTS.* series, London, 1910), p. 95 n. 1.

1 Mrs. Rhys Davids, "Soul Theory in Buddhism", *JRAS.*, 1903, pp. 587-591, says that there is apparent contradiction between nihilistic *anātmanism* and the belief in *karman* which implies a persistent continuity of the individual.

2 A.K. Coomaraswamy, *Buddha and the Gospel of Buddhism*, p. 109.

Makkhali Gosāla. Ajita also had denied the notion of consequences following from action.

According to Buddhism there are two types of actions *sāśrava* and *anāśrava*. The *sāśrava* actions are those which bring about good and bad consequences. On the other hand meditation on the four noble truths which leads to Arhatship is an *anāśrava* action and it does not generate good or evil consequences. Sometimes Buddhism is said to be *samkleśa-vyavadānika-dharma* according to which there is defilement by bad desires and purification by good desires. Buddha was a moral teacher who taught the path of *nirvāṇa* which could be attained through one's own efforts towards gnosis (*prajnā*) and meditative absorption (*samādhi*). He refused to accept the mediation of any gods and any priesthood. He taught the conservation of moral merit.[1] Buddha says : "My action is my possession, my action is my inheritance, my action is the womb which bears me, my action is the race to which I am akin, my action is my refuge."[2] He inculcated the supremacy of the purification of action and motivation. Through one's own efforts alone can one attain *nirvāṇa* and hence Buddha stressed vigilance, constancy of endeavours and a rigorous struggle against one's baser propensities. He vehemently condemned all those sceptics and sophists who repudiated the significance of actions. He said : "Just as, bhikkhus, of all kinds of woven robes, a hair-garment is known to be the least desirable, cold in cold weather, hot in the heat, unpleasant to the touch, so of all the many assertions by the recluses the Makkhali theory is the most undesirable. He, foolish man, believes and

[1] The Buddhist scriptures refer to the punishment of evil-doers in hell by Yama. The "*Devadatta Sutta*" of the *Aṅguttara Nikāya* (Vol. II, pp. 77-78 of the Nālandā ed.) says : "He is riveted to glowing iron, plunged in glowing seas of blood or tortured on mountains of burning coal, and he dies not until the very last residue of his guilt has been expiated." — H. Oldenberg, *Buddha*, p. 245 and M. Monier-Williams, "*Buddhism*", (London, John Murray, Albemarle Street, 1889), p. 114ff. The reference to Yama is specially predominant in northern Buddhism. — *Encyclopaedia of Religion & Ethics*. Vol. V, p. 375, (article "Eschatology").

[2] According to Hopkins, "Modifications of Karman Doctrine, *JRAS*. 1906, p. 583, the notion of *karman* "struck hard against the old belief in acrifice, penance and repentance as destroyer of sin."

declares there is no effective action (going on), no effected action (the result of effective action), no indwelling energy. Herein he rejects what all past Buddhas have declared, all future Buddha will declare, and which I now, the Buddha, declare. I, even I, declare that there is effective action, resultant action, indwelling energy."[1]

Buddha holds that the law of *karman* has a ubiquitous operation.[2] According to the *Vāsettha Sutta* of the *Majjhima Nikāya* (No. 98), the world is being impelled by *karman* and living beings are bound by their actions like the wheels of a chariot. According to the *Aṅgulimāla Sutta* of the *Majjhima Nikāya*, one has to live in hell for several hundreds and even several thousands of years for the sake of reaping the consequences of actions. In place of animistic superstitions and absolutist speculations Buddha put forward an explanation of human life and destiny in terms of *pratityasamutpāda* which is a representations of the working of the law of *karman* at the psychological and moral planes.[3] The predominance attached

[1] The *Aṅguttara Nikāya*, 1.1.286. It contains a sharp warning to the Ājīvikas.

[2] According to the *Milinda Panho*, only that death which occurs due to the working of *karman* is death in due season. But there may also be cases of death out of season :

"By hunger, thirst, by poison and by bites
Burnt, drowned, slain, men out of time do die;
By the three humours, and by three combined,
By heats, by inequalities, by aids
By all these seven men die out of time".

—*The Questions of King Milinda*,
(Pt. II, E.T. by T.W. Rhys Davids.
SBE. series, Vol. 36, 1894), p. 164.

There are some men who die through the working of some evil deed or other they have committed in a former birth. There are four causes of death according to Buddhism : (i) exhaustion of the force of reproduction (*janaka karma*), (ii) expiration of the life-term *āyukshaya*), (iii) combination of numbers one and two and (iv) action of a stronger arresting *karman* (*upacchedaka*) that suddenly cuts off the *janak karma* before the expiry of the life-term *āyukshaya*). — Narada, "Samsāra or Buddhist Philosophy of Birth and Death", *Indian Historical Quarterly*, Vol. III, 1927, pp. 561-70.

[3] A.B. Govinda, *The Psychological Attitude of Early Buddhist Philosophy* (Patna University Readership Lectures, 1936-37), pp. 80-81.

to the concept of *pratityasamutpāda* indicates that in Buddhism it enjoys almost a religious sanctity and is not a more psychological hypothesis for explaining human action.[1] Evil actions can catch hold of a man even in the sky, in the seas and in the recesses of mountains.[2] According to the *Aṅguttara Nikāya* there are two kind of actions — (i) Actions performed under the influence of *rāga*, *dvesha* and *moha* produce bondage. (ii) Actions performed without influence of *rāga*, *dvesha* and *moha* lead to emancipation. *Ahimsā*, *asteya* and *abhoga* are the constituents of *samyak karmānta* which is the fourth element in the *ārya ashṭāṅgika mārga*. Hence nobility of actions was to be the primary goal of a religious aspirant. Mere external ceremonialism and formal monasticism were regarded as being of no avail unless both the inner motives and external acts were purified. Buddha was a great teacher of moral idealism and he preached the enormous sanctity of the law of righteousness.[3]

[1] Cf. Edmund Holmes, *The Creed of Buddha* (London, John Lane. The Bodley Head, 1908), pp. 32-33 : "But, whereas in the West the conception of natural law has in the main been applied to the outward and visible world, in the East, where the outward and visible world owes such reality as it possesses to its own inward and spiritual life, the conception of law has not merely been applied to the inward and spiritual life, but has been more intimately associated with it than with any other aspect of Nature. In the Universe, as the popular thought of the West conceives of it, there are two worlds, — the natural, which is under the dominion of law, and the supernatural, which is under the sway of an arbitrary and irresponsible despot, who can also suspend or modify at will the laws of the natural world. But Eastern thought, in conceiving of the inward life as the real self of Nature, conceived of it also as the ultimate and eternal source of all natural law."

[2] According to the *Atthasālinī*, P.V. Bapat & R.D. Vedekar, eds., Poona, Bhandarkar Oriental Research Institute, 1942, p. 73, there are four kinds of *karma*. (i) Bad—producing impurity ; (ii) Good—producing purity : (iii) Partly Bad and partly Good—Producing both impurity and purity and (iv) Neither Bad nor Good — producing neither impurity nor purity but contributing to the destruction of *karman*. Sometimes the Buddhist writings make a three-fold distinction between *kuśala* (*puṇya*), *akuśala* (*apuṇya*) and *avyākrita* actions. See Poussin "Karma", *Encyclopaedia of Religion and Ethics*, Vol. VIII, pp. 673-77.

[3] S.K. Maitra, *Ethics of the Hindus* (Calcutta University Press, 1956), 2nd edition, p. 86. "...for the Bauddha there is no merit in *karma* or duty in an objective sense (as in the Mimānsā) and that it assumes a moral significance only as subjectively willed and accomplished and thus

He taught the efficacy of moral will.[1] At a time when the contemporary religious structure was subjected to the devastating onslaughts of scepticism regarding the metaphysical principle, and relativism regarding moral values, he preached the significance of holy life.[2] The *Samyutta Nikāya*, (I, 227), says :

> "According to the seed that's sown
> So is the fruit ye reap therefrom.
> Doer of good will gather good
> Doer of evil evil reaps
> Sown is the seed and thou shalt taste
> The fruit thereof."

The *Majjhima Nikāya* (I, 129) declares : "Our mind shall not waver. No evil speech will we utter. Tender and compassionate will we abide, loving in heart, void of malice within...and with that feeling (love) as a basis we will ever be suffusing the whole world with thoughts of love, far-reaching, grown great, beyond measure, void of anger and ill-will." Buddha taught ethical purity and perfection[3] and said that in heaven the man who

as modifying the subjective disposition of the agent. Hence according to him their is no inherent moral worth in *karma*, but only in its conduciveness to the purification of the mind. Thus the Shastric *karmas* have no inherent worth or excellence, their moral value being conditional only on their conduciveness to spiritual perfection."

[1] According to the *Aṅguttara Nikāya*, III, 415, "It is volition, O monks, that I call *karma*". This view of Buddha was misunderstood by Parivrājaka Potaliputta who took it to mean that according to him (Buddha) *manokamma* is true act and neither that which is vocal nor that which is bodily.— *Majjhima Nikāya*, III, 207. Vasuvandhu in the *Abhidharmakosha*, IV, 1, enormously stresses that in the Buddhist view *karman* is nothing but *cetanā*. *Abhidharmakosha*, IV. 1. C.A.F. Rhys Davids, *Buddhist Psychology*, *op. cit.*, p. 93 ; Th. Stcherbatsky, *Central Conception of Buddhism*, *op. cit.*, p. 19.

[2] The later Buddhist idealists like Śāntarakshita and Kamalaśila, however, who adhered to the theory of momentariness refuted the theory of action.— S.N. Dasgupta, *Indian Idealism*, *op. cit.*, p. 147.

[3] A.B. Keith, "The Buddha as a Master Mind", *Indian Culture*, Vol. V, pp. 229-238, is sadly mistaken in his *obiter dictum* that there is no proof in the Buddhist texts that Buddha held a view of the universe in which the moral law stood highest. Buddha might not have formulated the notion of a cosmic norm but there is no doubt that in individual lives he maintained the primacy of moral causation and moral retribution.

had acquired moral merit would be happily received as the kinsmen receive their relations who return after a long foreign sojourn.

The belief in the supremacy of *karman* as held by Buddha implies some kind of a non-mechanical and purposive universe. In a purely mechanistic conception there is no place for the belief that one's intention and will also receive their commensurate reward. Hence if there is no sanction in early Buddhist scriptures for the notion of an immanent spiritual teleology, it may also be safely held that neither could they sponsor a a conception of the universe as an unconnected chain of random facts and a conglomeration of disparate meaningless elements. Buddha firmly adhered to the law of causation. He said : "This, ye monks, is not your body, nor that of others. You have rather to see in it, ye monks, the old deeds (*kammam*), the result of actions, volitions and feelings (in former existences)."[1] In explaining the genesis of sorrow he subscribed to the notion of transitive causation. It is true that he did not advocate the concept of the soul as a substance but there can be no denial of the fact that he thoroughly adhered to the view that the human being could assert his superiority to the numerous oppositions of physically and psychologically deviant forces and thus vindicate his strength of purpose. The *Nikāyas* and the *Jātakas* contain the stories of sinners who wrought tremendous moral reformation in their lives. The personality of Buddha himself was a monumental example of the fact that in face of the firmness of a strong will, all obstacles vanish. He conquered the numerous allurements and temptations put forward by Māra and thus vindicated the superiority of the moral will.

The early Buddhist scriptures also stress the concept of *upādāna* as a propulsive force for *karman*.[2] The will to be, is the real cause of the terrestrial existence of a man. Explaining

His significance lies in having replaced the theonomic moral standard by the autonomic. As a moral autonomist, he reached higher standards that the aesthetic intuitionists.

[1] *The Samyutta Nikāya*, XII, 37.

[2] The Buddhist *upādāna* has some resemblance to Pareto's concept of "residues" or basic constellations of sentiments, and to the "interests" of Ratzenhofer-Small theory.

the Buddhist view about the body, Oldenberg says : "......[it is] the action of his past state, which then assuming a form realised through his endeavour, has become endowed with a tangible existence." The conjunction of *upādāna* and *karman* would show that early Buddhism adhered to the organic view of the universe.[1] The elimination of *upādāna*[2] is essential for the attainment of *nirvāṇa*. The older generation of Pali scholars was mistaken in maintaining that the exhaustion of *karman* would produce *nirvāṇa*. It may be pointed out that this is interpreting early Buddhism on the lines of Jainism.[3] According to the Jains, bondage is regarded as being produced due to the influx of subtle material *karman* - particles into the soul and consequently the *samvara* (arrest or stoppage) and *nirjara* (exhaustion or wearing out) of *karma* are viewed as leading to the liberation of the soul. But, according to Buddhism, not the mere stoppage of physical action but the neutralization of the psychological clinging to action is essential for *nirvāṇa*. Although Buddha is a great ethical teacher and inculcates the supremacy of moral living and righteous endeavours it will be incorrect to interpret him as the promulgator only of the sanctity of actions. Beyond actions he teaches the supremacy of knowledge. Although *karman* has a vital importance in

1 The relation of *upādāna* and *karman* has been analysed in the *Tathatā* philosophy of Aśvaghosha — S.N. Dasgupta, *Indian Philosophy*, I, p. 133.

2 According to the later Buddhist scholastics, the loss of *upādana* along with that of (a) *karma*, (b) *dṛshti*, (c) *śilavrata* and (d) *ātmavāda* follows from the loss of egoistic feelings.

3 James B. Pratt, *The Pilgrimage of Buddhism* (New York, The Macmillan Co., 1928), p. 73 : "It is *Tanhā*, craving, that keeps one on the weary wheel of rebirth and brings one back after the death of the body to birth in a new one. That one's *karma* was the cause of rebirth was a Brahmin and Jaina concept : hence the ideal of worklessness as a means of salvation, referred to so repeatedly in the *Bhagavad-Gitā*, and the attempt of the Jainas to extinguish acquired *karma through ascetic* practices and avoid the acquisition of new *karma*. Against these conceptions the Buddha set up his new psychological theory (if so we may style it) that rebirth was due not to *karma* but to craving ; and that by rooting out evil desire and the will to live one could escape from rebirth, regardless of the *karma* one had brought with one to this life. This, of course, was a much more hopeful and moral doctrine, and one for which a certain amount of empirical evidence based on analogy could be produced."

Buddhistic ethics and metaphysics, still the supreme way to enlightenment it not merely moral action but the knowledge of the four Aryan truths. Hence it will be incorrect to interpret Buddha as a mere practical moralist. Since he propounded a concept of emancipation based on knowledge he may be said to have attained the gnomic stage of moral reflection. Both the Upaniṣads and Buddhism stress knowledge for the attainment of the highest goal of a man. By knowledge or *vidyā* the Upaniṣads mean intuitive suprarational apprehension of the Absolute and not any analytical or dialectical learning. But knowledge according to the Buddhist, signifies the realization of the four Aryan truths. The last of the four truths is the *ārya ashtāṅgika mārga* and the last item in the *mārga* is *samādhi.*

6. *Sociological Implications of Moral Determinism*

Sometimes it is said that the Buddhist philosophy with its negativistic conceptions of *dukkha* and *nirvāṇa* is antithetical to any positive approach to life and politics. It is difficult to deny this charge completely. It is true that during the ages that Buddhism was culturally ascendant in India, great progress had been made in the secularistic departments of life. But it does not mean that the great examples of art, architecture, political administration and social organization of that epoch owe their construction to the Buddhist monks who were making endeavours for the attainment of *nirvāṇa* or who were experiencing the bliss of *samādhi*. England and U.S.A. are Christian countries but that does not mean that the achievements in the mundane domain in these countries are due to the efforts of Christian monks and theological preachers. The main problem is : Is the adherence to the Buddhistic ethical and spiritual code repugnant to a rigorous pursuit of political and social objectives ? It, certainly, is antithetical. The Buddhist 'way' is definitely and dominantly individualistic. On the other hand, the pursuit of social and political objectives is possible only through group cooperation, organization, diplomatic manipulation and compromise. Politics is a game of give and take and of expediency. This attitude, highly commendable in the mundane sphere, is not consistant with the austere character of the ethical norm. It is true that several prophets and teachers in the world have attempted to combine the technics of religious liberation with the conquest of social and political power. But the consequence has been that either they have failed in their endeavours or political considerations have engulfed the religious. The organization of political life assumes a positive, directed, instrumental and insistent approach to the world. This positivism may entail choices and decisions wherein the strict rigorous and ascetic ideals and norms may have to be sacrificed. Hence although the ethical and the religious man may excel in the acquisition of inner illumination, he may appear to be unsuccessful from purely social and secular considerations. The worldly attitude believes in the quantitative computation of goods. It adheres to the determinism of the cash nexus and allocation of power, status and respect for oneself. Thus there may be chances of radical antithesis between the conduct of the man who works for the sake of the emancipation of the soul and that of the man who is busy collecting the so-called 'good' things of the world through even unfair means. The truly ethical and religious man may even choose to enter the path of martyrdom for the sake of his convictions. But such a course will be thoroughly unmeaningful for the person engrossed in the world. Hence there can be no denial of the proposition that the path leading to *sambodhi* (illumination) and *prajnā* (gnosis) may be radically different from and sometimes even thoroughly opposed to the way of the mercantile magnet, the politician and the warrior. Religion and ethics are not worth the name unless they teach the subordination of self-interest and the egoistic considerations of the individual. But can a competitive society exist without the motivational commitments derived from a calculation of personal considerations of self-interest?

So far as Buddha himself is considered, it is true that if on the one hand he taught the resort to *appamāda* (non-sloth) and *viriya* (strenuous efforts) to realize one's supreme goal of life — *nibbāna,* he was also consulted sometimes on political questions and he tendered his advice. It appears thus that although he had renounced the world he was not absolutely indifferent to the appeal of peace and welfare of the people.

The advocacy of moral determinism had two significant political and sociological consequences. First, it provided a support for conservatism. All persons were supposed to belong to the station to which they were apportioned as a consequence of their past actions. The law of *karman* is fitted to the demands and *mores* of an agrarian[1] society. It suits the behaviour-patterns and need-dispositions of an agrarian dogma-ridden fatalistic people. Perhaps such a dogma was essential to buttress the foundations of *cāturvarṇya.* The example of Turkey substantiates this sociological generalization. In pre-Kemalist Turkey, the inhabitants believed in *kismet* but after the great transformation wrought by Kemal Pasha the same people began to believe in self-efforts. In ancient India, a rationale and justification was provided by *karman* theory for the incongruities and contradictions of social and political life. If certain sections enjoyed esteem, power or influence they were regarded as doing so because of the merit earned by them in previous lives. Thus the disparities of present social and political life were explained in terms of the antecendent past.[2] A philosophy of resistance against social oligarchy and political despotism could not arise in such an intellectual framework. A theoretical defence of disobedience to social and political superiors can be built only when the irrationalities of contemporary life are explained in terms of actions and behavior which can be put a stop to here and now. But the resort to the methodological device of unknown past actions to explain the present contradictions, minimizes and even virtually neutralizes the efficacy of any social theory which seeks to buttress individual efforts towards ending the regime of callous and irresponsible social and political autocrats.

But although I accept the conservative implications of the theory of *karman*, I think that the view of Marxian interpreters that the notions of *karman* and *punarjanma* were deliberately formulated by the exponents of the interests of the dominant

[1] Hegel, in *Philosophy of Right* (English trans. G.T.M. Knox, Oxford, The Clarendon Press, 1949), pp. 130-131 and 270, points out that the agrarian population has to depend on accidental rains and hence it is prone to an unreflective mode of life thanking God and living in faith and confidence that divine goodness will continue.

[2] D.T. Suzuki, *Outlines af Mahayana Buddhism*, *op. cit.*, pp. 186 ff. does not seem to be correct in his view that since the law of *karman* operates in the moral sphere only, hence cases of economic inequality and social injustice must not be explained by evil *karman*.

classes to "mystify" the suppressed strata is uncharitable. When there are alterative hypotheses to explain the emergence of the concept of *karman*, why should mean and sordid motives be attributed to some supposed ideologists who framed this notion to justify the *status quo* by means of this "superstructure" ? If the concepts of *karman* and *punarjanma* had the function of serving as ideological devices to hoodwink the exploited sections, there can be no reason whatsoveer as to why Buddha, whom the Marxists regard, to a certain extent as the heralder, of a social revolution against the exploitationist technics of the sacerdotal sections, should have preached this doctrine.

Secondly, the theory of moral determinism encouraged individualism. It sanctioned a course of noble conduct which, if assiduously followed, would ensure better station in the succeeding lives. By emphasizing a just apportionment of rewards in the present and in the succeeding lives the philosophy of moral determinism encouraged the pursuit of a course of action for the betterment of one's fate. If *karman* is interpreted in this sense of individual responsibility, then it can be the foundation of the doctrine of a sturdy individualism. It will strengthen the nerve to succeed in the struggle for existence. It makes the individual responsible for his fate and in this sense could be made to inspire a person like Herbert Spencer. But in ancient Indian thought, *karma* was mainly interpreted in a moral and religious direction although in modern India it has also been used by Tilak and Gandhi to support social idealism. The view that one's lot can be immensely bettered through one's own efforts is one of the cardinal implications of the theory of *karman*.[1] Both the *Dhammapada* and the *Bhagavadgitā* contain emphatic statements eulogizing one's individual efforts.[2] Thereby the gospel of spontaneity and self-determination is heralded. The stress on individual efforts was a great blow to the traditional system which inculcated social deference in

[1] Although the main emphasis of *karman* is on efforts, still only the efforts towards fostering social cooperation are lauded. But in the *Bhagavadgitā*, armed struggle also is praised as a part of the vocation of a particular *varṇa*.

[2] A charismatic conception of leadership is found in the view that through efforts made in several lives, was the Buddha able to attain "Buddhahood".

accordance with birth. Buddha declared that it is through *karman* that one becomes a Brahmin or a non-Brahmin.[1] This was a revolutionary statement and its implications for social democracy were drawn up later by the exponents of the *bhakti* movement like Nānak, Kabir and Chaitanya. In place of the superiority of birth, Buddha exalted the nobility of actions and thus he dealt a mighty counterblast to the speculations of the *purusha sūkta* which had sought to glamourize the four-fold division of society by providing it a divine origin. Therefore, the stress on personal efforts by Buddha was aimed not only against the notion of divine predetermination and election for the purpose of salvation but it stressed also that social esteem and prestige should go not to birth but to efforts meant to enhance one's moral personality.

Thus it is possible to draw a support both for conservatism and individualism from the concept of *karman*. It depends on which particular side of its teaching is taken into consideration. If its retrospective, retributive and deterministic aspects are stressed, it becomes a support for conservatism and strengthens the leaning to interpret one's present status in terms of previous actions. But if it is used to support strong energetic efforts in the present then its individualistic implications are stressed.

7. Conclusion

Buddha repudiated the conception of the spiritual self as a substance but he accepted the supremacy of the law of *karma*. This law of *karma* had been accepted since the Vedic times. The prevalence of the ritualistic cult strengthened the belief in the law of *karma* because the different sacrificial mechanisms and processes were supposed to operate with almost a deterministic certainty so far as the production of the intended result was concerned. It has been sponsored by some sociologists that the concept of causality is only a sophisticated version of the old primitive belief in the prevalence of the notion of retribution. The theory of *karma* served several purposes from philosophical and sociological standpoints. It inculcated the view of a purposive universe because it promised good results to the suit and evii to the wicked and the sinner. To impart a popular appeal

[1] *Vāsettha Sutta, Majjhima Nikāya.*

to the conception of the correlation and commensurability of means and ends which is implied in the law of *karma*, both the Upaniṣads and Buddhism accepted the existence of heaven for the virtuous and hell for the sinner. The operative pattern of the law of *karma* moving almost with an inexorable and inevitable power strengthens the belief in the religious view of the world to the extent that it is an aspect of the working of a divine providential justice. But although Buddhism dispensed with the conception of a theistic Godhead, nevertheless, it accepted the law of *karma* and this elemental and powerful law vindicates the religious view of the victory of the just and punishment to the wicked. Thus the law of *karma* operating as a universal, magniloquent, imperative world-order serves as a factor for the ethicization of human motivation. To be just, the action should not merely be a good action but the impulsion to it must also be an unconstrained disposition to effectuate the good for its own sake. In this way like the Upaniṣads, Plato and Kant, Buddha also has taught the purification of intentions and feelings and the spontaneous outflow of the noble determination — *samyak samkalpa*.

From the sociological standpoint, this cosmic force of operative necessity symbolized by the concept of *karma* serves to rationalize the existing social and political structure in terms of the operation of the actions of past lives. From the very nature of the case, the accumulated potency and efficacy of the deeds of past lives and the dynamics of their operative behaviour are not available for rational analysis and inspection and thus we find that the belief in the law of *karma* serves to incorporate a non-rational factor for social explanation. The existing structure of the society is sought to be justified not in terms of the impact of social, political and economic forces but in terms of individual action. While the concept of social forces is more impersonal and mechanical, the stress on individual action introduces a more introspective, organic and subjective element. Hence the approach to social and political history in the system accepting the law of *karma*, is radically different from the one accepted in a more mechanistic and materialistic scheme. When we stress social forces we do not mean to exclude the role of the individual participants in action, but we do not stress the dispositional orientation of the subjective role-takers. But in offering an analysis of history in terms of psychic motivation we necessarily stress the pragmatic dialectics of the subjective approach. From the standpoint of prediction and control also, the subjective forces, although amenable to the discipline inculcated by the Yogic system, are not capable of being controlled on a large social scale. A rational theory of social control tends to calculate and evaluate the results of action in terms of the actual realization of the proximate physical and financial goals of collective efforts. On the other hand, the theory of *karma* seeks to interpret even the institutionalized forces of authority and control in terms of the highly variable and non-experimental category of psychic dispositions generated on an existential scale by the interaction of the present balance of individual bio-mental structure and the dominant force of the unseen actions of the past lives. This type of explanation is immensely suited for a small-scale rural economy where it is possible to discuss the metaphysics of permanent spiritual ends. But from the sociological standpoint the law of *karma* seems unsatisfying in trying to explain the immensely mobile and dynamic structure of a large-scale competitive and industrial economy of the great society. To explain the enormous shifts in the residence of social, economic and political power in terms of the operation of the law of *karma,* whose main centre is the individual human person, does not appear adequate to the modern mind. But although the sociological implications of the law of *karma* may appear inadequate to the scientific mind, from the moral standpoint of vindicating the law of justice this law has philosophical and ethical significance.

CHAPTER 11

THE CONCEPT OF NIRVĀNA

1. *Conceptual Analysis of Nirvāṇa*

Nirvāṇa is regarded as the highest goal of the endeavours of a Buddhist aspirant. Hence it may be regarded as the central theme in Buddhist religion and philosophy.[1] In the words of the *Milinda Panha, nirvāṇa* is "profound like an ocean, lofty like a mountain peak, sweet like honey". Buddha claimed to have attained this climax of moral and mystical endeavours under the sacred Bodhi tree. In later philosophical works a great controversy raged about the nature of *nirvāṇa*.[2] Sometimes it is regarded as a positive fulfilment and sometimes as a negative extinction.[3]

From the etymological standpoint, *nirvāṇa* has three meanings.[4] The first is a naturalistic interpretation. It means cooling. Metaphorically, it can be used to indicate the cooling of the cravings and passions which produce disturbance,

[1] Suzuki, *Outlines of Mahayana Buddhism*, p, 331, holds a radically different view. C.A.F. Rhys Davids, *Buddhism*, p. 232 : "*Nibbāna* is likened by Nāgasena to a wonderful city of the Norm — *dhammanagara* — built for mankind by the Buddha as architect, lit up by the Norm, with moral conduct for its ramparts, prudence for its moat, knowledge for its gate battlements, energy for its watch-tower, and bazars where men come to exchange their *karma* for the intellectual and spiritual requisites of the *Arahant*."

[2] The *Nirvāṇa Sūtra* of the Mahāyāna School upon which Vasubandhu wrote comments. Also the *Nirvāṇa Upanishad*.

[3] J. Dahlmann, *Nirvana* (Berlin, 1897). Poussin, *The Way To Nirvana.* P.E. Foucaux, *Doctrine des Bouddhistes sur le Nirvāṇa*, Paris, 1864.

[4] Oldenberg holds that the idea of *nirvāṇa* originates from the idea of of *brahman*. But Poussin controverts it and says that there is no mention of the word *brahman* in the Tripiṭaka literature. The word *ātman* is also not used in a universal sense but always in an individual sense.

agitation and heat.[1] The second meaning of *nirvāṇa* is also naturalistic in its origin. It means the stillness produced by the absence of wind — *nirvāṇo avāte*. This is the sense attributed to this word by Paṇini. It is difficult to state categorically that the word *nirvāṇa* is pre-Buddhistic.[2] Even if it were pre-Buddhistic, Buddha gives to it an extended interpretation. There are passages in the Buddhistic literature which indicate that a third meaning of *nirvāṇa* as extinction is also present there.[3] In this context *nirvāṇa* means the extinction of pain and suffering.[4] It is also interpreted to mean the extinction of the psycho-physical complex — *nāmarūpa-skamdha* which is regarded as responsible for pain and sorrow.[5]

There are four possible interpretations of the concept of *nirvāṇa* and for each one of them some support can be obtained

1 The *Aggi-Vahchhagotta Sutta* of the *Majjhima Nikāya* says that as fire is extinguished (*nirvṛta*—attained *nirvāṇa*) due to the exhaustion, *paryādana*) of fuels and non-acquisition (*anupahāra*) of other fuels and it cannot be pointed as to which direction the fire went so also the Tathāgata free from *rūpa, vedanā, samjnā, samskāra* and *vijnāna* cannot be described in terms of predicative categories.

2 A.B. Keith, *The Sāmkhya System*, pp. 124-25, seems to be absolutely mistaken in holding that there is frequent occurrence of the word *nirvāṇa* in the epic literature and hence it was borrowed by Buddhists from Brahmanical speculation.

3 *Dīgha Nikāya*, II, 15ff. *Sutta Nipāta*, 235, :

> "As the extinction of a flame
> Even so was his mind's release."

In the *Mahābhāratam*, XII, 543, also, the simile of the fire that is extinguished after the fuel is consumed is used. Thus *nirvāṇa* signifies the extinction of lust, hatred and infatuation, false beliefs, passions and torments.

4 *Samyutta Nikāya*, I, :

> "My sense with passion burns, my mind's flame
> O well did Gotama Compassionate
> Speak of a putting out *nibbāpaṇa*."
>
> (Quoted in C.A.F. Rhys Davids, *Buddhism*, p. 175)

5 Poussin holds that the Pali texts represent *nirvāṇa* in different ways either as a happy state, as pure annihilation, as an inconceivable existence or a changeless state. Dasgupta, *Indian Philosophy*, I, p. 108.

from the vast body of Buddhistic literature.[1] (1) At the primary level, *nirvāṇa* means the extinction of pain and sorrow. (ii) At a more philosophical level, *nirvāṇa* means the extinction of the empirical phenomena. (iii) A third implication of *nirvāṇa* sanctioned in some parts of the Buddhistic literature is absolute extinction or total nihil. (iv) A fourth possible significance of *nirvāṇa* is the implication of the being of an absolute real. This interpretation is sanctioned in the *tathatā* philosophy of Aśvaghosa.[2] There *nirvāṇa* is identified with the real being of an Absolute. A few passages of the Tripiṭaka literature may possibly sanction this fourth interpretation.

Early Buddhism stresses constant efforts and endeavours — *appamāda* and *viriya.*[3] It teaches the immediate conquest of pain and sorrow.[4] It prescribes a rigid scheme of psychological and moral discipline for the end of suffering. Through progressive advance in this path the state of *arhat* is attained.[5] The attainment of the the state of the *arhat* is the same as the culminating realisation of the state of *nirvāṇa*. But there are suggestions in the Buddhist literature that the state of the *Tathāgata* is superior to the state of the *arhat.*[6] Perhaps this is to indicate the immensely superior, almost super-eminent position

[1] According to the *Ratan Sutta* there is a distinction between arhatship and *nirvāṇa.* C.A.F. Rhys Davids, *Buddhism,* p. 171, says that the ideal of arhatship may or may not, possibly have been formulated to interpret two factors : (i) Nature sacrifices quantity, for quality (ii) A genius dies out and does not reproduce, B.C. Law, "Eschatological Aspect of Nirvana," *The Cultural Heritage of India,* Vol. I.

[2] The *Brahmajāla Sutta* of the *Dīgha Nikāya* contains the term *drishtidharmanirvāṇavādi* which signifies not the end of existence but the highest goal. The accounts appear to B.M. Barua, to favor some kind of sensualism or positive hedonism. The entire picture is rather confused. But Barua is wrong because only the first point of the text refers to worldly pleasures, the four other points refer to contemplation and meditation.

[3] S.N. Dasgupta, *Indian Idealism*, pp. 87, ff.

[4] In the *Milinda Panho*, IV, 7, 13, Nāgasena definitely asserts that Buddha denied the origin of *nirvāṇa* although he pointed out several ways for its realization.

[5] The perfect *arhat* is called *nisklesha*, Monier-Williams, *Buddhism*, p. 124 says that in Buddhism the words *kleśa* (pain) and *akuśala* (demerit) take the place of sin.

[6] M. Govinda Pai, "Jain References in *Dhammapada*", *Indian Historical Quarterly*, 1927.

of the founder of the religion. In the *Ṛgveda*. [II, 3, 1 ; II, 3, 3 ; II, 33, 10] the word *arhan* is used. Perhaps the word *arhat* is related to the *argha*, a value. The Avestan form of the verbal root √*Arh* is *Arej*.

We have stated earlier that the primary meaning of *nirvāṇa* is the extinction of pain and sorrow.[1] It does not mean, however, the negation of all feelings and emotions. Buddha's heart is regarded as surging with deep compassionate love.[2] From very early times, he has been regarded as the embodiment of compassion.[3] Once it is said that two kshatriya clans were about to engage in a deadly combat for the possession of the waters of a certain river Rohini. Buddha placed himself in the middle of the raging militant crowds and thus prevented a violent holocaust. This instance would show that the attainment of *nirvāṇa* is consonant with noble emotions and with action for the good of the community. This aspect of compassion (*karuṇā*) was emphasized in Mahāyānism. There *nirvāṇa* signifies the annihilation of the notion of ego substantiality. It is produced by the actualization of the *bodhicitta*. Universal love is the concomitant of *nirvāṇa*. Hence *nirvāṇa* cannot be identified with the annihilation of mentation.

Nirvāna is attained in this life. Sometimes a distinction is made between *nirvāṇa* and *parinirvāṇa*.[4] *Nirvāṇa* means the

[1] C.A.F. Rhys Davids, "Basis and Ideal in Buddhism", *Kane Commemoration Volume*, makes an attempt to describe the historical transition in the ideals of life in Buddhistic days. The older phrase "becoming *brahman*" was no longer used, the formula of the *parinirvāṇa* of the *arhat* had not yet been reached, and the other formulas expressing the consummation of the *arhat* on earth were not yet present, the only phrase that was used was *dukhasyāntam*. But C.A.F. Rhys Davids seems to be guilty of fantastic imagination when she says that the ideal of *nirvāṇa* was not present in the original formula because in the early suttas it is not regarded as the *summum bonum* but is equated with *nirodha*.

[2] *Majjhima Nikāya*, (*Maluṅkyaputta Sutta*).

[3] Suzuki, *Outlines of Mahayana Buddhism*, pp. 50-52 says : "*Nirvāṇa* is the subjective and *Dharmakāya* is the objective phase of one and the same principle."

[4] It may be possible to identify *nirvāṇa* with *jivanmukti* and *parinirvāna* with *videhamukti* of the later Vedanta. The *Itivuttaka*, *op.cit.*, 44, makes a similar distinction between *upadhiśesha* and *anupadhiśesha nirvāṇa* (*upadhi* = support or substratum of pain. The term *sabbupadhipaparikkhayo* is applied to an *arhat*.

withering away of pain and sorrow. *Parinirvāṇa* means the state of the *arhat*,[1] after the disintegration of the physical body elements of the *arhat*.[2]

2. *Nirvāṇa as the Extinction of Pain*

(a) *Implication of the Extinction of Pain*

Nirvāṇa has two significant consequences. It implies the elimination and termination of pain and sorrow.[3] This neutralization of sorrow and egoistic indulgences and gratifications is engineered by the deep insight which the person obtains into the concatenation of the forces which produce pain.[4] *Nirvaṇa* means the end of all agonies.[5] One who has attained it is immune against all dualities and is not contaminated by the perversities of the ego.[6] He attains equanimity and peace.[7] The attainment of balance, poise and an unruffied state of the mind

[1] The sect of Sammitiyas upheld the heretical view that an *arhat* in possession of *nirvāṇa* can fall away. Poussin, "Sammitiyas", *ERE.*

[2] There is, however, no rigid separation between *nirvāṇa* and *parinirvāṇa*. *Sutta Nipata*, 358. In the *Cullavagga*, VI, 414, Buddha describes himself as *brahmano parinirvṛtah.* The *Majjhima Nikāya* at one place refers to a horse as *parinirvṛta.*

[3] Oldenberg, *Buddha*, p. 263 : "Difficult will it be for men to grasp the law of causality, the chain of causes and effects. And this also will be very hard for them to grasp, the coming of all conformations to an end, the loosening from everything earthly, the extinction of desire, the cessation of longing, the end, the *Nirvāna*." — (*Brahmayācanakathā*, *Mahāvagga*, p. 7 in Nālandā ed.).

[4] The *Milinda Panho* describes the technics through which *nirvāṇa* is attained. "*Nibbana* is to be realized, not by quiescent meditation only, nor in hypnotic trance, much less by mortification of desire, but by rational discontent, strong anguish, longing, followed by forward leap of the mind into peace and calm, then again by a vibrating zeal, in which the aspirant strives with might and main along the path." Quoted in C.A.F. Rhys Davids, *Buddhism*, p. 223.

[5] *Samyutta Nikāya*, IV, 251 : Sāriputta says to Jambukhādaka that *nirvāṇa* is the extinction of hatred, lust and ignorance.

[6] The *Aṅguttara Nikāya*, III, 55 raises the question of *sāmdrishtika nirvāṇa.* Buddha says that this is effected by the destruction of lust, hatred and stupidity and is *akālikam ehipassikam opaneyyikam paccattam veditabbam vinnūhi* — Vol. I, p, 46, Nālandā ed.

[7] In the Vijñanavādi school of later Buddhism, *nirvāṇa* is said to be the destruction of all root desires (*vāsana*). The *Lankāvatāra* says : "*vikalpasya manovijñanasya vyāvṛtih nirvāṇamityuchyate*".

is a positive gain.[1] In the statues of Buddha which have come down to us we find that a deep calm and peace pervade his face. In the representations of Buddha in the Gāndhara, Mathurā and Pātaliputra schools of art we find that a profound austere calm and stupendous sense of conquest of all feelings of agitation of the mind impart a supreme lustre to his face. This implies that in the succeeding six to seven centuries after the demise of Buddha the sculptors of the country conceived of his personality as a typification of calm, silence, austerity, self-conquest and supersensuous peace. In the rock-cut reclining figure of the dying Buddha in Polonnāruva, Ceylon, he is represented as being absolutely unperturbed in the face of imminent death. This artistic representation is in complete consonance with the character and personality of Buddha portrayed in the *Mahāparinibbāna Sutta* of the *Digha Nikāya.* Buddha's personality was a monument of complete integration. There was no trace of disquiet, disgust or mental contradiction in it. The *Aṅguttara Nikāya*, (II, 24) thus represents the personality of Buddha :

He hath discerned all this life o' the world,
In all the world the how and thus of things,
From all detached and leaning upon naught :
Who all hath mastered, from all bonds is loosed :
Touched is for him high peace and the blest calm,
Where no fear cometh more.

(Quoted in C.A.F. Rhys Davids, *Buddhism*, p. 225)

He represented peace, calm, dignity, repose, and conquest of passions.[2] Thus from the psychological standpoint *nirvāṇa*

[1] In the *Majjhima Nikāya*, I, 509, and *Sutta Nipāta*, 749, nirvāṇa is said to be productive of health and happiness. The *Srāmaṇyaphala Sutta* outlines the benefits of *nirvāṇa*.

[2] According to the *Cula-Gopālaka Sutta* of the *Majjhima Nikāya*, *nirvāṇa* is consequent upon the attainment of the status of *aupapātika deva* which is realized through the cessation of five *avara-bhāgiya-samyojana*. The *Abhidhammathasamgaha* states that *nirvāna* is not concerned with material entities and is realized through the knowledge of the four paths. "It is called *nibbāna* in that it is departure (*ni-vah*) from that craving which is called *vāna*." — C.A.F, Rhys Davids, *Buddhism*, p. 174. A.K. Coomaraswamy, *Buddha and the Gospel of Buddhism*, pp. 124-25 : " 'To say of a Brother thus set free by insight — He knows not, he

signifies extinction of all suffering.[1] *Nirvāṇa* is that state when there is the realization of the transitoriness and painfulness of all phenomena and this produces non-attachment. Thus there is freedom from erroneous judgments. This is the view of the Śrāvakas and the Pretyekabuddhas.

(b) *Nirvāṇa as Bliss*

According to the *Cullavagga*, *vimokkha* or *vimutti*, that is emancipation from the travail of worldly misery and ego-attitudinal conflicts, is the central concept in Buddhist philosophy.[2] *Vimutti* is not an aesthetic or epistemological concept but only refers to eschatological ontology, that is, it posits the continuity in freedom of the *arhat*. The Buddhist literature also makes a distinction between *cittavimukti* and *prajnāvimukti*. It is plausible to identify *vimokha* with *nirvāṇa*.[3] They are only the positive and negative methods of stating the urgency of the neutralization of pain.[4] According to the *Mahānidana Sutta* and the *Mahāparinibbana Sutta*, there are eight stages of deliverance (*Vimokha*) :

(i) Having oneself external form, one sees forms,
(ii) Unaware of one's own external form, one sees forms external
(iii) Aesthetic hypnosis (*śubha* or *śubhra*),
(iv) Abiding in *ākaśānantyāyatana*,
(v) Abiding in *vijnanānantyāyatana*,
(vi) Abiding in *ākimcanyāyatana*,
(vii) Abiding in *naivasamjñānāsamjñāyatana*,
(viii) Abiding in *samjñāavedayitanirodha*.

sees not — that were absurd' (*Mahānidana Sutta*, 32). In other words, it is clear that the emancipated individual after death does not cease to know things as they really are; the doors of perception being cleansed, he must continue to see things as they are."

[1] Dasgupta, *Indian Philosophy*, I, 151.

[2] *Cullavagga*, IX, 1, 4.

[3] Hindi Trans. of the *Dīgha Nikāya* by Rahula and Kāśyapa, pp. 116, 132-33.

[4] Schopenhauer taught repression of desires and contemplation. If an individual pursues this path "he may hope ultimately to enter a blissful state of existence, free from all desire and from everything that we think of as consciousness, similar to what Buddhists mean by *nirvāṇa*." — W.K. Wright, *History of Modern Philosophy*, p. 380

The Buddhist ethical discipline holds that freedom from *kāmāsrava, bhavāsrava, avidyāsrava* and *drishti* (metaphysical propositions) gives *vimukti.*

A more positivistic concept of *nirvāṇa* is prevalent in the *Theragāthā* and the *Therigāthā.*[1] There it is stated that the elders of the Buddhistic fraternity relish the bliss of *nirvāṇa.* In the *Therīgathā* we find :

One day, bathing my feet I sit and watch
The water as it trickles down the slope.
Thereby I set my heart in steadfastness,
As one doth train a horse of noble breed.
Then going to my cell, I take my lamp.
And seated on my couch I watch the flame ;
Grasping the pin, I pull the wick right down
Into the Oil......
Lo ! the Nibbāna of the little lamp !
Emancipation dawns ! My heart is free. (No. 72)

It may be said that the idea of a blissful *nirvāṇa* is due to the possible influence of the *Brihadāraraṇyaka Upaniṣad* or may be a compromise with the popular notions of the day. The *Dhammapada* also says that *nirvāṇa* is the highest happiness — *paramam sukham.*[2] This positivism of *nirvāṇa* can have two possible implications. The general sense is that *nirvāṇa* is not a state of vacuity or emptiness or emotional nihil.[3] It is a state of positive fulfilment of feelings and emotions and is absolutely uncontaminated with the least degree of actual or proximate or remote pain.[4] When the *Therigāthā*, the *Theragāthā* and the

[1] S.N. Dasgupta, *Hindu Mysticism*, pp. 85-91, points out that *nirvāṇa* is blissful in the sense that it stimulates spiritual cravings and strivings to the highest degree.

[2] *Dhammapada*, Verses 23 and 203-205, 197-200.

[3] Poussin, "Nirvāṇa", *ERE.*, IX, 376 : "It is difficult to find in the Brahmanic literature or even in the Upaniṣads feelings so fervid and enthusiastic." According to Poussin, the deep joy at the prospect of *nirvāṇa* indicates mystical and religious exaltation and does not have much metaphysical or doctrinal speculation in it.

[4] According to the *Milinda Panho*, although *nirvāṇa* signifies unalloyed bliss, the endeavours for its realization involve pain. *Nirvāṇa* is realized in consciousness "by freedom from distress and danger, by confidence, by peace, by calm, by bliss, by happiness, by sweetness, by purity, by coolness." — *Milinda*, II, 182.

Dhammapada speak of the happiness of *nirvāṇa*, they intend to stress the intensification of the neutralization of *dukkha* and the concentration on a state of super-emotional and super-mental happiness.[1] It is not possible to equate the bliss of *nirvāṇa* with the "beatitude" of Christianity and the state of fellowship with God or absolute — something like the "*sāyujya mukti*" of the Vedanta.[2] There is no sanction for this comparison because at least in the early Pāli literature there is no evidence for the recognition of a primordial spiritual entity with which dynamic supersensuous contact is sought.[3]

The delight and superior rapture associated with the state of *nirvāna* is also stated to be a fact in the *Mahāparinirvāṇa Sutra* of the *Dighā Nikāya*.[4] There it is stated that the spirit of the Buddha passes "from one state of ecstasy to another up and down through the stages of rapture until he passed into nirvāṇa."[5]

1 Childers, *Pali Dictionary*, p. 268, refers to an earthly *nirvāṇa* (bliss of *nirvāṇa*) before death. Rhys Davids also emphasizes this point. Also Poussin, "Nirvāṇa", Sāriputta is reported to have said: "Just that my friend is bliss, and there is no feeling there." *ERE.*, vol. IX, p. 378, With reference to Nirvāṇa.

2 The *Tevijja Sutta* of the *Dīgha Nikāya* identifies *nirvāṇa* with the union with Brahmā. A. K. Coomaraswamy, *Buddha and the Gospel of Buddhism*, p. 115, compares *nirvāṇa* with *moksha*, Tao and the Eternal Life of the Christians. Streeter, *The Buddha and the Christ*, pp. 84-85, also holds a similar view. He says that *nirvāṇa* consists in the realized identify with the Absolute and the peace ineffable which comes therewith and is not extinction.

3 According to Pfleiderer, *Philosophy of Religion*, Vol. III, pp. 70-71, the Buddhist *nirvāṇa* comes practically to the same thing as *moksha*; only that it lacks the metaphysical pantheistic background of the latter. F.S.C. Northrop, *The Meeting of the East and the West*, p. 347, interprets *nirvāṇa* as undifferentiated all-embracing aesthetic continuum. Evidently, he is trying to read the ideas of Plato's *Symposium* in Buddhist thought.

4 E. Obermiller, "The Account of Buddha's Nirvāṇa", *Indian Historical Quarterly*, Vol. VIII, 1939, pp. 781-84. According to L. Finot, the *Mahāparinirvaṇa Sutra* and the *Cullavagga* originally formed part of one work and only subsequently were dismembered. *The History of Buddhism* by the Tibetan Buston, (Vol. II, pp. 56-72 of Obermiller's translation, Heidelberg, 1932), borrows the account of the *nirvaṇa* of Buddha from the first volume of *Vinayakshudraka*, preserved in the Kangyr., H. Beck, Ed. Lehman, (in *Buddhismus*), N. Soderblom and Fr. Heiler, (in *Die Buddhistische Versenkung*), provide a mystic interpretation of Buddhism. Th. Stcherbatsky. *The Conception of Buddhist Nirvāṇa* (L ningrad, Academy of Sciences, 1927), p. 6n.

5 Oldenberg, *Buddha*, p. 202.

(c) *Nirvāṇa and Mysticism*

A positivistic interpretation of *nirvāṇa*, implying the negation of pain and sorrow and the attainment of a state of unperturbed super-emotional calm would receive further substantiation from the mystical descriptions of *nirvāṇa* that we find in the Buddhist literature.[1] It is said that the state of *nirvāṇa* cannot be adequately comprehended by logical categories.[2] It is a state which has to be intuitively felt and experienced. There is stated to be slender scope for logical discussions and theoretical statements regarding *nirvāṇa*. It is the climax of a series of *dhyāna*.[3] Hence it cannot be put in the subject-predicate categories of Aristotelian logic.[4] It requires subjective experience by the chastened mind.

(d) *Māra and Buddha's Parinirvāṇa : An Anthropological Study of the Nature and Personality of Māra*

In the life of Buddha there are two vitally significant stages. Under the Bodhi tree, by the practice of a series of *dhyāna* he obtained *nirvāṇa*. At the age of eighty when he had carried on his preaching ministry for forty-five years he is said to have decided to enter *mahaparinirvāṇa*.[5] It is said in the *Dīgha*

[1] According to Schrader, *Journal of the Pali Text Society*, 1905, "The Buddha held that those who sought to become identified after death with the soul of the world as infinite space or consciousness attained to a state in which they had a corresponding feeling of infiniteness without having really lost their individuality." Dasgupta, *Indian Philosophy*, p. 109, however, holds that this view amounts to a sensuous representation of *nirvāṇa*. In the *Ratana Sutta* of the *Khuddaka Pātha* the word *amatam* (immortal), and in the *Metta Sutta* of the *Khuddaka Pātha* the words *sāntam padam* have been used in connexion with nirvaṇa.

[2] *Samyutta Nikāya*, III, 109. Oldenberg, *Buddha*, p. 282. Warren, *Buddhism in Translations*, p. 138.

[3] Hence sometimes it is said that in *nirvāṇa, a* super-sensuous consciousness can be generated.

[4] The *Udāna* (Nālandā Ed., VIII, 10, 23), says :

"As the fiery sparks from a forge are one by one extinguished,
and no one knows where they have gone,
So it is with those who have attained to complete emancipation,
Who have crossed the flood of desire,
Who have entered the calm delight, of those no trace remains."

[5] W. Geiger, E.T. of the *Mahāvamśa* (London, *PTS.*, 1912), pp. xxii-xxviii. According to J.F. Fleet, "The Day on which Buddha Died."

Nikāya that Māra had requested Buddha to enter *mahapari-nirvāṇa* and the latter had agreed. The Buddhistic books do not provide any reason as to why had he agreed to this unusual proposal. It may appear surprising because one of the greatest exploits in the life of Buddha is to have vanquished the great Māra and all his entourage.

Māra is derived from √*Mri* (to die). Hence, sometimes, Māra and *Mṛtyu* are identified. According to Oldenberg, Senart and Vidhusekhar Bhattacharya, Māra = *Mṛtyu* = Yama. There are three possible explanations of the nature of Māra.[1] The first is that he is the god of death and is the Buddhistic version of of the gods Yama and Antaka.[2] The second is that Māra is the Buddhistic version of the god Kāma or Cupid. He is the embodiment of the power of lust. A third explanation of Māra is that he is the embodiment of ego and wickedness.[3] He is the representative not of any single human weakness but of all the baser passions, appetites and weaknesses of man.

Māra seems to be a popularly accepted evil spirit. He is comparable to the Satan of Christian mythology or the Ahriman

JRAS January 1909, the date of the *parinirvāṇa* of Buddha was 13 October, 482 B.C. (Kārtika śukla, 8). Saunders, *Gotama Buddha*, p. 80. B.C.J. Charpentier holds that Buddha died in 477 B.C.

[1] Windisch, *Māra und Buddha* Leipzig, 1895) Sometimes Māra is compared to the Vedic Namuci. Western Indologists like Oldenberg compare Māra and Lucifer. It is said that as worlds die and appear so also new Maras appear. The *Padhāna Sutta* of the *Sutta Nipāta* contains the conversation between Buddha and Māra before the attainment of *Bodhi*. There the epithet Namuci appears for Māra. This gives an indication of the Vedic origin of Māra. For references to Namuci, *R.V.* V, 10, 7-8 ; VI, 20, 6 ; VIII, 14, 13 ; the *Śatapatha Brāhmaṇa* V, 4, 1, 9 ; XII, 7, 3, 1 ; the *Pancaviśma Brāhmaṇa*, XII, 6, 8 ; the *Maitrāyaṇi Samhitā*, IV, 3, 4 ; IV, 4 ; the *Taittīrīya Samhitā*, I, 8, 14 ; the *Taittīrīya Brāhmana*, I, 7 : I, 6 ; VIII, 2. See also T.O. Ling, *Buddhism and the Mythology of Evil* (London, George Allen & Unwin, 1962).

[2] But in the *Cula-Gopālaka Sutta* of the *Majjhima Nikāya* (Hindi translation by R. Samkrityayana, p. 137), it appears that Māra and *Mṛtyu* are different because they are separately mentioned. I feel that there is slender evidence for identifying the *Māra* of Buddhist literature and the *Mṛtyu* referred to in the *Kathopaniṣad*, although some scholars incline towards identifying *māra pāpimmā* with *mṛtyuh pāpmā* of the Vedic texts.

[3] Māra first appears before Buddha at the time of the *abhinishkramana* on the Āsādha purnimā.

of Zoroastrian mythology. The figure of Māra seems to be one taken by early Buddhism from popular beliefs and superstitions.[1] It is pointed out that Māra is the lord of evil and not the originator of evil.

Buddha says to Ānanda that he (Buddha) had the supernormal power to extend his bodily existence for long aeons — *kalpa.*[2] But since he had told Māra that he would enter *nirvāṇa* he is bound to do so.

(e) *Nirvāṇa and a Philosophy of Life*

The attainment of the state of the *arhat* or of *nirvāṇa* does not mean a life of intense particularization and isolation. It does emphasize a quiet life of meditation and the enjoyment of the bliss of the extinetion of pain and sorrow. But it does not mean absolute withdrawal.[3] Buddha had a deep, profound and personal experience of the pervasiveness of pain and sorrow[4] but he does not lead a cloistered life of contemplation in some retreat[5] but spends the remaining forty-five years of his life in ltinerary and in preaching to the suffering-stricken multitude the way to the end of all suffering. He says:

> "But twentynine was I when I renounced
> The world, Subhaddha, seeking after Good—
> For fifty years and yet another year
> Since I went out, a pilgrim have I been
> Through the wide realm of System and of Law
> Outside thereof no victory can be won."

The early Buddhist literature is categorical on the point that Buddha had attained *nirvāṇa* under the Bodhi tree.[6] Hence it

[1] The large number of people in Burma whose Buddhism is tinged with Shamanism believe in a future life after the death of Tathāgata. Reported in, C.A.F. Rhys Davids, *Buddhism*, p. 195.

[2] The theosophists would identify *parinirvāṇa* with the *anupādaka* or monadic body and *mahaparinirvāṇa* with the *ādi* or the divine body.

[3] The *Sutta Nipāta* holds that only *srāmanya* can lead to *nirvāna*. But according to the *Majjhima Nikāya* and the *Milinda Panha*, *nirvāṇa* can be attained even by a householder.

[4] Melamed, *Buddha and Spinoza*, pp. 274, 348, says that Buddha attempted to escape not only from life but also from death and hence his yearning for *nirvāṇa* was so deep.

[5] Thus it is evident that *nirvāṇa* is not *naishkarmya*.

[6] Hence it is a positive proof that *nirvāṇa* is attainable in this life.

follows that even after the attainment of the state of *nirvāṇa*, a life of dynamic energy and action is possible. The way of life of Buddha is in consonance with the path followed by the *vānaprasthas* and *sannyāsins* of ancient India. They also preached among the people the truths they had realized.[1] Thus it may be said that the state of *nirvāṇa* is comparable to the state of the *jivanmukta*. Sāriputta is reported to have uttered :

> "It is not death, it is not life I welcome
> As the hireling his wage, so do I bide my time
> It is not death, it is not life I want
> Mindful and thoughtful I bide my time."

Gārgāyana held that contemplative life and active life were incompatible. On the other hand the *Ishopaniṣad*,[2] Yājnavalkya and Mahīdāsa Aitareya uphold that the realization of God and the performance of temporal works can be synthesized. According to early Buddhism, missionary activity and compassionate altruism are not antithetical to the pursuit of *nirvāṇa*.

Nirvāṇa implies the stoppage of the wheel of rebirth. Rebirth is brought about by the potency of clinging and the lust to become. The *Sutta Nipāta* refers to *nirvāṇa* as the end of the wheel of birth and death — *Jarāmaccu parikkhayam*.[3] In one verse (No. 1094) it says : "This matchless island, possessing nothing and grasping after nothing, I call the *nibbāna*, the destruction of decay and death." In the *Āryaparyeshaṇā Sutta* (*Pāsarāsi*, No. 26) of the *Majjhima Nikāya* it is stated : "There are two cravings oh, Bhikkhus," says Gotama, "the noble one and the ignoble one ...... we may have, oh Bhikkhus the case of one who himself subject to birth, old age, disease, death, sorrow, corruption, perceives the wretchedness of what is subject to these and craves for the incomparable security of the *Nibbāna* which is free from birth, old age, death, disease, sorrow, corruptions. This oh Bhikkhus, is the noble craving."

[1] The *Ishopaniṣad* stressed the conquest of delusion and sorrow ; the *Chhāndogya* IV, 14, 3, stated *pāpam karma na ślishyata* ; the *Muṇḍaka* III, 2, 3, stresses *karmapravilinatva* and the *Katha*, VI, 10-11, emphasizes peace as the goal to be realized by the spiritual aspirants. In course of time these ideals were preached amongst the people.

[2] Mantra No. 2.

[3] Hence it is said that *nirvāṇa* is not death but "death of death." (B.G. Tilak, *Gitā-Rahasya*, Hindi Trans. Ed. of 1950, pp. 575-76).

The Jātakas record the stories of the previous births of Buddha, before he finally embodied himself as the son of the king of the Sākyas. In later Mahāyana works it is recorded, however, that the Boddhisattva refuses to enter *nirāṇa,* until he had worked for the emancipation of the vast masses who are engrossed in suffering.

3. *Nirvāṇa as the Negation of Empiric Phenomena*

The primary meaning of nirvāṇa as used in the Buddhist literature is the extinction of pain and sorrow. This is the conception of *nirvāṇa* at the psychological level. It is a statement from the standpoint of the individual. There is, sometimes, an extension of this connotation. From the extinction of pain, it is not a very long step to argue for the extinction of all worldly phenomena which, to be sure, are the root of all pain.[1] According to the *Dhammapada*, the *arhat* is said to have perceived unconditioned deliverance through the perception of the void — *sunyato animitto ca vimokkho yass gocaro.*[2] Here it is stated that the perception of the voidness of empiric phenomena is a precondition of the attainment of the highest status of deliverance.[3] The *Udāna* says :

> "Where water, earth, heat and air do not find footing, where no light burns and the sun does not shine, the moon does not shed her radiant beams and darkness does not exist. When a Brāhmin has realized the truth by silent concentration, then he becomes free from form and formlessness, happiness and suffering."

4. *Nirvāṇa as Utter Extinction*

The sense of negation is implicit in *nirvāṇa.* But there is no foundation for interpreting *nirvāṇa* as perpetual death, a lifeless reality, in some sense comparable to the *avyakta prakṛti* of the

1 *Samyutta Nikāya,* II, 115, regards *nirvāṇa* as cessation of becoming. Sometimes it is stated that permanence and bliss of *nirvāṇa* are for the unregenerated while impermanence, selflessness and annihilation are for the trained. Poussin, *The Way to Nirvāṇa*, p. 137. Saunders, *Gotama Buddha*, p. 31. Cf. the *Chhāndogya,* VIII, 11, 1-2, — *vināśamevāpito bhavati.*

2 *Dhammapada,* Verse 93.

3 Nāgarjuna and Candrakīrti emphasize the meaning of *nirvāṇa* as the non-essential character of all phenomena. S.N. Dasgupta, *Indian Philosophy*, I, p. 215, states that according to Charaka also, in the state of Yoga there dawns the realization that "all are produced by causes, are transitory" and "all affection and knowledge become finally extinct."

Sāmkhya. The negation implicit in *nirvāṇa* can be conceived at three levels. First, the negation or extinction of pain. This is the predominant view of *nirvāṇa* sanctioned in an overwhelming number of passage in the Tripiṭaka literature. Second, the negation or extinction of empiric phenomena.[1] The second meaning is a further extension of the first meaning.[2] There are some passages which may sanction the second meaning. We see that almost as a corollary to this second interpretation, it is stated in the early Buddhist scriptures that there is something transcendent and profound and which has not been revealed to disciples. A few passages there are which even refer to the *nirvāṇa* as an absolute unconditioned entity.

The third meaning of *nirvāṇa* can be the negation of everything — both empirical and transcendent.[3] This is the conception of *nirvāṇa* as utter extinction, absolute nihil, zero or complete void.[4] There is slender sanction for this extreme interpretation of the negativism of *nirvāṇa* in early Buddhist literature.[5] The *Samyutta Nikāya* states that the identification of *nirvāna* with extinction is a deeply wicked heresy.[6]

1 The *Praśnopaniṣad,* I, 10, contains *etasmānna punarāvartanta ityesha nirodhah.* This word *nirodha* seems to be a remarkable forecast of the Buddhist view because it is used here not in the usual sense of moral restraint but signifies the cessation of all phenomenal activity (the transitory empirical world of becoming as the Buddhist would say).

2 S.N. Dasgupta, *Indian Idealism* (Cambridge Univ. Press, 1932), pp. 74-75, states that early Buddhism as interpreted in the Theravada school does not show any positive conception of *nirvāṇa.* The perceived elements have no reality. Everything is void and essenceless : there is no ground of the appearances and there is no substance.

3 Poussin, "Nirvāṇa", *op. cit.*, says that Buddha denied the soul and hence was forced to accept the annihilationistic notion of *nirvāṇa.* "The doctrine of annihilation was not an original purpose, it was a result."

4 Adolf Wutke holds that Buddhism accepts the view of phenomenal procession out of nothing and hence the phenomenal being must lapse into nothing. Oldenberg criticizes this standpoint. Edward Caird, *Evolution of Religian,* I, p. 34, holds that *nirvāṇa* is supposed to be the result of the self-negating process of the human mind.

5 In the later Mahāyānistic metaphysics this idea was expounded. S.N. Dasgupta, *Indian Idealism*, p. 78.

6 *Samutta Nikāya* (*PTS*. ed.), III, 109. The *Viśuddhimagga* also says : *Khayamatam eva na nibbanam ti vatabbam* (one must not say that *nirvāṇa* is mere extinction. According to the Vaibhāsikas, Buddha having attained final *nirvāṇa* by his death lost his being. S. Radhakrishnan, *Indian*

This interpretation of *nirvāṇa* as utter extinction would be against the spirit of Buddha who wanted to avoid the two extremes of eternalism and annihilationism.[1] The acceptance of *nirvāṇa* as non-being would amount to positing something like absolute nihil and this Buddha repeatedly wanted to avoid.[2]

5. *Nirvāṇa as the Absolute*

I have earlier referred to the four possible interpretations of the concept of *nirvāṇa* and for each one of them some scriptural sanction is possible. For the fourth interpretation we have mainly to turn to the later Mahāyāna literature.[3] In the *Dīgha Nikāya*, however, we find the use of *nirvāṇa*, in the fourth sense.[4] This particular passage of the *Dīgha Nikāya* states that the *nirvāṇa* is the beginning-point of all mundane phenomena and the worldly elements are dissolved in that.[5] This implies the

Philosophy I, 619. Th. Stcherbatsky, *Nirvāṇa*, p. 25, states that according to the Vaibhāsikas the essence of *nirvāṇa* is a materialistic lifeless reality. He compares the concept of nirvāṇa according to the Vaibhāsikas to the concept of Energy in modern science. — *Ibid*, p. 25.

[1] According to the Mādhyamika philosophers, *nirvāṇa* is *aniruddha-manutpannam* and is *amoshadharma* (not to be lost) and it signifies the absence of the essence of all phenomena (*prapancapravṛtti*). "By morality, knowledge and contemplation, attain the spotless dignity of the quieting and subduing *nirvāṇa*, not subject to age, death or decay, devoid of earth, water, fire, wind, sun and moon."—Wenzel's translation of Nagarjuna's *Suhrillekha's* Tibetan translation, quoted in Dasgupta, *Indian Philosophy*, p. 145.

[2] A. Schweitzer, *Indian Thought and its Developmant*, p. 99, clings to the interpretation of *nirvāṇa* as extinction and hence he says that Buddha deviates from his principle of *nirvāṇa* as extinction and expresses himself in a way that it looks like the eternal rest of Jainism and Sāmkhya. Edward Caird, *Evolution of Religion*, Vol. II, p. 1, also holds a similar view. According to him, the Upaniṣadic teaching is the euthanasia of objective religion. Buddhism starts from the fundamental subjectivism of the Upaniṣads and works out the conclusions fearlessly. It (Buddhism) represents the first and extremest recoil upon the subjective, the vehemence of which is clear in Schopenhauer. In Buddhism, first the destruction of the objective consciousness is posited and then there is the extinction also of the subjective. The con- cept of *nirvāṇa* represents the extreme of subjectivity because in the end even subjectivity loses its meaning.

[3] K. Kimura, *Origin of Mahayana Buddhism*, p. 97, says that Nirvāṇa is not extinction of something, but "eternal reality of cosmic existence."

[4] *Digha Nikāya*, II, 15.

[5] *Digha Nikāya, Kevatta Sutta*, the last lines. Here *nirvāṇa* is said to be *anidarśana* and *ananta*.

conception of *nirvāṇa* as Absolute.[1] Sometimes the absolute *nirvāṇa* is compared to the state of deep sleep when the dualities of subject and object are almost neutralized, *nirvāṇa* is called the state of pure consciousness and transparent luminosity. The realization of this subject-objectless pure transcendent *nirvāṇa* is consequent upon complete freedom from the phenomenal stream of becoming. Since it is absolute, it is superior to the operation of the normal laws of causality. There are a few passages which provide some sanction for the acceptance of some kind of an Absolute. In the *Udāna* (viii, 3) and the *Iti-Vuttaka* (43) there is the explicit recognition of a permanent principle.[2] These two passages together may reinforce the interpretation of *nirvāṇa* in an absolutistic sense.[3] In the *Sutta Nipāta* (verse 204), it is stated — *amṛtam śāntam nirvāṇam padamachyutam.*[4] This description reminds one of the description of the *brahman* in the Upaniṣads.[5]

The Tripiṭakas are a vast body of miscellaneous literature having different authorships. Hence there is nothing to be surprised at this absolutist concept of *nirvāṇa.* This particular passage of the *Sutta Nipāta* seems to be modelled upon the passages of the Upaniṣads which refer to the absolute *brahman.*

[1] Cf. the *Udāna* [No. 71 = VIII, 1,]. "For there is a sphere where there is neither earth nor water, light nor air, neither infinity of space nor infinity of consciousness, neither nothingness nor consciousness and unconsciousness, neither this world nor that world, neither sun or moon. I call it neither coming nor going nor standing, neither motion nor rest, neither death nor birth. It is without stability, without a footing. That is the end of sorrow."

[2] But Oldenberg takes a different view. He says, *Buddha,* p. 283 : "These words seem to sound as if we heard Brahmanical philosophers talking of the Brahma, the unborn intransient ... Yet these expressions, when viewed in the connexion of Buddhist thought, convey something wholly different ... For the Buddhists, the words : 'there is an uncreated' merely signify that the created can free himself from the curse of being created.' "

[3] *Aṅguttara Nikāya* : "There are O Bhikkhus, two Dhammas, permanent, eternal, everlasting, not changing, viz, ākāśa and *nibbāna.*"

[4] *Samyutta Nikāya,* IV, 362, 369ff. refers to "*sudurdarśam, ajaram, dhruvam, nishprapancam, amritam, śivam.*"

[5] A.A. Macdonell, "Buddhism", *Comparative Religion,* p. 77, says that the glowing colours in which the bliss of the first stage of *nirvāṇa* is described led to the transformation of the complete *nirvāṇa* into a positive paradise in Sanskrit Buddhism.

The word *nirvāṇa* seems to be substituted for the word *brahman.* It will not be out of the mark to suggest that some of these passages might have been composed in circles which bore the definite impress of the concepts and ideas and phraseology of the Upaniṣadic literature. But this absolutistic interpretation is certainly not the one which Buddha provided in his gospels.[1]

The identification of the Buddhist *nirvāṇa* and the Upaniṣadic Absolute is problematical. There is nothing definite to establish this hypothesis although in the later philosophical literature of India the *nirvāṇa* and the *brahman* were identified. The *Bhagavadgitā* refers to *brahma-nirvāṇam.*[2] In the *Rāmacharitamanās* of Tulsidāsa, the God Śiva is called *nirvāṇarupam.*

There is one strong point, however, which runs counter to this interpretation of *nirvāṇa* as the Absolute. It becomes tantamount to the fallacy or even heresy of *śāsvatavāda* or eternalism which Buddha was so anxious to avoid. Buddha persistently preferred to remain silent about any absolute primordial entity. Hence in consonance with the declared views of Buddha, this fourth interpretation of *nirvāṇa* as an Absolute remains only hypothetical and problematical.

In spite of the repeated statements of Buddha not to sanction eternalism and his constant disinclination towards entertaining metaphysical questions, in the later Mahāyāna philosophy in India as well as in some of the Buddhistic schools in China and Japan a positive absolutistic character began to be imparted to Buddha's teachings.[3] This is a vindication of the inability of the human mind to rest content in a state of confusion or

[1] Dr. Wallesar, *Der Altere Vedanta* (Heidelberg, 1910), states that by overemphasizing the negation of the reality of the external world Buddhism played up to the absolutist position of its Vedantist opponents.

[2] B.G., V, 24-26.

[3] Aśvaghoṣha holds that *nirvāṇa* signifies *tathatā* or pure *thatness* uncontaminated with any disturbing factor which would produce the manifold experiential structure. A person is said to have attained *nirvāṇa* when "the truth of the condition of defilements, their products and the mental disturbances are all annihilated." — S.N. Dasgupta, *Indian Idealism*, p. 87. According to Asanga, *nirvāṇa* signifies union with the Great soul of the Universe or Mahātma. S. Radhakrishnan, *Indian Philosophy*, I, p. 605. The Mahāyāna metaphysical equation is *Bhutatathatā = Dharmakāyā = Nirvāṇa = Bodhi.* In the Mahāyāna, *nirvāṇa* was regarded as synonymous with *aviprayāsatathatā, ananyatathatā, avitathatā* etc.

negativism.[1] The human mind yearns for some primal being, entity, or principle to which it can surrender itself. Thus if a spiritual Absolute was not explicitly provided in early Buddhism, it was provided later on almost by some kind of subterfuge — either in the shape of surrender to Buddha or by conceiving of an absolute primordial Dharma or by conceiving of the transcendent world of *Sukhāvatī*.

The assertion of the character or *nirvāṇa* as a positive Absolute would raise one serious problem. If *nirvāṇa* means a positive Absolute, then it will be difficult to deny the existence of the human soul. If *nirvāṇa* is a positive absolute entity and, if further, it is stated that it is attained by the human being by rigorous and arduous endeavours, then it follows logically that there must be some entity that experiences this Absolute. It seems ridiculous for a non-existent entity or an entity that could become non-existent in the process of experiencing, to work for the realization of an Absolute. If the universe is characterized by the teleological endeavour to attain *nirvāṇa*, which would logically follow from the acceptance of *nirvāṇa* as an Absolute, then there must be some sentient experiencing continuum that is to experience this entity.[2]

Hence in view of this difficulty of accepting for Buddhism a substantialist absolute continuum, I prefer to stress the first meaning of *nirvāṇa* as the extinction of pain and sorrow as the dominant import of this concept in the early Buddhist literature. There can be some sanction for each of the four meanings from some part or other of the Buddhist literature. But the vast majority of passages would sanction a conception of *nirvāṇa* as a state of the neutralization of all deviant and perverse psychological factors.[3] In this sense *nirvāṇa* would be tantamount to a profound psychological revolution. It is

[1] In the Mahāyāna philosophy, *nirvāṇa* is sometimes spoken of as possessing the four features, *nitya, sukha, atmā* (self-acting) and *śuchi.*

[2] Cf. Poussin, "Nirvana", *in Encyclopaedia Of Religion And Ethics*, Vol. IX.

[3] In Hinayāna religion *nirvāṇa* meant the negation of consciousness. It is no permanent substance. N. Datta, *Aspects of Mahāyana Buddhism and its Relation to Hinayāna* (London, Luzac & Co., 1930), pp. 203-09, says that the Mahāyanic *nirvāṇa* signifies the attainment of a state where the individual can no longer distinguish himself as such, as different from the infinite elements constituting the universe.

supposed to effectuate a change in the total psychological make-up of man. It postulates immense inner conquests. Man has to wage the real battle with himself. The enemy lies within. The objectivity of pain and sorrow is seen to be a delusion produced by man himself. Once the domineering passions and lusts have been conquered, the *summum bonum* has been realized.

6. *Nirvāṇa According to The Abhidhamma*

The *Abhidhamma Piṭaka* contains some aspects of the metaphysics of *nirvāṇa*.[1] In the *Dhammasangaṇi*, *nirvāṇa* is regarded as an *asamskṛta dhātu* or an unconditioned element. In this book various predicates are used for the *nirvāṇa* or the *asamskrita dhātu*. It says :

> "The latter is indeterminate (*avyākṛta* or *avyakta*), neither result nor productive of result (*vipakāvipaka dharma*), neither grasped at nor favourable to grasping, neither vitiated nor vicious, without applied or sustained thought, to be put away neither by insight nor by culture, that which makes neither for the piling up nor for the undoing of rebirth, neither appertaining nor not appertaining to training, infinite, excellent that which does not entail fixed consequences, invisible and non-reacting, not a root-condition, without root conditions as concomitants, not associated with a root-condition, without material form, supramundane, not an *Āsava*, not having Asavas, disconnected with the Asavas, not a fetter, unfavourable to the fetters, disconnected with the fetters, not a hindrance, unfavourable to the hindrances, disconnected with the hindrances, not a perverted belief, unfavourable to a perverted belief, disconnected with a perverted belief, disconnected with and unfavourable to a perverted belief, without concomitant object of thought, not mind, not mental property, disconnected with thought, detached from thought, not something coming into being because of thought, not something coming into being along with thought, not something to undergo change after thought, not derived, without the attribute of grasping, disconnected with grasping, disconnected with and not favourable to grasping, without the attribute of vice, not vicious, disconnected with the vices and not vicious etc."

This account of the *Dhammasangaṇi* indicates two funda-

[1] According to the *Kathāvatthu*, Vol. II, p. 583, "*Nirvāṇa* is the deliverance, the safety, the refuge, the highest path, the stability, the eternal cessation, the unfathomable." (In the translation of the passage by R. Kimura). The *Visuddhimagga* interprets *nirvāṇa* to be the highest teleology. "*Tattha visuddhi ti sabbamalavirahitam accantaparisuddham nibbanam veditabbam. Tassavisuddhiya maggo ti visuddhi-maggo. Maggo ti adhigamupayo vuccati.*" 1.5.

mental points about *nirvāṇa*. First, its at least partly positive character[1] is to be noted. *Nirvāṇa* is not utter extinction or absolute nihil. Second, there is stress on the indescribability of the state of *nirvāṇa*. Its negative descriptions have been applied in virtue of its transcendence.

7. *Factors for the Silence Regarding Nirvāṇic Metaphysics*

It may appear surprising that although *nirvāṇa* is the key concept in Buddhist religion and psychology, there are no clear statements about it in the Pali literature. This anti-metaphysical orientation differentiates Buddhism from the other religions of the world. In medieval Christian scholastic literature there are many discussions about the state of grace and beatitude. In the Purāṇas there are numerous discussions about the various regions — *lokas*, where the soul goes after death. Even in the Upaniṣads we find discussion about the two paths of *devayāna* and *pitṛyaṇa* and there are constant allusions in them to different lokas. But Buddha refuses to give explicit categorical answers about the nature of *nirvāṇa*.

Two explanations are possible as to why Buddha did not give clear statements about *nirvāṇa*.[2] First, the extreme sophist like A.B. Keith would point out that he did not know the answer himself. But this agnostic interpretation of the nature and attainment of Buddha as a teacher appears somewhat uncharitable.[3] He must have known the answer to his own satisfaction to justify at least the appellation of Buddha.[4]

[1] According to the *Kathāvatthu* and the *Abhidharmakosha*, *nirvāṇa* is regarded as *prāptam* (obtainable), *lokottara*, eternal, blissful and pure.

[2] In the conversations between Pasenadi and Khemā in the *Samyutta Nikāya*, it is stated that the categories of the finite and the conditioned cannot be applied to the unconditioned. The existence of Buddha is said to be unfathomably deep, like the ocean. Hence the state of Buddha after death can be said to be "No being in the ordinary sense, but still assuredly not a non-being : a sublime positive, of which thought has no idea, for which language has no expression." — Oldenberg, *Buddha*, p. 280.

[2] Saunders, *Gotama Buddha*, pp. 31 ff. states that Buddha was an agnostic so far as *nirvāṇa* is concerned.

[4] H.O. Taylor, *Ancient Ideals* (New York, The Macmillan Co., 1921), Vol. I, p. 103, says that Indian thought reaches not conclusions but catastrophes. The theory of *ātman* and *brahman* was one leap in the void, *nirvāṇa* was the second leap. Like Oldenberg, Taylor would say that

He claims to have known many more truths than he had taught to the disciples. But he did not consider it wise to reveal these transcendent truths because they were not relevant to the immediate goal of the attainment of *nirvāṇa.* When Buddha himself claims that he has attained *nirvāṇa*, implying that he had known the truths leading thereto, then the agnostic interpretation does not appear convincing. Sometimes instead of the agnostic interpretation, the pragmatic answer is given.[1] Buddha was a teacher of dynamic psychological morals. He noticed the futile conclusions of a speculative philosophy. He found to his dismay that vague cogitations and disquisitions about ultimate problems which are really speaking *avyākṛta* or indescribable constitute a danger to man's rigorous application to ethical endeavours. Hence he preached the urgency of ethical efforts. Instead of giving discourses on the metaphysical problem of the origin of the cosmos, he felt it was wiser and better to follow and teach the path leading to *nirvāṇa.* Thus the positivistic and morally pragmatic orientation to the problems of man is regarded as the factor responsible for the disinclination of Buddha to engage in discussions about the real nature of *nirvāṇa.* This radical moral pragmatism of Buddha would distinguish him from other Vedantic teachers like Śamkara and Rāmānuja. The later also subscribe to the Upaniṣadic formula for *neti neti*, but nevertheless do indicate some predications about the Absolute. Buddha, on the other hand, is radically committed to the fact that no logical predication is possible regarding the *avyākṛta* questions and hence gives no clues to their answers. However, the dominant metaphysical trend proved victorious and several forms of *nirvāṇa* were differentiated in later thought. Suzuki refers to four forms : (i) absolute *nirvāṇa* (= *Dharmakāya*), (ii) *upadhiśesha nirvāṇa*, attained by Buddhists in their life-time, (iii) *anupadhiśesha nirvāṇa* (supramundane bliss) and, (iv) the *nirvāṇa* that has no abode. The Yogācharas developed the concepts of *apratisthita nirvāṇa* and *prakṛtśuddha*

Buddhism was neither a religion nor philosophy but a philosophical way of life.

[1] F.C. Schrader, "On the Problem of Nirvāṇa", *JPTS*, (1904-1905). Schrader holds that in an age of great speculative ferment, the silence of the Buddha with regard to *Nirvāṇa* was pragmatic.

nirvāṇa.[1] The logical and metaphysical discussions about *nirvāṇa* appear also in the *Lankāvatara Sūtra* according to which *nirvāṇa* is neither of these four factors as conceived by the heretics : (i) *bhavasvabhāvābhāva*, (ii) *lakshanavicitrabhāvabhāva*, (iii) *svalakshanabhāvābhāvāvabodha*, and (iv) *svasamānyalaksha-nasamtati-prabandhavyuchheda*.

8. *Sociology of Nirvāṇa*

The political philosopher or the sociologist is interested in the problem of *nirvāṇa* for two reasons. (i) He wants to know if there was anything specific in the social, economic, political and cultural background of the country which made possible the emergence of a concept like *nirvāṇa*. If *nirvāṇa* were the mere goal of an isolated individual, it would not have been a significant problem for the social scientist. But if it becomes the goal of aspiration of a large number of persons, the question of the possible correlation of the emergence of this concept with the objective external situational background becomes relevant.

I think that the factor responsible for the insistence on suffering and despair in the first Aryan truth proclaimed by Buddhism is the registration of a philosophical vision and it is not possible to trace its immediate causal roots in the decline in the political vitality or economic prosperity of northern India. *Dukhavāda* in Buddhism is a philosophical world-view and does not seem to be the necessary symbolization of physical or political-economic misery. *Nirvāṇa* is the extinction of suffering but it refers to phenomena which are not political or economic. It means the end of misery produced by birth, disease, old age and the chain of rebirth. These phenomena are bound to recur even if there is unprecedented political power or economic prosperity. Hence I think that the roots of the concept of *nirvāṇa* should be traced in the tradition of philosophical and ethical enquiry and not in the decline of political and economic prosperity.

It is possible to argue, however, that although the sufferings which *nirvāṇa* wants to put an end to emerge from natural phenomena which are operative with a deterministic inexorable-

[1] Suzuki, *Outlines of Mahayana Buddhism*, pp. 343-46. N. Datta, *Hinayana and Mahayana*, pp. 193 ff.

ness and cannot be put an end to by the increase in the number of hospitals or by an increase in national wealth or by the growth of imperialistic power, still the growth of prosperity enables individuals and groups to become unmindful of them. Death, every person after his teens is acutely aware, is bound to occur, but he is enabled to forget it if he is prosperous. On the other hand adversity of any kind reminds him of the dark fateful end. Any disturbance in the scale of adjustment tends to remind man of the ultimate misery and final tragedy. If we study the sociology of *nirvāṇa* from this standpoint then also I think that the explanation is more psychological than sociological. The deep adversities and unprecedented calamities in the careers of several individuals prompted them to renounce the prospects of worldly life and endeavour to attain *nirvāṇa.* But the Buddhistic literature does not refer to any social or political calamity that would explain the large-scale acceptance of the creed of Buddhistic *nirvāṇa.*

Although I recognize the limitations of the methodology of the sociology of religion and advocate its supplementation by the psychological study of religion, in which greater stress is put on the study of the inner frustrations, inhibitions, complexes and contradictions of the person in quest of religion, I would refer to a few factors that might have created an atmosphere favorable to the acceptance of the Buddhist theory of *nirvāṇa.* From the sixth century B.C. onwards the political situation of the country was one of disquiet characterized by external depredations from the Janapadas and the kingdoms and there must have been occasions for frequent bloodshed. This was a tremendously shocking situation and sensitive souls must have felt a desire to get out of it.

Another socio-economic factor that would have made the situation favorable for the acceptance of the Buddhist truths and formulas was that the younger sons of the kshatriya aristocracy had no political career ahead of them. The eldest sons obtained some power by virtue of primogeniture. Some or most of them got possession of the landed wealth and were something like feudal magnates. But the younger sons had no career ahead of them commensurate with their ambitions. It may be suggested, therefore, that they joined the Buddhistic Samgha where they could seek peace and emancipation or *nirvāṇa.*

The second problem for the student of sociology of religion is to examine the possible social, economic, political and cultural consequences, following, either directly or incidentally, from religious concepts, propositions and dogmas. It can not be doubted that the Buddhist ideal of *nirvāṇa* intensifies a non-secularist outlook. Social. economic and political goals and quests lose much of their meaning by the acceptance of this world-view. True it is that eventually death and disaster overtake all things human. But from the standpoint of organized collective existence, if strength, security and prosperity are our desired objectives then they cannot be obtained by sheer indifference. An exaggerated stress on philosophical resignation, stoic indifference and the cultivation of the yogic *dhyāna* would generate an attitude that would regard political happenings as if of no concern. Hence, the proclamation and wide acceptance of the formula of *nirvāṇa* did weaken the nerves for political resistance and fight. In place of strengthening the goals of liberty, political independence and economic prosperity, the ideal of life became extremely individualistic.

CHAPTER 12

EARLY BUDDHIST MYSTICISM

ACCORDING TO the Vedanta and Buddhism the advance of physical and chemical researches cannot pronounce the final word on epistemology, ontology, and ethics. From the Ṛgvedic seers to Bergson and Aurobindo,[1] and from Buddha and Plato to Nāgārjuna, Śamkara and Gandhi, we find confirmations of sources of knowledge higher than perceptual realism and positivist scientific conceptualism.[2] The Vedic cults,[3] the Egyptian ritualistic rites, the Orphic and the Pythagorean sects,[4] the Buddhistic and the medieval Christian brotherhoods had

[1] Cf. Sri Aurobindo, *The Life Divine* (Calcutta, Arya Publishing House, 1943), 2nd edition, Vol. I, p. 5.

[2] H. Bergson, *The Two Sources of Morality and Religion*; Evelyn Underhill, *Mysticism*; William James, *The Varieties of Religious Experience*. In Christianity also we find discussion of the mystic experiences of St. Teresa, St. Catherine of Siena (1347-1380) and Rulman Merswin and others. For the ideas of St. Catherine of Siena and Rulman Merswin, see Rufus M. Jones, *Studies in Mystical Religion* (Macmillan, London, 1923), pp. 301-305, 245-254. Plotinus also used to experience hypnosis or ekstasis. Hegel was a determined opponent of mysticism but there is a passage in the *The Philosophy of Religion*, Vol. 3, p. 8, which seems to support the mystic thesis of the unity of the subject and the object. He says: "Thought is pure unity with itself, from which all that is obscure and dark has disappeared. This kind of thought may also be called pure intuition, as being the simple form of the activity of thought, so that there is nothing between the subject and the object as these two do not yet really exist (spirit is not yet particularized or dirempted). This kind of thought has no limitation, it is universal activity, and its content is no other than the Universal itself; it is pure pulsation within itself."

[3] Since the days of the *Atharvaveda*, technics of Yoga were developed in India. But it is not possible to trace any direct connexion between the specific Yogic technics of the *Atharvaveda* and those of Buddhism. The *Ṛgveda* 1, 164, 4 : 1, 164, 31 ; 1, 164, 38.

[4] A.B. Keith, *The Samkhya System*, pp. 75-77, refers to the doctrine of ecstasy in the Bacchic religion, in Pythagoras, in Plotinus (206-69) and also in Abammon, a later contemporary of Porphyry (232-304).

esoteric processes of doctrinal transmission. Stoicism stresses rigorous moral endeavours and philosophical contemplation. Christianity emphasises the cultivation of the virtues of hope, faith and charity and even when mystically-oriented, it does not give up faith in Jesus Christ as an intermediary between man and God. But the Upaniṣadic and the Buddhistic mystics stressed personal efforts for mystical illumination. Buddha never claims to be a mediator as Christ and Mohammad do. Rāmakrishna, who claimed an intimate personal and intuitive realization of the cosmic and transcendent reality[1] influenced Vivekananda only due to his possession of mystic occult knowledge. History does contain records of the degeneration of mystery worships but that certainly does not amount to a challenge to all forms of higher mysticisms. We are concerned in this chapter with showing the elements of mysticism in the original teachings of Buddha.[2]

The Tripiṭakas are a vast body of literature and if one emphasizes stray references there, it is possible to attribute numerous view-points to Buddha. There are passages which can support paralogism or atheism and agnosticism. There are also passages which indicate his role as a critical rationalist (*bibhajjavādi*) who wanted to demolish the foundations of orthodox beliefs and Brahmanical superstitions. The *Brahmajāla sutta* of the *Dīgha Nikāya* convincingly shows that Buddha wanted to elaborate a dialectical framework to demonstrate the fallacious character of the contemporary philosophical stand-points. But there are also references to the attainment of the

[1] It is believed by devout followers that Sri Rāmakrishna had the realization of the *nirvikalpa samādhi* or the *asamprajnāta samādhi* in the terminology of Patanjali's *Yoga-Sutra*, *The Life of Sri Ramakrishna*, (Almora, Advaita Ash rama, 1936), 4th edition, p. 181.

[2] The *Tevijja Sutta* of the *Dīgha Nikāya* and the *Alagaduupama Sutta* of the *Majjhima Nikāya* contain references to the Upaniṣadic mystical doctrines like *brahmasahavyatā* (the *Tevijja*) and the unity of world and soul (the *Alagaduupama*). These doctrines are refuted by Buddha but nevertheless the Tripiṭakas do contain elements of mystical teachings. Louis Valle de la Poussin, "Attā in the Pali Canon", *Indian Culture*, Vol. II, p. 35, says that Buddhism was mystical (How can I escape from the realm of death) ? before being philosophical (what is the nature of I ?) The *Majjhima Nikāya* (Hindi translation by R. Sānkrityāyana) pp. 249-50, stresses *ānapāna-sati bhavana* and the control of inhalation and exhalation.

bliss of *nirvāṇa* which indicate that Buddhism did not remain a mere negative movement of critical protest. Original Buddhism is regarded as a rationalistic[1] protest against Upaniṣadic absolutism,[2] Brahmanical ritualistic sacrificialism, sophistic speculative wrangling and the crude animistic cults and practices of the masses. But rationalism does not exhaust the content of Buddhism.[3] Original Buddhism was a vast system which had the capacity to cast a tremendous influence over Eastern Asiatic thought and culture. The twelve Nidānas (causational formulas) or *Pratityasamutpāda*, as explained earlier, are the greatest contribution of Buddhism to the origins of world science because in place of a "theodicy they set up a rational cosmodicy." Buddha resorted to keen dialectical arguments when he had to refute the propositions of his opponents. But there was the suprarational side too. A religion is not a mere adventure of the empirical and critical reason, much less so an ethically-oriented meditative religion of the type of Buddhism.[4]

According to the *Bhayabherava Sutta* and the *Mahāsaccaka Sutta* of the *Majjhima Nikāya*, on the night of enlightenment the following three Vidyās dawned on Gautama as a result of

[1] S.N. Dasgupta, "Message of Buddhism", *Philosophical Essays*, (University of Calcutta, 1941), p. 268, refers to the "sturdy universal rationalism of Buddhism.

[2] Otto Pfleiderer, in *The Philosophy of Religion*, Vol. III, pp. 65, 73-74, says that since Buddhism denied God and soul, it became a religion which completely lacks motive-power both for progressive and deepening knowledge and for action for the reform of society, state and commonwealth. "For only out of the depths of the divine mystery do the never-ceasing streams of living spiritual power issue forth ; the streams which spring from the mere surface of experience do not flow to the life eternal." (*Ibid.*, p. 65).

[3] According to H. Kern, *A Manual of Buddhism*, "For Buddhism is professedly no rationalistic system, it being a superhuman (*uttarimanussa*). Law founded upon the decrees of an omniscient and infalliable Master, and in such a creed mysteries are admissible." He refers to the "idealistic nihilism of original Buddhism." In the *Brahmajāla Sutta* of the *Digha Nikāya* (Hindi translation by R. Sānkrityāyana), pp. 6-7, *cittasamādhi* is regarded as an alternative method to *tarka* for the knowledge of dualistic eternalism.

[4] Cf. Saunders, *Gotama Buddha*, p. 88 : "Whilst Gautama himself lived they (disciples) had no doubt, a sense of personal devotion which in some measure made up for the sense of that presence of the "Divine Lover" which is so real a thing to the Christian mystic."

deep *samādhi* :[1]

(i) *purvanivāsānusmṛti* — knowledge of past births. This knowledge is contained in the *Jatakas*.

(ii) through the *divya caksu*, the process of the attainment of heaven and hell according to one's actions (or *sattavānam chyuti-utpāda jnāna*). This knowledge is contained in the *Apadāna*.

(iii) Knowledge of the Four Aryan Truths (including the *pratityasamutpāda* (dependent origination). In some versions it is said to be *āśravakshaya jñāna*. This knowledge is contained in the Mātikās.

Buddha had gained enlightenment[2] as a result of the practice of the severest ascetic discipline and philosophic abstraction[3] and meditation. He had fathomed the depths of human heart and intellect[4] through elevated attainments (*samāpatti*) and as a result of the dawn of noetic *prajnā* had brought forth the saving truths. In the *Brahmajāla Sutta* of the *Dīgha Nikāya* there is the assertion of the eternal dualism of the world and the soul based upon the remembrance of previous lives in *cittasamādhi*. There are also logical (*tarka*) grounds for the

[1] Barua, "Early Buddhism", *The Cultural Heritage of India*, pp. 237ff.

[2] Expounding the tenets of later Buddhism, Th. Stcherbatsky "The Dharmas of the Buddhists and the Gunas of the Sāmkhya", *The Indian Historical Quarterly*, 1934, p. 759 says : "... the extinction of the *kleśas* not only makes a man dispassionate, but converts him into a Buddha, hence it converts phenomenal life into the absolute. The *samkleśas* are the 12 *nidānas* or phenomenal life as contrasted with the absolute and are produced by transcendental illusion (*Avidyā — mukhyā bhrāntih*). The *kleśas* are therefore transcendental forces creating and controlling phenomenal life (*samsāra*)."

[3] H. Oldenberg, *Buddha*, p. 315 : "The devotion of abstraction is to Buddhism what prayer is to other religions."

[4] In later Buddhism, as for example in Vasubandhu's *Trimśikā*, the processes of the attainment of the extinction of vicious tendencies were thoroughly elaborated. S.N. Dasgupta, *A History of Indian Philosophy*, Vol. II, p. 22, says : "When a saint's mind becomes fixed (*pratisthita*) in this pure consciousness (*vijñapti-mātra*), the tendency to dual thought of the subjective and the objective (*grāhya-grāhakanuśaya*) ceases and there dawns the pure indeterminate (*nirvikalpa*) and transcendent (*lokottara*) consciousness. It is a state in which the ultimate pure consciousness returns from its transformations and rests in itself. It is divested of all afflictions (*kleśa*) or touch of vicious tendencies and is therefore called *anāśrava*."

assertion of the dualism of the world and soul. Gautama Buddha claims that he is familiar with both these bases of dualistic metaphysics. Thus it appears that he was an expert both in dialectics and in concentration. He stated that the ineffable truths he had found out were not demonstrable to the ordinary intellect. In the *Samyutta Nikāya*, by the analogy of the leaves of the *Simsapā* tree,[1] Buddha indicates that he had given out to the disciples only what was necessary for the elimination of pain but he knew much more. The great teachers like Christ and Śamkara and Rāmakrishna claim to possess such a superior knowledge which they reserve for themselves and do not impart that to the ordinary disciples. We can refer to some basic elements in early Buddhist philosophy[2] which indicate its mystical character.

(i) The *prajñā*[3] which is attained as a consequence of the culmination of the spiritual[4] and moral efforts of a Bhikkhu is not the result of any more rational enquiry but is preceded by ethical discipline, faith in the certitude of the Buddha's teachings as leading to *nirvāṇa*, and the practice of the various kinds of highest concentrative disciplines — the Samādhis. The concept of *prajñā* is the first mystic element in early Buddhism.[5]

[1] H. Oldenberg, *Buddha*, pp. 201.5.

[2] According to M. Hiriyana, *Outlines of Indian Philosophy*, pp. 150-51, the eight steps of the *ārya ashtāṅgika mārga* which is the central element of early Buddhist ethics are sometimes equated with the trichotomy of *śīla, samādhi* and *prajña*. Sometimes the *ārya ashtāṅgika mārga* is regarded as being parallel to the *daśa bhumi* of Mahāyana. These are (i) *pramuditā bhūmi* (thought of *bodhi*), (ii) *vimalā bhūmi* (stage of purification) ; (iii) *prabhākari* ; (iv) *āicismati* ; (v) *sudurjayā* ; (vi) *abhimukhi* ; (vii) *duramgamā* : (viii) *acalā sthiti* (characterized by *anutpattika dharmacakshuh*) ; (ix) *sādhumati* and (x) *tathāgata* (*dharmamegha*). This supreme realization of the stage of the *tathāgata* is attained by the deepest concentration and the practice of the most universal altruistic compassion (*maitrī* and *karuṇā*).

[3] According to S.N. Dasgupta, *Hindu Mysticism*, p. 91, the mysticism of the Buddhists consists in the belief in the essenceless state of *nirvāṇa* as the ultimate. perfect, realisable state to be attained by the extinction of *tṛshṇā* (*tanhā*) and by the super-intellectual *prajnā* gained by Yoga.

[4] C.A.F. Rhys Davids, *Buddhist Psychology*, p. 130, says that besides intuitive knowledge, *prajña* signifies any intelligent exercise. It comprehends cognitive functions from research and analysis to insight.

According to Buddhaghosha, the study of the *Suttas* leads to the realization of *samādhi*, while the study of the *Abhidhamma* leads to the

(ii) The Buddhist records contain a number of instances of the display of supernormal powers of Buddha. "I, brethren, according as I desire, enjoy manifold mystic power [the six super-knowledge — *abhijnā*] : being one I become many, being many I become one ; here visible, there invisible, I go without let or hindrance through wall, through rampart, through hill as if through air ; I dive into earth and up again as if in water ; I travel seated cross-legged through air as if I were a bird upon the wing ; I can handle and stroke with the hand this moon and sun, mighty and powerful though they be ; I can control the body even to Brahma-world."[1] The modern intellect may not believe in these[2] but the ancient sages did believe in them

attainment of *prajñā*. B. M. Barua, "Early Buddhism", *The Cultural Heritage of India*, Vol. I, pp. 237ff makes a distinction between *samādhi* and *prajñā*. *Samādhi* (or *śamathayāna*) refers to man's psychical, psychological, intuitional and mystical aspects of life. *Prajñā* (or *vipaśyanāyāna*) comprehends man's ratiocinative, logical and reflective aspect. *Prajñā* is further sub-divided into (a) *śrutamayi* or book-learning, (b) *cintāmayi* or original reflection and (c) *bhavanāmayi* or systematic knowledge. I think that this distinction between *samādhi* and *prajñā* worked out by B.M. Barua is incorrect for two reasons. First, since *prajñā* succeeds and not precedes the attainment of *samādhi*, hence it cannot be mere reasoning. It is, rather, the culmination of reason, in the attainment of the direct awareness or vision of truth. Secondly, by translating *bhavanāmayi* as systematic knowledge he neglects the role of absolute concentration also of feelings and emotions as a prior condition of the realization of supreme knowledge. Sometimes the word *abhijñā* is also used for supernormal insight and sometimes for supernormal powers.

1 *The Book Of The Kindred Sayings* (*Samyutta-Nikāya*), Part II, English translation by Mrs. Rhys Davids, assisted by F.L. Woodward (London, Luzac & Co., 1952), p 143.

2 H. Oldenberg 'poses' to speak in an ultra-modern 'superior' manner when he says in *Buddha*, p. 316 : "The descriptions in the prose Sutras which deal with these conditions of the mind, although the scholastic accessions of doubtful or imaginary psychological categories materially impair the objectivity of the picture, leave no room to doubt that here circumstances of the picture, leave no room to doubt that here circumstances of a pathological kind also, as well as qualities which a sound mind is in a position to induce, must have played a part. The predispositions to those were superabundantly at hand. In men who were by the power of a religious idea torn from existence in the regular relations of home-life, the physical consequences of a wandering mendicant life, combined with spiritual over-excitement, exhaustion of the nervous system, might easily produce a tendency to morbid phases of this kind.

and cultivate them. From the inspired hymn of the Vedic *muni* to the Patanjala *Yoga-Sutra*,[1] we find reiteration of the belief in these powers. The Purāṇas contain instances of the supernormal powers of the saints and heroes obtained by the practice of tremendous askesis.[2] Buddha gains hold over the band of a thousand Jatila ascetics of Gayā headed by the three Kassapa brothers, — Uruvela Kassapa, Nadi Kassapa and Gayā Kassapa, due to the display of his superior powers.[3] He has the faculties of clairvoyance and clairaudience. In contests with the heretical teachers he uses them. The existenee of these powers is a matter of certain belief for the Buddhist but Buddha warns the Bhikkhu not to use them.[4] The belief in the supernormal powers or *riddhibala*[5] is a second mystic element in early Buddhism.

The Buddhist scriptures refer to a legion of gods and

We hear of hallucinations of the sight as well as of the hearing, of 'heavenly visions' and 'heavenly sounds'. From the days when Buddha aspired to enlightenment, it is related how he sees 'a ray of light and the vision of forms,' or even a ray of light alone and again forms only. The appearances of deities also, or of the tempter of whom the legends have so much to relate, betray the existence of hallucinations."

1 Both Buddhism and Yoga stress the elimination of sense impressions. But Yoga is more rigorous in always emphasizing the distinctness of the individual aspirant, than Buddhism with its destructive cult of the *anātman*. Furthermore, while in Buddhism there is no place for a personal God, the *Yoga-Sūtra* of Patanjali is attached to the notion of *Iśvarapraṇidhāna*. S. N. Dasgupta, *Philosophical Essays*, p. 268, says : "The whole of Patañjali's *Yoga-Sūtra* with its *Vyāsa-bhāshyam* does not seem to me anything more than a Hinduised version of Buddhist Yoga."

2 Cf. the experience of Sri Rāmakrishna. *The Life of Sri Rāmakrishna*, *op. cit.*, pp. 107-08.

3 Buddha used *dhyāna* as the best method for conversing with people born in the higher realms.

4 Madame Guyon, St. John of the Cross and Walter Hilton also criticized the display of such powers. Hilton (14th century) wrote *The Ladder of Perfection.*

5 Louis de la Vallee Poussin, "Buddhist Mysticism", *The Encyclopaedia of Religion and Ethics* : "Anyone who sits near me", says Gautama Buddha, in the *Aṅguttara Nikāya*, "and touches my garment, if he does not see the Law is far from me." Thereupon Udayi rebukes Ānanda, "Why do you care for the cosmical power of the Master". Then Buddha rebukes Udayi — If Ānanda were to be reborn, he would obtain owing to his confidence in my power, seven heavenly births, seven births as king but he will be in this life liberated from existence."

Gandharvas, Yakshas and celestial spirits. When Buddha is reluctant to preach at Gayā, he is solicited by Indra and Brahmā to carry on evangelisation for universal welfare. Times without number the gods come and solicit his advice. The Devas are not divine immortal beings but belong to a superior species who had attained their dignity due to their moral and spiritual efforts. These beings are at the beck and call of Buddha and aid him in his propaganda work. The acceptance of the existence of superhuman beings who live for thousands of years is a third mystic element in early Buddhism.

Much more important for Buddhist mysticism is the insistence on *dhyāna*[1] and *samādhi*.[2] The four stages of *rūpa dhyāna* and the four stage of *arūpa dhyāna* are processes of absorption into the deepest fathoms of reality.[3] These eight jhānas (*dhyāna*)

[1] E.J. Thomas, *The Life of Buddha*, pp. 180-81, points out that *dhyāna*, is a term wider than "mystic meditation" which is also vague. Nor is it possible to equate the jhanas (*dhyāna*) with ecstasy which is an inexpressible experience and is the culmination of the whole process of mystic experience. The *jhānas* are only four stages in a much more extended scheme. According to the *Samyutta Nikāya*, III, 235ff. Sāriputta was an expert in jhāna (*dhyāna*). "Now Ānanda saw Sāriputta coming afar off and ... he said to him : 'Serene and pure and radiant is your look, brother Sariputta ! in what mood has Sāriputta been today.' 'I have been alone in first *jhāna*, brother, and to me came never the thought : I am attaining it, or I have got it or I have emerged from it." This same terminology is repeated with reference to Sāriputta expressing his attainment of the second *jhāna*, the third *jhāna*, the fourth *jhāna*, the infinity of space, the infinity of consciousness, the sphere of nothingness, the sphere of neither perception nor non-perception and the state of cessation of perception and feeling. See *The Kindred Sayings*, *op. cit.*, Vol. III, pp. 186-191.

[2] E.J. Thomas, *The Life of Buddha*, p. 184-85 says : "It is usually held that the practice of concentration is borrowed from the methods of the Yoga philosophy. This is probable, but little direct evidence is available. A more important cause of the resemblance between Buddhist practice and Yoga is that they developed side by side... It is possibly owing to the rivalry of systems that we find included among the Buddhist methods the acquisition of exceptional psychical powers ... But in Vipassin's enlightenment there is no word of special mystical processes." According to the *Abhidharmakosha* 1, 39 and 40, only *samādhi* and not *jnāna* can suppress material entities and phenomenal consciousness.

[3] These four *arūpa jhāna* may be compared to "formless visions" of St. Angela and St. Teresa, the interior silence of Molinos (Evelyn Underhill, *Introduction to Mysticism*, p. 387). According to the *Samyutta Nikāya*, XXXVI, 19, the meditative processes produce happiness.

can be thus represented :

(A) *Rūpa Jhāna*

1. Thinking (in its initial state) destroys sloth and torpor (*thina-middha*).

2. Reflecting (or sustained thought) destroys *vicikicchā*.

3. Joy (or rapture) destroys hatred (*dosha* or *vyāpāda*).

4. Happiness destroys restlessness and mental worry (*uddhacca-kukkucca*). Concentration destroys greed (*lobha*).

(B) *Arūpa Jhāna*

5. The realm of the infinity of space (*ākāsānancāyatana*).

6. The realm of the infinity of consciousness (*viññāṇañcā-yatana*).

7. The realm of 'no-thing-ness' (*ākincannāyatana*).

8. The realm of the ultimate limit of perception (*nevasannā-nāsannāyatana*).

The realm of the suppression of consciousness and the knower (*samjnā-vedayita nirodha*) is also categorized. It is said that the four stages of *rupa-jhāna* and the four stages of *arūpa jhāna* (or the eight *samāpatti*) were known to the Yogins before Buddha. His original contribution in this field was the attainment of the *samjñā-vedayita nirodha*. The four *arūpa jhāna* lead to rebirth in formless worlds where the dwellers have no physical form.

The four (and at times five if *samjñā-vedayitanirodha* process is also included) stages of *arūpa dhyāna* are stages when supramental vision dawns on the Bhikkhu and he visualises Infinity of space, Infinity of consciousness, Infinity of nothingness, and Infinity of neither perception nor non-perception.[1]

[1] According to F. Heiler, *Die Buddhistische Versenkung, Eine Religionsgeschichtliche Untersuchung*, Habilitationsschrift for the Ludwig Maximilian University in Munich, 1918, (referred to in E.J. Thomas, *The Life of Buddha*, p. 187), one who has reached the fourth *jhāna* is an *arahat*. This stage of perfect equanimity (perfect balance between different emotions) is parallel, according to Heiler, to Plotinus's union with the One, Spinoza's *amor Dei intellectualis*, and the mystic death of Madame Guyon. I may, however, point out that a reading of Spinoza's *Ethics* would convince a person that he is not at all referring to any mystical experience in his 'intellectual love of God' but only wants to stress the rational cognition of the substance. It is true, however, that Spinoza also refers to a third mode of apprehension, the intuitional.

The four *arūpa dhyānas* are higher than the four rūpa dhyanas which represent a lower stage of ecstatic contemplation. Buddha had attained the cessation of consciousness and thus he surpassed his two old guides Ālāra Kālāma and Uddaka Rāmaputta who had taught him only *samāpatti* but he was in quest of the higher *mahāpadhāna* (the *samjnā-vedayita nirodha*).

Another factor proving the mystic element in original Buddhism is that the various categories like *samskāra* and *vijñāna*[1] are subdivided into a number of processes which cannot be demonstrated by the logical method alone. (e.g. *vijñāna* has 89 subdivisions). They involve mystical experience for their comprehension.

Nirvāṇa is the culmination of Buddhist mysticism. Its mystic character is evident from the fact that Buddha refused to speculate on the proposition about the eschatology of the Tathāgata.[2] Nirvāṇa is a logically indemonstrable state. We cannot be absolutely certain as to whether *nirvāṇa* is an unqualified extinction into void and nothingness, or whether it is only the Advaitic union with the supreme absolute[3] described negatively or whether it is the extinction of mere empiric phenomena. But this much is clear that it is a logically indemonstrable state. It can be felt and realised but cannot be rationally cogitated upon. The insistence on a supramundane *nirvāṇa* as the supreme goal of human life and the prescription of means and measures for the attainment of that reveals in an abundant measure the mystical character of Buddhism.

[1] Elliot, *Hinduism and Buddhism*, Vol. I, pp. 190ff.,— there are fifty two divisions of *samskāra*, mostly mental or at least subjective states. This list includes contact, sensation, perception, thought, reflection, memory, attention, effort, joy, torpor, stupidity, fear, doubt, lightness of body or mind, pity, envy, worry, pride etc. There are eighty nine divisions of *vijñāna* (good, bad or indifferent). It is admitted that *vijñāna* cannot be disentangled and sharply distinguished from feeling and sensation.

[2] According to Schrader, "Vedānta and Sāmkhya in Primitive Buddhism", *The Indian Historical Quarterly*, 1934-35, pp. 543ff., the references to *arūpa brahmaloka* in Buddha's system are not directly based on the pantheistic Vedanta doctrines current at that time. The four *brahmavihāra* exercises, however, indicate Vedantic influence.

[3] Sri Rāmakrishna, Vivekananda and M. Gandhi put forward a theistsic interpretation of Buddha's teachings.—*The Life of Swami Vivekananda by his Eastern and Western disciples* (Almora, Advaita Ashrama 1933), pp. 170-71.

Gautama Buddha's attitude in not giving any positive categorization of *nirvāṇa* is at times criticized and it is said that it is surprising that although he recognizes the efficacy of the mystical technics of *dhyāna*, *samādhi* and *prajñā*, he refuses to give any explict hints regarding the highest principles. The Upaniṣadic teachers also indicate their reluctance to discuss final problems and show their weariness by saying *anatipraśnyām vai devātāmatipṛchasi*, but nevertheless, they never waver in their explicit enunciation of an absolute real spiritual being. Śamkara also stresses that the *brahman* is to be realized by one's own endeavours but he also does acknowledge his full faith in the reality of the *saccidānanda brahman* on the basis of the records of the sages contained in the *śruti*. According to the Hindu tradition the sages were perfect beings and had drunk of the 'nectar of spiritual immortality'. But Buddha's attitude is absolutely different. There is no denying that he was a very great holy man. He engaged in *dhyāna* and *samādhi* and even while living in the physical body he had attained *nirvāṇa* (after the extinction of the body he attained *mahāparinirvāṇa*). Nevertheless, he was averse to any dialectical and metaphysical discussions of any ultimate truth and reality. The Upaniṣads inculcate the possibility of final realisation through *manana* and *nididhyāsana*. Buddha teaches the rejection of the transitory temporal phenomena, and adheres to the concept of the *anātmān*. But he does not provide any knowledge of the 'noumena'. The Vedantic seers, Socrates and Plato and the Christian teachers also taught the prevalence of sorrow in the spatio-temporal realm but they also did give positive and explicit hints regarding the Absolute or God. Early Buddhism and, later on, the school of Vijñanavāda and Śunyavāda tended to pulverise and negate the empirical objective world but did not explicitly and categorically posit any highest spiritual reality. Hence although rigorous ethical endeavours are enjoined in Buddhism and although the glories of mystical Yogic processes are exalted, *nirvāṇa* is not positively categorised and hence there is no concept of a transcendent absolute *nirvāṇa* in Buddhism.

From the presence of mystical elements in early Buddhist thought one should not jump to the conclusion that Buddha accepted a metaphysical ultimate principle.[1] Early Buddhist thought is mystical only to the extent that it does recognize supra-intellectual and intuitional sources of knowledge. It does not, however, believe in a supreme real.

Buddha regards as futile any discussion of the ultimate origin of suffering. Instead, he adopts a more ethically realistic attitude and is concerned with the elimination of pain and sorrow. But he does recognize that suffering has a cause and the fact of psychological suffering is linked up with the universally prevalent law of causation. The formulation of the law of causation or dependent origination does not owe itself to logical argumentation but according to the *Vinaya Piṭaka* it dawned on the Buddha in the process of the attainment of illumination on the night when he became the Buddha under the Bodhi tree. The Upaniṣads (the *Muṇḍaka*, for example) also state that metaphysical discussions and argumentative ratiocinations are not the path to realisation. Their philosophic quest also starts with the recognition of suffering and misery in the world (*lokadukha*) but, unlike early Buddhism, they finally inculcate the oneness of the psychic and the cosmic and transcosmic principles. But Buddha, regardless of the recognition of *samādhi* and *prajñā*, does not teach any metaphysical real or any transcendental unity of apperception. Some critics point out that Buddha himself does advance to a metaphysical level and adopts a 'transcendental' attitude when from some perceived cases of the operation of causality he passes to the affirmation of an ubiquitous law of dependent origination or an inexorable law of *karman* and in their support they state that the Cārvāka realists have criticized *vyāpti* and the positing of a categorical law of invariable concomitance. It is true that

[1] Louis Valee de la Poussin and E.J. Thomas, "Buddhist Mysticism", *The Encylopaedia of Religion and Ethics*, Vol. IX, pp. 85-87, say that since Buddhism either in its Hīnayāna or Mahāyāna forms does not accept any Absolute, hence, strictly speaking, there is no mysticism in it. Christianity, Bhāgavatism and Islam accept a personalistic Absolute; Vedānta and neo-Platonism accept an impersonalistic Absolute. But although Buddhism does not accept any absolute real, it is mystical in the sense of emphasizing the absolute aim of realising, the *asamskṛta* by destroying the *samskṛta*. Poussin's and Thomas's statement, however, that the merging into Nothingness of Buddhism is comparable to the merging into One of Vedānta and neo-Platonism is without any foundation.

there are discussions of metaphysical problems in early Buddhism. The concepts of *dukha, anātman, pratityasamutpāda, karman, nirvāṇa* etc. do involve metaphysical discussions. But there is nothing in early Buddhism to prove that, like the Upaniṣadic teachers, Buddha taught the existence of any omnipresent soul as the substratum of empirical phenomena which is intuited in mystic visions.

SECTION FOUR

YOGA, SĀMKHYA AND BUDDHISM

CHAPTER 13

YOGA AND EARLY BUDDHISM

CULTURE IS A complex totality involving symbolization and evaluation. It is interrelated organic whole. But there may be some elements in a culture which are dominant and they may significantly influence the rest. Religion has been the predominant component in ancient Indian culture in spite of the multifarious achievements of the ancient inhabitants of this country in the secularistic sectors of existence. Yoga is one of the dominant aspects of the esoteric and mystical side of Indian religion.[1] It has added an uniqueness and distinctness to Indian culture.[2] The significance of Yoga is two-fold. First, it involves a tremendous degree of moral and physical training. It is a profound psychological discipline. Yoga, in its highest phases, represents absorptive concentration and deep meditation on the secrets of cosmic existence. Second, this enormous training is regarded as the path to divide illumination. Even those systems of thought which do not explicitly acknowledge the existence of a superior Godhead, like the Jaina,[3] the Buddhist and the Sāmkhya, accept the supreme validity of Yoga as a technic for the realization of wisdom.[4]

The developed psychology and philosophy of Yoga that we find in the systems of Pātañjala Yoga and Buddhism has had a long history behind it. Sometimes it is said that the roots of

1 Yoga is comparable to German *Joch*, Latin *Jugum* and Anglo-Saxon *Geoc*.

2 Even the highly logical and dialectical Nyāya system accepts the efficacy of Yoga. See *Nyāya-Sutras*, iv, 2,38-42.

3 The Jaina technics of Yoga meant for the chastening of the mind are different from those of the Buddhists and the Pātañjala system. See S. N. Dasgupta, *A History of Indian Philosophy*, Vol. I, p. 203.

4 Richard Garbe (1857-1927), *Sāmkhya Und Yoga* (Strassburg, Verlag von Karl J. Trubner, 1896).

Yoga can be traced to pre-Aryan antiquities.[1] This pre-Aryanism of Yoga, receives additional confirmation from the statues or figures unearthed at Mohenjodaro and Harappā. Some of the most remarkable of these figures are a white steatite head and bust and a seal-amulet which is considered as a representation of Paśupati Śiva, possibly in a Yogic mood.[2] In later mythology and literature, Siva is the god *par excellence* of Yoga. Śiva is regarded as the lord of the Yogis — Yogīśwara. It is remarkable that at the busy mercantile centre of Mohenjodaro, the founders and builders of this culture could conceive of the ideal of Śiva in a Yogic posture.

Yoga, in its earlier aspects, was conceived not so much as a path of spiritual trans-substantiation, as a magical technic for the enhancement of vital powers. It was calculated to increase the powers of endurance and to foster the acquisition of dynamism and vigor. This side of Yoga has been perfected by the school of Hathayoga which develops the practice of Yoga as a means to control the effects and impacts of some elements of nature.

1. *Yogic Ideas in the Vedic Literature*

There are numerous references to the practices of Yoga as well as to the word Yoga in the Vedic literature.[3] This indicates that although the roots of Yoga may be pre-Aryan and even aboriginal in some of their crude aspects, by the time of the composition of the Vedic literature, they were assimilated into the priestly religion. This is an illustration of popular ideas and notions being transformed into hieratic concepts. According to later Yogic practices, the control of breath or *prāṇāyāma* is an essential stage of Yoga. In the *Atharvaveda* the great immanental power of *prāṇa* is recognized. The names of some

[1] According to G.W. Brown, the terms Yoga, Sāmkhya and even Upaniṣad are of Dravidian origin.

[2] Ernest Mackay, *The Indus Civilization* (London, Lovat Dickson, 1935), pp. 66-70. S. Radhakrishnan, *Eastern Religions and Western Thought*, pp. 36, 118.

[3] Cf. Maryia Falk, *Nāma-Rūpa and Dhamma-Rūpa* (Calcutta Univ. Press, 1942. This book is reviewed in *JBRS*, Sept.-Dec. 1944, p. 261). also Gopinath Kaviraj, "Yoga Kā Vishaya Paricaya" (In Hindi), See *Kalyāṇa* : *Yogāṅka*, (Gita Press, Gorakhpur, 1935). Tuxen's *Yoga*.

of the *prāṇas* are also found in the early Vedic literature. Although no specific mention of *prāṇāyāma* is found in the Vedic literature, it is possible that the idea of the control of breath must have developed in those days because in the Vedas there is explicit mention of the control of the mind and the intellect.[1]

There are other Vedic references to ideas associated with the Yoga.[2] In the *Ṛgveda* the word Yoga is used in various sense ; viz : (a) accomplishing the unaccomplished, (b) yoking or harnessing, (c) relation or combination etc. In the *Ṛgveda* there is mention of mysterious Uttānapād as a cosmic power.[3] It may be a possible reference to the notion of assuming the position of an embryo in the womb as a means of realizing mystical rebirth. This interpretation receives substantiation from what the *Ṛgveda* says about Vāmadeva. There, there is an explicit enunciation of the idea that mystic vision and consciousness can be attained even in the womb. The later interpreters and exegetists of Vedānta like Bādarayaṇa and Śamkara also put a mystical interpretation on the Vāmadeva hymn. This implies that according to the contemporary ideas, some exceptional souls were regarded as gifted with Yogic powers from their very birth. This conception becomes very important later on and Buddha has been credited with omniscience from the very birth. In the Ṛgvedic hymn of Lopāmudrā and Agastya, the powers acquired by continence are referred to.[4] The practice of continence is an important element in Yoga. The famous *brahmacarya sūkta* of the *Atharvaveda*[5] is a classic eulogy in praise of the power of continence. It asserts that with the aid of *brahmacarya* and *tapas* the gods were able to conquer death.[6] Western Indologists, trained in and imbued with different cultural values, have thoroughly misunderstood the significance

[1] Cf. "Ṛgveda Me Prāṇa Vidyā", *Kalyāṇa Yogāṅka*, *op.cit.*

[2] *Ibid.*

[3] *R.V.* X, 72, 3. It is not valid to hold Uttānapad as a primitive creator Yogin.

[4] *R.V.*, 1, 179.

[5] In the *Atharvaveda*, XX, 26, I, there is the word *Yogeyoge*. Charpentier, Z *DMG*, Vol. LXV.

[6] Referring to the *Brahmacāri*, the *Ṛgveda*, X, 109, 5, says *sa devānām bhavatyekamangam.*

of this theme. Some critics tend to dismiss Yoga as mental aberration or a pathological nervous reaction. But in India, some of its greatest men, from the times of the Vedas to Dayānanda and Rāmakrishṇa, have recognized the superiority of the technics of Yoga for mental peace and quiet. Some of the western thinkers like Pythagoras, Plato, Plotinus and the Gnostics accepted the efficacy of mental concentration. In ancient India, the belief prevailed that spiritual exercises of an esoteric character reveal the fullness of inner life. Yoga incorporates, in immensely powerful terms, one of the essential elements of the higher ethics and culture of India which unfailingly advocates the efficacy of discipline, austerities and sex control. The advocacy of purity and continence is the perennial theme of Indian ethics and spirituality. In the later developed theory and practice of Yoga, great stress has been laid upon the cultivation of the status of *Urdhvaretas* — that is, one who succeeds in transforming his lower sensual energy into higher spiritual power. In the technical language of the Yoga it is called the elevation of *virya* from the *mulādhāra cakra* to the *sahasrāra cakra*. It will not be historically wrong to guess that the exaltedness and emotional fervour with which the efficacy of the technics of *brahmacarya* and *tapas* are lauded in the *Atharvaveda* indicate that the germs of the later ideas of Yogic mysticism were prevalent at the time.

The goal of the various processes and technics of Yoga in later Indian thought is either the realization of the emancipated transparent character of the *purusha* or the mystic unitive realization of the supreme spirit. Although, in the early stages of Indian thought, the aim of Yoga was the enhancement of the physical and mental powers of the person who employed those technics, there are some references in the Vedic literature which can be regarded as forestallings of the later notions regarding mystic union with the Godhead. In one of the hymns of the *Ṛgveda* there is a reference to two *purushas* who are *sayujā* and *sakhāyā*.[1] This may imply that enlightened fellowship with the Godhead, on the part of the individual soul, is mentioned in this particular hymn. This interpretation gains ground from the fact that this hymn is also mentioned in the *Muṇḍaka Upaniṣad*.

1 *R.V.*, I, 164, 20.

The famous *muni sūkta* of the *Ṛgveda* is also important from the standpoint of later development of ideas regarding the Yoga.[1] The *muni* is regarded as traversing the path of Apsaras, the Gandharvas and the beasts of the wild forests. He is regarded as dwelling in the eastern and western oceans. This power of the *muni* to roam at will in different regions and paths may be the root of the later notion prevalent both in the *Yoga-Sutras* of Patanjali as well as in the Buddhist literature that the Yogi developes supernormal powers which generate the faculty of untrammelled movement at will. Buddha claims to have the capacity to move in celestial and atmospheric regions. In this *sūkta* of the Ṛgveda the hairs of the *muni* are said to be long. His garments have a yellow appearance. This reference to the yellow garments of the *muni* perhaps forestalls the later monastic dress of the Buddhist monks. The *Ṛgveda* also refers to the dirt spread over the person and garments of the *muni*.[2] This dirt may be the ashes which are spread over the bodies of Yogins. Some of the Jaina antiquarians hold that this Vedic reference has relevance to the Jaina Sādhus.[3] Although the *muni sūkta* is an isolated production of its type and does not fall in line with the worship of gods and the performance of the sacrifices that occupy so large a part of the Vedic religious system,[4] it is remarkable in the definite hint that it explicitly provides for the existence of a class of people who can safely be considered the prototypes of the later Sannyasins and Bhikkhus. Researches into ancient history and archaeology are pointing out to us the remote and antique character of monasticism as an institution. In ancient Babylonia there used to be virgin priestesses who devoted themselves to intellectual and cultural pursuits. The institution of these sacred virgins was developed to so great an extent that for maintaining their independent economic status they even carried on trade and commerce. Madame Blavatsky has pointed to the existence of mystic rites and esoteric cults in ancient Egypt in her book *Isis*

1 *R.V.*, X, 136.

2 *R.V.*, X, 136, 2.

3 References to Jaina Yoga are contained in *the Ācārānga, the Uttarādhyāna*, Umāswati's *Tattvārthidhigamasutra* etc.

4 In the *Ṛgveda*, VIII, 17, 14, occurs *Indro munīnam sakhaā*.

Unveiled. Sri Aurobindo also refers to the existence of mystery sects in ancient Egypt. Seen in the context of the religious life of Babylonia and Egypt, the *muni sūkta* of the Ṛgveda may point to the existence of a class of people who later become important in Indian religion as Yāyāvaras, bhikkhus etc.

The Vrātyas referred to in the *Atharvaveda* represent another institution of the religious world.[1] The Vrātyas are somewhat like the Yogi. Sometimes the Vrātyas are represented as pre-Aryans and sometimes as Indo-Aryans. They have been also represented as Kshatriya Yogins or mendicants. They are referred to as flourishing in the eastern regions. This also is a remarkable hint from the standpoint of the origins of Buddhism because it was in eastern India that the monastic sects of Buddhism and Jainism flourished.[2] The Vrātyas engaged themselves in ecstatic practices. Most probably the Vrātyas operated outside the pale of Brahmanism and were recipients of the favour and patronage of the Kshatriya kings. According to Haraprasad Sastry, the Vrātyas were of Aryan stock but were considered degraded.[3] They could be taken back into the Aryan community by undergoing some purificatory ceremonies. Such re-Aryanized, and other non-Aryanized Vrātyas were a fruitful source for the production of anti-Aryan heterodox ideas. The existence of the Vrātyas in eastern India made it a fit place for the growth of the unorthodox speculations of the Buddhists, the Jainas and Ājīvikas.

Another significant idea about Yoga referred to in the *Atharvaveda* is the mention of the "eight chakras." *Cakra* or plexus is a key concept in the later philosophy and practices of Hathayoga. The Atharvavedic reference to the eight cakras and nine doors of the human body is of considerable significance in so far as it proves that the *Atharvaveda* is not merely a work of magic but it also has theosophic and mystic-philosophic doctrines. The *Atharvaveda* has a syncretic character. It contains the roots of : (i) theosophic and cosmogonic ideas, (ii) the ideas of asceticism and of Yogic practices which were

[1] *Ath.*, V. 15, 1 ; XV, 8, 1 ; XV, 9, 1.

[2] H.P. Sastry, *Indian Historical Quarterly,* Vol. IX, No. 1 (March, 1933), pp. 340 ff.

[3] *Ibid.*

later developed in Hathayoga, (iii) other notions and ideas and religious practices that were later developed by the school of the Tantra in medieval India, and (iv) primitive magical notions.

Fasting is an important element in the practice of Yoga. It is resorted to for the control of the body and for mental purification. Fasting is a Vedic idea[1] and also appears as an important preparation for the various sacrifices in the *Śatapatha Brāhmaṇa*.[2] Buddhism also stressed fasting on certain days.

The Brāhmaṇas contain formulas and technics about sacrifices. They do not develop the notions regarding Yoga.

Even the *Āraṇyakas*, of which only some have come to light, do not contain any additional information regarding Yoga although it is possible that one of the teachers of the Āraṇyakas — Mahīdāsa Aitareya lived for one hundred and sixteen years and resorted to some of the practices of Yoga.[3]

2. *Yoga and the Upaniṣads*

With the advance of the Upaniṣadic philosophy, there was the rise of the idea of spiritual absolutism. The realization of the transcendent bliss of the ultimate spiritual real through philosophical and mystical contemplation is the central tenet of the Upaniṣads and it is this idea that has been developed in the system of Vedānta.[4] In his comments on one of the *Vedānta-Sūtras*[5] Śamkara has recognized the supremacy of the Vedāntic methodology to the practices inculcated in the dualistic system of Sāmkhya-Yoga. But it is made clear from Śamkara's comments on another *Vedānta-Sūtra*[6] that he means to criticise only the dualistic metaphysics of the Sāmkhya-Yoga philosophy and is willing to recognize the efficacy of Yogic technics referred to in some of the Upaniṣads like the *Kaṭha* and the *Śvetāśvatara* as preparations for the knowledge of the supreme

[1] *R.V.*, 1, 179.

[2] The *Chhāndogya Up.*, vi, refers to the fast undertaken by Śvetaketu.

[3] Vidhusekhara Bhattacharya, *The Basic Conception of Buddhism*, p. 6, strongly advocates the pre-Buddhistic origins and development of Yoga. See also S.N. Dasgupta, *Indian Philosophy*, Vol. I, p. 227.

[4] In the Upaniṣadic triple formula of *śravana, manaṇa* and *nididhyāsana*, it can be argued that the last refers to the intensity of Yogic absorption.

[5] The *Sutra* is *yoginah prati ca smaryate smārte caite* (*B.S.*, 4, 2, 21).

[6] See Śamkara's commentary on the *Vedānta Sutra* : *etena yogah pratyuktah* (*B.S.*, 2, 1, 3).

reality.[1] The essential teachings regarding Yogic practices of the Pātañjala system and of the Upaniṣads like the *Kaṭha* and the *Śvetāśvatara* are similar. It is to be stressed, however, that the fundamental emphasis of the Upaniṣads and of the Vedānta is not on external practices but on inner contemplation and meditation. In the *Chhāndogya Upaniṣad* there is the mention of the practice of establishing all the sense-organs in the *Ātma—ātmani sarvendriyaṇi sampratisṭhāphya.*[2] This practice is similar to the concept of *pratyāhāra* mentioned in the Yoga system of Pātañjali.

The *Kaṭha Upaniṣad* inculcates the restraint of the external workings of mind and speech.[3] Mind should be merged in the knowledge Self (*Vijñāna Ātmā*), and the knowledge self into the Great Self (*Mahān Ātmā*).[4] This ideal of progressive merging into the spheres of ever-inclusive realities is considered the essence of Upaniṣadic Yoga. The stoppage of the operations of mind and intellect is the consummation or the highest fulfilment —*paramām gatim*. The teachings of the *Kaṭha Upaniṣad* are comprised by it under two words, *vidyā* and *yogavidhi.*[5] This implies a synthesis of the highest luminous knowledge and the technics of the Yoga. This Upaniṣad also refers to the *sushumnā* through which the soul of the Yogi is supposed to depart to the higher worlds.[6] Some of the Upaniṣads are very rich in physiological researches[7] and here we find one instance. These physiological insights and researches were latter systematized in the medieval systems of Hathayoga and the works of Ayūrveda.

[1] According to the Upaniṣads, the technic of *tapas* is the way for the attainment of the *loka* or region of the fathers and does not lead to emancipation. The *devayāna* is the way leading to the realization of *brahman*. In the *Maitrāyaṇi Upaniṣad*. 1, 2, King Bṛhadratha even after rigorous austerities is represented as being far from attaining the liberating gnosis. Vijñānbhikshu, however, tries to link the Yoga system with the spiritual knowledge of the Upaniṣads.

[2] *Ch. Up.*, viii, 15.

[3] Cf. the *Kaushitakī Upaniṣad* where Pratardana is said to have discovered a novel method of self-control known as *antaram agnihotram.*

[4] *Kaṭha Up.*, III, 13.

[5] *K.U.*, VI, 18.

[6] *K.U.*, VI, 16.

[7] The *Brihadāraṇyaka Upaniṣad*, II, 1, 19 refers to seventy two thousand channels called *hitā* which lead from the heart to the pericardium.

The *Kaṭha* and the *Śvetasvatara* are later productions in the field of Upaniṣadic literature[1] and that accounts for the fact that they have incorporated many new elements of Yogic practices which had gained popularity. The second chapter of the *Śvetāśvatara Upaniṣad* contains the psychology and technics of Yoga. The chapter begins with prayers to the god Savitā, adapted from the *Taittirīya Saṁhitā*. According to the *Śvetaṣvatara* (1, 14), *svadeha* and *praṇava* are regarded as the two *araṇi* for *dhyānanirmathanābhyāsa*. This amounts to the advocacy of the middle path which is intermediate between physical askesis and meditation. The *Śvetāśvatara*[2] states that the place where Yogic practices are to be cultivated should be level, and free from pebbles, fire or gravel. It also recommends that the presence of water is conducive to thought.[3] It regards a secluded place as necessary for contemplation. In the Ṛgveda, Vipras are said to have attained intellectual perfection in the crevasses of mountains and at the confluence of rivers. The *Śvetāṣvatara* refers to the attainment of physical experiences which are preliminary to the attainment of *brahman* — the experiences of fog, smoke, sun, winds, fire, fireflies, lightning, crystal and the moon.[4] It emphatically states that the Yogi conquers disease, old age and death.[5] It may be pointed out that these (three) are the specific occasions of deep sorrow which had made Gautama Buddha restless. Buddha left his ancestral home to find a way out of sorrow and here the Upaniṣad also categorically states that through the mystic union with the Godhead the terror of these elements — disease, old age and death, is neutralised and the Yogi becomes immune against their attacks.

The *Maitrāyaṇī* (VI, 18), refers to the *shādanga* (six limbs) of Yoga. *Tarka* or deliberative reasoning is included here as one

[1] E.H. Johnston, *Early Sāmkhya*, (London, Royal Asiatic Society, 1937), p. 3, points out that the relevant parts of the *Kaṭha Upaniṣad* are hardly earlier than the 4th cent. B.C., while the sixth Valli may be a later addition.

[2] Some of the Upaniṣads are emphatic in their belief that Yoga leads to illumination — *Jāgrivadbhih*. They also refer to the practice of *prāṇāyama* and mention the concept of *vāmana*.

[3] *SV. Up.*, II, 10.

[4] *Ibid.*, 11.

[5] *Ibid.*, 12.

of the elements of Yoga.[1] The *Maitrāyaṇī Upaniṣad* marks a further step in the advancement of the ideas and technics of Yoga. Here we find the ideal of superconsciousness or *turīyāvasthā* referred to.[2] It refers to the process of a "higher concentration." It states that by pressing the tip of the tongue against the palate, by controlling voice, mind and speech, one can see the *brahman* through contemplation. Here we find the idea of synthesis between the technics of Yoga and the Vedāntic method of meditation.[3] The *Maitrāyaṇī* also refers to other Yogic practices like closing the ears by the thumb.[4] In the tradition of the Upaniṣads which exalt the contemplation of the *udgītha* and the *praṇava*,[5] the *Maitrāyaṇi* also inculcates the merit of repeating the sacred syllable *Om*.[6] Pātañjali's *Yoga-Sūtra* also recognizes the efficacy of meditating on *Om*.[7]

3. *Yoga and Early Buddhist Religion and Philosophy*

After leaving his ancestral home in Kapilavastu, Gautama restlessly searched for truth and wisdom. For the satisfaction of his quest, he tried numerous methods. He also practised Yoga.[8] Ālāra Kālāma taught him the technics leading to the realization of *ākincanya-āyatana* (the realization of the realm

[1] The *Brahmajāla Sutta* of the *Dīgha Nikāya* also refers to meditation of three degrees or through reasoning.

[2] *Maitrāyaṇī* Up., VI, 19.

[3] Vijñānabhikshu in later times attempted to bring the technology of Yoga in affiliation with the theosophy of the Upaniṣads.

[4] *Maitrāyaṇī*, VI, 22.

[5] The Upaniṣads refer to the concentration on other mystic words as *tadvanam* and *tajjalān*.

[6] *Maitrāyaṇī*, VI, 24. For references to *Om* in the Upaniṣads *Ch. Up.*, 1, 1. *T. U.*, 1, 8. *Kaṭha Up.*, II, 17, and *Sv. U.* 1, 14.

[7] It is a little disturbing to find that some of the later Upaniṣads like the *Jābāla*, 5, and the *Kaṇṭhaśrutī*, 4, should sanction religious suicide.

[8] For details of early Buddhistic Yoga the following Suttas of the *Majjhima Nikāya* may be consulted : *Ānāpāna Sati*, *Kāyagatā Sati*, *Cula-Sunyatā*, *Mahā-Sunyatā*, *Uddesa-vibhanga*, etc. The *Sati-Patthāna Suttana* of the *Majjhima Nikāya* which belongs to the oldest portions of the Buddhist literature also contains important ideas regarding self-concentration. In Zen Buddhism there was increasing stress on *dhyāna*. In the Yogāchara school of thought, Buddhistic ideas were combined with the practice of Yoga.

of Nothingness).[1] Uddaka Rāmaputta taught him a further stage of Yoga. He taught him the mystic process leading to *naivasamjñā-nāsamjnā-āyatana* (the realm of neither consciousness nor unconsciousness).[2] Gautama was not satisfied with these technics. He regarded them inadequate for the realization of *nirveda, virāga, nirodha, abhijñā, sambodha* and *nirvāṇa.* Hence he fell back upon his own efforts.

Buddha's historicism and traditionalism were fully revealed by his adherence to the technics and practices of Yoga.[3] The famous Aryan eight-fold way refers to *dhyāna*[4] and *samādhi.* The early Buddhist scriptures refer to the four *dhyāna.* (i) In the first *dhyāna* the Yogi concentrates his mind on reasoning (*vitarka*) and investigation (*vicāra*) and this leads to the joy of detachment and serene thought. (ii) In the second *dhyāna*, there is a stoppage of conscious reflection. Concentration, however, continues and the consequence is the attainment of ecstasy and serenity. (iii) The third *dhyāna* produces a state comparable to what is termed *udāsinavat āsīnah* in the *Bhagavad-gitā.* In this stage the joy which attends on concentration in the first and second *dhyāna* is also transcended. In this stage the Yogi attains perfect tranquility, equanimity and bodily ease. Lust of self is completely conquered in this stage. (iv) The fourth *dhyāna* results in the absolute conquest of all sense of elation and joy. It is a state of total indifference to all kinds of feelings. It is the state of the *arhat.* The full absorption in this stage results in the attainment of *nirvāṇa.* According to the *Mahā-Saccaka Sutta* and the *Bodhirājakumāra Sutta* of the *Majjhima Nikāya.* Buddha had undergone the experience of

[1] According to Saunders, *Gotama Buddha*, reprint of 1959, p. 15, "eight stages of meditation were taught by Ālāra to Gautama, (*Jatakas*, Vol. I, pp. 65-69)." (The reference to the Jātakas is inaccurate.)

[2] For a different view see E. J. Thomas, *Life of Buddha*, pp. 184-5. Cf. the concept of *śunya-cintana* in the *Sutta Nipāta*, 1117 and 1119 and *Majjhima Nikāya*, III, 294.

[3] According to H. Beckh, *Buddhismus*, Buddhism is through and through nothing but Yoga.

[4] C.A.F. Rhys Davids, "The Unknown Co-founders of Buddhism," *Journal of Royal Asiatic Society*, April 1927, pp. 193-208, says that originally *dhyāna* (the practice of rapt musing) was a mode of converse with the other world, later on it was regarded as a mode of mental exercise only.

caturdhyāna prior to his enlightenment under the sacred tree.[1] The *Pāsa-rasi Sutta* of the *Majjhima Nikya*, on the other hand, only refers to the fact that Buddha sat at a place in Uruvela Senani Nigama near a river that was flowing nearby and attained *nirvāṇa.* Here there is mention of his having resorted to *dhyāna* but the four-fold scheme of *dhyāna* is not mentioned.

The four-fold *dhyāna* is one of the significant contributions to the psychic science of Yoga.[2] Its systematic presentation and its explicit mention of mental categories indicate the deep researches that must have been made in this field.[3] In the *Yoga-Sūtras* of Pātañjali also a scheme almost the same as the one discussed here is found and that raises the historical problem of the relative priority of the Buddhistic or the Pātañjala scheme. It is not far-fetched to hold that both may have borrowed from a third common source. According to Senart,[4] Buddhism is undoubtedly the borrower from Vishnuism and Yoga. He says that the moral tendencies of the Yoga when transported in metaphysical domain could easily give rise to the nihilism of Buddhism. He also points out that it is due to the prominence of the elements of Yoga in Buddhism that Asoka calls the faithful *yuta* and *dhammāyuta.* It is a

[1] According to C.A.F. Rhys Davids, "A Dynamic Conception of Man", *Indian Culture,* Vol. VI (1939-40), pp. 235 ff., *dhyāna* or *jhana* is a preparation for developing the *abhijñā* of clarirvoyance and clairaudience. It necessitates the cultivation of *sati* or *avilapanatā* which indicates absence of superficiality of mind and the attentive alertness of will and cognition. In another paper "Dhyana in Early Buddhism", *Indian Historical Quarterly* (1927), Vol. III, pp. 689-715, C.A.F. Rhys Davids denies that *dhyāna* means meditation. According to her, early Buddhist *dhyāna* is a deliberate putting off (*pahāna*) of applying and sustaining thought. What is stated to be left is *sati* (*smṛti*) or lucid awareness. It seems that C.A.F. Rhys Davids is unnecessarily trying to appear too clever. Heiler accepts a mystical interpretation of *dhyāna.*

[2] The *Lankāvātārasūtra* has given a different scheme of the four *dhyāna* — *arthapravicaya, bālopacārika, tathatālambana* and *tāthāgata.* (See *BST* ed., p. 41, verse no. 159).

[3] In the early Buddhist literature, Anuruddha, Revata and Subhuti are regarded as experts in *dhyāna.* See the *Theragatha,* CCLVI, 3, 1. Sāriputta, Moggallāna and Nanda also were adepts in *dhyāna.*

[4] E. Senart, *Origins Bouddhiques,* Paris, Ernest Leroux, 1907 (translated into English by M. Roy, *Indian Historical Quarterly,* Vol. VI, 1930).

testimony to the persistent recollection of the origin of Buddhism from Yoga system. Senart asserts that Gautama Buddha was a Yogin brought up in the practices of a Yoga-system which received its final form in the cult of Vishnu-Krishna.

Besides the four-fold *dhyāna*, a second categorical scheme in the field of Buddhistic Yoga is that of the four *brahmavihāra* or sublime occupations. Buddha in the *Tevijja Sutta* of the *Dīgha Nikāya* refers to the cultivation of four exalted psychological moods : love and kindness (*maitrī*), compassion (*kāruṇā*), cheerfulness (*muditā*) and impartiality (*upekshā*).[1]

Buddhaghosa is one of the great systematizers of the teachings of early Buddhism. He states in the third section of the *Visuddhimagga* that the higher life has three phases — (i) *adhicitta* or concentration. There are forty subjects (*karma-sthāna*) noted by Buddhaghosa on which concentration can be practised. There are ten *kasiṇa*, ten impurities (*aśubha*), ten reflections (*anusmṛti*), four *brahmavihāra*, four *arūpadhyāna*, one perception or *samjnā* (that all nourishment is impure) and one analysis or *vyavasthāna* (the analysis that all things consist of four elements). These constitute the forty entities on which *adhicitta* is to be practised. But *adhicitta* is not indispensable for *nirvāṇa*. (ii) *Śamatha* or peace constitutes the second phase of the higher life. (iii) The third phase is *adhiprajṇā* or *vipaśyanā*. It provides insight and is indispensable for *nirvāṇa*. This triology of *adhicitta*, *śamatha* and *adhiprajṇā* established by Buddhaghosa seems to be a reformulation of the earlier Buddhist triology of *śila*, *samādhi* and *prajnā*. *Śamatha* is exactly the same as *samādhi*. *Adhiprajṇā* or *vipaśyanā* is only another term for

[1] Cf. the *Indrīya-Bhāvanā Suttanta* of the *Majjhima Nikāya*. According to Warren, *Buddhism in Translations*, pp. 282-283, "The states (*samāpatti*) in the Buddhist system of meditation were of importance not merely as a means for arriving at *nirvāṇa*, but the release they afforded from the sense-percepts and the concrete was so highly esteemed that they were looked upon as luxuries and enjoyed as such by the saints and by the Buddha himself." C.A.F. Rhys Davids, *Buddhist Psychology*, (London, Luzac & Co., 1924), p. 104, points out that the exercise of the *Brahma-vihāra*, according to the testimony of the Nikāyas (*SN*, V, 115 ff.) were not originally or at least not exclusively Buddhist.

prajṇā.[1] There are differences, however, between *adhicitta* and *śila.* While *śila* is the name of a code of moral rules for the lay adherents as well as for the bhikkhus, *adhicitta* is a system of concentration and thus it pertains not to the field of ethics but to that of Yoga and mysticism. Buddhaghosa's contribution in heaving formulated this scheme lies not in the field of original construction but in that of systematization of a large body of ideas regarding mental discipline.[2]

4. *Buddhism and Pātañjala-Yoga*

There are some remarkable resemblances between the conceptions of Yoga of the Pātañjala system and the Buddhistic thought.[3] Both accept that through Yoga there is the extinction of pain. In both the systems the practice of Yoga is defined and stressed without any reference to a Godhead. Buddha is silent about a Godhead if not absolutely atheistic. According to Pātañjali, belief in God is one of the alternative paths to the attainment of *samādhi.* Both the systems, however, accept the concept of *samādhi.* According to Pātañjali, through the practice of Yoga there is a loss of the sense of *asmita* or egoism. In Buddhism there is no recognition of any soul substance.[4] But it also states that with the perfection in the practice of

[1] According to the *Sutta Piṭaka, prajñā* is allied to *vijñāna.* The Abhidharma would comprehend *prajñā* under the comprehensive category of *samskāra.* The view that one form of *prajña-divyacakshu,* can be classed under *rūpa skandha* is considered a heretical proposition according to the *Kathāvatthu,*

[2] For the Sautrāntika and Vasubandhu's conception of *samāpatti,* see Th. Stcherbatsky, *The Central Conception of Buddhism,* p. 23.

[3] J.H. Woods, *The Yoga-System of Pātaūjali,* Harvard Oriental Series, Vol. XVII (Harvard University Press, 1914), Indian Reprint of 1967, pp. XII-XIX points out the historical importance of Yoga texts as forming a bridge between the philosophy of ancient India and the fully developed Indian Buddhism and the religious thought of to-day in Eastern Asia. He also says that the Yoga system, together with the Nyāya, and Vaiśeshiska systems, when grafted upon the simple practical exhortations of practical Buddhism, serves as an introduction to the logical and metaphysical masterpieces of Mahāyāna. According to Jacobi, the *Yoga-Sūtra* is definitely influenced by Buddhist *Vijñānavāda* and is probably later than Vasubandhu.

[4] In Buddhism the stress is on the purification of mind. In the Brāhmanical schools of Yoga, on the other hand, the substantialist conception of man is always adhered to.

Yoga, the least clinging to any egoism or any false sense of attachment is neutralized.[1] Moreover, there is both ideological and terminological similarity between the Buddhist ideal of *nirvāṇa* and Patanjali's view that Yoga is practised for the *nirodha* — suppression or ultimate extinction of the mental states. The ideal of the elimination of sense-impressions is accepted in both the systems. Both the schools use *bhumi* to mark the progress made in religious endeavours. From the numerical standpoint there is some parallelism between the Aryan eightfold way and the *ashtānga* Yoga of Pātañjali, because the number eight is exalted in both.

It has been sometimes stated that the methodology of the fourfold Aryan truth of suffering — predication, predication of its origin (*samudaya*), cessation (*nirodha*) and the way to cessation, have been taken from the contemporary medical science. According to Vyāsa's *Bhāsya* on Patanjali's *Yoga-Sūtras*, (Y.S., II, 15), there are four sections of medical science : (a) disease — *roga*, (b) the cause of disease — *rogahetu*, (c) health — *ārogyam* and (d) medicinal treatment—*bhaishajyam*. Vyāsa states that in the philosophy of Yoga also there are four sections (*caturvyūha*) : (a) the world — *samsāra*, (b) the cause of the world — *samsārahetu*, (b) emancipation — *moksha* and (d) the path to emancipation — *mokshopāya*.

5. *Sociological Approach to Yoga*

In the early periods of the development of Yoga, it was resorted to mainly for exhilaration and for the enhancement of physical and vital powers. From the beginning, Yoga had an individualistic orientation because it resulted in the production of mighty individuals who could assert themselves against the taboos and commands of the community. In the later phases of its development, Yoga became a tecnnic of intellectual illumination. The use of Yoga for increasing physical and vital powers became more and more associated with the practices of Hathayoga. According to the Upaniṣads, the attainment of supreme wisdom is the aim of the spiritual

[1] According to E.H. Johnston, *Early Samkhya*, the Buddhist view of Yoga is not the suppression of the senses while in the Brāhmanical view the stress is on complete suppression of the sense (see the Bhāsya on *Yoga-Sūtra*, II, 55).

aspirant. According to Buddhism, the final goal of moral efforts (*śila*) and concentration (*samādhi*) is the attainment of *prajñā* or cognitive illumination. In the school of Pātañjali also, there is the acceptance of the ideal of the attainment of *ritambharā prajñā* through the practice of the processes of Yoga. Thus in all the three schools of thought — the Upaniṣads, Buddhism and Pātañjala Yoga, the aim, of Yoga is considered to be cognitive perfection. This dominantly intellectual orientation of Yoga further intensifies its original individualistic character. Perfection in Yoga is consequent upon an increasing isolation not only from the claims and obligations of the society but also from the physical proximity of other citizens. In place of the king's court or the republican motehall, or the sacrificial altar, the places that the Yogi frequents aie the caves of the mountains, the confluence of rivers, burning ghats and other secluded quarters. Thus the Yogi is the representation of the ideal of extreme individualism. Yoga, thus, has significantly contributed to the growth of individualism in Indian culture.

Chapter 14

SĀMKHYA AND EARLY BUDDHISM

A. ORIGINS OF SĀMKHYA THOUGHT AND PHILOSOPHY

1. *Introduction*

LIKE BUDDHISM, the Sāmkhya is a very important system of Indian philosophical thought.[1] Rationalistic intellectualism and dialectical subtlety[2] characterize this system throughout. According to Vivekananda, Kapila is the founder of Indian rationalism.[3] The Sāmkhya enjoys a very reputable position in Indian philosophic thought and the *Bhagavadgitā* calls Kapila to be a perfect sage.[4] Kapila was regarded as having attained perfection from his very birth. Modern critics interpret the word Kapila occurring in the *Śvetāśvatara Upaniṣad*[5] as referring to the world-soul (*hiranyagarbha*).[6] But Śamkara and Vivekananda take the word 'Kapila' there as a reference to the founder of the Sāmkhya thought[7] and from a perusal of the context I agree with them. Śamkara was busy demolishing the claim of the Sāmkhya to be based upon the scriptures but even he too had to acknowledge it as a *smṛti*. Bādarayaṇa had also called

1 R. Sarma, *Vedantism*, (Sreegopal Basu Mallick Fellowship Lectures, 1907-1908. Calcutta, Wilkins Press, Publisher J.N. Bose, 1909), p. 8.

2 John Davies, "On the connection of the Sāmkhya System with the Philosophy of Spinoza", (pp. 139-143), "On the connection of the system of Kapila with that of Schopenhauer and Von Hartmann" (pp. 143-151), *Hindu Philosophy : The Samkhya Karika of Iswara Krishna* (London, Trubner & Co., Ludgate Hill, 1881).

3 *The Complete Works of Swami Vivekananda*, Mayavati memorial edition, Part II (Almora, Advaita Ashrama, 1945), p. 443.

4 *Bhagavadgitā*, X, 26.

5 *Śvetāśvatara Upaniṣad*, V, 2.

6 The *hiraṇyagarbha* of the Vedas may be compared to the Demiurgus of Plato's *Timaeus*.

7 *The Complete Works of Swami Vivekananda*, *op. cit.*, p. 443.

Sāmkhya a *smṛti*.[1] So great was the premium put upon the Sāmkhya metaphysics and its emphasis on contemplation that the way of the Sāmkhyas came to be considered synonymous with the contemplative life as opposed to the active energistic life, in the *Bhagavadgitā*.[2] Some of the elements of the Buddhistic thought have been considered to be the legacy of the Sāmkhya. The Pythagorean philosophy of "Numbers" was regarded as having been formulated as a result of the misunderstanding of the Sāmkhya thought.[3] Garbe has also called attention to the influence of Sāmkhya thought on the Gnostics and on Plotinus.[4] Garbe held that Pythagorean arithmology was the result of his misunderstanding the fact that the Sāmkhya owed its name to the enumeration of principles for the notion that the Sāmkhya made number the basis of nature. Keith does not agree with this. Garbe accepts the influence of the Sāmkhya also on the *Mahābhārata*, the *Purāṇas* and the *Manusmṛti*. He regards Kapila as a clear and practical thinker, as distinguished from the Upaniṣadic sages. The Sāmkhya, he considers, as the oldest system of Indian philosophy which launched a reaction against the idealistic monism of the Upaniṣads.

The Sāmkhya,[5] as the name suggests, pursues an analytical methodology based on numerical classification. It also emphasises contemplation and reason, hence the word *pratisāmkhyā-nirodha* is stressed in the later Buddhistic philosophy.[6] The

1 *Brahma-Sūtra*, II, 1, 2.

2 *Bhagavadgitā*, II, 39 ; III, 3.

3 A.B. Keith, *The Samkhya System* (London, Oxford University Press, 1924), 2nd ed., p. 76, refers to Von Schroeder in his *Pythagoras Und, die Inder*, pp. 72-76 and to Richard Garbe, who upheld the influence of the Sāmkhya upon Pythagoras.

4 Richard Garbe, "Sāmkhya", *The Encyclopaedia of Religion and Ethics*, Vol. XI. In his book *Outlines of Indian Philosophy*, pp. 10ff., Garbe pronounces the Sāmkhya to be the "oldest real system of Indian Philosophy" and says that it supplies in main outlines the foundations of Jainism and Buddhism. For scepticism regarding the influence of Indian thought on Plotinus, A. Berriedale Keith, "Plotinus and Indian Thought", *Indian Culture*, Vol. II, July 1935-April 1936, pp. 125-130.

5 The word *Sāmkhya* has two meanings : (i) enumeration and (ii) thinking.

6 *Pratisamkhyānirodha* (or *nirvāṇa*) means conscious universal destruction of *saśrava dharma* and *apratisāmkhyānirodha* means unconscious

Sāmkhyan categories show the attempt of the human mind to analyse the empiric phenomena. Even as early as the *Ṛgveda* we find attempts at numerical analysis and the classification of cosmic phenomena. We shall see that the Sāmkhya has made the most comprehensive attempt to categorize both the objective external and subjective psychic phenomena and to reduce them all to the indeterminate original *prakṛti*, a concept comparable in some respects to the *apeiron* of Anaximander, or to the Matter of Haeckel.

Otto Pfleiderer has represented five parallel dialectical stages in the development of thought from naturalistic pantheism and atheism in India and Greece.[1]

(i) The concepts of the primal principle as primal germ and emanation from it were enunciated.

(ii) The second stage saw the denial of the reality of the becoming and many, and the world of appearance was considered as an illusion as in the Vedānta and Parmenides.

(iii) The question arose, why are there many ? — No answer was given to it either by the Brāhmin speculations or by the Eleatics. Hence against abstract monism arose abstract pluralism.

(iv) In opposition to the doctrine of unity arose the Sāmkhya theory of multiplicity of souls (in a spritualist manner) paralleled by the theory of multiplicity of atoms in Leucippus and Democritus (in a materialist manner).

(v) The Buddhist doctrine of the flux and becoming also arose as a reaction against the concept of the motionless Being. Similarly the Ephesian Heraclitus reacted to the Eleatic doctrine of "all-one" with his doctrine of "all-flows."

Fundamental and epoch-making landmarks in human thought are the products of long years and even decades and in some rare cases even centuries, of deep pondering. We may find dominant notions crystallised in one pesonality or being propounded in one era but they require previous periods of long preparation. It is not logical to hold that so momentous a thought-system as the Sāmkhya would appear suddenly. The fundamental ideas of the Sāmkhya were developing from very

universal destruction. These two categories are terms of the Sarvastivadī school.

1 Otto Pfleiderer, *The Philosophy of Religion* : *On the Basis of Its History*, translated from the German of the second and greatly enlarged edition by Alexander Stewart and Allan Menzies (London, Williams & Norgate, 1886-1888), 4 Vols., Vol. 3, pp. 240-241.

old times.

First I shall summarise the leading tenets of the Sāmkhya and then try to trace their historical-philosophical antecedents. We find the following dominant principles and concepts in this school :

(I) A very clear-cut recognition of the ultimate duality of the subject and the object.

(II) *Prakṛti* or objective, super-sensual, unconscious nature. In the words of B. N. Seal it is 'an undifferentiated manifold, an indeterminate infinite continuum of infinitesimal Reals'.[1] Guṇaratna (14th Cent. A.D.) in his commentary on the *Sad-darśanasamuccaya* called the *Tarkarahasyadīpikā*, says that there are two schools of the Sāmkhya. (i) Those who maintain that there are different *pradhāna* (prakṛti) for each *purusha*. (ii) They who maintain the existence of only one eternal *pradhāna*. (Maulikya Sāmkhya).

(III) *Guṇas*[2] —There are the three *guṇas* or constituent forms or powers of prakṛti and not its qualities. *Sattva* is of the nature of illuminating light, *rajas* produces action and energy and *tamas* is an obstructing element.[3] According to the *Sāmkhya-Karikā*, *sattva* is of the type of light (*prakāśa*), *rajas* is the source of motion (*pravṛti*) and *tamas* has the character of being heavy

[1] Brajendra Nath Seal, *The Positive Sciences of the Ancient Hindus* (London, Longmans & Co., 1915). Just as B.N. Seal has tried to interpret the Sāmkhya concept of *guṇa* in the light of modern physics, so also, Th. Stcherbatsky, "The Dharmas of the Buddhists and the Gunas of the Sāmkhya", *The Indian Historical Quarterly*, Vol. X, 1934, pp. 737-760, and p. 749 says that the gunas and their phenomena are momentary flashes of instantaneous infra-atomic quanta charged wlth some energy. S. N. Dasgupta, "Sāmkhya as Non Vedic", *Indian Culture*, 1934-1935, holds that according to the Sāmkhya matter is the product of a course of successive emanations from a fundamental pre-matter (*prakṛti*). There does not seem to be any support for this interpretation.

[2] A.B. Keith, *The Sāmkhya System*, p. 20n, has controverted the view of P. Oltramare as stated in his *L' historie des Idees Theosophiques*, that the *guna* doctrine is a later accretion to the Sāmkhya.

[3] S.N. Dasgupta, *A History of Indian Philosophy*, (Cambridge University Press, 1922, Reprint of 1957), Vol. I, p. 221 : "originally the notion of gunas was applied to different types of good and bad mental states, and then they were supposed in some mysterious way by mutual increase and decrease to form the objective world on the one hand and the totality of human psychosis on the other."

and producing impediments (*niyama*). The *Bhagavadgitā*, (Chapter XVII) and Vācaspati in the *Sāmkhyatattvakaumudī* follow a similar interpretation. But Vijnānabhikshu in his *Sāmkhyapravacanabhāsyam* categorically interpreted the gunas as reals. B.N. Seal, has accepted this interpretation.[1] According to him these Reals are termed Gunas, and are classed under three heads : (a) *sattva*, essence or intelligence-stuff ; (b) *rajas*, energy, and (c) *tamas*, matter characterised by mass or inertia. But he also incorporates the Spencerian notions of (a) increasing integration and increasing differentiation within the evolving whole and (b) the law of dissipation of energy, and the Aristotelian distinction of *potentia* and *actualisation* in his sophisticated version of the Sāmkhya. In the historical interpretation of the Sāmkhya it is safe to confine to the interpretation provided in the *Sāmkhya-Karikā*. B.N. Seal has made the most determined attempt to interpret the Sāmkhya on modern lines. He says that the *tanmātra* is infra-atomic particle of subtile matter, characterized by (a) quantum or mass, (b) physical characters and (c) potentials of energies. Ākāśa is the link between the infra-atomic particles (*tanmātra*) and the atoms. The proto-atomic *ākāśa* integration resides in the ubiquitous non-atomic *ākāśa*.

(IV) A plurality of *purushas* who exercise tremendous but silent influence over the cosmic procession, and the *prakṛti* keeps working for their final liberation.

2. *The Vedic Roots of the Sāmkhya*

(a) *Materialism or Hylozoism in the Nāsadiya Sūkta*

With these broad tenets of the orthodox Sāmkhya in our mind, if we analyse the older literary and philosophical texts, we arrive at valuable conclusions. I feel that a very great drawback in our studies of the ancient Vedic texts is a fundamental prejudice that these books are primitive and hence unphilosophical. But the late B.G. Tilak has pointed out that there has been no appreciable major advance in the philosophical thought of the world, upon the *nāsadiya sūkta*, although more and more arguments and counter-arguments have been advanced

[1] B.N. Seal, *Positive Sciences*, pp. 17ff.

for and against the monism contained there. The vital truth of all spiritual monism is declared there in powerful language. I have the conviction that the Vedas contain the elementary roots of genuine philosophical ideas. Those scholars who have worked upon the origins of the Sāmkhya system of thought mainly start with the Upaniṣads. Dr. S. N. Dasgupta, for example, says: "The origin of the Sāmkhya system of thought is rather obscure. We find almost nothing regarding the Sāmkhya course of thought in the Samhitā literature or the Brāhmaṇas." But the learned professor is sadly mistaken here because he too shares the same old prejudice. It has now been substantially accepted that the *Ṛgveda* contains elements of ontological realism and that may be regarded as the basis of the Sāmkhya.

The Vedas recognize the existence of *prakṛti*. Just as the hylozoistic philosophers of Ionia and the Greek mainland considered water, air, or fire as the '*arche*', so also in the Vedas one finds that physical elements are posited as the original constitutive ground of the entire universe. One of the hymns of the *Ṛgveda* states that water was the *arche*. Rāmāvatāra Śarmā says with regard to the *nāsadiya* hymn: "The *arche* suggested by this ancient hymn is already very subtle. It is something like Anaximander's *Apeiron* and appears to be the prototype of the Sāmkhya conception of Prakṛti. This hymn also refers to *salila*, *tamas*, *tapas*, or water, chaos, and heat as the primal elements from which the world has evolved. But these appear to be later evolutions of that one (*tad ekam*) which breathed without air (*avātam*) through its self-sustaining power of *svadhā*."[1] But I differ from the view of Prof. Sarmā. This hymn raises the fundamental question as to the breathing of the *ekam* and it says that he breathed from out of his cosmic power. The power of breathing shows that the 'one' was a living being. Thus it means that the *ekam* of the *Nāsadiya* invested with the *svadhā* is a sentient power and hence it cannot be the origin of the Sāmkhya *prakṛti* which is inconscient. Therefore, we should make other attempts to locate the Sāmkhya trends of thought in the Vedas.

[1] Ramavatara Sarma, *Vedantism*, *op. cit.*, pp. 2-3.

(b) *Origin of the Concept of Prakṛti in the Vedas*

I suggest the following hymns as the possible sources of the idea behind the concept of *prakṛti* :

"Two birds associated together, and mutual friends, take refuge in the same tree ; one of them eats the sweet fig ; the other, abstaining from food, merely looks on ... In the tree into which the smooth-gliding (rays), feeds on the sweet (produce), enter, and again bring forth (light) over all ; they have called the fruit sweet, but he partakes not of it who knows not the protector (of the universe) ... I wage war with (hostile) men, I pervade heaven and earth ... my birthplace is in the midst of the waters ; from thence I spread through all beings, and touch this heaven with my body ... I breathe forth like the wind, giving form to all created worlds ; beyond the heaven, beyond this earth (am I), so vast am I in greatness." (*Ṛgveda* : I, 164, 20ff. and *R.V.* X, 125. Wilson's Translation, Vol. II, pp. 74-75).

Vṛksha here stands as the symbol of the original energy and matter-stuff wherefrom the cosmos proceeds.[1] In the Sāmkhya thought nature enjoys a very important position, so much so that it is termed *pradhāna*. In the *Ṛgveda*, 1, 164, quoted above in translation, we find that both the cosmic and individual souls adhere to the same 'tree' and this shows the importance nature symbolised by the 'tree' enjoyed in the Vedic thought. Doubtless, nature during the Vedic period was not considered autonomous but was regarded as being governed by the famous gods like Prajāpati, Bṛhaspati or Viṣvakarman, unlike in the Sāmkhya, but the idea of nature, apart from spirit, is present there.

In the *Ṛgveda*, X. 125, quoted above in translation, we find *vāgāmbhṛṇī* being thoroughly eulogised without any theological taint. *Vāgāmbhṛṇi* is a prototype of the *śakti* of medieval Tantricism, which is the concentrated stuff wherefrom the cosmos proceeds.[2] In the *Ṛgveda* there is thus the germinal conception of the Sāmkhyan *prakṛti*.

[1] Cf. Sri Aurobindo, *The Life Divine*, Vol. I, (Calcutta, The Arya Publishing House, 1943), 2nd edition, p. 305 : "... in the ancient Vedic formula Earth, type of the more solid states of substance, was accepted as the symbolic name of the material principle." Cf. the *Pṛthvi Sukta* of *Atharvaveda*.

[2] The *Vāgāmbhṛṇi* may be compared with the *aditi*. With regard to the *aditi*, see S. Radhakrishnan, *Indian Philosophy*, Vol. I, p. 82.

(*c*) *The Vedic Origins of Guṇavāda, Naturalism and Dualism*

The *Prakṛti* of the Sāmkhya is constituted of the three *guṇa.* The *Atharvaveda* (X, 8, 43) refers to the three *guṇa.*[1] Thus a Vedic source for the concept of the three *guṇa* is found. Hence not only the germs of the concept of *prakṛti* but even the concept of the three *guṇa* can be traced to the *Atharvaveda.*

> "The lotus flower of nine doors,
> Covered with three strands,
> What prodigy there is within it,
> That the Brahman-knowers know.

(The *Atharvaveda*, X, 8, 43.)

In the *Ṛgveda* X, 72. 3 it is said :

> "In the first age of the gods the existent was born of the non-existent ; after that the quarters (of the horizon) were born, and after them the upward-growing (trees)."

(*Ṛgveda*, Wilson's translation, Vol. VI, p. 130)

Macdonell says that the conception of the origination of the existent (*sat*) from the non-existent (*asat*) as formulated in the *nāsadiya sūkta* is "the starting-point of the natural philosophy which developed into the Sāmkhya system."[3] This notion of the emanation and manifestation of the existent from an original Nothing is referred to also in the *Chhāndogya* and may be the precursor of the later nihilistic systems of thought. Contemporary with the Vedic thought there was a heterodox tradition. The *nāsadiya sūkta* refers to that, and the *Ṛgveda* X. 72, is the classic example of that. This anti-Vedic doctrinal tradition was the fountain of all antagonistic creeds which sought to undermine the foundations of orthodox wisdom. But according to Śamkara, the *asat* in the Śruti (like the *Taittirīya Upaniṣad*) refers only to an apparent non-existence and not to

1 Sometimes Upaniṣadic origins are ascribed to the three concepts, *tamas, rajas* and sattva. The *Brihadāraṇyaka* says : *tamaso mā jyotir gamaya.* The *Munḍaka* refers to *virajam brahma nishkalam* and *viśuddha-sattvah kāmayate.* But I may point Vedic origins of at least the *tamas* and the *rajas.* In the Ṛgveda X, 129, there is mention of *tama āsita tamasā guḍham* and of *nāsidrajo na vyomā.*

2. A.A. Macdonell, *The Vedic Reader* (Oxford, Clarendon Press, 1928), p. 207.

a total denial of ultimate reality. There is no doubt, however, that this naturalistically oriented hymn of the *Ṛgveda* prepares the background for the metaphysical propositions of tne Sāmkhya which seek to explain the universe without positing any supreme spiritual being. There is no direct connexion between this particular hymn and the non-theistic cosmology of the Sāmkhya. But this hymn is an indication of the type of philosophical mentality which resulted, later on, in the naturalistic, materialistic and anti-spiritualistic schools of Indian thought.

It would be an inaccurate attempt to trace the root of the Sāmkhya dualism in the Vedas. S. Radhakrishnan says :

> "There are hymns which stop wlth the two principles of *Purusha* and *Prakṛti*. In X. 82. 5-6 of the hymn to Viśvakarman, we find it said that the waters of the sea contained the first or primordial germ. This first germ is the world-egg floating on the primeval waters of chaos, the principle of the universe of life. From it arises Viśvakarman, the first-born of the universe, the creator and maker of the world."[1]

But it is not plausible to trace in this hymn the root of a fundamental principle of the Sāmkhya thought—dualistic metaphysics. Although in this chapter we are trying to demonstrate the Vedic origin of the Sāmkhya, we find it difficult to regard this particular hymn as even the indirect source of Sāmkhya dualism. Undoubtedly, the *nihareṇa pravṛtā jalpyā*[2] may be ragarded as a parallel to the Sāmkhya *prakṛti*. In the Sāmkhya conception both the *purusha* and *prakṛti* are eternal, but since this hymn asserts the birth of the Visvakarman from the world-egg, hence any comparison with Sāmkhya thought is absolutely negated.

As regards the origins of Sāmkhya thought in the Vedas we have indicated the following points so far :

(1) In the *Ṛgveda*, 1.164, the human ego is regarded as separate from the cosmic ego. This *mantra* is reproduced in the *Muṇḍaka* and the *Śvetāśvatara*.[3] This notion of a disinterested participant in the cosmic process refers to an importnt point and possibly might have led to the formulation of the Sāmkhya

1 S. Radhakrishnan, *Indian Philosophy*, Vol. I, p. 102.
2 *Ṛgveda*, X, 82, 7.
3 *Muṇḍaka Upaniṣad*, III, 1, 1, *Śvetāśvatara Upaniṣad*, IV, 6.

conception of *purusha.* It is peculiarly important as a radical contrast, in the context of the later developments of the Upaniṣadic monism, which made the cosmic and the psychic selves identical.

(2) The mention of the three *guṇa* is found in the *Atharvaveda.*

(3) Gertain words like *vṛksa,* which may be the root of the conception of *prakṛti* as a unity are found in the *Ṛgveda.* This notion can prepare the way for Sāmkhya *prakṛti* and for the realism of Sāmkhya. The intellectual legacy of the dominant realism of the Vedas must have been of vital importance in face of the great danger to Sāmkhya theory from the Upaniṣadic idealism with its implied premise of the world as *māyā.* The Sāmkhya ontological realism could well derive support from the Vedas. Even if we cannot trace any other ideas of the Sāmkhya in the Vedas, these three points are not insignificant. In face of them we can well realise the absurdity of the attempt of modern scholars like Deussen and Keith to start with the Upaniṣads in tracing the roots of Sāmkhya ideas.

3. *The Upaniṣads and the Sāmkhya*

After the Vedas we pass on to the Brāhmaṇas. These books, especially the *Śatapatha,* contain cosmogonic passages. Johnston holds that the Sāmkhya is rooted in the speculations of the Brāhmaṇas and the oldest Upaniṣads with regard to the constitution of the individual.[1] He came to the conclusion that Buddhism originated before Sāmkhya. Sāmkhya arose at a time when primitive Buddhism was transformed by the first growth of dogmatism. The Buddhist records preserve two elements of speculation dealing with the analysis of the individual — (i) *nāmarūpa* (this word occurs in the *Atharvaveda* X, 2, 12 ; XI, 7, 1 and XII, 5, 9) and (ii) the categories of *dṛsta, śruta, mata,* and *vijnāta.* These can be traced to remote sources, that is before the time when early Sāmkhyan categories had been gathered together. These older categories of pre-Upaniṣadic and Upanisadic times, which had lost their comprehensive

[1] According to E.H. Johnston, *Early Sāmkhya* (London, The Royal Asiatic Society, 1937), pp. 18-19, the *Śatapatha* X, 1, 3, 4, which contains mention of five mortal and five immortal parts may be a starting-point for early Sāmkhya. (pp. 23-24, *Ibid.*)

connotation, and for which reason they were later replaced, would not have been adopted by Buddha, had the more accurate Sāmkhyan categories been available to him. Hence Johnston holds that "Buddhism originated before Sāmkhya, which should be placed in the epoch when the primitive teaching of the Buddha was being transformed by the first growth of dogmatism."[1] The cosmogony and cosmology of the Brāhmaṇas are the precursors of a realistic system of thought. In the orthodox Sāmkhya we find the elaboration of the evolution of categories from *prakṛti*. The Sāmkhya scheme is realistic because it traces all physical entities and psychic transformations to one fundamental *prakṛti*. In the Brāhmaṇas also all spatio-temporal entities are regarded as having emanated from one basic principle, sometimes called the Prajāpati. The fundamental difference between the Sāmkhya and the Brāhmaṇas, however, is that while the former stresses nature as the originating real, the latter refer to a spiritual or a theological principle. Nevertheless, the fundamental attempt in both cases is to stress one supreme originating matrix for the multiple phenomena of the world. Thus in spite of differences in positing the nature of the originating principle, the procedure is similar. It is possible that the cosmogonic speculations of the Brāhmaṇas might have helped that trend of thinking which is interested in finding the one primal root of multiple temporal phenomena.

The Upaniṣads are a veritable storehouse of philosophic wisdom and in spite of the various attempts of the different Ācāryas to construe a harmonious philosophy out of them it remains a fact that the Upaniṣads contain a collection of different types of philosophical ideas, although the central note is one of spiritual monistic idealism. The Upaniṣads do contain references to divergent schools of thought and consider materialistic, naturalistic and nihilistic ideas as the views of opponents which are subsequently refuted. I have a feeling that a great mass of literature intermediate between the Brāhmaṇas and the Upaniṣads, which would have been the source of the Upaniṣadic ideas has been lost. In the Brāhmaṇas we find a very detailed sacri-

[1] The *Chhāndogya Upaniṣad*, VI, 2, contains mention of *asat* (non-being) as the source of the origination of being. This idea is subsequently refuted. But this shows that materialistic conceptions were in the air.

ficial ritualistic mechanism. But in the Upaniṣads we see a developed idealism and there does not seem to be any logical procession of thought from ritualism to idealism. Rāmāvatara Sarma[1] also upholds a similar view from a different standpoint.

(a) *Refutation of the Views of Deussen, Dahlmann, Keith and Barua*

Attempts have, so far, been made by Western and Indian scholars to trace the development of Sāmkhyan ideas from the Upaniṣads, but our thesis is that the Sāmkhya had a Vedic source and it developed as an important branch of thought along with the Upaniṣads and the Upaniṣadic references to Sāmkhya, as in the *Kaṭha* and the *Śvetāśvatara* are not the sources for the Sāmkhya but indicate the attempt of the Upaniṣadic writers to bring the Sāmkhyan ideas into harmony with the Upaniṣadic monism.

Deussen says : "The rise of the Sāmkhya system...is one of the most difficult and obscure problems in the region of Indian philosophy."[2] His point of view is that the Sāmkhya thought emerges due to a natural disintegration of the doctrine of the Upaniṣads.[3] We shall briefly state his thesis and then enter into its criticism. He says that although the idealism of the Upaniṣadic teachers culminated in the formulation of the notion of a supreme absolute or *brahman*, nevertheless the empirical consciousness of man continued to cling to material phenomena and a place had to be found for matter.[3] Cosmogonic researches

[1] Sarma, *Vedantism*, pp. 3-4.

[2] Paul Deussen, *The Philosophy of the Upaniṣads*, p. 239.

[3] Paul Deussen, "Outlines of Indian Philosophy", *The Indian Antiquary*, Vol. XXIX, December 1900, pp. 365-70 and 393-399. Deussen also says that the *Bhagavadgitā*, the *Sanatsujātiya*, the *Moksha Dharma* sections and other texts of the *Mahābhārata*, though in an earlier form than that attained by them in the present *Mahābhārata*, have formed the common basis of Buddhism and the Sāmkhya. In the philosophical system of the *Mahābhārata*, whether it is called epic Sāmkhya or realistic Vedānta, the *prakṛti* is opposed to the plurality of souls but both are, more or less, dependent on the *brahman*. This is the starting-point both of the Sāmkhya and Buddhism. The *Mahābhārata*, XII, 318, 319 mentions three schools of Sāmkhya :

(i) Those who admit 24 categories—this is the teaching of Kapila. In it the *avyakta* in the state of *purusha* (= *purushā-vasthā*) is the ultimate

were conducted and the *Chhāndogya* and the *Taittirīya* contain the cosmological argument for the existence of a Godhead. The Absolute which according to the rigors of philosophical argumentation was regarded as a category for contemplation and mystical realisation came to be regarded as a personal God for purposes of worship and the *Māṇḍukya* contains such notions. The Godhead was also conceived as immanent in the world. Cosmogonic and pantheistic attempts, really speaking, spell the death of monistic idealism. According to Deussen, the pantheism of the Upaniṣads develops into theism because the *brahman* entering the created world as soul is faced with the individual soul which gains a reality of its own as the method of empirical knowledge gains acceptance. The Upaniṣadic theism later developed into atheism. The division of the *ātman* between the supreme and the individual souls led to the destruction of the supreme soul because it had derived its vital force solely from the *atman* existing in me, which indeed alone exists.[1] After its separation from the latter it could only with difficulty be maintained at all. The creative faculties were attributed to matter and God became superfluous and ultimately the Sāmkhya realism ousted God. Deussen concludes by saying that the Sāmkhya system is nothing but the result of the degeneration of the Upaniṣadic Vedānta through the growth of realistic tendencies. There seems to have been a time when Vedānta thought lived only in its Sāmkhya form and the Yoga based itself on it because no other base was available.

According to Paul Deussen, there are, thus, six succeeding stages of Indian philosophical evolution which can be thus

reality. (ii) Those who admit 25 categories—they maintain the dualism of *purusha* and *prakṛti*. This is the teaching of Pancaśikha, who is said to be the pupil of Āsuri who was Kapila's pupil. (iii) Those who admit 26 categories—they accept also the reality of *Iśvara*.

[1] Paul Deussen, "Outlines of Indian Philosophy", *op. cit.*, and *The Philosophy of the Upaniṣads, op. cit.*, says that when these cosmogonic attempts were emphasized and stressed, matter assumed a prominent shape and came to be regarded as the great *arche* of all objects (which is the fundamental thesis of the Sāmkhya). Because Upaniṣadic idealism had taught the identification of the cosmic and the psychic principles, hence, it was easy to oust the absolute and invest each of these psychic selves with the same creative and other functions of the absolute.

summarized[1]:

(a) Idealism	—	The *ātman* is the sole reality.
(b) Pantheism	—	The Universe is real, and yet the *ātman* is the sole reality, for the *ātman* is the entire universe.
(c) Cosmogonism	—	The *ātman* is regarded as the cause which produced the universe from itself as the effect.
(d) Theism	—	After creating the universe the *ātman*, as soul, entered into it. Also, a distinction is drawn between the *ātman* as the creator of the universe and the *ātman* entering into the creation.
(e) Atheism	—	By the separation of God and the individual soul the reality of God was questioned. The soul was contrasted with God, was ascribed an independent existence and even regarded as apart from God. In this scheme the main function of God was to create an universe as a field where the independent souls could obtain rewards and punishments for their actions. If the powers necessary for this purpose could be transferred to matter itself, God as creator of the universe becomes superfluous. Henceforward there remain only souls and primitive matter. This is the transition from Vedāntism to the Sāmkhya.
(f Deism	—	On considerations of practical utility, the doctrine of a personal God is attached in the Yoga system to the atheistic Sāmkhya in a purely external manner. Thus the Yoga restores the conception of God which had been eliminated by the Sāmkhya.

[1] P. Deussen, *The Philosophy of the Upaniṣads*, pp. 237-39. The first five stages are also discussed in Paul Deussen, "Outlines of Indian Philosophy", *The Indian Antiquary*, *op. cit.*, pp. 394-95.

Artificiality is writ large upon the face of Paul Deussen's theory. The development of panthestic idealism into theism and of theism into atheism is a queer theory unsubstantiated by any parallel example from the history of any system of philosophy in any country. It is certainly true that the *Sāmkhya-Kārikā* establishes the plurality of selves on empiric grounds, for which it has been the target of attack, but never do the Upaniṣads establish the identity of the cosmic and empirical selves. Whenever the point of unity is emphasized in the Upaniṣads it is always between the absolute and the *ātman* (the *ātman* = the *jiva* divested of all realistic, materialistic and dream-state traits). Hence this process of the derivation of Sāmkhya dualism from Upaniṣadic idealism as attempted by Deussen is not convincing. It is more simple to assert that the Upaniṣad idealism is a philosophical advance upon the Sāmkhya dualism than to hold that the latter is a natural disintegration from the former. Certain parallels for my suggestion can be referred to in European thought. The dualism of Descartes was succeeded by the monistic conception of Substance in Spinoza and the ontological dualism (between the things-in-themselves and the percipient subjects with their intuitions and categories) and the epistemological dualism (between perceptual sensibility and understanding) of Kant were succeeded by the monistic conceptions of the Absolute and reason in Hegel. If we base our hypotheses upon a logical view of the natural procession of human thought we may say that the Sāmkhya dualism should precede Upaniṣad monism; because dualism is more natural for the empirical human consciousness than monism.

The view of Dr. Deussen regarding the incorporation of cosmogonic theories after the formulation of pure idealism seems to be artificial. There is no doubt that the intellectual formulation or intuitional apprehension of one supreme reality is a brilliant philosophical achievement. What then is the rationale of destroying the philosophical worth of this notion by introducing confusing conceptions? In religious movements it may be possible to incorporate folk elements in cults and practices. But no serious philosopher will like to compromise the philosophical subtlety of his system by consciously introducing into it contrary or incongruent elements.

Joseph Dahlmann derives nearly four of the later Indian systems of philosophy from the early speculations of the Upaniṣads[1] which are, in his view, more or less dualistic, since they accept the *ātman* (the *brahman*) and also what is the not-*atman* (the *prakṛti*). His thesis is that when the unity of the universe was emphasized and the existence of *prakṛti* as real denied, illusionism naturally resulted and hence *mayavādi* Vedāntism came to the front. But when the *ātman* was emptied of all empirical reality and the *prakṛti* was emphasized, materialism resulted. For the logical intellect it was difficult to conceive of the doctrine of release on the basis of one absolute *ātman* and hence to rationalize the doctrine of release it was necessary to search for the plurality of selves and thus the Sāmkhya system resulted. Lastly, the subjectivism involved in the *ātman* doctrine led to scepticism and then to the philosophical indifference of early Buddhism.[2] Thus Dahlmann's attempt is to trace both the Sāmkhya plurality of selves and the Buddhist philosophic indifference from the same parental roots — the early speculations of the Upaniṣads, which have close touch with the expressions of the Brāhmaṇas as to the process of creation. Although I appreciate the suggestiveness of Dahlmann's hypothesis, it must be stated that his original starting-point is wrong. There is slender justification for his statement that the early Upaniṣadic metaphysics was, more or less, dualistic. It appears that Dahlmann has arrived at untenable propositions because his initial assumption is open to question.

A.B. Keith has stated that the Sāmkhya is a system built on the basis of the Upaniṣads for various reasons.[3] (i) When the Absolute created the plurality and entered that as *jiva*, the functions of the Absolute remained confined to creation

[1] Dahlmann, referred to in A.B. Keith, *The Religion and Philosophy of the Veda and the Upaniṣads*, Vol. II, pp. 540-41, considers the Brāhmaṇas and the early speculations of the Upaniṣads as the source of four philosophical schools : (i) the Sāmkhya (ii) the Vedanta and *mayāvada* (illusionism), (iii) materialism and (iv) scepticism, Buddhism and subjectivism. He holds that the *Mahābhārata* contains, not eclecticism as is supposed by Hopkins and Deussen but represented the oldest stage of Sāmkhya philosophy. He regards the *Mahābhārata* as prior to Pāṇini.

[2] Joseph Dahlmann's views are summarized in Keith, *op. cit.*, pp. 541-52.

[3] A.B. Keith, "The Sāmkhya in the Upaniṣads", The *Sāmkhya System* (London, Oxford Univ. Press, 1924), pp. 5-12.

and matter and jiva became more important. When the *Brihadāraṇyaka Upaniṣad*, 1, 4, 6, says that 'food' and the 'eater' make up the entire universe, the path is prepared for the elimination of the *brahman* (p. 8). (ii) According to the *Ṛgveda* (X, 121), *hiranyagarbha* is produced from the primeval waters. According to the Upaniṣads, the Absolute as first-born reappears in matter. The Sāmkhya view that *mahān* emerges from *prakṛti* is similar to these Upaniṣadic views. (iii) The *Praśnopaniṣad*, in the discussion of the fourth *praśna*, mentions *manas*, *buddhi*, *chitta* and *ahamkāra*. Keith says : "It is perfectly clear that the *Praśnopaniṣad* is not an exposition of the Sāmkhya, but the elements of the Sāmkhya derivation are present." (p. 10).

The first argument of Keith is a mere re-statement of Deussen's. In the second argument he has tried to equate the production of *mahān* to the re-appearance of *brahman* in matter, which is without any basis. The categories that are mentioned in the *Prasnopaniṣad* belong not to the original Sāmkhya but to the later developed form of it. Hence my own view that the Sāmkhya had Vedic roots and that some of the concepts that are common to the Upaniṣads and the Sāmkhya may express the synthesizing attempt of the writers of the Upaniṣads to incorporate Sāmkhya categories in their scheme is not refuted by the statement of Keith. In the eighth, seventh and sixth centuries B.C., the question of conscious borrowing of philosophical categories and notions is not so significant because a large mass of common ideas were permeating the atmosphere.

Dr. Keith has made an attempt to stress the derivative character of the Sāmkhya thought on the ground of the doctrine of deliverance. His point of view is that only in the context of the false apprehension of multiplicity is there a real ground for saving knowledge being applauded. But in the Sāmkhya, between the subjective selves and the objective nature, both being independent, there is no connexion there and hence there is no need of saving knowledge. Hence Keith argues that the doctrine of knowledge as a means of salvation has been borrowed by the Sāmkhya from an older system.[1]

[1] A. B. Keith, "The Sāmkhya and Buddhism and Jainism", *The Sāmkhya System*, pp. 23-34, says that the Sāmkhya which is a believer in the dualism of *purusha* and *prakṛti* could not develop from Buddhism

But here Keith seems to have deviated from the main point. In the Sāmkhya the objective nature (*prakṛti*) and the subjective selves are at least real entities, and hence there can be grounds for false connexions. It might have been argued with more plausibility that in the monistic spiritualistic Upaniṣadic doctrine, there is really no ground for any saving knowledge. All phenomenal plurality pertains to the domain of *māyā*, hence there is no real evil or sin from which one could desire deliverance. But when a rigorous monism can accommodate the concept of saving knowledge, why cannot the Sāmkhya dualism do so ? The doctrine of emancipation is no spurious external creed implanted on the Sāmkhya. According to the comprehensive conceptions of the Indian mind, all knowledge, whether it be of biology or botany, physics or paleontoloy, medicine or mechanics, is for the salvation of the soul, and hence the Indian thinkers, generally, start with stressing the necessity of the deliverance of the human self enchained in the net of *māyā*. Hence there is no wonder that the Sāmkhya also should accept the doctrine of emancipation from the ills of the world.

We shall examine some other inaccurate attempts to trace the Upaniṣadic origin of Sāmkhyan thoughts. Dr. B.M. Barua[1] traces the root of Sāmkhyan dualism in the *Praśnopaniṣad*.[2] There a question is raised regarding the origination of the *prajā* and the answer is that Prajāpati produced a pair (*mithuna*) of Matter (*rayi*) and Vital Force (*prāṇa*) with the object that these

which only believes in a law of movement (pp. 23-24). But the possibility, according to him, of deriving both Buddhism and Sāmkhya from the Upaniṣads, each borrowing from the Upaniṣads independently without the direct influence of the other cannot be denied (p. 24).

[1] According to Benimadhava Barua, *A History of Pre-Buddhistic Philosophy*, p. 214, there are 4 stages of the development of the Sāmkhya, considered, in general, as a rational theory of the universe. (i) The *Purusha-sūkta* of the *Ṛgveda* ascribed to Nārayaṇa, (ii) The *Purusha-vidha Brāhamaṇa* of the *Brihadāraṇyaka* I, 4, (iii) The doctrines of Pancaśikha as stated in the *Śanti-Parva* of the *Mahābhārata*, and (iv) Iśvarkrishṇa's ideas.

[2] Benimadhava Barua, *A History of Pre-Buddhistic Indian Philosophy*, pp. 233-34. There seems to be no foundation for the identifications arrived at by Barua between *prāṇa* and *purusha*, *rayi* and *prakṛti*, *mūrta* and *vyakta*, *amūrta* and *avyakta*, and *mātra* and *tanmātra*.

two would produce manifold creatures.[1] But to trace in the *rayi* and the *prāṇa* either the origin of, or the parallel to, Sāmkhyan dualism is without solid foundation. According to *Praśnopaniṣad* the list of Matter (*rayi*) and Vital Force (*prāṇa*) is as follows[2] :

Matter (*rayi*)	*Vital Force* (*Prāṇa*)
1. Moon (*Candramā*)	1. Sun (*āditya*)
2. Dark-half (*krishṇapaksha*)	2. Bright-half (*śuklapaksha*)
3. Night (*rātri*)	3. Day (*ahan*)

It is apparent that this is an attempt at the classification of similar facts which is a natural adventure of the human mind and it has no pertinent resemblance to the Sāmkhya.[3]

Another attempt has been made to trace the Sāmkhya conception of the psychic body (*linga śarīra*) to the sixteen *kalā* in the *Praśnopaniṣad* (the sixth question in the *Praśnopaniṣad*).[4] The *Praśnopaniṣad* says : "He created life (*prāṇa*) ; from life, faith (*sraddhā*), space (*kha*), wind, light, water, earth, sense-faculty (*indriya*), mind, food; from food, virility, austerity, sacred sayings (*mantra*), sacrifice, the worlds ; and in the worlds, name."[5] But here too we do not find that integral connexion among the various elements mentioned here, which is a preponderant characteristic of the Sāmkhya idea of psychic body. This notion of the sixteen-fold (*shodaśakala*) *purusha* is a disjointed conglomeration and hence there does not seem to be any valid ground for holding that this conception was borrowed

[1] *Praśna Upaniṣad*, 1, 3-4.

[2] *Praśna Upaniṣad*, 1, 9, 12-13.

[3] Another attempt to find the root of Sāmkhya dualism in the *Chhāndogya Upaniṣad* has been made by Barua. He says in his *Pre-Buddhistic*, *op. cit.*, p. 137 that, in the *Chhāndogya*, VI, where Uddālaka says that there are earth, fire and water on one side and therein there is the penetration (*anupraviśya*) by the *jivenātmanā*, we have the roots of dualistic metaphysics. But actually we have here not two but four entities (three plus one) referred to. There is no attempt to point out the emergence of earth, fire and water from one unitarian material principle.

[4] B.M. Barua, *History*, *op. cit.*, p. 236. Barua says that the sixteen phases (*shodaśa kalā*) denote the sixteen successive changes in the later Sāmkhya nomenclature. This is an example of fanciful guess and the two schemes have no sound resemblance at all.

[5] *Praśna Upaniṣad*, VI, 4. English translation by Robert E. Hume, *The Thirteen Principal Upaniṣads*, translated from the Sanskrit (Oxford University Press, 1931), p. 389.

from the *Praśnopaniṣad* by the Sāmkhya because the latter contains no such scheme.

Attempts have also been made to locate Sāmkhya thought in the following verses of the *Kathopaniṣad*[1] :

> Higher than the Senses are the objects of sense ;
> Higher than the objects of sense is the mind (*manas*) :
> And Higher than the mind is the intellect (*buddhi*).
> Higher than the intellect is the Great Self (*Atman*).
> Higher than the Great is the Unmanifest (*avyakta*).
> Higher than the Unmanifest is the Person.
> Higher than the Person there is nothing at all.
> That is the goal. That is the highest course.[2]

The three highest categories in this scheme represent the topmost points of any philosophical scheme—*purusha* (absolute), *avyakta* (*prakṛti*) and *ātman* (human self). But this scheme contains some vital fallacies. (i) In no sense can the *avyakta* (indeterminate unconscious matter) be regarded as superior to the *mahān ātman*. If the *ātman* is conscious, and if still the *avyakta* is regarded as superior to it, then it is an attack on the fundamental thought of the Upaniṣads. (ii) There seems to be a logical flaw in mentioning *artha* or the objects of sense-perception between the *manas* and the *indriya*. (iii) *Buddhi* is not used in this scheme in the Sāmkhya sense of a cosmic determinant but as a mere conscious functioning entity. (iv) The attribute *mahān* applied here to the *ātman*, becomes the synonym of *buddhi* as a cosmic principle and is then used as a substantive. But there does not seem to be much logic in regarding *ātman* as *mahān* when in this scheme two further categories, the *avyakta* and the *purusha* have been rated as superior to the *ātman*.

The *Kaṭha* further states :

> Higher than the senses (*Indriya*) is the mind (*manas*) ;
> Above the mind is the true being (*sattva*).
> Over the true being is the Great Self [i.e. *buddhi*, intellect] ;
> Above the Great is the Unmanifest (*avyakta*).
> Higher than the Unmanifest, however, is the Person (Purusha),
> All-pervading and without any mark (*a-linga*) whatever.

[1] B.M. Barua, *op. cit.*, p. 276.

[2] *Kaṭhopaniṣad*, I, 3, 10-11. English translation by Robert E. Hume, *op. cit.*, p. 352.

Knowing which, a man is liberated
And goes to immortality.[1]

Both the Sāmkhya and Buddhism had pre-Upaniṣadic beginnings but are only to a certain limited extent, influenced by the Upaniṣads. In our view, the *Kaṭha* version is not the source of Sāmkhya psychology. Its scheme pointing out the transcendent superiority of the *parah purusah* to all psychic and physical factors definitely shows that an attempt is being made to bring a harmony between the Upaniṣadic and Sāmkhya teachings. These two poetic passages cannot be adequately explained either on the basis of the orthodox Sāmkhya conception of the categories or of the Upaniṣadic idealistic model. They indicate the attempt to synthesize the Sāmkhya theory of evolution with the Upaniṣadic spiritual monism. The first scheme of categories of the *Kaṭhopaniṣad* represents a deliberate and conscious effort to affiliate the Sāmkhya evolutionary scheme with that of the Upaniṣads. The entire scheme, however, instead of being harmonious and organic, betrays an element of rough agglomeration. In the second scheme of categorisation in the *Kaṭhopaniṣad* (VI, 7-8), the word *sattva* has been used as a synonym for *buddhi*. This synonymous identification could be only possible when the Sāmkhya scheme of the three gunas had been developed. Hence this second scheme also supports my contention that the two schemes of categories in the *Kaṭha Upaniṣad* have been formulated after the growth of the Sāmkhya evolutionary series. Hence instead of tracing the roots of the Sāmkhya in the *Kaṭhopaniṣad* it is more plausible to say that the developmental scheme of the Sāmkhya is prior to the *Kaṭhopaniṣad* and the latter tries to synthesize its own categories with those of the Sāmkhya. The distinction between the *arthāh*, the differentiated diversity of material phenomena and *avyakta*, the harmonious continuum of matter is remarkable and is definitely a Sāmkhyan notion.

(b) *Vedic, and not Upaniṣadic, Roots of the Sāmkhya*

We shall briefly state our own thesis now. Any attempt to trace the roots of Sāmkhya ideas in the Upaniṣadic literature

[1] *Kaṭhopaniṣad*, II, 3, 7-8. English translation by Robert E. Hume, *op. cit.*, p. 359.

does not appear plausible. The Upaniṣads inculcate idealism; the Sāmkhya teaches realism. The Upaniṣads advocate monism; the Sāmkhya teaches dualism. The Upaniṣads accept theism; the Sāmkhya is atheistical. In spite of this fundamental disparity, Indian scholars have tried to follow the lead of Western scholars in tracing Sāmkhya ideas to the Upaniṣads. The main factor perhaps as to why the Western scholars stress the Upaniṣadic genesis of the Sāmkhya is that they work under the fantastic notion that the Hindu genius did not produce anything remarkable except the Vedāntic idealism.

The Sāmkhya is an original system of thought expounded and developed by a long line of scholars and thinkers. We have tried earlier to attribute a Vedic origin to some of the leading conceptions of the Sāmkhya, but that does not mean that the Sāmkhya teachers make a conscious borrowing therefrom. In the pre-Upaniṣadic ages, Hindu philosophy was not systematized, and hence different sets of ideas were prevalent then, and the Sāmkhya thinkers could very well be influenced by the realistic, materialistic, naturalistic and sceptical elements of the Veda.

The founders and the thinkers of the Sāmkhya take a bold stand. The atheism of the Sāmkhya shows its boldness in relation to the philosophy of those days. The Sāmkhya atheism and the insistence on the evolutionary methodology indicate the rationalism of the founder. The *prakṛti* of the Sāmkhyas is an intellectual product of the same kind of unity-seeking speculation which led to the idea of the *brahman*. Just as the spiritual thinkers arrived at the ultimate unity of the *brahman*, so too the naturalistic thinkers arrived at the *prakṛti*. There is some doubt as to whether the *ajāmekām lohitaṣuklakrishṇām* as discussed in the *Śvetāśvatara*[1] referred to the *prakṛti* constituted of three gunas, or to the earth, fire and water of the *Chhāndogya*.[2] If it is a reference to the *prakṛti*, it shows not a source of the Sāmkhya, but is an attempt to incorporate this

[1] *Śvetāśvatara Upaniṣad*, IV, 5.

[2] *Chhāndogya Upaniṣad*, VI, 2, 3, 4; VI, 4, 6. According to Paul Deussen, *The Philosophy of the Upaniṣads*, *op. cit.*, p. 189ff., in the threefold division (*sthavishtha*, *madhyama* and *aṇistha*) of the primitive elements—food, water and heat, "lies the earliest germ" of the conception of *tanmātra* and the gross elements (p. 192).

great discovery of the Sāmkhya in the later Upaniṣadic philosophical scheme.[1] The Upaniṣads were developing the *māyā* theory and the Sāmkhya had formulated the concept of *prakṛti* and the *Śvetāśvatara* identifies them. The disinterested non-attached (*asamga*) *purusha* of the Sāmkhya is paralleled by the similar conception in the *Brihadāraṇyaka Upaniṣad* about the *brahman*,[2] but there is no reason for any borrowing.[3] There might be independent speculation.

B. *Buddhism and Sāmkhya*

The problem of the influence of the Sāmkhya on Buddhism[4] has been widely debated. The Sāmkhya is regarded as one of the dominant sources responsible for the emergence of Buddhism.[5]

[1] According to E.H. Johnston, *Early Sāmkhya, op. cit.*, p. 19, there is a distinct possibility that the dialogue between Yājñavalkya and Maitreyī which contains the detailed mention of five *karmendriya* (organs of action), was, in its final form at least, "composed by some one acquainted with the Sāmkhya categories." S.N. Dasgupta, "Sāmkhya as Non-Vedic", *Indian Culture*, 1934-35, pp. 79-81, also holds that the apparent Sāmkhya ideas in the *Kaṭha* and the *Śvetaśvatara* have no organic connexion with the Upaniṣadic scheme of thought. These are doctrines probably current in the local circles and then adapted by the Upaniṣads.

[2] *Brihadāraṇyaka Upaniṣad*, IV, 3, 15 ; III, 8, 8 ; III, 9, 26.

[3] Some words which are dominant concepts in the Sāmkhya system are, at times, traced to the Upaniṣads. For example, the word *linga* occurs in the *Brihadāraṇyaka*, IV, 4, 8, *ahamkāra* occurs in the *Chhāndogya*, VII, 25, 1, and *sattva* occurs in the *Chhāndogya*, VII, 26, 2

[4] A. B. Keith in his *The Sāmkhya System, op. cit.*, pp. 25-26, has summarized the views of Hermann Jacobi regarding the influence of the Sāmkhya on Buddhism. Keith's own view, (*op. cit.*,) pp. 27-28), is more moderate and he says that some Buddhist conceptions are "very closely allied" to the Sāmkhya. First, he says that the use of *samskāra* is possibly a direct borrowing in Buddhism. Second, the conception of casuality is found in both. Third, just as Buddhism propounds that nothing or no aggregate is *attā* so Sāmkhya-Yoga teaches freedom from empiric phenomena (*op. cit.*, p. 20).

[5] F. Otto Schrader, "Vedānta and Sāmkhya in Primitive Buddhism", *The Indian Historical Quarterly*, 1934-35, pp. 543ff. Hermann Jacobi, "Der Urspruing des Buddhismus aus dem Sāmkhya-Yoga", *Gott. Nachrichten*, 1896, pp. 1ff. and "Uber das Verhaltniss der Buddhistischen Philosophie zum Sāmkhya-Yoga und die Bedeutung der Nidana", *ZDMG.*, 52, pp. 1ff. According to R. Pischel, *Leben und Lehre des Buddha*, pp. 22,62,65,67,69, 75, "theoretical Buddhism rests entirely on Sāmkhya-Yoga", "it has borrowed from Sāmkhya-Yoga almost everyth-

Both the Sāmkhya and Buddhism are heterodox[1] in their nature and they repudiate the static immobile transcendent *brahman* of the Upaniṣads, either through overt statements or by deliberate silence. There are several common points between these two systems.[2] Some of the Western scholars, however, have gone too far astray in their romantic attempt to trace the influence of the Sāmkhya on Buddhism. Albrecht Weber, for example, came out with the romantic suggestion that Gotama Buddha and Kapila, the traditionally recognized founder of the Sāmkhya system, were one and the same person.[3] In quest of their identity some scholars went to the extent of hazarding that Buddha's birth in the town of Kapilavastu is a corroboration of this fact.[4]

The tendency to emphasize the gloom and misery of the world is found both in the Sāmkhya and Buddhism. Just as there are four cardinal truths in Buddhism—pain, diagnosis

ing", "Buddha has converted into religion what his teachers had taught before as a philosophy". According to E. Senart, "Bouddhisme et Yoga", *Revue de l' histoire des Religions*, Vol. 42, 1900, pp. 345 ff., Buddhism is dependent on the Sāmkhya for the practical teaching of the path to salvation. He, however, also stated that Buddhism is more dependent on the Yoga than on Sāmkhya. The views of H. Jacobi R. Pischel and E. Senart have been quoted in Th. Stcherbatsky, "The 'Dharmas' of the Buddhists and the Gunas of the Sāmkhya", *The Indian Historical Quarterly*, Vol. X, 1934, pp. 737-760. See also B.H. Kapadia's English trans. of Pischel's book with the title *Life and Doctrines of Buddha* (Gujrat University, 1965), pp. 80, 82 and 90.

1 Th. Stcherbatsky "The Dharmas of the Buddhists and the Gunas of the Sāmkhya", *The Indian Historical Quarterly*, Vol. I, 1934, p. 749.

2 Richard Garbe, *Die Sāmkhya Philosophie*, Eine Darstellung des Indischen Rationalismus Nach den Quellen, Leipzig, Verlag von H. Haessel, 1894, 2nd edition, p. 10, holds that Sāmkhya preceded Buddhism not in the shape of detached ideas but as a complete closed systems. The view of Garbe is referred to in Th. Stcherbatsky "The Dharmas of the Buddhists and the Gunas of the Sāmkhya", *op. cit.*, p. 753. According to Hermann Jacobi, from Kautilya's *Arthaśāstra* it can be inferred that by the 4th century B.C., the Sāmkhya and Yoga systems as well as the Purva-Mimānsa and the Cārvaka Lokāyata schools were in existence. A. B. Keith, *The Religion and Philosophy of the Veda and the Upaniṣads, op. cit.*, Vol. II, p. 505.

3 Weber, *Indische Studien*, I, 436. Referred to in Max Müller, *Ancient Sanskrit Literature*, p. 52n.

4 *Ibid.*

and cause of pain, extinction of pain and the Aryan eight-fold way for the cessation of pain, so also in Vijñānabhikshu's *Sāmkhyapravacanabhāsya* four truths are inculcated : "(1) That from which we deliver ourselves is pain. (2) Deliverance is the cessation of pain. (3) The cause of pain is want of discrimination between *prakṛti* and *purusha*, which produces the continued union. (4) The means of deliverance is discerning knowledge." But there is nothing to indicate that early Buddhism is indebted to the Sāmkhya for the theory of pessimism. The roots of pessimism are found in the Upaniṣads.[1] Furthermore, the poignancy and depth of world-sorrow are far more elaborately and deeply portrayed in the Buddhist scriptures than in the Sāmkhya. Hence only this much can be said that both Buddhism and the Sāmkhya accept the concept of sorrow but there is nothing definite to indicate any borrowing from the Sāmkhya tenets by Buddhism. The Sāmkhya traced suffering to intra-organic, extra-organic, supernatural and extra-organic natural causes. By painting the transcendent self-luminosity of the *purusha*, it, by contrast, brought the sense of cosmic suffering to a great prominence. In both Sāmkhya and Buddhism, suffering is due to *avidyā*. In the former case, *avidyā* is non-discrimination of the *purusha* and *prakṛti*, in the latter it is ignorance of the Aryan way. The Upaniṣads had tended to exalt the monastic tendency and showed the worthlessness of all mundane desires and ambitions. The Vedic prayer for sons had become a thing of the past. At this same time, the wandering preachers and saints, the Tāpasas, the Śramaṇas, the Parivrājakas and the forest-dwellers, all taught the doctrine of suffering. The teachings of most of the six Tirthakas are permeated with a sense of weariness and disgust of the empirical world. These six teachers were the contemporaries of Buddha, a few of them slightly senior to him. The weariness present in the Upaniṣads is a consequence of the supreme insistence on the vanishing nature of the world. The pessimism of original Buddhism is not a direct legacy of the Upaniṣads but is partly

[1] Paul Deussen, *Philosophy of the Upaniṣads, op. cit.*, p. 140, says that pessimism is the latent underlying view of the Upaniṣad teaching, in the sense of being the presumption of deliverance and the later systems of Buddhism and Sāmkhya which are founded upon it, dwell upon this theme.

due to the influence of the then socially and politically tense atmosphere and the impact of the doctrine of the ascetic teachers.

There are some other common elements in the Sāmkhya and Buddhism.[1] In neither is there any place for a personal God. Although they both accept the existence of lower deities, they do not sanction any prayers to them nor do they advocate any ritualistic sacrifices for them. The Buddhist literature contains references to gods and deities but only for the purpose of showing the superiority of Buddha to them.

Buddhism is definitely later than the Sāmkhya, because it represents a more radical disintegration of the Upaniṣadic thought than the Sāmkhya.[2] The latter subscribes to the notion of multiplicity of selves. But Buddhism is defiantly an adherent of the cult of *anātman.*[3] Oldenberg, Pischel, Garbe and Jacobi say that the *anātman* was originally a Sāmkhya theory. The conception of the Sāmkhya *purusha* represents an attenuated form of the Upaniṣadic *ātman* and from this attenuation, its dissolution into five component states as represented by the Buddhist *anātman*, is only a logical step. The Upaniṣads inculcate the superabundant reality (*bhūma*, of a transcendent and immanent being and identify the psychic selves with the *brahman*. But, while both the Sāmkhya and Buddhism are similar in their repudiation of the infinite spirit, Buddhism appears more nihilistically radical in having reduced the self to a psycho-physical complex process,[4] while the Sāmkhya, all the

[1] Th. Stcherbatsky, *op. cit.*, p. 751.

[2] According to Pfleiderer, *The Philosophy of Religion, op. cit.*, the Sāmkhya theory shares the abstract, unspiritual notion of substance of the Vedānta. In Buddhism there was a natural reaction and the notion of substance was replaced by the law of becoming.

[3] Mrs. C.A.F. Rhys Davids in the *Sakya or Buddhist Origins* (London, Kegan Paul, Trench, Trubner & Co., 1931), held that Buddha taught neither the Four Aryan Truths, nor *nirvāṇa,* nor *anātman*. These, she calls, later accretions to the original gospel. In this book I have used the entire Tripiṭakas as the documents of early Buddhism, though there can be no doubt that layers of successive development in thought can be traced in them.

[4] Th. Stcherbatsky, "The Dharmas of the Buddhists and the Gunas of the Samkhya", *The Indian Historical Quarterly*, Vol. X, 1934, (pp. 737-760), pp. 750-51 : "Sāmkhya admits besides the moving gunas a motion-

while, retains its adherence to the principle of the multiplicity of selves.[1]

In the *Brahmajāla Sutta* of the *Dīgha Nikāya* there is reference *sassatavāda*[2] and *ekacasassatavāda* — "On what grounds and for what reasons do the recluses and the brahmins, who are believers in the eternity of existence declare that both the soul and the world are eternal," and "the souls are many also." Here two dominant tenets of the Sāmkhya — the eternality of nature and the purushas and the multiplicity of the purushas are definitely foreshadowed. The *Brahmajāla Sutta* is amongst the oldest portions of the Buddhist literature and hence it can be stated that some Sāmkhya ideas were known to the earliest Buddhist teachers and possibly to Buddha himself. The mention of dualistic eternalists is to be construed as a very definite mention of the Sāmkhya. According to Hermann Jacobi and

less (*niskriya*) soul. This soul is degraded in Buddhism, it is converted into simple consciousness (*vijñāna*) which is also a *dharma*, an Element having the same sense as all other Elements. In Buddhism as well as in Sāmkhya the human personality consists of an infinite number of point-instants of *gunas* or *dharmas* which are held together in Sāmkhya by a pervading Matter (*pradhāna*) and an eternal soul, in Buddhism exclusively by causal laws (*pratitya-samutpāda*)." Keith is of the opinion that the Sāmkhya cannot be derived from Buddhism because the latter represents a further disintegration of the Upaniṣadic doctrine. The Sāmkhya accepts the self of the Upaniṣads but Buddhism pulverises the psychic entity and reaches a subjective atomism.

1 Richard Garbe, *Der Mondschein der Sāmkhya Wahrheit*, Munich, 1892, pp. 9-10, quoted in Th. Stcherbatsky's paper, *op. cit.*, pp. 753-54, seems to be incorrect when he tries to show that the concept of *anātman*, in its origin, is a Sāmkhya and not a Buddhist idea.

2 According to Schrader, "Vedānta and Sāmkhya in Primitive Buddhism", *Indian Culture*, Vol. I, 1934-35, pp. 543ff., the reference to *sassato attā ca loka ca ... kutthako esikattha citthito,* means that the self and the world are eternal for the *Kutastha* (According to Schrader, this word is not an adjective but is a substantive and signifies an entity like the *purusha* of the Sāmkhya), is unproductive, as a pillar firmly fixed and the beings run through births, transmigrate, pass away and spring up. Here, thus, Schrader finds the duality of *prakṛti* and *kutastha.* He says that Buddha modified this Sāmkhya view and used that for the purposes of his own teaching. Schrader's view is that the influence of the Vedānta on Buddhism is peripheric while that of the Sāmkhya is central and the basis of Buddhism is the metaphysical dualism inherited from the Sāmkhya.

Richard Garbe, the Sāmkhya dualism is older than Buddhism. Early Buddhism has made no sustained attempt to explain the evolution of the phenomenal world. But the elucidation of the processes of cosmic evolution is a cardinal tenet of the Sāmkhya. Both Buddhism and Sāmkhya, however, stress the aspects of change, differentiation and transformation.

It is also possible that the *pratityasamutpāda* scheme has been partly modelled upon the Sāmkhya evolutionary series.[1] The conception of schematic evolution as present in the Sāmkhya philosophy might have influenced the formulation of dependent origination.[2] Certainly there are vital differences between the two schemes also because while the Sāmkhya formulates the notion of evolution at the cosmic level, Buddhism is more concerned with the emergence of individual suffering. The Sāmkhya is an adherent of *satkāryavāda*[3] since the idea of the evolution of the differentiated cosmos from the undifferentiated *prakṛti* is accepted by it. Buddhism, on the other hand, is more

[1] According to Schrader, "Vedānta and Sāmkhya in Primitive Buddhism" *Indian Culture*, Vol. I, 1934-35, pp. 543-552, the *pratityasamutpāda* is the academic reply of Buddha to the doctrine of *satkaryavāda.* There is, strictly speaking, not even a causation in this dependent origination but simply a succession brought about by laws that are inherent in the links themselves of the chain. This formula of *pratityasamutpāda* arose in contrast to the Sāmkhya evolution series. Buddha opposed the *pariṇāmavāda* of the Sāmkhya and almost cancelled the very idea of transmutation of substance (*pariṇāma*). C.A.F. Rhys Davids, "The Relations between Early Buddhism and Brahmanism, "*The Indian Historical Quarterly*, Vol. X, 1934, (pp. 274-87), p. 285, says : "... whenever you see, the man cannot be got at save through the mental items of *dharmas*, you have the working of the new psychology called Sāmkhya or Analysis : the Human phase in Buddhism."

[2] Th. Stcherbatsky, "The Dharmas of the Buddhists and the Gunas of the Samkhya", *The Indian Historical Quarterly*, Vol. X, 1934, (pp. 737-760), p. 755.

[3] According to Liebenthal, referred to in A.B. Keith, "Pre-canonical Buddhism", *The Indian Historical Quarterly*, Vol. XII, 1936, p. 15, the concept of *satkāryavāda* was first formulated in Vācaspati's *Sāmkhyatattvakaumudī* and hence it may not belong to the early Sāmkhya. But this is not substantiated since in the *Sāmkhya-kārikā* (No. 9) we find *śaktasya śakyakaraṇāt kāraṇābhāvācc satkāryam* and *sarvasambhavābhāvat*. See also Harrison, *The Philosophy of the Sāmkhya-Kārikā.* The notion of *pariṇāmavāda* was also not a part of the original Sāmkhya and even in the *Sāmkhyatattvakaumudī* its significance is not great.

concerned with the emergence of subtle psychic forces and tendencies. The Sāmkhya scheme is a cosmic one, stressing the doctrine of causation, technically called *satkāryavāda* because the undifferentiated *prakṛti* developing into the spatio-temporal-phenomenal cosmos, through the mechanism of differentiation and integration, is governed by the general rule of the conservation of energy. But the Buddhistic scheme is basically a psychological one. It has reference only to growth of subtle psychic forces and tendencies through the formula of dependent origination. The Sāmkhya, on the other hand, makes an attempt to fuse the psychic and the physical in a comprehensive standpoint. Cosmic intelligence (*mahat*) and individuation (*ahamkāra*) produce the elements as also the psychic and physical organs. Nevertheless, it may be held that some of the categories of *pratityasamutpāda*[1] might have been derived from the Sāmkhya.[2] The following table may indicate the parallelism[3] :

Sāmkhya Evolution	*Buddhist Pratityasamutpāda*
1. *Prakṛti* (or *pradhāna*)	1. *Avidyā*
2. *Mahat* (or *buddhi*)	2. *Samskāra*
3. *Ahamkāra* (Individuation)	3. *Vijñāna*[4] (Parallel to *buddhi* of the Sāmkhya)

1 Louis de l' Vallee-Poussin in reviewing Oltramare's book says that the number 'Twelve' was a pre-Buddhist datum and to fill the twelve sections synonymous phrases were in use. C.A.F. Rhys Davids, "The Unknown Co-Founders of Buddhism", *The Journal of the Royal Asiatic Society*, Part II, April 1927, pp. 193-208, points out that the teacher Assaji who was an enthusiast of natural causation was more responsible for the emphasis on the concept of *pratityasamutpāda* than Buddha. See also the *Cula-Saccaka Sutta* of the *Majjhima Nikāya*.

2 S. Radhakrishnan, *Indian Philosophy*, I, p. 472n, says that there is close resemblance between the Buddhist *pratityasamutpāda* and the Sāmkhya *pratyayasarga*. There are fifty sub-divisions of *pratyayasarga* : 5 kinds of *viparyara*, 28 kinds of *aśakti*, 9 kinds of *tuṣṭhi* and 8 kinds of *siddhi* (Gaudapādaswami's *Bhāsyam* on the *Sāmkhya-Kārikā*). To me, there does not seem to be any resemblance, terminological or ideological between the *pratityasamutpāda* and the *pratyayasarga*.

3 Cf. also Kern, *A Manual of Indian Buddhism*, p. 47, fn 6.

4 According to H. Jacobi, summarized in A.B. Keith, *The Sāmkhya system*, *op. cit.*, pp. 23-24, the derivative character of Buddhism is clearly shown because for both *avidyā* and *samskāra* "an intellect must be assumed, which Buddhism merely admits after the *samskāra*, in the form

4. *Tanmātra*[1]	4. *Nāmarūpa* (Individualisation) Parallel to *ahamkāra* of the Sāmkhya)
5. *Indriyāṇi*	5. *Shadāyatana* (Parallel to Gross world—five gross elements)

Sparsa, *vedanā* and *tṛshṇā* are common to both the schemes.

The Sāmkhya deals with the modifications (*pariṇāma* or *visṛsti*) of *prakṛti*. Buddhism, on the other hand, is a theory of matter without materiality or of sense-data without any substance.

The concept of *nirvāṇa* in one of its formulations has resemblance to the Sāmkhya.[2] Nirvāṇa is a state realisable through great *dhyāna* (intellectual and meditative efforts) but at one place in the *Dīgha Nikāya* it is said to be a vast cosmic force wherein all the elements eventually merge. Hence, just as in the Sāmkhya, *prakṛti* is the ground-repository of the physical elements and psychic organs, so also the Buddhistic *nirvāṇa*, at least at one place, is regarded as the ultimate final ground where all beings merge.[3]

Although Sāmkhya ideas must have been current when Buddha flourished, the theoretical architectonic structure that the Sāmkhya attains in the *Sāmkhya-Sūtra*, which is regarded

of *vijñāna*". In the Sāmkhya scheme, from *ahamkāra* (Individuation) the tanmātraṇi are derived and therefrom the derivation of the five gross elements is correct because of the acceptance of the cosmic principle of individuation for each world-period. In the Buddhist scheme there is no justification for the derivation of the gross world from the individual. Deussen, on the other hand, (referred to in Keith, *op. cit.*, p. 29n), holds that *vijñāna* is cosmic and produces all reality.

[1] Sometimes a parallel is drawn between the *tanmātra* and the *rūpa dharma.*

[2] Keith has made an ingenious attempt to trace a parallel between the concept of *nirvāṇa* and the notion of the Sāmkhya *purusha.* Arthur B. Keith, "Pre-Canonical Buddhism", *The Indian Historical Quarterly,* Vol. XII, (pp. 1-20), pp. 19-20.

[3] S.N. Dasgupta, *A History of Indian Philosophy*, Vol. I, *op. cit.*, pp. 215 and 215n (footnote No. 2) says that Caraka's concept of *brahma. bhūta* which is like absolute annihilation without any sign of existence (*alakṣaṇam*) resembles Nagārjuna's *Nirvāṇa.* This resemblance is being noted here because Dasgupta regards Caraka's *Samhitā* (which is called *Ātreyasamhitā* or *Ātreyatantra*) as an "early school of Sāmkhya".

as a much later work than the *Sāmkhya-Kārikā*,[1] is a post-Buddhistic development.[2] The *Sāmkhya-Sūtras* condemn the Buddhist doctrine of momentariness (*kshaṇikavāda*). They are critical also of the Buddhist doctrine which denies the substantial character of entities and regards that entities exist only because of the operation of the perceptual mechanism. The nihilistic notions of Nāgārjuna are also sharply rebuked as being antithetical to the universal experience of the reality of external nature and the inner self.

One fundamental distinction between the classical Sāmkhya and Buddhism is that while the former recognizes a gap between mind and consciousness, in the latter, between the intellect, mind and consciousness no such gap exists. *Nyāya-Sūtra* IV, 1, 25 (*sarvamanityamutpattivināśadharmakatvāt*) refers to the Buddhist position, while the *Nyāya-Sūtra*, IV, 1, 27 (*sarvam nityam pancabhutanityatvāt*) refers to the Sāmkhya position,

1 The *Sāmkhya-Kārikā* is ascribed to the 5th century A.D.

2 S.N. Dasgupta, *A History of Indian Philosophy*, Vol. I, p. 78, says that although the classical Sāmkhya and Yoga treatises were written decidedly after Buddhism "it may be that there is some truth in such a view that Buddhism drew much of its inspiration from them." Dasgupta concedes that it may be possible that in the Upaniṣadic stage of its development, the Sāmkhya "also gave some suggestions to Buddhism or Jainism" (*Ibid.*, p. 210). He is categorical in his view that the Sāmkhya works, as we have them now, are post-Buddhistic (p. 78). He also says that "the Sāmkhya-Yoga philosophy as we now get it is a system in which are found all the results of Buddhism and Jainism in such a manner that it unites the doctrine of permanence of the Upaniṣads with the doctrine of momentariness of the Buddhists and the doctrine of relativism of the Jains". (p. 210). Dasgupta thus accept Buddhist influence on the classical Sāmkhya. A.B. Keith, *The Sāmkhya System, op. cit.*, p. 31, says that "classical Sāmkhya was not the source of Buddhism" because, (i) in Buddhism, there is the entire rejection of the *prakṛti* as an original foundational entity, (*op. cit.*, p. 30) ; (ii) there is no acceptance of *sattva* or goodness because of the great emphasis on misery (*op. cit.*, pp. 30-31) and (iii) in Buddhism there is a total denial of a transcendent self. On these grounds Keith holds that classical Sāmkhya is not the source of Buddhism and opines that either both had a common heritage or Buddhism may have derived to some extent from the epic (Mahābhārata) Sāmkhya. Keith goes to the extent of maintaining that Buddhism may fairly be regarded as the lineal ancestor of the classical Sāmkhya, since it suggests the existence during the period of it philosophical development of a doctrine, which denied the Absolute.

thus indicating the ontological difference between Buddhism and Sāmkhya. The Sāmkhya did not adhere to the atomic theory in the early times. The Tripiṭakas are silent with regard to *aṇuvāda.* But both the Vedānta and the Sāmkhya as well as the Mahāyāna Buddhist thinkers repudiate atomism.

4. *Summary and Conclusions*

(i) In this chapter we have traced the Vedic roots of the concepts of *prakṛti* and *guṇavāda* — two of the central notions of the Sāmkhya. (ii) It has also been maintained that the Upaniṣads like the *Kaṭha* and the *Śvetāśvatara* are not the sources of the categories of the Sāmkhya but represent attempts to synthesize the tenets of the Sāmkhya with the dominant Upaniṣadic philosophy of spiritual idealism.

(iii) There are fundamental philosophical similarities between the Sāmkhya and Buddhism. Both refuse to subscribe to an impersonal absolute or to a spiritual Godhead and both believe in the elimination of pain and suffering which are the characteristics of mundane phenomena. But there are radical dissimilarities between (a) the Sāmkhya Purushas and the Buddhist *anātman*, and (b) the Sāmkhya isolation of the Purushas and the Buddhist *nirvāṇā*. Both the Sāmkhya and Buddhism were developing almost simultaneously as is apparent from the reference to dualistic eternalists in the *Brahmajālasutta* and from the prevalent legend that Buddha's teacher Ālāra Kālāma was the exponent of Sāmkhya. But the Sāmkhya, in the formulation of its basic ideas, seems to have preceded Buddhism, in its (the latter's) development, by about a century because Buddhism is far more removed from the Vedic atmosphere than the Sāmkhya. So far as the question of borrowing is concerned, it is by Buddhism, howsoever minor in extent, from the Sāmkhya.

PART TWO

BUDDHISM AND THE SOCIAL SCIENCES

Chapter 15

THE ECONOMIC FOUNDATIONS OF EARLY BUDDHISM

1. *Economic Causation and Religion*

The economic factor has great importance both for individual life and social history. Through the command of economic instrumentalities and resources, man obtains increasing facility in the struggle for existence. But the economic factor is never the sole factor in a man's life. There are four dominant factors in human existence : (i) the physiological factor, (ii) the economic factor, (iii) the desire for honour, esteem, power and prestige and (iv) artistic, idealistic and transcendental interests. These four factors express themselves with varying intensity and in different magnitude in different individuals. Historical movements are propelled through the activities of individuals who have, in varying degrees, these four-fold factors and interests and manifest them in the external social and physical environment. In certain individuals or for certain classes or civilisations the economic factor can become very important but it is always one factor and never the sole factor.

So far as the origin of religious truth is concerned, the economic factor may not have any or much relevance. The processes of logical and philosophical thinking and intuitive meditation that went into the formulation of the main teachings of Buddhism — the four Aryan truths, twelve-fold causational formula, the eight-fold path, the four *dhyāna* or the four *brahmavihāra* etc., — are not economically determined in the least. But when I make this statement, I do not intend to deny the commonplace truth that before Buddha and his disciples could meditate on these truths they must have had something to eat and for producing the articles and materials of food there must have been prevalent some process of production within a social and economic system. What I mean to deny is that the processes and conclusions of religious and philosophical thought are determined by the economic process. We must eat before we can think but the method and processes of food production do not determine whether one is to think about *nirvāṇa* or about relativity or about factors resulting in the decline of the empire of the Mauryas.

It is not possible to trace the economic foundations of the Buddhist doctrines of *anātman*, *pratityāsamutpāda*, and *nirvāṇa*. It is true that the rise of the nihilist movement in Russian thought can be linked up with the despair experienced by the Russian workers and revolutionaries. It is possible to correlate the Nietzschean cult of the superman with the triumphant political and economic mood of imperial Germany. But this kind of correlation is possible only for sociological philosophy. Speculative philosophy, on the other hand, is, more or less, independent of the economic and political situation. One would have to venture into the abstract, rarefied, and even illusory regions of speculations for searching the economic and political background of the nihilism of Nāgārjuna or of the idealism of Asaṅga and Vasubandhu. It is more plausible to interpret a system of thought with reference to its intellectual antecedents. The fine and subtle distinctions pointed out by philosophical minds are not determined by the cash nexus or the economic changes in trade values. It will be very difficult to find a correlation between Kant's categorical imperative, categories of the understanding and the Ideas of Reason and the changing conditions of the economic and political life of Germany. But although the economic and political roots of philosophical concepts, categories and propositions may not be accurately traced, it is possible and even worthwhile to find out the influence of economic and political factors on religious movements.

But although the origination of religious truths is not determined by the economic process, the influence of the economic factor is tremendous on the organisational phase of religion as discussed below.

(a) The spread of a religious movement like that of other social movements is facilitated by economic patronage. The richer sections can shower their munificence in various ways on the religious organization. They can build rest-houses and buildings where the monks can reside. They can arrange for the food of the monks and teachers. In times of illness of the religious aspirants they can arrange for medical facilities to them. Thus the influence of the economic factor is very important on the organizational side of a religion.

(b) It is also a fact that several adherents join a movement being tempted by its economic attractions. Some individuals who might have failed to make out a living in other spheres may sometimes find an easy means of subsistence in the religious congregation. In several such cases, however, the economic motive may not overtly work. It may be a subconscious motivation and in some cases it may be suffused with highly idealized feelings of reverence for the founder of the religion and his teachings.

(c) A third way in which the economic factor operates in a religious movement is that aid, subventions and donations can be utilized in sending preachers for missionary work. This factor is becoming more important in modern religious movements than in the ancient because of the increased facilities for transportation.

(d) A fourth way in which the impact of the economic factor is felt on religious systems is the establishment of congruity between the demands of the economy and the possible economic implications of the religious teachings. If the demands of the economic system require that interest should be charged on capital investments, then between two religious movements, one of which supports the lending of money at interest and the other which condemns usury, the chances of the first one being patronized by the holders of economic power are great. To take another example — if a religious system, even by implication, suggests the concept of economic equality, the chances are that the economic magnates would try to suppress it. Thus it is evident that the study of the correlation between the structure of economic power and the economic ethics of religious movements can significantly advance our knowledge.

2. *The Economic Background of Buddhism*

It will be worthwhile to analyse some of the dominant features of the contemporary economic life and to find out if directly or indirectly they could foster or retard the progress of the Buddhistic movement.

(a) *Trade and Commerce*

During the days of the Indus civilization some amount of trade was carried on between India, Sumer and Egypt. Some seals of common design have been unearthed in Ur and Mohenjodaro. The trade between these countries must have resulted in a clash of ideas and have promoted a wider orientation and outlook. The Vedic civilization which is depicted in the Samhitās, the *Aitaraya* and the *Satapatha* Brāhmanas and the Upaniṣads is more agrarian and secluded in outlook as contrasted to the urbanism of the Indus civilization. There are some references to the sea in the Vedic literature but there is no reference to trade outside India. The *Atharvaveda* exalts sea-faring and there are some references in the Vedic mythology to persons saved in the sea by some kind deity. There is also the mention of the Paṇis who probably are the ancient Phoenicians. Some words of proto-Australoid origin have been found in the Atharvaveda but, by and large, the civilization depicted in the Vedic literature is characterized by localism and an intra-country outlook.

The foundation of the Median empire, however, resulted in a change and commercial activities were once again started between Western Asia and north-west India. The Jātakas contain explicit references to the trade of India with Babylon. The Babylonian markets offered fabulous prices for some of the luxury articles exported from India. One of the Neo-Babylonian emperors specially constructed a new harbour for the landing of the vessels engaged in Indian trade. The trade in luxuries points out that the cultures of the countries engaged in that must have been, at least partly, aristocratic. On the other hand, it is the necessary concomitant of an aristocratic or semi-aristocratic culture that it must be supported at the base either by slaves or by some other sections of the plebian strata.

The growth of trade and commerce had two significant consequences. First, it promoted a broader outlook. This wider orientation is seen in the attitude of Buddha. Buddha hopes that his message should spread in all quarters and corners. This missionary outlook of Buddha would have been possibly influenced by the dynamic economy of the day. The ritualistic cult of the Brahmins had fostered a local and restricted outlook. It was complicated and required for its performance a trained priesthood. Hence its spread in countries outside India was difficult. The predominantly agrarian economy on which the Vedic civilization was based also fostered a local outlook. The village has been always the centre of localism. Hence there must have been some other material base for the missionary zeal manifested by Buddhism. It may be stated that there must have been some correlation between the expansion of trade and commerce from the 7th century B.C. onwards and the missionary zeal of the new religions. A second consequence of expanded trade and commerce is that it increases the wealth of the country and accelerates the production process. In the early Buddhistic works there is reference to great mercantile magnates. These magnates substantially helped in the strengthening of the Buddhistic movement. I do not mean to suggest that the merchants who helped Buddhism were actually engaged in or derived their wealth from foreign trade and commerce. I only state that the increase of trade and commerce is an index of the economic prosperity of the richer sections, and the merchants who helped Buddhism must have been indirect sharers in the expanded wealth of the country. Thus it appears that the increase of trade and commerce had two consequences for the new movement of Buddhism. It fostered the acceptance of a wider missionary outlook and it prepared the ground for the expansion of wealth which made it possible at least in some cases that large gifts could be extended to the religious movements.

The *Arthaśāstra* of Kautilya also contains references to the expansion of trade and commerce with the countries of eastern and western Asia. But since the date of Kautilya is controversial and since there is a tendency to regard the *Arthaśāstra* as post-Mauryan, this book cannot be referred to in connexion with the economic life of northern India from about the seventh to the fourth centuries B.C. It will not be wide of the mark to suggest, however, that the correlation between extended economic activity and the growth of a missionary outlook was maintained for a long time in India.

(b) *Economic Position of the Brahmin Class*

The *Majjhima* and the *Dīgha Nikāya* contain references to *brahmadeya*[1] — gifts for Brahmins.[2] This term refers to a prevalent custom in the contemporary society of providing gifts and charities to the Brāhmin caste. For a long time the Brāhmins had been solidifying their social position.[3] They had the boldness to proclaim the vicious theory of the origin of the four varṇas from the four organs of the *purusha.* For themselves, they had claimed that they were the mouth of the *purusha.* The Brāhmins also solidified their economic position. The rituals brought a large amount of fees or *dakshiṇā* to them. Although the wealth of the Brāhmins can in no way be regarded to be as fabulous as that of the medieval Church in Europe, it is a fact that, more or less, the Brāhmins depended for their subsistence on the charity of the laity. Some of the sacrifices conducted by the Brāhmins were continued for months and they must have brought large fees to the priests who were in charge of these rites. *Brahmadeya* and *dakshiṇā*, thus, must have been of significance in enabling the Brāhmin caste to maintain its economic position.[4]

Another way in which the Brahmin caste fortified its economic position was that it maintained educational institutions. Uttara and Śaila are reported to have their educational centres in Mithilā. Yājñavalkya, the reputed teacher of monistic

[1] *brahmadeya* = tax-free gift of land.

[2] Even during the days of the Upaniṣads, liberality and generosity were recognized as great virtues. The *Brihadāraṇyaka*, III, 8, 9 says *dadato manushayāh praśamsanti yajamānam devā darvīm pitaroanvāyattāh*: According to the *Brihadāraṇyaka*, III, 9, 21, *yajña* is based upon *dakshiṇā.*

[3] In the *Brihadāraṇyaka*, III, 8, 10, the knower of the *akshara* is called a *brāhmaṇa* and is contrasted to a *kripaṇa.* Because of the sameness of the term *brāhmaṇa*, both for the *brahmin* class and for the knower of *brahman*, in practice, this was bound to increase the social status of the brahmin class. In the *Brihadāraṇyaka*, II, 1, 21, the *mahāraja* and the *mahābrāhmaṇa* are treated, on an equal footing. This indicates that the *mahābrāhmaṇa* had a socially covetable position. It is also said, *Ibid.*, II, 1, 15, that Ajātaśatru took Bālāki Gārgya by the hand and rose (*paṇāvadāyottasthau*). It may indicate that Ajātaśatru and Gārgya were on intimate terms.

[4] Cf. Max Weber, *The Sociology of Religion* (E. T. by E. Fischoff, London, Methuen & Co., 1965), p. 213.

philosophy, had a large band of students. The gifts of Janaka[1] in the shape of gold and cows were of considerable help to him in maintaining himself and his devoted pupils. King Janaka used his great wealth for sacrificial purposes. A great sacrificial congregation was held at his court and Brahmins, even from a distance, assembled there. After the costly sacrifice, Janaka offered ten thousand gold pieces (ten pādas of gold were bound to the horns of each cow and there were one thousand cows) for the victor in the scholarly combat in the science of *brahmavidyā*.[2] There are references to other teachers having set up educational institutions under them for initiation in the Upaniṣadic literature. In the Buddhist literature there is reference to several Brāhmin teachers having under them *mānavaka* or young students. Although not very affluent, these educational institutions must have been at least able to maintain the teachers and the pupils. They would be financed either by the gifts of the people or, to some extent, by the daily begging of the students and sometimes of the teacher also. This tradition must have been continued in Buddha's time also. It it true that the 7th, 6th and 5th centuries B.C. were not the epochs of people's enlightenment or mass culture. The literacy figures in those days must have been very small. But although not politically significant as the third or the fourth estate, it may be guessed that the middle classes must have attended the sermons of Buddha and must have made some financial contributions to the movement.

It is true that the economic position of the Brahmins as a caste was not covetable. Some *mahāśāla* Brahmins might have been prosperous but, by and large, the Brahmins as a caste were only able somehow to maintain themselves. The important point to note about them is that they were not a producing class. They generally depended for their maintenance on the gifts and charities of the believers who accepted the

1 Cf. the word *brahmagavi* in the *Brihadāraṇyaka*, III, 7, 1.

2 Yājñavalkya must have been maintaining a vast educational centre, otherwise he would not have taken one thousand cows. It may also be pointed out that the structure of the educational establishments must have been large because otherwise one thousand cows could not have been housed. From these it may be inferred that in the 'academy' of Yājñavalkya there must have been at least one thousand students. He charged his student Sāmaśravā to conduct the cows to his āśrama.

prevalent religious theology and rituals. The laity who contributed these gifts did so because they adhered to a system of beliefs wherein charity to Brāhmins was inculcated. Their gifts might not be so considerable as to finance what may be regarded as a decent standard of life but slender, though they might have been, the important point is that on their basis a non-producing caste had been generally able to maintain its physical existence. The point to be emphasized is that the means of subsistence of the Brahmin caste were integrally connected with a system of traditional theological beliefs.[1]

Buddhism challenged the contemporary Brahmanical theology. It does not accept any metaphysical Absolute. It ridicules the notion of a supreme creative power. It undermines the position of the traditionally venerated gods of the Vedic pantheon. It says that the gods like Brahmā and Indra are subordinate to Buddha and even supplicate him for favour. It denied the efficacy of the fee-giving sacrifices, some of which involved even the slaughter of animals. Instead, it preached that the due performance of one's duties towards parents and the giving of help to the needy were the true sacrifices. We have discussed earlier the nature and religious implications of the Buddhistic attack on Brāhmanical theology and ritualism. At this place it is only essential to point out that the attack against contemporary theology and ritualism was a direct challenge to the social and economic position of the Brahmin caste. If the creative primordial principle or *Iśvara* himself was a non-entity, what significance could be attached to being the "mouth" (*brāhmano asya mukhamāsit*) of such an agency? The vehemence with

[1] According to the *Brihadāraṇyaka Upaniṣad*, 1, 4, 11, the Brahmins are regarded as the *Yoni* of the political rulers. "Verily, in the beginning this world was Brahma, one only. Being one, he was not developed. He created still further a superior form, the Kshatrahood, even those who are Kshatras (rulers) among the gods : Indra, Varuṇa, Soma, Rudra, Parjanya, Yama, Mrityu, Iśāna. There is nothing higher than Kshatra. Therefore at the Rājasuya ceremony the Brahman sits below the Kshatriya. Upon Kshatrahood alone does he confer this honor. This same thing, namely Brahmanhood (*brahma*), is the source of Kshatrahood. Therefore, even if the king attains supremacy, he rests finally upon Brahmanhood as his own source. So whoever injures him [i.e. a Brahman] attacks his own source. He fares worse in proportion as he injures one who is better."

which the Brahmin protagonists opposed Buddhism in post-Asokan India was based on the fact that their entire economic position was sought to be undermined by the success of the Buddhist creed.

(c) *Economic Support to Buddhism*

We have earlier pointed out the four possible ways in which, in its organizational form, a religious movement can be supported by the economic leaders. A good financial basis does constitute a dominant source of strength to any religious movement. The temples of Egypt and Babylonia could play such a significant role in the political, educational and religious life of these countries because they had considerable economic assets. They even received some state subsidies for carrying out their various activities. In a sense they could be regarded as states within states. In ancient Palestine also, David and Solomon (10th century B.C.) rendered help to the growing Israelite religion by constructing the 'Great temple.'

Before the rise of Buddhism, as we have mentioned earlier, the kings had developed the practice of making grants to individual Brāhmin teachers.[1] King Bimbisāra of Magadh made grants to the Brāhmin Brahmadatta of Anga. There are other such references in the contemporary Buddhistic literature. Buddhism also received the support of kings[2] and financial magnates.[3] Prasenajit, the king of Kośala, is stated to have professed his adherence to Buddhism. But Ajātaśatru did not possibly render any support to the Samgha in Buddha's life-time. But according to the *Mahāparinirvāṇa Sūtra* of the *Dīgha Nikāya*, he is reported to have built a *stupa* over some portions of the relics of Buddha. Perhaps one of the factors why the five heretical teachers could not succeed in organizing any big movement was that they did not receive adequate financial support.

1 In the *Brihadāraṇyaka*, II, 1, 1, Ajātaśatru, King of Kāśi promises to give a thousand cows to Dṛpta Bālāki for a speech on *brahman*. Janaka's magnificent munificence was the subject of talk in the contemporary metropolises and rural areas.

2 T.W. Rhys Davids, *Buddhist India*, pp. 7-8 (Indian edition).

3 Contrasting early Buddhism and Christianity, Monier-Williams, *Buddhism*, pp. 554-55, says that while Jesus Christ was despised and rejected by kings and princes and followed by poor ignorant fishermen, Buddha was honoured by kings and princes and followed by rich men.

Buddhism was more fortunate in the gifts and grants that it received from kings[1] and rich merchants.[2] It may be hazarded that possibly the support of the mercantile community of Rājagir to Buddha might be a counteracting step to the royal pressure on them because Rājgir being the capital of Magadhan kings, due to physical proximity, the kings might have exercised pressure on the setthis. Bimbisāra made liberal grants to Buddhism.

One institutional change came with the pouring in of gifts and grants. Originally the bhikkhus used to reside in very ordinary and sequestered places exposed to all kinds of privations. But when devoted followers began to build Vihāras, Buddha allowed the bhikkhus to reside even in these comfortable dwellings. Some famous Vihāras presented to Buddha were Veluvana Kālandakanivāpa, the Jetavana at Srāvasti, Jivaka's Āmravana and Maddakuchchi Mrigadāva.

(d) *The Influence of the Contemporary Economy Upon Buddhism*

We have earlier referred to the growth of trade and commerce in the country after the seventh century B.C. But that should not lead us to infer that the economy was industrial. The trade and commerce was in agricultural products and not in industrial commodities. There was no large-scale manufacturing system prevalent at the time in spite of the mention of "śreshthis." The prevailing economy of the time was rural.[3] Though there is the

[1] According to the *Sāmaññyaphala Sutta* of the *Dīgha Nikāya* (Hindi translarion by R. Sāmkrityāyana) p. 22, it appears to have been a practice of contemporary kings to take care of the clothing, food, shelter, medicine, protection, watch and ward of the *bhīkkhus*. It may be possible that the religious philanthropy of the contemporary kings might have been one of the factors for the development of monasticism.

[2] N. Datta, *The Spread of Buddhism*, points out that the Vaiśya community in Rājagir furnished the largest number of converts. Buddha is said to have allowed the use of sugar to the bhikkhus when one merchant offered to give sugar to the Samgha.

[3] C.A.F. Rhys Davids, "Economic Conditions According to Early Buddhist Literature", *The Cambridge History of India*, Vol. I, ed. by E.J. Rapson, p. 176 : "The rural economy of India at the coming of Buddhism was based chiefly on a system of village communities of landowners, or what in Europe is known as peasant proprietorship. The Jātaka bears very clear testimony to this. There is no such clear

mention of towns like Rājagir, Champā, Pataliputra, Vesali, Kāsi, Śrāvāsti, Ujjine, Taxilā, etc. in the Buddhistic literature,[1] these towns were not renowned for any industry. Some of them derived their importance from being only capital towns. The development of big towns in Europe is a consequence of the Commercial Revolution during the latter part of the Middle Ages. The Indian towns associated with early Buddhism were much smaller compared to the towns of the 16th century in Europe. The vast bulk of the population lived in the countryside. Even in the Buddhistic literature the recognition of the physical existence of the villages is pronounced. The imagery and the metaphors, and some of the setting and the scenes in the Tripiṭakas are taken from the countryside.

Perhaps a village economy and population are more receptive to religious ideas and movements. Towns, on the other hand, breed a materialistic and sensate outlook. The reason for this is that in the towns the struggle for existence is very hard. There is keen competition and hence the minds of the townspeople are in constant tension. Most of the time their minds are engaged in the quest of material goods. They have to devise new ways and means to ascend in the economic ladder. After the end of the Middle Ages and with the growth of the Renaissance, science, technology and commerce have become

testimony in it to isolated large estates, or to great feudatories, or to absolute lords of the soil holding such estates. In the monarchies, the king, though autocratic and actively governing, had a right to a tithe on raw produce, collected as a yearly tax ; and only to this extent could he be considered the ultimate owner of the soil. All abandoned, all forest land the king might dispose of (D. I, 87) ; and under this right was included the reversion to the crown of all property left intestate or 'ownerless' [S. I, 89 (*Kindred Sayings*, I, 115). *Jāt*. III, 302 ; cf. IV, 485 ; VI, 348] a custom which may or may not be a survival of an older feudalism. The sovereign was moreover entitled to 'milk money', a perquisite paid by the nation when an heir was born to him (*Ib*. IV, 323), and he could declare a general indemnity for prisoners at any festal occasion (*Ib*. IV, 175 ; V, 285 ; VI, 327)."

1 During the day of early Buddhism, Pātaliputra had not yet become a big town. It seems that Śrāvasti, Rājagriha and Gayā were the Mecca and Medina of early Buddhism. H. Oldenberg, *Buddha*, p. 197, refers to the "opulent and brilliant free, town Vaiśali." It is certainly true that Vaiśali plays a more important part in the development of Buddhism than Kapilavastu, the birth-place of Gautama Buddha.

the foci of general attention in the West. We do have churches, sects and denominations in the Western countries but the overwhelming quest for religious values and symbols that we find in the Middle Ages has never been repeated on any similar magnitude in the West. There seems to be some definite correlation between the growth of urban civilization and the generation and fostering of a materialistic outlook.

The villages, on the other hand, have always been more receptive to religious ideas and values. The cynic may say that this is due to the acceptance of superstitions, magic, ghost-stories and priestcraft amongst the village population. But in sociological terms, it seems that the village population is more receptive to the acceptance of religious ideas because they have a fatalistic outlook, since agriculture, their very source of existence, is almost absolutely dependent on rains except in those areas where modern technology has been able to provide for irrigational facilities. Whether in a particular year there will be rains or not is entirely a matter of chance. This, almost absolute, dependence on chance makes the village population fatalistic. The essence of fatalism is the supreme acceptance of a higher power and almost utter resignation to it in face of its inexorable decrees. But this fatalism did not result in generating any pessimistic strain of gloom or frustration. The social collectivity as a total structure can never be given to any permanent attachment to sorrow. In spite of numerous privations the people experience a tremendous amount of pleasure in the sheer face of physical continuity. Physical existence, in itself, is so absorbing that political and economic convulsions and their social and moral repercussions do not count as significant categories in their scheme of calculation and evaluation. This kind of political apathy is a normal feature of people's life everywhere. Even at the time of the rise of Macedon and of the threatened invasion from her, the people of Athens and Sparta were not specially desperate and thinking of death. The condition of the Roman people at the time of the Teutonic invasions or of the people of England, France and the other countries of Western Europe at the time of Norman invasions would corroborate this generalisation regarding popular psychology. The Indian people throughout their history would offer numerous examples to substantiate this point of view. Thus pessimism is a personal outlook and not a collective experience. The village economy dependent on chance rainfall fosters a mentality suitable to the acceptance of religious creeds, dogmas and rituals. What I am stating receives substantiation from the performance of great sacrifices—*yajña*, even in modern India to please the rain-god for the grant of rains.

A second factor which might have made the village population of north India during the centuries preceding the rise of Buddhism receptive to religious values is that the struggle for existence had not been acute. The wants of the population were simple and their demands were slender.[1] Besides, the population was not large and hence the pressure on land was not great. Hence people had some leisure. Leisure is essential for providing to the people the time when they can listen to religious discourses.[2] The absorbing and compulsive demands of the economic organization have made the modern man almost

[1] H. Oldenberg, *Buddha*, p. 164, says : "...the merchant Anāthapiṇḍika, who had presented to the order the garden of Jetavana, Buddha's favourite place of resort. In all important place which Buddha touched in the course of his wanderings, he found bands of such lay-believers, who went out to meet him, arranged for assemblies, in which Buddha spoke, who gave him and his companions their meals, who placed their residences and gardens at their disposal, or made them over to the order as Church property. If he went wandering about with hundreds of his disciples, pious votaries were sure to accompany him on his journey with carts and waggons, and they brought necessaries of life, salt, and oil with them, for each in his turn to prepare the wanderer a meal, and crowds of needy folk followed in their train to snatch the remains of these provisions." The last part of the sentence is a baseless and even nonsensical attack against the contemporary economic condition of India and it shows that even so-called objective Western Indologists could be 'brutal' in their depiction of the situation of 'colonial' India.

[2] Max Weber, *The Religion of India* (Illinois, The Free Press of Glencoe, 1958), E.T. by H.H. Gerth and Don Martindale, pp. 204-205, takes a somewhat different view and connects the rise of Buddhism with the growth of towns. Weber says: "Like Jainism, but even more clearly, Buddhism presents itself as a product of the time of urban development, of urban kingship and the city nobles.... Oldenberg drew attention to the fact that rural surroundings, cattle and pasture, were characteristic of the ancient Brahmanical teachers and schools, at least in the early times of Upaniṣads, whereas the city and the urban palace with its elephant-riding kings were characteristic of Buddha's time."

leisureless. But the very fact that in the seventh and sixth centuries B.C. several religious teachers were roaming in the country and getting large audience for their sermons is a testimony to the fact that the people had relative rest and freedom and all their energies were not taken up with the drudgeries of the struggle for economic subsistence.[1]

Buddhism flourished at a time when a large section of the people had some amount of leisure at their disposal. Hence it is that whenever Gautama Buddha would pass through the village, the people would come out to receive him and the group of bhikkhus. They would spend considerable time in his services and arrange for the food of the august religious visitors.[2]

[1] A. Bose, *Social and Rural Economy of Northern India* (Calcutta, Firma K.L. Mukhopadhyay, 1961), p. 83 : "The entertainment of Buddha with his Fraternity by the faithful which became a general custom in the Gangetic provinces was performed sometimes by individuals, sometimes by families, sometimes by *gamas* and even whole clans. A single family might make a house to house collection of food materials (*Jāt.* II, 85 : Mv. VI, 37) or all the villagers might come forward (*ibid.*, 282 ; 33. 1). The Mallas of Kusināra even make compacts that whoever does not join the reception shall be fined and that the members should regale the Saṃgha by rotation (*ibid.*, 36). Sometimes it was the turn of a section or assembly viz., the *puga* (Cv. 6.2 ; VIII. 4. 1). The corporate unity and homogeneity of faith among the villages facilitated the conversion of villages *en masse* by Buddha repeatedly claimed in the Pali canon." I have doubts regarding this last statement.

[2] T. W. Rhys Davids, *Buddhist India*, pp. 43-44 (Indian edition) : "Of want, as known in our great cities, there is no evidence. It is put down as the direst misfortune known that a free man had to work for hire. And there was plenty of land to be had for trouble of clearing it, not far from the settled districts. On the other hand, the number of those who could be considered wealthy from the standards of those times (and of course still more so from our own) was very limited. We hear of about a score of monarchs, whose wealth consisted mainly of the land tax, supplemented by other dues and perquisites; of a considerable number of wealthy nobles, and some priests, to whom grants had been made of the tithe arising out of certain parishes or countries or who had inherited similar rights from their forefathers; of about a dozen millionaire merchants in Takkasilā, Sāvatthi, Benares, Rājagaha, Vesāli, Kosāmbi, and the seaport, and of a considerable number of lesser merchants and middlemen, all in the few towns. But these were the exceptions. There were no landlords. And the great mass of the people were well-to-do peasantry, or handicraftsmen, mostly with land of their own, both classes ruled over by local headmen of their own selection."

But in spite of the receptivity to the acceptance of religious values and dogmas implicitly present in the mentality of the village population due to the compresence of these two factors—(i) a rain-dependent economy and (ii) an economy providing some amount of leisure — early Buddhism never became an agrarian movement. Nor did it provide any program for the economic betterment of the village population. Its attitude was too much taken up with ethical quests and psychological perfections. Hence, directly or indirectly, it did not provide any economic program for the village population. If any person was economically thwarted then he could join the Samgha and thus escape the stigma and the privations of the economic world but there was no relief provided by Buddhism to him if he continued to remain in his previous station. A more significant sense in which Buddhism never became an agrarian movement was that its membership was not constituted to any considerable extent by the vast bulk of the inhabitants of the villages. Early Buddhism had some very important royal converts, it had some significant groups of rich men to finance its activities and operations and it also succeeded in organizing a vast body of bhikkhus in its Samgha. These were, no doubt, sources of great strength. But in spite of all these avenues of strength, a very grave weakness of Buddhism was that it never became an agrarian mass movement in India. It was, in its beginnings, to a considerable extent, an urban lower middle class and bourgeois-aristocratic movement. Nowhere in the records of Pali Buddhism or in other sources of historical information for nearly twelve hundred years from the sixth century B.C. to the sixth century A.D. do we find any evidence to show that any large area, in northern India, was ever fully converted to Buddhism or entirely subscribed to the three-fold formulas of surrender. Buddhism, essentially, was a movement of protest, it was heterodox in its orientation, and its tone was critical. Its abstruse metaphysics and subtle subliminal psychology were meant only for a small coterie of the bhikkhu group. But early Buddhism or even later Buddhism did not reach the mass of the people on a very large scale. There is no evidence to prove that an entire janapada or the majority of the population in any republican Samgha or *rājya* ever accepted Buddhism completely. It is surprising that Buddhism never became a popularly accepted movement even amongst the Sākiyas or the Koliyas. This non-popular character of Buddhism explains the ease with which it almost faded out of organized existence from India.

CHAPTER 16

THE POLITICAL FOUNDATIONS OF EARLY BUDDHISM

1. *Buddhism as an Eastern Indian Movement*

PANJAB AND THE Middle country had been the main centres of the Vedic and Upaniṣadic culture.[1] But the early Buddhists made Magadha and also Kosala[2] the centre of their propaganda.[3] In Magadha the influence of the Brahmin teachers was

[1] Discussing the term *Vrātya* in his book *Darshana Digdarshana*, Rahula Sāmkrityāyana says that it (*vrātya*) was a term applied to the Aryans of Kabul-Swat and the Saptasindhu and the Mallas and the Vajjis, by the Aryans of the 'middle country' because the former people (the vrātyāh) wanted to stick to the manners and customs they had brought from their homeland, while the Aryans of the 'middle country' wanted to introdue innovations. Rahula regards the Kuru-Pāñchāla land as the centre of Vedic culture because therein flourished Divodāsa and Sudās and (b) to that region belonged Uddālaka Āruṇi. But the third argument advanced by Rahula to prove, that Kuru Pañchāla land was the centre of Vedic culture, that the *Mahāsatipatthāna Sutta* and the *Mahānidāna Sutta*, the two philosophical discourses were delivered there, is facile and unconvincing if not ridiculous.

[2] T. W. Rhys Davids, "The Buddha's Residences", *JRAS*, 1891, p. 339. R.S. Hardy, *A Manual of Buddhism*, p. 356. According to *Uvasagadasao*, Srāvasti, the capital of Kośala was the headquarters of the Ājivika sect. According to Buddhaghosa, the Bhadravargiyas were the brothers of the kings of Kośala.

[3] T.W. Rhys Davids, *Buddhist India*. B.C. Law, *The Geography of Early Buddhism*. Th. Stcherbatsky, "The Dharmas of the Buddhists and the Gunas of the Samkhya", *IHQ*, Vol. X, 1934, pp. 737-60, has thus described the evolution of Buddhist thought:

(a) Sarvāstivāda	=	in ancient Magadha
(b) Mahāyānism	=	in Andhradesha in 2nd cent. A.D.
(c) Vijñānavāda	=	in Peshawar in 4th cent. A.D.

Hara Prasad Sastry, *IHQ*, Vol. IX, No. 1, March 1933, holds that a favourable atmosphere for the rise of Buddhism resulted from the impact

probably not as strong as in Middle India.[1] European indologists stress the point that Buddhism and Jainism arose and flourished in eastern India because the influence of Brāhmanism was not strong in this region. The *Śatapatha Brāhmaṇa* also states that the ritualistic cult of sacrifice did not extend beyond the river Sadānirā. Prince Mathva took his abode east of the Sadānira, a land unillumined previously by Agni Vaiśvānara. His descendants later became the rulers of Mithilā. According to the Buddhist literature, the Brahmins of eastern India trace their descent from the Brahmins of the northern regions of India which means that the north and not the east was the source of brahmin nobility and culture. There were some regions, however, in eastern India where Branmanical influence had been substantial. In Mithilā at the court of King Janaka, important contributions were made to the monistic theory of Upaniṣadic idealism.[2] Gayā, as has earlier been pointed out, was the centre of the sacrificial cult and one thousand Jatila teachers lived there. It is said that the *Atharvaveda*, which in spite of having some important mystic theosophic hymns con-

of the culture of the three civilized tribes, the Vangas, the Vagadhas and the Cheras (*Aitareya Āraṇyaka*) upon the Aryans. The place of this favourable development was between the eastern limit of the region occupied by the Aryans and the western limit of tract of land occupied by the Vangas, the Vagadhas and the Cheras The Tharuns living near Kapilavastu may be a branch of the Cheras, while the Vagadhas may be Magadhans.

[1] See R. Fick, *The Social Organization in N.E. India*, pp. 34, 40, 213. The groups of Brahmins who flock to the court of Janaka, the Videha King, are, with the exception of Yājñavalkya from the West — *Kurupañcālānam brāhmanah* (*Śatapatha*, XIV, 6, 1, 1.). Oldenberg, *Buddha*, p. 398, says that even Yājñavalkya was a pupil of Āruni who was a Pāñcāla, E.J. Thomas, *Life of Buddha*, 3rd ed., reprint of 1960, p. 174, says that Brahmanism was probably recent enough in the extreme east of India to have met with opposition and counter-claims. This would explain the origin of reform movements in this land against the view taken by Brahmins regarding their own functions. In the Upaniṣadic age, there are references to Gandhara, that is, the north-west portion of India, to Kuru-Pāñchāla and to Videha, but there is no mention of the area extending from modern Gorakhpur and Chapra to Muzaffarpur.

[2] In the Upaniṣads, Kekaya, Madra and Gāndhāra are mentioned. According to the *Kaushitaki Upaniṣad*, IV, 1, Gārgya Bālāki goes to the Kurus and the Pāñchālas, Kasis and Videhas, Vatsas and Matsyas and Usinaras.

tains a very large number of hymns referring to magic and charms, spells and incantations, shows the lower side of religion which must have prevailed amongst the contemporary masses.[1] In the *Tevijja Sutta* of the *Dīgha Nikāya* and other places, Buddha refers to Brahmins versed in the three vedas but surprisingly, there is no mention of the *Atharva.* It seems Buddha was also influenced by the dominant emphasis only on the *trayī.* The *Atharvaveda* has some hymns singing the splendours of the supreme spirit,[2] but it is full of magical formulas. In it significance is attributed not so much to the rituals and sacrificial cult as to magic. Because this veda is supposed to have been composed in eastern India, it can be said that since the olden times Brahmanical ritualistic influence had been weak in this area.[3] Some Austro-Asiatic and Malayo-Polynesian influences, specially on language, are traceable in eastern India. If any validity has to be attached to Pargiter's researches then it would appear that eastern India was not anti-Brahmanical because the Angirasas flourished in north Bihar and the Kaśyapas in Anga. Philosophers and sociologists have also pointed out the influence of race, culture, geography and environment on

1 The Vratyas, according to one interpretation, were Yogins in eastern India.

2 Cf. also the "Kāla" hymns of the *Atharvaveda*, XIX, 53-54.

3 *Atharvaveda*, V, 22, 14. In this hymn fever is said to be sent to the Gandharas, the Mujavant, the Angas and the Magadhas. Perhaps this would indicate that Magadha was beyond the recognized domains of Brahmanism. C.A.F. Rhys Davids says: "Buddhism was born in the eastern half of the so-called Middle country, or watershed of the Ganges and Indus, not in the western. There is silence in the Buddhist scriptures about the country west of the junction of the Ganges and Jumna, save only in a rare sporadic way, such as reference to Ujjeni. I have it on scholar's authority that, eastern Middle country Brahmanism was in a more morally lax, less organised state than was western Middle country. Brahmanism, hence, may be, the birth and growth of new reform movements in cult in the eastern half, such as Jainism and Brahmanism. The Suttas (Refer: *Brāhmanadhammika Sutta* in the *Sutta Nipāta*) do not hesitate to hint that Brahmin morals were lax; where the first Buddhists taught (at Sravasti: *Brahmanadhammika Sutta* of the *Sutta Nipāta*) albeit the class-respect claimed by Brahmins was none the weaker for that [Buddhists laid the supremest emphasis on moral conduct. In fact for them morality meant religious life]......"

thought.[1] Thus the hypothesis that climate and the natural and social environment influence the philosophical, religious and ethical ideas of teachers should not appear strange.[2] It is but natural that the peculiarities of the situational context of eastern India, as distinguished from those of western India, should find expression in some aspects of Buddhistic teachings,[3] and have influenced its anti-Brāhmanical tendency.[4] If this hypothesis of geographical influence is correct then Buddhism must have been moulded by the riparian influence of the Gangetic Valley as distinguished from the continental culture of what Manu has called "Brahmarshideśa." According to tradition as recorded later on, Vena and Prithu were opposed to Brāhmanism. If the chronological conclusions of Pargiter (*Ancient Indian Historical Tradition*), are correct, then it may be possible to consider Vena and Prithu as precursors of the Buddhist and Jain movements. It is remarkable that the scene of the activities of Vena and Prithu is the same eastern India where Buddhism and Jainism originated. The distinction in the culture of Eastern India, Western India and specially of Magadh and the Western Gangetic plains is definitely recognized in the ancient literature.

2. *The Political Background of Buddhism*

In the Tell-el-Amarna tablets (1400 B.C.), Aryan and Sanskritic names are found. If these indicate an early migration of Aryan tribes from India to the north-west regions then that could

[1] Melamed, *Spinoza and Buddha*, regards it as a general law of history that races create and environment modifies culture and civilization.

[2] Cf. the methodology followed in S.J. Case, *The Social Origins of Christianity* (Chicago, 1923) and Alfaric, *L'evolution intellectual de St. Augustine* (Paris, 1918).

[3] Rapson, *Ancient India*, p. 11 : "...fertile plains of the Jumna and the Ganges...birthplace of its [Brāhmanism] rival religions, Jainism and Buddhism." The *Manusmṛti*, VII. 41 and IX, 66, 67, refers to Vena as an arrogant monarch who resisted the authority of the Brahmins. According to Monier Williams, *Buddhism*, p. 423, probably Vena was a Buddhist. There is a Stupa of Vena in Kesaria, in North Bihar and Buddhists claim that this Stupa commemorates the spot where Buddha once preached.

[4] According to the *SB*, III, 2, 3, 15 : "Among men the speech is best in the country of the Kuru Pāñchālas and the Asuras and barbarians alike talk a bad speech."

be regarded as an early precursor of the trans-Indian movement of Buddhist religious missionaries after the 2nd century B.C. In the pre-Buddhist ages and specially in the history of Babylonia and Assyria, we get some instances of the imposition of the religion of the victors on the defeated people, but Buddha initiated the ethico-intellectual method of large-scale conversion.

Territorially speaking, the early Buddhist movement was confined to north-east India. Gautama Buddha was roughly the contemporary of the Achaemenian (Persian) emperors Cyrus and Darius,[1] having flourished from 560 B.C. to 480 B.C., or according to another method of reckoning, from 603 B.C. to 523 B.C.[2] The general period of Cyrus was from 558 to 530 B.C. and that of Darius from about 522 to 486 B.C. The Achaemenian emperors had succeeded in conquering Gāndhāra, in the extreme north-west of India.[3] They employed Arameans for administrative purposes in that area and they introduced the Aramaic script in that part of the country. The success of the ancient Persian empire in conquering Gāndhāra showed that the north-western portion of the country was vulnerable. It is surprising that no organised attempt was made to repulse the Persians. During this period the empire of Magadha was slowly extending its political strength and in those days of undeveloped transportation it could not be expected to play a vital political role in that remote territory. It is also possible that the news of foreign penetration in north-west India did not create any stir in northern and north-eastern India.

In Persia, Zoroaster started his movement of monotheism and ethical reform slightly earlier than the beginning of the Buddhist movement in north-east India. He propounded an ethical dualism and taught the existence of a continuous fight between Ahur Mazda, the typification of cosmic Good and Angra Mainyu, the embodiment of Evil. It is possible that the liberal teachings

[1] Croesus of Lydia and Nabonidus, the neo-Babylonian ruler, were also contemporaries.

[2] It is not correct to equate the Sakiya (Sākya) clan from which Gautama Buddha came with any Scythian tribe. According to Aśvaghosa, the word Saka denotes a kind of Śāla tree.—Hara Prasad Sastry, *IHQ*, Vol. IX, No. 1, March 1933, pp. 348 ff.

[3] In the *Chhāndogya Upaniṣad*, Gāndhāra is mentioned, possibly as an integral part of the then India.

of ethical idealism of Zoroaster aided the political career of the Achaemenian empire. The political teachings of early Buddhism also sponsored the concept of the *cakkavatti.*[1] It is true that there are dominant elements of idealism, gloom and asceticism in the metaphysics and ethics of Buddhism so far as it concerns the problem of individual redemption from sin and sorrow. But the political philosophy of the Tripiṭakas is, in no way, anti-terrestrial. The *Lakkhana Sutta* of the *Dīgha Nikāya* inculcates a similarity between the ideal of Buddhahood and the ideal of *cakkavattī.* In the *Cakkavattī Simhanāda Sutta*, the old imperial rulers are mentioned. The *Aitareya Brāhmana* first formulated the ideal of a *cakravarti* (*cakkavattī*)[2] but, more or less, it was conceived, in its practical operation, as being confined to upper India.[3] But the missionary movement of Buddha succeeded in giving an expanded territorial connotation to this term. It is possible that Asoka was influenced by the political philosophy of the Tripiṭakas and he wanted to be a *cakkavattī* emperor. Hence it may be stated that just as the ethical movement of Zoroaster imparted some sort of a political enthusiasm to the Achaemenian emperors, so also the Buddhist missionary propaganda succeeded in imparting an expanded territorial field of action to the Magadhan empire. Vidudabha carried a war against the Sakiyas only a year before the death of Gautama Buddha (i.e. 481 B C. or 532 B.C.). Eight years before the death of Buddha, Bimbisāra died by starvation. Ajātaśatru made a subsequent visit to Buddha. Ajātaśatru carried an imperialistic war against the Lichchavis. It may be stated that both Vidudabha and Ajātaśatru repudiated the Buddhist doctrines of *maitrī* and *karuṇā*, because they tried forcibly to destroy the independence of free states. The indirect incentive, however,

[1] In the *Sela Sūtta* of the *Sūtta Nipāta*, III, 7, 7, Buddha says : "A king am I, Sela, the king supreme of righteousness. The royal chariot wheel of righteousness do I set rolling on that wheel that no one turn back again."

[2] In the *Brihadāraṇyaka* there occurs *yā hutā adhiśerate manushya-lokameva tābhirjayati* which implies that there must have been a notion of universal supremacy (manushyaloka) which could be acquired by sacrifice (*BRU*, III, 1, 8).

[3] In the *Brihadarāṇyaka* there is also reference to the Madra land which was visited by some of the wandering (*carakāh*) people. The latter, however, were not yet crystallized into a definite group.

that Buddhism gave to monarchical imperialism was only through suggesting the view that just as there was an expansive missionary movement so also there could be an expansive political movement. Thus, although political imperialism, based on coercion, is an explicit repudiation of the Buddhist doctrine of compassion, and although the organisation of the Buddhist Samgha was, generally republican, nevertheless, the success of Buddhism as a movement, of course, very indirectly, aided the cause of political expansion. The political horizon of those days was confined either to the monarchical janapadas[1] or to the republican Samghas.[2] According to the *Aṅguttara Nikāya* there were sixteen Mahajanapadas:

1. Kāśī	9. Kuru
2. Kośala	10. Pāñchāla
3. Aṅga	11. Matsya
4. Magadha	12. Surasena
5. Vajji	13. Assaka (in the Indus Valley)
6. Malla	14. Avanti
7. Cheḍi (Ceti)	15. Gāndhāra
8. Vamsa (Vatsa)	16. Kamboja

[1] In the *Brihadāraṇyaka* II, 1, 18, it is said : "As a great king, taking with him his people, moves around in his own country as he pleases, even so here this one, [the man] taking with him his senses, moves around in his own body as he pleases." This referes to something like a political tour by the kings of those days and may be considered a precursor of the *dharma-yātrā* introduced by Asoka. Such an inspection tour appears to be the contemporary monarchical ideal. Ajātaśatru of Kāśī seems to be an advocate of this monarchical practice as he uses it as an ordinary instance of comparison. The phrase *jānapadān gṛhitvā* would indicate the smallness of the territorial dimension of the ruler who could move around in his country taking with him his people. But the word *gṛhitvā* smells of dictatorial significance and may signify something of a political autocracy. The monarchical ideal is supreme in the Upaniṣads. The sleep of the *vijñānamaya purusha* in the *puritata* is compared to the sleep of the *kumāra* or the *mahārāja* or the *mahābrāhmṇa.*

[2] Except for recognizing the supreme leadership (śāstā) of Buddha, the Buddhist Samgha was based on the republican pattern. Possibly this pattern was borrowed from the contemporary republican clans. There is no Brahmanical parallel for this Samgha congregation which is more or less a confederacy of autonomous monks bound together by the loyalty to *Dharma* and *Samgha* and *Buddha*. In view of the statement "*rājā mukham manussānām nadinām sāgaro mukham*", in the *Sela Sutta* of the *Sutta Nīpāta,* it will not be correct to regard Buddha as an anti-monarchist.

Early Buddhism succeeded in extending its field of missionary operations almost in the whole of modern Bihar and the Uttara Pradesha.[1] This crossing of the inter-janapada and inter-gaṇa lines provided a considerable field of action to the Buddhist preachers. It may be possible that the expansion of the religious theatre of action might have, at least indirectly, aided the expansion of the territorial field of action for the Magadhan emperors also. Generalizing from the experiences of Zoroastrianism and Buddhism, it may be possible to say that religious movements aid the political action of governmental structures.

The older Upaniṣads were composed against a monarchical background. Early Buddhism, on the other hand, flourished against the background of the republicanism of the Licchavis, the Mallas and the Sakiyas as well as the monarchy of the Kosalans and the Magadhans. It may be possible to trace some correlation between the monarchical background of the Upaniṣads and their concept of the Absolute. In Judaism, a similar phenomenon can be seen. It exalts Jehova as an autocratic monotheistic God. Parallel to this monotheism, we have, at the social and political levels, the supreme leadership of Moses and the imperialism of David and Solomon. But it will be far-fetched if we hazard the proposition that there could be some correlation between the republican backgrouud of Buddhism and its concept of dynamic reality. In the *Brahmajāla Sutta* of the *Dīgha Nikāya*,[2] Gautama Buddha says that he is not interested in political matters, army and battles, nor in the problems of *grāma*, *nigama*, *nagar*, *janapada*, nor in economic matters of clothes, chariots etc. He is also condemnatory of those Sramanas and Brahmins who acted as the emissaries of kings, ministers, princes etc. Buddha thus denies that he has any

[1] C.A.F. Rhys, Davids, *Buddhism*, p. 11 says that in Kosala the Buddhist movement took firmest root. Śrāvasti in Kosala was also the chief centre of the Ājivikas. Hence Kosala appears to have a prominent place in the 7th and 6th centuries B. C. intelletual movements. In those days Kāsī was an important centre of Upaniṣadic metaphysics, while Gayā was an important centre of sacrificial ritualism associated with the Jatilas. (See the *Mahāvagga*, *Vinayā Piṭaka*).

[2] The *Dīgha Nikāya*, Hindi translation by R. Sāmkrityāyana and J. Kashyap, p. 4.

interest in these things. In the *Sāmaññyaphala Sutta* of the *Dīgha Nikāya*,[1] the contemporary Śramanas and Brahmins are stated to have been interested in politics and in problems of war, conquest, victory and defeat and transfer of monarchs. Gautama Buddha absolutely disclaims any interference by him in such matters. This may indicate that his movement was mainly concerned with ethical advancement and psychic illumination and not with political affairs. But, nevertheless, political repercussions did ensue from the movement of Buddhism. In spite of this disclaimer, in the *Brahmajāla Sutta*, Gautama Buddha emphatically states that he is vitally interested in social cohesion and co-operation and in the act of reconciling those people who are divided.

From the later Mahāyānist transformations of Buddhism also, political consequences followed. In Tibet, Lamaism established a theocracy which sought to unite *imperium* and *sacerdotium*. In Mongolia also, similar developments took place. Melamed has strongly emphasized the non-political character of Buddhism. He says that 'Neither slain nor slayer, neither oppressed nor oppressor' is a Buddhist figure of speech and this would imply that there is no cause for resistance in the world of illusion.[2] He opines that Buddha was not concerned with the lot of the lower castes, was disinterested in man and his welfare and was equally indifferent to political, economic or social justice. Just as there is no Buddhistic theory of state, so there is no Buddhistic theory of sociology and economics. Melamed's views are grossly exaggerated. The Tripiṭakas do contain social, political and economic teachings. Gautama Buddha, himself, associated with kings and princes. Early Buddhism did have significant political consequences.

A de-politicizing consequence of the Buddhist movement is stressed by Melamed, when he says, "Buddha destroyed the Roman Empire."[3] Palestine was the meeting-ground of the East and the West. The triumph of Buddhism in Palestine led to the greatest religious upheaval in world's history resulting in (i) the destruction of Judea, (ii) the rise of Christianity and

[1] *Ibid.*, p. 22.
[2] Melamed, *Spinoza and Buddha*, p. 272.
[3] *Ibid.*, p. 302.

(iii) the destruction of ancient Rome. Almost all historians and scholars, except St. Augustine, agree that the rise of Christianity spelled ruin to ancient Rome. Not the aggressive barbarians but the ascetic monks, the destroyers of the fighting spirit and the planters of Eastern holiness, destroyed Rome. But I think that Melamed makes a surprising statement when he says that not Caesar but Buddha destroyed Judea. Not Roman forces but the ideas of redemption, salvation and self-negation destroyed the ideal of the ancient Hebraic culture. The fabric of Hebrew life was destroyed by the formation of the Buddhistic sects of the Essenes, Mandeans and the Nazareans. Melamed's entire hypothesis rests on two historically uncorroborated propositions. First, that Buddhism inspired the rise of Christianity and secondly that monkish ideas and notions led to the enervation of the aggressive conquering spirit of the Romans. These propositions, to say the least, are highly subjective and for their corroboration require further researches into ancient history and social psychology.

Chapter 17

THE SOCIAL FOUNDATIONS OF EARLY BUDDHISM

1. *Introduction*

It is possible to decipher two trends in Indian history and culture. The one was dominantly sacerdotal, conservative, dogmatic, hieratic and externalistic. Its spokesmen have been Brahmins from the times of Vaśistha, Bhāradvāja, Kaśyapa, Yājñavalkya and Śamkara. The other trend was more liberal, rationalistic and critical and stressed inner culture and subjective thinking. Its spokesmen have been the Vedic sceptics, Gosāla, Mahāvira, Buddha and Kabir. There is a tendency to minimize the radical nature of the Buddhist protest against traditional sacrificialism and theology. The exact extent of the Buddhist protest may be a matter of debate but it would be running counter to the entire historical perspective if the protestant character of the Buddhistic reformation movement is sought to be denied by interpreting Buddha as a democratizer of Upaniṣadic idealism. It is true that Buddha did not organize a crusade for the liquidation of the iniquities of the caste oppressions and slavery but there can be no denial of the fact that he prepared the foundations of a more liberal and critical approach in matters of metaphysics and sociology.

Gautama Buddha, the gentle, kind and dignified prophet, may not have been a protagonist of social revolution in the radical sense in which a classless millenium is sponsored by Rousseau, Marx or Kropotkin but in the context of Indian society with its deep roots in hoary tradition his words of social wisdom did have a momentous value.

The fact that a leader of unchallenged intellectual preeminence like the late Dr. B. R. Ambedkar found solace in becoming a Buddhist shows that the ethical and social teachings of the *Dhammapada* contain vital meaning even for a trained economist and sociological scholar.[1] Buddha was faced with the problem of caste at the social and religious levels. In the *Assalāyana Suttanta* of the *Majjhima Nikāya*, Gautama Buddha condemns the traditional *Varna* system while expounding the concept of *Cātuvanni suddhi*.[2] He substantiates his arguments by referring to Asita Devala's teachings which were meant to controvert the claims of Brahmanical superiority. It is not certain whether this reference can be historically validated, but it, at least vaguely, indicates a trend to challenge the priestly claims to superiority. Gautama Buddha advances nine arguments to substantiate his concept of *Cāṭuvanni suddhi*—the arguments are either historical, biological, physical, ethical, eschatological etc. In this *suttantta* Buddha appears as a great champion of the masses. He gives equal right to the sudras for meditation. He accepts not only the claims of the sudras to ritualistic sacrifices, but also of the *cāndāls, nishāds, basor, rathakara, pukkusa* etc. In this *Sutta*, Gautama Buddha appears as a precursor of Christ and Ramanuja in his championship of the cause of the lowest in the social strata. His zeal in putting forward their claims to the most cherished thing of that day— admittance into the sacrificial system, is almost Marxian. The insight of the great man who first heralded an emphatic protest against the sacerdotal[3] and hieratic aspects of life and attempted to free man from the dominance of the cunning manipulating tactics[4] of the contemporary priesthood,[5] can still have social significance.

[1] In 1961, I saw that in Manmad (Bombay) a marble bust of Ambedkar has been set up and in the inscription thereon, the Scheduled Caste leader has been addressed as a *Boddhisattva*.

[2] Hindi Trans. by Rahula, pp. 386-390.

[3] E. J. Rapson, *Ancient India*, p. 48 : "The tremendous spiritual power which the sacrifice placed in the hands of the priestly caste, was no doubt the cause which directly led to the predominance of this caste in the social system." Also *ibid.*, p. 54; "The coronation ceremonies referred to in the eighth book of the *Aitareyā Brāhmaṇa* show how completely the priestly caste had, in theory at least, gained supremacy over the kingly caste."

[4] As early as the *Atharvaveda* there are references to the supremacy of the Brahmin caste. The entire *Sūkta*, V, 19, of the *Atharvaveda* is an exaltation of the Brāhmin caste.

[5] Jawaharlal Nehru, *Discovery of India* (Calcutta, Signet Press, 1946. 2nd edn.), p. 141 : "He [Buddha] did not claim to be an uprooter of the

2. *Buddhism as a Social Movement : The Relation between the Vedicists and the Early Buddhists*

It may appear surprising that although Buddha stood against the contemporary system of Vedic religion, the attitude of the Brāhmins towards him was not one of persecution. In the Tripiṭaka literature we get plenty of references to meetings between Brāhmins and Buddha.[1] Although these Brāhmin teachers do not have the metaphysical subtlety and intellectual brilliance of an Uddālaka or a Yājñavalkya, nevertheless, the teachers like Uttara, Śailya and Āsvalāyana are persons of intellectual maturity. In the *Kuṭadanta Sutta* and the *Tevijja Sutta*, Buddha bitterly and openly condemns the contemporary Brāhmanical sacrificial system and the practice of invoking the deities and the notion of seeking identity with Brahmā, but, surprisingly enough, we find no mention in the Buddhist literature of any policy of Brāhmanical discrimination against Buddha. Nor is there any evidence to point out that there was any organized counter-revolt of Brāhmins against him. Times without number, Buddha stayed in places which were the strongholds of Brāhmanical influence but instead of any organized hostile demonstrations against him, we find that eminent Brāhmin teachers flocked to him and looked up to him as a person of enlightenment and moral perfection. According to the *Māgandiya Suttanta* of the *Majjhima Nikāya*, Buddha occupied the *agniśalā* of a Brāhmin belonging to the Bharadvāja gotra. The masses regarded him as a great religious figure and looked up to him with awe and veneration. There are, roughly speaking, about one hundred Suttas which refer to meetings between Brāhmin teachers and Buddhist missionaries. In almost all of them we find that cordial exchange of views takes place between the two sides. In several Suttas it is found that although there is no serious

existing social order or economic system, he accepted their basic premises and only attacked the evils that had grown under them. Nevertheless he functioned, to some extent, *as a social revolutionary* and it was because of this that he angered the Brahmin class who were interested in continuance of the existing social practices." (Our Italics)

[1] Monier-Williams, *Buddhism*, p. 71 : "He [Buddha] himself was a Hindu of the Hindus and he remained a Hindu to the end." He never required his followers to make a formal renunciation of Hinduism.

intellectual discussion on an advanced theoretical plane, still the Brāhmin *brahmacārins* accept the discipleship of Buddha.[1] The *Brahmāyu Sutta* of *Majjhima Nikāya* contains the story of the conversion of Brahmāyu Brāhmin to Buddhism. It appears that during the days of early Buddhism there were Vedic centres in Mithilā because famous Brāhmin Vedicists like Brahmāya and Uttara lived there. Another famous Vedic seat was in Aṅguttarapa where three hundred Vedic students resided and studied under Śaila. Śaila Brāhmin and his entire band of three hundred students were converted to Buddhism. The writers of the Tripiṭakas also are considerate enough and they never refer to any humiliating defeat of the Brāhmins at the hands of Buddha. These points are enough to indicate that the relations between early Buddhism and contemporary Brāhmin teachers were cordial. The Buddhist ceremony of *upostha* was patterned on the Vedic ceremony of *upavasatha* which means fasting. This indicates a spirit of sympathetic appreciation manifested by early Buddhism.

The principal Upaniṣads being pre-Buddhistic, it is not at all surprising that we should find no mention there of Buddhist teachers. In the *Maitrāyaṇi Upaniṣad*, however, there is one passage[2] which ushers in a different note. This passage states: "men are saying that there should be attention to *dharma*, which is destructive of the Vedas, and of other teachings (Sāstras), hence one should not attend to this." Deussen held that this passage contained a reference to Buddhism. Except for this isolated reference, the contemporary literature would imply that the relations between early Buddhism and Brāhmanism were generally cordial. Kautilya's *Arthaśāstra* is the first important work where we find a pronouncedly anti-Buddhist attitude. Kautilya wants to safeguard his Janapada from the ravages of Buddhist monasticism. His book contains the injunction that legal action should be taken against those

[1] Burnouf, quoted in Max Müller, *Ancient Sanskrit Literature*, says: "Buddhism soon grew into a system of easy devotion, and found numerous recruits among those who were frightened by the difficulties of Brahmanical science. At the same time that Buddhism attracted the ignorant among the Brāhmans, it received with open arms the poor and miserable of all classes." (Cf. p. 18, *ibid.*)

[2] *Maitrāyaṇi*, VII, 9.

teachers who persuaded the householders to assume the path of monasticism. The Rock Edict XII of Asoka emphasizes universal concord and lays down that all sects should have freedom of settlement wheresoever they liked. This injunction may contain an implicit reference to the pacification of any disputes that might have been arising among the Brāhmins and the Buddhists. But the main problem of Asoka was not so much to bring about amicable relations between the Brāhmins and Buddhists as to prevent schism and disruptions in the body of the Buddhist Samgha itself. The fact that in the period from the death of Buddha to the times of Kanishka, four councils were held to settle doctrinal disputes is an eloquent testification to the growth of divisive tendencies in the Buddhist Samgha. From the days of the Indus civilization and the Vedas down to its later phases, Hinduism has been a vast body of spiritual and cultural codes of discipline. Hinduism never assumed the pattern of an organized religion like the Christian Church and the Islamic Caliphate and hence it never betrayed that kind of arrogance and fanaticism which are associated with the organized sects. Non-conformity and dissensions have never been considered offences in Hinduism as they were during the days of Edward VI, Mary, Elizabeth, James I, James II etc. Hence C.A.F. Rhys Davids says : "There was nothing in Brāhmanism resembling the ecclesiastical autocracy of the Holy Roman Church of the Middle Ages."[1] It was an indication of the toleration of ancient Indian religions that teachers of nihilistic morals like Prakruddha Kātyāyana and Kassapa and naturalistic metaphysicians like Ajita Keśakambala and sceptical epistemologists like Samjaya Belatthaputta were accorded honourable social place and hailed as teachers and professors in the contemporary social and cultural life. It may however be pointed out that Brahmanism is a name coined by European scholars and is rather unfortunate because it imparts to the entire complex of ancient Indian notions, cults, ceremonies etc. an exaggerated Brāhmin character and tends to minimize the role of the other sections.

The supreme concept of the Upanișadic philosophy is the

[1] C.A.F. Rhys Davids : "The Relations between Early Buddhism and Brahmanism", *IHQ*, Vol. X, 1934, p. 276.

unity of the *brahman* and the *ātman* and the divinity of man. But it appears utterly surprising that Buddha should remain silent about this dominant theme. Even if in his personal talks he would not have been silent, he is made to remain silent in the accounts about him that we get in the Tripiṭakas. Some of the disciples of Buddha like Sāriputta and Moggalāyana are said to be desirous of immortality—an ideal lauded since the days of the Ṛgvedic concept of *amṛtam*.[1] Nevertheless, it is utterly surprising to find that Buddha and his early disciples keep silent about the theme of *brāhman*, whose knowledge is supposed to impart immortality according to the Upaniṣadic teachers.[2] The *Tevijja Sutta* of the *Dīgha Nikāya* refers to a controversy between Vasistha Mānavaka and Bhāradvāja Mānavaka about the method for the attainment of *brahmasālokya*. Failing to convince each other they resort to Buddha. This shows that the contemporary intellectual opinion felt that an enlightened person or Buddha should answer such metaphysical questions. Even in the list of ten indescribable problems — *avyākṛta*, this concept of *brhaman*-identity is conspicuous by its absence. Even in the *Brahmajāla Sutta* which refers to sixty-two metaphysical views, this doctrine of monistic idealism is left out.[3] According to some interpreters, the sixty-two views are not metaphysical conceptions but indicate the experiences of the progressive degrees of ecstatic enlightenment of a person on the path of the realization of supreme truth. According to Mrs. C. A. F. Rhys Davids, on the contrary, that

1 S. N. Dasgupta, *Indian Idealism*, is guilty of reading exalted philosophical notions in the Upaniṣadic conception of *amṛtam*. He says that *amṛtam* of the Upaniṣads means not individual survival over infinite time but deathless and indestructible spiritual experience.

2 R. Sāmkrityāyana, *Buddha-Charyā*, p. 203.

3 E. J. Thomas, *Life of Buddha*, p. 199, states that not one of the sixty-two hypotheses can be definitely identified with that of any Indian system as now known. Datta, "Brahmajāla Sutta in the light of Nāgārjuna's Expositions", *IHQ*, Vol. VIII, 1932, pp. 706-46, says that since the views of the six Tirthakas, the Jainas and the Upaniṣads are outside the scope of this Sutta, hence it should not be regarded as a bird's eyeview of non-Buddhist opinions. According to Eliot, *Hinduism and Buddhism*, I, p. 97, there is the enumeration of 363 views, comparable to the 62 views of the *Brahmajāla Sutta*, in the Jain literature.

this vital point has been left out, is a crucial instance proving that cordial relations existed between early Buddhism and Brāhmanism. But to me it appears that Buddha has left out the discussion of absolutistic idealism perhaps because he did not know much about it since he did not have much of metaphysical knowledge.[1] Some interpreters like Radhakrishnan would say that if the analysis of the *pratityasamutpāda* formula is made then it appears that the logical nexus of *avidyā*, which is the starting-point of the series, remains incomplete without belief in some kind of an Absolute. But to me it seems that if Buddha had known deeply of the Upaniṣadic absolutistic metaphysics then he must have spoken his mind about it.[2] The later tradition, however, credits Buddha with a full knowledge of the ancient religions and philosophies. In the eyes of the orthodox Buddhist believers it may appear preposterous to assert, as Oldenberg and Keith do, that a man of the intellectual equipments of Buddha hankering after final truth had no systematic knowledge, perhaps not even a rudimentary one, of the Upaniṣadic truths. For the Buddhist believers it is only a truism to say that Buddha had knowledge of the Upaniṣads. Unfortunately we do not have any accurate old biography of Buddha. It is possible to say that Buddha may have had some general ideas about the Upaniṣadic doctrine although he might not have known them formally and systematically. To try to show that he had knowledge of that idealism through circuitous processes does not appear convincing. Hence I do not agree with the view that the absence of the discussion of the problems of absolutistic metaphysics is an indication of the cordial relations between the early Buddhists and the Brāhmins. It only shows that Buddha did not have any deep training in problems of metaphysics and cosmology. But although the early Buddhist literature gives no explicit criticism of the absolutistic philosophy of the Upaniṣads and is silent about the word *brahman*,

[1] Cf. Oldenberg, *Buddha*, p. 52 : "......Of all the texts in which the Brahmanical speculations as to the delivering power of knowledge are contained, perhaps not even one was known except by hearsay to the founder of the Buddhist community of believers."

[2] Przyluski, quoted in Keith, "Pre-Canonical Buddhism", *IHQ*, Vol. XII, pp. 12-13, holds that there is little speculation in original Buddhism.

still it constantly mentions the God Brahmā. According to the *Muṇḍaka Upaniṣad*, Brahmā is the first-born amongst the gods and is the first created being according to the *Śvetāśvatara*. Brahmā is equated with the Vedic Hiraṇyagarbha. But the Brahmā who appears in the Pali literature as a mere supplicator of Buddha has little in common with the Vedic Prajāpati, or Viśvakarman or Hiraṇyagarbha.[1] Thus it is not possible to draw any significant sociological conclusion from the absence in the Tripiṭakas of the discussions of *brahman*-metaphysics.

In the *Appannaka Suttanta* of the *Majjhima Nikāya* (No. 60) there is reference to a class of Brāhmins and Sramanas who refused to acknowledge any fruits of charity or sacrifice or heaven, who had no faith in *pāpa* and *pūṇya*. Buddha criticizes them on ethical grounds and says that they are liable to take recourse to physical and mental evils. The *Ghoṭamukha Suttanta* of the *Majjhima Nikāya* (No. 94), refers to two kinds of Brāhmins : (i) those engrossed in house and wealth and gold and (ii) those non-engrossed in house and wealth and gold. One aspect of the relation between early Buddhism and Brāhmanism is revealed by the ethicization of the word *Brāhmana* itself which early Buddhist scriptures provide.[2] We find that in the Upaniṣads, sometimes this word 'Brāhmaṇa' has lost its old caste or class connotation and is used to indicate the person who has achieved spiritual enlightenment. Buddha also, at many places, used the word Brāhmaṇa in an ethical fashion. This ethicization of the term shows the cordial relation between early Buddhism and Brāhmanism and also reveals the implicit antipathy of Buddha and his disciples towards the

[1] C. A. F. Rhys Davids says: "And the lively presentation of a Brahmā ... is due to the renascence of Deity as personal that was going on in India when the Piṭakas were taking shape as literary compositions, perhaps some three hundred years after the birth of Buddhism. With Brahmā as personal, was coming up a masculine not a neuter Siva and the Vedic Vishnu was reborn......And the later Buddhism was only conforming to the diction of its day, when it referred to this regal Brahmā in terms befitting a universal monarch..."

[2] Oldenberg, *Buddha*, p. 172n, says that the word 'Brāhmana' as used in the Pali scriptures does not connect with this word the idea of an enemy of Buddhism, in the way that in the New Testament Pharisees and scribes appear as the standing enemies of Jesus. Cf. *Dhammapada*, 419.

assumption of social superiority on the mere basis of caste.[1] In the *Ambaṭṭha Sutta* we find that Buddha engages himself in an unrestrained and violent polemic against the Brāhmins. In the *Tevijja Sutta* we find that he makes a scathing ridicule of the Brāhmin morals. Thus what Buddha means by appropriating the term *Brāhmaṇa* into his own vocabulary is not the incorporation of or adherence to Brāhmanical views but it is only the use of a term prevalent in society and giving to that a more moral connotation. He frankly derides the caste and class connotation of the term. He says in the *Dhammapada* : *na jaṭāhi na gotehi na jaccā hoti brāhmaṇo/yamhi saccañca dhammo ca so sukhi so ca brāhmaṇo*. It may, however, be noted that when Sahapati Brahmā requests Buddha to adopt the preacher's career, it is not in the name of the redemption of the Kshattriyas only, nor is it for leading a protestant movement against Brāhmanical egoism and orthodoxy but for the salvation of the suffering-stricken people.

Sometimes Buddhism is regarded as a movement of social protest.[2] Vivekananda interpreted Buddhism as a religion invented by the Kshattriyas and as a crushing rejoinder to Brāhmanism. It is supposed to herald the Kshattriya revolt against the Brāhmanical stronghold, because Buddha, a member of the clan of the Sakiyas was the leader of the protest against Brahmanical metaphysics, Brahmanical theology and Brāhmanical ritualism.[3] According to V. A. Smith, Buddhism was promoted by the Kshattriyas of Mongolian origin but this "Mongolian"

[1] The *Tevijja Sutta*, *Dialogues of Buddha*, pp. 309-11, refers to the contemporary Brāhmins who clung to five things predisposing to lust — forms, sounds, odours, taste and substance. 'Infatuated by these, attached to them, they do not see the danger of them and know not how unreliable they are.'

[2] *Life of Swami Vivekananda*, p. 690, and *Complete Works*, Vol. IV, p. 378. S. N. Dasgupta, *Indian Philosophy*, I, pp. 208-11, regards Buddhism and Jainism as anti-sacrificial Kshattriya movements. Cf. Jawaharlal Nehru, *The Discovery of India*, 1946, p. 95 : "Although in origin a Kshattriya movement and representing a conflict between the ruling class and the priests...."

[3] M. N. Roy, *From Savagery to Civilization*, p. 9, regards Buddha as a social revolutionary and Buddhism as a gigantic social upheaval. He says that Buddha was the personification of revolt against parasitic luxury. The conversions to Buddhism of Pukkusatti of Taxila, Bodhi Rajkumara, the son of Udayana of Vatsa and of Bimbisāra and Prasenjit indicate the

hypothesis is, more or less, an exploded view. According to Edward Caird, in the early Vedic age, there was the supremacy of the Kshattriyas but later on there was the supremacy of the Brāhmins. But in the Vedas and the *Śatapatha* there is recurrent prayer and fervent wish for the reconciliation of *brahma* and *kshatra*. There is no mention in ancient Indian religious history of a Papal-Imperial conflict although legends refer to the struggle of Viśvāmitra and Vaśishtha. The *Aitareya Brāhmaṇa*, VII, 27, refers to the quarrel of Janamejaya with the Brāhmins. The *Aitareya* also states that the Kasyapas were the priestly opponents of Janamejaya, the son of Parikshita. Some scholars are of opinion that during the days of the *Śatapatha* and *Aitareya Brāhmaṇas* and early Buddhism, the Brāhmin and the Kshattriya social orders were in a fluid state and the literary mention of them is more the representation of a philosophical ideal than the statement of a concrete social fact.[1] But there is exaggeration in this hypothesis. Since the eighth century B.C. the various castes were undergoing a process of solidification and during the period of early Buddhism, castes did constitute the dominant element in the Indian social structure.[2] Of the twelve chief disciples of Buddha the following eight were Brāhmins — Sāriputta, Moggalāna, Kotthita, Kaccāna, Kassapa and two brothers of Sāriputta, i.e. Cuṇḍa and Revata. The four important Kshattriya disciples were Anuruddha, Kappina, Ānanda and Rāhula. The Brāhmin disciples do not appear to have made

active Kshattriya support rendered to Buddhism. Cf. T. W. Rhys Davids, *Buddhist India*, pp. 1-6.

[1] A. K. Coomaraswamy, *Buddha and the Gospel of Buddhism*, (London, George G. Harrap & Co., 1916), pp. 216-17, says that the caste system as it now exists had not crystallized in the days of Buddha and what already existed was a classification of men according to complexion in the *cāturvarṇya* or colours. Each of these included many groups which afterwards crystallized as separate castes. But he is exaggerating the colour differentiation of a racially mixed population.

[2] *Evolution of Religion*, Vol. I, pp. 262-63. See also Pargiter, *Ancient Indian Historical Tradition*, p. 114. The policy of persecution adopted by Pushyamitra and the anti-Buddhistic injunctions of Kauṭilya belong to a later era. A. K. Coomaraswamy, *Buddha and the Gospel of Buddhism*, pp. 216-17, states that the status of the Brāhmins in the age of Gautama was somewhat lower than that of Kshattriyas. (All the references to this book are to the London edition of 1916, unless otherwise stated.)

a deliberate intellectual and emotional break from the contemporary philosophies and creeds.[1] According to the *Mahāvagga*, Sāriputta was converted after having listened to the formula of causation. Sāriputta and Moggallāna had the same vital impulse to explore the immortal as the seers of the Ṛgveda. They could not get satisfaction from the sceptical and destructionist teachings of Samjaya Belatthaputta because their quest was not merely logical and dialectical but concerned the deepest recesses of the human heart. They finally found the solution of their spiritual riddles under Buddha, but there is no indication of their having revoked or renounced their aspiration for immortality. This would indirectly point out that they were not conscious of any deep break between the tradition they originally belonged to and the teachings of Buddha.[2] This would thus strengthen the view that Buddhism was not regarded in those days as a movement of deliberate schism and protest against the caste arrogance of the Brāhmins.[3] But it is not to be doubted that early Buddhism was, to a considerable extent anti-Brāhmanical in its social philosophy[4] and more democratic

[1] For the relation between Buddhism and Brāhmanism at a later period see, Stevenson, "Intermixture of Buddhism with Brāhmanism in the Religion of the Hindus of the Deccan, "*JRAS.*, 1845 and "Analysis of the *Ganesha Purāna* with special reference to Buddhism", *JRAS.*, 1846. Ratilal Mehta, *Pre-Buddhist India* (based entirely on the *Jātakas*).

[2] But C. A. F. Rhys Davids is guilty of gross exaggeration when she says that the early Buddhist disciples accepted the Upaniṣadic doctrine of Immanence. She says : "····the first Sakyans were as far from denying the Immanence accepted and taught in their days as were say, John and Charles Wesley from denying the Central teaching of Christianity."

[3] According to Monier-Williams, *Buddhism*, p. 72, although Buddha was the first to establish some kind of a "universal monastic communism", he had no aim to deliver men from the tyranny of caste, nor did he claim to be a champion of social equality. Oldenberg, *Buddha*, pp. 152 ff., denies to Buddha the role of a social reformer. He stresses the otherworldliness of Buddhism to which things of the world and society were of no concern. He regards it incorrect to interpret Buddha as a democratic champion of the oppressed. He says that Buddhism did not mark a social upheaval. Nevertheless, it cannot be denied that Buddha's disciples were recruited from all the four castes and no social distinction operated in the Samgha. Furthermore even previous slaves and servants who joined the Samgha were accepted and respected by monarchs.

[4] C. A. F. Rhys Davids, "The Norm as Moral Law", *Buddhism*, (London, Williams & Norgate), p. 115. "And the frequency with which

than contemporary Brāhmanism. The *Ambattha Sutta* of the *Dīgha Nikāya* contains references to (i) the origin of the Sākyas from the King Ikshvāku, (ii) to the prevalence of brother-sister marriage among the Sākyas for the preservation of racial purity and (iii) to Krishna rishi, the founder of Kārshṇyāyana Gotra, who was born of the maid-servant of Ikshvāku. This *Sutta* contains definite and explicit statements by Buddha regarding the superiority of the Kshattriyas to the Brāhmins. Silavat Thera (or Sunita Thera) who confesses his humble origin and poverty is accorded place of high esteem in the Samgha and Buddha says that a man becomes a Brāhmin by *tapas* and *brahmacarya.* Oldenberg, however, points out that the Buddhist records contain no mention of a *Cāndāla* as being accepted in the Samgha.

3. *The Social Foundations of the Buddhistic Movement*

The work of Buddha is interpreted in two ways. The devout believers in his creed look upon him as a world teacher who wanted to preach the gospel of emancipation to all the suffering-stricken multitude. He is regarded primarily as a spiritual and religious leader who taught the transcendent worth of *dhyāna, samādhi, prajñā* and *nirvāṇa.*

But some historians and some social scientists consider Buddha as a democratic crusader against the iniquities of the caste system and the empty pretensions of the Brāhmanical theology.[1] He is regarded as having weakened the foundations

we find the Buddha consulted on the growing social claims of the Brāhmins, shows that these claims were a burning question of the day. His own positions tracing the origin of social divisions or 'classes' to some primitive norm or standard (*dhamma*) arising through division of labour, and recognising only an aristocracy of intellect and virtue, must have appealed strongly to those who were dissatisfied with the Brāhmins' assumptions." According to B. M. Barua, the pre-Buddha-Mahāvira sophistic movement originated with Uddālaka Āruni. Cf. the case of Ushasta Cākrāyaṇa. Ridiculing the attitude of Brāhmins, Buddha, *Majjhima Nikāya* (Hindi Translation p. 397), refers to "the *andha-veṇu paramparā.*"

[1] *Aggañña Sutta,* (*Dīgha Nikāya Dialogues of Buddha,* Vo. II) p. 78 : "On the contrary, brahminees, the wives of brāhmins, are known to be fertile, are seen to be with child, bringing forth and nursing children. And yet it is these very womb-born brāhmins who say that ... brāhmins are

of the prevalent religious and social structure by having repudiated the revelatory character of the Vedas and having challenged the arrogant claims to dignity, importance and merit of the Brāhmin priests.[1]

There is truth in both the views. Buddha taught the philosophical theories of anātman, *prātityasamutpāda* and *nirvāṇa.* But as the supreme leader (*śāstā*) of the samgha and as an eminent prophet who, although a *bhikkhu,* lived amongst the people, he got numerous opportunities to challenge the unfounded claims to superiority of the Brāhmins.[2] Hence although his ethical and religious teachings demanded great intellectual penetration and moral endeavours for which only a few selected people could have the adequate prerequisites, still his fight against the Brāhmin monopoly of spiritual gnosis and ritualism, imparted some aspects of social and democratic character to his religious mission.

Social, economic and political consequences do follow, sometimes directly and sometimes indirectly from religious teachings. Śamkara was a great teacher of monistic spiritual

genuine children of Brahmā, born from his mouth; his offspring, his creation, and his heirs ! By this they make a travesty of the nature of Brahmā."

[1] R.S. Copleston, *Buddhism : Primitive and Present* (London, Longmans Green & Co., 1882), pp. 228-29, stresses the fact that according to the *Buddhavamsa* all the previous Buddhas had been either Brāhmins or Kshattriyas. Hence he says : "It is therefore an exaggeration to describe Gotama as a champion of equality against caste tyranny. On the other hand, both his system and his teaching were indirectly opposed to it. All castes (of well-born men) were equally admissible to the Community ; it is not clear that any outcast would have been admitted. The idea of caste being a claim to *status* within the Community is repudiated ; all such distinctions are merged in the Community as the rivers in the sea. And as regards the dominion of caste outside the Community, his teaching was calculated to undermine it."

[2] *Aggañña Suttanta, Dīgha Nikāya* (*Dialogues of Buddha,* Vol. II), p. 89 : "Now it occurred, Vasettha, to some of those beings, as follows : Evil deeds, sirs, have become manifest among us, inasmuch as stealing, censure, lying, punishment can be noticed, and banishment. Let us now put away from us evil and immoral customs. And they put away from them such customs. They put away (*bāhenti*) evil, immoral customs, Vasettha, is what is meant by Brahmins, and thus was it that Brahmins became the earliest standing phrase [for those who did so]. They, making leaf huts in woodland spots, meditated therein."

metaphysics. But in spite of his pronounced and dominant other-worldly and acosmic philosophical teachings, his movement indirectly stabilized the foundations of the Brāhmanical theology and the caste structure based on endogamy and hereditary role-taking. The medieval teachers like Nānaka, Chaitanya and Kabir taught the gospel of devotion. Their appeal was to the emotions of the heart. But although they taught absorption in divine splendours, they became the heralders of the cult of social equality. If the Vedantic *ācāryas* taught the sanctity of the traditional social system, the Bhakti movement stood for popular claims to equal participation in the bliss and grace of God. The Sanskrit language contains some of the profoundest expressions of universalism and human equality but the difficult structure of its language and literature and its message are aristocratic. It requires long years of preparation for its mastery and the complicated network of its concepts, its logical argumentative apparatus exemplified by the Nyāya system and the jungle of the mysterious cult of the eternality of the Vedic and Vedantic scriptures, all tend to breed a conservative, if not a reactionary, outlook upon the problems of life, society and politics. The Vedic Samhitās, the Brāhmaṇas and the Upaniṣads have a conservative philosophy of life and society. They exalt the mighty, vague and mysterious formulas of godhood, sponsor a complicated ritualism and by implication tend to exalt the unfounded and baseless claims of Brāhmanical superiority. All this is clothed in the garb of the relatively inaccessible Sanskrit language. But in Buddhism we get a freshness of atmosphere. Buddha begins the practice of teaching the highest truth in the spoken vernacular language.[1] This was a tremendous revolt. Gautama Buddha, however, cannot be credited with having formulated the gospel of an all-India-nationalism. He spoke in the language of Kosala and Magadha. Later on, in Asokan inscriptions we find that Pali is used even in those found in Orissa and Hyderabad. But Asoka was also a cautious politician and he used the Kharosthi script for his inscriptions in the remote north-west. The immense barriers and fortifications of the difficult rules of Sanskrit grammar

[1] E.J. Rapson, *Ancient India*, p. 14, compares the linguistic liberalism of Jainism and Buddhism to that of the reformed Churches in Europe.

that had guarded the so-called revealed and concealed treasures of the Brahmanical priests and writers were attacked, by the early Buddhistic teachers, at their basic roots by popularization of Pali. On the day that Buddha taught the message of the *dhamma-chakkapavattana* at Sāranath, in Pali, he delivered a stupendous counterblast against the traditional theology, speculative metaphysics and the fossilizing trends of the caste structure.[1] Hence although the declared purpose of Buddha's mission was not social and although he had left his ancestral palace to seek a way of emancipation and the conquest of death, in the course of his preaching career, directly and indirectly, social and economic and political consequences did follow from his propaganda and mission.

[1] Cf. The following lines from the *Bhuridatta Jātaka* (*The Jataka*, Vol. VI, No. 543), E.T, by Cowell & Rouse, *op. cit.*, pp. 109-10 :

"These Veda studies are the wise man's toils,
The lure which tempts the victims whom he spoils;
A mirage formed to catch the careless eye,
But which the prudent passes safely by.
The Vedas have no hidden power to save
The traitor or the coward or the knave ;
The fire, though tended well for long years past,
Leaves his base master without hope at last.

To worship fire, the common drudge of all,
Senseless and blind and deaf to every call,
And then one's self to live a life of sin, —
How could one dream that this a heaven could win?
These Brahmins all a livelihood require,
And so they tell us Brahma worships fire;

Doctrines and rules of their own, absurd and vain,
Our sires imagined wealth and power to gain;

These greedy liars propagate deceit,
And fools believe the fictions they repeat;
He who has eyes can see the sickening sight;
Why does not Brahma set his creatures right?
If his wide power no limits can restrain,
Why is his hand so rarely spread to bless?
Why are his creatures all condemned to pain?
Why does he not to all give happiness?
Why do fraud, lies, and ignorance prevail?
Why triumphs falsehood, — truth and justice fail?

Some scholars think that Buddha was a spiritual redeemer of mankind who taught the philosophy of the negation of empirical phenomena in the silence of *nirvāṇa* and was indifferent to the social, economic and political struggles going on in the country. But this is not the whole truth. It is true that in the vast Tripiṭaka literature, there are passages which can be interpreted to support idealism, agnosticism and even scepticism. Whatever might have been the essential basis of Buddha's philosophical teaching — an idealism of ultimate moral values or a negativistic creed of rationalistic and naturalistic atheism —, it cannot be denied that he had to operate in a social environment. He was in close touch with the kings of Magadha, and Kosala, and he had to bring to his fold rich mercantile magnates like Yasa and Anāthapiṇḍika[1] and he also had to spread his teachings far and wide. Thus it is evident that his religious mission did have an extended social dimension. Jesus Christ and St. Paul also propounded social teachings, and a social gospel is attached in the religious philosophy of Śamkara and Dayānanda. Buddha was a leader in the field of morals and spiritual wisdom of a transcendent kind, but he was also busy in framing the minutest rules for the organization of his Samgha. He also laid down rules for the safety of a republican constitution. Hence it can be said that manifold activism characterized the prophetic personality of Buddha. It is true that original Buddhism was never a purely temporal movement. It was a gospel for the emancipation of the suffering humanity. But being a gigantic moral and religious movement, it did have profound social and economic repercussions. Max Weber has pointed out that Buddhism began as the salvation doctrine of an intellectual class and in the beginning, at least, cannot be considered the religion of the non-privileged classes.[2] But it may be stated that Buddhism did prepare those foundations

I count your Brahma one th' injust among,
Who made a world in which to shelter wrong."

[1] Cf. The lines quoted in P. Lakshmi Narasu, *The Essence of Buddhism* (Madras, Srinivasa Varadachari & Co., 1912), p. 140 : "The time of the full sway of the guilds coincides with the period of the greatest Buddhist influence and it was in the provinces where Buddhism was strongest, that the merchant guilds were most firmly established,. . . ."

[2] Max Weber, *The Sociology of Religion* (London, Methuen & Co., 1965), pp. 116-117.

upon which a more radical prophet might have built, if he so desired, the superstructure of egalitarianism and democracy. Buddha did denounce the ultimateness of economic and political values and regarded them as much inferior to the soteriology of *nirvāṇa.* Thus it could have been possible to argue that the holders of economic and political status and dominance did not have any legitimate foundations to stand upon and, by this kind of reasoning, prepare the background for equality. Weber, nevertheless, is correct in emphasizing that early Buddhism should not be considered as having arisen in response to the feelings of resentment experienced by the numerous components of the vaisyas and the shudras.

The most important social force in India's history in the three centuries preceding the era of Buddha was the growing caste consolidation. The pre-Vedic and early Vedic social structure was diffusive, pliant and mobile. But towards the later Vedic days, the trend towards caste consolidation based on hereditary allocation of power, status and esteem become significantly marked. The *puruṣa sūkta* contains the first reference to the division of the contemporary society into four classes. The great *puruṣa* is regarded as the source of the origin of this quadruple division. The ascription of a divine origin to the caste differentiation shows that selfish Brāhmin ingenuity was at work.[1] If there would not have been any sacerdotal and selfish motive, all the castes would have been simply stated to have had a similar divine origin but to say that the different castes "were" (*āsita*) or were "created" (*krṭah*) and born (*ajāyata*) from the different limbs of the gigantic *purusha* was bound to imply a sense of superiority and subordination in accordance with the primacy and purity attached to the different limbs. In the pre-Buddhistic times the social structure had become much more rigid.[2] Buddha had to take into account the factor of

[1] Contrast A. E. Gough, *The Philosophy of the Upaniṣads and Ancient Indian Metaphysics*, (London, Trübner & Co. 1882), p. 2-3, "Negroid aborigines, Tatar hordes, and successive Aryan swarms have severally contributed their blood to mould the Brahman theosophist."

[2] According to Gilbert Slater, *The Dravidian Element in Indian Culture*, Brahmins are the products of those people who brought the heliolithic culture from Egypt with the Dravidians. Slater has adduced three arguments for the Egypto-Dravidic origin of the caste. (i) The Brāhmins

the growing caste consciousness demanding the patternization of status-roles on hereditary basis, in the contemporary Indian society.[1] There is ample evidence for this in the Upaniṣadic and the Tripiṭaka literature. The Upaniṣads claim to teach the immutable super-reality of the supracosmic *brahman*. But even the Upaniṣadic teachers themselves are tremendously caste-conscious. In the *Chhāndogya Upaniṣad*, Ajātaśatru, the king of Kasi remarks to Uddālaka that it was paradoxical (*pratiloma*) for the Brāhmin (Uddālaka) to seek intellectual shelter under a Kshattriya. Pravāhaṇa Jaivali claims that the Kshatriyas had the monopoly of metaphysical wisdom in the past and he indirectly appears to be desperately keen on saving the intellectual prestige of his caste. During the age of Mahāvira and Buddha caste arrogance had mounted to a high pitch.[2]

Buddha had to face this great factor — intensifying caste-consolidation.[3] He cannot be regarded as the defiant and declared spokesman of the Kshatriyas but it is clear from the Buddhist dialogues of the Tripiṭakas that he had anti-Brāhmani-

of the south are distinguished from the rest of the population. (ii) The Namboodiri Brahmins worship cobras and the *brahman* as a solar deity. (iii) The Brāhmins used the sacred thread of cotton. But cotton spinning and weaving was not prevalent according to the Veda.

[1] E. J. Rapson, *Ancient India*, p. 55 : "The interesting fact, that the Brahmanical religion did not include all the tribes of Aryan descent, is gathered from the account given in the *Tāndya Brāhmaṇa* of certain sacrifices (in *vrātyastomas*) which were performed on the admission of such Aryans into the Brahmana community. The description of these non-Brahmanical Aryans—'they pursue neither agriculture nor commerce., their laws are in a constant state of confusion ; they speak the same language as those who have received Brahmanical consecration, but call what is easily spoken hard to pronounce' (trans. in Weber : *Ind. Lit.*, p. 67) — show that they were freebooters speaking the Prakrt or dialects allied to Sanskrit."

[2] *Ambattha* (*Dīgha Nikāya*), *Madhura Sutta* (*Majjhima Nikāya*), *Vāseṭṭha Sutta* (*Sutta Nipāta*) and *Svetaketu Jataka*. According to the Jatakas, instances of intermarriage are also there. From the Jatakas, it appears that the terms vaisya and sudra were only generic ideal-types and that the actual components of the social structure were a large number of 'sub-castes,' and professional groups.

[3] L. Barnett, *Antiquities of India*, p. 7 : "Society (the Vedic) showed the same contrasts and discrepancies as in modern times. The rich rode on horses and in chariots, and lived in lordly ease, while the poor struggled to wrest a meagre livelihood from the capricious powers of Nature."

cal prejudices and was interested in addressing his sermons to the Kshatriya youths of good family status (*kulaputra*). It is not possible to be certain about the caste origin of teachers like Purna Kassapa, Makkhali Gosāla, Ajita Kesakambala, Prakruddha Katyāyana and Sanjaya Belatthaputta. But both Buddha and Mahāvira belonged to the Kshatriya clans of eastern India. Hence they could not act as the conscious exponents of the interests of the proletariat and the agricultural laborers who formed the numerous assemblage of the Shudras.

It is true that Gautama Buddha as a spiritual and ethical teacher was not a declared champion of the suppressed sections. But he did indirectly foster the cause of social democracy and egalitarianism by his outspoken condemnation of the Brāhmanical and Kshatriya claims to superiority. In the famous *Ambattha Sutta* he says that some of the Brāhmins are descended from a slave-girl and among some of the Kshatriyas there was the prevalence of brother-sister marriage. In other words, Buddha condemns some Brāhmins and Kshatriyas as mongrels or varnasamkaras. Gautama states :

"Then the Blessed One thought thus : 'This Ambattha is very set on humbling the Sakyas with his charge of servile origin. What if I were to ask him as to his own lineage.' And he said to him :

'And what family do you then, Ambattha, belong to ?'

'Yes, but if one were to follow up your ancient name and lineage, Ambattha, on the father's and the mother's side, it would appear that the Sakyas were once your masters, and that you are the offspring of one of their slave girls. But the Sakyas trace their line back to Okkaka the king.

'Long ago, Ambattha, King Okkaka, wanting to divert the succession in favour of the son of his favourite queen, banished his elder children — Okkamukha, Karanda, Hatthinika, and Sinipura — from the land. And being thus banished they took up their dwelling on the slopes of the Himalaya, on the borders of a lake where a mighty oak tree grew. And through fear of injuring the purity of their line they intermarried with their sisters.

'Now Okkaka the king asked the ministers at his court : "Where, Sirs, are the children now?"

'There is a spot, Sirs, on the slopes of the Himalaya, on the borders of a lake, where there grows a mighty *oak* (sako). There do they dwell. And lest they should injure the purity of their line they have married their *own* (*sakahi*) sisters.'

'Then did Okkaka the king burst forth in admiration : "Hearts of oak (*sakya*) are those young fellows ! Right well they hold their own (*paramasakya*) !"

'That is the reason, Ambattha, why they are known as Sakyas. Now Okkaka had a slave girl called Disa. She gave birth to a black baby. And no sooner was it born than the little black thing said, "Wash me, mother, Bathe me, mother. Set me free, mother, of this dirt. So shall I be of use to you."

'Now just as now, Ambattha, people call devils "devils," so then they called devils "black fellows" (kanhe). And they said : "This fellow spoke as soon as he was born. 'Tis a black thing (kanha) that is born, a devil has been born !" And that is the origin, Ambattha, of the Kanhayanas. He was the ancestor of the Kanhayanas. And thus, is it, Ambattha, that if one were to follow up your ancient name and lineage, on the father's and on the mother's side, it would appear that the Sakyas were once your masters, and that you are the offspring of one of their slave girls."[1]

The caste-structure of some of the important personages associated with early Buddhism was as follows:

Kshatriyas	*Brāhmins*	*Vaishyas, Shudras and Others*
Buddha	Sāriputta	Upāli
Ānanda	Moggallāna	Ambapāli
Prajāpati Gautami	Mahākassapa	Yasa
Rāhula	Kappina	Vidudabha
Nanda	Kaccāna	Anāthapiṇḍika
Bimbisāra	3 Jatila Brāhmins and their 1000 disciples	Jivaka Kumārabhṛtya
Udayana		Cuṇḍa
Prasenajit		Viśākhā
Anuruddha		Dhania (herdsman)
Bodhi Rājakumar (son of Udayana)		60 "rich youth" of Vārānasi
Pukkusātti (of Taxila)		Culakhandaka
Sumanā (aunt of Prasenajit)		Mahākhandaka
		Subhuti
		Rāshtrapāla
		Krishā Gautami
		Ugra

[1] T. W. Rhys Davids, *Dialogues of Buddha* (E.T. of the *Dīgha Nikāya*), Vol. I, pp. 114-15.

The occupation and caste-belongingness of some monks, nuns and other persons associated with early Buddhism are as follows :

Angulimāla	...	Robber (Possibly he was an Ābhira)
Thera Sunita	...	Of low caste. He was a temple sweeper
Thera Svapāka (Sopaka)	...	Used to cook dogs
Thera Svāti	...	Fisherman
Nanda	...	Cow-keeper (Ābhira)
Campā	...	Daughter of a hunter
Purnā	...	Daughter of a slave
Sati	...	Fisherman
Khujjuttara	...	Daughter of a female-servant

4. *Buddha's Technics for Social Integration and Assimilation*

The first important technic for social integration and coordination prescribed in Buddha's social thought was the cultivation of a sense of universal compassion (*metta*)[1] and creative altruism. We cannot characterize Buddha as having begun with the explicit intention of challenging the Brahmin priesthood and raising the economic and social status of the downtrodden, the slaves and the outcastes But he stressed the cultivation of those elevated sentiments, the fostering of which was bound to reduce social exploitation and social tension. It is important to remember that Buddha, in advocating the deepening and ennoblement of character produced by *metta*, was not impelled by any secular considerations. The following verses from the *Metta Sutta* of the *Sutta Nipāta* illustrate Buddha's emphasis on compassionate altruism:

> May creatures all abound
> in weal and peace; may all
> be blessed with peace always;
> all creatures weak or strong,
> all creatures great and small;
> creatures unseen or seen,
> dwelling afar or near,
> born or awaiting birth,
> — may all be blessed with peace!

1 Buddhist *metta* is parallel to the Biblical *agape* (or *caritas* that is, charity).

Through the cultivation of compassion it is possible to rise superior both to the drives of physical nature and also to the socially antipathetic forces of opposition, conflict and antagonistic competition.[1] Social accommodation and adaptation are bound to follow as consequences of the practice of *metta.* In Buddhism, with its notions of *maitrī* and *karunā* man is taught to cultivate that softness of feelings which shudders to commit the least injury to the creatures.

A second important social technic prescribed by Buddha is to instal qualitative achievement in place of birth. He refused to sanction ascriptive superiority based on the physical fact of birth in a particular *gotra* and family.[2] In the *Brāhmanavagga* of the *Dhammapada* we find some of the classic verses eulogizing the moral attributes of a Brāhmin.

"I do not call a man a brāhmaṇa because of his origin or of his mother ; he is indeed arrogant, and he is wealthy. But the poor who is free from all attachments, him I call indeed a brāhmaṇa.

Him I call indeed a brāhmaṇa who does not cling to sensual pleasures, like water on a lotus-leaf, like a mustard seed on the point of a needle."[3]

If we have to translate the message of Buddha in the language of modern social sciences, we can say that merit has to replace all kinds of subjective considerations like bias, caste preference and prejudice etc. The *Madhuriya Sutta* of the *Majjhima Nikāya* propounds absolute equality of all the four orders so far as the punishment for evil deeds and reward for meritorious actions, both in this secular world and beyond, are concerned. It

[1] Like Buddha, Thomas More in his *Utopia* also stressed the cultivation of altruism. Auguste Comte stated that in antiquity the practice of altruism was limited to the family, the tribe and the *polis*; in the medieval period it received a further extension while the good of humanity demands that in the modern scientific age it is universally practised.

[2] Cf. *Samyutta*, VII, 1, 9 :

"Ask not of race, but ask of conduct,
From the stick is born the sacred fire;
The wise ascetic though lowly born
Is noble in his modest self-control."

[3] *Dhammapada* (Nalanda Ed. of the Tripiṭakas) Nos. 396-401. Max Müller's E.T.

ridicules the claims of Brahmanical superiority as unfounded and illogical.

A third important technic for social integration on Buddhist lines would be not to give any place to caste in associations, groups and organizations. Caste-consciousness generates sometimes dysfunctional stresses. Though the factor of caste as the determinant of status-sequence was rampant in the contemporary social universe, Buddha ignored it completely for entrance into the Samgha.[1] The Samgha was a religious association built for the solidification of efforts in quest of the higher life of spiritual freedom and emancipation. Its dominant purpose was the achievement of moral and spiritual certainty. Hence, other considerations became irrelevant. It included persons of different caste origins like the Brāhmin Kassapa, the Kshatriya Ānanda and the barber Upāli. The allegiance and loyalty to the Samgha took absolute precedence over other sectional loyalties.

5. *The Sociology of Buddhist Monachism*

A religious movement, regardless of the nature and significance of the original truth either revealed to or intuitively perceived by the founder, in the process of its historical growth, partly assumes the character of a community.[2] The Samgha was not merely an association oriented to the specificity of functional performance but was almost a deliberate exercise in total living. In other words, from the moment the Bhikkhu joined the Samgha he could lead a full life under the guidance of the Samgha and through the friendship and companionship of other fellow-members. Hence so far as the Bhikkhu was concerned, he could lead an organic and full life in the Samgha from the moment he joined it to the time of his death. The Bhikkhu could spend the rainy season at a certain place, he could wander in the different parts of the country, at times he could be absorbed in quiet contemplation in a cave or on the bank of a river or near a place where dead bodies were crema-

[1] *Vinaya Piṭaka*, II, 239 : "As the rivers lose their individual distinctions after falling into the ocean, so the monks lose all their distinctions as regards social status after joining the monastic order."

[2] J. Wach, "Expression in Fellowship", *The Comparative Study of Religions* (New York, Columbia University Press, 1958), p. 142.

ted, but, nevertheless, he was under the supervision of the Samgha which was a congregation of ascetic virtuosi specializing in the art of liberation from the pain of the world. Thus the Samgha was an exercise in the art of collective community living. It is true that times without number, Buddha warned the disciples to seek their own emancipation and refused to obtain vicarious salvation for them and the Samgha also refused to guarantee emancipation to anybody. Emancipation or *nirvāṇa* was conceived as the product of concentrated efforts and dedication to the different types of *dhyāna* and *samādhi* but, nevertheless, the Samgha as a social community served to accentuate the individual sentiments towards moral redemption. It served to reinforce the element of individual resolve and determination with the weight of collective beliefs, aspirations and traditions.

In early Buddhism, the Samgha enjoyed a dominating place and the disciple had to accept the surrender also to the Samgha. But the dominance of the Samgha[1] as a community showed that it was postulated on the acceptance of the nominalistic conception of the social universe. Society in the sense of an organic coherent body of social selves living in functional and organisational interdependence does not seem to have possessed any meaning and significance for early Buddhism. Early Buddhism is oriented to the quest of the way of emancipation. It puts the primacy on revulsion, dispassion, release and redemption. Hence it taught the transcendence of an individual's obligations to the family, the society and the state. Creative participant citizenship based on the performance of one's allotted duties in the scheme of the social structure had not much worth in the Buddhist world-view whose basis was the fact of misery and which taught the way to end that misery. The persuit of a cultural life and the enjoyment of aesthetic delight in leisure—this ideal was inadequate for early Buddhism. All the possible goals of individual and social efforts were found unsatisfactory and even meaningless because the dismal force of all-encompassing destruction was there to overtake

[1] Alice Getty, *The Gods of Northern Buddhism* (Oxford, Clarendon Press, 1914), p. 19, says with reference to later Buddhism: "In China, Dharma and Samgha are personified and form a popular triad with the Buddha. They symbolize the generative power (Buddha), the productive power (Dharma), and the active power of creation (Samgha)."

them all. Hence the only satisfying teleology was the one which taught the immediate realization of the state of the *arhat*. This stress on monasticism as a consequence of the prevalence of misery and gloom and death, did, in fact, imply that, for Buddhism, society as an organic totality had no reality. Hence I have said that early Buddhism did not accept the view of society as a real organic structure with a social and ethical significance of its own. To it society was a mere agglomeration of individuals. It was a mere name. The aim of man was to attain *nirvāṇa* and not to waste the precious human life in the accumulation of money or the pursuit of political power. The implicit repudiation by early Buddhism of the realistic organic character of the society implies that early Buddhism was a creed of individualism. It started with the view of moral personalism that the individual as a person was the master of his own destiny and the realization of his mission of life consisted in mendicancy and Arhatship. Buddha having renounced his ties and obligations to his family and parents and society is the supreme example of a moral and spiritual individualist. Hence we can say that early Buddhism did not teach the rational organization and structural solidarity of the society and the state by inculcating the theory of social self-realization but it emphasized the necessity of spiritual endeavours oriented to the supreme and ultimate teleology of *nirvāṇa*. Since the most significant pursuit of an individual was of a private and ethereal character, the primacy of the society and the state declined seriously as a matter of logical consequences.[1]

Early Buddhism taught the transitoriness and evanescence of

[1] Edward Conze in his *Buddhist Thought in India* (London, George Allen & Unwin, 1962), has stressed the four *brahma-vihāra* as representing "the cultivation of social emotions" (pp. 80-91) and as "the graded training of social behaviour" (p. 90). But even Conze says: "On reaching its perfection, the social attitude also seems to become distinctly a-social ...They [the brahma-vihāras] are concerned with the social world and with living beings, who represent a deceptive, diminished and alienated reality, and the final effect of the Brahma-Vihāras is to push them out of the way and to allow the yogin to peacefully withdraw from them. Deliverance depends on the ability to break out of this charmed circle in which non-existent individuals are constantly interfering with one another, and to penetrate to the dharmic reality which lies beyond them." (pp. 90-91).

worldly phenomena and a retreat from them. This attitude is based on the acceptance of the vanity of the world. To the philosopher who contemplates the final extinction of all things, the world can never provide final satisfaction and solace. So long as the structure of the world appears perfectly satisfying, one does not meditate on the nature and destiny of things. Buddha was highly sensitive and the pleasures and attractions of the world had no charm for him. I think that the source of the supreme stress on suffering in early Buddhism is psychological because it had its roots in the sensitive temperament of Buddha and of kindred souls. An attempt has been made to find the roots of his emphasis on suffering in the contemporary social, political and economic situation. The *Aṅguttara Nikāya* says that within the memory of the people then living, many populous cities had been devastated. Wars, famines, lawlessness, tyrannies etc. had made the people frustrated and desolate and to such a people the gospel of the vanity of things appeared natural. It is possible that the external factors leading to disenchantment and sorrow may have been present, but the internalization of these factors of gloom and sorrow into personal motivations of the leaders and disciples of the Buddhist fraternity is significant. The same objective and external forces generated in Buddha an attitude of gloom and detachment and in the contemporary sceptical and materialistic thinkers an attitude of enjoyment. Death overtakes all but the sensualist thinks that since he has to die one day it is best to enjoy to the maximum the pleasures of the world, while the ascetic shuns them because for him the world is fleeting. Hence the real problem is not only to find out the possible external factors which would lead to gloom, despair and sorrow but also to analyze the dynamics of psychological operation through which these forces become transformed into the personal motivating entities of individuals.

In course of its historical and institutional development, an intuitional and transcendentally-oriented religion becomes mixed up with diverse types of sociological factors. The deep and fundamental problem for Buddha was to search a way of escape from cosmic misery and he discovered a norm of release to his satisfaction. He did not find solace and satisfaction in the contemporary Brāhmanical ritualism and theology. He also criticized the Brāhmanical creeds and cults. He was a Sakya Kshattriya and some of his important disciples were Kshatriyas. To some extent, Buddhism became associated with the anti-Brāhmanical movement of the Kshatriyas and Vaisyas but a social revolution was never the aim of Buddhism. The finances of the early Buddhist movement received considerable stability from Anāthapinḍika who is stated to have bought the Jetavana park for eighteen Kotis of goldpieces and built a huge Vihara there. Viśākhā, the daughter of the Vaisya Dhananjaya and Sumanā of Anga, was instrumental in the conversion of her father-in-law Mṛgāra to Buddhism. She also built a Purvārāma near Sāketa for the use of the monks. But to interpret Buddhism as predominantly a movement of anti-Brāhmin reaction is to be guilty of exaggeration. In the Samgha, no social distinctions were maintained and to this extent social equality was practised. But Buddhism did not preach an open revolution against the existing hierarchical organization, privileges and status of a class-and-caste-ridden society. Hence to interpret Buddhism as a socialist and democratic movement is also far-fetched. The teaching of Buddha, especially its psychological metaphysics and gnoseological analysis is very subtle and ingeneous and is not meant for the masses but could be suitable only for an elite. It is wrong to say that Buddha wanted to popularize the teachings of the Upaniṣads. It could have been somewhat possible to understand the metaphysics of the identity of the human self and the Brahman but to expect that the masses could understand the formula of the *pratityasmputpāda* is unrealistic. Buddha was the teacher of an ethical gospel and it is unnecessary to credit him with being the democratic popularizer of Upaniṣadic teachings. It is being unjust to the man who had made such a fundamental revolt against the Upaniṣads. The Buddhist Samgha was based on a republican structural model. It did not have any theocratic head comparable to the Roman Catholic Pope. After the death of Gautama Buddha, a council was held at Rājagir to settle the religious canon. The second Council held at Vaiśāli in about 380 B.C. consisted of 700 Arhats. The third Council was held in Pātliputra around 242 B.C. under Asoka's inspiration. The fourth Council was held around 70 A.D. at Jālandhar at the initiative of Kanishka. The last three Councils show the interaction between temporal political authority and the custodians of religious wisdom and schismatics. In the Buddhist church, we do not find the development of any doctrine of apostolic succession derived from the personality of the founder. There was no sacrosanct keeper of the keys of heaven in the Buddhist Samgha. The Samgha did not preach any open crusade against monarchy. The economic structure of the Samgha in the early days was also very simple. It was based on individual begging and the occasional gifts of the rich magnates of the commercial community. Hence there could be no question of economic rationalization based on the organization of the motive of self-interest resulting in the realization of common good. In such a simple and austere system of economic life, the problem of economic accountability and responsibility does not arise. The basic and fundamental concern remains ethical with transcendental orientations towards *nirvāṇa*.

Buddhism was the most potent religious movement in the whole of Asia. The emergence and growth of this religious system was indicative of the maturation of the human intellect.

CHAPTER 18

THE ANTHROPOLOGICAL FOUNDATIONS OF EARLY BUDDHISM

1. *Introduction*

IF WE EXAMINE the Vedic literature and the Tripiṭakas with a critical eye, we shall find that along with some of the loftiest conceptions of mysticism, metaphysics and ethics they also contain the records of concessions to the primitive ideas, magic,[1] rites and practices of the common mass of people.[2] This should not appear surprising, it is only an evidence of the catholic, assimilative and comprehensive character of Hinduism. Even today, along with the sublime ethics of *karmayoga*, there is a place in popular Hinduism for veneration for the small-pox, the cow, the serpent and the dog.[3] Hence for a thorough sociological and philosophical study of religions we can neglect neither the higher theoretical and doctrinal speculations of the philosophers or the rites, ceremonies, cults, practices and myths of the vast number of inhabitants.[4] Only thus can the intermixture of the exalted philosophico-ethical ideas and the crude and barbaric notions of the masses can be adequately studied.

The Upaniṣads inculcate, in some passages, monistic

[1] The *Atharvaveda*, XI, 8, 19 and VI, 26 refers to *pāpman* as impersonal evil. There is mention of *takman* as actual fever disease ; — *Atharvaveda* VII, 10 ; II, 25. L. Thorndike, *The History of Magic*. Frazer, *The Golden Bough* (One vol. edition).

[2] Cf. S. Radhakrishnan, *Eastern Religions and Western Thought*, pp. 307-8.

[3] The *Śitalā-pujā*, *Gopujā*, *Nāgapañcami* and *Bhairav-bābā*.

[4] The *Vaitāna Sutra* and the *Gopatha Brāhmana*. Richard Garbe, *Vaitāna Sūtra* (German translation), Strassburg, 1878. Victor Henry, *La Magie Dans L'Inde Antique*, Paris, 1904. Alfred Hillebrandt, *Ritual-litteratur : Vedische Opfer und Zauber*. B.C. Law, *The Buddhist Conception oi Spirits* (1923).

idealism, and in some, pantheistic immanence. But there are references to many primitive notions as well, in them.[1] The *Brihadāraṇyaka Upaniṣad* refers to the possession of a human being by a ghost-spirit. Kabandha Atharvana is said to possess (*gṛhitā*) the daughter of Patanjala Kāpya.[2] It is also possible to hold that the Upaniṣadic descriptions of the various regions (lokāh) are also borrowed from the popular mythological store. The reference to *gandharvaloka* is one example.

The Upaniṣadic eschatology also contains reference to primitive ideas.[3] In describing the disintegration of the organs of a dead person the Upaniṣad describes the various elements to which they are reduced:[4]

Organs of the person		*Elements & Entities to which reduced*
Speech (*vāk*)	...	Fire (*agni*)
Vital spirit (*prāṇa*)	...	Air (*vāta*)
Eye (*cakshush*)	...	Sun (*ādityah*)
Mind (*mana*)	...	Moon (*candrah*)
Ear (*srotram*)	...	Space (*diśah*)
Body (*śariram*)	...	Earth (*pṛthivī*)
Soul (*ātman*)	...	Ether (*ākāśa*)
Hairs (*lomam*) (on the body)	...	Medicinal plants (*auṣhadhi*)
Hairs (*keśā*) (of the head)	...	Plants (*Vanaspatih*)
Blood (*lohitam*)	...	Water (*āpah*)

In this scheme it appears that a queer mixture of some elements of the products of mass consciousness and some kind of rudimentary logical causation in the field of eschatology has been brought together.

[1] A. E. Gough, *Philosophy of the Upaniṣads*, pp. 1-4 opines that the demerits of the Upaniṣads are due to racial intermixture.

[2] *Brihadāraṇyaka Upaniṣad*, III, 3, 1.

[3] In the *Chhāndogya Upaniṣad*, VIII, 8, 5, in the conversations of Prajāpati and Virocana, there is a reference to animistic or primitive view: "*pretasya śariram bhikshyā vasanenālamkāreṇeti samskurvantyetena hyamum lokam jeshyanto manyante.*" In the early pre-Buddhistic periods as well in the days when the Buddha flourished the people believed in the possibility of the resurrection of the physical or the subtle (sūkshma) form of a religious leader.

[4] *Brihadāraṇyaka Upaniṣad*, III, 2, 13.

There are in the Upaniṣads other references as well which have their origin in primitive notions. One passage says that the *jīva* leaves a branch of the tree when it is cut from the main tree. The Upaniṣadic gods are regarded as assuming different forms at will (*tān Indro suparṇo bhutvā vāyave prāyachat tanvāyuratmani dhṛtva tatrāgamayat*).[1] The famous description in the *Kaṭhopaniṣad* of Naciketā being taught by Yama, the god of death, is also reminiscent of days when the appalling character of physical destruction was sought to be deified.[2] Some of the personal names in the Upaniṣads also indicate relics of primitivism, *e.g.* Indradyumnna Bhāllaveya and Vudila Āsvatarāśvi and also Vaiyaghrapadya.[3] Another primitive notion is that due to the curse of a victorious knower of the absolute, the head of the defeated disputant will fall (*murdhā te vipatishyati*).

These points serve to establish it conclusively that the Upaniṣads as they are, (which do contain the records of some of the sublimest conceptions of spiritual monism) also preserve some of the crude notions of the masses who were absorbed in the worship of animal and nature entities. The Vedantic mystics and sages were tolerant enough not to purge the primitive notions and practices of the people.

2. *Anthropological Foundations of Early Buddhism*

The Buddhistic *Vinaya Piṭaka* and the *Sutta Piṭaka* contain many features and ideas which seem to have been derived from the prevailing practices and beliefs of the masses. In spite of the attempts of modern philosophical ingenuity and logical intellect to put a positivistic interpretation on the Buddhist *anātman*, it is difficult to deny that the two Piṭakas, teach a doctrine of soullessness. The Buddhist *anātmavāda* is a counterpoise not only to the Upaniṣadic absolutism but also to the prevailing animistic notions.[4] The Buddhist *anātman* thus

[1] *Brihadāraṇyaka Upaniṣad*, III, 3, 2.

[2] Cf. the primitive belief of Naciketā that his longevity would depend on the blessings of Yama.—*jīvishyāmo yāvadīsishyasi tvam.*

[3] Also the name of the snake seer—Arbuda Kādraveya.

[4] G. W. Brown in his article in *Studies in Honour of Bloomfield*, pp. 75 ff., (quoted in A.B. Keith, *Religion and Philosophy of the Veda*, p. 631), claims that the Dravidians upheld animistic beliefs and that in it Buddhism and Jainism bear clear resemblance to Dravidian notions, repudiating the Aryan gods.

represents not an incorporation of primitivism but a refutation of it. If we examine critically the ideas of the common man regarding the human soul, we shall find that really he adheres not to the concept of a spiritual soul-entity as taught in the Nyāya-Vaiśeshika and the Yoga philosophies but he adheres to some kind of animistic idea. This is the situation today and it is possible to guess that this must have been the situation in the sixth century B.C. also. It is true that some of the Buddhist Mādhyamika philosophers like Nāgārjuna and Candrakīrti and some modern thinkers like James and Russell try to refute the notion of an abstract metaphysical human self but the criticisms of Buddha were aimed largely not so much against a metaphysical or substantialistic conception of the self as against the prevailing animistic view of the human soul. The main point in the animistic conception is that "there is recognized in nature no aristocratic class of soul-possessing beings; everything dignified by thinghood, has its own power or function, however insignificant, and therefore its own soul."[1] Tylor says: "Plants partaking with animals the phenomena of life and death, health and sickness not unnaturally have some kind of soul ascribed to them. In the lower ranges of culture the souls of plants are much more identified with the souls of animals."[2] The Jaina conception of *ahimsā* flourishes on such a theory of universal animism. Jainism promulgates not so much a metaphysics of absolute love flowing from the acceptance of a personal lord. It teaches non-violence because it regards all beings and entities as souls. The Jaina animistic notion of the soul is not a deterioration of degeneration of the Upaniṣadic pantheism.[3] It is very definitely an acceptance of the prevalent popular view of the masses. The early Buddhist doctrine of *anātman* is also levelled against the Jaina notions of animism. According to Buddhism it indicated hollowness of intellectual strength and futility of philosophic endeavours if one adhered to the notion of a soul which could

[1] "Animism", *Encyclopaedia of Religion and Ethics.*

[2] Tylor, *Primitive Culture*. Also Jevons, *Comparative Religion.*

[3] The nakedness of the Acelaka ascetics, the Ājīvakas, their leader Gośālaka Makkhaliputta and the Digambara Jainas is a relic of primitive days. According to the *Kausika Sutra* (XXXVIII, 4) a day of ill omen can be expiated by sitting naked (nagna) and rubbing the forehead.

be possessed by all entities.[1] By attempting to demonstrate the weakness of animism, Buddha did a great service to the advancement of logical rationalism. Even some of the early Greek philosophers were not able to attain to this critical psychological standpoint. Even the Ionics believed in hylozoism—the doctrine that matter (*hyle*) has a soul (*Zoon*). It shows the profundity of Buddha's philosophical researches and his strength of mind that he was able to apply the critical gaze of rationalism to the animistic notions of the Jainas and the masses. He thus opened the way for the advance of philosophical rationalism. But it will be a mistake to interpret Buddha as a complete rationalist and a perfect repudiator of animism. He not only believed in mysticism but the Tripiṭakas do contain several statements and passages which are themselves definitely animistic. Hence while partly acknowledging the services of Buddhist *anātmavāda* in the refutation of Jaina animistic notions, we should take note of the animistic and primitive elements in Buddhist thought. It is possible that the picture of *nirvāṇa* as blissful may be due to a compromise with the popular notions of heaven. In the *Cullavagga*, there is reference to the use of *Sutrapātha* for the safety of Buddha when Devadatta was planning his (Buddha's) death.

It can also be said that in the context of Upaniṣadic absolutism the entire doctrine of the transmigration of the soul appears as a concession to the empirical consciousness.[2] When the infinite *brahman* is the sole real, then transmigration is a purely phenomenal process.[3] Here I am not concerned with the

[1] In some passages, however, Buddha himself is made to uphold a popular view of the soul.

[2] A.B. Keith, *Religion and Philosophy of the Veda*, II, p. 415 : "The idea of the incarnation of men as snakes is clearly to be accepted for the later period (Winternitz, *Der Sarpabali*, p. 37. *contra*, Paton, *Spiritism*, pp. 96 ff), but for the actual Vedic period it is not demonstrated, and it must in all likelihood be deemed to be an idea which entered the religion of the Veda with the advance of aboriginal influences. A more interesting case is recorded in the ritual for the final burial of the bones of the dead (*Kauc*. Lxxxiii. 22 ff.) ; if they cannot be found, then a garment is spread out, and, if a beast alights on it, it is treated as representing the bones of the dead."

[3] *The Śatapatha Brāhmaṇa* contains popular ideas regarding eschatology. *SB*, IV, 6, 1, 1, states that the pious rise in the world with all their

examination of the veracity or soundness of the concept of transmigration. I only mean to stress, what has even been recognized by Śamkara himself, that transmigration of the soul is a concept relevant to the empirical realm and has no absolute reality. Buddhism does contain idealistic elements and to some extent even doctrines sanctioning illusionism. But even Buddhism had to make concessions and accept some or other of the prevailing primitive notions of the masses. The appearance of Māra at several significant periods in the life of Buddha as well as the conversations of Buddha with Indra and Brahmā Sahampati are indications of the influence of the prevailing notions of the masses on the compilers of the Tripiṭaka literature. In Buddhism, although on grounds of logic and experience, the substantial independent character of the soul has been repudiated, still the *Dhammapada* says that the liar goes to hell (*abhutavādī nirayam upeti*).[1] In the Tripiṭakas there is mention of an elaborate realm of heavens and hells.[2] There is allusion to the Tushta heaven.[3] What logical or scientific evidence can be adduced for accepting this idea? Where is this Tushta *loka* situated and who are its inhabitants? Sometimes the early Buddhist writings would condemn a non-believer to habitation in damned infernal hell—the Hades of the Greek mythologies or the sunless regions (*asuryā nāma te lokāh andhena tamasāvṛtāh*) of the Vājasaneyins. Ghosts and spirits are legion.[4] There is mention of the

limbs complete. *SB*, X, 1, 5, 4, states that the pious can dispense with food due to the good consequences produced by the sacrifice.

1 Melamed, *Spinoza and Buddha*, p. 256 : "Desire and action are the two sources of evil which bind man to this world of finiteness, manifoldness, illusion and misery, and pursue the soul from existence to existence. When Buddha formulated his doctrines, he took over bodily this popular view."

2 According to Hiriyanna, *Indian Philosophy*, p. 136, the references in the Buddhist literature to other worlds and their inhabitants are due to two factors: (a) people upheld those beliefs and (b) Buddha's beliefs in the doctrine of Karma with its definite eschatological reference. According to A.B. Keith, *Buddhist Philosophy*, p. 26, the Buddha himself was a great divinity in the eyes of his followers in a "barbarous age."

3 According to the *Cullavagga*, Kakudha Koliyaputra was born in a *manomaya loka*. (Manomaya Kāya, acc. to Nalanda ed. pp. 283-284),

4 B.C. Law, The Buddhist Conception of Spirits. *The Pārājika* I, 10, l 4; II, 6, 4 and the *Pettavatthu*. A.B. Keith, *Religion and Philosophy of the Veda*, II, pp. 414-15: "there is no reasonable doubt that some of the

gandharva.[1] These views which appear in recognized Buddhist scriptures cannot be lightly brushed aside by the superior pose of a philosopher. Some explanation has to be found for their existence in scriptural works of recognized religious worth and value. The incorporation of these elements was done as a concession to the enormous weight of the views and notions which were thoroughly held by the masses for centuries. The belief in the potency of the *tapas* of the Shāstā to work miracles is another example of popular superstitions. At the house of the Kassapa brothers Buddha works out 3500 miracles. Even the mystic and the aristocratic philosopher cannot isolate himself entirely from the beliefs and superstitions of people. Thus Buddhism which proclaimed its intellectual boldness by at least silently repudiating the absolute *brahman* of the Upaniṣads and by denying the personal God of the Brahmin priests and the soul of the Jain animists, had, in its own scriptures to accept several ideas and doctrines which were the property of the unregenerate masses. This is a testimony to the dominance of the force of race consciousness.

Buddhist ghosts are transmutations of tree and water spirits due to the growing animism which treated the spirit as merely living in, and not having its life in the tree or the waters. But it is worth noting that in many cases the Buddhist ghosts are to die and go to hell in a certain period (*Petavatthu*, i. 10, 12 ; ii. 7, 12.) : it is natural to see in this the record of the condition before final damnation of the preta."

[1] *The Majjhima Nikāya, "Mahātaṇhāsamkhaya Sutta"* (No. 38). The *gandharva* is 'exciting impulse' and is called *pratisandhivijñāna* in the *Abhidhamma. Gandharva = antarābhavasattvah gandham bhukte.*—Narada, "Samsāra or Buddhist Philosophy of Birth and Death, "*Indian Historical Quarterly*," Vol. III, 1927, pp. 561-70.

CHAPTER 19

EARLY BUDDHISM AND THE METHODOLOGY OF SOCIAL AND POLITICAL RESEARCH

EARLY BUDDHISM has been discussed from various standpoints. It has been investigated as a system of ethical religion and salvationistic ethics. The significance of the Buddhist ethical imperative, comparable in some respects to the Kantian good-will, has been emphasized as an antidote to the rampant contemporary disquiet, nihilism and despair. It is considered a system of soteriology by Max Weber and a scheme of Nirvanistic eschatology by Dahlmann. Some hold it to be a promulgator of the law of causation and thus a precursor of science. Spengler regarded Buddhism, Stoicism and Socialism as examples of intellectual movements during the era of civilization, coming at the end of 'late culture' and characteristic products of megalopolitanism and rationalism. He interprets Buddha as a nihilist and asserts that there is no ethic of will in Buddhism and Epicureanism. Toynbee in his *Civilization on Trial* states that according to Buddha, Stoicism, one school of Christianity and some forms of Platonism, the truth lies beyond history. Albert Schweitzer has drawn attention to the ethic of compassion in Buddhism. Northrop has drawn our attention to the stark realism and positivism involved in the concept of *dukkha* and has interpreted *nirvāṇa* along the lines of the notion of an undifferentiated aesthetic continuum.[1] Buddhism had also deep social repercussions and profound political consequences. Gautama Buddha did prescribe some social and political formulas relevant to the contemporary setup. For a comprehensive study of early Buddhism the social and political teachings of early Buddhism must be analysed.[2] This will also

[1] F.S.C. Northrop, *The Meeting of East and West*, p. 347.

[2] Even if Gautama's primary interest was not in politics and although he did not formulate an explicit social philosophy still in its institutional phases early Buddhism did inculcate social and political notions.

be a contribution to the history of social and political thought.

If a comprehensive history of social and political thought in the world is to be attempted, then Indologists, Sinologists, Egyptologists, Babylonologists, Assyriologists and other specialists in the ancient civilizations of Africa and Asia and Europe will have to specify the social and political speculations that were attempted in those countries. This will be a commendable enterprise not only from the historical standpoint but will also provide ideas and data which will be yardsticks for comparing modern ideas and data with them.[1]

In the evolution of social and political categories we can distinguish three stages. The first is the stage of speculations, ideas and vague formulations. In this stage categories appear as unsystematized and have all the marks of a difficult birth. Sages, religious leaders, prophets, magicians, poets, political rulers take the initiative in the formulation of categories and ideas in this stage. In India the Vedas may be said to belong to this stage. The *second stage* is that of social and political thought. In this stage philosophers, idealists and thinkers, either singly or as the spokesmen of a generation, take the initiative in the formulation of utopias, systems and codes. The Upaniṣads, the Tripiṭakas, the Smṛtis and the writings of Śamkara, Rāmānuja, Vijñanabhikshu, Kautilya, Kāmandaka, Śukra may be said to belong to this stage. In the West, Plato, Aristotle, Aquinas, Machiavelli, Hobbes, Hegel, Comte, Marx, Spencer, Green may be said to belong to this stage. With reference to creations of these writers and system-builders we use the terms *philosophy*, *thought* and *theory* almost interchangeably although there may be and are some differences even among these terms but for the purpose of broad typologization they may be used synonymously. The *third stage* is that of scientifically-oriented social and political theories which use not only the methods of observation and classification as the old philosophers also did but are more concerned with the technics of correlation and inductive behavioral research. This stage is marked by the decline of norms-setting and prescription ideals and prognosis. It is more fascinated by data-collection and analysis and claims to be objective and at least to a considerable extent 'value-free.'

[1] The UNESCO should undertake this project.

Generally, writers on the history of social and political thought in the West would relegate the social and political ideas and speculations of early Buddhism to the first stage—the stage of utterance of *obiter dicta*. If they were a little more comprehensive in their orientation and less prejudiced then they would concede that early Buddhism is also a system of social thought or social philosophy. It is the contention of this chapter that early Buddhism is of interest not only as a bundle of disjointed social categories and speculations and is not only, at least partly, also a system of social and political thought, but it is also possible to apply to it the technics of modern social and political research. It will certainly be unfounded to call the early teachers and writers on Buddhism as sociologists and political scientists. But it is possible to apply the methods of sociology of knowledge and sociology of religion to the study of Buddhism. Furthermore, a student of political science who has studied the modern behavioral theories of political power and leadership can also apply the modern concepts to the study of power relations in the Buddhist Samgha. He can study the technics used by Gautama Buddha for the maintenance of his leadership. He can study the situational data provided by the then society and polity and find out to what extent were they congruous with the emergence of authoritarian or democratic types of personality. He can also study the technics, if any, provided by Gautama to fight tyranny and for the furtherance of solidarity. In this short chapter I could not undertake this kind of empirical study, nor did I intend to do it. My only purpose is to make a case for the study of aspects of early Buddhism by students and teachers of sociology and political science. Due to their ignorance of Indian history and philosophy as well as of the comprehensive developments in the social sciences in the West, some Indian teachers and students of political science are reluctant to study Buddhism. They will say that it is a subject outside the domain of political science. It is the contention of this chapter that with the maturation of Indian independence, we should evolve our own political science and sociology. In that connection the contributions of early Buddhism should not be lost sight of.

According to Albion Small, the beginnings of modern sociology are to be traced not to Comte and Spencer alone but to the "drive towards objectivity" in German historical research. He tried to trace the beginnings of sociology in the "drive towards objectivity" in German historiology about 1800 AD. We can examine if the quest for objectivity was present in the system of ideas of the early civilizations.

It cannot be denied that the researches of indologists have brought to light the elements of positivistic, objective, inductive and empirical thought and methodology in the Hindu and Buddhist philosophies.[1] Hence it can be stated that the methodological foundations of empirical social enquiry were present in ancient India. It should not, however, be imagined that the sophisticated clarifications of the experimentally-oriented scientific method and mathematical logic can be traced in ancient India. But it must be stated that the methodological foundations of ancient Indian and Buddhist speculations were at least similar to those of the Greeks.

Max Weber holds that the period since the sixteenth century in Western Europe is era of 'disenchantment'. The magical and enveloping theological creeds of the Middle Ages with the dominance of Christian *Weltanschauung* were now ending due to the rise of Renaissance humanism and secularistic science. This 'disenchantment' provided the mental framework necessary for the emergence of social and political thought which was oriented more to the problems of worldly organization and social control than to speculation regarding an ideal republic or the best form of polity. We can examine if in the Indian context there ever appeared eras of disenchantment necessary for the growth of intensive social and political thought.

It can be stated that in Indian history there have been ages and epochs which bear some resemblance to the European period of disenchantment. The period from the middle of the seventh to the beginning of the fourth century B.C. can be considered such an age. I do not want to imply that the intellectual achievements[2] of this period of 'somewhat of disen-

[1] Brajendra Nath Seal, *The Positive Sciences of the Ancient Hindus*. B. K. Sarkar, *Positive Background of Hindu Sociology* (Allahabad. Panini Office). S. C. Vidyabhusana, *A History of Indian Logic*. V. P. Varma, *Studies in Hindu Political Thought and its Metaphysical Foundations*. Satya Prakash's book on Indian Science.

[2] B. K. Sarkar, *Political Institutions and Theories of the Hindus*

chantment' are comparable in substantial value to the European achievements in science and sociology following in the wake of the period of sixteenth century disenchantment to which Max Weber has referred. My aim is only to point out that mental phenomena resembling disenchantment are characteristic of the evolution of all great cultures and civilizations. Eras of scepticism, intellectualism, mental and emotional frustration and questioning and repudiation of theological systems can be found in the cultural history of all peoples.[1] They are not the specific and monopolistic characteristics of Western culture alone although it is absolutely correct to maintain that the sustained emphasis on disenchantment may be peculiar to the West. In the modern era of world understanding which necessitates the appreciation of the cumulative achievements of mankind in the development of thought, it is necessary to give up the kind of ethnocentrism which characterizes most of the writers of the history of social and political thought in Europe and America. Dunning, Sabine and MacIwain are absolutely innocent of any information regarding Asian contributions to political thought. Lichtenberger makes no mention of Asian contributions to social thought.[2] Although I differ from the

(Leipzig, 1922), p. 150 says : "In an inventory of India's contributions to the spirit of inquiry and the progress of mankind, the epoch of republics (c. 600 BC.-AC. 350) interspread no doubt with monarchies, must be recognised as responsible for the anatomy, therapeutics and medicine of Charaka's academy, the linguistics and methodology of Panini and his scholars, the metallurgy and alchemy that found patron-saints in Patanjali and Nagarjuna, the philosophical speculations of the atomists, monists, sensationalists, and sceptics, the schools of political science that came to be finally absorbed in the systems of Kautilya and Sukra, the legal and sociological theories associated in the long run with the *nom-de-Plumes* of Manu and Yajnavalkya, the elaboration of the Jataka folklore and of the Ramayana and Mahabharata epics, dramaturgy and the fine arts of the Bharata and Vatsyayana cycles, the mystical militarism and the *niṣkāma karma* or "categorical imperative" of the Gita, and last but not least the *sarva-sattvamaitrī* (humanitarianism and universal brotherhood) of Śakya, the preacher of *appamāda* (strenuousness) and apostle of *viriya* (energism)."

[1] E.W. Hopkins, *Religions of India*, pp. 298 ff., refers to the growth of "searching scepticism" in India, Greece and Palestine (*Ecclesiastes*) in the 5th century BC.

[2] The chapters on Asian social thought in Becker and Barnes, *Social*

main propositions and conclusions of *The Decline of the West*, I would appreciate Spengler's methodological approach. He says:

> "The most appropriate designation for this current West-European scheme of history, in which the great cultures are made to follow orbits around *us* as the presumed centre of all world-happenings, is the *Ptolemaic system* of history. The system that is put forward in this work in place of it I regard as the *Copernican discovery* in the historical sphere, in that it admits no sort of privileged position to the classical or the Western culture as against the cultures of India, Babylon, China, Egypt, the Arabs, Mexico—separate worlds of dynamic being which is of mass count for just as much in the general picture of history as the classical, while frequently surpassing it in point of spiritual greatness and soaring power."[1]

I definitely feel that such a Copernican revolution must be attempted in the history of the social sciences. The contributions of the ancient and medieval civilizations which were outside the context of the Western sector should be studied by students and teachers of the social sciences. P. A. Sorokin in his famous text-book *Contemporary Sociological Theories* has, on occasions, referred to the insights into social problems of the ancient thinkers of China and India. He says:

> "...in my opinion, the formal school is very old. Its founders were neither Tonnies, nor Simmel, as Dr. Vierkandt claims; nor Kant, Hegel Herbart, Ferguson, Fichte, L. Von Stein, Gneist, Jelleinek, nor Spencer, as G. Richard indicates more rightly. Its founders were all lawgivers who formulated the first rules of social relations, and especially all juriconsults and theorizers of law. Beginning at least with Confucius and the Roman juriconsults, who so brilliantly formulated the principal forms of social relations, and ending with the theorizers of law, all have 'been formal sociologists'."[2]

I do not agree with the views of Sorokin on this particular point but I have cited these lines to indicate that the Copernican revolution in the history of the social sciences is essential and this requires a comprehensive frame of reference wherein

Thought from Lore to Science 3rd ed. are absolutely inadequate but they do indicate a new trend.

[1] Oswald Spengler, *The Decline of the West* (Alfred A. Knopf), Vol. I, p. 18.

[2] P. A. Sorokin, *Contemporary Sociological Theories* (New York, Harper & Co., 1928), pp. 497-98.

Simmel has to be studied along with Confucius and Comte along with Gandhi. If the concept of natural law has to be studied then not only the contributions of Cicero, Thomas Aquinas and Grotius but also those of Lao-Tse, Buddha[1] and Patañjali should be taken into consideration. Hitherto historians of social and philosophical thought in the West have not only been ignorant of the Eastern contributions but have shown almost a contemptuous indifference towards them. It is for new research scholars to dispel this vast mist of ignorance, indifference and prejudice and discuss the contributions of early Buddhism to the concepts of individualism, liberty, internationalism etc. Certainly this comparative study has to be done not at the emotional but at the scientific level. The ancient literature of India is too vast and the dimensions of its social and political contributions have to be specifically spelled out.

Several sociologists have adopted a broad framework for the science of sociology. Small's earlier contention was that sociology is the philosophical synthesis and organization of the results of the specialized social sciences. This view of Small resembles the view of Giddings. According to the latter, a sociological type of approach to the study of social phenomena was "predicted" if not created by Auguste Comte. Giddings holds that sociology is the elemental and basic social science, studying society in its broadest and most fundamental aspects. Small's views, however, later underwent a transformation and in the article on the "Future of Sociology" he said:

> "In proportion as sociology becomes responsibly objective it will leave behind its early ambition for a hegemony over social sciences, and it will realize its destiny of functioning within a federation of scientific activities. With widening and clarifying of social consciousness, it must become progressively evident that a single technique, no matter how penetrating, can at most lay bare only certain constituent aspects of the total social process."[2]

Znaniecki considers "activities-intentionally-affecting others"

[1] Gautama Buddha was opposed to dogmatic superstitions and denied supernatural intervention in the operation of the law of causation. He accepted the uniformity of natural phenomena and hence denied the role of chance.

[2] Quoted in Harry E. Barnes (ed.), *An Introduction to the History of Sociology* (University of Chicago Press, 1948), p. 779.

as the central or exclusive object of sociology. Prof. L. T. Hobhouse holds that even after social psychology, cultural geography, history and the special social sciences have developed there would be need, for sociology as a discipline of interpretative correlation—to bring facts into perspective even though it may not discover any facts. Prof. Hayes also accepts a broad general conception of sociology although in 1902 he defined sociology as "study of a particular type of causation, the casual relations between the activities of associates." He thinks that Comte and Spencer were not wholly wrong in their comprehensive conception of sociology as a philosophy of super-organic or social life.

I favour a broad comprehensive standpoint for social sciences. I do not think that sociology as a specialized discipline of social organization and social disorganization can rest content only with the study of family, criminology, human ecology and demography. The attempt to confine sociology to a study of "institutions" as some recent social theorists propose would result in the ignoring of vital infra-institutional and even supra-institutional dynamics of human behaviour. Buddhist psychology as formulated in the Tripiṭaka and by Vasuvandhu and others is full of reference to subliminal, mystical, introspective and supra-intellectual layers of consciousness. Early Buddhism, in analysing the psychic structure (*skandhacatushtaya*) refers to four categories — feeling (*vedanā*), ideation (*samjñā*), will or volitional cognition (*samskāra*) and sensation or 'conscientness' (*vijñāna*). These also have to be studied. I agree with Sorokin when he says: "Sociology has been, is, and either will be a science of the general characteristics of all classes of social phenomena with the relationships and correlations between them; or there will be no sociology."[1]

If a broad approach is favoured towards the subject-matter of social sciences then it becomes relevant to analyze early Buddhist literature from this standpoint. Thus it becomes essential to find out the Buddhist views on society, community, primary groups, factors for social solidarity, causes of social disorganization, role of amity (*maitli*) as a social bond, social

[1] Sorokin, *Contemporary Sociological Theories*, p. 761.

change, leadership etc.[1]

When I conceive of sociology as the broad science treating of all the diverse forms of social relationships I do also emphasize a quantitative, empirical, and inductive research methodology. But I distrust any mere Humean scepticism towards the acceptance of the role of rationalism in sociology. Inductive researches are highly necessary for the formation of large empirical and historical generalisations. But in spite of the attacks on the rational (metaphysical) method of philosophy by Russell, Wittgenstein and Carnap, I still think that mathematical rationalism cannot be avoided either by sociology or by philosophy. Some of the basic contributions of the Nyāya philosophy of the Hindus and of Kant, still are noteworthy. Inductive and historical empiricism can procure data but the transformation of the empirical generalisations into the conceptualized framework of a theoretical system requires the employment of rational techniques. Once 'theories' have been formulated we may begin to deduce therefrom further implications through the help of the Platonic geometrical-mathematical method or the logical-analytical method of the Hindu philosophers. Against the scientific empiricists, Max Planck tried to argue that science cannot proceed further unless the statistical laws are transformed into causal laws and the formulation of causal hypothesis is necessarily based on a rational insight. Because I accept a combination of rational-mathematical and historical-empirical methods both in the social sciences and philosophy, hence I strongly advocate that the speculations, generalizations and theorisations of the early and medieval social thinkers and philosophers cannot be dismissed on the ground they do not furnish huge statistical tables.

While analyzing the explicit teachings of Gautama Buddha

[1] A comprehensive study of the Buddhist social and political teachings may expose the hollowness of such extreme statements : "Buddhism not being concerned with man and his welfare, was equally disinterested in man and his interests. Hence *jurisprudence, politics and economics were not within the purview of Buddhistic ethics*. Its indifference to the caste system, which is iniquity personified, can thus be understood. Buddha was indifferent to the *status quo*. He did not condemn the burdensome and demoralizing domestic rituals, although they were meaningless to him." (Melamed, *Spinoza and Buddha*, p. 272. Our Italics).

and his disciples with regard to political and social questions, it is possible to obtain numerous insights which have a socio-political relevance if the methods evolved by the school of sociology of religion are accepted. One may disagree with Marx regarding his statement that religion is the "reflex" of the social relations but it cannot be doubted that it is essential to be aware of the situational factors amidst the context of which religious propositions have their emergence and their norms get institutionalized. The study of the interrelations of the situational data and the intellectual and moral responses to them does provide notions which are extremely significant for the political and social scientist. Max Weber tried to study the sociology of religion and in the three volumes of his "*Gesammelte Aufsatze zur Religionssoziologie*" he tried an analysis of this type.[1] His broad attempt was to judge the general character of the social structure as being "favourable" or otherwise to the development of the characteristic institutional patterns. I have attempted in some of my papers to demonstrate the interrelations between the contemporary social and economic and political situations and the dominant trends of Buddhist moral teachings.[2] Troeltsch attempts the task "of solving the problem of how far the origin, growth and modifications of Christianity as well as the arrest of that growth in modern times were sociologically determined." He wanted to make comprehensive analysis of the social structure where in particular religious systems arise. My contention is that now is the time not to rest content with merely an intuitive supra-cognitional prophetic attitude to religion but to take up a scientific attitude. If Buddhism and Hinduism are analyzed from the standpoint of sociology of religion, this will be a contribution not only to the history of social and political philosophy but also to the scientific study of the social science. If only the social and political teachings of Buddhism are described in a historical

[1] The second volume deals with Hinduism and Buddhism.

[2] V.P. Varma, "The Sociology of Early Buddhist Ethics", Buddha Jayanti Volume of the *Journal of Bihar Research Society*, 1956. "The Origins and Sociology of Buddhist Pessimism", *JBRS*, Vol. XLIV, June 1958, "The Origins and Sociology of the Early Buddhist Philosophy of Moral Determinism", *Philosophy : East & West* (University of Hawai, April 1965).

fashion then that study pertains to the history of social and political ideas. But if the task of correlation between the environmental data and the emergence of theoretical propositions is attempted then this method has a scientific appearance.

A systematic approach to the study of social and political problems postulates the formulation of the distinction between the observer and the observed. Furthermore the conception of man as an actor and participant in the multiple network of significant activity—patterns is essential. To anyone who has been a student of metaphysics it is clear that the central point at dispute between realism and idealism is this relationship of the percipient and the object. We find this problem dealt with in Buddhism, Berkeley and Einstein. A student of sociology who has never been a student of metaphysics cannot appreciate the implications of this distinction and its significance for the study of the sciencc of sociology. In early Buddhism we can find that the question of epistemology and ontology have been discussed at an advanced level. These discussions provide the theoretical background for social and political insights also. In a traditionalist custom-bound conservative society it is essential to challenge first the metaphysical and religious norms before any attack can be made on customs, conventions and *mores*. This is imperative because social and political practices are rooted in and enveloped by religious ideas and practices. Absolutism tends to support the concept of a motionless being. Since the highest reality is motionless, by analogy, it may be argued that social and political transformations are illusory. The ascendant classes may use absolutism as a philosophical cloak to hide the process of social and political exploitation. The Upaniṣads and Permenides and Plato inculcated sometimes pantheism and sometimes absolutism. This philosophy may sometimes be a method for resisting social and political change. By and large, Indian philosophical absolutism has been hostile to social and political changes. On occasions it may make concessions to ideas which some modern exponents of Brahmanism may exalt into a theory of resistance on behalf of popular rights. The Upaniṣadic idealism supports a philosophy of *status quo* in society. But early Buddhism by its resistence to pantheism and idealism sponsored a point of view which might have supported a dialectical transformation. I do not maintain that early Buddhism was an explicit movement for Kshatriya ascendancy in opposition to the Brahmanical ecclesiasticism.[1] But it is also a historical fact that in the tide of Buddhist advance the people of the lower classes also got opportunities to share in religious movements. The case of Upali, the barber, is a classic example. Individuals and groups tend towards the acceptance of ideas which, at least indirectly, support their interests. I do not uphold the thesis of dialectical materialism which pleads for the view that ideas are the superstructure raised on the basis of the relations of production. Nor do I hold it possible to maintain that all types of acceptance are determined by interests. Ideas, specially in abstract realms of the natural sciences and in logic, are capable of receiving acceptance on their inherent theoretical standing. But conclusions of the historical and social sciences, in the process of the acceptance either by individual research workers or by groups, can be said to bear the impact of one's interests. For example, regardless of the soundness of the historical data and evidence, we find that British imperialist historians tend to regard the Indian movement of 1857 as a local Sepoy Mutiny. But younger Indian intellectuals are on the look out of evidence to substantiate its character as an independence movement. Thus it is possible to argue that towards the teachings of Buddhism the people of those groups must have tended to flock who felt that in some way or the other they were deprived. It will be unrealistic to negative the role of consciously felt deprivations in the acceptance of ideologies. The complicated ritualism as propounded in the *Brāhmaṇas* like the *Aitareya* and the *Śatapatha* as well as the metaphysical absolutism taught in the Upaniṣads were congruous with the interests of the intellectual elite. The latter could alone participate in them. The protest of Gautama Buddha against Vedic revelation, Brahmanical liturgy and the Upaniṣadic absolutism and his enunciation of simple moral

[1] Oldenberg, *Buddha*, seems correct in his view that the relation of Buddhism to Brahmanism is not comparable to that of Lutheranism to Papacy. There was at that time no Brahmanical organised Church, nor did Brahmanism enforce its commands through the instrumentality of the state. The presence of several religious sects in eastern India makes it possible to argue that Gautama did not find himself in the presence of a Brahmanical hierarchy embracing the whole popular life.

truths meant for the extinction of sufferings of the multitude were bound to evoke sentiments of acceptance in the non-privileged sections.[1] If the statements in the Tripiṭakas are to be accepted as authentic propositions regarding Gautama Buddha's theories then it is undoubted that he was hostile to the claims of the Brahmins. He wanted to ridicule the claim of descent from the mouth of Brahmā. But it will also be an unfounded generalisation to maintain that Gautama Buddha was the declared spokesman of the interests of the Kshatriyas. Only this much can be legitimately argued that from his teachings, the under-privileged sections among the Kshatriyas, the Vaisyas and the Sudras got relief.[2] Thus it is possible to utilize the insights gained from the discipline of sociology of knowledge to enquire into the social impact of philosophical teachings.[3]

[1] According to Hermann Oldenberg, *Buddha*, pp. 25ff, it will be an error to consider Gautama Buddha as a declared and conscious champion of the spiritual rights of the poor and the humble. Gautama did not aim at a war against the privileged. Oldenberg would view it as historically untrue to conceive of "Buddha as the victorious champion of the lower classes against the haughty aristocracy of birth and brain." But even Oldenberg cannot deny that the Buddhist confraternity or Samgha was patterned on the principles of equity and justice and that admission to the band of Sramanas was far more open and liberal in contrast with the closed group of the Brahmins. Oldenberg, however, seems correct in his statement that he is not aware of the admissions of *chāndal* and pariahs in the Samgha. Oldenberg tries to minimize the social significance of the ascendancy of Upali in the Samgha by saying that he (Upali) was a barber of the Śakyas and hence was a courtier and friend of the Śakyas, Ed. Caird, *Evolution of Religion*, Vol. I, p. 372, states that Buddhism did not seek to everthrow caste but treated it as an external and indifferent distinction. It dealt with it in the same way in which St. Paul deals with slavery (1 *Corinthians*, vii, 21).

[2] Buddha did condemn some of the Brahmanical practices of the day, for example, astrology Even his indirect opposition to Brahmanical sacerdotalism was calculated to undermine the status of the Brahmins. The opposition to Brahmanism meant that people of the lower strata would be freed from the economic exactions of the Brahmins in terms of *dakshinā* etc. But, of course, Gautama did not contemplate in open revolt against the state and society for the emancipation of the slaves. He missed the chance of becoming an Abraham Lincoln, twenty-five hundred years ago.

[3] Cf. Hegel : "Only in the presence of a given form of religion can a given form of state structure exist, only in the presence of a given state structure can a given philosophy and a given art exist." (Quoted in *Text-*

I think that sociology in its methodological aspects has to lean heavily on science and philosophy. Sociologists are busy these days with the problem of social causation, but if they do not know the metaphysical problems associated with causation, they cannot go deep into their investigations. A sociologist or political scientist who dabbles with positivism and does not know the phenomenalist physics of Mach, Avenarius, Petzoldt etc. is not well-equipped. Causation, for a comprehensive knowledge, has to be studied with reference to the works of Buddhist and Nyaya philosophers of India, Aristotle, Hume and Russell as well as the conclusions of statistics and science. Viewed in this light, if the problem of social and political causation has to be analyzed, then the contributions of Buddhist philosophers also have to be studied.[1] A social and political philosopher in India cannot afford to be ignorant of the Buddhist philosophy. Similarly, if the social and political philosopher wants to investigate the problem of social and political freedom he cannot be blind to the ethical dimensions of the case. If this task has to be approached, then some probe into Buddhist researches regarding determinism and the autonomy of the will have also to be carried on.

MacIver[2] and Hertzler[3] (especially the former) think that there may be social speculation in the ancient (thus including the Buddhist) classics but there is not anything of "sociology" in them. I do hold that the amount of scientific detachment from all theological orientation which is necessary for the development of sociology and a scientifically-oriented empirical theory of political science was not present in Early Buddhist

Book of Marxist Philosophy).

[1] Th. Stcherbatsky, *The Conception of Buddhist Nirvāṇa* (Leningrad, 1927). p. 14, in commenting on the concept of *karman* in the *Abhidhamma-kosha*, II, states that it (*Karman*) is the driving force of nature, which, may correspond with the notion of Evolution or *Elan Vital*. But there does not seem to be present any old textual authority for this "scientific" interpretation. If the Hinayāna metaphysics is interpreted as teaching radical pluralistic momentariness, then it will be absolutely incongrous to reconcile it with the concept of an immanental continuous Energy.

[2] R.M. MacIver, "Sociology", *Encyclopaedia of the Social Sciences*, Vol. XIV.

[3] Joyce O. Hertzler, *The Social Thought of the Ancient Civilizations* (New York, 1936).

India (6th to 4th cent. B.C.) but I do maintain that Buddhist philosophy makes certain vital contributions which should be and can be utilized for the development of a science of sociology and politics. I will summarize them:

(I) Against the Upaniṣadic metaphysical conception of immobile reality, Buddhism formulated the conception of a dynamic reality.[1] Ceaseless becoming is what is real. Illusion or false knowledge is responsible for the view that an entity is perdurable. Buddha, thus, was, in some sense the precursor of Heraclitus, Marx, Engels, and Bergson. A philosophy of historical and cultural change can be constructed only on such a view of mutation and transformation as the constituent of reality.

(II) Against the Vedic theological cosmology,[2] Buddhism, as for example in the *Aggañña sutta* of the *Dīgha Nikāya* tried to construct a naturalistic scheme of the origins of the universe. In some Buddhist passages we find a remote and indirect forestalling of the Kantian Nebular hypothesis. It was unfortunate that this quasi-scientific insight of Buddha was lost sight of by later Hindu philosophers who once again tried to substantiate a completely theistic view of the universe.

(III) Against any theological, metaphysical or intuitive basis of ethics, Buddha tried to forestall Herder, Auguste Comte, Ludwig Feuerbach and the humanists by his view of a non-transcendental religion unconcerned with theology. In his philanthropic concern for human welfare and the extinction of misery without any reference to an extra-cosmic Godhead, he was setting up the theoretical pattern of a somewhat egalitarian society and polity.

(IV) I concur with Small and Ward in their view that sociology is also a science of social betterment. In his *Between Eras: From Capitalism to Democracy* Small advocated the substitution of service for profit as the dominant motive of economic relationships. At one place he condemns the German professors for their support for the first World War. The social telesis of

[1] Against the dominance of absolutism in the Upaniṣads which made their writers sometimes unmindful of ethics, Buddhism and Jainism have been considered "ethico-pluralistic" reactions.

[2] E. Caird, *Evolution of Religion*, Vol. I, pp. 361 ff., holds that Buddhism is primarily a protest against superstitious polytheism with the social disorganization which accompanied it.

Lester Ward deals with the conscious improvement of society. In his *Psychic Factors of Civilization* Ward deals with the prerequisites for the concretisation of collective telesis through governmental agencies. Hence insofar as Buddhism, in its ethics, emphasises norms for real collective advance towards the achievment of individual and social peace and resolution of political tensions it has to be studied by students of sociology also and not left as being only the battle-ground of ethicists quarreling over the problems of pain and moral evil.

(V) Moreover, even for a sociological study of the present day Indian social and political movements which are inspired by the teachings of Mahatma Gandhi, it is necessary to study Buddhist ethics[1] which was the most determined attempt to inculcate the concept of a moral natural law governing the world upon the minds of the Indian population.

(VI) There is an attempt in modern sociology to understand the structure and dynamics of human action in terms of interests, subconscious layers of the psychic structure, feelings etc. In this connection, I think, the study of the Buddhist view of "Dependent Emergence" (*pratityasamutpāda*) would provide a related field.[2] The significance of the "*Upādāna*" or doing action with desire or egoistic motivation has to be grasped. *Bhava* (previous existence), *Jāti* (birth) and *Jarāmaraṇa* (old age and death) depend sequentially on it. It, thus, stresses the notion of psychic structuralization as an antecedent to the actual occurrence of concrete action. It emphasizes that motivation has to be taken account of. It may even be partly compared with Ratzenhofer — Small formula of "interests."

It is clear that the application of the modern methodological approaches to the study of early Buddhism reveals important insights. It indicates the ways in which the students of political science and sociology can study early Buddhism and make contributions to their own disciplines. Some of these standpoints can be thus summarized:

[1] V. P. Varma, *The Political Philosophy of Mahatma Gandhi and Sarvodaya* (Agra, 1965), 2nd ed., pp. 83-84.

[2] The doctrine of *svabhāvavāda* inculcates the production of effects out of the immanent teleology of the causes. But while accepting the universal effectiveness of the law of causation, *pratityasamutpāda* accepts the dependence upon certain condition as necessary for the effect to happen.

(1) A contribution to the "sociology of Buddhist religion" can be attempted and this would be in line with the sociological attempts of Max Weber and Troeltsch with regard to Christianity.[1]

(2) Such a study will be a contribution to "sociology of knowledge" insofar as it tries to trace the genesis of some of the concepts of Buddhist ethics and psychology in the contemporary economic and political conditions.[2] So far Buddhist scholars have attempted only a historical genesis of its philosophy.

(3) The Buddhist emphasis on moral actionism can be the necessary background for the concretisation of the aspirations behind the United Nations. It is very true that Buddhism cannot provide the detailed solution of social and political problems at institutional levels. No recipie can be obtained from it for the resolution of day-to-day affairs of a complicated world. But the immense value of Buddhism lies in stressing the moral background of political, economic and social problems. Its plea for the elevation of moral personality can alone be the solid citadel on which political, economic and social peace can be built. Thus alone can stability be obtained in the structure

[1] Th. Stcherbatsky, *Nirvāṇa*, pp. 11-12 has discussed the Buddhist cosmography according to the *Abhidhammakosha* of Vasuvandhu. The inhabitants of the *chaturdhyānaloka* do not need clothes because they are born with a light ethereal covering that lasts all their very long life through. They do not want any residential constructions because *karman* provides to the newly born houses. The phenomenon of sex is spiritualized, so to say, and the new born baby is apparitional (*upapāduka*) and does not come out of the matrix of a female. No coercive governmental mechanism is needed because in the absence of gross passions there are no crimes. The feeling of hatred is absolutely non-operative. In commenting upon these details Stcherbatsky opines that this scheme is constructed with the notion that physical labour is the curse of humanity. Hence a state of existence is imagined where food, clothes and dwelling-houses do not present any problem. Dharma is the sole incentive to action. Among the inhabitants, however, there is not absolute equality. Sometimes a *pṛthagjana* can appear among them.

[2] Some correlation has been attempted between the feudal social structure of Egypt and its feudal conception of the hierarchy of gods. Similarly it is said that the Temple organisation in Babylon was paralleled by the similar organisation of the state.

of civilization. The moral and psychological aspects of even such concrete events as the proletarian and peasant revolts in Asia and Russia or the national upsurge in Africa cannot be lost sight of. The Buddhist scriptures, and specially the *Dhammapada* and the *Sutta Nipāta* preach in moving terms the concepts of charity, humility, love for the human kind and exalted philanthropy. Their stress on the neutralization of the ego can alone be the background for the solution of the detailed social, economic and political problems. According to Buddhist teachings individual betterment is the means of and basis for socio-political advance. If early Buddhism is interpreted in this way then its outlook has resemblance to the philosophy of the UNESCO which holds that war begins in the minds of men and hence necessarily preaches the primacy of culture and education for the remaking of human personality. Early Buddhism would also advocate that good men are social assets. Mere hedonistic utilitarianism which is the generally prevalent psychological view of most of modern professors of sociology and political science in the West and of the quantitative statisticians has to be supplemented with the moral insights of Buddhist philosophers. It will be a contribution to political science and sociology as applied disciplines if the Buddhist technics for the elimination of conflict and the enforcement of social solidarity and cooperative mutualism are found out and investigated.[1] After their theoretical meaning and implications have been spelled out, it will be possible to implement them in action.

(4) By its treatment of metaphysics and sociology together. this type of intellectual enterprise is a warning to the narrow academic dogmatists who care only for specialized researches. These are most welcome but an integration of the propositions formulated by the specialized sciences has also to be attempted if man is to be viewed as an integrated being and society an integrated unit. To understand the theories of climatic, racial or physical determinism it is essential for the student of the social sciences also to know the metaphysical meaning and implication of determinism. Similar is the case for causality.

[1] Monier-Williams, *Buddhism*, pp. 51-52, says that the preaching of the doctrine of universal brotherhood open to all constituted the corner-stone of his popularity.

causation demands knowledge also of the philosophies of causation.

(5) It is correct that the application of the modern technics would clarify the nature of early Buddhism as social philosophy but it is to be noted that social sciences have to borrow the "rational" method of social and political philosophy. Moreover, sociology would lose much of its historical vitality if it traced its origin only with Comte or Spencer or the Scottish moralists. The ancient Hindu, Buddhist and Western philosophies — both metaphysical and social — can make substantial contributions in the shape of their insights. Hence it will not be worthwhile to neglect the theories and propositions of the social and political philosophers of the world on the ground that they do not follow the value-free methods and technics of the modern behavioural sciences and systems analysis.

Thus the relevance of the study of early Buddhism for the student of the social sciences is evident. Such a study will be a contribution to the history of social thought. If a comprehensive conception of the science of sociology is upheld, then such a study may also be conceived as pertaining to the domain of sociology. At least, so much may be conceded by all that this study will be a contribution to the history of sociological theory. Even the most sophisticated advocates of a "pure" objective science of sociology will grant that early Buddhism will provide a fertile field for the application of the methods and technics of sociology of religion and sociology of knowledge. The student of political science may undertake a study of the power structure and leadership in the Buddhist Samgha. He may try to differentiate between the approaches to political power of Gautama Buddha, Machiavelli and Hobbes. A comparative study of the Buddhist and Marxian dialectic may also be undertaken.

APPENDICES

APPENDIX 1

BUDDHIST NIHILISM

1. *Philosophical Factors for the Emergence of Nihilism*

THE PHILOSOPHIC intellect has been busy throughout the centuries in unravelling the nature of cosmic and supracosmic reality. Indian thought from the days of the *Ṛgveda* to modern times has been concerned with the quest of the supreme real. When the thinker, however, sees the futility of all his endeavours to find out the supreme truth he is driven towards nihilism (*śunyavāda* or *sarvavaināśikavāda*) which is the cry of philosophic despair. It is very difficult for a thinker to remain content with the position that knowledge of the final reality cannot be obtained. He wants to go beyond the *causa efficiens* and to comprehend the infinity of God as the *causa finalis.* Those aspects of religious theism which preach the absolute transcendence of God for man's intellect engender in him a spirit of futility and despair. For T.H. Huxley and Otto Neurath metaphysics may be futile but both the human mind and the human heart hanker after final metaphysical knowledge. To Kant the noumena are unknowable, and Hamilton and Bradley have drawn agnostic implications from the view that all knowledge is relative but even today we find that metaphysics has revived in the forms of neo-Thomism, existentialism, neo-Vedāntism etc. Thus it appears that if one supposes that agnosticism can be a permanent attitude he is mistaken. The natural consequence of agnosticism, if held long, is nihilism. It may be hazarded that Buddhism arose as a natural corollary to the agnosticism present in some passages of the Tripiṭakas. Thus nihilism may emerge as the culmination of the weariness engendered by upholding an agnostic position. The human heart has an inherent and persistent desire to grasp the utter truth and hence probings into the nature of the *sat* and the *asat* keep on going regardless of the warning of some thinkers that the real is indeterminable.

In the *nāsadiya* hymn of the *Ṛgveda* all determinations like *asat*, *sat*, *rajas*, *vyoman* etc. are denied so far as the primal state is concerned. In spite of the predication of *tadekam* as *ānīdavātam*, the hymn ends on a note of scepticism when it says that the absolute superintendent (*adhyakshah*) of the cosmic process seated in the highest heavens even, may not know how the *visṛishti* has eventuated. The Upaniṣads also could not afford a logically satisfying answer to the quest for eternal reality (*nāyamatmā pravacanenā labhyah na medhyā*) and hence they stressed the necessity of mystic realizations. The infinite magnitude of absolute *brahman* or of the *tathatā* who is beyond all empirical predications and cognitive categorisations does not satisfy the 'hard-boiled' realist and the intellectual who wants something more palpable and concrete than an indeterminable indescribable real which is removed from the *catushkoti — sat*, *asat*, *sadasat* and *nasadnāsat*. It is said by the supporters of the mystic view that supersensuous realizations would satisfy all doubts and convince the aspirant of the futility of mundane endeavours. But the human intellect refuses to be satisfied with abstract mysticism which points an entity so rarefied and ethereal[1] as to elude all solid concrete grasp of it.[2] Its utter abstraction repels the concrete intellect. Hence Hegel says:

> "But this mere Being, as it is mere abstraction, is therefore the absolutely negative: which, in a similarly immediate aspect is just Nothing. Hence was derived the second definition of the absolute; the absolute is the Nought. In fact this definition is implied in saying that the thing-in-itself is the indeterminate, utterly without form and so without content, — or in saying that God is only the supreme Being and

[1] Some Hindu interpreters with Advaitic leanings interpret Nāgārjuna to be the exponent of a transcendental reality and truth (*Paramārtha-satya*) which is utterly beyond mental and extra-mental predications and is so indeterminable that it cannot be said even to be real or sat.

[2] Sri Aurobindo seems to be aware of this danger implicit in abstract mysticism. Hence he interprets the *Chit* (free and all-creative self-awareness of the Absolute) as a power not only of knowledge but of expressive will, not only of receptive vision but of formative representation; the two are indeed one Power. For *Chit* is an action of Being, not of the *Void.*

nothing more ; for this is really declaring Him to be the same negatively as above. The Nothing which the Buddhists make the universal principle, as well as the final aim and goal of everything, is the same abstraction."[1]

Even if one were not to accept any kind of naïve corporeal materialistic realism, one cannot help feeling that Advaitic mysticism lands one into an abstract forced unity and when the concrete intellect cannot lay claim to any mystic vision of the transcendent it comes to beware of the formidable reality of the *brahman*.

There is a further sense in which mystical absolutism may directly foster the development of nihilism. By positing the total loss of all sensation and empirical cognition in the super-conscious state, a mystical metaphysics necessarily prepares the ground for the denial of all empirical phenomena. The logical criticism of all empirical categories makes the worldly phenomena appear divested of all solidity.[2] Thus both the affirmation of the supernal absolute and the rigorous denial of all empirical particularities appear to be very near nullity and so the concrete intellect finds itself completely forlorn and hence at last it may seek shelter in nihilism. This nihilism applies only to the particularities of the phenomenal world. Both in the mysticism of Eckhart and the highest *jhāna* (concentration) of Buddha there are such negativistic implications so far as the mundane sphere is concerned.[3]

Thus, in a sense, both agnosticism and mysticism generate nihilism. Agnosticism fails to satisfy the realist. It can never be an abiding attitude. On the other hand, the concrete intellect does not find satisfaction in mysticism either, and may not feel enamoured of the technics of Yoga for the development of a transcendent vision. Similarly, it is also unbelievable that after

1 Hegel, *Logic* (E.T. by Wallace), p. 161.

2 Physical science demonstrates the presence of a harmonious rhythm in the cosmos but idealistic philosophy denies the absoluteness of the world. Even a modern neo-Hegelian like F.H. Bradley criticized the reality of the world and showed that the various categories are infested with contradictions. The concrete intellect feels bewildered when the reality of the world is sought to be challenged and in despair it lands himself in nihilism.

3 George Grimm, "Christian Mysticism in the Light of the Buddha's Doctrine", *Buddhistic Studies* (ed. by B.C. Law, Calcutta, Thacker Spink & Co., 1931), pp. 776-777.

death the soul contemplates the archetypal ideas as Plato imagines in several of his dialogues.

A third method to unravel the nature of the world and the source of its origination is intellectual riddle. Zeno's criticism of motion appear dogmatic and his attempt to demolish the notion of motion from human experience only excites a sense of curiosity but does not satisfy the intellect.[1] Thus along with Spencerian-Kantian agnosticism, and Upaniṣadic-Aśvaghosian mysticism, the riddles of Zeno also cannot assume the satisfying character for which the human heart aspires and for which the human mind has an inherent urge. The failures of agnosticism, mysticism and Zenoism at different periods in the history of human thought prepare the atmosphere in which nihilism arises.

There are sociological factors also for the emergence of nihilism. Nihilism appeared in the writings of Pisarev, Dobrolubov and Chernyshevsky in Russia. Russian nihilism was a natural reaction to the failure of the reformist plans of the Russian politicians. Nihilists, hence, preached a crusade against all cultural values.

2. *Origins of Buddhist Nihilism and Nāgārjuna*

The roots of Buddhist nihilism[2] lie not merely in the sporadic statements of the Tripiṭakas where absolute negation is sanctioned, but in the further past where non-existence is posited, sometimes even as an entity. The *Ṛgveda* says that in primeval times existence was born out of non-existence.[3] The *Chhāndogya*, at least in one of its passages contains such a view.[4] The *Kathopanisad* contains a reference to eschato-

[1] H. Jacobi (*JAOS*, XXXI, No. 1, p. 1), has suggested a comparison between the Mādhyamika dialectics of Nāgārjuna and the sophisms of Zeno.

[2] A.B. Keith, "Pre-Canonical Buddhism". *The Indian Historical Quarterly*, Vol.XII, March 1936, pp. 1-20, mentions three consecutive stages of Buddhist thought-*pudgalanairātmya, śunyavāda* and *vijñānavāda.*

[3] *Ṛgveda*, X, 72.

[4] B.M. Barua, *A History of Pre-Buddhistic Philosophy*, pp. 264ff, says that Uddālaka made an advance upon the notions of Parameshthin (*nāsadiya* hymn of the *Ṛgveda*). Parameshthin approached the problem of Being entirely from the physical standpoint while in the hands of Uddālaka the query *katham asatahsadajāyata* came to be formulated as a logical

logical nihilism.[1] These notions may have strengthened the belief in non-existence or negation as a category. Early Buddhism mentions *samjnāvedayita-nirodha* and this concept prepares the ground for the negation of the percipient consciousness and even for its extinction.

There is parallelism between the nihilistic notions of Buddhism and some of the propositions of Sāmkhya-Yoga. In the Sāmkhya there is a description of the human self when there is a complete cessation of the fluctuations of the mind-stuff. In the Pātañjala-Yoga there is the description of the *asamprajñāta samādhi* when the experiencer realises almost the nothingness of his empirical self (*svarūpaśunyamiva arthamātranirbhāsam*).

Nāgārjuna tries to establish his nihilistic position through the demonstration of the falsity of all concepts[2] like *gati* (motion), *sambhava* (origination), *vibhava* (extinction), casuality, *samsarga* (contact), *jāti* (general characteristics), perception, *samskārāh* (composite entities), time (*kāla*), *svabhāva* (inner essence) , etc.[3] He cannot only propounds the unsubstantiality of the external world of momentary relations but, like the dialectician Nāgasena, rids the self of all autonomous subsistence and denies the reality of fleeting impalpable transient sensations which are in a state of terrific flux. He pursued the dialectical method with a devastating finality till he ended in universal scepticism and denied any specific predication regarding any

doctrine. But, to me, Barua seems to be guilty of hair-splitting. He is wrong in saying that Uddālaka is discussing a logical proposition only. To me, Uddālaka seems to be discussing a cosmological question.

[1] *Kathopanishad*, 1, 21.

[2] Cf. Bradley's critique of empirical categories like things and qualities, space and time, self, motion and causality, relations etc. Hence Stcherbatsky in *The Conception of Nirvāṇa*, p. 52, says: "From the Indian standpoint Bradley may be characterized as a genuine Mādhyamika." See also A.C, Mookerjee, "The Dialectic Method in Nāgārjuna, Bradley and Śriharsha", *The Nature of Self*, pp. 300-304. Mookerjee points out that Bradley steers clear of Nāgārjuna's agnosticism by means of the Hegelian doctrine of degrees in truth and reality. But it is, more or less, an unconvincing subterfuge.

[3] The criticism of causality by the Buddhist philosopher Nāgārjuna would remind the reader of modern Machian positivism and phenomenalistic physics.

entity.[1]

Nāgārjuna argues for the *śunyatā* of all entities and categories[2] from the fact of their dependent origination—*pratītya-samutpāda*. This dependence or conditional character imparts an element of contingency and thus makes the essences (*svabhāva*) unascertainable. In a contingent universe nothing certain can be predicated.[3] The context of the phenomenal universe is constituted by hypostatised relations which lack any fundamental essentiality and substantiality. *Pratyaya* or antecedent determination being only a cluster of momentary *dharmas*, it is the height of anthropomorphic vanity and egoism to search for any absolute self-essence. Eternal nothingness is the primal stark fact in existence.[4] While the Sarvāstivādins (or the Vaibhāsikās) had accepted seventy-five

[1] M. Anesaki, "Buddhist Docetism", *Encyclopaedia of Religion and Ethics*, Vol. IV, (pp. 835-840), p. 838.

[2] In expounding the *Mādhyamika* philosophy, Y. Sogen, *Systems of Buddhistic Thought*, pp. 195-97, refers to three kinds of *śunyatā*: (i) *samaskṛta śunyatā* or the ever-changing state of the phenomenal world, (ii) *asamaskṛta śunyatā* or absolute unrestrictedness of the *noumenal* side of the universe and (iii) *ālamba śunyatā* or transcendental truth. Sogen further says: "we may only grasp the absolute reality or transcendental truth if we earnestly cultivate our mind and body." Poussin, *Journal of Royal Asiatic Society*, 1910, p. 129 and A.B. Keith, *Buddhist Philosophy in India and Ceylon*, pp. 240-245, emphasize the distinction between the *śunya* of Nāgārjuna (as interpreted by Candrakīrti, as distinct from the interpretations of other Buddhists like Bhāvaviveka), and the *vyāvahārika sattā* as posited by Śamkara.

[3] Stcherbatsky, *Nirvāṇa*, p. 52, institutes a comparison between Nāgārjuna's method and that of Nicolas Cusanus and G. Bruno who insist upon the negative method of cognising the absolute. Thus Stcherbutsky imparts a positive interpretation to Nāgārjuna's *śunyatā*. He says that Nāgārjuna made a transition from original Buddhist pluralism to monism. I, on the other hand, repudiate the modern attempt to make Nāgārjuna a positivist. In his enthusiasm, Stcharbatsky criticizes Keith and Wallesar who say that Nāgārjuna denies the reality of the empirical phenomenality of the world and stops at negation and he (Stcherbatsky) goes to the extent of saying that Nāgārjuna believes in a direct intuition of *Dharmakāya* or *brahman* or the One-without a second (*Nirvāṇa*, pp. 52-54).

[4] *anirodhamanutpādamanucchedamaśāśvatam*
anekārthamanānārthamanāgamamanirgamam (*MK, VI*, 1.)
Atmetyapi prajñāpitam anātmetyapi deśitam
Buddhairnatmā na cānatmā kaściditya pi deśitam (*MK, XVIII*, 6.)

infra-atomic subtile elements, the Mādhyamikas took the fatal last step and the *dharmas* were shown to be unreal, illusory and non-existent. Hence while the Sarvāstivādins developed the realistic implications of *pratityasamutpāda* as inter-relationism, the Mādhyamikas interpreted interdependence to imply the negation of intrinsic reality.[1]

Summarizing the position of the Buddhist *śunyavāda of* Nāgārjuna and his various followers the *Sarvadarśanasamgraha* says:

> "The venerated Buddha then having taught that of the illusorily superposed (silver etc.), the basis, the connexion between them, the act of vision. and the *videns*, if one or more be unreal, it will perforce ensue that all are unreal, all being equally objects of negation; the Mādhyamikās excellently wise explain as follows, viz., the doctrine of Buddha terminates in that of total void (universal baselessness or nihilism) by a slow progression like the intensive steps of a mendicant, through the position of momentary flux and through the (gradual) negation of the illusory assurances of pleasurable sensibility, of universality, and of reality."[2]

3 *Criticism of the Positive Interpretation of Mādhyamika Philosophy*

The older orthodox view about *Śunyavāda* has been that it is a nihilistic system and it promulgates the conception of total non-existence. But with the discovery of the Chinese, Japanese and Tibetan Buddhist sources, a re-interpretation of the Mādhyamika system has been made and it is now being imparted a positive connotation. It is being stated now that the *Śunya* of Nāgārjuna is a concept akin to the concepts of *Tathatā* and *Tathāgatagarbha* (as found in the *Lankāvatārasutra*) and all of them either state or imply an Absolute. A second factor responsible for the positive interpretation of the Mādhyamika system has been the unfortunate reading of Hegelian and Bradleyian notions in the dialectic of Nāgārjuna.[3]

I am a conservative in the matter of the interpretation of the

1 But Th. Stcherbatsky seems to be going off the track when he says that *śunyatā-pratītyasamutpāda* is *advayavāda* or monism. While there are monistic and absolutistic elements in the school or *vijñānavāda*, I adhere to the nihilistic emphasis in Nāgārjuna's teachings and am opposed "to interpolate" elements of monistic idealism in Nāgārjuna's philosophy.

2 Cowell, *Sarvadarśanasamgraha* (English translation), p. 22.

3 Stcherbatsky, *Nirvāṇa*, p.52.

Mādhyamika philosophy. The main aim of this system is to propound a middle way between the polar positions of eternalism and annihilationism. Hence I think that it is not possible to identify the *Śunya* of Nāgārjuna and *brahman* of the Vedānta.[1] This system emphatically teaches the absolute futility of all logical predications and categories to characterize either the nature and contents of the objective external continuum or the modality of internal cognition. Hence although this system never sanctions absolute nihilism, its rigorous criticism of logical categories amounts to the acceptance of an almost negativistic position about reality.[2] If the thinkers of this school had even implicit or lurking faith in some form of Being, there was no necessity for them to show shyness or reticence. I do not concur with that view which interprets the concept of *catushkotivinirmukta* as implying some form of Absolutism as the necessary foundation for the experiential continuum to which the concept of *catushkotivinirmukta* is being applied. It is not accurate from a philosophical standpoint to equate the *samsāra* of Nāgārjuna with the "modes" of Spinoza or the "appearances" of Bradley. Nāgārjuna does not refer at all to any absolute nor does he affirm any thing concrete about the world. Hence I feel that in spite of the Buddhist view that annihillationalism is a heresy, Nāgārjuna's position is perilously bordering upon nihilism. It is ridiculous to draw a parallelism between the *Brahman-Māyā* equation of Śamkara and the *śunya-samvṛti* equation of Nāgārjuna.[3] Śamkara's position is far more positive, clear and categorical than that of Nāgārjuna.

There is no validation for the view that the Mādhyamika philosophers believe in an Absolute and also in a trans-empiric state of *nirvāṇa* which was attained by the Tathāgat. The

[1] According to Sri Aurobindo, on the other hand, *Śunya* is that which exceeds our idea or experience of existence.—*The Life Divine*, (New York·ed.), p. 29.

[2] Cf. the criticism of *śunya* by Udayana, Sri Harsha and Vidyāraṇya. The Yogācāras had attacked the notion of the reality of the phenomenal world. Nāgārjuna argued that both the phenomenal (*samsāra*) and the psychic worlds are unreal since both are conglomerations and associations of unreal transient momentary dharmās.

[3] Ashokanath Sastri, "Śunya and Brahman", *Indian Culture*, Vol. I, (1938-39), pp. 271-77. Poussin, *JRAS*, 1910, pp. 129-140.

Mādhyamikas seem to carry the original Buddhistic view of the dynamic fluxional character of the apparent world almost to a position where the phenomenal world seem to evaporate into nothingness.[1] Although technically they seems to characterize the world as belonging to the lower phenomenal *sāmvṛtika* stratum, there is nothing snbstantial and foundational left behind which could have acted as the substructure for this phenomenal world.

I want to repeat that if the Mādhyamika philosophers wanted to show that the world was only partly real and not absolutely non-real, than the word *śunya* that they chose to indicate their position is unfortunate. *Śunyavāda* does not offer any textual ground for the interpretation that it accepts the traditional idealistic theory of a transcendent higher reality and an empirical phenomenal layer which is not definable according to the categories of logic. This view is Vedāntism and not Mādhyamika theory. If the philosophers of this school did believe in some kind of Absolute whose reality they were so anxious to prove indirectly through the rigorous criticism of sensuous experience, I feel amazed as to why they should have felt shy in saying so. It is preposterous to build up a system of absolutistic metaphysics from the *Mādhyamika Kārikā* of Nāgārjuna.[2] Later Buddhist logicians and philosophers obtained from him not absolutism but a devastating dialectic applied to the almost dismissal of the phenomenal world. Hence I do not think it accurate to interpret Nāgārjuna as a metaphysical precursor of Śamkara's Advaitism although the latter was influenced by his philosophical methodology. According to me, the *Mādhyamika Kārikā* either teaches nihilism or is very near such a position.[3] If we impute

[1] M. Anesaki, "Buddhist Docetism" *Encyclopaedia of Religion and Ethics*, Vol. IV, p. 838.

[2] S. Radhakrishnan, in *Indian Philosophy*, Vol. I, p. 644, says that Nāgārjuna offers a more critical account of experience than the Sautrāntikas and the Yogācaras. From the Buddhists he derives a sceptical mood and from the Upaniṣads he has drawn absolutism. I think that the "Vedantification" of Buddhism attempted by Radhakrishnan is a gross betrayal of the critical revolt carried on by Buddha against the Vedantic tradition. If idealistic monism or spiritual mysticism is a valid view it should stand in its own right and it should not require the crutches provided to it by reading these notions in Nāgārjuna's *śunyavāda*.

[3] Śamkara was influenced by the Mādhyamika dialectics and sometimes

positivistic and absolutistic doctrines to Nāgārjuna, we are implying that the great philosopher (Nāgārjuna) was untrue to himself and was a past literary master in concealing his own ideas.

4. *Critique of Nihilism*

There are several inadequacies of the nihilistic thesis. Samkara in the *Brahma-Sūtra-Bhāśhyam*, and Descartes have said that it is impossible to doubt the existence of the self-conscious *ātman* or of the experiencing cogniser. The Sāmkhya dualism is established on the basis of the felt and cognised reality of both the experiencing continuum and the vital potentiality of *prakṛti.* Thus non-existence appears to be a philosophical abstraction. Hence among the exponents of the Vaiśeshika philosophy there was disagreement as to the existence of *abhāva* as a separate primal category.

On epistemological grounds also nihilism appears unsatisfying. It is difficult to ignore the fact of sensation and cognition and these presuppose a dualism. How much soever one may ponder speculatively and condemn the empiric consciousness to *samvṛti* or may regard it as mere appearance (*abhāsamātram*) or mere phenomena (*vyavahāra*) it is difficult to hide from one's self the fact that empirical phenomena thrust themselves upon the thinker every moment of his life and even his death is a demonstration of the portentous sway of physical nature on the too aggressive denying mind. The Naiyāyika realists emphasize the point that the non-controllability of our perceptions and sensations is a demonstration of the might of the external world on the subjectivist thinker. The agonizing and tormenting experiences of the world are too powerful to make any thinker, who claims to have a conscience and is truthful, shudder to maintain the position that the content of the waking world is as intangible, impermanent and unreal as the dream-world. Philosophy should provide a cogent scheme of the universe but mere logical denials of experienced subtotalities and worldly phenomena lead us nowhere. It is difficult for a sane mind to negate the fact of the existence of the atoms and of the Himalayas. Even the *Taittiriyopaniṣad* which is other-

he is regarded as a *prachhanna Bauddha*, S. N. Dasgupta, *Philosophical Essays*, p. 269.

wise idealistic says that *annam* or matter is *brahman* and hence should not be treated with contempt (*annam na nindyāt*). Cosmic phenomena are a vital, even preponderant fact of epistemological cognition and they cannot be denied and neglected since they are concretely experienced. Even on pragmatic and melioristic grounds it can be said that the way for human welfare lies in viewing the world as the manifestation of a supreme spirit rather than in denying the existence of the world.

The religious history of Mahāyāna Buddhism itself is a demonstration of the inadequacy of nihilism. The attempts of Nāgārjuna, Āryadeva and other nihilistic writers could not check the growth of a transcendent conception of super-soul in Buddhism. Even Buddha was regarded as a supernal and immanental highest deity in Mahāyānism. While on the one side, *śunyavādī* philosophers were pointing out the inadequacy of all kinds of positivism, the followers and supporters of Mahāyāna were fabricating a cluster of cults and deities and were raising Buddha himself to the supreme devahood.[1] Thus it appears that although nihilism might have satisfied the intellectual curiosities of a few abstract philosophers there must have been some grave lacuna in it as a consistent philosophy of life.

Sometimes attempts are made to interpret nihilism as a formulation of relativity.[2] But it can be said that if the law of relativity itself is an omnipresent operative existence then it almost assumes the shape or form of an Absolute. Thus total nihilism whether at the highest philosophical level or at the empirical level cannot be substantiated.

[1] In the medieval sect of Mahasukhavādins like the Vajrayāna and the Sahajayāna, *śunyatā* was conceived not only as *anirvacanīya sat* and *chit* but also as *anirvacanīya sukha.* Hara Prasad Sastry traces the influence of the Magi priests, who came to India from the regions round the Caspian Sea, Lake Van and Aral, having fled from these places due to Moslem persecution, in the symbolization of *Mahasukha* in *śunyatā* (*The Indian Historical Quarterly*, Vol. IX, No. 1, March 1933, pp, 340 ff).

[2] Stcherbatsky, *The Conception of Buddhist Nirvāṇa* (Leningrad, Academy of Sciences, 1927), pp. 52-53, stresses the likeness between Nāgārjuna and Hegel. In the *Phenomenology of Mind*, Hegel challenged common sense and said that all that we know of the object is its 'thisness', all its remaining content being only relation. This is the exact meaning of *Tathatā* and relativity is the exact meaning of *Śunyatā.*

It cannot be denied that nihilism shows a spirit of weariness and exhaustion. Nāgārjuna and his followers were keen dialecticians and the subtlety of their thought is remarkable but the element of unsatisfactoriness is writ large upon their thought. Science which probes into the mysteries of nature and reveals its secrets staggers the concrete imagination when it demonstrates the working of laws and the presence of stages and rhythms in the cosmic phenomena. The hair-splitting attempts of the nihilists, on the other hand, showing the inadequacy of the experienced continuum because of the inadequacy of the logical categories appear futile. Not only the concrete intellect but the man of faith who accepts the genuineness of religious experience feels repelled by it. Hence what is needed is a more positive philosophy which can offer a satisfying explanation of the world and man's place in it and can point out the technics through which man can gather the experiences on which he can build an adequate way of life.

APPENDIX 2

ASOKA AND BUDDHISM

POLITICS AND SPIRITUALISM, both, are vital responses to the fundamental instincts and aspirations of humanity. The political process shows the manifestation of man's wish for power, domination and influence and also his pugnacity. Spiritualism indicates the wish for inner culture, moral illumination, inward self-enlightenment and also the aspiration after infinity and immortality. It is possible both at the personal and institutional levels to combine both these types of experiences in a modified form. In ancient Israel, one finds the growth of a theocracy where the secular ruler had some kind of headship over the religious organization and occasionally the religious leader also exercised some political influence. In the Vedas and the Brāhmaṇas there is stress on the synthesis of the *Brahman* and the *kshatra* or the *sacerdotium* and the *regnum*. The Egyptian pantheon of gods was conceived on a feudalistic hierarchical pattern and just as there were nomarchs[1] in the secular world so also the various gods were regarded as being ranged in power and authority.[2] The Mesopotamian temples were several time ravaged because they were also big secular institutions and custodians of wealth. These four examples from the Israelite, Vedic, Egyptian and Mesopotamian history and religious literature are indications of the comingling of politics and religion.

In world history, on the other hand, it is also possible to find moral, religious and spiritual leaders who sometimes participate in the political process and may even cast deep influence over the course of political and social history. Moses,

[1] Nomarchs refer to feudal heads.

[2] Refers to the great temples at Karnak.

Jeremiah, Christt, St. Peter, St. Bernard, Savonarola, Muhammad, Lao-Tse, Confucius, Buddha and Gandhi are such leaders and figures. The impact of these men has been marked on political life, thought and institutions. Sometimes we may also notice the opposite trend when leaders in the secular departments of existence also influence the religious life and activity. In Egyptian history, King Akhnaten led a famous religious movement in favour of monotheism symbolized by the Aten cult. David and Solomon, it appears from the Old Testament, were men of very devout religious feeling but their accesion to political supremacy signified the growth of centralized Hebrew religion. Nebuchadnezzar of the neo-Babylonian empire put a large number of Jews in captivity and placed them within various centres of his empire. It appeared that Judaism was being crushed almost. Cyrus was more liberal and he permitted the return of the Jews from the Baylonish Captivity. After the return, in the post-Exilic period, we find that Judaism was divided into two groups — the old and the new, partly as a consequences of the exile, and this bipartite division had further repercussions on the religious history of the Jews. Charlemagne, although a great political figure, made attempts to convert the Avars and other sections to Christianity.

It is in this comprehensive world-historical perspective that the relations between Asoka (273-232 B.C.) and Buddhism[1] have to be visualized.[2] Asoka's conversion to Buddhism[3] is a phenomenon not only in Indian but in world history. According to Max Weber, the special position of Asoka in the Buddhist Samgha resulted in the emergence of "the beginnings of political

[1] Alfred Hillebrandt, *Alt Indien* (Breslau, 1899), chapter VII, "Konig Asoka".

[2] From various inscriptions it appears that Buddha who in the Tripiṭakas is regarded as *śāstā* and *sārthavāha* was during the time of Asoka represented by the elephant symbol. In the Rock Edict XIII at Girnar occurs "*sabba seto hatthi*", in the Rock Edict VI occurs *seto* ('the White One') and in the Kalsi Rock Edict occurs *gajatame*.

[3] V.A. Smith, *The Oxford History of India*, (1941 ed.), p. 101: "Northern tradition, which was much more likely to be well founded than the tales composed by the Ceylon monks and distorted by theological bias, testifies that the instructor of Asoka in Buddhism was Upagupta of Mathura, son of Gupta the perfumer of Benares."

theory."[1] The pacifistic-moral orientations and implications of the policies of Asoka led to the development of "patriarchal ethical and charitable ideal of a welfare state."[2] The acceptance of the gospel of Sakyamuni[3] had immense political and social effects.[4] The extent to which Asoka impeded the growth of a pan-Asiatic Indian empire and his indirect responsibility for bringing upon the north-west regions of India the invasion of the Bactrian Greeks, because of having neglected the defence of the country under the impact of *ahimsā*, are controversial subjects of historical debates. In this chapter I shall confine myself to analyzing the influences of Asoka upon Buddhists religion and history only — in other words, an attempt will be made here to examine the moral and religious influences of the conversion.[5]

One major influence of Asoka's conversion to Buddhism was the check to the increasing trend towards monasticism.[6] From the 7th and the 6th centuries B.C. monasticism was being lauded as the ideal of life. Jainism and Buddhism exalted renunciation. Early Buddhism painted the terrific predicaments and grim horrors of a man's tragic life in over-rated colours. Henceforth household life was regarded as fraught with miseries only and meant, therefore, only for the ignorant. Kauṭilya in his *Arthaśāstra* banned unlicensed mendicancy and forbade the appearance of Buddhistic monks at sacred ceremonies.[7] If the *Arthaśāstra* is regarded as pre-Asokan, then it would imply that in the centuries previous to the conversion of Asoka, Buddhist

[1] Max Weber, *The Religion of India*, pp. 237-238.

[2] *Ibid*, p. 238.

[3] E. Hulztsch, *Inscriptions of Asoka* (1925), pp. xliii-xliv, says: "Asoka's inscriptions fully corroborate the tradition that he favoured Buddhism, and show that he was intimately acquainted with its tenets, legends, and literature."

[4] For Asokan inscriptions, Hultzsch, *Corpus Inscriptionum Indicarum*, Vol. I. E. Senart, *Les Inscriptions de Piyadasi* (2 Vols., 1886). R. Śarmā, *Priyadarshi Prasastayah*.

[5] B.K. Sarkar, *Sociology of Race, Cultures and Human Progress*, p. 275, is mistaken in his exaggerated views when he asserts: "Nor can the famous edicts of the emperor be regarded as manifestoes in favour of Shakyaism. His own cult of Dharma or Duty again was distinct from though based on Shakya's tenets."

[6] Cf. Bal Gangādhar Tilak, *Gita-Rahasya*, p. 582.

[7] *Arthaśāstra*, II, 1.

monasticism had been on the ascendant and must have been occupying the attention of the sensitive souls. There may be some exaggeration in Jayaswal's statement that the birth of Buddhist Samgha was the birth of organized monasticism in the world[1] but his view represents substantial truth. It is difficult to deny the monastic tendency of early Buddhism; Buddha himself typifies the monastic trend in a supreme way. In the great personality of Buddha, the superiority of the monastic life to the householder's way of existence, according to the contemporary opinion, is indicated. But Asoka's conversion to Buddhism is a landmark in the history of Buddhism because it signified the definite ascendancy of the laity.[2] It is true that earlier also that were important lay figures associated with Buddhism. Bimbisāra (if he was a convert to Buddhism), Ajātaśatru, Pukkusāti of Taxilā,[3] Anāthapiṇḍaka, the famous merchant who did quite a good deal for the economic advancement of the Buddhist Church and Kālāsoka Kākavardhana during whose regime the Buddhist Council met at Vaisāli, had been important lay figures in the history of Buddhism but Asoka was able to establish almost an overwhelming sway on the Buddhism Samgha. If it is not a 'royal rodomontade', then Asoka's pronouncement in Sarnath Minor Pillar Inscription shows that it emanates from a person who claims to wield supreme authority.[4] Asoka's claim seems comparable to the claim made in the title, 'Defender of the Faith'. It is not possible to say if Asoka belonged to any particular sect either of the Theravāda or of the Mahāsamghikas.[5] In the Bhabra

[1] K.P. Jayaswal, *Hindu Polity* (3rd ed. Bangalore), p. 42.

[2] D.R. Bhandarkar, *Asoka*, p. 84, hazarded the fantastic hypothesis that in the tenth year of his reign Asoka became a "*Bhikshu-gatika*." According to the Buddhist tradition, however, about 240 BC Asoka is said to have become a monk.

[3] *Majjhima Nikāya*. According to the *Atthakathā* he was a convert to Buddhism.

[4] V.A. Smith, *Asoka*, pp. 83-84, regards Asokan systems based on Dharma as a theocracy without a god. J.M. Macphail, *Asoka*, (Calcutta, The Association Press), p. 43, "Monk or layman, however, Asoka was evidently the temporal and spiritual head of the Church; he was a Pope with temporal power; he magnified his office as Defender of the Faith."

[5] H. Kern, *A Manual of Indian Buddhism*, pp. 110-112. Asoka stressed amity and concord or *samavāya* and the growth of the essence or

Edict where he expresses his feelings of adoration for the Samgha[1] it appears that he has in his mind the entire Buddhist Samgha as one big organization. Asoka is regarded having summoned the Third Buddhist Council for suppressing heretical trends in the Samgha. From the Sānchi Minor Pillar Inscription it appears that he introduced an amount of officialism in the Church because not only he issues proclamations — *Dhamma-sāvana* and *Dhammānusathi*, and commands (*śāsana*) but he prescribes punishment for those who disrupt the Samgha.

Another influence of Asoka's conversion to Buddhism was the supremacy attached to the ethical factors in religion. In early Buddhism ethical idealism was lauded and this is clear from the stress on the *ārya āshtāṅgika mārga*, the noble eight-fold Aryan path. But the doctrines of the *nāmarūpaskam-dha* and the *pratītya-samutpāda* would indicate that analytical psychology and causationalistic philosophy were also important in early Buddhism. It may even be said that early Buddhistic ethics partly follows from the psychology of the Tripiṭakas. But in the inscriptions of Asoka the ethical side primarily is stressed. The humanist and syncretist teachings of the Asokan inscriptions contain pointed references to the betterment of social relations and stress loyalty and fidelity to one's superiors.[2] According to Rock Edict Eleven, slaves and servants are the objects of kind consideration—*dāsa phataka-mbhi samyapratipati*. Although there is no reference to the extension of *maitrī* in the inscriptions as in the Tripiṭakas, still Asoka emphasizes universalism, philanthropy, benevolence and

sāravriddhi, of religion. He wanted that sectarian spirit — *ātma pāshamda-Vṛdhi*, should be checked. In the pre-Asokan ages, Buddhist sects were multiplying and they claimed to find support for themselves in the different sections of the Buddhist literature. But the Asokan inscriptions have a more liberal spirit. They stress *dhammashadipanā* or religious illumination and transformation.

[1] "You know, Reverend Sirs, how far extend my respect for and faith in the Buddha, the Sacred Law, and the Church. Whatsoever, Reverend Sirs, has been said by the Venerable Buddha, all that has been well said."

[2] The Rock Edicts stress :

(a) *Mātari pitari suśrushā*
(b) *thaira-suśrushā*
(c) *gurūnām apachiti*
(d) liberal and courteous treatment to friends, acquaintances, relations, Brahmanas and Śramanas.

beneficence. He stresses *samavāya bhāva-śuddhi* and the conquest of *pāpa* and *asinava*. Therе is one difference between the ethical teachings or early Buddhism and Asoka. Early Buddhism lays stress on meditation and cognition as preparing the basic foundation for moral conduct and for the transcendence of *avidyā*. There is no mention in the Asokan inscriptions of *nirvāṇa* which has been considered the highest goal or ideal of the *arhat* and which is also the object of the highest endeavours of the *Upāsaka*. This may imply that the ideal of *nirvāṇa* could not be popular. There is reference in the inscriptions to *svarga* or heaven and from this it may be inferred that the pre-Buddhistic popular faith in some spatial superterrestrial land of bliss could not be shaken by years of preaching about *nirvāṇa*. In the Tripiṭakas also there are references to hell and heaven. In the inscriptions the practical and social content of morality is emphasized and the deeper aspects of introspective and subliminal psychology as expounded in the *Abhidhamma Piṭaka* are not mentioned.[1] Asoka does, however, put stress on *Pativekkhā* or self-introspection for purposes of inner purification. These are some aspects of Asoka's positivism and he may be said to have propounded ethical idealism and social betterment of relations without any explicit or implicit acceptance of a metaphysical notion of reality. Asoka's positivism is farthest removed from any deliberate neutralization of the will to live or any exaltation of abnegation. He shows real foresight in having stressed the significance of the ennoblement of social relations and thus having hinted at the significance of social self-communion. His aim is not merely individual emancipation but also the enhancement of the social good or *kalyāṇa-āgama*.

Asoka should not be regarded as a boastful imperialist nor was he a mere superficial royal devotee of Buddhism.[2] He selects six sections or *Dhamma-pariyāya* from the canonical

[1] In view of the fact that there are scholastic elements in the *Abhidhamma Pitaka*, Senart, *Indian Antiquary*, 1891, pp. 264-5, is not correct in stating that till the time of Asoka, Buddhism was "a purely moral doctrine, paying little attention to particular dogmas or to abstract theories, little embarassed with scholastic or monkish elements."

[2] Max Weber, *The Religion of India*, pp. 238, 237 compares Asoka's position to that of the Byzantine monarchs. He also compares Asoka's officers in charge of morals (Dharma) and *stri-adhyaksha-mahāmātras* to

literature[1] and this shows the keenness of his intellect and his firm attachment to moral idealism. These six pieces are ethical in tone. An analysis of them would show that they are normative injunctions to strengthen the social bonds of people and the moral fabric of character. They are not ritualistic or credal in orientation. Asokan inscriptions are resonant with moral and humanist teachings and are singularly free from the superstitious accretions of later Buddhology.

As a Buddhist, Asoka followed the path of non-violence in practical life—*anārambho prānānām avihisā bhutānām*. It is true that Buddha never appreciated the extreme obsession of the Jainas with non-violence, but, nevertheless, he bitterly denounced the bloody sacrifices of the day. In Pillar Edict V, Asoka advocates a moderate and practical view of non-violence.[2] In Rock Edict I, he says that no animal should be sacrificed here (*iha*). The word *iha*, according to some interpreters, refers only to Pataliputra while according to others it contains an injunction forbidding violent sacrifices in entire kingdom. If this latter interpretation is correct then it is a great illustration of the use of political power to implement a species of social and moral reform that was so dear to the moral personality of Buddha.

A third influence of Asoka on the Buddhistic movement was felt in the great advance of the tide of evangelical propaganda.[3]

"Carolingian systems of emissaries and judicial censorship" and to Cromwell's estate of saints.

1 The literary pieces referred to by Asoka are the following:

(*i*) *Vinaya-samukasa*
(*ii*) *Aliya-Vasani* = Ariya-Vamsa (*Aṅguttara Nikāya*, II, 27*i*
(iii) *Anāgata-bhayāns* (*Aṅguttara*, III, 103)
(iv) *Muni-gāthā*=*Muni-sutta* (*Sutta Nipāta*)
(v) *Moneya-sute* = *Nālaka-sutta* (*Sutta Nipāta*)
(vi) *Upatisa-pasina* = *Rathavinita sutta* (*Majjhima Nikāya* I, 146-51).
(vii) Laghulovāda—*Rahulovāda-sutta* (*Majjhima Nikāya*) See D.R. Bhandarkar, *Asoka* (1925 edition), p. 86.

2 V.A. Smith, *The Oxford History of India* (1941), pp. 102-103, "The fifth Pillar Edict expresses the emperor's matured views on the subject of *ahimsā*, or abstention from injury to or slaughter of animals. He indicates his disapproval of the practice of castration or caponing, and publishes many rules for the protection of living creatures."

3 According to the *Census of India*, 1911, Vol. I, p. 125, there were 10,700,000 Buddhists in India including Burma, of which all but one-third of a million were in Burma.

It is difficult to determine the exact number of the inhabitants of India who had embraced Buddhism under the impact of Asokan propaganda. It is doubtful if the majority of the people ever became Buddhists either during the time of Asoka or later. He was no doubt a person of lofty moral idealism and aspirations who renounced unlegitimized coercion but he had also political skill and diplomatic foresight and he utilized the resources of an imperial power to raise Buddhism from a north-east Indian movement eventually to the position almost of a pan-Asiatic religion. In one sense it can be said that Asoka's religious propaganda signified the fulfilment of the prophecy of Brahmā Sahāpati in the *Mahāvagga.* From the time of the *dhammacakkapavattana* to the great decease at Kusinagar, Buddha was engaged in incessant preaching for nearly forty-five years and his wish was that his gospel should spread for the happiness and good of large numbers of people and should enkindle compassion to all living beings.[1] According to Rock Edict VIII, Asoka undertook *Dharmayātra* in place of *Vihāra-yātrā.* In the Nigliva Pillar inscription Asoka states that in the twentieth year of his reign (249 BC.), he visited that place (Nigliva) and had earlier got the *stupa* of Buddha Konkamana enlarged (243 BC.). This shows that the creed of "previous Buddhas" had flourished in the days of Asoka. Asoka, it appears from the inscriptions, made vigorous efforts for making Buddhism a success not only in India but even in foreign lands like Greece and Macedon. His mission to Ceylon sent under the leadership of his son Mahendra and daughter Sanghmitrā was an epoch-making event (between 258 to 230 BC.). It may be that Buddhist preachers were also sent to Tibet. If so, then it is possible to state that Tibet had received the impact of early Hinayānistic Buddhism also, besides receiving in later periods the influence of developed Māhāyanism. Tibet in that sense may be said to have served the mirror where the successive developments of Buddhism in India were also reflected.

Asoka established cordial relations between India and the

[1] H.G. Wells, *The Outline of History* (1931 edition), p 451 : "Moreover, in the third century BC when King Asoka was ruling India in light and gentleness, the Romans were reviving on Etruscan sport, the setting on of slaves to fight for their lives."

countries of western Asia. His agents carried missionary operations in Syria, Egypt and Cyrene, and Macedonia and Epirus. Asoka claims to have effected 'conquest by the Law of Piety' in the realms of the Greek king Antiochos and of Ptolemy (Turāmaya), Antigonās (Aṃtekina), Magas and Alexander. His missionary activities thus extended to Western Asia, North Africa and Eastern Europe. In these countries efforts were also made for the spread of Buddhism. Christian writers complain against the lack of ethical element in Buddhism because it taught a philosophy of world-and-life negation. But it can be pointed out that original Buddhism taught universal compassion and Asoka's evangelical work and his successful efforts for establishing two kinds of *cikitsā* (building hospitals) for men and even animals show that he made concrete efforts to give to the Buddhist teachings a positive social shape. The propaganda of Buddhism in Western Asia had some influence also over Judaism. The pre-Christian monastic sects of the Essenes and the Theraputae (often identified with the Theras or elders of Judaism) bore some amount of Buddhist influence.

Nevertheless, it is a historical fact that the success of Buddhist propaganda in Western Asia was not so effective. It is a great problem of historical research to find out as to why Buddhism which flourished so successfully and so widely in China, Japan, Tibet, Siam, Burma, Ceylon and other areas of the East failed to obtain a foothold in Western Asia. This appears still more intriguing a problem because from the Asokan inscriptions it appears that preaching activities for the spread of the Buddhist gospel were carried on only in Western Asia and the adjoining regions. They contain no reference to any evangelical activity in the eastern lands. Thus the historical problem is to determine all those reasons, as to why in spite of the evangelical efforts of Asoka in Western Asia and despite some initial success attained in the shape of Buddhist influence on the Essenes and the Theraputae and possibly also on Christianity, it was Eastern Asia which became the real home and centre of Buddhism for nearly over a millenium and half.

Two possible hypothesis in this connexion may be suggested here which, of course, would need further exploration. First, it might be that Buddhist propaganda in Western Asia might have been looked upon with an eye of doubt and suspicion because it was associated with the religious efforts of a powerful monarch of a big neighbouring country. The religious and moral import of the evangelical movement might have been thus lost sight of and doubts and fears might have been entertained regarding its possible adverse political consequences. The second hypothesis, of greater historical relevance, may also be suggested. In the post-Asokan period Bactria and Parthia developed as powers and there were foreign invasions from these areas on the north-west regions of India. It seems believable that the daughter Buddhist centres in Western Asia lost touch with the fountain-spring of the mother country and in the absence of the continuity of inspiration brought about by the protracted political conflicts in the north-west portions of India they possibly perished and thus the story of the Buddhist evangelization in Western Asia was brought an end to.

Another area in which Asoka sought to introduce Buddhism was that of the Atavyās — the foresters.

After the death of Asoka who had done so much for the strengthening of the power and authority of the Buddhists Samgha as also for the evangelical propaganda of this creed, there was a Brahmanical Revival.[1] The *Mahābhārata* in its present form as redacted for the second time after the intrusion of the foreigners in India from the 2nd century B.C. to the 2nd century A.D., shows definitely signs of the reassertion of the old ritualistic creed and cult. The Renupali inscription of the Sungas shows signs of Brahmanical revival. One possible reason for the reaction against Buddhism and the revival of the Brahmanical creed may be that possibly due to its being associated with the monarchical patronage of Asoka, the Samgha became contaminated with regal and aristocratic affiliations and thus, to some extent at least, it might have forfeited the sympathies of the people.[2] Thus, at least partial secularization of the Buddhist Samgha, due to its having

[1] James M. Macphail, *Asoka*, p. 49, is of the view that the prohibition of animal sacrifice "must have given great offence to his Hindu subjects."

[2] T.W. Rhys Davids, *Buddhism*, p. 222, holds that Asoka's conversion to Buddhism and his large-hearted benefactions and donations to the Samgha were "the first step on the downward path of Buddhism; the first step on its expulsion from India."

accepted the superiority of Emperor Asoka was a factor also of weakeness and might have led to the loss for the Buddhist cause of some amount of popular sympathy.[1]

[1]Max Weber, *The Religion of India*, p. 240, discusses the linkage of Buddhism to patrimonial kingship. For patrimonial kingship, Buddhism appears valuable as "a means of mass domestication" and it was related to Asoka's policy of purposeful opposition to the ruling strata.

APPENDIX 3

BUDDHA AND DAYĀNANDA

THE POWERFUL personality of Buddha effected a social, intellectual and moral revolution in the East. Some scholars find even on Christianity and West Asiatic religion and philosophy Buddhist influence.[1] Vaishnavite Hinduism made him an 'Avatāra'. Dayānanda (1824-83) the iconoclast has not met with that amount of popular recognition but impartial critics do acknowledge his services as a saviour of Hinduism and as a prophet of Indian Nationalism.

1. *Vedism and Anti-Vedism*

These two personalities had fundamentally different approaches to the problems of human life and destiny. Buddha was an ethical idealist and a Nirvānist. He had no belief in any dogmatism or supernaturalism or revelation.[2] He hurled a great challenge against the theory of Vedic infallibility. He was shocked at the contemporary cult of violent sacrifices and the degeneracy of the Brahmins — the self-appointed and selfish custodians of Vedic scholarship. The practice of invocations to the various Vedic and popular deities did not attract him.[3] He

[1] According to Richard Garbe, the story of Simeon, the Temptation, the reference to Peter walking on the ocean and the miracle of the loaves and the fishes are illustrations of the borrowings by the writers of the Gospel from Buddhist mythology. — "Some Aspects of the Philosophy of Buddha", *Proceedings of the Eighteenth Indian Philosophical Congress*, 1943 (Lahore).

[2] Both Buddha and Hegel were opposed to pure transcendentalism. Hegel ridiculed ethereal transcendentalism. Buddha also rejected the notion of a transcendent extra-cosmic Godhead. Kern, on the other hand, in *A Manual of Indian Buddhism* (1898), refers to the 'mystical and transcendental systems of Vedanta and Buddhism.

[3] H. H. Wilson, "Buddha and Buddhism", *Journal of the Royal Asiatic Society*, 1856, pp. 259-60, 357.

compared belief in the Vedas to *andhaveṇu-paramparā*.

Dayananda's cry was perfect Vedism. He proclaimed the revelatory character of the Vedic Samhitās and wanted to solve the problems of life in accordance with the Vedic canons. His seer-vision found in the ancient code of Aryan wisdom the words of God himself and hence emerged his rock-like faith in the Vedas.[1] We feel that since the days of the Vedic Samhitās there has not appeared in the world any greater emotional protagonist of the Veda (Vedic Samhitās) than Dayānanda. With the zeal and energy of a St. Paul and Luther combined, his whole life was a concentrated dedication at the altar of the Veda. I personally do not uphold the doctrine which Dayānanda proclaimed — that the Veda contains the entire amount of knowledge. But we do acknowledge that the Vedas have something important to say about mysticism, philosophy and social organisation. Buddha's criticisms of the Vedas seem partial and one-sided and indicate his dialectical orientation.

2. *Metaphysics and Mysticism*

Dayānanda was a devotee and a theist, He, like Rāmānuja and Mādhva, repudiated the Advaita Vedāntic distinction between the absolute of metaphysics (*nirguṇa*) and the God of theology (*saguṇa*) — impersonal and personal God. The God of Dayānanda has all the essence and all the predicative determinations of the Vedāntic *brāhman* and *iśwara* combined. He believed that the highest degree of *asamprajñāta samādhi* revealed *almost* the identification of the human ego and the transcosmic Godhead. But even in the states of highest *mukti*, there does exist a separation between the soul and God. Hence the ancient Upaniṣadic formulas which state *ayamatmā brahman*, and *tattavamasi* are only metaphorically[2] but not literally correct.

Buddha believed in *samādhi*. He was a Yogi and meditative contemplation culminating in the loss of a finite ego-sense is

[1] Cf. A. J. Davis (of America), *Beyond the Valley*, p. 382 (quoted in *Dayānanda Commemoration Volume*, p. 283).

[2] Regarding the four great statements, *prajñānam brahman, aham brahmāsmi, tattvamasi* and *ayamatmā brahman*, Dayānanda views them as examples of *tātsthyopādhi* and *tatsāhacaritopadhi*. Dayānanda, *Satyārtha-prakāsha*, Chapter VII.

the final step in his Yogic system.[1] He was not explicit with regard to any ultimate being which, possibly, is intuited in the state of *samādhi.* Mystics all the world over testify to the realisation of some universal truth in the state of suprarational consciousness. But Buddha gives no hint that he accepted the possibility of the cognition or realization of an ultimate existent in the state of Yogic *samādhi.* He has explicitly denied the primal creative agency of a personal God. It seems that his Yoga is comparable to the Yoga contemplated in the atheistic Sāmkhya which teaches that meditation results only in a discrimination between "Matter and Purusha."[2]

3. *Psychology*

Dayānanda dismissed the Vedantic theories of the soul, which maintain it to be either one in essence with *brahman,* or only partially different from *brahman.* He advocated the eternal difference of soul and God and pointed out that even in the state of Mukti, the soul retains its distinction from Brahman, due to its possessing the "powers of the internal organs". He believed in a theory of return from Mukti — which may be considered a new contribution to eschatological thought. Unlike the Sāmkhya-Yoga and Mimāmsā, Dayānanda believed in the soul as being of atomic size. He ruthlessly did away with the Jaina conception of a soul which views it as equal in size to the structure of the body.

Buddha did not believe in a separate psychic ego. He denied the concept of a spiritual human soul. Instead of the extreme standpoints of annihilation (*ucchedavāda*) and the permanent continuity of the soul (*śāsvatavāda*) he advocated a via media — the procession of a stream-of-consciousness-states (*vijñāna-*

[1] E. J. Thomas, *The Life of Buddha,* p. 173, says that it is this "way of escape fram pain, with the attaining of a permanent state of repose which, as a course of moral and spiritual training to be followed by the individual, constitutes Buddhism as a religion."

[2] The Yoga of Buddha may have also some resemblances with the pre-Buddhistic religious system of China because there too, belief in ethical life was maintained without reference to any supreme Deity. Stressing the difference of the Buddhistic system of salvation from the Jaina or Brahmanical, E. W. Hopkins, *The Religion of India,* p. 298 ff. says that knowledge is wisdom to the Brahmin, asceticism is wisdom to the Jaina, while purity and love is the first wisdom to the Buddhist.

saṁtāna). Some of the later Buddhistic sects like the Vātsiputriyas and the Sāmmitīyas believed in a soul. But Buddha did not believe in any kind of soul although it is clear that the doctrines of transpsychosis and *karmaphala* do not legitimately suit a doctrine of soullessness. The Buddhist view of a consciousness-stream without any spiritual substratum has been compared with the doctrines ("psychology without a soul") of William James and Bertrand Russell.

We feel that human thought is still groping in the dark about the concept of the human soul and the reality of an absolute spirit. The Islamic and Christian religions believe in the creation of the soul by God and accept only one terrestrial life. More or less, they adhere to the notion of the destruction of the living soul after death, but maintain simultaneously its mysterious survival in the grave, which may appear to be a revival of the belief of the Egyptians that the 'double' inhabited the pyramidal grave. Modern scientists are accepting some kind of an all-pervasive energy and the electro-magnetic theory has changed the former notion of static matter-stuff. Materialism in the old eighteenth century sense is no longer recognized. On the other hand, it will be hazardous to state that modern science gives any hints for the acceptance of a spiritual ultimate. There is no objective evidence for the survival of the soul as a substance after physical extinction. They who blieve in a spiritual continuity after death do so either on the basis of scriptural testimony or on the authority of religious teachers or on the basis of unverified subjective experience. If the soul were such a persistent spiritual entity there must have been more concrete evidences of its continuity after the destruction of the physical tenement. In my sceptical moods I sometimes tend to view the doctrine of the soul as a gigantic long-continued attempt at self-deception. Man is terrified at the prospect of extinction and hence he believes in a spiritual continuity after death. The concept of the human spiritual soul as ultimately only a reflection or limitation of the Brahman is also not satisfying to the realistic intellect.

4. *Views Regarding the Universe*

Dayānanda was a realist. He believed in an independent eternal *Prakṛti* as did the Sāmkhyas. But he also believed in a creator God who arranges matter. He believed in the cosmological argument for theism. He also advocated that the manifest immanental teleology and purposiveness of the world is a very strong ground for the support of theism. He stated (like Aristotle) that there was a cyclic recurrence of creations and destructions on the basis of the Vedic authorities — *suryācandramasau dhatā yathāpurvamakalpayat*. He refuted the Semitic conception of only one creation as unsatisfying to the logical intellect because it could not explain moral differences. The *Purusha Sūkta* which is the basis of Dayānanda's cosmology is unscientific because it makes all creatures and all castes spring from the supreme sacrifice. The sun and the moon are made to appear simultaneously; this is another scientific incongruity.

Buddha also believed in a realistic cosmogonic scheme. But the various processes of the growth of the universe which have been outlined in the *Aggaññya Sutta, Dīgha Nikāya* are comparable to the notions of the Greek thinker Empedocles and they do not have much value in the light of modern scientific knowledge with regard to cosmogony and cosmology. There is a passage in the *Samyutta Nikāya* which refers to the eternity of the world process:[1] "The pilgrimage (*samsāra*) of beings, my disciples", Buddha says, "has its beginning in eternity. No opening can be discovered, from which proceeding, creatures, mazed in ignorance, fettered by a thirst for being, stray and wander."

5. *Ethical Idealism*

Buddha's main contribution to world thought was a supreme insistence on suffering and on the purity of a moral life to be attained by psychological culture. The Vedāntic doctrine of the realised saint as being free from "*pāpa*", and "*pūṇya*" was unfortunate because the people could not understand its metaphysical significance, and ethical transcendence from the philosophical standpoint could be vulgarised to sanction ethical nihilism and a life of moral anarchy. We find mention of the

[1] The following passage from the *Viśuddhi Magga* (quoted in S. N. Dasgupta, *A History of Indian Philosophy*, p. 88 is, however, more nihilistic: "but just as when a lute is played upon, there is no previous store of sound; and when the sound comes into existence it does not come from any such store; and when it ceases it does not go to any of the cardinal or intermediate points of the compass....in exactly the same way all the elements of being, both those with form and those without forms, come

non-ethical and even immoral doctrines of Pūrṇa Kaśyapa and Ajita Keśakambala in the *Dīggha Nikāya.* But to Buddha, the four Āryan truths were meant not merely to distract man's minds from a worldly life by emphasizing cosmic suffering as is fancied by scholars like Radhakrishnan, but were gospels to be even mystically comprehended in the processes of *dhyāna* and *samādhi.* Hence early Buddhism teaches the absolutism of the eight-fold path and the luminous reconciliation and integration of ethics and metaphysics. The *Yoga-Sūtra* of Patañjali also says that cosmic suffering is realised not by the ordinary individual but by the discriminating intellect.

Dayānanda also believed in the great importance of ethics.[1] He never believed in the transcendence of ethical categories because his conception of the supreme Godhead is comparable to Rāmānuja's notion — *aśeshakalyāṇauṇah.* The God of Dayānanda and Rāmānuja is not the attributeless Nirguṇa Brahman but the reservoir of all noble attributes and hence Dayānanda prescribes that one of the ways of the attainment of moral life is the contemplation of the divine attributes.

6. *The Social Philosophy of Buddha and Dayānanda*

The *Purusha Sūkta* seeks to stereotype the contemporary social organisation because it makes the four social divisions spring from the cosmic and the trans-cosmic *Purusha.* But Buddha — the social reformer, the great repudiator of the Brahmanical citadel of orthodoxy and conservatism, accepted only a social and historical origin of the castes.[2]

into existence after having previously been non-existent and having come into existence pass away..."

[1] T.L. Vasvani in his *The Torch-Bearer* points out that Dayānanda was a greater person than Aristotle, Schopenhauer and Tolstoy because he (Dayānanda) was a *tapasvi* and practised the moral norms while the latter were only thinkers and artists. Dayānanda's life is an exemplification of immense will-power directed to the practice of *vairāgya, brahmacarya* and *tapasyā.* Vasvani points out that in the *tapasyā* of his life, Dayānanda was greater than Martin Luther.

[2] K.P. Jayaswal, "Swami Dayananda and Hindu Social Revaluation", *Dayananda Commemoration Volume,* ed. by H.B, Sarda, Ajmer, 1933, pp. 161-63, p. 162, "Dayananda emphasized, on the other hand, the traditional conservative regard for the Vedas and the Vedic culture, but he did not have the limitation of Śankara and rose above it and pronounced

He did not provide any divine sanction for social stratification. To him *varṇa* was a human institution. But *varṇavyavasthā*, since it is contained in the Vedas, which for Dayānanda are the words of God (*apaurusheya*), has a super-human sanction for the latter. I regard Buddha as the greater social revolutionary. Although Dayānanda preached against the doctrine of caste-stratification on the basis of birth, he accepted the four-fold nomenclature — *brahmin, kshatriya, vaiśya* and *shudra*. It is very true that he emphatically maintained that this nomenclature is assumed on the basis of qualitative development and never on the basis of birth, but the very acceptance of the nomenclature itself, which is suffused with centuries-old traditions of caste exploitation, is bound directly and indirectly to lead to the perpetuation of the old legacies of caste dominance and arrogance. Buddha although not a democratic and socialist equalitarian of the modern type, fought more trenchantly against Brahmanical iniquites and false claims to caste superiority.[1]

7. *The Political Philosophy of Buddha and Dayānanda*

Dayānanda was an advocate of Aryanism. He accepted the view of Kaṇāda according to whom the true Dharma was that which gave both mundane prosperity (*abhyudaya*) and soul's salvation (*nihśreyasa*). The ideal of this great Samnyasin was universal political paramountcy (*cakravartī sāmrājya*) as also God-realisation. Dayānanda's programme for social consolida-

that the theory of caste was false, un-Vedic and un-Hindu. Such a thing which was the negation of the laws of Manu and contradiction of the accepted view of the *Purusha sūkta*, would not have been accepted by Hindu society, unless it came from a national type as Swami Dayananda...who could consume the cause of injustice with the fire of his speech like the Buddha, and who could be irresistible in polemics like Śankara."

Dr. Jayaswal is not fully correct because Dayananda interpreted Manu and *Purusha Sūkta* to support *Guṇakarmavāda*. He did not accept the traditional interpretation which brings the *Purusha-Sūkta* and the *Manusmṛti* in support of a hereditary caste system.

[1] E.W. Hopkins, *The Religions of India*, pp. 298 ff. says: "And at the same time the old caste-system oppressed and insulted them. It is evident that the times were ripe for a more human religion and a new distribution of social privileges"

tion and his political and sociological conclusions are contained in the sixth chapter of the "*Satyārtha Prakāsha.*"

The ideal of Buddha was to an extent, one-sided — a recoil from terrestrial life and almost the extinction of all normal worldly life. But Dayānanda prescribed means and measures for political greatness also. The political injunctions of Dayānanda can also be found in his criticism of the Europeanisation of the Brahmo Samaj. Dayānanda had a national instinct and vision and was an advocate of Svadeshi. Buddha lived in days of the full and vigorous independence of India.[1] Both Dayānanda and Buddha had the most intense concern for the good of all life, human and sub-human, as is indicated by their lives of selflessness and dedication.[2] Dayānanda's nationalism was no narrow cult. He wanted the universalisation of the Aryan creed but that was not a programme of political conquest but only signified a scheme of spiritual, moral and intellectual reformation. Like Buddha, Dayānanda also was a missionary.

It was possible that Buddha's desire for the universal spread of his doctrines could be narrowly capitalized to mean political unification of India and its domination over others. Napolean had selfishly capitalized the French revolutionary gospel of universal fraternity to mean only French nationalism. But the extreme Buddhist insistence on the transitoriness and the

[1] B.K. Sarkar, in *The Sociology of Races, Cultures and Human Progress*, pp. 275-76, points out that Buddha was not a recluse. He taught diplomats, merchants, consuls and governors also and offered advice to the confederacy of the Vajjians. He says: "The regular monks and ascetics of the Buddhist organization, they also did not keep wholly aloof from politics. They knew how to take part in intrigues and promote revolutions. They were tried as "*seditionists*" by some rulers and worshipped as "*king makers*" by other. They would band themselves into military orders to be qualified as partisans in civil wars. They were adepts in Jesuitical casuistry too. During the 7th and 8th century e.g. under Harsha, Śaśānka, Dharmapāla and others the political interferences of monk generals were constantly in evidence. The medieval history of China and Japan also afford instances of warfare conducted by Buddhist monks as politico-military divines."

[2] The *Jātakas* contain several stories which represent Buddha as ready to immolate himself for saving the lives of even lower animals. Dayānanda also in his personal career of a *samnyāsin* practised the maxim of nonviolence even with regard to the animals.

momentariness of the world led to an attitude of resignation which weakened the sense of social cohesion and political consolidation in India and hence Asoka and Harshavardhana could not play the roles of Napolean.

Dayānanda's insistence on the independent reality of the world, as opposed to viewing it as a mere game or *māyā* or phantasmagoria has a very great national importance. His plan and programme of social reform and rehabilitation became the precursor of national political progress in modern India. His gospel of the equal rights of all (including the untouchables and the peoples of all the world over) in the Vedic gospel and Vedic studies also has a great national meaning.[1]

8. *Conclusion*

Both Dayānanda and Buddha are great figures in Indian history. Buddha organised the great Samgha which spread over the whole of Asia. Dayānanda founded the Arya Samaj which also has plans for universal evengelisation. Dayānanda had the spirit of the warrior-prophet fiercely battling against all odds and his writings reflect his power and prowess. Buddha was the incarnation of love and compassion and his personality was a great factor in the spread of the Dharma. We feel that the Buddhist doctrines of Godlessness and soullessness could find some great advocates in the tradition-bound, priest-ridden and superstition-dominated land of India only due to the power of his moral personality. Among the great religious teachers of the world Buddha was perhaps the sole dominant figure who almost dispensed with God and soul. From the normal standpoint, this appears as a quaint combination of contradiction. It is a problem as to how could Buddha attain moral eminence and spiritual illumination without the explicit acknowledgement of a God and a soul. How could people be drawn to this system? His personality was the convincing factor for the truth of his teachings. He could not have succeeded if his appeal would have been only intellectual or dialectical.

[1] K.P. Jayaswal, *op. cit*, p. 163: "He wisely, like the Buddha, composed in the most popular vernacular Hindi — the present day imperial Magadhi..." This is another national contribution of Dayananda. He challenged the Brahmanical monopoly of Vedic wisdom and as an intellectual democrat opened its gates to all.

Dayānanda's *tapasyā* cast a halo over his personality. Both Buddha and Dayānanda have infused the might of their stupendous personalities in the make-up of the Indian nation. The synthesis of the character and asceticism of Buddha with the physical might and moral intellectual light of Dayānanda is a great ideal to be achieved.

APPENDIX 4

BUDDHA AND SRI AUROBINDO

Introduction: Personality and Influence

GAUTAMA BUDDHA was the most dynamic personality of the ancient world and there are only a few great men of history who can be placed in his rank. His greatness and the supremacy of his overwhelming goodness have imparted to him a position and status almost unchallenged. His influence still pervades over and permeates the thought and civilization of the East. His critical revolt against the Vedic tradition almost revolutionized the concepts of Indian philosophy. His magnanimity and depth of personality touched the consciousness of the masses: There is no doubt that even traditional Brahmanism which was being ossified into moribund ritualism was enriched by the impact of Buddhist thought. The dynamic character of the Buddhist gospel expressed its power in having transcended the barriers of oceans and mountains. Buddha was indeed a gigantic and mightly personality.[1]

Sri Aurobindo has been perhaps the foremost scholar-mystic of modern India. His philosophy has appeared also as a message for several people and some of his ardent followers and admirers have expressed the view that eventually *The Life Divine* is bound to revolutionize the thought of the East and the West.

[1] Sri Aurobindo himself has paid the most eloquent tributes to Buddha, "Thus it was possible for the Buddha to attain the state of *nirvāṇa* and yet act puissantly in the world, impersonal in his inner consciousness, in his action the most powerful personality that we know of as having lived and produced results in the world." (*The Life Divine*, Vol. I, p. 36). I may point out that synthetic was also the type of Sri Krishna. He was a great Yogi and philosopher but at the same time he was a puissant worker for the political salvation of the Pandavas and the Yadavas.

Buddha and Sri Aurobindo, both, have attempted the construction of a philosophy of life. Both are creative thinkers but they are not primarily scholastic academicians. Their thought maintains a living contact with the dynamism of life. They want that the philosophical and ethical propositions should be concretely realised in life. Buddha placed before his disciples the supreme goal of *nirvāṇa* in which there is attained the extinction of all lower particularizations and attractions. Sri Aurobindo has placed before us the ideal of the divinization of the cosmos which will mean a fusion of matter and spirit. In their emphasis on the transcendence of the gratifications of the lower ego, Buddha and Sri Aurobindo remind us of the traditions of the great saints of humanity. But in their endeavours to put their teachings in the framework of a philosophical architectonic, they also remind us of the traditions of the German idealists. Hence it can be said that both these thinkers represent in their personality and teachings a picture of Christ and Hegel combined — emotional detachment, a deep concern for the sorrows and afflictions of tormented humanity and a philosophic mind which is out to make a theoretical scheme providing for the explanation of the cosmos and of life.

It is true that of all spiritual thinkers, Buddha and Sri Aurobindo are perhaps the most fundamentally different in their attitudes. Hence this comparative study attempted here is mostly a study of contrasts rather than of common elements. But there is one dominant common point and that is the emphasis on ethical discipline. Both maintain that spiritual pursuits require discipline, inner strength and a firm will. However, Sri Aurobindo would not sanction the rigorous asceticism associated with early Buddhism. His emphasis is more on the cultivation of a divine-mindedness than on the negative cult of restraint.

2. *Methodology of Superior Knowledge: Rationalism and Intuitionism*

Both Buddha and Sri Aurobindo are partly rationalists and partly intuitionists. Buddha was a rationalist to the extent that he attempted to shatter the foundations of Brahmin orthodoxy by resorting to the faculty of critical reason. He attempted to destroy the unfounded superstitions of the people. But so far as the concrete realization of the supreme truth was concerned, it was to be attained by meditation and concentrated absorption. Hence Buddha called it as *takānavacara* or incapable of logical and ratiocinative comprehension. Thus it may be stated that Buddha was partly a rationalist and partly an intuitionist.

Sri Aurobindo ascribes a very important place to reason in socio-political evolution and metaphysical constructions and he says that a spirituality which negates reason is bound to become petrified. Hence in his own personal career as well as in his writings he attempted to combine intellectual scholarship and deep mystical orientation. He pays tribute to reason and science for having liberated Western humanity from the sway of dull superstitions.[1] But the top points in his spiritual metaphysics are the concepts of illumined mind, intuition, overmind and supermind. He says that the three Vedantic standpoints of *dvaitavāda*, *viśishtādvaitavāda* and *advaitavāda*, although difficult of synthesis through the operations of the logical mind, can be shown to be reconciled through spiritual realizations wherein the three standpoints would represent three layers of the ascent of consciousness.

Sri Aurobindo's belief in layers of super-rational consciousness is also testified to by his belief in the *devayāna* and the *pitṛyāṇa.*

3. *Ontological Speculations*

A momentous problem of philosophy throughout the ages has been to determine the nature of the ultimate reality.[2] But so far as ontological questions are concerned, Buddha was a pragmatic utilitarian. He keenly saw that contemporary metaphysicians were engaged in futile intellectual discussions and vain wranglings. He was opposed to the identification of the metaphysical quest with empty sophistry and eristic dissertations. He wanted to elevate the tone of moral life and in place of metaphysical essays he placed before man the supremacy of a

[1] Sri Aurobindo, *Evolution* (Calcutta, Arya Publishing House, 1921), 4th edition, 1944, p. 29 : "Reason is not the supreme light, but yet is it always a necessory light-bringer and until it has been given its rights and allowed to judge and purify our first infra-rational instincts, impulses, rash fervours, crude beliefs and blind prejudgments, we are not altogether ready for the full unveiling of a greater inner luminary."

[2] Sri Aurobindo, *Heraclitus* (Calcutta, Arya Publishing House, 1947), 2nd edition, pp. 10-11.

scheme of ethical discipline. But in spite of Buddha's ban on metaphysics, early Buddhism does contain a good deal of abstruse philosophy. The notion of the *pratītya-samutpāda* which propounds the dependent origination of cosmic and psychic phenomena and illustrates this idea through the twelve-fold causal categories — the *dvādaśāyatana*, is a stupendous formulation for those days although from the modern standpoint it is a vague forecast of the scientific view of universal causality and the ubiquitous sway of natural law. It is true that the *avidyā*, the first element in the causal chain of *dvādaśayatana* cannot be interpreted to signify cosmic energy, nevertheless the *dvādaśāyatana* does contain the dim and inexplicit rudiments of a law of universal causation. The *pratītyasamutpāda* may be regarded as a more detailed exemplification of the law of *karman* which in its inexorability and its cosmic operation almost assumes the necessitarian character of a rigid natural law.

Besides stressing the operation of a natural law of moral retribution in the world, the *dvādaśāyatana* formula is based on the acceptance of the primacy of ideal factors and forces over the material. It states that the *samskāra* and the *vijñāna* — tendencies and impressions of past actions and consciousness lead to the generation of *nāmarūpa*. It asserts that *upādāna* and *bhava* (tendency to become) lead to *jāti* (birth). At one place Buddha says that the body is more permanent than the mind. Hence sometimes it is said that contrary to the prevalent opinion, Buddha regards the mental to be more shadowy than the physical.

Sometimes it is said that although Buddha's main aim was ethical reformation,[1] his teachings do implicitly point out to some belief in an absolute of the Upaniṣadic type. The exponents of this school maintain that Buddha stressed the significance of four-fold *dhyāna* and *five-fold dhyāna* (*Caturdhyāna* and *Pancadhyāna*) and also believed in the realisability of *samādhi*, and they state that these supernormal Yogic visions receive their proper fulfilment only in the context of the reality

[1] Buddha is reported to have said, 'Philosophy purifies none, peace alone does'. (Quoted in M. Hiriyanna, *Outlines of Indian Philosophy*, p. 137).

of an absolute spiritual real. But I put a negativistic meaning on Buddha's silence. If an absolute spiritual real were acceptable to Buddha, he should have said so. A great teacher does not fight shy of reiterating the central theme of his teachings. What moral right the modern "Vedantificators" of early Buddhism have in ascribing to Buddha the faith in an absolute when the entire Tripiṭakas save for a few lines in the *Udāna* and a stray line or word here and there contain no mention of it ? The occurrence of such words as *brahmabhuta*, *brahmavihāra*, *brahmakāya* and *brahmacarya* is not a positive indication of Buddha's belief in the Upaniṣadic *brahman* as a supreme spiritual real but is only the acceptance of a traditionally prevalent vocabulary.

Sri Aurobindo insists on the attainment of an integral consciousness or a supramental vision through which alone the omni-present supreme spirit can be realized. But in the line of Indian mystics like Yājñāvalkya and Śamkara he has also attempted an intellectual formulation of the eternal infinite being which can be said to be the *sachchidananda* or the *purushottama*. It is claimed that in Sri Aurobindo's metaphysics the impersonal *brahman* of the Advaitins and the matter of the scientists are reconciled since they both are regarded as aspects only of the supreme truth. Sri Aurobindo had a good grasp of eastern and western thought and hence if on one side he is aware of the stupendous importance of a supernal absolute in the Vedāntic tradition, he is also conscious of the role of an energising and vitalising cosmic creative and executive power. His disciples credit him with having provided the logical consummation to the dominant trends of eastern and western thought. He attempts a synthesis at a higher level of the propositions of Vedāntism and science. He says: "A Consciousness-Force everywhere inherent in Existence, acting even when concealed, is the creator of the worlds, the occult secret of Nature."[1]

Sri Aurobindo would feel repelled by the concept of an annihilationistic *nirvāṇa* as upheld by some Buddhist extremists. His notions regarding the relation of the human self and the supreme self seem to be coloured with the Vaishnava classifications of *mukti* as *sāmīpya*, *sālokya*, *sārūpya* and *sāyujya*. He

[1] Sri Aurobindo, *The Life Divine*, Vol. II.

does not subscribe to that conception of *mukti* as held in the Advaita Vedanta which posits an identification of the human and the absolute self. To him the summits of divine life are synchronistic with the status of a spiritual awareness of both the static and the dynamic aspects of the absolute. There is some similarity between the Mahāyāna concept of collective liberation through the efforts of the Boddhisattva and Sri Aurobindo's notions of a race of gnostic beings.

4. *Anātman and the Human Self*

Buddha denied the reality of an empirical ego-identity as well as of a spiritual soul-monad. He frankly denies the existence of a transmigrating soul-monad. He definitely repudiates the ascription of the character of *ātman* to *rūpa*, *samskāra*, *vijñāna* etc. The various conceptions of the human self upheld in the *Viśishtādvaita* and *dvaita* schools of latter Vedānta as well as in the Nyāya and Yoga systems do not find any support in the books of early Buddhism. But just as in the cosmological field Buddha did not want to adhere to the extremes of eternalism and annihilationalism. (*śāśvatavāda* and *ucchedavāda*), so also in the field of psychology he was reluctant to sanction the extinction of the human self because it would land the generations in a morass of nullity and despair, since they would become desperate at the thought, 'I am not.'

We seem to find a great amount of vagueness and even contradiction in the philosophy of the original Pali Buddhism. There is no God and no soul but still the law of *karman* and the notions of *punarbhava*, *samādhi*, *purvanivāsānusmṛti* and *sattvānam chyuti utpādavijñāna* are accepted and at a more empirical and popular level the belief in a number of gods and devils, heavens and hells is maintained. Buddha's insistence on the realization of the supreme truths in profound contemplation and mystic absorption would appear utterly dissatisfying if there is no persistent self to act as the continuum for these experiences. If the various sections of the *Vinaya* and *Sutta Piṭaka* are not explained away as concessions to the popular psychology, then we have to face the fact that in a system which is predominantly atheistic and adheres to the notion of a 'psychology without a soul' there is the profession of a serious belief in ghosts and goblins, spheres of heaven and hell and a succession of births and deaths according to the merits and demerits accumulated in previous lives. Hence at times the modern critical research scholar of Buddhist philosophy is constrained to utter in disgust that original Buddhism is one of the most unsatisfying systems in the world. If man is deprived of some immanental spiritual principle, it can be conductive neither to his moral life and perfectibility of character nor would it urge him to pursue a scheme of spiritual liberation or final emancipation. If the concept of *anātman* or the doctrine of the negation of the soul is accepted then its logical implication will be a view of *nirvāṇa* as total extinction. It will necessarily prepare the foundations of a belief in complete *śunya* or utter nihil and void (or the *sarvavaināśikavāda* of Śamkara's terminology). The negativism of early Buddhism as seen in its repudiation of God and soul, if pressed fully, may become the necessary foundation of a total nullification of all life and culture, religion and philosophy. I think that to construct intellectually the panorama of a supreme void, as is done by Nāgārjuna, is a vain theoretical effort, utterly disgusting to the heart and dissatisfying in its blindness to the value of freedom, justice and beneficence.

The human self, according to Sri Aurobindo, is, in essence, the absolute. The microcosm is one with the macrocosm. In its inmost essence the individual is one with the universal spirit and at the empirical level also it can be said that the individual is the limitation or the finite particularization of the supreme real.

5. *The Problem of Pain*

The fundamental difference between the two thinkers is seen in their attitude towards pain and suffering. Buddha's supreme realism is seen in his attempt to reveal the stupendous fact of pain and suffering amidst all external attractions, ceremonies and splendours. Of all great thinkers and reformers, Buddha was most concerned with the phenomena of cosmic pain and this shows his enormous realism, if visualized in a philosophic context wherein previously Yājñavalkya and Uddālaka were preaching the notion of the supernal bliss in their advocacy of absolute idealism. Buddha was in this sense a philosopher of the people because comparatively speaking the lower strata of the population are more prone to physical misery than the elite. The seriousness and depth of urgency with which Buddha stressed the dismal element of suffering shows that to him *dukkha* was not a mere psycho-physical-pathological problem but it was almost a stupendous fact of the phenomenal world.

Regarding the purpose of the cosmic process Aurobindo says: "The Movement with all its formed objects has been created in order to provide a habitation of the spirit...The object of Habitation is enjoyment and possession." This notion is comparable to the Vedāntic doctrine of *lokalīlā* and the myth of the cosmic dance of Krishna in the Vaishnava theology. But the reality of suffering is too potent a fact in the phenomenal world to be explained away by the juggleries of pantheistic Vedānta which revels in singing the melodious tunes of a trancendent self. Any Vedāntic or mystical-philosophical attempt to deny the existence of all-pervasive misery, especially in the lands of Asia and Africa, looks like a child's joke. The omnipotent sway of historical and sociological forces and the stark facts of bitter social and economic exploitation spelling enormous misery for the masses cannot be dismissed by the endless parade of sonorous words depicting the bliss of the beyond, which go on nullifying the existence of misery by regarding it merely as the interpretation or construction of the limited self. It may be remembered that the great philosophers of the mystical and nihilistic schools had also to meet with final death and the destruction of their physical tenement. Because of an undue absorption in the transcendent and the non-mundane *ānānda* and a blindness to the social and political fact of power politics and exploitation, the social philosophy of India looks dull and gloomy and leaves a sense of emptiness. This defect is present in Aurobindo too. You may describe the cosmic misery as the dance of Rudra or you may negate all worldly suffering in the context of the peace of the absolute *brahman*, — it is the same story of Rome burning and Nero fiddling. You go on singing the hymns of *ānānda rūpamamṛtam yad vibhāti*, but taht will give no consolation to the masses.

6. *Conclusion: A Plea for Increasing Synthesis*

Human knowledge about the phenomenal universe is increasing at an unprecedented speed. Deeper probings into the realms of mental operations are also going on. At such a time in the evolution of human thought one cannot afford to be dogmatic and cling to his narrow conclusions. Hence the synthesis of the abstractions of science with the humanistic and valutational insights of world religions can alone be a fruitful endeavour in the field of knowledge. Quite early in the course of his philosophical development Aurobindo had visualized the necessity of a philosophical synthesis and had written in his *The Ideal of the Karmayogin*:

> "The religion which embraces Science and faith, Theism, Christianity, Mahomedanism and Buddhism and yet is none of these, is that to which the World-Spirit moves. In our own, which is the most sceptical and the most believing of all, the most sceptical because it has questioned and experimented the most, the most believing because it has the deepest experience and the most varied and positive spiritual knowledge, — that wider Hinduism which is not a dogma or combination of dogmas but a law of life, which is not a social framework but the spirit of a past and future social evolution, which rejects nothing but insists on testing and experiencing everything and when tested and experienced turning it to the soul's uses, in this Hinduism we find the basis of the future world-religion."

What we need in Indian thought today is a reconciling construction on the basis of eastern and western knowledge and the insights gained through the experiences of the thinkers themselves.

Appendix 5

SRI AUROBINDO'S INTERPRETATION OF BUDDHIST PHILOSOPHY

Buddhism is one of the most significant and powerful intellectual creations of the speculative mind. In the history of ancient Indian thought it appeared as a great idea-force and it rendered necessary the reconstruction of the Vedāntic philosophy to meet its challenge. In the movement of modern renaissance also Buddhism has played an important role. Vivekananda, Aurobindo and Gandhi have been deeply influenced both by the personality and the teachings of Buddha. They have also attempted to emphasize those aspects of Buddhist philosophy which indicate its affiliations with the traditional current of Vedāntism. In his philosophical books Aurobindo has tried to minimize the role of Buddhism as a critical and sceptical school of thought and has stressed the notion of Buddhism being an ethical system of mystical discipline. He interprets it as a system inculcating the concept of spiritual redemption.

The lofty and towering character of Buddha has cast a deep and profound influence on the minds of modern Indian thinkers. Buddha's personality symbolizes the supreme synthesis of puissant dynamic action and the calm silence of inner impersonality. Vivekananda in his book *Karma Yoga* has called Buddha to be the greatest typification of the essential concept of *Karma Yoga* because he (Buddha) followed the path of disinterested actionistic altruism. Aurobindo tries to build the metaphysical foundation of this kind of Karmayogic synthesis which is the essence of the personality of Buddha. According to Aurobindo, it is possible to make two types of assertions regarding the supreme reality. It is possible to conceive it as the Pure Being, as the foundational and fundamental primal principle which permits the diverse play of multiple becomings and mutations.

But it is also possible to regard this same Pure Being from an alternative standpoint. It can be also called *Asat* — implying not absolute non-being but only freedom from limitation by its own determinations. It also implies its freedom from all conceptual formulations of its own existence. Hence Aurobindo says:

> "The Non-Being permits the Being, even as the silence permits the activity. By this simultaneous negations and affirmations, not mutually destructive, but complementary to each other like all contraries, the simultaneous awareness of conscious Self-being as a reality and the unknowable beyond as the same reality becomes realisable to the awakened human soul. Thus was it possible for the Buddha to attain the state of Nirvāṇa and yet act puissantly in this world."[1]

Thus it appears that because both positivistic and negativistic formulations of the supreme reality are valid hence it is possible to attain the stillness of spiritual realisation and also to be active and dynamic in the world. I agree with Aurobindo and Vivekananda in thinking that Buddha combined the silence and calm of the realized spirit with the capacity to perform immense amount of actions but the metaphysical argument advanced by Aurobindo to explain this synthesis does not seem plausible and convincing to me. It does not appear rational to establish an analogue and parallelism between the Pure Being and action on the one hand and between Non-Being and the silence of *nirvāṇa* on the other. If the primal reality is conceived as pure being, there is no reason why the person who has attained an awareness of such a reality should engage himself in action. Vedāntic seers accept the supreme reality of the *sachchidānanda*, but inculcate not action but the profundities of contemplations for the human aspirant and the sage. Action and stillness of the individual person on the terrestrial level are not dependent on the alternative formulations about the supreme reality but are dependent to a very great extent on the environmental situation, on the capacity of the human physique and the social and economic requirements of the times. Psychological make-up also plays a part in this orientation of the human body. Hence although I regard Buddha as a mighty Karmayogi, I do not consider Aurobindo's attempt to explain this combination of

1 *The Life Divine* (American ed.), pp. 29-30.

Nirvanic silence and dynamic action on metaphysical grounds as valid.

Aurobindo has emphasized the significance of compassion in the gospel of emancipation heralded by Buddhism. Buddha enshrined in his personality the perfection of love not only for human beings but for all living beings. Legend has it that while he was on the threshold of *nirvāṇa*, his soul recoiled and he made up his mind not to attain individual emancipation so long as there was one being on earth who was enmeshed in suffering. The Buddhist view of ethical perfection and universalistic compassion introduced a dynamic element in the culture of India, and the world, and when Buddhism penetrated into Western Asia and when its teachings were carried to the Mediterranean regions, then it, according to some authorities, became a potent influence in the rise of Christianity. To the Hellenic and Roman cultures of beauty, harmony, law and integration, Buddhism added the concepts of love, justice, reciprocity and spiritual mutuality. Aurobindo rightly believes that if Europe is to recover her soul and is to be saved from the engulfing crisis of an expansive and corroding commercial and scientific civilisation, she should once again emphasize the old Eastern Ideal. He is critical of the fetish made of science. He points out:

> "This was the Eastern ideal carried by Buddhism and other ancient disciplines to the coasts of Asia and Egypt and from there poured by Christianity into Europe. But these motives, burning for a time like dim torchlights in the confusion and darkness created by the barbaric flood that has submerged the old civilizations, have been abandoned by the modern spirit which has found another light, the light of Science."[1]

Aurobindo pleads for a synthesis of the different values enshrined by the religions of the world and the Buddhistic insistence on love and compassion calls forth his earnest admiration. Buddha not only taught compassion but represented its concrete embodiment. I agree with Aurobindo in holding that it is necessary to add the Buddhist note of compassion to our growingly sophisticated and materialistic civilization.

Buddhism pleaded for the moralisation of our values and existence. It taught the transitory character of the charms

[1] *The Life Divine*, Vol. II, p. 923.

and pleasures of life and it preached the urgency of *nirvāṇa* with a supreme vehemence.[1] This kind of supra-terrestrial ideal was very commendable from the standpoint of a few subjectively-oriented individual but it could become disastrous from the standpoint of the community and the nation. Vivekananda regarded this extreme emphasis of Buddhism on Ahimsa as a factor for the national decline of India. According to Aurobindo, the old Aryan mind as exemplified in the Vedas accepted a synthesis of the values of this world and the values of the other world. It formulated a synthesis between the demands of rational existence in this world and the quest of the supernal bliss beyond. But Buddhism over-emphasized the miseries of this world and the consequent stress on world-weariness and disenchantment was a destructive force from the standpoint of political growth and social development. Aurobindo says:

> "And the mind when it passes those gates suddenly, without intermediate transitions, receives a sense of the unreality of the world and the sole reality of the silence which is one of the most powerful and convincing experiences of which the human mind is capable. Here, in the perception of this pure self or of the Non-Being behind it, we have the starting-point for a second negation, — parallel at the other pole to the materialistic, but more complete, more final, more perilous in its effects on the individuals or collectivities that hear its potent call to the wilderness, — the refusal of the ascetic. It is this revolt of spirit against matter that for two thousand years, since Buddhism disturbed the balance of the old Aryan world, has dominated increasingly the Indian mind."[2]

I agree with Aurobindo in holding that the over-emphasis of

[1] "In India the philosophy of world-negation has been given formulations of supreme power and value by two of the greatest of her thinkers, Buddha and Shankara. There have been, intermediate or later in time, other philosophies of considerable importance, some of them widely accepted, formulated with much acumen of thought by men of genius and spiritual insight, which disputed with more or less force and success the conclusions of these two great metaphysieal systems, but none has been put forward with an equal force of presentation or drive of personality or had a similar massive effect. The spirit of these two remarkable spiritual philosophies — for Shankara in the historical process of India's philosophical mind takes up, completes and replaces Buddha, — has weighed with a tremendous power on her thought, religion and general mentality : everywhere broods its mighty shadow, everywhere is the impress of the three great formulas, the chain of Karma, escape from the wheel of rebirth, Maya" — *The Life Divine* by Sri Aurobindo, Vol. II, p. 147.

[2] *The Life Divine*, Vol. I, p. 28

Buddhism on cosmic misery and the impermanence of the worldly phenomena, to a certain extent, weakened the nerves of the Indians in carrying on successfully a political struggle for competitive success against the West Asiatic and Central Asiatic races. It exalted the moral values but did create the fatal sense of recoil from this world. Hence I believe that to the Buddhistic stress on ethics we should add the Vedic and Platonic stress on the reformation and transformation of this world.

Buddhism is a gospel of emancipation from the ills of this world. It teaches the necessity of the negation of the worries and frustrations that engulf human existence. Buddha wanted to teach the ethical way. He regarded metaphysical dialectice about the being and origination of this world as nerve-exhausting and useless. In the famous *Brahmajāla Sutta* Buddha ridicules the diverse schools of cosmological metaphysics and almost in the spirit of a modern pragmatist and positivist, stresses the urgency of moral redemption. Aurobindo, commenting on the anti-metaphysical temper of Buddha, says:

> "Buddha refused to consider the metaphysical problem; the process by which our unreal individuality is constructed and a world of suffering maintained in existence and the method of escape from it is all that is of importance. Karma is a fact; the construction of objects, of an individuality not truly existent is the cause of suffering: to get rid of Karma, individuality and suffering must be our one objective; by that elimination we shall pass into whatever may be free from these things, permanent, real: the way of liberation alone matters."[1]

But although Buddhism tried to banish metaphysics it could not do so. The explanation of the chain of psychic becoming by the intricate mechanism of the formula of the *pratītyasamutpāda* is only one example of a subtle metaphysical construction in early Buddhism. Some of the later Buddhist philosophers like Nāgārjuna and Śāntarakshita were great metaphysicians. Metaphysics does try to satisfy a very urgent and insistent aspiration of the human mind to know the inmost reality of things. It is an attempt to satisfy the longing of man to know the origination of the cosmos and to have a plausible account of human destiny. Aurobindo rightly points out:

[1] *The Life Divine*, Vol. II, p. 234 note no. 1, or p. 435 note no. 1. American ed.).

"But our mind cannot remain satisfied — the mind of Buddhism itself did not remain satisfied — with this evasion at the very root of the whole matter. In the first place, these philosophies, while thus putting aside that root question, do actually make far-reaching assertions that assume, not only a certain operation and symptoms but a certain fundamental nature of the Ignorance from which their prescription of remedies proceeds and it is obvious that without such a radical diagnosis no prescription of remedies can be anything but an empiric dealing."[1]

I endorse Aurobindo's standpoint that no gospel of ethical redemption can ever be satisfying without substantial metaphysical foundations. Even the most anti-metaphysical creeds have to assume some sort of metaphysics. Metaphysics is of primary importance to the human being. The human intellectual cannot sustain himself without some metaphysics. The Marxists engage in bitter fulminations against the speculative excesses of Hegelian metaphysics, but even the positivist Marxists make a parade of their attachment to scientific and dialectical materialism and on its basis try to give an explanation of the cosmic process and human destiny. I believe that a philosophy that tries to eradicate metaphysics is a half-philosophy and is bound to fail. Hence I agree with Aurobindo in holding that the failure of Buddhism to offer a systematic metaphysics was a radical flaw.[2]

But in spite of the persistent desire to eliminate metaphysical propositions from his discourses, Buddha did give vent to certain views which are metaphysical. The concept of *karman* had a great place in the Upaniṣadic philosophy. It was regarded not merely in the sense of physical action but also in the sense of the psychological force of disposition to action. It had also assumed the shape of a cosmic law of conservation of energies. Buddha took over from the Upaniṣads the concept of *karman* and tried to explain the personality and destiny of man in its terms. He inculcated the inexorability of the operative mechanism of *karman*. The law of *karman* worked with inevitable

1 *The Life Divine*, Vol. II, p. 235 (p. 436 of American ed.).

2 T.W. Rhys Davids and Paul Carus stressed the negativism of Buddhism. But Edmund Holmes in his *The Creed of Buddha* (New York, John Lane Co., 1908), has strongly pleaded for a positive interpretation by attempting to understand Buddha in the context of Upaniṣadic idealism. Hence he states that *nirvāṇa* should be conceived as "a state of self-realisation through union with the Divine or Universal soul." (p. 229). S. Radhakrishnan seems heavily indebted to Holmes.

finality and was the supreme determinant of the life of a man. In face of such a law of elemental power it was unnecessary to believe in the God of the theists. Aurobindo says:

"And seeing that moral evil is in reality a form of mental disease or ignorance, who or what created this law or inevitable connection which punishes a mental disease or act of ignorance by a recoil so terrible, by tortures often extreme and monstrous ? The inexorable law of *Karman* is irreconcilable with a supreme moral and personal Deity, and therefore the clear logic of Buddha denied the existence of any free and all-governing personal God; all personalty be declared to be a creation of ignorance and subject to *Karma*."[1]

It is true that Buddha does not accept the reality of a personal God but I think that the reason of this is not the incompatibility of the concept of a personal God with the law of *karman* as Aurobindo thinks but the possible fact that Buddha did not have the realisation of a personal Godhead. In the Old Testament we find the acceptance of the significance of actions simultaneously with the fervour of the belief in a monotheistic Godhead. Even in modern times we find that Dayānanda and Gandhi have simultaneously upheld the exalted belief in a personal Godhead with the acceptance of the law of *karman*. I think that Buddha was fundamentally an ethical teacher who perhaps did not personally experience the exalted state of profundities consequent upon firm belief in God — profundities which we find in the lives of Nānaka, Tukārama, Ramadas, Rāmakrishna and other theistic saints of India and abroad.

Aurobindo stresses the nihilistic elements in Buddhism. He says: "Or else, like the Buddhist, one comes to regard even that eternal self as an illusion, a representation, a subjective image, a mere imagination of false sensation and false idea of being."[2] In early Buddhism the negativist orientation is pre-eminent. Buddha does not refer to the absolute of the Upaniṣads. But in later Buddhist philosophy we do find some kind of absolutism. Aśvaghosha believes in the supreme concept of *Tathatā*. It is possible to give at least a half-absolutistic interpretation of the Mādhyamika metaphysics of Nāgārjuna. Hence Aurobindo's statement about the denial of the eternal self in

[1] *The Life Divine*, Vol. I, p. 113.
[2] *Ibid*, Vol. II, p. 259 (p. 454 of American ed.).

Buddhism represents only a partial truth and needs considerable reservations in the light of the development of later Buddhist philosophy.

Early Buddhism denied the infallibility of the Vedas, it condemned the ritualistic ceremony of the sacrificial cult and it ignored the supreme Brahman of the Upaniṣads but it could not do away with the belief in rebirth. The acceptance of the doctrine of rebirth was an essential adjunct of and supplement to the theory of *karman*. The operative efficacy of *karman* needed the acceptance of previous and future lives to make it appear rational, meaningful and acceptable to the people. Hence to make his ethical gospel significant Buddha accepted the concept of rebirth. But a further difficulty presented itself. Buddha denied the concept of the substantial character of the soul as a spiritual monad. He put reliance only in some form of psycho-physical personality constituted by the complex of the *nāma* and *rūpa*. Buddha denied both the Upaniṣadic and the Sāmkhya theories of the human self.

> "The Buddhists took this last step and refused reality to the self on the ground that it was as much as the rest a construction of the mind ; they cut not only God but the eternal self and impersonal Brahman out of the picture".[1]

According to Aurobindo this denial of the self is an illustration of the workings of toe surface-mentality. He says:

> "Those who live in this surface Time-self and have not the habit of drawing back inward towards the immutable or the capacity of dwelling in it, are even incapable of thinking of themselves apart from this ever self-modifying mental experience. That is for them their self and it is easy for them, if they look with detachment at its happenings, to agree with the conclusion of the Buddhist nihilists that this self is in fact nothing but a stream of idea and experience and mental action, the persistent flame which is yet never the same flame, and to conclude that there is no such thing as a real self, but only a flow of experience and behind it Nihil...."[2]

Buddhism repudiates the concept of a spiritual substance and hence there is no possibility of the acceptance of the rebirth of the immortal principle into another body after the extinction of the present body But Buddhism accepts the rebirth not of the soul but of personality. The principle of *karman* provides some continuity to the ever incessantly changing consciousness. This

[1] *The Life Divine*, pp. 418-419. (American ed.)
[2] *Ibid*, p. 458. (American ed.)

repudiation of the spiritual self and the acceptance of the rebirth of personality in the shape of the changing psycho-physical complex leads to the conception of what Aurobindo calls "Vitalistic Buddhism." He says:

> ".....a sort of vitalistic Buddhism, admitting *Karma*, but admitting it only as the action of a universal Life-force; it would admit as one of its results the continuity of the stream of personality in rebirth by mental association, but might deny any real self for the individual or any eternal being other than this ever-active vital becoming."[1]
>
> Thus in Buddhism the concept of rebirth did not imply the real rebirth of a real spiritual substance into the forms and patterns of terrestrial existence. Hence in face of the denial of the existence of the self the Buddhist rebirth only meant "a continuity of the ideas, sensations and actions which constituted a fictitious individual moving between different worlds, — let us say, between differently organised planes of idea and sensation; for, in fact, it is only the conscious continuity of the flux that creates a phenomenon of self and a phenomenon of personality."[2]

I agree with Aurobindo's interpretation of the Buddhist theory of rebirth. I may add my own conviction that the Buddhist conception is very unsatisfying to me. In the *Milinda-Panho* several analogies have been given to indicate how rebirth is possible even in the absence of a soul substance. But I think it illogical to accept the rebirth of mere consciousness which is regarded as ever-changing. In order to make any sense out of the theory of rebirth we have to accept the concept of a soul as a spiritual substance which provides the synthetic unity to the apparently diverse movements of consciousness. To accept the notion of rebirth and to repudiate the conception of the spiritual self makes the Buddhist attempt almost ludicrous from the standpoint of serious philosophy.

The problem of *nirvāṇa* has been one of the most controversial issues in Buddhist metaphysics and eschatology. There are at least three views about it. First, *nirvāṇa* implies utter extinction of the human personality and is consequent on the complete neutralization of egoistic attachments and conformations. Secondly, *nirvāṇa* is regarded as the negation of empirical particulars and determinations. But the trans-empirical is regarded as unfathomable and unknowable. The only statement that

[1] *The Life Divine*, p. 668. (American ed.).
[2] *Ibid*, p. 669. (American ed.)

can be made is that *nirvāṇa* is something which can be only realized by the sage who has cognized the depths of the supreme truth by a rigorous discipline in the Aryan way. The third view about *nirvāṇa* is that it is a definite and specific stage of spiritual realization. Aurobindo adheres to this third view. He says that the *nirvāṇa* of Buddhism represented a luminous attempt of man to reach the height of Non-Existence. It Implied unspeakable peace and gladness for the consciousness of the liberated being, yet on earth. It indicated the extinction of all suffering, sorrow and misery and "the nearest we can get to a positive conception of it is that it is some inexpressible Beatitude (if the name or any name can be applied to a peace so void of contents) into which even the notion of self-existence seems to be swallowed up and disappear."[1] Aurobindo has tried to give a poetic representation of the state of spiritual realization which *nirvāṇa* is:

> "All is abolished but the mute Alone.
> The mind from thought released, the heart from grief
> Grow inexistent now beyond belief;
> There is no I, no Nature, known-unknown.
> The city, a shadow picture without tone,
> Floats, quivers unreal; forms without relief
> Flow, a cinema's vacant shapes; like a reef
> Foundering in shoreless gulfs the world is done.
>
> Only the illimitable permanent
> Is here. A Peace stupendous, featureless, still
> Replaces all, — what once was I, in It
> A silent unnamed emptiness content
> Either to fade in the Unknowable
> Or thrill without the luminous seas of the Infinite."[2]

According to Aurobindo *nirvāṇa* is a state of spiritual consciousness but not the highest consciousness. He claims to have attained the silence and stillness of *nirvāṇa* very early in his career as a Yogi.

It is very difficult to pronounce my own views about *nirvāṇa* because it is a super-intellectual problem. I disagree with the concept of *nirvāṇa* as utter and absolute extinction and nihil because moral endeavours cannot be stabilized on the basis of

[1] *The Life Divine*, p. 48.
[2] Sri Aurobindo, *Collected Poems and Plays*, Vol. II, p. 298.

such dark and dismal prospects. A true moral life postulates the conservation of our efforts towards the concretization of moral norms. Hence there can be a *nirvāṇa* of human sufferings but not of the human personality. To the believers in the spiritual destiny of mankind Aurobindo's claims to have realized *nirvāṇa* will appear as a source of consolation because it is confirmation of a fundamental spiritual teleology amidst the attacks of atheism, nihilism and agnosticism. But it is open to the critic of Aurobindo to minimize the value of his egoistic claim to have not only realized the state of *nirvāṇa* but to have gone beyond even the Nirvanic consciousness and to have attained still more transcendent vistas of supramental splendours. However, Aurobindo's interpretations of the concept of *nirvāṇa* indicate that he favours a more positive interpretation of it — a trend which we find in Mahāyānism.

This positive interpretations of *nirvāṇa* by Aurobindo necessarily postulates a positive interpretation of *śunya* and *asat* also. Aurobindo says: "......the dissolution of our present state by *nirvāṇa* may be reaching to some highest state beyond all notion or experience of self even, an ineffable release from our sense of existence."[1] Hence the affirmation of non-being or nihil which is left after the elimination of the percipient and the perception and the percept, amounts not to absolute non-being but only to the negation of the applicability of the highest human concepts and particulars to that *śunya* implies nihil but only from the human standpoint. *Asat* implies non-existence but also from the human standpoint. Thus according to Aurobindo the formulations about *nirvāṇa*, *śunya* and *asat* are only the indications of the incapability of the human mind to know the supreme truth and to convey that adequately in terms of verbal concepts and phraseology. He thinks that the Vedāntic trend in certain-senses represents the attempt of the human mind to go still further and to comprehend the positivistic fullness of the supreme being. He says:

"The Buddha applied his penetrating rational intellect supported by an intuitive vision to the world as our mind and sense see it and discovered the principle of its construction and the way of release from all constructions, but he refused to go farther. Śankara took the farther

[1] *The Life Divine*, p. 507. (American ed.).

step and regarded the suprarational truth, which Buddhism kept behind the veil as realisable by cancellation of the constructions of consciousness but beyond the scope of the reason's discovery."[1]

Hence according to Aurobindo *śunya* and *asat* do not imply complete and utter unreality and extinction but indicate a positive being. Sometimes Aurobindo regards the *sat* and *asat* as only too equally valid formulations about the supreme truth. But in this particular context he claims a higher ontological status for the Vedāntic category of absolute being, in comparison to the Buddhist category of *śunya* and *asat*. I agree with Aurobindo on this point. Instead of saying that for the highest reality, being and non-being are equally valid predications, I think, that it is better to say that being stands higher than non-being. When we say that the highest reality is non-being we are speaking from the human standpoint but when we say that the highest reality is being we are speaking from the standpoint of the highest reality itself.

Aurobindo is not a serious scholar of Buddhist philosophy. Hence his statements and conclusions are not substantiated by erudite and scholarly documentation. As an interpreter of Buddhist philosophy he will not rank with savants like Oldenberg or Stcherbatsky or Dr. Otto Rosenberg. But his significance lies in a different direction. Aurobindo is a profound thinker — one of the greatest thinkers of the modern East. The value of his interpretations of Buddhist philosophy lies in the way he has used some of the dominant Buddhist ideas and concepts in the construction of his own elaborate system of spiritual metaphysics. Aurobindo has attempted to create an integral philosophy on the basis of the synthesis of eastern wisdom and western metaphysics. He is not an antiquarian interested in objective historical research but is a philosopher interested in the validity and usefulness of concepts and notions. Hence the significance of Aurobindo's interpretations of Buddhist philosophy is notable. He has made an original and pioneer attempt to erect a metaphysical system of his own on the foundations of ancient disciplines and teachings. He has, thus, gone beyond the compass of a mere scholar. A similar attempt at integral synthesis was made by Hegel in his

[1] *Ibid*, pp. 415-416. (American ed.).

book *The Phenomenology of Mind.* Hegel's interest in Christianity lay not in the field of scholarly research but in the domain of finding out those vital elements which he could use for perfecting his own metaphysical system. Aurobindo has rendered a great service to Indian thought. He has indicated to us that we should study other systems of thought also from a similar standpoint and should find out precious elements for creating systems of thought-constructions. Schopenhauer had made some minor attempt to incorporate some Upaniṣadic and Buddhistic notions in his book *The World as Will and Idea.* But Aurobindo is an important thinker of the modern world who has pioneered in the field of making a detailed application of some of the prime concepts of Buddhist philosophy like *karman, nirvāṇa, śunya* etc. in the framework of his own intellectual-spiritual system of thought.

Appendix 6

BUDDHA AND MARX

1. *Introduction*

To the pragmatic intellect, a comparative study of Buddha, the typification of the supernal enlightenment and calm of the supramental Nirvanic status and Marx, the promulgator of the proletarian creed of economic epicureanism and revolutionary conquest of political power will not appeal. To the devout Buddhist, Buddha, the incarnation of *bodhicit*, or the truth-consciousness of the Ṛgvedic seer, should not be compared with the profane Red German intellectual of the 19th century. To the Marxist, Buddha was the enemy of the proletarian classs because he was the initiator of the pessimistic philosophy of cosmic illusionism[1] and suffering. Still some of the fundamental points of similarity and differences between these two creative thinkers will be presented here.

Buddhism has exercised potent influence on the creative thought of the East. Christian ethics and philanthropic doctrines, the asceticism of the Alexandrian Therapeutae and the Essenes, the mysticism of Plotinus and the sacred path of the Gnostics, bear at least partial Buddhistic traces. Korea, Japan, Tibet, China, Siam, Burma, and Ceylon owe their religion to the Sākyamuni. The *advaita* Vedānta of Śamkara is said to be inspired by the *śunyādvayavāda* of the Mādhyamikas and *vijñānādvayavāda* of the Yogācaras. The philosophy of Schopenhauer and Hartmann owe some debt to the Buddhistic insistence on *tṛshnā* and *dukkha*. The American New Humanistic philosophy bears some resemblances to Buddhism, and Babbit

[1] Rosenberg contends that illusionism can be traced to early Buddhism. So also does Edward Caird. But Stcherbatsky contrasts the half-way illusionism of early Buddhism with the radical illusionism of Nāgārjuna and Śamkara.

acknowledges his indebtedness more to Buddha than to Plato.[1] Marx has considerably changed the entire outlook of the proletarian workers, and the hope for a communistic classless society has replaced the former Christian fervent ardour for the kingdom of heaven, or the Hebrew belief in the return of David or the Muslim faith in Resurrection. Technology and Economics have replaced the philosophic Absolute and triumphant Russian Marxism has been installed in place of the God of the theologians and the Upāsakās.

2. *Ontology and Dialectics*

The problem of all systematic cosmological thinking is to determine the exact relationship between the supracosmic Absolute One and the manifold plurality and diversity. The *Iśopaniṣad* of the Vājasaneyins formulates an idealistic philosophy of history. It says *sa paryagāt* — 'The Absolute traverses the cosmos', and further *sarvāṇi bhutāni ātmaivābhuta.* The concrete ultimate Reality of the Upaniṣads, bifurcated into the subjective and objective dualistic ultimates of the Sāmkhyas, was later reduced into the pulverised psychic-subjective atomism — the five psycho-physical *nāmarūpa* complexes of early Buddhism. Kant and E. Haeckel have dealt with the cosmological problem. Hegel formulates his philossophy of the Concrete Determinate Absolute, in the fashion of Rāmānuja, and calls history the march of the Absolute on earth. Marx adopts the Hegelian philosophy of history along with the anti-theological materialism of Ludwig Feuerbach. The impersonal ideas of Hegel are replaced by preponderant technological and economic forces in the Marxist philosophy of historical materialism. But neither Marx nor Buddha is greatly interested in analysing the nature of the primal substance-energy. Marx is anxious to emphasize the cash-nexus in human history. Buddha accepts a realistic cosmogony in the *Dīgha Nikāya* but his vital concern is with the elimination of pain and sorrow.

Both Marxism and Buddhism inculcate a dynamistic view of the world. To the exponents of socio-economic change the Upaniṣadic and the Hegelian Absolute seems to impart an

[1] S. Radhakrishnan: "The Teaching of Buddha by Speech and Silence," *Hibbert Journal*, April, 1934.

immutable appearance to society. Hence Buddha in the *Mahāvagga* formulates the philosophy of motion. Heraclitus and Nietzsche propounded a dynamic theory of reality. Engels (in the *Anti-Dühring*) and Lenin (in *Materialism and Empirio-Criticism*) equate matter and motion and thus arrive at a complete antithesis of the point of the Eleatic Zeno. The disintegration of the atom into electro-magnetic energy — the great discovery of modern physics — is in consonance with the dynamic view of the universe. Lenin was over-confident that researches in science will support the Marxian theory. He says: 'Modern physics is in travail, it is giving birth to dialectical materialism'.[1] On the other hand, the advances in modern physics are interpreted in an idealistic fashion by other thinkers.[2]

The dynamic theory of the universe tends towards the dialectical philosophy. In Europeon thought, the dialectic was supposed to indicate the logical procession of thought. In *The Science of Logic*,[3] Hegel has traced the evolution of the dialectic. He says that the Platonic dialectic (even in *The Parmenides* and still more in the other dialogues) is sometimes intended merely to dispose of, and refute through themselves, limited assertions, and sometimes again has nullity for its result. Hegel proceeds to state that Kant set the dialectic higher, and this part of his work is the greatest of his merits—for he freed dialectic from the semblance of arbitrariness attributed to it in ordinary thought. Kant in the Antinomies of Pure Reason vindicated that (a) objectivity of appearance and (b) necessity of contradiction belong to the very nature of thought-determinations. On its positive side this is merely the inherent negativity of these thought-determinations and may be considered their self-moving soul and may also be deemed to be the principle of

1 *Materialism and Empirio-Criticism*, p. 222.

2 Shri Aurobindo says: "Wireless telegraphy is Nature's exterior sign and pretext for a new orientation. The sensible physical means for the intermediate transmission of the physical force is removed; it is only preserved at the points of impulsion and reception. Eventually even these must disappear, for when the laws of the supraphysical are studied with the right starting-point, the means will infallibly be found for Mind directly to seize on the physical energy and speed it accurately on its errand". — *The Life Divine*, Vol. I, p. 19.

3 Hegel, *The Science of Logic*, Vol. I, pp. 66-68.

all physical and spiritual life. Hegel asserts that if people stop short at the abstract-negative side of the dialectic, they reach only the familiar result that reason is incapable of comprehension of the Infinite. Hence, according to him, the genuine dialectical procedure is that the concept carries within itself the negative.

Marx derived the dialectical method from Hegel. Lenin characterizes the Hegelian dialectics as "that pearl......from the dung-heap of absolute idealism.[1] But instead of the idealistic dialectic of Hegel, Marx formulated the materialistic and historical dialectic, and in his philosophy the notion of advance due to the imbalance between the forces and relations of production occupies a prominent place.

Buddha also adopted, although to a very minor extent, the dialectical methodology. Both Buddha and Marx are similar in this that they had idealistic-spiritual antecedents and they both revolted against them. The analytic philosopher of ancient India, Kapila, had formulated some elements of a dialectical philosophy. In the *Ṛgveda* we find the mention of the *pravatā* and *yatyudvatā* (path) of Savitā[2] — a path and its reverse. This may be considered a rudimentary formulation of the dialectic. The Socratic method of questions and counter-questions is also found in the Veda (*kah svidekākī carati—suryah ekākī carati.*) and the Upaniṣads. Just as Socrates tried to overwhelm his opponents with argumentative skill, so too Buddha was a past master in the dialectical art of controversial polemics. This use of the dialectic is in the Platonic sense. With regard to the Hegelian use of the terms thesis, antithesis, and synthesis, we see in the Sāmkhya the scheme of the three guṇas, and this may be considered as a rough approximation to the dialectic. *Tamas* is the mass and the *rajas* is the dynamic pulsating energy-stuff. These two clash and that culminates in the triumph of the *sattva*, the intelligence-force. Harmony and reconciliation (*sattva*) or synthesis appears after the energy-stuff (*rajas*) or the antithesis (in Hegel's terminology) has broken the darkness of the original mass (*tamas*), the thesis.[3]

[1] *Materialism and Empirio-Criticism*, p. 170.

[2] The *RV*, 1,35,4.

[3] The *Bhagavadgitā* says: *rajastamascābhibhūya sattvam bhavati Bhārata.*

If we accept this dialectical point of view of the Sāmkhya the following historical illustrations can be noted. At certain times when *tamas* prevails, we find decadent rulers, *e.g.*, the later Pārikshitas, the later Mauryas, the later Mughals, or the decadent days of Russian Czardom. When *rajas* prevails in history we find vigorous and violent action, *e.g.*, the days of the Kauravas and the Pāndavas, the Guptas, the Pratiharas, or the days of Charlemagne, Napoleon, or Hitler, or the days of the Mongols. When these two have been exhausted we find either king-prophets like Rāma and Aśoka or idealistic thinker-workers like Marcus Aurelius, or Rousseau, or Mazzini, or Mahatma Gandhi.

Buddha modified the Samkhya dialectic. He accepts the transiency and mutations of the cosmic phenomena, but derives them from *avidyā* energised by powerful *samskāra* and dynamised by the *vijñāna*. The *pratitysamutpāda* also partly proceeds on the dialectical procedure, because it posits the consequence of one thing upon the antecedence of another.

Hegel accepts the role of ideas and mind in the cosmic procession. Bergson traces the evolution of the entire world to the primal *elan vital*. The Taittirīyas of ancient India conceived of the cosmos as the transmutation of the will-energy of the *ānanandamaya brahman*. Kapila traces universal transformation to the '*purushasannidhi*.' Buddha also accepts the role of psychic forces in evolution, and this is the significance of the *tṛshnā* and the *bhava* in the *dvādaśayatana*.

Both Buddha and Marx repudiated faith in an Absolute Being. Although, the later Mahayānistic writers were absolutists, in the *Dīgha Nikāya*, Buddha derides the concept of a primordial creative agency. He is critical of the personal God of the theologians. But Buddhism, though it repudiates the concept of a creator and though it pulverises the *purusha* of the Sāmkhyas into almost a psychic atomism of the five-fold Skandhas, is far from being a materialistic creed.

But Marxism is a defiant materialistic creed in the sense of acknowledging the birth of consciousness from primal matter. Lenin says: "The Idealist philosophers have always sought to change this latter name (*i.e.*, God)... Absolute Idea, universal spirit, world-will... are different formulations of one and the same idea."[1]

Lenin is distrustful of all schools of idealism as indirectly preparing the ground for religious fiedism. But it is to be borne in mind that against the materialism of the eighteenth and nineteenth centuries, Bergson has formulated his gospel of creative evolution. The Taittirīya philosophers of ancient India had attempted to formulate a scheme of universal evolution wherein life, mind, intellect and spirit were also recognized as four dominant entities along with matter. These four were considered as already involved entities using matter as their foundational receptacle. The Vedāntic idealistic philosophy is getting some supporters both in modern America and modern Europe. Other philosophical schools like existentialism, neo-vitalism, realism, neutralism and Whitehead's organism are also critical of some of the assumptions of materialism. Hence it will be only a species of dogmatic fanaticism to hold that dialectical materialism is the sole correct philosophical world-view.

Marx's rationalism constituted a vigorous revolt against all kinds of mystical consciousness. When he flourished (1818-1883), Europe was passing through the nationalistic convulsions in France, Italy, Germany and Austria. It was a period of action — *rajas*. Christianity at that time, shorn of a St. Peter and a St. Francis, had no mysticism to offer. The historical epoch of contemporary Europe was characterized by nationalism, rationalism and materialism. Hence a mystical and contemplative *Weltanschauung* could not find favor. But Buddha was a Yogi, an adept in *dhyāna* and *samādhi* and a believer in clairvoyance and clairaudience, — in short, he claimed to be gifted with the supernormal powers of Yoga. Hence the Buddhist rationalism is supplemented by transcendentalism and mysticism. Marx was a believer in a philosophical and logical rationalism. He did away with all traces of belief in scriptural testimony. But the Buddhistic rationalistic epistemology does believe in higher truths being acquired by *śamatha* and *vipaśyanā*. Later devout Buddhists believed in the revelatory character of Buddhistic teachings, and the Mimānsakas condemned them for this.

[1] V. I. Lenin, *Materialism and Empirio-Criticism*, p. 222.

3. *Philosophy of Religion*

Marxists say that the great religions of the world arise in consonance with the demands of contemporary economic conditions. Engels calls Christianity to be a religion of the slaves and the oppressed.[1] The main reason for this is the pragmatism and the materialistic positivism of the Marxists. But Buddha always claimed that the truths he preached were revealed to him in a supernormal state. They were not due to speculative cogitation or keen dialectical ratiocination on philosophical topics but were born of direct super-rational intuitive perceptions. Swami Vivekananda has vigorously asserted the thesis that all great religions arise in the superconscious state Hence the idealistic school will maintain that the economic origin of religion is a myth. Buddha was an adept in the art and practice of self-introspective meditation (*sallayana*) of the Palī scriptures. But Marx held the view that religion was a recognition of the infra-rational aspect of man and is the opium of the people. Lenin, like Hobbes, held that religion is born of fear. The views of Buddha are in direct opposition to them. Recent researches into the origins of the ancient religions reveal its primitive unsophisticated roots. Totemism, fetishism, ancestor-worship, plant-worship in certain religions, (cf. the sacredness of the *tulsi* plant, the *dhatura*, etc.), zoomorphism and zoolatry practised in the Egyptian and Indus civilizations, worship of nature-spirits and deification of powerful objects of nature do show that religion in its origins is definitely a repudiation of the rational faculty. But there is the other side of the picture also. Religion also, sometimes, registers the immanent wish to transcend the sense of the finitude of man. It often indicates a mystic consciousness. It vindicates the inherent urge of man to comprehend the Absolute. Hence one finds in the *Ṛgveda* the deification of the Aditi — the infinite. In the *Piṭakas* one finds the concept of *ānantyāyatana* (infinity). The great prophets and the enlightened mystics of the world give their unequivocal opinion that religion is the search for the infinite. This search is present in the *Ṛgveda* and the older Upaniṣads. Hegel has regarded religion as the representation of the Absolute. Kant had recognised the place of the Transcendental Infinite in religion. Buddha,

[1] F. Engels, *Anti-Dühring*, p. 98.

would accept the origin of religion to be in the natural trend of the human mind to transcend the limitations of sorrow and death. One finds this tendency also in the ancient forms of Egyptian mysticism. Maspero has pointed out that the ancient temples of Babylonia were supposed to be the cosmos in miniature. Thus they were attemps to transcend the limitations imposed on man.

But there is an element of truth in the analysis of Marx with regard to the support rendered to political rulers and dominant social classes by religious groups. At times religion, certainly, has been misused. David and Solomon, the 'chosen sons of Jehovah', utilized the Jewish religion for practical political ends. Constantine and Charlemagne sought support from Christianity. The Orthodox Church of Russia was always a great bulwark of the autocratic Czarist regime. Austria maintained her reactionary despotism in Italy and Germany in the first half of the 19th century and in this game she received, to some extent, the support of religion. As a keen student of history, Marx, drew pointed attention to the role of religions as an ideological buttress of political and economic power-holders.

4. *Philosophy of History*

Buddha and Marx differ radically in their historical philosophy. Marx has overrated the role of the economic factor in human history. Buddha, whose whole life of renunciation was an emphatic challenge to all kinds of materialistic pomp and exaggerated worship of Mammon, could never accept economics as the supreme determinant of human movements. Renunciation or *sannyāsa* repudiates the pre-eminent value of economics in human life.

The Hegelian dialectic unduly exaggerates the role of 'impersonal forces' and points out that great men are the products and not the creators of the time-force. But in the *Śānti Parva* of the *Mahābhārata*, Bhisma formulates the theory that the great man is the creator of the time-force. Krishna calls himself to be the *Zeit-geist* (*kālosmi*). The Marxists adopt the Hegelian standpoint and would argue that if there would have been no Luther, somebody else would have produced the Reformation. It is true that in the making of an individual, Buddha accepts the enormous power wielded by the past *samskāra*. But he accepts the freedom of the human will to surmount them and create a new transformed man of changed consciousness. No doubt, traditions and historical forces are mighty. It has been said of the First World War that it was not due either to the Kaiser or to any one statesman or to all of them, but the leaders were being goaded by imponderable forces of history. But the Vedāntic and the Buddhistic theory of history will not accept this type of objective determinism. According to the Vedānta, the human ego, in its essence, is identical with the cosmic and supracosmic Eg. Hence a human individual who realises his identity with the World-soul can be said to be omniscient. Rāmānuja accepts that a *mukta ātman* is omniscient. Buddha, times without number, calls himself omniscient. Owing to this faith in himself he wielded superhuman moral power over his disciples. The great prophets also claim some kind of extraordinary power and charisma. Thus it may be said that in several schools of philosophy more importance will be attached to the role of the creative moral and spiritual individuals in history than the Hegelians and Marxians will be willing to accept.

5. *Assessment of the Roles of Buddha and Marx in History*

Marx's main aim was to give a revolutionary programme to the proletarian workers. Hence, in his materialistic interpretation of history, he condemned all religions. But Marxists are fundamentally wrong in their technological and economic interpretation of history. The great movements of the world are not the products solely of economic struggles. I realize that the French and the Russian revolutions were motivated by tremendous economic forces, but there were other forces too. Napoleon said that what made the Revolution was vanity. In other words, the French bourgeoisie was jealous of the aristocracy in that country. Several scholars unhold the view that the modern national state is a product of the Reformation. The latter, to be sure, was a religious movement. Asoka had political power to extend Indian imperialism in eastern and western Asia, but he was checked in his conquering adventures by an ethical sense of universalistic fraternity as inculcated by Buddhism. The tremendous social and moral upheaval engendered by the personality of Buddha had its source in the extraordinary meditations and castigations of Buddha beneath the sacred tree and not in the solutions of economic riddles. Hence the role of non-economic forces should be recognized in the study of historical dynamics. Economics has assumed the terrific importance it wields today only after the agricultural and industrial revolutions of the 18th century. Furthermore, the difference between economic "determinism" and economic "influence" or "impact" on non-economic aspects of existence or the "conditioning" role of economic factors has also to be noted. The dynamics of social and historical causation is too intricate a process to be revealed solely by treating the material forces and relations of production as the causal category and the other entities of human life as the effect thereof. In the study of the motivations and determinants of the historical process the significant role of human intelligence which probes into the processes of the workings of nature and which, thereby, dynamically assesses and defines the conjuncture of operative categories in a specific situation has to be recognized. It is not the material or the economic or the political entities in themselves which are socially causal categories but the entities as present to the human mind and as understood by it.

Buddha and Marx were not pure speculative philosophers. Buddha condemned all dialectical problems as *avyākṛta* and philosophizing was a heresy for a Bhikkhu. Marx became the advocate of a practical sociological and revolutionary philosophy and was not vitally concerned with keen ontological metaphysics. But Buddha ushered in a train of revolutionary thought which led to the systems of Asanga, Āryadeva, Vasuvandhu and Nāgārjuna. Marxists want to buttress their arguments with philosophic concepts.[1] Marx's faith in the omnipotence of economics was immense. His belief in the ultimate victory of the workers is comparable to the Buddhist belief in *nirvāna* being the birth-right of all.[2] The Marxists go a step further and they attribute to the dynamic economic

[1] N. Bukharin, *Marxism and Modern Thought*, Chapter I.

[2] Max Weber holds a different view. He says : "The supreme sacred values, which are promised by religion......have not necessarily been the most universal ones. Not everybody had entree to Nirvana, to the contemplative union with the divine, the orgiastic or the ascetic possession of God." (*Essays in Sociology*, *op. cit.*, p. 287).

forces such a deterministic certainty that it inspires the socialists with the same religious fervour as inspired the early Islamics.

The gospel of freedom has been emphasised by both the doctrines. The Vedic and Upaniṣadic doctrine of *mukti*[1] and self-realisation or the Buddhistic tenet of *nirvāṇa* does imply spiritual and moral freedom. Buddhism wants the relinquishment of the egoistic desires of the partial self. The socialistic world revolution as contemplated by Marx also pleads for political, economic and social liberty. Marx hoped for the eventual realization of the classless society when the state as machine of exploitation would wither away. The truly religious man cares not for the worldly powers and is, in a way, an anarchist. A Christ, a Dayānanda, or a Gandhi does not bow before the powers that be. Marx also was unyielding in his resolute defiance to political autocrats.

In India today one sees the phenomenon of the clash of the ideals of the different civilizations. India geographically belongs to Asia but she is not purely Asiatic. For the last two centuries and more she has been exposed to the political, economic and cultural impact of the West. Hence although revivalistic trends in modern India plead for the reincorporation of the Vedic and Buddhistic ideals of moral and spiritual freedom, one cannot minimize the constructive role of the ideals of social and economic justice which Marx has championed. He wanted to change the world which philosophers had only interpreted. The pragmatism, positivism and revolutionary realism of Marxism have proved a powerful dissolvent of the old conservative traditions, irrational customs and pretensions of social oligarchy. Marx's doctrine of all extinction of governments is more assuring than the traditional, partly monarchical and partly republican, political philosophy of Buddha.

[1] The European scholars hold that the Vedic seers did not have the belief in Mukti.

APPENDIX 7

NARENDRA DEVA'S INTERPRETATION OF BUDDHIST PHILOSOPHY

Bauddha Dharma-Darsana[1]. By Late Acharya Narendra Deva Patna, Bihar Rashtrabhasa Parishad, 1956, pp. 72+616+76, Rs. 17/-.

THIS BOOK which incorporates the results of the studies of the learned author for a number of years has been hailed as a very significant, almost monumental, production in the field of Buddhist scholarship. It has received two prizes — one by the U. P. Government and the other by the Sahitya Academy, New Delhi. It brings together the various Buddhistic research essays of the author published in the Kashi Vidyapitha Journals. The large Chapter on the idealism of Vasubandhu (pp. 422-487) was originally published in the *Sampurnānanda Abhinandana Grantha.*

Narendra Deva accepts that a social structure must have an ethical foundation. He subscribes to the potency of the concept of *karman* — the belief that actions must produce consequences commensurate with their moral worth — both for social organizations and for personal conduct (p. 2). To this extent it appears that although a Marxist, he has modified the Marxist view which interprets ethics in terms of class relations. He interprets Buddhism as a canon of universalistic ethics (pp. 14-16).

The author has penetrated deeply into the original works of Buddhist philosophy. He has made available to the student and research scholar the main propositions of Vasubandhu's idealism on the basis of his *Vimśatikā,* and the *Siddhi* of Hiuen-Tsang which is a commentary on the *Trimśikā.* He has also sum-

[1] This Review originally appeared in *The Indian Journal of Political Science,* Vol. XXI, No. 3, July-Sept. 1960, pp. 284-85.

marized the views of Poussin and Stcherbatsky on Nirvāṇa and other abstruse concepts of Buddhist philosophy. He accepts that Hīnayānism is a system of pluralistic realism (p. 303). Here he seems to be influenced by Stcherbatsky' interpretation of *Dharma* as element. It may not be possible to concur with the learned author in his view that Mahāyanism is monistic. (p. 303). How can the *śunyavāda* of Nāgārjuna be called unreservedly monistic ? The last chapter of the book contains a subtle discussion of time, space, ether and the problems of logic.

The method followed in this book is one of summarizing the main tenets of a school as embodied in the classics of that school. This method has great merit from the standpoint of accuracy although the style of the book at times becomes heavy due to the acceptance of too many technical Sanskrit terms. Many a time it appears that the writer is adopting verbatim Sanskrit sentences and adding Hindi articles, verbs and prepositions only. From a worshipper at the shrine of dialectical materialism that the late Acharya was, it would have been legitimately expected that he would have made some tentative attempt at correlating the tenets of Buddhist philosophy ("superstructure") with the basic forces and relations of production ("substructure"). Furthermore, the absence of adequate documentation of statements made in the book would also detract from its usefulness as a reference work for the serious students of Buddhism. But we have also to remember that this is a posthumous publication.

The book is not a systematic treatise. It is mainly a collection of papers written at different periods which have been brought together. Hence it suffers from some serious omissions which would not have been possible if it had undergone a thorough scrutiny by the author. The whole of early Buddhist philosophy as embodied in the *Tripiṭakas*, the *Milinda-Pañha* and the works of Buddhaghosa like the *Viṣuddhi-magga* is finished in one hundred pages. There is an unjustifiable neglect of the philosophy of the Abhidhamma. Similarly the *Tattvasamgraha* of Śāntarakshita which is a monumental and epoch-making book in the field of Buddhist thought, is dismissed in five lines. The discussion of Dharmakirti's *Nyāyavindu* is also extremely unsatisfactory.

From the historical point of view objections may be taken to the author's unwarranted characterization of the period from the 5th to the 7th centuries AD as the golden age of Indian Culture (p. 565). Similarly controversial is the author's statement that the older elements of Buddhism are preserved more in the Mahāyana than in the Hīnayāna (p. 574). The author seems to accept the rather unfounded generalization of European indologists that there were throughout ancient Indian history two streams of culture — the Brāhmaṇa and the Śramana (p. 1).

These shortcomings, however, do not vitally affect the claim of the book to rank as a major work, almost a landmark, in the study of Buddhist philosophy in the Hindi language. I will even say that there is no book even in the Western languages which provides so much information about Buddhism in one single volume. I earnestly hope that this book will raise the standard of Hindi scholarship. The Bihar Rashtrabhāshā Parishad should be congratulated for having published this important book.

BIBLIOGRAPHY

Primary Sources

Tripiṭakas : Texts & Translation

Tripiṭakas, Edited in Devanagari Script by J. Kashyapa, 41 volumes, Nalandā Pāli Mahāvihara.

Tripiṭakas, Edited in Roman Script. (Pali Text Society, London).

Vinaya Piṭaka, Hindi translation by Rāhul Sāmkṛtyāyana.

Dīgha Nikāya, Dialogues of the Buddha, trans. by Thomas William Rhys Davids, Vol. I, 1899.

Dialogues of the Buddha (*Dīgha Nikāya*), trans. by Thomas William Rhys Davids and Mrs. Caroline Augusta Foley Rhys Davids, Vol. II, 3rd ed., 1952.

Dialogues of the Buddha (*Dīgha Nikāya*), Vol. III, 1921.

Dīgha Nikāya, Hindi translation by Rahul Samkṛtyāyāna and J. Kashyapa, Sarnath, Mahabodhi Sabha, 1936.

Dhammapada, Hindi trans. by Bhadanta Ānanda Kauśalyāyana.

Jātakas, (A) E.T. by R. Chalmers, W. Rouse etc. under the editorship of E.B. Cowell, 6 vols. and Index. Cambridge 1895-1913. (Complete except for the *Nidānakathā*,

——, (B) E.T. by T.W. Rhys Davids, London, 1880. New edition by C. A. F. Rhys Davids, 1925. (Contains the *Nidānakathā* and the first 40 stories of the *Jātakas*).

Dhammasaṅgaṇi, E.T. under the title *A Buddhist Manual of Psychological Ethics* by C.A.F. Rhys Davids, London, 1900.

Atthaśālinī (Buddhaghosha's Commentary on the *Dhammasaṅgaṇi*), E.T. under the title, *The Expositor*, by Maung Tin and C.A.F. Rhys Davids, 2 Vols., London, 1921-2.

Other Primary & Secondary Sources

ALLEN, G.F., *The Buddha's Philosophy*, London, 1959.

Abhidhammattha-sangaha, by Aniruddha, E. T. under the title

Compendium of Philosophy, by Shwezan Aung, revised and edited by Mrs. C.A.F. Rhys Davids, London, 1910.

ARNOLD, EDWIN, *The Light of Asia.*

AŚVAGHOSHA, *Buddhacarita*, translated by E.W. Cowell in *S.B.E* Vol IL.

BAPAT, P.V., ed. *Atthaśālinī*, Poona, 1942.

BARTHELEMY ST-HILAIRE, J., *Le Bouddha et sa religion*, Paris, 1860, translated into English under the title *The Buddha And His Religion* by Laura Ensor, London and New York, George Routledge and Sons, 1895.

BARUA, B.M., *Prolegomena to the History of Buddhist Philosophy*, Calcutta University, 1918.

——, *A History of Pre-Buddhistic Indian Philosophy*, Calcutta University, 1925.

BASAK, R.G., *Lectures on Buddha and Buddhism*, Calcutta, 1961.

BEAL, SAMUEL, *The Romantic Legend of Sakya Buddha*, from the Chinese Sanskrit, London, 1875. (Said to be a translation of the *Abhinishkramaṇa-sutra.*)

——, ed. and trans. *Texts from the Buddhist Canon Commonly Known as Dhammapada.* London, Trubner, 1878.

BHAGWAT, N.K., *Theravada Buddhist Philosophy.* (Patna University Readership Lectures).

BHATTTACHARYA, VIDHUSEKHARA, *The Basic Conception of Buddhism.* Calcutta University, 1934.

——, "Evolution of Vijñanavāda" (*IHQ*, X, pp. 1-11).

BUDDHAGHOSA, *Viśuddhimagga*, English translation under the title *The Path of Purity* by Pe Maung Tin, 3 vols. Vol. I, 1922, Vol. II, 1928, 1929 and Vol, III, 1931. London, Pali Text Society.

BURTT, E.A., ed. *The Teachings of the Compassionate Buddha*, New York, The New American Library, 1955.

BUSTON (of Tibet), *History of Buddhism*, translated from the Tibetan by E. Obermiller. Part I, *The Jewelry of Scripture.* Part II, *The History of Buddhism in India and Tibet*, Hiedelberg, 1931-1932.

CARUS, PAUL, *The Gospel of Buddha*, First Indian edition issued by the Publications Division, Government of India, 1961, Originally published by the Open Court, Chicago.

CHILDERS, R. C., *A Dictionary of the Pali Language.*

ÇONZE, EDWARD, *Buddhism, its Essence and Development.*

Oxford, 1951.

——, *Buddhist Thought in India*, London, George Allen & Unwin, 1962.

COOMARASWAMY, A.K., *Buddha and the Gospel of Buddhism*, London, 1916.

COPLESTON, R.S., *Buddhism, Primitive and Present, in Magadha and Ceylon*, 1892. 2nd ed. 1908, London.

CSOMA DE KOROS, ALEXANDER, *The Life and Teachings of Buddha*, Calcutta, Susil Gupta, 1957.

DAHLKE, PAUL, *Buddhismus als Religion and Moral*. Munchen, English translation from the German by Bhikkhu Śilāchara under the title *Buddhist Essays*, London, 1908.

——, *Buddhismus als Weltanschauung*. English translation from the German by Bhikkhu Śilāchara under the title *Buddhism and Science*, London. 1913.

DAHLMANN, JOSEPH, *Nirvāṇa*, Berlin, 1896.

DATTA, N., *Early History of the Spread of Buddhism and the Buddhist Schools*, Calcutta, 1925.

——, *Aspects of Mahāyāna and its Relation to Hīnayana*, Calcutta, 1930.

——, *Early Monastic Buddhism*, Calcutta, Oriental Book Agency, 1960.

——, "The Brahmajāla Sutta exposited in the light of Nāgārjuna", (*IHQ*, III, 1932).

DASGUPTA, S.N., "Buddhist Mysticism", *Hindu Mysticism*, London, The Open Court, 1927, pp. 85-109.

——, "Buddhist Idealism," *Indian Idealism*, Cambridge University Press, 1962, pp. 76-108.

——, "Buddhism and Croce", *Philosophical Essays*, University of Calcutta, 1951, pp. 117-150.

——, "Buddhist Philosophy", Chapter V of *A History of Indian Philosophy*, Cambridge University Press, reprint of 1957, pp. 78-168.

——, "Is Sāmkhya Non-Vedic?", *Indian Culture*, 1934.

DATTA, SUKUMAR, *Early Buddhist Monachism* (600 BC-100 BC), Trubner's Oriental Series, London, Trubner, 1924.

ELIOT, SIR CHARLES, *Hinduism and Buddhism*. 3 vols. London, Edwin Arnold, 1921.

FAUSBOLL, V., Ed. *Jātakas*. 6 volumes and an index vol. London, 1877-97.

GAUR, HARI SINGH, *The Spirit of Buddhism.* N.C. Seth, Calcutta.

GOVINDA, A.B., *The Psychological Attitude of Early Buddhist Philosophy*, Patna University Readership Lectures, 1936-37.

GRIMM, GEORGE, *The Doctrine of Buddha ; The Religion of Reason* (Leipzig, Druglin, 1926, 2nd Revised ed., 1958). (This book is the English translation of the author's *Die Lehre des Buddha, die Religion der Vernunft*, Munchen, 1925).

HAR DAYAL, *The Bodhisattva Doctrine.* London University Ph. D. thesis. London, Kegan Paul.

HARDY, R. SPENCE, *Eastern Monachism*, London, Partridge & Oakey, 1850.

——, *A Manual of Buddhism in its Modern Development.* London, Williams & Norgate, 1853. 2nd ed., 1880.

——, *The Legends and Theories of the Buddhists.* London, Frederick Norgate, 1881. 2nd ed.

HOLMES, E.G.A., *The Creed of Buddha*, New York, John Lane, 1908.

HOPKINS, E.W., "Buddhism", *History of Religions.*

——, "Buddhism", *Religions of India.*

HORNER, I.B., *The Early Buddhist Theory of Man Perfected.* London, Williams & Norgate, 1936.

JAYATILEKE, K.N., *Early Buddhist Theory of Knowledge*, London, George Allen & Unwin, 1963.

JENNINGS, J.G., *The Vedantic Buddhism of the Buddha*, London, 1947.

KASHYAP, J., *The Philosophy of Abhidhamma*, Sarnath, Mahabodhi Society, 1942-43. 2 vols.

KEITH, A.B., *Buddhist Philosophy in India and Ceylon*, Oxford, Clarendon Press, 1923.

KERN, J. HEINRICH C., *A Manual of Indian Buddhism*, Strassburg, 1896.

KHANṬIPALO, PHRA, *Tolerance*, London, Rider & Co, 1964.

KIMURA, RYUKAN, *The Original and Developed Doctrines of Indian Buddhism*, (in charts), University of Calcutta, 1920.

——, *A Historical Study of the terms Hinayana and Mahayana and the Origins of Mahayana Buddhism*, University of Calcutta, 1927.

KING, W.L., *Buddhism and Christianity*, London, 1963.

KRETPER, BRYAN DE, *Man in Buddhism and Christianity.* Calcutta, 1954. (Edinburgh Ph. D. thesis)

LAKSHMI NARSU, P., *The Essence of Buddhism*, Bombay, Thacker & Co., 1907. 2nd ed. revised and enlarged, Madras, S. Varadachari & Co., 1912.

LAW, B.C., *History of Pali Literature*, 2 vols. London, Kegan Paul, 1933.

——, (ed.) *Buddhistic Studies.* Calcutta, Thacker Spink, 1931.

LING, T.O., *Buddhism and the Mythology of Evil*, London, 1962.

MALASEKHARA, G.P., *Dictionary of Pali Proper Names*, 2 Vols. London, 1931-38.

MELAMED, SAMUEL MAX, *Spinoza and Buddha.* University of Chicago Press, 1933.

MONIER-WILLIAMS, M., *Buddhism : in Its Connection with Brahmanism and Hinduism*, London, John Murray, 1890.

MUKHERJEE, SATAKARI, *Buddhist Philosophy of Universal Flux*, Calcutta University Press, 1935.

MURTI, T.R.V., *The Central Philosophy of Buddhism*, London, George Allen & Unwin, 1955.

NAGARJUNA, *Mādhyamaka-Karikā*, edited along with the Prasannapadā commentary of Chandrakīrti by Poussin in *BB* 1903 ff, in *BST* Darbhanga, 1960.

NARENDRA DEVA, *Bauddha-Dharma-Darshana*, in Hindi, Patna, Bihar Rashtrabhāsā Parishad, 1956.

——, *Abhidharma-Kosha*, In Hindi (Hindi Trans. of Poussin's French volumes.) Allahabad, Hindustani Academy, 1958.

OLDENBERG, H., *Die Lehre der Upanishaden Und die Anfange des Buddhismus*, Gottingen, 1915.

——, *Buddha : sein leben, seine Lehre, seine Gemeinde*, Berlin, 1881. 8th and 9th ed., 1921. English translation of first ed. by William Hoey, London, 1882. French translation of 3rd ed. Paris, 1903.

OLTRAMARE, PAUL, *L' histoire des Theosophiques Bouddhique*, Paris, Paul Geuthner, 1923.

PANDE, G.C., *Studies in the Origins of Buddhism*, University of Allahabad, 1957.

PISCHEL, RICHARD, *Leben und Lehre des Buddha*, Leipzig 1905. 3rd ed., by H. Luders, 1916. English translation by B.H. Kapadia, Vallabh Vidyanagar, 1965.

POUSSIN, LOUIS DE LA VALLEE, *The Way to Nirvāna: Six Lectures on Ancient Buddhism as a Discipline of Salvation*, Cambridge, University Press, 1917.

——, *L. Abhidharmakosa*, 6 Vols. Paris, 1923ff.

PRATT, J.B. *The Pilgrimage of Buddhism and a Buddhist Pilgrimage*, New York, Macmillan, 1928.

RADHAKRISHNAN, S., *Gotama the Buddha*.

——, "The Ethical Idealism of Buddhism", Chap. VII, (pp. 340-476), "Buddhism as a Religion" (Chap. X, pp. 581-610, "The Schools of Buddhism" (Chap. XI, pp. 611-669), in *Indian Philosophy*, Vol. I.

——, "The Teaching of Buddha by Speech and Silence." *Hibbert Journal*, 1934.

RHYS DAVIDS, C.A.F., *Buddhism, a Study of the Buddhist Norm*, New York, Henry Holt, 1912; revised, *Buddhism : Its Birth and Dispersal*, London, Thornton Butterworth, 1934.

——, *Buddhist Psychology*, 2nd ed., The Religious Quest of India Series, London : G. Bell, 1914; London, Luzac & Co., 1924. *The Birth of Indian Psychology and its Development*, Revised ed. of *Buddhist Psychology*, London, Luzac & Co., 1936.

——, *Gotama the Man*. London, Luzac, 1928.

——, *Sakya or Buddhist Origins*, (London, Kegan Paul, 1931).

RHYS DAVIS, T.W., *Buddhism*, London, 1877, last revised, 1910. London, Society for the Promotion of Christian Religion, 1925.

——, *Lectures on the Origin and Growth of Religion as illustrated by Some Points in the History of Indian Buddhism* (Hibbert Lectures, 1881), 4th ed., London, Williams & Norgate, 1906.

——, *Buddhism, its History and Literature*, New York, 1896, Indian edition, Calcutta, Susil Gupta, 1952.

——, *Buddhist India* (1903), Indian ed., Calcutta, Susil Gupta, 1950, 3rd ed., 1957.

——, *Buddhistic Birth Stories*, London, Trubner, 1880.

——, "Early History of Buddhists" in *The Cambridge History of India*, Vol. I, 1922.

——, & STEDE, W., *Pali-English Dictionary*, London, 1921.

ROKOTOFF, NATALIE, *Foundations of Buddhism*, New York, 1930, pp. 137.

SAMKRITYAYANA, RAHUL, *Bauddha-Darshana.*

——, *Buddha-Charyā*, Kashi, Sevā Upavana, 1931.

SENART, EMIL, *Essai sur la legende de Buddha, son caractere et ses origines.* Paris, Imprimerie Nationale, 1882, first appeared in (*J.A.*) August-September 1873ff.

SOGEN, YAMAKAMI, *Systems of Buddhistic Thought*, University of Calcutta, 1912.

STCHERBATSKY, TH. *The Central Conception of Buddhism and the Meaning of the Word Dharma*, London, 1923, Indian edition, Calcutta, Susil Gupta, 1956.

——, *Buddhist Logic*, 2 vols. (Bibliotheca Buddhica. Vol. XXVI, Parts I & II), Leningrad, Academy of Sciences of the USSR, 1930-32, Paperback, Dover, New York.

——, *The Conception of Buddhist Nirvāna*. Leningrad, Academy of Sciences of the USSR, 1927. This book contains a translation of Chap. I (on causality) and Chap. XXV (on *Nirvāṇa*) of Nāgārjuna's *Mulamadhyamik-a-akarikās* and of Chandrakīrti's *Prasannapadā* commentary thereon.

STREETER, BURNETT HELMAN, *The Buddha and The Christ*, London, Macmillan, 1932.

SUZUKI, D.T., *Outlines of Mahayana Buddhism*, London, Luzac, 1907.

TACHIBANA, *The Ethics of Buddhism*, Oxford, 1926.

TAKAKUSU, J., *The Essentials of Buddhist Philosophy*, Honolulu, 1945.

THOMAS E. J., *The Life of Buddha ; as Legend and History*, Kegan Paul, London, 1927, 2nd ed., 1931.

——, *Early Buddhist Scriptures.*

——, *The History of Buddhist Thought*, Routledge & Kegan Paul, London, 1933, 2nd ed., 1951.

UPADHYAYA, BHARAT SINGH, *Buddha-Darshana Tathā Anya Bhartiya Darshana*, in Hindi, 2 vols.

VARMA, VISHWANATH PRASAD, *Studies in Hindu Political Thought and its Metaphysical Foundations*, Delhi, Motilal Banarsidass, 1959, 2nd ed.

——, "Buddha and Marx", *Patna College Magazine*, April, 1946.

——, "The Gospel of Buddha", *The Patna University Journal*, September, 1946.

——, "Sri Aurobindo's Interpretations of Buddhist Philosophy." Buddha Jayanti Special Issue Vol. I, of *The Journal of Bihar Research Society*, 1956.

——, "Buddha and Dayananda", *The Uttara Bharati*, Vol. X, No. 2 (Agra University).

——, "Buddha and Aurobindo", *The Uttara Bharati*, Vol. IX, No. 2 (Agra University).

——, *Bhartiya Darshana*, in Hindi, Agra, Laxmi Narayan Agrawal, 1967.

——, *Rajniti Aur Darshana*, in Hindi. Patna, Bihar Rashtra-bhāsha Parishad, 1956.

VIDYABHUSANA, S.C., "The Buddhist Logic" (pp. 57-144) in *History of the Medieval School of Indian Logic*, Calcutta University, 1909. (Calcutta University Ph. D. Thesis).

VIDYABHUSANA, S.C. "The Buddhist Logic" (pp. 225-353) in *A History of Indian Logic*, Calcutta University, 1921.

VASUBANDHU, *Abhidharmakosha*, ed., with the commentary entitled Nālandikā of R. Sankrityayana. Varanasi, Kashi Vidyapitha, 1931.

WEBER, MAX, *The Religion of India ; The Sociology of Hinduism and Buddhism*, Trans. from German and ed. by Hans H. Gerth and Don Martindale. Glencoe, Ill., Free Press, 1958.

WINTERNITZ, W., *Geschichte der Indischen Litteratur*. 3 Volumes, Vol. 2, *Die buddhistische Litteratur und die heiligen Texte der Jainas*, Leipzig, 1920.

INDEX